AF680755

THE EU LAW ON CRYPTOASSETS

This book provides a comprehensive guide to EU regulation of cryptoassets and FinTech regulation more broadly. The authors explain the need for regulation in an accessible manner and against the background of the instances now dubbed the 'Crypto Winter' – when millions of crypto investors lost billions of value due to technical malfunctions, misconduct, and fraud – and place the EU regulation in the context of the recent rebound and institutionalization of cryptoasset markets. They combine an in-depth perspective on the bespoke regulations of cryptoassets provided in the EU's Markets in Crypto-Assets (MiCA) Regulation and Pilot Regulation with the EU's revised Anti-money Laundering and Counter-Terrorism Financing (AML/CTF) legislation, digital operational resilience regulation (DORA), and private law. They conclude by analysing how the combined new EU financial regulation addresses the causes of the Crypto Winter and which risks remain despite the plethora of new policy action. Authored by world-leading FinTech experts, the book will be a go-to source for researchers and practitioners and a crucial guide for those navigating the field of cryptoassets.

Dirk Zetzsche is Professor in Financial Law and holds the ADA Chair in Financial Law (inclusive finance) at the Department of Law, Faculty of Law, Economics and Finance, University of Luxembourg. Professor Zetzsche co-leads Luxembourg's National Centre of Excellence in Research in Financial Technologies, the FinTech Working Group of the European Banking Institute, as well as the House of Sustainable Governance & Markets at the Faculty of Law, Economics and Finance, University of Luxembourg. As member of the Consultative Working Group of ESMA's Investment Management Committee and the Cryptoasset Task Force of the European Systemic Risk Board, Professor Zetzsche is one of the globally most well-known authors on FinTech regulation, a frequent consultant to regulators and parliaments, and a regular guest at all the leading universities and academic conferences across the globe.

Jannik Woxholth is a senior research scientist at the ADA Chair in Financial Law (inclusive finance), Department of Law, Faculty of Law, Economics and Finance, University of Luxembourg. He combines, in a unique fashion, academic and practical experience in law, finance, and technology. He holds a PhD on shareholders' agreements, was a junior partner with McKinsey & Company, and functions as an institutional technology investor.

The EU Law on Cryptoassets

A GUIDE TO EUROPEAN FINTECH REGULATION

DIRK ZETZSCHE
University of Luxembourg

JANNIK WOXHOLTH
University of Luxembourg

CAMBRIDGE
UNIVERSITY PRESS

CAMBRIDGE
UNIVERSITY PRESS

Shaftesbury Road, Cambridge CB2 8EA, United Kingdom

One Liberty Plaza, 20th Floor, New York, NY 10006, USA

477 Williamstown Road, Port Melbourne, VIC 3207, Australia

314–321, 3rd Floor, Plot 3, Splendor Forum, Jasola District Centre, New Delhi – 110025, India

103 Penang Road, #05-06/07, Visioncrest Commercial, Singapore 238467

Cambridge University Press is part of Cambridge University Press & Assessment, a department of the University of Cambridge.

We share the University's mission to contribute to society through the pursuit of education, learning and research at the highest international levels of excellence.

www.cambridge.org
Information on this title: www.cambridge.org/9781009196321

DOI: 10.1017/9781009196338

© Dirk Zetzsche and Jannik Woxholth 2025

This publication is in copyright. Subject to statutory exception and to the provisions of relevant collective licensing agreements, no reproduction of any part may take place without the written permission of Cambridge University Press & Assessment.

When citing this work, please include a reference to the DOI 10.1017/9781009196338

First published 2025

A catalogue record for this publication is available from the British Library.

Library of Congress Cataloging-in-Publication Data
NAMES: Zetzsche, Dirk, author. | Woxholth, Jannik, author.
TITLE: The EU law on crypto-assets : a guide to European fintech regulation / Dirk Zetzsche, University of Luxembourg; Jannik Woxholth, University of Luxembourg.
OTHER TITLES: European Union law on crypto-assets
DESCRIPTION: 1. | Cambridge, United Kingdom ; New York, NY : Cambridge University Press, 2024. | Includes bibliographical references and index.
IDENTIFIERS: LCCN 2024029089 (print) | LCCN 2024029090 (ebook) | ISBN 9781009196321 (hardback) | ISBN 9781009196338 (ebook)
SUBJECTS: LCSH: Cryptocurrencies–Law and legislation–European Union countries. | Digital currency–Law and legislation–European Union countries. | Cryptocurrencies–Law and legislation–European Union countries–Criminal provisions. | Money laundering–Law and legislation–European Union countries.
CLASSIFICATION: LCC KJE7051 .Z435 2024 (print) | LCC KJE7051 (ebook)
LC record available at https://lccn.loc.gov/2024029089
LC ebook record available at https://lccn.loc.gov/2024029090

ISBN 978-1-009-19632-1 Hardback

Cambridge University Press & Assessment has no responsibility for the persistence or accuracy of URLs for external or third-party internet websites referred to in this publication and does not guarantee that any content on such websites is, or will remain, accurate or appropriate.

Contents

Acknowledgements

We thank sincerely our co-authors on the research who have shaped our thinking in this field profoundly and provided the groundwork for this book, including Filippo Annunziata, Linn Anker-Sørensen, Douglas Arner, Ross Buckley, Maurits van Ek, Areti Nikolapoulou, Maria Lucia Passador, Eriks Selga, Julia Sinnig, and Andreas Wehrli.

This earlier foundational research has been expressed in the following publications:

1. D. A. Zetzsche, R. P. Buckley and D. W. Arner, 'The Distributed Liability of Distributed Ledgers: Legal Risks of Blockchain', *University of Illinois Law Review*, (4) (2018): 1361–406.
2. D. A. Zetzsche *et al.*, 'The ICO Gold Rush: It's a Scam, It's a Bubble, It's a Super Challenge for Regulators', *Harvard International Law Journal* , 60(2) (2019): 267–316.
3. R. P. Buckley *et al.*, 'TechRisk', *Singapore Journal of Legal Studies*, (2020): 35–62.
4. D. A. Zetzsche, D. W. Arner and R. P. Buckley, 'Decentralized Finance', *Journal of Financial Regulation*, 6(2) (2020): 172–203.
5. L. Anker-Sørensen and D. A. Zetzsche, 'From Centralized to Decentralized Finance: The Issue of "Fake-DeFi"' (Working Paper, University of Luxembourg, 2021).
6. D. A. Zetzsche *et al.*, 'DLT-Based Enhancement of Cross-Border Payment Efficiency: A Legal and Regulatory Perspective', *Law and Financial Markets Review*, 15(1) (2021): 70–115.
7. D. A. Zetzsche *et al.*, 'The Markets in Crypto-assets Regulation (MICA) and the EU Digital Finance Strategy', *Capital Markets Law Journal*, 16(2) (2021): 203–25.
8. D. A. Zetzsche and J. Woxholth, 'The DLT Sandbox under the Pilot-Regulation', *Capital Markets Law Journal*, 17(2) (2022): 212–36.
9. D. A. Zetzsche *et al.*, 'Remaining Regulatory Challenges in Digital Finance and Cryptoassets after MiCA', Study for the European Parliament's ECON Committee (May 2023), PE 740.083. Website IPOL_STU(2023)740083_EN.pdf (europa.eu).
10. J. Woxholth *et al.*, 'Competing Claims to Crypto-assets', *Uniform Law Review*, 28(2) (2023): 226–46.
11. D. A. Zetzsche, J. Sinnig and A. Nikolakopoulou, 'Crypto Custody', *Capital Markets Law Journal*, 19(3) (2024): 207–29. Website https://doi.org/10.1093/cmlj/kmae010.
12. J. Woxholth, *Kryptoeiendeler i formueretten* (Oslo: Gyldendal, 2024).

13. D. Arner *et al.*, 'The financialisation of Crypto: Designing an international regulatory consensus', *Computer Law & Security Review* 105970, (July 2024) 53. Website https://doi.org/10.1016/j.clsr.2024.105970.
14. J. Sinnig and D. A. Zetzsche, 'Traditional and Digital Limits of Collective Investment Schemes', *European Company and Financial Law Review* , 21(2) (2024): 57–191.
15. D. A. Zetzsche, F. Annunziata and J. Sinnig, 'Digital Assets, MiCA and EU Investment Law', *European Business & Organization Law Review* , (2024)– in press. Website https://ssrn.com/abstract=4670918.
16. J. Sinnig and D. A. Zetzsche, 'La notion d'organisme de placement collectif à l'égard des phénomènes numériques récents' (co-authored article) *Banque & Droit*, (2024) – in press.
17. D. A. Zetzsche and J. Sinnig, 'The EU Approach to Regulating Digital Currencies', *Law and Contemporary Problems* 87(2) (2024)– in press. Website https://ssrn.com/abstract=4707830.
18. D. A. Zetzsche and A. Nikolakopoulou, 'Crypto Custody and Crypto Wallets – An Empirical Assessment', University of Luxembourg Working Paper (March 2024). Website https://ssrn.com/abstract=4769396.
19. J. Woxholth and D. A. Zetzsche, 'DORA on DeFi', University of Luxembourg Working Paper (June 2024). Website https://ssrn.com/abstract=4874057.

We would also like to express our gratitude to the several postdoctoral research fellows, doctoral students, and research assistants who have supported us in finalizing this book, especially in the final intensive stage of manuscript polishing and preparation. In particular, in alphabetical order, we thank: Diletta Blangero, Maurits van Ek, Jenna Hensen, Luisa Künzel, Kate Lamb, Areti Nikolakopoulou, Julia Sinnig, Cedric Strobel, Stamatia Stylianopoulou, and Marian Unterstell.

This research was funded in whole, or in part, by the Luxembourg National Research Fund (FNR), grant reference NCER22/IS/16570468/NCER-FT, as well as the ADA Chair in Financial Law (inclusive finance), University of Luxembourg.

Table of Cases

Case *Dixon et al.* v. *Bovill* [1856] 3 Macqueen HL 1, 16.

Case *Edelstein* v. *Schuler & Co* [1902] 2 KB 144, 154.

Case C-270/12, *United Kingdom* v. *Council of the European Union and European Parliament* [2014].

Case C-264/14, *Skatteverket* v. *David Hedqvist* [2015] ECR 718.

Case E-9/17, *Edmund Falkenhahn AG* v. *The Liechtenstein Financial Market Authority (Finanzmarktaufsicht)* [2018] EFTA.

Case C-19/11, *Geltl v. Daimler AG* [2012] ECJ of 28 June 2012.

Case C-628/13, *Lafonta v. AMF* [2015] ECJ of 11 March 2015.

Case *Ion Sciences Ltd. and Duncan Johns* v. *Persons Unknown and others* [2020].

Case *Commodity Futures Trading Commission* v. *Ooki DAO* [2022] US District Court, Northern District of California, 3:22-cv-05416-WHO.

Case *Osbourne* v. *(1) Persons Unknown and (2) Ozone Networks Inc.* [2022] EWHC 1021.

Case *Tulip Trading Ltd.* v. *Bitcoin Association for BSV and Others* [2022] EWHC 667.

Case *Commodity Futures Trading Commission (CFTC)* v. *Changpeng Zhao, Binance Holdings Limited, Binance Holdings (IE) Limited, Binance (Services) Holdings Limited, and Samuel Lim.* [2024] US 1:23-cv-01887. www.courtlistener.com/docket/67092867/commodity-futures-trading-commission-v-zhao/ (last accessed on 1 October 2024).

Case 9-56, *Meroni & Co., Industrie Metallurgiche, SpA* v. *High Authority of the European Coal and Steel Community*, ECJ [1957]

Case 10-56, *Meroni & Co., Industrie Metallurgiche, società in accomandita semplice* v. *High Authority of the European Coal and Steel Community*, ECJ [1958]

Table of Legislation

Unfair Terms in Consumer Contracts Directive. Council Directive 93/13/EEC of 5 April 1993 on unfair terms in consumer contracts

ICSD: Directive 97/9/EC of the European Parliament and of the Council of 3 March 1997 on investor-compensation schemes

SFD: Directive 98/26/EC of the European Parliament and of the Council of 19 May 1998 on settlement finality in payment and securities settlement systems

MiFID: Directive 2004/39/EC of the European Parliament and of the Council of 21 April 2004 on markets in financial instruments amending Council Directives 85/611/EEC and 93/6/EEC and Directive 2000/12/EC of the European Parliament and of the Council and repealing Council Directive 93/22/EEC

TD: Directive 2004/109/EC of the European Parliament and of the Council of 15 December 2004 on the harmonisation of transparency requirements in relation to information about issuers whose securities are admitted to trading on a regulated market and amending Directive 2001/34/EC

Unfair Commercial Practices Directive: Directive 2005/29/EC of the European Parliament and of the Council of 11 May 2005 concerning unfair business-to-consumer commercial practices in the internal market and amending Council Directive 84/450/EEC, Directives 97/7/EC, 98/27/EC, and 2002/65/EC of the European Parliament and of the Council and Regulation (EC) No. 2006/2004 of the European Parliament and of the Council

VAT Directive: Council Directive 2006/112/EC of 28 November 2006 on the common system of value added tax

PSD1: Directive 2007/64/EC of the European Parliament and of the Council of 13 November 2007 on payment services in the internal market amending Directives 97/7/EC, 2002/65/EC, 2005/60/EC, and 2006/48/EC and repealing Directive 97/5/EC

TFEU: Consolidated version of the Treaty on the Functioning of the European Union created on 17 December 2007 (Treaty of Lisbon)

UCITSD: Directive 2009/65/EC of the European Parliament and of the Council of 13 July 2009 on the coordination of laws, regulations, and administrative provisions relating to undertakings for collective investment in transferable securities

EMD II: Directive 2009/110/EC of the European Parliament and of the Council of 16 September 2009 on the taking up, pursuit, and prudential supervision of the business of electronic money institutions amending Directives 2005/60/EC and 2006/48/EC and repealing E-money Directive I 2000/46/EC

Solvency II Directive: Directive 2009/138/EC of the European Parliament and of the Council of 25 November 2009 on the taking-up and pursuit of the business of Insurance and Reinsurance

Commission Directive 2010/43/EU of 1 July 2010 implementing Directive 2009/65/EC of the European Parliament and of the Council as regards organisational requirements, conflicts of interest, conduct of business, risk management, and content of the agreement between a depositary and a management company

EBA Regulation (EU) No. 1093/2010 of the European Parliament and of the Council of 24 November 2010 establishing a European Supervisory Authority (European Banking Authority), amending Decision No. 716/2009/EC and repealing Commission Decision 2009/78/EC

AIFMD: Directive 2011/61/EU of the European Parliament and of the Council of 8 June 2011 on Alternative Investment Fund Managers and amending Directives 2003/41/EC and 2009/65/EC and Regulations (EC) No. 1060/2009 and (EU) No. 1095/2010

Consumer Rights Directive: Directive 2011/83/EU of the European Parliament and of the Council of 25 October 2011 on consumer rights, amending Council Directive 93/13/EEC and Directive 1999/44/EC of the European Parliament and of the Council and repealing Council Directive 85/577/EEC and Directive 97/7/EC of the European Parliament and of the Council

SSR: Regulation (EU) No. 236/2012 of the European Parliament and of the Council of 14 March 2012 on short selling and certain aspects of credit default swaps

EMIR: Regulation (EU) No. 648/2012 of the European Parliament and of the Council of 4 July 2012 on OTC derivatives, central counterparties, and trade repositories

AIFMR: Commission Delegated Regulation (EU) No. 231/2013 of 19 December 2012 supplementing Directive 2011/61/EU of the European Parliament and of the Council with regard to exemptions, general operating conditions, depositaries, leverage, transparency, and supervision

CRR: Regulation (EU) No. 575/2013 of the European Parliament and of the Council of 26 June 2013 on prudential requirements for credit institutions and investment firms and amending Regulation (EU) No. 648/2012

CRD: Directive 2013/36/EU of the European Parliament and of the Council of 26 June 2013 on access to the activity of credit institutions and the prudential supervision of credit institutions and investment firms, amending Directive 2002/87/EC and repealing Directives 2006/48/EC and 2006/49/EC

SSMR: Council Regulation (EU) No. 1024/2013 of 15 October 2013 conferring specific tasks on the European Central Bank concerning policies relating to the prudential supervision of credit institutions

MAR: Regulation (EU) No. 596/2014 of the European Parliament and of the Council of 16 April 2014 on market abuse (market abuse regulation) and repealing Directive 2003/6/EC of the European Parliament and of the Council and Commission Directives 2003/124/EC, 2003/125/EC, and 2004/72/EC

MAD: Directive 2014/57/EU of the European Parliament and of the Council of 16 April 2014 on criminal sanctions for market abuse (market abuse directive)

DGSD: Directive 2014/49/EU of the European Parliament and of the Council of 16 April 2014 on deposit guarantee schemes

SSM Framework Regulation: Regulation (EU) No. 468/2014 of the European Central Bank of 16 April 2014 establishing the framework for cooperation within the Single Supervisory Mechanism between the European Central Bank and national competent authorities and with national designated authorities

MiFID II: Directive 2014/65/EU of the European Parliament and of the Council of 15 May 2014 on markets in financial instruments and amending Directive 2002/92/EC and Directive 2011/61/EU

UCITSD V (Latest Version): Directive 2014/91/EU of the European Parliament and of the Council of 23 July 2014 amending Directive 2009/65/EC on the coordination of laws, regulations, and administrative provisions relating to undertakings for collective investment in transferable securities (UCITS) as regards depositary functions, remuneration policies, and sanctions

MiFIR: Regulation (EU) No. 600/2014 of the European Parliament and of the Council of 15 May 2014 on markets in financial instruments and amending Regulation (EU) No. 648/2012

CSDR: Regulation (EU) No. 909/2014 of the European Parliament and of the Council of 23 July 2014 on improving securities settlement in the European Union and on central securities depositories and amending Directives 98/26/EC and 2014/65/EU and Regulation (EU) No. 236/2012

ELTIF: Regulation (EU) 2015/760 of the European Parliament and of the Council of 29 April 2015 on European long-term investment funds

AMLD: Directive (EU) 2015/849 of the European Parliament and of the Council of 20 May 2015 on the prevention of the use of the financial system for the purposes of money laundering or terrorist financing, amending Regulation (EU) No. 648/2012 of the European Parliament and of the Council and repealing Directive 2005/60/EC of the European Parliament and of the Council and Commission Directive 2006/70/EC

PSD2: Directive (EU) 2015/2366 of the European Parliament and of the Council of 25 November 2015 on payment services in the internal market, amending Directives 2002/65/EC, 2009/110/EC, and 2013/36/EU and Regulation (EU) No. 1093/2010 and repealing Directive 2007/64/EC

Commission Delegated Directive (EU) 2017/593 of 7 April 2016 supplementing Directive 2014/65/EU of the European Parliament and of the Council with regard to safeguarding of financial instruments and funds belonging to clients, product governance obligations, and the rules applicable to the provision or reception of fees, commissions, or any monetary or non-monetary benefits

Commission Delegated Regulation (EU) 2017/565 of 25 April 2016 supplementing Directive 2014/65/EU of the European Parliament and of the Council as regards organisational requirements and operating conditions for investment firms and defined terms for the purposes of that Directive

GDPR: Regulation (EU) 2016/679 of the European Parliament and of the Council of 27 April 2016 on the protection of natural persons with regard to the processing of personal data and on the free movement of such data, and repealing Directive 95/46/EC (General Data Protection Regulation)

NIS I: Directive (EU) 2016/1148 of the European Parliament and of the Council of 6 July 2016 concerning measures for a high common level of security of network and information systems across the Union

Prospectus Regulation: Regulation (EU) 2017/1129 of the European Parliament and of the Council of 14 June 2017 on the prospectus to be published when securities are offered to the public or admitted to trading on a regulated market, and repealing Directive 2003/71/EC

MMFR: Regulation (EU) 2017/1131 of the European Parliament and of the Council of 14 June 2017 on money market funds

UNCITRAL Model Law on Electronic Transferable Records adopted by the United Nations Commission on International Trade Law on 13 July 2017

Regulation (EU) 2017/2402 of the European Parliament and of the Council of 12 December 2017 laying down a general framework for securitisation and creating a specific framework for simple, transparent, and standardised securitisation and amending Directives 2009/65/EC, 2009/138/EC, and 2011/61/EU and Regulations (EC) No. 1060/2009 and (EU) No. 648/2012

Virtual Financial Assets Act: An Act to regulate the field of Initial Virtual Financial Asset Offerings and Virtual Financial Assets and to make provision for matters ancillary or incidental thereto or connected therewith, drafted on 1 November 2018

Blockchain I: Loi du 1er mars 2019 portant modification de la loi modifiée du 1er août 2001 concernant la circulation de titres.

Regulation (EU) 2019/2088 of the European Parliament and of the Council of 27 November 2019 on sustainability-related disclosures in the financial services sector

Regulation (EU) 2020/852 of the European Parliament and of the Council of 18 June 2020 on the establishment of a framework to facilitate sustainable investment and amending Regulation (EU) 2019/2088

SFDR: Regulation (EU) 2019/2088 of the European Parliament and of the Council of 27 November 2019 on sustainability-related disclosures in the financial services sector

Blockchain II: Loi du 22 janvier 2021 portant modification de la loi modifiée du 5 avril 1993 relative au secteur financier et de la loi du 6 avril 2013 relative aux titres dématérialisés.

AMLD6, adopted on 20 July 2021 replacing the existing Directive 2015/849/EU (AMLD4 directive, as amended by Directive 2018/843, AMLD5 directive)

PilotR: Regulation (EU) 2022/858 of the European Parliament and of the Council of 30 May 2022 on a pilot regime for market infrastructures based on distributed ledger technology and amending Regulations (EU) No. 600/2014 and (EU) No. 909/2014 and Directive 2014/65/EU

ELI Principles on Blockchain Technology and Smart Contracts approved by the ELI Council on 5 July 2022 and by the ELI Membership on 8 September 2022

DORA: Regulation of the European Parliament and the Council adopted in November 2022 on digital operational resilience for the financial sector and amending Regulations (EC) No. 1060/2009, (EU) No. 648/2012, (EU) No. 600/2014, and (EU) No. 909/2014

Directive (EU) 2022/2464 of the European Parliament and of the Council of 14 December 2022 amending Regulation (EU) No. 537/2014, Directive 2004/109/EC, Directive 2006/43/EC, and Directive 2013/34/EU, as regards corporate sustainability reporting

NIS II: Directive (EU) 2022/2555 of the European Parliament and of the Council of 14 December 2022 on measures for a high common level of cybersecurity across the Union, amending Regulation (EU) No. 910/2014 and Directive (EU) 2018/1972 and repealing Directive (EU) 2016/1148

Directive (EU) 2022/2557 of the European Parliament and of the Council of 14 December 2022 on the resilience of critical entities and repealing Council Directive 2008/114/EC

UNIDROIT Principles on Digital Assets and Private Law adopted by the International Institute for the Unification of Private Law on 10 May 2023

Directive (EU) 2022/2464 of the European Parliament and of the Council of 14 December 2022 amending Regulation (EU) No. 537/2014, Directive 2004/109/EC, Directive 2006/43/EC, and Directive 2013/34/EU, as regards corporate sustainability reporting

MiCA: Regulation (EU) 2023/1114 of the European Parliament and of the Council of 31 May 2023 on Markets in Crypto-Assets and amending Directive (EU) 2019/1937

TFR: Regulation (EU) 2023/1113 of the European Parliament and the Council of 31 May 2023 on information accompanying transfers of funds and certain cryptoassets and amending Directive (EU) 2015/849

EU Data Act, Regulation (EU) 2023/2854 of the European Parliament and of the Council of 13 December 2023 on harmonised rules on fair access to and use of data and amending Regulation (EU) 2017/2394 and Directive (EU) 2020/1828 (Data Act)

AMLAR: Regulation (EU) 2024/1620 of the European Parliament and of the Council of 31 May 2024 establishing the Authority for Anti-money Laundering and Countering the Financing of Terrorism and amending Regulations (EU) No. 1093/2010, (EU) No. 1094/2010, and (EU) No. 1095/2010

Abbreviations

AIF	Alternative Investment Fund
AIFMD	Alternative Investment Fund Managers Directive
AIFMR	Alternative Investment Fund Managers Regulation
AMF	FR: Autorité des marchés financiers
AML/CTF	Anti-money Laundering and Counter-Terrorism Financing
AMLA	Anti-money Laundering Authority
AMLD	Anti-money Laundering Directive
AMLR	Anti-money Laundering Regulation
AMLAR	Anti-money Laundering Authority Regulation
API	application programming interfaces
ARTs	asset-referenced tokens
BaFIN	GER: Bundesanstalt für Finanzdienstleistungsaufsicht
BAT	Basic Attention Token
BIS	Bank for International Settlements
CAS	cryptoasset service
CASP	cryptoasset service provider
CBDC	central bank digital currencies
CDD	Customer Due Diligence
CeFi	centralised finance
CER	resilience of critical entities
CEX	centralised exchanges
CFTC	Commodity Futures Trading Commission
CIU	Collective Investment Undertaking
CRA	credit rating agency
CRD	Capital Requirements Directive
CRR	Capital Requirement Regulation
CSD	central securities depository
CSDR	Central Securities Depositories Regulation
DAO	Decentralised Autonomous Organisation
dApps	decentralised Applications
DDOS	distributed denial of service
DeFi	decentralised finance
DEX	decentralized exchanges

DFS 2020	Digital Finance Strategy 2020
DGSD	Deposit Guarantee Schemes Directive
DLT	distributed ledger technology
DORA	Digital Operational Resilience Act
DPoS	Delegated Proof of Stake
DTCC	Depository Trust and Clearing Corporation
e-money	electronic money
EBA	European Banking Authority
ECB	European Central Bank
EEA	European Economic Area
eEUR	Stablecoin by e-money A/S
EFTA	European Free Trade Association
EIOPA	European Insurance and Occupational Pensions Authority
ELTIF	European Long-term Investment Funds
EMIR	European Market Infrastructure Regulation
EMD	E-money Directive
EMTs	e-money tokens
ENISA	European Network and Information Security Agency
ERC-20	Ethereum Request for Comment 20
ESA	European Supervisory Authority
ESMA	European Securities and Markets Authority
ETF	exchange-traded fund
ETH	Ether
EU	European Union
EU FSAs	Financial Supervisory Authorities in the EU
EURS	Stasis Euro
eWpG	GER: elektronisches Wertpapier Gesetz
FATF	Financial Action Task Force
Finfluencer	financial influencer
FinTech	financial technology
FIU	Financial Intelligence Unit
FMI	Financial Market Infrastructure
FSAP	Financial Stability Action Plan
FSB	Financial Stability Board
FTX	Futures Exchange (company)
GDP	gross domestic product
GDPR	General Data Protection Regulation
GmbH&Co	GER: Gesellschaft mit beschränkter Haftung & Compagnie Komm
KG	anditgesellschaft
ICO	initial coin offering
ICSD	Investor-Compensation Schemes Directive
ICT	information and communication technology
IOSCO	International Organization of Securities Commissions
IPO	Initial Public Offering
ITS	implementing technical standards
KYC	know your customer
LEI	Legal Entity Identifier

MAD	Market Abuse Directive
ManCo	management company
MAR	Market Abuse Regulation
MiCA	Markets in Crypto-Assets Regulation
MiFID	Markets in Financial Instruments Directive
MiFIR	Markets in Financial Instruments Regulation
ML	Money-Laundering
MMFR	Money Market Funds Regulation
MMoU	Multilateral Memorandum of Understanding
MTFs	multilateral trading facility
mUSD	mStable US Dollar
NCA	national competent authority
NFT	non-fungible token
NIS	Network and Information Systems Regulation
OJEU	*Official Journal of the European Union*
PAXG	Pax Gold stablecoin
PilotR	Pilot Regulation
PoS	Proof of Stake
PoW	Proof of Work
PR	Prospectus Regulation
PSD	Payment Services Directive
PSP	payment service provide
RegTech	Regulatory Technology
RTS	regulatory technical standards
SEC	U.S. Securities and Exchange Commission
SEO	Search Engine Optimisation
SFD	Settlement Finality Directive
SICI	systemically important crypto intermediaries
SMEs	small and medium-sized enterprises
SPV	special-purpose vehicle
SS	Settlement System
SSM	Single Supervisory Mechanism
SSR	Short Selling Regulation
SSS	Securities Settlement System
STO	Security Token Offering
TIBER-EU	European framework for Threat Intelligence-Based Ethical Red-teaming
TCP/IP	Transmission Control Protocol/Internet Protocol
TD	Transparency Directive
TF	Terrorist Financing
TFEU	Treaty of the Functioning of the EU
TFR	Transfer of Funds Regulation
TLPT	threat-led penetration testing
TSS	Trading and Settlement System
UCITSD	Undertakings for Collective Investment in Transferable Securities Directive
UNCITRAL	United Nations Commission on International Trade Law
UNIDROIT	International Institute for the Unification of Private Law

USD	United States dollar
USDC	United States dollar coin
USDT	US dollars by Tether
VASP	virtual asset service provider
VAT	value-added tax
VC	venture capital

1

Introduction

1.1 SUBJECT MATTER: CRYPTOASSETS

At the time of writing, more than 10,000 different cryptoassets are listed on a popular website.[1] The regulatory treatment of cryptoassets has been an area of concern since the launch of Bitcoin in 2009; regulators' activities then accelerated against the background of the crypto bubble of 2018[2] and Facebook's proposal for the creation of Libra in 2019, now renamed 'Diem', a stablecoin project with potentially global reach and dimensions.[3] Attention increased further in response to the 2022–23 Crypto Winter that followed a piling up of malfunctions, hacks, and frauds since 2021 and resulted in prominent systems malfunctioning, billions of US dollars' worth of losses spreading through decentralised finance (DeFi) systems, and eventually the collapse and bankruptcy of several prominent market participants including FTX Trading Ltd. (FTX), Silicon Valley Bank, and Signature Bank.[4]

While a globally uniform definition is lacking, the EU's Market in Crypto-Assets (MiCA)[5] Regulation defines cryptoassets as 'a digital representation of a value or of a right that is able to be transferred and stored electronically using distributed ledger technology [DLT] or similar technology',[6] where a distributed ledger is 'an information repository that keeps records of transactions and that is shared across, and synchronised between, a set of DLT network nodes using a consensus mechanism'.[7] The various nodes together function as one ledger.[8] Coupled

[1] CoinMarketCap.com, 'Today's Cryptocurrency Prices by Market Cap'. Website https://coinmarketcap.com/ (last accessed on 1 October 2024).

[2] See D. A. Zetzsche, R. P. Buckley, D. W. Arner and L. Föhr, 'The ICO Gold Rush: It's a Scam, It's a Bubble, It's a Super Challenge for Regulators', *Harvard International Law Journal*, 63(2) (2019): 267.

[3] See D. A. Zetzsche, R. P. Buckley and D. W. Arner, 'Regulating Libra', *Oxford Journal of Legal Studies*, 41(1) (2021): 80; D. W. Arner *et al.*, 'Stablecoins: Risks, Potential and Regulation', Working Paper No. 905. Bank for International Settlements (2020). Website www.bis.org/publ/work905.htm (last accessed on 1 October 2024).

[4] See D. A. Zetzsche *et al.*, 'Remaining Regulatory Challenges in Digital Finance and Crypto-Assets after MiCA', Committee on Economic and Monetary Affairs (ECON) (2023). Website http://dx.doi.org/10.2139/ssrn.4487516 (last accessed on 1 October 2024).

[5] Regulation 2023/1114 of the European Parliament and of the Council of 31 May 2023 on Markets in Crypto-Assets, and amending Regulations (EU) No. 1093/2010 and (EU) No. 1095/2010 and Directives 2013/36/EU and (EU) 2019/1937, OJ 2023 No. L150, 9 June 2023.

[6] Article 3(1)(5) of MiCA, Regulation 2023/1114, OJ 2023 No. L150.

[7] Article 3(1)(2) of MiCA.

[8] D. Mills *et al.*, 'Distributed Ledger Technology in Payments, Clearing, and Settlement', Working Paper No. 2016-095. Federal Reserve Board, Finance and Economics Discussion Series (2016), pp. 10–11.

with cryptographic solutions and a blockchain protocol,[9] distributed ledgers may curtail the risk of data manipulation and increase transparency for all ledger participants (nodes), thereby offering a solution to the perennial trust problem with regard to the content of stored data.

This allows for new, disintermediated models of finance (i.e., DeFi)[10] and financial services where the defining element is the type of technology used rather than the economic features of the assets or services itself, which we discuss throughout this book. In particular, Chapter 2 introduces the technical concept, after which Chapters 3 and 4 outline the legal definitions underlying MiCA.

Academics have classified cryptoassets into the following categories:[11]

Currency/payment tokens aim to fulfil the economic purpose of money, which is to serve as a means of exchange, storage of value, and unit of account.[12] While Bitcoin is the most widely known example in this category, many other currency tokens exist, including *stablecoins*, which are designed to keep a stable value against other assets – typically (a basket of) fiat currencies. Meanwhile, central bank digital currencies (CBDCs) are payment tokens issued by central banks that substitute for fiat currency and are characterised by the respective central bank(s) functioning as the issuer.[13] Given their public background, CBDCs are often exempted from cryptoasset regulation, as provided for in Article 2(2)(c) MiCA.

Security/financial/investment tokens are tied to an underlying asset and represent ownership of a share of the overall asset – just like conventional shares and bonds. Hence, they are typically treated by financial regulation as financial instruments.

Utility tokens are the collective term for other fungible tokens that provide some sort of access or right(s) to a company's ecosystem, goods, or services.[14] Examples include a licence to use

9 See, for example, P. De Filippi and A. Wright, *Blockchain and the Law: The Rule of Code* (Cambridge, MA: Harvard University Press, 2018), pp. 13–57 (describing blockchains) and 136–40 (arguing that widespread deployment of the blockchain will lead to tech-based business practices that could prompt a loss in importance of centralised authorities, such as government, and urging a more active regulatory approach); M. Finck, *Blockchain Regulation and Governance in Europe* (Cambridge: Cambridge University Press, 2019), pp. 12–14; see also S. Davidson, P. De Filippi and J. Potts, 'Blockchains and the Economic Institutions of Capitalism', *Journal of Institutional Economics*, 14 (4) (2017): 639, 641 (arguing that blockchain technology is a new governance institution that competes with other economic institutions of capitalism, namely, firms, markets, networks, and even governments).

10 See D. A. Zetzsche, D. W. Arner and R. P. Buckley, 'Decentralized Finance (DeFi)', *Journal of Financial Regulation*, 6(2) (2020): 172–203.

11 See P. Hacker and C. Thomale, 'Crypto-Securities Regulation: ICOs, Token Sales and Cryptocurrencies under EU Financial Law', *European Company and Financial Law Review*, 15(4) (2018): 645, 652–53; F. Annunziata, 'Speak If You Can: What Are You? An Alternative Approach to the Qualification of Tokens and Initial Coin Offerings', *European Company and Financial Law Review*, 17(2) (2020): 129, 136–37; I. M. Barsan, 'Legal Challenges of Initial Coin Offerings', *Revue trimestrielle de droit financier*, 3 (2017): 54, 62 (identifying only "currency like" and "security like" tokens); P. Maume and M. Fromberger, 'Regulations of Initial Coin Offerings: Reconciling U.S. and E.U. Securities Laws', *Chicago Journal of International Law*, 19 (2019): 548, 558; Zetzsche *et al.*, 'The ICO Gold Rush', 267, 276 (arguing for a functional approach). See also the distinction between 'app tokens' and 'protocol tokens' by J. Rohr and A. Wright, 'Blockchain-Based Token Sales, Initial Coin Offerings, and the Democratization of Public Capital Markets', *Hastings Law Journal*, 70 (2019): 463, 469.

12 B. Geva, 'Cryptocurrencies and the Evolution of Banking, Money, and Payments', in C. Brummer (ed.), *Cryptoassets: Legal, Regulatory, and Monetary Perspectives* (Oxford: Oxford University Press, 2019), p. 12.

13 See Committee on Payments and Market Infrastructures and Markets Committee, 'Central Bank Digital Currencies', Papers No. 174, Bank for International Settlements (2018). Website www.bis.org/cpmi/publ/d174.htm (last accessed on 1 October 2024).

14 The term is now defined in Article 3(1)(9) MiCA as 'a type of crypto-asset that is only intended to provide access to a good or a service supplied by its issuer'.

a software program (i.e., a usage token) or membership in a community (i.e., a community token).

Beyond these three broad categories, non-fungible tokens (NFTs) represent a unique personalised digital item such as digital art, audio, videos, or items in video games.

We discuss the classification of cryptoassets in the context of EU financial law as well as MiCA's scope in Chapters 3 and 4 of this book.

1.2 OPPORTUNITIES ASSOCIATED WITH CRYPTOASSETS

1.2.1 *Opportunities for Issuers*

1.2.1.1 Access to Finance

With digitalising of the process of issuing and transferring financial assets, cryptoassets may be instrumental in streamlining capital-raising processes for companies and enhancing competition among financial intermediaries, effectively offering small and medium-sized enterprises (SMEs) the option to raise money from the public in ways that were only available to large companies in the past.[15] Framed in political jargon, one may coin this phenomenon as the 'democratisation of finance'. Yet, the issuance of tokens is no panacea: discounts of up to 50 per cent are often offered to early lead investors, and issuers now increasingly also realise that they must engage legal and other professional advisors in the process.[16]

1.2.1.2 New Types of Investors

Traditionally, SMEs often rely on venture capital (VC) firms for funding. This is a challenge for many companies because VCs frequently have strict criteria for what companies to invest in and typically force investor-friendly terms upon them.[17] Further, in some regions, VC funds are small, prompting the need to tap into foreign institutional VC funds with their own expectations (for instance, a listing at a US exchange in case an initial public offering (IPO) takes place in the future of the company). Hence, the option of issuing tokens instead now offers companies an alternative source of capital,[18] which also provides some leverage in negotiations with VCs. Through borderless online sales, tokens also offer access to global capital without the typical legal and business hurdles encountered in conventional VC financing.[19]

1.2.2 *Opportunities for Investors*

1.2.2.1 Access to Capital Markets

Just as companies get access to new types of investors, retail investors also gain access to investment opportunities in highly innovative businesses usually not accessible to these investor classes, given that VC investing tends to be reserved for institutional investors and high-net-worth individuals. Hence, retail investors can access a global pool of investment opportunities with potentially higher returns (and higher risk) than they would in the conventional capital markets.

[15] See Zetzsche *et al.*, 'The ICO Gold Rush', 267, 304; ESMA, 'Advice: Initial Coin Offerings and Crypto-Assets', ESMA50–157-1391 (2019). Website www.esma.europa.eu/document/advice-initial-coin-offerings-and-crypto-assets (last accessed on 1 October 2024). The concept of token offerings is further discussed in Chapter 2.

[16] See W. A. Kaal, 'Digital Asset Market Evolution', *Journal of Corporation Law*, 46(4) (2021): 909, 919.

[17] For details, see P. A. Gompers and J. Lerner, *The Venture Capital Cycle*, 2nd ed. (MIT Press, 2014).

[18] See Kaal, 'Digital Asset Market Evolution', 909, 919.

[19] See Kaal, 'Digital Asset Market Evolution', 909, 919.

1.2.2.2 *Enhanced Trust, Transparency, and Liquidity*

Conventional, centralised ledgers require that market participants trust an intermediary to manage the ledger of rights to and transactions of assets. Modern well-functioning markets have established institutions that have earned a high level of trust, including central counter-parties,[20] but such markets are often not available to SMEs and their investors. Now, however, they can reap many of the same benefits through DLT and the trading of tokens on crypto exchanges, which provide liquidity to investors in early-stage companies.[21]

Furthermore, even the well-functioning capital markets of today still come with an ever-present risk of financial default, human error, crime, and external (cyber) attacks. Here, cryptoassets, launched via DLT, potentially offer transparency to ledger participants. This transparency then fosters trust among ledger participants. For instance, by providing indisputable proof of ownership, cryptoassets solve the 'double-spending problem' because the buyer can be assured that they will receive the asset and that nobody else has claims to the same asset.[22]

1.2.2.3 *Freeing Collateral through Shorter Settlement Times*

Just as cryptocurrencies can be swiftly transferred, DLT financial market infrastructures may reduce settlement times from the typical T+1 days – in some markets even T+3 days – to nearer T+0.[23] This could reduce counterparty risk;[24] in turn, less collateral would be necessary during the settlement period.[25] On the other hand, it is also argued that 'most current settlement cycles are not long because of technological limitations but because of banks' back-office processes, legal arrangements, and liquidity management practices'.[26] Sometimes, parties need time to make available their liquid assets required for the transaction.[27]

1.2.3 *Opportunities for the Financial System*

1.2.3.1 *Cost Savings from Disintermediation*

Conventional financial market infrastructures rely on a central securities depository (CSD) that holds a master copy of the centralised ledger, while intermediaries having an account with the CSD hold partial copies of the master copy. These CSD account-holding intermediaries then function as a centralised ledger for other sub-level intermediaries that have access only to these

[20] See Zetzsche *et al.*, 'Decentralized Finance', 172–203.

[21] See Kaal, 'Digital Asset Market Evolution', 909, 918.

[22] See Zetzsche *et al.*, 'Decentralized Finance', 172–203; W. A. Kaal and S. Evans, 'Blockchain-Based Securities Offerings', *UC Davies Business Law Journal*, 20(1) (2020): 89, 98–99.

[23] For example, by streamlining reconciliation and reducing the number of intermediaries. See M. Bech *et al.*, 'On the Future of Securities Settlement', *Bank for International Settlements Quarterly Review* (March 2020), pp. 67 and 75.

[24] See Bech *et al.*, 'On the Future of Securities Settlement', pp. 67 and 75.

[25] However, the cost of overnight collateral for settlement is small relative to the total cost of trade processing. See M. Mainelli and A. Milne, 'The Impact and Potential of Blockchain on the Securities Transaction Lifecycle', Working Paper No. 2015-007. SWIFT Institute (2016), p. 28.

[26] E. Benos, R. Garratt and P. Gurrola-Perez, 'The Economics of Distributed Ledger Technology for Securities Settlement', *Ledger*, 4 (2019): 121, 130.

[27] Some proposed DLTs offer differentiated settlement times for different customers. See H. Van Steenis *et al.*, 'Blockchain in Banking: Disruptive Threat or Tool?' Morgan Stanley Global Insight (2016), p. 7; Mainelli and Milne, 'The Impact and Potential of Blockchain', p. 27.

intermediaries.[28] This 'hub and spoke' system requires regular reconciliation between the various ledgers. A synchronised and shared ledger potentially enables automatic clearing, settlement, and recording of transactions without intermediaries in one step.[29] If DLT-induced transparency ensures that the same transaction information is available to everyone, clearing agents,[30] reconciliation, and back-up systems across multiple ledgers will become superfluous.[31] However, unless DLT enables netting – the practice of balancing accounts following multiple trades before clearing only the net amount owed between market participants – automated clearing would miss out on significant liquidity savings.[32]

1.2.3.2 *Enhanced Cybersecurity*

DLT has the potential to improve cybersecurity because it enables other nodes to continue operations even if one or more of the nodes are compromised. For instance, if there are n nodes (instead of one concentrated ledger) and e describes the effort necessary to compromise any single server, all other conditions being equal (safety per server, etc.), the effort needed to manipulate all of the linked servers will be $n \times e$ rather than $1 \times e$. However, despite its overall resilience, DLT is also vulnerable to certain types of attacks because it relies on a number of (potentially weak) links. For example, data are often generated by just two entities, buyer and seller, so individual trades are exposed to cyberattacks at these dual points of failures.[33] Similarly, distributed denial-of-service attacks have at times brought Bitcoin mining to a halt.[34]

1.2.3.3 *Decentralisation as a Goal in Itself?*

Many cryptoasset proponents see decentralisation as a goal in its own right, setting out to create a financial system beyond the realms of regulators and central banks.[35] This is part of a broader political agenda characterised by distrust in central institutions, including the sovereign. For example, while conventional money supply has increased through monetary policy interventions (i.e., low interest rates and bond purchases by central banks, known as 'quantitative easing') in the aftermath of the 2007–8 financial crisis and the COVID-19 pandemic, creating a potentially substantial inflationary pressure, Bitcoin supply is predetermined by algorithms and cannot be influenced by any central authority. Similarly, control over the settlement of fiat currency transactions has increasingly been used as a policy tool, most notably as part of

[28] See Mills *et al.*, 'Distributed Ledger Technology', pp. 6–7.

[29] Optimistic estimates see the cost savings potential at USD 20 billion annually, while estimates assuming increasing efficiencies in traditional systems result in no savings at all. See M. Belinky *et al.*, 'The FinTech 2.0 Paper: Rebooting Financial Services', Santander InnoVentures, Oliver Wyman, Anthemis Group (2015), p. 15.

[30] Benos *et al.*, 'The Economics of Distributed Ledger Technology', 121, 130.

[31] Benos *et al.*, 'The Economics of Distributed Ledger Technology', 121, 129–30.

[32] For example, the Depository Trust and Clearing Corporation (DTCC) is currently able to reduce the volume of trades for final settlement through netting by approximately 97 per cent. See Mainelli and Milne, 'The Impact and Potential of Blockchain'; J. Chapman *et al.*, 'Project Jasper: Are Distributed Wholesale Payment Systems Feasible Yet?' *Bank of Canada Financial System Review* (2017), p. 130. Website www.bankofcanada.ca/wp-content/uploads/2017/05/fsr-june-2017-chapman.pdf (last accessed on 1 October 2024).

[33] See D. A. Zetzsche, R. P. Buckley and D. W. Arner, 'The Distributed Liability of Distributed Ledgers: Legal Risks of Blockchain', *University of Illinois Law Review*, 4 (2018): 1361, 1377.

[34] See Zetzsche *et al.*, 'The Distributed Liability of Distributed Ledgers', 1361, 1380–81.

[35] See Zetzsche *et al.*, 'Decentralized Finance', 172–203; Kaal, 'Digital Asset Market Evolution', 909, 912; S. Nakamoto, 'Bitcoin: A Peer-to-Peer Electronic Cash System'. Website https://bitcoin.org/bitcoin.pdf (last accessed on 1 October 2024).

American foreign policy.[36] Such developments have led certain people to demand a more decentralised global financial system, which cryptoassets could help to facilitate.

1.3 CHALLENGES ASSOCIATED WITH CRYPTOASSETS

1.3.1 *Information Asymmetry*

While information asymmetry is prevalent in all financial investments to some degree, the highly innovative cryptoasset markets are characterised by an *enhanced* degree of information asymmetry between, on the one hand, issuers and service providers, which possess the most knowledge about the financial assets they offer, and, on the other, the clients and investors that provide the funds for cryptoassets. Basic documentation is often misleading or completely lacking in cryptoasset offerings,[37] and it is difficult for investors to verify if the underlying computer code is compatible with the promises made by the issuer. Illustratively, some token offerings have been unmasked as scams and Ponzi schemes.[38]

1.3.2 *Legal Uncertainty*

EU financial law has evolved into multiple pieces of legislation, each with limited scope and applying to different types of financial assets and service providers. The emergence of cryptoassets raises the question of whether and to what extent this existing legislation applies to cryptoassets as a new type of financial asset. The answer depends on the definitions of existing financial products which were not drafted with cryptoassets in mind. This serves, for instance, as background for the discussion on whether stablecoins qualify as financial instruments, transferable securities, derivatives, collective investment schemes, units of account, e-money, commodities, or deposits, or more than one of these simultaneously.[39]

[36] See, for example, *The Economist*, 'America's Aggressive Use of Sanctions Endangers the Dollar's Reign' (18 January 2020). Website www.economist.com/briefing/2020/01/18/americas-aggressive-use-of-sanctions-endangers-the-dollars-reign?utm_medium = cpc.adword.pd&utm_source = google&ppccampaignID = 18151738051&ppcadID = &utm_campaign = a.22brand_pmax&utm_content = conversion.direct-response.anonymous&gad_source = 1&gclid = EAIaIQobChMIjrOEkrTjhwMVCQqiAxofQxDGEAAYASAAEgKQb_D_BwE&gclsrc = aw.ds (last accessed on 1 October 2024); For a detailed analysis see D. W. Arner, R. P. Buckley, D. A. Zetzsche, and A. N. Didenko, 'Monetary Hegemony, Technological Evolution and the International Monetary System', *Boston University Journal of International law*, 42 (2024) (in press).

[37] See Zetzsche *et al.*, 'The ICO Gold Rush', 267, 287.

[38] See, e.g., Munchee Inc., 'Securities Act of 1933, Release No. 10445', U.S. Securities and Exchange Commission (2017). Website https://perma.cc/ET52-T99G (last accessed on 1 October 2024); U.S. Securities and Exchange Commission, 'SEC Exposes Two Initial Coin Offerings Purportedly Backed by Real Estate and Diamonds', Press Release (2017). Website https://perma.cc/4GJW-QSWU (last accessed on 1 October 2024); U.S. Securities and Exchange Commission, 'SEC Emergency Action Halts ICO Scam', Press Release (2017). Website https://perma.cc/SG8A-YXRY (last accessed on 1 October 2024); Swiss Financial Market Supervisory Authority ('FINMA'), 'FINMA Closes Down Coin Providers and Issues Warning about Fake Cryptocurrencies', Press Release (2017). Website https://perma.cc/B8TD-TW7N (last accessed on 1 October 2024). Cf. Bitcoin Exchange Guide News Team, 'Top 5 Biggest 2018 ICO Scams, Ponzi Schemes, Crypto Thefts & Hacks So Far Bitcoin Exchange Guide' (2018). Website https://perma.cc/UPY4-FT8M (last accessed on 1 October 2024); A. Tomasicchio, 'Top 5 Cryptocurrency Scams', Bitcoin Chaser (2023). Website https://bitcoinchaser.com/top-5-cryptocurrency-scams (last accessed on 1 October 2024).

[39] See V. Burilov, 'Regulation of Crypto Tokens and Initial Coin Offerings in the EU', *European Journal of Comparative Law and Governance*, 6(2) (2019): 146 (arguing that EU regulators shall first ensure legal certainty by defining the scope of tokenised financial instruments).

1.3.3 *Regulatory Arbitrage*

Legal uncertainty, combined with deviations in how EU directives are implemented into national law, leads to divergence in the enforcement of EU financial law across Member States. This again results in a significant risk of regulatory arbitrage, where issuers and service providers seek out the most favourable and possibly laxest regulatory environment for their purposes, potentially at the expense of effective financial supervision and enforcement.

1.3.4 *Innovators as Intermediaries*

As is the case in other FinTech domains, many leading participants operating in the cryptoasset space tend to be newly established innovators. Consequently, they typically lack capital buffers, experience, and any reputation or track record. This makes it difficult for regulators to assess the real risks involved and to focus the attention of law enforcement on the riskiest sub-domains of the cryptoasset space.

1.3.5 *Ledger and Data Governance*

Given that DLT relies on algorithms and a potentially large number of nodes, questions arise as to who is practically and legally accountable for its operations. At least from a practical perspective, such problems may not be immediately apparent, but DLT often relies on code that is constantly rewritten to improve performance and security.[40] Therefore, over time, fewer and fewer experts will understand the structure, leading to an increased risk of coding errors.[41] At the same time, the standardisation and automation inherent to DeFi mean that any coding error may spread and affect the entire system more easily as compared to centralised finance (CeFi).[42] Such operational risks further pose the question of legal accountability. Moreover, if the servers are located in different jurisdictions with no central entity, there is also uncertainty as to which laws apply and which courts could rightfully assert jurisdiction.[43]

In addition, there are data governance and privacy concerns, given that DLT relies on data storage across multiple nodes, so each node operator has access to data stored on the ledger.[44] This arouses new worries over data privacy, insider trading, and market abuse.[45] Because DLT is supposed to be immutable, there are also concerns over how to change falsified information, for instance, in response to a court decision that requires the title to an asset to be updated on the ledger.

1.3.6 *Illegal Activities*

Due to the anonymity enabled by identity verification through cryptographic keys, cryptoassets have, since their infancy, been widely used to facilitate illegal activities.[46] This includes the

[40] See A. Walch, 'The Bitcoin Blockchain as Financial Market Infrastructure: A Consideration of Operational Risk', *New York University Journal of Legislation and Public Policy*, 18 (2015): 837, 865–67.

[41] Zetzsche *et al.*, 'The Distributed Liability of Distributed Ledgers', 1361, 1381; Q. DuPont and B. Maurer, 'Ledgers and Law in the Blockchain', *King's Review* (23 June 2015). Website www.kingsreview.co.uk/essays/ledgers-and-law-in-the-blockchain (last accessed on 1 October 2024).

[42] See ESMA, 'The Distributed Ledger Technology Applied to Securities Markets' (2017), para. 36.

[43] See P. Athanassiou, 'Impact of Digital Innovation on the Processing of Electronic Payments and Contracting: An Overview of Legal Risks, Legal', Working Paper Series No. 37, 16. European Central Bank (2017), pp. 30–31.

[44] For example, the DLT supporting Bitcoin stores all data except the identity of the owners, which requires a private key.

[45] See Zetzsche *et al.*, 'The Distributed Liability of Distributed Ledgers', 1361, 1375.

[46] S. Foley, J. R. Karlsen and T. J. Putnins, 'Sex, Drugs, and Bitcoin: How Much Illegal Activity Is Financed through Cryptocurrencies?', *Review of Financial Studies*, (2018): 26. Website http://dx.doi.org/10.2139/ssrn.3102645 (last accessed on 1 October 2024).

transacting of illegal goods and services (e.g., weapons, drugs, and counterfeit documents, typically through 'darknet' marketplaces online), money laundering, evasion of capital controls, ransomware attacks, and theft.[47] Furthermore, the cryptographic keys may themselves be obtained through fraudulent behaviour, theft, or otherwise, while there is currently no satisfactory system for recovering or replacing such keys.[48]

1.4 REGULATORY OBJECTIVES

MiCA, the Pilot Regulation (PilotR), the Digital Operational Resilience Act (DORA), and the revised Transfer of Funds Regulation (TFR) adopted in the context of the Digital Finance Strategy 2020 (DFS 2020) policy agenda[49] pursue six objectives which reflect, all in all, the regulatory objectives of all EU financial regulations.[50]

1.4.1 *Legal Certainty through Technology Neutrality*

First and foremost, the DFS 2020 aims to enhance legal certainty for three reasons. First, legal certainty reduces regulatory arbitrage. Second, legal certainty may be useful in related domains such as valuation for tax purposes, identification of ownership for Anti-money Laundering (AML) purposes, and the application of data protection rules (i.e., General Data Protection Regulation, GDPR). Third, legal certainty reduces transaction costs and thus enhances the efficiency of the European Single Market (see Section 1.4.6). The DFS 2020 thus seeks to establish a 'future-proof' legal framework, which is 'technology-neutral' by addressing the underlying realities of financial products and services rather than the use of a specific technology.[51] While we approve of technology neutrality as a general approach, it does not, however, solve the underlying problem of determining which pieces of EU financial law apply to which types of cryptoassets (cf. Chapter 4 on MiCA's scope).

1.4.2 *Consumer and Investor Protection*

The DFS 2020 sets out to ensure that 'prospective retail holders of cryptoassets should be informed of the characteristics, functions and risks of the cryptoassets that they intend to purchase',[52] by requiring extensive disclosures. Yet, some commentators argue that this purpose could have been achieved more effectively by expanding the scope of the mostly stricter existing EU financial legislation to cover cryptoassets. Less fundamental concerns surround the possibility that tech-savvy crypto-investors may anyway be more inclined to seek information elsewhere than in legal disclosure documents, while issuers face strong market incentives to provide information.[53]

[47] R. Houben and A. Snyers, 'Crypto-Assets: Key Developments, Regulatory Concerns and Responses', Committee on Economic and Monetary Affairs (ECON) (2020).

[48] See Benos *et al.*, 'The Economics of Distributed Ledger Technology', 121, 132–33.

[49] See European Commission, 'Communication on a Digital Finance Strategy for the EU', COM (2020) 591 Final.

[50] See MiCA Regulation Proposal, Explanatory Memorandum, COM (2020) 593 Final, pp. 2 and 3; PilotR Regulation Proposal, Explanatory Memorandum, COM (2020) 594 Final, p. 2.

[51] See, for example, Recital para. 9 of MiCA.

[52] Recital para. 24 of MiCA.

[53] See G. Ferrarini and P. Giudici, 'Digital Offerings and Mandatory Disclosure: A Market-Based Critique of MiCA', in E. Avgouleas and H. Marjosola (eds.), *Digital Finance in Europe: Law, Regulation and Governance* (Berlin, Boston: De Gruyter, 2022), pp. 87–207.

1.4.3 *Financial Stability*

While at the time of MiCA's adoption, EU legislators believed the threat to financial stability posed by cryptoassets to be low,[54] the potential for the emergence of global stablecoins – with Facebook's Diem being the most notable example – has since raised serious concerns.[55] In addition, the large losses suffered through scandals, frauds, and malfunctions during the Crypto Winter prompted negative spillover effects into the regulated financial sector.[56]

The DFS 2020 recognises the risks created by stablecoins 'which aim to stabilise their price by linking their value to a specific asset or a basket of assets' if characterised by a large customer base, high market capitalisation, and/or a large number of transactions. These features 'could raise additional challenges to financial stability, monetary policy transmission or monetary sovereignty'.[57] Moreover, if the share of cryptoassets in financial markets grows, the network character of DLT may also pose risks to financial stability from a 'too connected to fail' perspective.[58] For instance, if many smart contracts self-execute in response to an event, this could trigger contagion and adverse feedback loops.[59] In fact, as was vividly shown in the Terra/Luna stablecoin system, with the largest operational loss ever experienced in finance to date amounting to USD 50 billion in a couple of days,[60] frauds, hacks, and reliance on external data sources can all create these adverse feedback loops.

1.4.4 *Market Integrity*

Legislation seeking to enhance market integrity aims at establishing markets free from illicit behaviour, such as insider trading and market manipulation.[61] It intends to ensure that markets, overall, serve society rather than individuals by excluding profits from illegal activities. The DFS 2020 addresses this matter from three different angles.

First, since the extensive rules of the Market Abuse Regulation (MAR) (EU) No. 596/2014 could be overly burdensome for the typically small companies involved in crypto-markets and some concepts rely on the corporate hierarchy absent in some crypto ecosystems, Title VI MiCA provides tailor-made legislation to counter market abuse and insider trading. Second, the revised TFR (see Section 1.5.1 and Chapter 14) seeks to abolish anonymous cryptoasset transactions in

[54] See Recital para. 5 of MiCA.

[55] Financial Stability Board, 'Regulation, Supervision and Oversight of "Global Stablecoin" Arrangements' (2020), p. 13. Website www.fsb.org/2020/10/regulation-supervision-and-oversight-of-global-stablecoin-arrangements/ (last accessed on 1 October 2024); International Organisation of Securities Commission, 'Global Stablecoin Initiatives, OR01/2020' (2020), p. 17. Website www.iosco.org/library/pubdocs/pdf/IOSCOPD650.pdf (last accessed 1 October 2024); International Monetary Fund, 'Global Financial Stability Report' (2021), p. 44. Website www.imf.org/-/media/Files/Publications/GFSR/2021/October/English/text.ashx (last accessed on 1 October 2024).

[56] Cf. Zetzsche *et al.*, 'Remaining Regulatory Challenges in Digital Finance'.

[57] Recital para. 59 of MiCA.

[58] See Recital para. 3 of DORA, Regulation 2022/2554, OJ 2022 No. L333; R. P. Buckley, D. W. Arner, D. A. Zetzsche and E. Selga, 'Techrisk', *Singapore Journal of Legal Studies*, (2020): 35; Zetzsche *et al.*, 'Decentralized Finance', 172–203.

[59] See Committee on Payments and Market Infrastructures, 'Distributed Ledger Technology in Payment, Clearing and Settlement, No. 157', Bank for International Settlements (2017), p. 13.

[60] H. Uhlig, 'A Luna-tic Stablecoin Crash', Working Paper No. 2022-95. Becker Friedman Institute for Economics, University of Chicago (2022). Website http://dx.doi.org/10.2139/ssrn.4163038 (last accessed on 1 October 2024).

[61] See N. Moloney, E. Ferran and J. Payne (eds.), *The Oxford Handbook of Financial Regulation* (Oxford: Oxford University Press, 2015), p. 634.

an effort to counter a range of criminal activities. Finally, DORA[62] (see Chapter 15) is aimed at digital operational resilience, which is 'vital for ensuring financial stability and market integrity in the digital age'.[63]

1.4.5 *Innovation and Competition*

Legal uncertainty, together with high transaction and regulatory costs, could undermine efforts to use cryptoassets for digital innovation.[64] Following more recent approaches observed among regulators worldwide,[65] the DFS 2020 also seeks to enhance innovation and competition. Adopting this approach, the EU legislation finds itself in a conflict between ensuring low barriers for (new and innovative) companies to enter the market and at the same time forming regulation indispensable for other policy objectives, including consumer protection and financial stability. The DFS 2020 aims to support innovation and fair competition while ensuring a high level of consumer protection and market integrity in cryptoasset markets. An example of this balancing act is provided by virtue of the disclosure (whitepaper) rules in Title II MiCA, which are generally lighter than their Prospectus Regulation equivalents (see Chapter 5), and at the same time forego any product regulation which Titles III and IV MiCA foresee for asset-referenced tokens (ARTs) and e-money tokens (EMTs). Another example is PilotR's so-called 'sandbox' approach where EU legislators have created a controlled space with temporary derogations from existing rules to facilitate innovation while giving regulators an opportunity to learn (see Chapter 12).

1.4.6 *Efficiency of the European Single Market*

MiCA, PilotR, DORA, and the revised TFR have all been adopted as regulations (rather than directives) based on Article 114 TFEU, emphasising the harmonisation perspective.[66] The harmonisation of legislation and enforcement is a precondition for a well-functioning cross-border European Single Market, in general,[67] and, in particular, for a 'passport' regime based on the jurisdiction of the national competent authority (NCA) in the home Member State of the issuer or service provider. In turn, both MiCA and PilotR have established a 'passport' regime and an elaborate system for coordinated enforcement across NCAs, organised by the European Banking Authority (EBA) and the European Securities and Markets Authority (ESMA). This is part of the general EU agenda of increasing market efficiency

[62] Regulation (EU) 2022/2554 of the European Parliament and of the Council of 14 December 2022 on digital operational resilience for the financial sector and amending Regulations (EC) No. 1060/2009, (EU) No. 648/2012, (EU) No. 600/2014, (EU) No. 909/2014, and (EU) 2016/1011, OJ No. L333, 27 December 2022, pp. 1–79.

[63] Recital para. 8 of DORA.

[64] See Recital para. 5 of MiCA.

[65] See R. P. Buckley, D. W. Arner, R. Veidt and D. A. Zetzsche, 'Building Fintech Ecosystems: Regulatory Sandboxes, Innovation Hubs and Beyond', *Washington University Journal of Law and Policy*, 61 (2020): 55; D. A. Zetzsche, R. P. Buckley, D. W. Arner and J. N. Barberis., 'Regulating a Revolution: From Regulatory Sandboxes to Smart Regulation', *Fordham Journal of Corporate and Financial Law*, 23 (2017): 31.

[66] See MiCA Regulation Proposal, Explanatory Memorandum, COM (2020) 593 Final, p. 5; PilotR Regulation Proposal, Explanatory Memorandum, COM (2020) 594 Final, p. 2; Recital paras. 11 and 105 of DORA.

[67] Cf. M. Lehmann, 'National Blockchain Laws as a Threat to Capital Markets Integration', *Uniform Law Review*, 95 (2021): 148–79.

within the European Single Market by enhancing market liquidity and depth while intensifying cross-border competition.

1.5 LEGISLATIVE HISTORY

1.5.1 *The EU's AML/CTF Legislation*

At the EU level, the first legislative step observed with regard to cryptoassets was the EBA's recommendations in 2014 to bring virtual currency-to-fiat exchanges and providers of virtual currency custodian wallet services into the scope of the Anti-Money Laundering Directive (AMLD) in order to mitigate the risks of money laundering and terrorist financing.[68] These recommendations were ultimately passed into law as part of the AMLD5 with 10 January 2020 set as the implementation deadline.[69] Hence, virtual currency-to-fiat exchanges and virtual currency custodian wallet services are since part of the AMLD's scope,[70] and Member States have a specific duty to ensure that the respective service providers are registered.[71]

Following the AML/Counter-Terrorism Financing (CTF) Action Plan of 7 May 2020,[72] four legislative acts were proposed on 20 July 2021.

Among the legislative acts, the revision of the TFR was adopted in April 2023 together with MiCA. It expands the entities covered by the previous TFR to cover cryptoassets, effectively enabling the tracing of cryptoasset transfers and thus ensuring alignment with Financial Action Task Force (FATF) recommendations and inhibiting the provision and custody of anonymous cryptoasset wallets.

The three remaining regulatory projects came into force in July 2024: (1) the EU's 'Single Rulebook' Regulation[73] harmonises rules on conducting due diligence on customers, transparency of beneficial owners, and the use of anonymous instruments such as cryptoassets, came into force in July 2024; (2) the AMLD6[74] provides national rules on supervision and financial intelligence units (FIUs), as well as on the access of competent authorities to information, such as beneficial ownership registers and assets stored in free zones; (3) the regulation establishing the European Anti-money Laundering Authority (AMLA)[75] equips the AMLA with supervisory and investigative powers to ensure compliance with AML/CTF requirements and shall ensure that the AMLA becomes the focus point of EU AML/CTF activities. We discuss the EU's AML/CTF crypto initiatives in Chapter 14.

68 EBA, 'Opinion on "Virtual Currencies"', EBA/Op/2014/08 (2014).

69 See Article 1(3)(g) and (h), cf. Article 3(18) and (19) of AMLD, Directive 2015/849, OJ 2015 No. L141.

70 Article 1(3)(g) and (h), cf. Article 3(18) and (19) of AMLD.

71 Article 47(1) of AMLD.

72 European Commission, 'Communication from the Commission on an Action Plan for a Comprehensive Union Policy on Preventing Money Laundering and Terrorist Financing', C (2020) 2800 Final.

73 See Regulation (EU) 2024/1624 of the European Parliament and of the Council of 31 May 2024 on the prevention of the use of the financial system for the purposes of money laundering or terrorist financing, OJ L, 2024/1624, 19.6.2024.

74 See Directive (EU) 2024/1640 of the European Parliament and of the Council of 31 May 2024 on the mechanisms to be put in place by Member States for the prevention of the use of the financial system for the purposes of money laundering or terrorist financing, amending Directive (EU) 2019/1937, and amending and repealing Directive (EU) 2015/849, OJ L, 2024/1640, 19.6.2024.

75 See Regulation (EU) 2024/1620 of the European Parliament and of the Council of 31 May 2024 establishing the Authority for Anti-Money Laundering and Countering the Financing of Terrorism and amending Regulations (EU) No 1093/2010, (EU) No 1094/2010 and (EU) No 1095/2010, OJ L, 2024/1620, 19.6.2024.

1.5.2 *The EU's FinTech Action Plan (2018)*

Running parallel with the revisions to the AML/CTF legislation, the European Commission launched the EU's FinTech Action Plan on 8 March 2018.[76] As part of this plan, the Commission instructed the European financial supervisory authorities (namely, the EBA, the European Insurance and Occupational Pensions Authority (EIOPA), and the ESMA) both to examine the applicability of EU financial law to cryptoassets and to provide guidance on best practices for regulatory sandboxes. This laid the groundwork for what would later become MiCA and PilotR, respectively.

Notably, in their reports on cryptoassets that were published on 9 January 2019, both the ESMA and the EBA emphasised that cryptoassets posed non-negligible consumer protection, operational resilience, and market integrity risks.[77] Furthermore, the ESMA noted that many cryptoassets would qualify neither as financial instruments nor as e-money and, hence, fall outside the boundaries of EU financial law altogether.[78] In response, the ESMA suggested a bespoke regulatory regime for cryptoassets and outlined a scope similar to what would later become MiCA.[79]

1.5.3 *The EU's Digital Finance Package (2020)*

The launch of Facebook's stablecoin Diem (formerly Libra), together with the experience gleaned from the AMLD5, led the European Commission to take a broader approach to the future development of digital finance and innovation in the EU, which on 24 September 2020 resulted in the new Digital Finance Package,[80] which comprised the DFS 2020 and a renewal of the retail payments strategy, in an effort to 'boost Europe's competitiveness and innovation in the financial sector, paving the way for Europe to become a global standard-setter'.[81]

The DFS 2020 presented three legislative proposals on cryptoassets and digital operational resilience: MiCA, PilotR and DORA. Together, these legislative acts filled the identified gaps in EU law with respect to cryptoassets: MiCA establishes a financial law framework for cryptoassets that were not already covered by existing EU financial law; PilotR creates a regulatory sandbox to facilitate innovation in DLT market infrastructures; and DORA puts in place a digital operational resilience regime to ensure that the necessary safeguards are in place to mitigate cyberattacks and other risks.

It is worth noting that the EU's regulatory approach stands out from attempts by other regulators globally, in the sense that it is both elaborate and explicitly seeks to promote innovation. In comparison, some regulators have imposed outright bans on cryptoassets or

[76] European Commission, 'Communication on a FinTech Action Plan: For a More Competitive and Innovative European Financial Sector', COM (2018) 109 Final.

[77] EBA, 'Report with Advice for the European Commission on Crypto-Assets' (2019), para. 71, p. 29; ESMA, 'Advice – Initial Coin Offerings and Crypto-Assets', para. 178.

[78] ESMA, 'Advice – Initial Coin Offerings and Crypto-Assets', para. 179.

[79] ESMA, 'Advice – Initial Coin Offerings and Crypto-Assets', paras. 182–87.

[80] Directorate-General for Financial Stability, Financial Services and Capital Markets Union, 'Communication on the Digital Finance Package', European Commission (2020). Website https://ec.europa.eu/info/publications/200924-digital-finance-proposals_en (last accessed on 1 October 2024).

[81] European Commission, 'Digital Finance Package: Commission Sets Out New, Ambitious Approach to Encourage Responsible Innovation to Benefit Consumers and Businesses', Press Release (2020). Website https://ec.europa.eu/commission/presscorner/detail/en/IP_20_1684 (last accessed on 1 October 2024).

statements of disapproval (e.g., China[82] and South Korea[83]), others have issued general warning notices (e.g., NCAs in various EU Member States,[84] the Singapore MAS[85] as well as initially, the U.S. Securities and Exchange Commission (SEC)[86] with litigation[87] leading to a court-induced turn-around on 10 January 2024[88]), while some have instilled supportive and light regulatory regimes (e.g., Liechtenstein,[89] Switzerland[90] and Singapore[91]).

1.6 REGULATORY TECHNIQUES

MiCA, PilotR, DORA, and the revised TFR, with accompanying L2 and L3 legislation, are built on a set of distinct regulatory techniques.

1.6.1 *New and Better Definitions*

Because there has been extensive legal uncertainty related to whether some cryptoassets qualify under the different parts of EU financial law,[92] the DFS 2020 promises better definitions and that 'interpretative guidance on the application of existing rules will improve regulatory clarity, enabling the financial sector to reap efficiency gains through wider use of distributed ledger technology (DLT) in capital markets, while continuing to respect the safety and security rules and maintaining a high level of user protection'.[93]

This interpretative guidance is needed, and MiCA introduces a new legal taxonomy for cryptoassets. First, by explicitly excluding from its scope cryptoassets that qualify under existing

[82] See L. Y. Chen and J. Lee, 'Bitcoin Tumbles as PBOC Declares Initial Coin Offerings Illegal', Bloomberg (2017). Website www.bloomberg.com/news/articles/2017-09-04/china-central-bank-says-initial-coin-offerings-are-illegal (last accessed on 1 October 2024).

[83] See Y. Nakamura and S. Kim, 'Cryptocurrencies Drop as South Korea Bans ICOs, Margin Trading', Bloomberg (2017). Website www.bloomberg.com/news/articles/2017-09-29/cryptocurrencies-drop-as-south-korea-bans-icos-margin-trading (last accessed on 1 October 2024).

[84] See AFM, 'AFM waarschuwt voor grote risico's bij Initial Coin Offerings' (2017). Website https://perma.cc/JE4R-ZWXW (last accessed on 1 October 2024); Federal Financial Supervisory Authority ('BaFin'), 'Consumer Warning: The Risks of Initial Coin Offerings' (2017). Website https://perma.cc/JM49-XZEN (last accessed on 1 October 2024); Financial Conduct Authority ('FCA'), 'Consumer Warning about the Risks of Initial Coin Offerings' (2017). Website https://perma.cc/Y69C-SLLB (last accessed on 1 October 2024).

[85] See Monetary Authority of Singapore, 'MAS Clarifies Regulatory Position on the Offer of Digital Tokens in Singapore', Media Release (2017). Website https://perma.cc/W9KS-BLX6 (last accessed on 1 October 2024).

[86] See U.S. Securities and Exchange Commission, 'SEC Statement Urging Caution around Celebrity Backed ICOs', Public Statement (2017). Website https://perma.cc/2Q69-KJ73 (last accessed on 1 October 2024) (demanding compliance with US disclosure rules).

[87] At the time of writing, more than 100 cases are either taken to court or settled by the SEC. Website www.sec.gov/securities-topics/crypto-assets (last accessed on 1 October 2024).

[88] See U.S. Securities and Exchange Commission, Release No. 34-99306, January 10, 2024 re the listing of Grayscale Bitcoin Trust at NASDAQ.

[89] See Gesetz vom 3. Oktober 2019 über Token und VT-Dienstleister (Token- und VT-Dienstleister-Gesetz; TVTG), LGBl. 2019.301.

[90] See FINMA, 'Regulatory Treatment of Initial Coin Offerings' (2017). Website https://perma.cc/VB7B-L259 (last accessed on 1 October2024).

[91] See S. Supaat, 'Reply to Parliamentary Question on the Prevalence Use of Cryptocurrency in Singapore and Measures to Regulate Cryptocurrency and Initial Coin Offerings', Notice Paper No. 869. Monetary Authority of Singapore (2017). Website https://perma.cc/W9KS-BLX6 (last accessed on 1 October 2024). For more on ICOs in Asia, see D. W. Arner *et al.*, 'Cryptocurrencies, Blockchain and ICOs: Policy and Regulatory Challenges of Distributed Ledger Technology and Digital Assets in Asia', in C. Brummer (ed.), *Cryptoassets: Legal, Regulatory, and Monetary Perspectives* (Oxford: Oxford University Press, 2019).

[92] See Sections 1.3.2 and 1.3.3, with further details in Chapter 4.

[93] European Commission, 'Communication on a Digital Finance Strategy for the EU', p. 9.

EU financial law,[94] MiCA implicitly reaffirms that investment tokens do indeed typically qualify under the existing legislation. Then, within its scope, MiCA differentiates between cryptoassets that reference the value of an underlying asset and those that do not. Roughly put, if the reference value is one fiat currency that is legal tender, the cryptoassets qualify as EMTs, while if the reference value is several fiat currencies, commodities, and/or other cryptoassets, then the cryptoassets in question qualify as ARTs. Finally, if there is no reference value, the cryptoassets simply qualify as tokens that are neither EMTs nor ARTs, which de facto mostly comprise utility tokens given that investment tokens are already excluded from MiCA's scope. The details of this taxonomy and its challenges are laid out in Chapter 4.

The ESMA and the EBA have released interpretative guidance for MiCA.[95] Yet, as explained further in Chapter 4, the initial guidance remains vague. This is expected until a substantial number of cryptoassets have been classified by NCAs assisted by the opinions of the ESMA and the EBA, on which basis the initial guidance will be reshaped and made more granular. Until then, the challenge of legal classification under the existing EU financial law is likely to persist for some years even after MiCA has come into force.

1.6.2 *An Extended Authorisation Regime*

MiCA imposes an authorisation requirement on issuers of ARTs and EMTs; only issuers of 'other tokens than ARTs and EMTs' in the scope of Title II MiCA do not require authorisation. For ARTs, Title III MiCA provides a bespoke authorisation regime; Article 17 MiCA allows for some easing of the requirements to authorised credit institutions. Meanwhile, Title IV MiCA for EMTs is modelled on the E-money Directive (EMD) and requires authorisation as a credit institution or electronic money institution to issue EMTs. These requirements are discussed in Chapter 6.

In addition, Title V MiCA imposes a bespoke authorisation regime on in-scope cryptoasset service providers (CASPs), which we discuss in Chapter 7.

1.6.3 *A Risk-Adjusted Disclosure Regime*

MiCA aims to strike a balance between risk mitigation and the promotion of digital innovation through a simplified disclosure (whitepaper) regime, as compared to the prospectus regime under the Prospectus Regulation. MiCA's disclosure requirements are tailor-made for EMTs, ARTs, and 'other cryptoassets', respectively. Notably, issuers of other in-scope cryptoassets are under no requirement for pre-approval of the whitepaper, and requirements on the content and form of cryptoasset whitepapers are also differentiated for utility tokens, EMTs, and ARTs, respectively. These rules are covered in more detail in Chapter 5.

1.6.4 *Detailed Operating Conditions*

MiCA, PilotR, and DORA establish a set of operating conditions for the entities that fall under their scope which are covered in more detail throughout this book.

[94] See Article 2(4) of MiCA.

[95] See ESMA, 'Markets in Crypto-Assets Regulation'. Website www.esma.europa.eu/esmas-activities/digital-finance-and-innovation/markets-crypto-assets-regulation-mica (last accessed on 1 October 2024).

Here too, Title II MiCA takes a risk-based approach with a limited set of obligations for issuers of other in-scope cryptoassets and a more comprehensive set of rules for ART issuers in Title III, including a regulatory regime for own funds and reserve assets. For EMT issuers, MiCA largely relies on the operating conditions laid down in EMD, while for issuers of ARTs and EMTs that qualify as 'significant', a stricter regime applies, as laid down in Title III, Chapter 5 and Title IV, Chapter 2 MiCA. Finally, Title V MiCA includes a separate set of detailed operating conditions for CASPs.

In line with the regulatory sandbox concept, PilotR offers a scheme of exemptions and requirements. The regulatory technique here is the same for both multi-lateral trading facilities (MTFs) and securities settlement systems (SSSs).[96] For MTFs, the Markets in Financial Instruments Directive (MiFID) and Markets in Financial Instruments Regulation (MiFIR) apply, while for SSSs, the Central Securities Depository Regulation (CSDR) applies, unless the operator (a) has requested and been granted an exemption from certain provisions, (b) complies with a set of general obligations to set the rules and meet minimum standards for DLT market infrastructure operations, and (c) adheres to a set of conditions and, at the discretion of the NCA, additional compensatory measures.

Finally, DORA is in its entirety a set of detailed operating conditions for financial entities, including cryptoasset issuers and service providers.[97] These operating conditions span the entire digital operational resilience space, including information and communication technology (ICT) risk management; incident management, classification, and reporting; digital operational resilience testing; managing of ICT third-party risk; and information-sharing arrangements.[98]

1.6.5 *PilotR: The Regulatory Sandbox and 'Business Plan Approach'*

DLT and crypto-assets constitute a new space where many important questions can be answered only through trial and error. Hence, PilotR foresees a regulatory sandbox approach for the European Single Market, offering firms a set of exemptions from EU financial law that allow them to test DLT in certain activities related to trading and settlement, while regulators also gain experience in DLT market infrastructures.[99] Since its first adoption for financial services by the UK's Financial Conduct Authority,[100] the regulatory sandbox concept has been applied in more than seventy-three countries.[101] Prior to PilotR's inception, several EU Member States had adopted various regulatory approaches for experimentation, yet concerns over deviations from mandatory EU financial law that put the main privilege of EU membership (i.e., the 'EU Passport') at risk limited the space for doing so. Hence, the PilotR constitutes a recognition of the need to take action at EU level.

Moreover, the PilotR is characterised by an innovative 'business plan approach' whereby the DLT operator itself defines 'the rules under which the DLT market infrastructures and their operators are to operate, including the legal terms defining the rights, obligations, responsibilities and liabilities of operators of DLT market infrastructures, as well as those of the

96 See Articles 4–6 of PilotR, Regulation 2022/858, OJ 2022 No. L151.

97 See Article 2(1)(f) of DORA.

98 See Chapters II–VI of DORA, respectively. See Chapter 15 on details of DORA.

99 See Recital para. 6 of PilotR, Proposal 2020/0267.

100 Fca.org.uk, 'Regulatory Sandbox' (2022). Website www.fca.org.uk/firms/innovation/regulatory-sandbox (last accessed on 1 October 2024).

101 For an updated list of running sandboxes as of November 2020, see The World Bank, 'Global Experiences from Regulatory Sandboxes' (2020). Website https://documents.worldbank.org/en/publication/documents-reports/documentdetail/912001605241080935/global-experiences-from-regulatory-sandboxes (last accessed on 1 October 2024).

members, participants, issuers and clients using their DLT market infrastructure'.[102] This marks a substantial departure from the status quo where financial market law tends to define the role of each type of intermediary, and each of them is explicitly accountable for their activities as defined by their intermediary activity or entity status. Through this business plan approach, PilotR promotes innovation while demanding business-specific risk mitigation through carefully managed self-regulation, avoiding one-size-fits-all approaches. (We discuss the PilotR in Chapter 12.)

1.6.6 *An EU 'Passport' Regime*

The most valuable privilege of the European Single Market in financial services is the right to operate across borders. Hence, both MiCA and PilotR entail an EU 'Passport' regime based on the jurisdiction of the NCA in the home Member State of the issuer or service provider. Specifically, if issuers of utility tokens comply with MiCA, they can offer such tokens to the public and seek admission to trading 'throughout the Union'.[103] Similarly, authorisation for issuers of ARTs and CASPs is also valid for the entire EU[104] (issuers of EMTs must be authorised as a credit institution or e-money institution and that authorisation comes with an EU Passport). Finally, a specific permission under PilotR to operate DLT market infrastructures is valid throughout the Union for up to six years,[105] meaning that the operator is granted a time-bound EU Passport.

1.6.7 *Supervisory Cooperation and ESMA/EBA Coordination*

Given the objective of harmonisation across the European Single Market, MiCA, PilotR, and DORA provide a framework for supervisory cooperation, where NCAs are provided supervisory powers under a collaborative process coordinated by the ESMA and the EBA (and in the case of DORA, the EIOPA as well).[106] For instance, before an NCA can make a decision, there are processes to follow for the collection of advice from NCAs in other Member States and the so-called 'non-binding opinions' of the ESMA and the EBA, as well as sometimes the European Central Bank (ECB) and central banks in Member States.[107] To promote consistent enforcement across the European Single Market, there are also rules on the publishing of NCAs' decisions on official websites.[108] Finally, for ARTs and EMTs that are classified as 'significant', Title III, Chapter 5 and Title IV, Chapter 2 MiCA transfer supervisory authority from NCAs to the EBA. We discuss supervisory matters in Chapter 11.

[102] Article 7(1) and (2) of PilotR.
[103] Article 11(1) of MiCA.
[104] Articles 16(3) and 59(7) of MiCA.
[105] Articles 8(11) and 9(11) of PilotR for DLT MTFs and DLT SSSs, respectively.
[106] See Title VII of MiCA and Articles 8(5–8) and 9(5–8) of PilotR.
[107] See, for example, Articles 20(5) and 120(2) and Recital para. 45 of MiCA; and Articles 8(7), 9(7), and 10(8) of PilotR.
[108] See Article 114 of MiCA.

2

The Setup of Cryptoasset Schemes

2.1 THE TECHNOLOGY

2.1.1 *Purpose and History*

Distributed ledgers are a digital solution to the perennial puzzle of how to establish a single source of truth which is trusted by all parties involved. This is essential for all kinds of business transactions, and humans have used ledgers for this purpose since the advent of agriculture some 10,000 years ago when keeping a record of food and animals became necessary. The Sumerians used clay tokens before they came up with the bulla – essentially a spherical clay envelope in which tokens were sealed.[1] Because the bulla had to be cracked open to access the tokens inside, it helped to prevent dishonest tampering with the data stored on this ancient ledger.

Later versions included engravings on the outside of the bulla itself, a precursor to the development of writing, which in turn led towards the establishment of written ledgers that are used to this day, along with various types of seals, stamps, and signatures to prevent forgery.[2] A similar evolution took place in the development of money from precious metals to banknotes, which are essentially a type of ledger giving title to whoever is in possession of the notes. Of specific interest to this book, the same concept was applied to bearer securities during the seventeenth century, essentially creating one source of truth that – with the backing of the legal system – could be trusted by all parties involved.

Of course, modern ledgers are now in digital formats, but this exacerbates the old issue of forgery and double spending because digital data entries by their very nature can easily be altered or multiplied into an unlimited number of exact copies. That is why today we rely on trusted third parties to keep a master copy of the ledger and thereby act as arbiter to preserve a single source of truth, at least until the advent of cryptoassets that enable digital equivalents to cash or bearer securities.

2.1.2 *Centralised vs. Distributed Ledgers*

Examples of centralised ledgers include government property registers, banks' ledgers of amounts outstanding on their customers' bank accounts, and financial market infrastructures

[1] See A. Welfare, *Commercializing Blockchain: Strategic Applications in the Real World* (Chichester: Wiley, 2019), Chapter 4.

[2] By the term 'ledger', we here also include written contracts, which are essentially a listing of rights and obligations.

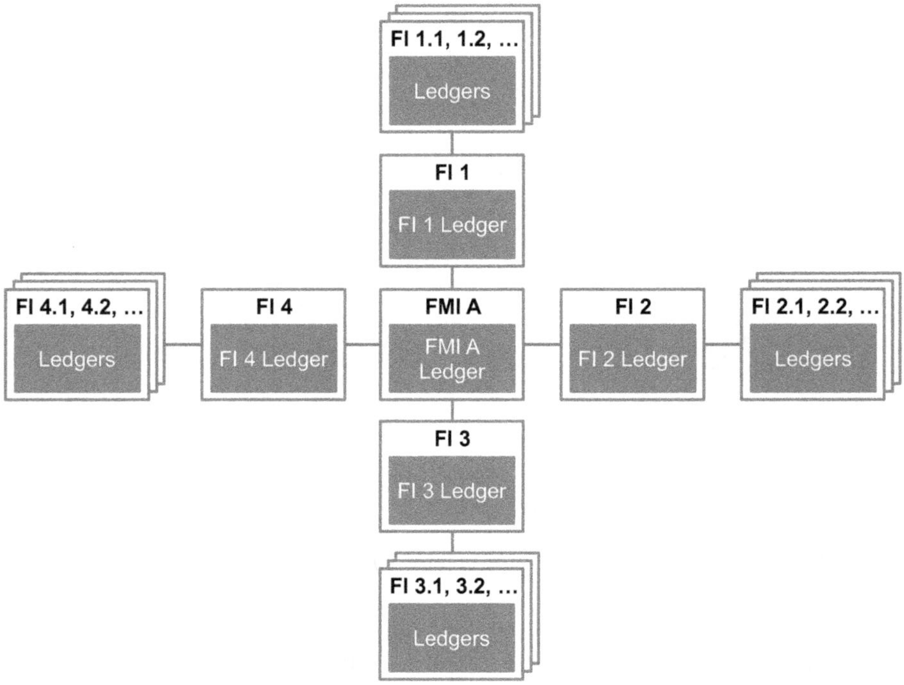

FIGURE 2.1 Centralised hub-and-spokes ledger

(FMIs). It is common with a central entity to hold a master copy of the ledger and for intermediaries to hold copies thereof (i.e., a hub-and-spokes system, as depicted in Figure 2.1).[3]

With DLT, in comparison, multiple entities (nodes) all hold an equivalent copy of the ledger, and authorisation for the recording of a given piece of information results from the software-driven consensus of many nodes (Figure 2.2). This is now possible, of course, due to the falling cost of data storage along with high bandwidth internet. It makes the ledger incredibly resilient because as long as at least one computer in the network is operational, the entire ledger will continue to exist. Coupled with cryptographic solutions, storage of the same data across multiple nodes also curtails the risk of data manipulation, thereby alleviating the need to trust any third-party data-storage service provider.[4] This enables peer-to-peer transactions, as A's private–public key pair is used to send cryptoassets to an account represented by B's public key without the need for any one trusted intermediary.

2.1.3 *Blockchain and Proof of Work: The Bitcoin Solution*

To work effectively, a distributed ledger must solve 'the double spending problem', essentially preventing malicious actors from altering or copying data entries on the ledger to spend the same tokens more than once. This was achieved in late 2008 by one or more anonymous developers

[3] See Mills *et al.*, 'Distributed Ledger Technology', pp. 6–7.

[4] See Finck, *Blockchain Regulation*, pp. 12–14; see also Davidson *et al.*, 'Blockchains and the Economic Institutions of Capitalism', 639, 641 (arguing that blockchain technology is a new governance institution that competes with other economic institutions of capitalism, namely, firms, markets, networks, and even governments); De Filippi and Wright, *Blockchain and the Law*, pp. 136–40 (arguing that widespread deployment of the blockchain will lead to tech-based business practices that could prompt a loss in importance of centralized authorities, such as government, and urging a more active regulatory approach).

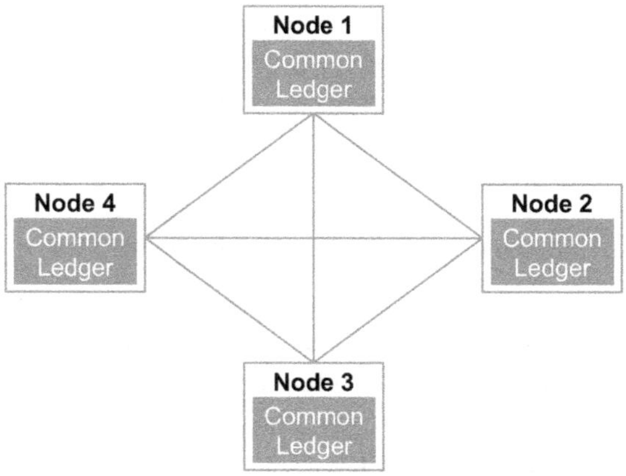

FIGURE 2.2 Decentralised ledger technology

under the pseudonym of Satoshi Nakamoto, who published their solution in a nine-page concept paper titled 'Bitcoin: A Peer-to-Peer Electronic Cash System'.[5]

The Bitcoin ledger stores data in bundles ('blocks') in a time-sequenced series ('blockchain'). Each block is time-stamped and, importantly, connected to the previous block through a cryptographic hashing function. To protect the integrity of the blockchain, Bitcoin entails an ingenious system that makes it expensive to add new data entries to the ledger and close to impossible to modify or delete information once it has been recorded. To this end, the Bitcoin protocol requires the hash of each block to begin with a specified number of zeros. To generate a valid hash, the nodes must solve a mathematical puzzle. While the puzzle can typically be solved only through random trial and error, once the solution is found it can then easily be verified.[6] The first node to arrive at the solution then broadcasts the new block with the valid hash to the entire network, and each node then validates the hash and adds the new block to their local copy of the ledger. To incentivise nodes to take part in this process, the first node to devise the solution and have its block validated by the network is rewarded with newly minted Bitcoins, which is why the process is called 'mining'.

Occasionally, the blockchain forks, whereby different nodes adopt different versions of new blocks, and the chain divides into branches. This can happen, for instance, due to disagreement among the nodes on certain update features. In such an event, the Bitcoin protocol mandates the nodes to agree on the longest chain, which is typically the one with the most blocks but technically defined as the chain that needed the most computing power to produce (i.e., to solve the mathematical puzzles required).[7] Through this process, the network can preserve a *consensus* as to what constitutes a single source of truth for the entire Bitcoin ledger.

The fact that the nodes with the most computing power have the highest chance of solving the mathematical puzzle first, and thereby of adding new blocks to the ledger, is representative of this consensus mechanism being called *proof of work* (PoW). It is also why the Bitcoin ledger consumes energy equivalent to that of a medium-sized country to operate, with the associated environmental impact. While this feature of the Bitcoin protocol is per se an unnecessary guessing game, it is also what prevents malicious actors from tampering with the ledger because

[5] Bitcoin.org, 'A Peer-to-Peer Electronic Cash System'. Website https://bitcoin.org/bitcoin.pdf (last accessed on 1 October 2024).

[6] See, for example, De Filippi and Wright, *Blockchain and the Law*, pp. 23–24.

[7] See, for example, De Filippi and Wright, *Blockchain and the Law*, p. 24 (and further detailed in note 60).

it would require an enormous amount of computing power to outpace the entire Bitcoin network in this way. Because the time-sequenced blockchain goes back to the very first block (the genesis block), a successful cyberattack would require simultaneously corrupting not just one set of data but multiple sets (i.e., the whole blockchain) as well as the time stamps.

2.1.4 *Other Consensus Mechanisms*

While the PoW consensus mechanism is an ingenious way of maintaining one source of truth and preventing cyberattacks on a distributed ledger, it comes with some important drawbacks. For instance, it requires both time and computing power to solve the mathematical puzzle, so the process to reach a consensus is inherently costly, energy-intensive, and slow. It also adds economies of scale to mining, benefiting large miners with plenty of computing power and thereby working against the very idea of a truly distributed network. To mitigate these drawbacks, alternative consensus mechanisms are being deployed to different distributed ledger networks.

Proof of stake (PoS) is the most obvious alternative, and the Ethereum ledger migrated to this consensus mechanism in 2022.[8] Instead of using computing power to prove one's eligibility to update the ledger, PoS uses proof of one's stake in upkeeping the network. For instance, the probability of adding a new block could be determined by the total amount of tokens or cryptocurrency each node holds.[9] A subset of PoS consensus mechanisms is called delegated proof of stake (DPoS), where network participants select (e.g., through voting) some nodes to be trusted to verify transactions between everyone else.[10] Similarly, *proof of importance* (PoI) represents another subset of PoS consensus mechanisms, where a score based on a number of factors determines each node's support in the network and, hence, the probability of being chosen to validate a new block. This is used, for example, by the New Economy Movement (NEM) cryptocurrency.[11]

Other consensus mechanisms are linked neither to computing power nor to the node's stake in the network. An example here is *proof of elapsed time* (PoET), which features a secure software allowing nodes to prove that they are waiting for a truly random time period before being picked as the first node to validate a new block. Essentially, the node is selected at random, which is a suitable consensus mechanism for permissioned ledgers.[12]

2.1.5 *Permissioned and/or Private Ledgers*

DLTs can be either permissioned (closed) or permissionless (open) and either public or private.[13] The first distinction (closed/open) reflects which entities can operate a node and thereby join in the consensus mechanism of validating transactions and add new datapoints to the ledger (referred to as 'miners' in Bitcoin terminology). The second distinction (public/private) reflects who can view the information on the ledger and initiate transactions on it (the owners of a 'wallet' according to Bitcoin terminology). Applying this taxonomy, the Bitcoin

[8] See Ethereum.org, 'Proof-of-Stake (POS)' (2023). Website https://ethereum.org/en/developers/docs/consensus-mechanisms/pos/ (last accessed on 1 October 2024).

[9] See Welfare, *Commercializing Blockchain*, Chapter 2.

[10] See Welfare, *Commercializing Blockchain*, Chapter 2.

[11] See Investopedia.com, 'All About NEM (XEM), the Harvested Cryptocurrency' (2022). Website www.investopedia.com\\tech\\meet-nem-xem-harvested-cryptocurrency (last accessed on 1 October 2024).

[12] See Welfare, *Commercializing Blockchain*, Chapter 2.

[13] See Benos *et al.*, 'The Economics of Distributed Ledger Technology', 121, 126–27.

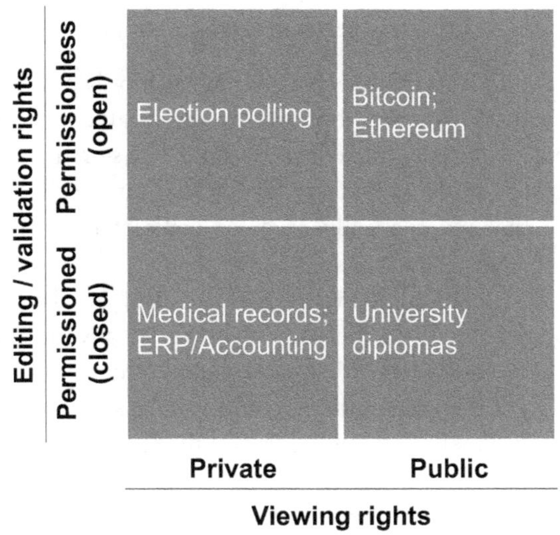

FIGURE 2.3 Example DLT use cases

ledger is both permissionless (open) and public. However, since they avoid the governance and accountability issues prevalent in Bitcoin-style public ledgers, permissioned (closed) and private DLTs so far have the greatest potential in many areas, such as FMIs.[14] One can imagine, for instance, DLT financial infrastructures that are permissioned (closed) and private to a group of existing financial intermediaries, such as custodian banks, clearing houses, or even security-holder registry providers like Computershare.

Looking beyond the financial system, permissioned and/or private ledgers may also have the greatest potential in many other domains (Figure 2.3).[15] For instance, it may be desirable to have a shared and trusted ledger for medical records, where only doctors are entitled to add information, which is then viewable only by each individual patient. Similarly, large organisations typically struggle to maintain trusted 'one source of truth' datasets across departments, so they may prefer an internal distributed ledger for enterprise resource planning (ERP) and accounting purposes. Therefore, permissioned (closed) ledgers are sometimes referred to as 'enterprise blockchains'. A different example is election polling, where an immutable, Bitcoin-style permissionless ledger might be more suitable, but where individual polling data remains secret. Finally, to prevent forgery of university diplomas, it may be preferable to establish a distributed ledger where only university personnel can add information, which is viewable to anyone.

One important argument against permissioned (closed) ledgers is that they miss out on DLT's main selling point, namely, the immutable data record with no need to trust a central data storage provider. By definition, permissioned (closed) networks reintroduce a set of central nodes, and one can argue that it would then be easier to simply use a conventional centralised ledger instead. Such questions will be answered over time, and the main point here is simply that we may see future DLTs and cryptoasset schemes that are significantly different from those that are prevalent today.

[14] Compliance becomes difficult if anyone can take part in validating transactions. Public ledgers are difficult to reconcile with privacy, insider trading, and market abuse legislation. Permissioned systems require less extensive consensus mechanisms because the nodes are pre-approved (trusted), which enables faster and cheaper processing of transactions. See, for all, Benos *et al.*, 'The Economics of Distributed Ledger Technology', 121, 127–28.

[15] See Welfare, *Commercializing Blockchain*.

2.1.6 *Ethereum and Smart Contracts*

While ledgers can be used to store transaction and ownership data on assets, they can also be used to store computer code. This makes it possible to run small computer programs, known as decentralised applications (dapps), on the ledger. Because data stored on a blockchain is close to immutable, so too is the code inherent in dapps. This allows for so-called smart contracts, which refer to computer code that automatically executes contract terms upon the fulfilment of specified conditions.[16]

At the time of writing, Ethereum is the prevailing ledger for dapps and smart contracts. Dedicated coding languages for the Ethereum platform let anyone build their own dapps, essentially opening a whole new world of cryptoassets and other DLT use cases. For instance, a crypto-bond traded on the Ethereum platform could entail a smart contract that automatically transfers interest (coupon) payments to bondholders on the ledger when they are due. Similarly, just as traditional shareholdings are often accompanied by elaborate shareholders' agreements, tokens issued by companies on the Ethereum platform are routinely accompanied by smart contracts that stipulate various elements such as anti-dilution protection and vesting periods.[17]

Crypto-proponents tend to see the Ethereum network as analogous to one global, decentralised computer – the 'Ethereum Virtual Machine' (EVM) – on which the applications powering 'Internet 3.0' will run. Just as the large, centralised tech firms used TCP/IP (the protocol on which today's internet runs) to take us from the nascent internet of the early 2000s to the data-driven Internet 2.0 of today with social media, targeted marketing, and online shopping, Ethereum is supposed to become the platform that underpins new business models and decentralised data ownership.[18] While Ethereum is currently both a slow and potentially expensive platform for running computer code, it is constantly improving and being coupled with new overlay networks that extend its usefulness.[19]

Whatever one believes about the future of blockchain and the internet, an important point for the purposes of this book is that the Ethereum platform has already empowered anyone to issue new cryptoassets enabled by smart contracts. While this type of automation may also occur on centralised ledgers, DLTs such as Ethereum open new ground for financial innovation by allowing users to enter into such contracts and even offer them as tokenised assets to the public without relying on a central authority.[20]

2.1.7 *Various Degrees of Decentralisation in Finance*

Smart contracts enable the decentralised provision of financial services without the need for conventional intermediaries (DeFi). Yet, the degree of such decentralisation on DLT varies from fully centralised to fully decentralised. For instance, the lending function may be provided by a pool of users' funds (functioning collectively like a credit institution, with interactions executed by smart contracts), while a single trading intermediary (i.e., functionally, an

[16] The term is somewhat misleading because mart contracts are probably neither smart nor actual contracts but merely a non-smart computer code (as opposed to artificial intelligence) that typically executes terms in existing contracts that pre-date the code itself. See Athanassiou, 'Impact of Digital Innovation'.

[17] See S. Cohney, D. A. Hoffman, J. Sklaroff and D. A. Wishnick, 'Coin-Operated Capitalism', *Columbia Law Review*, 119(3) (2019): 591, 612–15.

[18] See Welfare, *Commercializing Blockchain*, Chapter 2.

[19] See De Filippi and Wright, *Blockchain and the Law*, pp. 27–31.

[20] Bech *et al.*, 'On the Future of Securities Settlement', pp. 67 and 74 (who further notes that DLTs can also be set up in ways that would let only a central authority to facilitate smart contracts).

exchange) handles the trading. Furthermore, what is understood as the substance of decentralisation varies. Financial services marketed as DeFi are often not DeFi *stricto sensu*.

DeFi *stricto sensu* is characterised by peer-to-peer transactions and a lack of any centralised intermediary where smart contracts execute all transactions between supply and demand automatically. All servers that support the operation of the protocols (nodes), or token holders as the case may be, have equal access to data and equal governance rights (or technical equivalents of governance rights). Such a setup is also referred to as a decentralised autonomous organisation (DAO). If a trading platform is governed by a DAO, the crypto jargon refers to decentralised exchanges (DEXs). However, centralised intermediaries often deliver important functions to the DeFi ecosystem. From the DeFi sector's perspective, these constitute a type of CeFi. Centralised exchanges (CEXs), for instance, handle most of the trading volume for tokens issued under the DeFi maxim and influence the valuation of cryptoassets, which may then be relied upon by DeFi protocols.

Whether a service is partially or fully decentralised will be hard to determine in practice, and this may impair the effectiveness of EU financial regulation because certain fully decentralised services without an intermediary are outside of MiCA's scope, while partly decentralised ones are inside it (see Sections 4.2.4 and 7.2.3.4.)

2.2 TOKEN OFFERINGS (ICOS, STOS, AND BEYOND)

2.2.1 *Definitions and Characteristics*

The first token offerings were typically labelled *initial coin offerings* (ICOs). These are somewhat similar to their namesake initial public offerings (IPOs) in the sense that they entail an offering to invest in a project. However, unlike IPOs, token offerings do not typically involve the sale of traditional equity instruments.[21] Instead, investors buy tokens that may resemble shares but most commonly constitute tokens that give holders the right to use and take part in the governance of the products or services that the promoters plan to develop. To use a fitting analogy, '[i]t would be as if Coca-Cola had funded its initial deployment of vending machines through the sale of tokens its machines might one day require'.[22] Other tokens resemble traditional securities, and the offerings of such tokens have consequently been labelled *securities token offerings* (STOs). Other similar labels also exist, but for simplicity, we will use the term *token offering* for any offer of cryptoassets to the public.

Contrary to most cryptocurrencies, like Bitcoin which is issued in a decentralised fashion through mining fully determined by algorithms, token offerings require, in most cases, a central, identifiable issuer. Hence, the cryptoassets are centrally created, even if they are typically stored and settled on a fully decentralised permissionless (open) and public ledger, such as Ethereum.

2.2.2 *Early History*

Many token offerings to date have been internet-based and open to the public, albeit with variations as to the participants involved and amounts invested. The first very large token offering took place in early 2018 when Telegram raised over USD 1.7 billion,[23] followed by Block One

[21] See Cohney *et al.*, 'Coin-Operated Capitalism', 591, 593.

[22] See Cohney *et al.*, 'Coin-Operated Capitalism', 591, 593.

[23] See C. Russo and I. Khrennikov, 'Big Investors Circle Telegram's ICO While Veteran Crypto Insiders Pass', Bloomberg (2018). Website www.bloomberg.com/news/articles/2018-02-02/big-investors-circle-telegram-offering-as-crypto-insiders-pass#xj4y7vzkg (last accessed on 1 October 2024). The token offering was later 'reversed' as illegal

that unexpectedly raised USD 4.1 billion in a year-long token offering that culminated in June 2018.[24]

Compared to their current profile, token offerings came from very humble roots: initially, they began as a mechanism among the blockchain community to attract financial support for new ideas, and they involved small amounts of money and small numbers of investors. However, as the raised amounts increased, so did the interest in using token structures to gather money for ever broader purposes among ever broader groups of investors, with issuances in 2017 and 2018 forming a large portion of the early-stage fundraising globally.[25]

To begin with, investors often personally knew the technologists who were seeking funding, and information about the promoters and the technologists behind the entity raising the funds as well as financial information about it were often absent. As the market has expanded, this scarcity of information provided to investors has unfortunately become something of a market norm – typically consisting of a whitepaper (with varying levels of information) and a digital marketing campaign performed through social media. Combined with many failed ventures, leading to significant losses for investors and even some prominent scams or Ponzi schemes,[26] this has given the very term ICO a bad reputation.

2.2.3 *The Token Offering Process*

Entrepreneurs start with an idea, which they build into a product that can be tested with early users/customers and gradually improved. At least historically, ventures that have sought funding through token offerings were themselves oftentimes trying to build DLT-based or at least digital products. To achieve this, it would be necessary to recruit advisors, new team members, and external support, for which capital must be raised. It is at this point where the token offering process begins (Figure 2.4).

First, the initiators must define the purpose of a token offering.[27] This entails building a business plan to identify the product's revenue potential together with the time and costs required to deliver it, which again determines the associated capital needs. Based on this, the team evaluates alternative sources of funding, where a token offering is one of several options. Other alternatives are typically to issue traditional equity or convertible debt to investors that they find through their network or, for instance, through a crowdfunding platform.

Once a token offering is chosen, it is necessary that the team reviews and understands the applicable legislation, evaluates alternative jurisdictions (if relevant), and identifies the legal requirements that apply specifically to the planned token offering. Historically, this has often been neglected by the cryptoasset community though.

by the U.S. Securities and Exchange Commission (SEC). See SEC press release, 'Telegram to Return $1.2 Billion to Investors and Pay $18.5 Million Penalty to Settle SEC Charges' (2020). Website www.sec.gov/news/press-release/2020-146 (last accessed on 1 October 2024).

[24] See T. Magee, 'Biggest Initial Coin Offerings Techworld' (2018). Website https://perma.cc/W4WL-FXXW (last accessed on 1 October 2024). We have chosen to exclude the RedCab ICO from our analysis as we could not secure reliable consistent data about it, and our information requests to its initiators went unanswered. For some information on it, see TrackICO, 'RedCab (REDC)'. Website https://perma.cc/N7AA-K8T5 (last accessed on 1 October 2024).

[25] See Zetzsche *et al.*, 'The ICO Gold Rush', 267.

[26] See Zetzsche *et al.*, 'The ICO Gold Rush', 267.

[27] See The Corporate Finance Institute Team, 'Initial Coin Offering (ICO)?' The Corporate Finance Institute. Website https://corporatefinanceinstitute.com/resources/knowledge/trading-investing/initial-coin-offering-ico/ (last accessed on 1 October 2024).

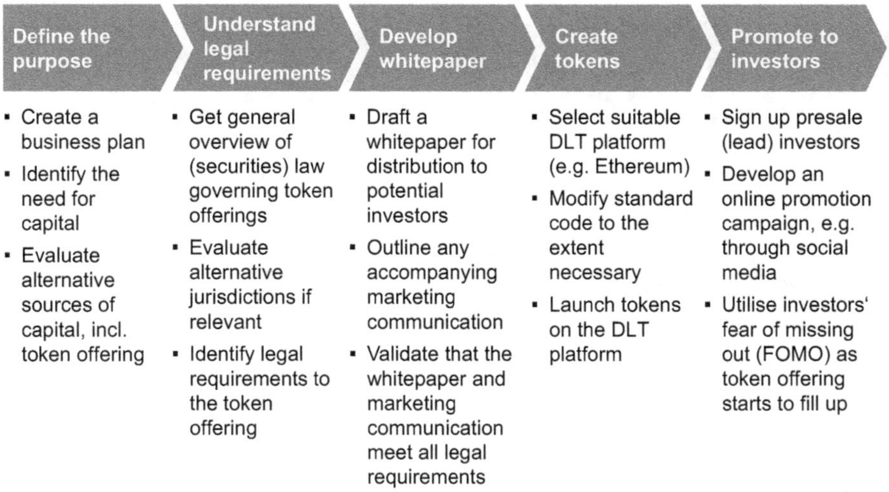

FIGURE 2.4 The token offering process

Then, the entrepreneurs must develop a cryptoasset whitepaper for distribution to potential investors. Typically, this should explain at least the vision, technology, team, business activities, token offering, and technology roadmap.[28] The whitepaper is mostly accompanied by marketing communication, for instance, a YouTube video. The draft whitepaper and marketing communication are then validated by a select audience, usually comprising early investors, industry insiders, and technical advisors.[29] It is also critical to validate that the whitepaper and marketing communication meet all legal requirements (see Chapter 5 on prospectus rules).

The next step is to create the tokens. This involves identifying a suitable DLT platform, modifying that platform's standard code to build a new token that meets the objectives of the offering, and then launching that token on the platform.[30] Ethereum is the most common platform for token offerings, where community-built standards like 'ERC-20' provide simple templates to create ('mint') and operate entirely new cryptoassets on the Ethereum system with a minimum of approximately fifty lines of code and three decision components: the asset's name, its ticker code, and the number of tokens issued ('minted').[31]

Finally, the token offering must be promoted to investors. This often entails a pre-sale,[32] where early (lead) investors sign up. This signals to other investors that the token offering is popular, creating a so-called fear of missing out among the broader set of investors whose funding will be necessary to fill up the entire offering. A broad marketing campaign is often required, typically through channels like Reddit, Telegram, Slack, Medium, online ads, blog posts, and webinars.[33] In the end, the cryptoassets are sold to investors in exchange for other cryptoassets or, more rarely, fiat currency.[34]

[28] See The Luxembourg House of Financial Technology, 'Understanding Initial Coin Offerings: Technology, Benefits, Risks, and Regulations' (2017), p. 8.
[29] See The Luxembourg House of Financial Technology, 'Understanding Initial Coin Offerings', p. 8.
[30] See The Corporate Finance Institute Team, 'Initial Coin Offering?' Website https://corporatefinanceinstitute.com/resources/knowledge/trading-investing/initial-coin-offering-ico/ (last accessed on 1 October 2024).
[31] See Cohney *et al.*, 'Coin-Operated Capitalism', 591, 612–15.
[32] See The Luxembourg House of Financial Technology, 'Understanding Initial Coin Offerings', p. 8.
[33] See The Luxembourg House of Financial Technology, 'Understanding Initial Coin Offerings', p. 8.
[34] See Cohney *et al.*, 'Coin-Operated Capitalism', 591, 620.

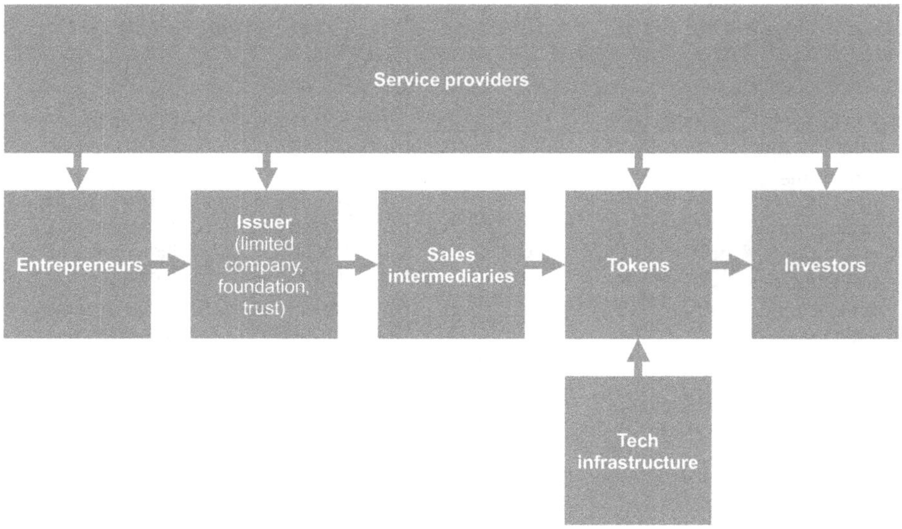

FIGURE 2.5 Typical parties involved in a token offering

2.2.4 *Legal Implications*

The EU law that applies to token offerings is covered in depth elsewhere in this book. Here, we simply emphasise that issuing a commitment to the public and accepting considerations on this basis is (of course) legally relevant conduct. In the past, however, token offerings have frequently been structured with an aim to avoid existing legal and regulatory requirements, or token issuers have simply ignored legal requirements altogether.[35] While avoiding any legal effects was never successful with regard to private law relations,[36] from a regulatory perspective, this has become increasingly difficult with increased supervisory attention and the passing of EU cryptoasset legislation.

2.3 PARTIES OF RELEVANCE TO A TOKEN OFFERING

A number of parties may be involved in a token offering (Figure 2.5), although the involvement of service providers varies considerably. In this sub-chapter, we describe the involvement of each party.

2.3.1 *Issuer*

Issuers of cryptoassets have so far typically been startups (or a special purpose vehicle functioning on the behalf of startups) at a stage where the token offering provides an alternative to angel or VC funding.[37] The issuing entity is most often a limited company, a foundation, or a trust.[38] MiCA applies a risk-based system where issuers of ARTs must either be an authorised credit

[35] Zetzsche *et al.*, 'The ICO Gold Rush', 267, 276–80.
[36] Cf. Zetzsche *et al.*, 'The Distributed Liability of Distributed Ledgers', 1361 (placing DLT into the private laws of various countries).
[37] See R. Fahlenbrach and M. Frattaroli, 'ICO Investors', *Financial Markets and Portfolio Management*, 35 (2021): 1, 24.
[38] See Zetzsche *et al.*, 'The ICO Gold Rush', 267, 281.

institution or have been granted special authorisation as an ART issuer,[39] issuers of EMTs must be authorised either as a credit institution or an e-money institution[40] (which comes with further requirements as defined at both EU and Member State level),[41] while issuers of other cryptoassets must simply be 'a legal person'.[42]

From a legal perspective, the token offering vehicle makes a set of promises to the investors, the terms of which vary between offerings. For instance, the promises can 'range from an exclusive right to use a certain IT service under development, to the right to participate in a community or to vote upon the future development of the software design underlying the token, or to participate in the future cash flow generated by the ICO vehicle'.[43] Furthermore, insofar as the tokens are made transferrable, the promise extends to any future holder of tokens, who consequently can request fulfilment from the token offering vehicle.[44]

2.3.2 *Sales Intermediaries*

Cryptoassets are frequently marketed and sold through sales intermediaries. This may typically be the case when the issuer resides outside of Europe, and indeed, we expect this practice to become increasingly common following the adoption of MiCA and the associated increase in regulatory scrutiny by EU and Member States' authorities. MiCA is already addressing this practice, for instance, through obliging the operator of a trading platform to publish a cryptoasset whitepaper in the event that the issuer has not already done so (see Section 5.4.2).

2.3.3 *Investors*

Tokens are typically offered to the public, raising money from a large number of token holders, investing mostly small amounts while speculating on an increase of the token value. Indeed, one study suggests that a typical token offering attracts around 4,700 investors, while the median investor invests just USD 1,200.[45] From a regulatory perspective, it is worth noting that financial law typically seeks to extend special protection to such retail investors. Yet, some token holders are of course more experienced than others. According to another study, around a quarter of investors take part in more than one token offering and some invest more than USD 1 million in total.[46]

Pre-sale investors, in particular, usually invest larger amounts and also tend to receive significant discounts compared to the regular token offering investors.[47] This allows for quick returns, similar to when conventional IPO investors flip their share allocations on the first trading day to profit from under-pricing. In fact, both small and large investors seem to trade extensively in the immediate aftermath of a token offering. One study suggests that around half of the initial investors had sold parts of their holdings within ninety days of the token offering,

39 Article 16(1) of MiCA, Regulation 2023/1114, OJ 2023 No. L150.
40 Article 48(1)(a) of MiCA.
41 See Title III of CRD, Directive 2013/36, OJ 2013 No. L176, and Title II of EMD, Directive 2009/110, OJ 2009 No. L267.
42 Article 4(1)(a) of MiCA.
43 See Zetzsche *et al.*, 'The ICO Gold Rush', 267, 281.
44 See Zetzsche *et al.*, 'The ICO Gold Rush', 267, 281.
45 See Fahlenbrach and Frattaroli, 'ICO Investors', 1, 2.
46 See D. Boreiko and D. Risteski, 'Serial and Large Investors in Initial Coin Offerings', *Small Bus Economics* (2021), pp. 1053–54.
47 See Fahlenbrach and Frattaroli, 'ICO Investors', 1, 23.

amounting to net sales (excluding purchases by the same investors) of more than 40 per cent of the tokens subscribed in the token offering.[48]

Investors take part in token offerings for ideological, technological, and financial reasons.[49] While the financial goals are common for all types of investments and technological reasons drive much of the traditional VC market, token offerings stand out for the ideological motives of many of their investors. Individual reasons, of course, vary, but it is clear that the cryptoasset investor base, at least in its early days, has been partly driven by a vision of a decentralised financial system with less government intervention. As more conventional investors enter the cryptoasset market, it is yet unclear what role VC firms and institutional investors, for instance, will play in this space.[50]

At least since the first quarter of 2024, driven by the U.S. SEC's decision to permit Bitcoin-linked exchange traded funds and exchange traded products under the U.S. Securities Act, an increase in institutional participation is noticeable in crypto markets, with a focus on the largest crypto ecosystems, Bitcoin and Ether. This creates results like the emergence of new crypto investment funds, large-scale industrial stablecoins such as the one by global payment service provider Paypal,[51] Twitter/X's announcement to enter into crypto and payments services, exchange traded products drawing on Bitcoin and Ether,[52] and custody solutions offered by traditional financial service providers (e.g., Fidelity[53]). This ongoing intermediation and institu tionalization of crypto makes the need for a sophisticated crypto custody framework even more apparent. We analyse the respective impacts in Chapters 8 and 9 of this book.

2.3.4 *Tech Infrastructure*

The tokens offered through a token offering must, naturally, be stored on a distributed ledger. Here, the most prevalent solution, by far, is to use the Ethereum platform,[54] where new cryptoasset schemes can be created with ease (see Sections 2.1.6 and 2.2.3). Other options also exist, including the creation of a completely separate ledger for the new cryptoasset. This choice may have legal implications because setting up a new ledger may entail the assumption of responsibilities associated with running FMIs (see Chapter 12). It is also unclear to what extent existing platforms, like Ethereum, could be liable for any loss caused by the malfunctioning of their platform and, due to their decentralised nature, which legal entities would be liable in such an event (see, e.g., Sections 4.2.4, 14.5, 15.5.3, and 15.5.4).

2.3.5 *Service Providers*

Many token offerings have taken place without the use of service providers, often fulfilling an underlying vision of the decentralisation and democratisation of finance. However, just as

48 See Fahlenbrach and Frattaroli, 'ICO Investors', 1, 21.

49 See C. Fisch, C. Masiak, S. Vismara and J. H. Block, 'Motives and Profiles of ICO Investors', *Journal of Business Research*, 125 (2021): 564, 569–70.

50 See Zetzsche *et al.*, 'The ICO Gold Rush', 267, 281–82.

51 See Paypal, 'Paypal Stablecoin' (stating that, 'PayPal USD is a stablecoin that's fully backed by US dollar deposits, US treasuries, and similar cash equivalents. You can buy and sell 1 PYUSD for 1 USD on PayPal'). Website www.paypal .com/us/digital-wallet/manage-money/crypto/pyusd#:~:text=PayPal%20USD%20is%20a%20stablecoin,for%20example%2C%20the%20U.S.%20dollar. (last accessed on 1 October 2024).

52 Binance/The News Crypto, 'X (Twitter) Gets License for Crypto Wallet Services in One U.S State', 20 August 2023. Website www.binance.com/en/square/post/1052807 (last accessed on 1 October 2024).

53 Fidelity Digital Assets, 'Digital Asset Custody and Trading Platform Built for Institutions'. Website www .fidelitydigitalassets.com/trading-custody (last accessed on 1 October 2024).

54 See Coindataflow.com, 'What Is an ICO – Initial Coin Offering Meaning – The Best Full 2021 Guide' (2021). Website https://coindataflow.com/clue/what-is-an-ico (last accessed on 1 October 2024).

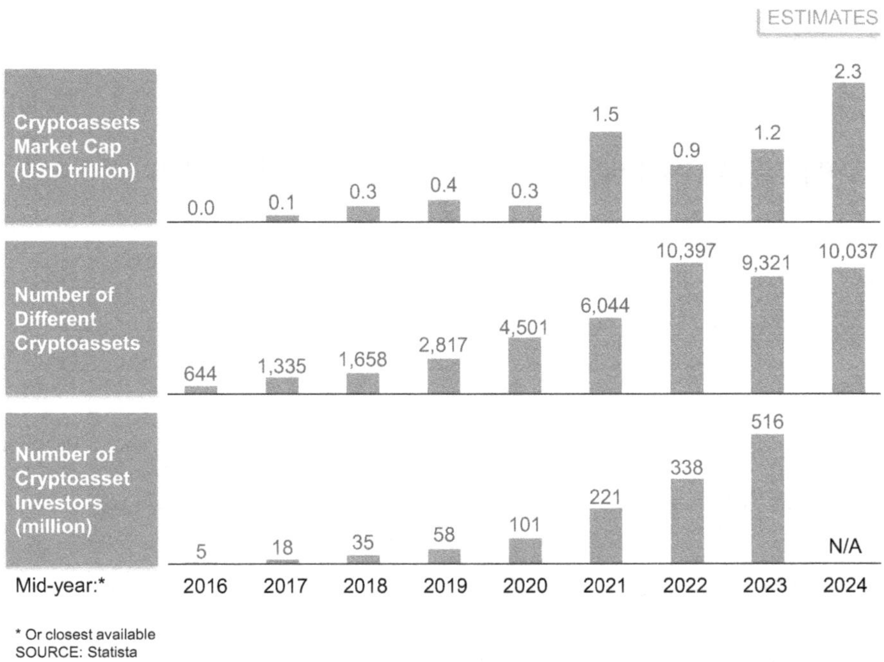

FIGURE 2.6 The cryptoasset market

several service providers tend to support conventional IPOs, well-run token offerings also tend to rely on third parties to, for instance, establish the token offering vehicle in accordance with legal and tax considerations, prepare the documents, sometimes function as the vehicle's director(s) or trustee(s), and market the token offering to attract investors.[55]

One example here is where the token offering is overseen by a cryptoasset exchange, often called initial exchange offerings to emphasise the support of a professional service provider. Typically, the exchange would perform a pre-screening of prospective token offerings to verify their quality, scrutinise the cryptoasset whitepaper and accompanying marketing information, and finally help to attract investors. This role taken by crypto exchanges is similar to the one performed by stock exchanges in the nineteenth century (leading to the development of modern securities law) and contemporary crowdfunding websites, which also provide a path to raising capital for small businesses, but typically through conventional equity and (convertible) debt instruments rather than cryptoassets. The organizational and hierarchical separation of trading and custody services, however, which is a hallmark of securities regulation, is yet to materialize in crypto. See Chapter 8.

2.4 THE CRYPTOASSET MARKET

New cryptoassets are launched all the time, and their market value is exposed to significant volatility. Hence, it would make little sense to discuss the absolute size of the cryptoasset market in this book. However, over several years we note a rapid market growth in terms of total market capitalisation, the number of different cryptoassets, and the number of investors (see Figure 2.6). It is fair to assume that the vast majority of these cryptoassets were launched through some type of token offering, which partly explains why MiCA focuses on issuers and service providers.

[55] See Zetzsche *et al.*, 'The ICO Gold Rush', 267, 281.

3

Cryptoasset Regulation in the System of EU Financial Law

3.1 MICA AS GAP-FILLING LEGISLATION WITHIN EXISTING EU FINANCIAL LAW

MiCA has become a pressing matter amid various scandals and crises that formed part of the ICO bubble of 2017–18 and also against the background of Member States developing their own cryptoasset legislation, putting the European Single Market agenda at risk. For instance, France introduced its 'DLT Order' in 2017,[1] allowing issuers of some securities to register them on a distributed ledger with the same legal effect as if they were registered on a conventional securities registry. The French regulator Autorité des marchés financiers (AMF) also launched a programme dubbed 'UNICORN', which should guide token offering organisers to operate under the AMF's guidance.[2] Thereafter, the AMF also launched a comprehensive set of token offering rules in September 2018 to attract innovators globally.[3] In the same year, Malta passed its token offering rules with the Virtual Financial Assets Act.[4]

In 2018, the Government of Liechtenstein issued a proposal on cryptoassets.[5] In a far-reaching move, the corresponding act, which was adopted on 16 October 2019 and entered into force on 1 January 2020,[6] included all types of tokens, their issuers, and associated intermediaries (named 'trusted technology service providers'), with rules on private law and insolvency matters also laid out. In a similar vein, on 25 September 2020, the Swiss parliament passed the so-called DLT Act (DLT-Gesetz),[7] which amends ten existing acts to accommodate cryptoassets.[8] It covers, for

[1] Order No. 2017-1674, 8 December 2017. Website www.legifrance.gouv.fr\\loda\\id\\JORFTEXT000036171908 (last accessed on 1 October 2024).

[2] See AMF, 'L'AMF lance une consultation sur les Initial Coin Offerings et initie son programme UNICORN', Press Release (2017). Website https://perma.cc/G75E-88JT (last accessed on 1 October 2024).

[3] See A. Berman, 'France Finalizes New ICO Framework to "Attract Innovators Globally"', Cointelegraph (2018). Website https://perma.cc/AG6C-BUJ2 (last accessed on 1 October 2024); I. M. Barsan, 'Regulating the Crypto World – New Developments from France', *Revue Trimestrielle de Droit Financier*, 4 (2019): 9, 12–24.

[4] See Legislation.mt, 'Virtual Financial Assets Act'. Website https://legislation.mt/eli/cap/590/eng/pdf (last accessed on 1 October 2024).

[5] Liechtenstein Government, 'Vernehmlassungsbericht betreffend die Schaffung eines Gesetzes über auf vertrauenswürdigen Technologien (VT) beruhende Transaktionssysteme' (Blockchain-Gesetz; VT-Gesetz; VTG), 16 November 2018.

[6] Act of 3 October 2019 on 'Token und VT-Dienstleiter', Liechtenstein OJ (Liechtensteinisches Landesgesetzblatt) 2019 No. 301, 950.6, 2 Dezember 2019.

[7] Bundesgesetz vom 25 September 2021 zur Anpassung des Bundesrechts an Entwicklungen der Technik verteilter elektronischer Register, No. RO 2021 33.

[8] See R. H. Weber, 'Neue Blockchain-Gesetzgebung in der Schweiz', *Recht Digital*, 4 (2021): 186.

instance, the order of priority among competing rights to cryptoassets and the collateralising of cryptoassets while also adding a whole new chapter on DLT trading platforms, including a new authorisation regime.

The more focused Luxembourg Blockchain I, II, and III legislation of 2019, 2021, and 2023[9] allowed securities first to be registered on DLT-based accounts and then permitted the issuance and circulation of dematerialised securities directly using DLT; in 2023, while implementing the PilotR (see Chapter 12), Luxembourg also allowed the use of DLT for financial collateral arrangements since the concept of book-entry transferable financial instruments now includes "financial instruments registered or existing in securities accounts held within or through the secured electronic registration mechanisms, including distributed electronic ledgers or databases". Germany followed suit on 9 June 2021 with its act on electronic securities (eWpG), allowing for legal ownership of securities to be documented by recording on a distributed ledger rather than through conventional paper certificates.

Against this background and given the large variety of cryptoassets, MiCA shall create a technology-neutral regulatory framework. Therein, assets that qualify under existing EU financial law should be treated as such even if they use DLT and thereby also qualify as cryptoassets,[10] while MiCA itself specifically covers the remaining cryptoassets that are otherwise not subject to EU financial law.

This is achieved through a regulatory technique where MiCA at the outset applies to all cryptoassets but then explicitly excludes from all or some of its scope cryptoassets or institutions that are covered by various parts of EU financial legislation.[11] In essence, this means that MiCA covers cryptoassets that fall outside of existing EU financial law, as well as EMTs, which are covered by both MiCA and EMD.[12] As much as this approach makes sense, it also makes it notoriously difficult to determine the exact scope of MiCA because it depends on the interpretation of various pieces of EU financial law to identify where their scope ends and where that of MiCA begins. Here, in Chapter 3, we address the boundaries between MiCA and other parts of EU financial law from a conceptual point of view. Further details for various types of cryptoassets are considered in Chapters 4 and 6, while the scope regarding cryptoasset services is discussed in Chapter 7.

3.2 INVESTMENT ASSETS VS. BANKING ASSETS

The most notable exemptions from MiCA's scope are the categories of cryptoassets listed under Article 2(4) MiCA, which are essentially cryptoassets that qualify as MiFID

9 See Law of 1 March 2019 amending the General Securities Law (Blockchain I); Law of 22 January 2021 modifying (1) the law of 5 April 1993 on the financial sector and (2) the law of 6 April 2013 on dematerialised securities (Blockchain II); Law of 15 March 2023 (1) amending (a) the law of 5 April 1993 on the financial sector, as amended; (b) the law of 5 August 2005 on financial collateral arrangements, as amended; (c) the law of 30 May 2018 on markets in financial instruments, as amended; and (2) implementing Regulation (EU) 2022/858 of the European Parliament and of the Council of 30 May 2022 on a pilot regime for market infrastructures based on distributed ledger technology, and amending Regulations (EU) No. 600/2014 and (EU) No. 909/2014 and Directive 2014/65/EU (Blockchain III).

10 Recital para. 6 of MiCA Regulation Proposal, COM (2020) 593 Final. This corresponds to the 'same activity, same risk, same rules' principle under the EU's Digital Finance Strategy (DFS) 2020.

11 See Article 2(1), cf. Article 2(2) and (4) of MiCA, Regulation 2023/1114, OJ 2023 No. L150.

12 That EMTs are regulated both by MiCA and by EMD2 constitutes an exception from MiCA's "technology neutrality" principle, presumably justified by MiCA's particular aim of regulating stablecoins, which may have economic implications beyond those of conventional e-money.

financial instruments, deposits, structured deposits, funds (unless they qualify as EMTs), securitisation, or certain insurance and pension products. This list highlights that the variety of cryptoassets spans across the whole spectrum of financial law from typical investment assets (like financial instruments) to typical banking assets (like deposits) and hybrids (like structured deposits). This is because cryptoassets are defined by their use of DLT rather than the characteristics of the assets themselves (see Section 1.1), and it means that gap-filling legislation like MiCA necessarily complements very different types of existing financial legislation.

Fundamentally, the purpose of the financial system is to facilitate transactions and to fund investments in the real economy by exchanging capital today for capital tomorrow. This is achieved through the issuance and trading of financial assets, where the financial system can assume two fundamentally different roles.

First, financial firms can be pure intermediaries, facilitating the issuance and trading of financial assets issued by others (so-called 'off-balance sheet intermediation'). This is, for instance, the case with financial instruments, such as shares and bonds. Here, the primary risk for investors is fiduciary and, depending on the economic performance of the issuing firm in the real economy, lies outside of the financial system. Hence, the role of financial law for these assets is primarily to prevent market abuse and ensure that investors are provided with the information they need to evaluate risks in relation to both the issuance and secondary trading of financial assets.

Second, financial firms can carry the risk involved on their own balance sheets (so-called 'on-balance sheet intermediation'). This is the core business of banks, which borrow money from depositors and lend it out to clients in need of financing. Here, the main risk involved is the insolvency of the financial entity itself, meaning that the risk sits inside the financial system and, hence, under the scope of financial law. Therefore, banking legislation mitigates risk primarily through regulating what banks and bank-like entities can and cannot do, with the aim to protect their balance sheets against excessive risk-taking. The backing of a "strong" balance sheet means that banking assets typically retain a stable value relative to that of the more volatile investment assets. Therefore, banking assets are suitable as a unit of exchange, much like cash, underpinning transactions involving bank transfers, and e-money, for example. This implies that financial legislation for banking assets must also mitigate risks associated with the handling of payments.

Because of the fundamentally different risks that financial law aims to mitigate for investment assets and banking assets, the type of financial regulation also varies considerably. This explains why MiCA, as gap-filling legislation for all cryptoassets, entails very different rules for the different types of cryptoassets under its scope. Essentially, the rules for ARTs and EMTs under Titles III and IV MiCA, respectively, regulate some features of cryptoassets akin to banking assets, in that the issuer promises a stable value (akin to a bank deposit), albeit this stable value may be realised by a type of asset swap through redemption only (similar to open-ended investment funds, an archetypical investment asset). Hence, these MiCA rules lean to some extent on EU banking legislation, such as the Capital Requirements Regulation (CRR) and EMD. On the contrary, other cryptoassets under MiCA's scope are regulated under Title II MiCA. Together with Title V on cryptoasset service providers and Title VI on market abuse, which both apply to all cryptoassets, Title II MiCA resembles EU legislation on investment assets, such as MiFID and the Prospectus Regulation (PR). The role of MiCA vs. existing EU financial law for investment assets, banking assets, and hybrids thereof, respectively, is the focus of the following sub-chapters.

3.3 INVESTMENT ASSETS

3.3.1 *Legal Coverage under EU Financial Law*

MiCA exempts from its scope both financial instruments as defined by MiFID[13] and securitisation as defined and specifically regulated by Regulation (EU) 2017/2402 (STSR). While the reference to MiFID financial instruments covers the bulk of investment assets under EU financial law, securitisation refers to securitisation schemes standardised by STSR that pool other investment assets, namely, various types of debt such as residential mortgages, commercial mortgages, auto loans, or credit card debt.[14] STSR covers by far not all types of securitisation schemes,[15] yet the common feature of securitisation schemes is that they issue transferable securities and thus fall, as a default option, under the term financial instruments.

Large parts of EU financial law apply to financial instruments that are traded or admitted to trading on a trading venue – and sometimes also to financial instruments irrespective of trading on such venues. For example, MiFID sets authorisation, capital, organisational, and operating requirements for investment firms, MiFIR requires transparency from trading venues, the Market Abuse Regulation (MAR) and Market Abuse Directive (MAD) deal with inside information and market abuse, the Short Selling Regulation (SSR) covers short selling, while the CSDR and the Settlement Finality Directive (SFD) regulate settlement activities. Because this legislation applies to 'financial instruments' as defined in MiFID, many cryptoasset service providers (CASPs) may find themselves under the stricter regulatory regime of this EU financial regulation (compared to MiCA's more lenient rules) if the tokens qualify as financial instruments.[16]

Some parts of EU financial law apply specifically to certain subsets of MiFID financial instruments, most notably 'transferable securities'. In fact, important pieces of EU financial law apply to transferable securities only, such as the PR and, for the most part, the Transparency Directive (TD). Similarly, the European Market Infrastructure Regulation (EMIR) entails separate rules for certain derivatives, while units in collective investment undertakings (CIUs) are regulated specifically by the Undertakings for Collective Investment in Transferable Securities Directive (UCITSD),[17] the Alternative Investment Fund Managers Directive (AIFMD),[18] the Money Market Funds Regulation (MMFR),[19] the European Long-Term Investment Funds Regulation (ELTIFR),[20] as well as the European Venture Capital Funds

[13] See Article 4(1)(15), cf. Section C of Annex I of MiFID, Directive 2014/65, OJ 2014 No. L173.

[14] See Article 2(1) of Regulation 2017/2402, OJ 2017 No. L347.

[15] For an in-depth discussion, see D. A. Zetzsche and S. N. Hooghiemstra, 'Securitizations and SPVs under STSR and AIFMD', in D. A. Zetzsche (ed.), *The Alternative Investment Fund Managers Directive* (Alphen aan den Rijn: Wolters Kluwer, 2020), 3rd ed., pp. 375, 376–86.

[16] ESMA estimated in 2019 that up to 30 per cent of all cryptoassets outstanding qualify as financial instruments. See ESMA, 'Advice – Initial Coin Offerings and Crypto-Assets', para. 82.

[17] Directive 2009/65/EC of the European Parliament and of the Council of 13 July 2009 on the coordination of laws, regulations, and administrative provisions relating to undertakings for collective investment in transferrable securities (UCITS), OJ 2009 No. L302, 17 November 2009.

[18] Directive 2011/61/EU of the European Parliament and of the Council of 8 June 2011 on Alternative Investment Fund Managers and Amending Directives 2003/41/EC and 2009/65/EC and Regulations (EC) No. 1060/2009 and (EU) No. 1095/2010, OJ 2011 No. L174, 1 July 2011.

[19] Regulation 2017/1131 of the European Parliament and of the Council of 14 June 2017 on money market funds, OJ 2017 No. L169, 30 June 2017.

[20] Regulation (EU) 2015/760 of the European Parliament and of the Council of 29 April 2015 on European long-term investment funds, OJ 2015 No. L123, 19 May 2015.

(EuVeCa) Regulation[21] and the European Social Entrepreneurship Funds (EUSEF) Regulation.[22] Note that not all units issued by collective investment schemes, or which they invest in, qualify as financial instruments; it is here that MiCA and EU investment fund law overlap (cf. Chapter 9).

3.3.2 *MiFID Financial Instruments: Challenges*

While we discuss cryptoassets under the various parts of MiFID's "financial instrument" definition in Section 4.4.2, the ESMA's 2019 report clearly articulates the broader challenge of achieving a harmonised application of EU financial law for cryptoassets.[23] Based on a survey of twenty-nine NCAs,[24] the ESMA found wide discrepancies as to whether they considered a set of six real cryptoasset examples to qualify as MiFID financial instruments under their respective national laws. In fact, in just one of the six cases did all NCAs agree on the legal qualification, and even then, there were different opinions as to which of the criteria under the MiFID definition that were or were not met. In the other five cases, the NCAs were split with at least a significant minority deviating from the majority view.

The discrepancies across NCAs were driven partly by different interpretations of the same terms, but also by twelve out of twenty-nine NCAs reporting to have national criteria that deviate from the definition of 'financial instruments' under MiFID.[25] For example, German law considers 'units similar to foreign currencies and not of legal tender' to be financial instruments, a category that is not recognised by MiFID. This has led the German regulator BaFin to treat cryptocurrencies as financial instruments under this uniquely German category.[26] On the other hand, three of the NCAs in the ESMA's survey reported that they have in their national legislation a compulsory book-entry recording requirement, which does not allow them to qualify securities other than those explicitly classified as such by law.[27] Similarly, while MiFID itself has no definition of 'instruments of payment' (but explicitly excludes such instruments from the definition of 'transferable securities'),[28] ten NCAs reported having national definitions.[29] These broad discrepancies in the treatment of cryptoassets under the definition of MiFID financial instruments translate into different views on the scope of MiCA as gap-filling legislation for cryptoassets other than MiFID financial instruments.

3.3.3 *MiCA's Gap-Filling Function*

A number of cryptoassets with investment asset characteristics do not qualify as MiFID financial instruments. The most obvious example is so-called utility tokens, which grant some sort of

[21] Regulation (EU) No. 345/2013 of the European Parliament and of the Council of 17 April 2013 on European venture capital funds, OJ 2013 No. L115, 25 April 2013.

[22] Regulation (EU) No. 346/2013 of the European Parliament and of the Council of 17 April 2013 on European social entrepreneurship funds, OJ 2013 No. L115, 25 April 2013.

[23] ESMA, 'Advice – Initial Coin Offerings and Crypto-Assets', with the associated ESMA, 'Annex 1: Legal Qualifications of Crypto-Assets – Survey to NCAs', ESMA50-157-1384 (2019).

[24] 27 Member States, Liechtenstein, and Norway.

[25] ESMA, 'Annex 1: Legal Qualifications of Crypto-Assets', para. 24.

[26] See N. Vandezande, 'Regulating Initial Coin Offerings and DAO Tokens under the EU's Financial Instruments Framework', *Law and Financial Markets Review*, 14(1) (2020): 33, 36.

[27] ESMA, 'Annex 1: Legal Qualifications of Crypto-Assets', para. 25.

[28] See Article 4(1)(44) of MiFID.

[29] ESMA, 'Annex 1: Legal Qualifications of Crypto-Assets', para. 39. (The ten countries had transposed in their legislation the definition of 'payment instrument' in Article 4(14) of PSD2, Directive 2015/2366, OJ 2015 No. L337.)

access or right(s) to use ecosystems, goods, or services, such as a licence to use a software program (usage token) or a membership in a community (community token).[30] These are often issued by companies to raise capital and traded by investors much like transferable securities, but they often do not qualify as such under MiFID. Other examples could be, for instance, tokens similar to shares or bonds, but with a lock-up mechanism that prevents them from being 'negotiable on the capital market' and thereby also from qualifying as transferable securities. Furthermore, tokens can represent derivatives that may not qualify as MiFID financial instruments, such as commodity derivatives for physical settlement that are not traded on a regulated market. Similarly, cryptoassets that represent ownership of other non-financial assets, like a property deed, would also not qualify as MiFID financial instruments.

The examples from the ESMA's survey of NCAs, as described in Section 3.3.2, show that it is often far from simple to determine whether a cryptoasset either qualifies as a MiFID financial instrument or falls under the scope of MiCA.[31] In such cases, the very fact that MiCA applies to all cryptoassets that fall outside the scope of existing EU financial law also means that the definitions become less important in practice. There is little to gain for private parties from having their assets classified as one type or another insofar as MiCA and EU financial law for MiFID financial instruments provide a similar set of rules.

3.4 BANKING ASSETS

3.4.1 *Legal Coverage under EU Financial Law*

MiCA exempts from its scope funds (unless they qualify as EMTs) and deposits, along with a variety of insurance products, which also have banking asset characteristics.[32] Moreover, certain bank-like institutions are exempted altogether from MiCA, namely, the European Central Bank and national central banks of Member States when acting as a monetary authority.[33] These institutions are similar to banks in the sense that they carry financial risks on their own balance sheets.

Generally, banks and other credit institutions are authorised and supervised under the Capital Requirements Directive (CRD), and they must adhere to prudential requirements under the CRR. Similar rules exist for insurance undertakings under the Solvency II Directive.[34] In addition, according to the Deposit Guarantee Schemes Directive (DGSD) and the Investor Compensation Schemes Directive (ICSD), Member States must establish guarantee schemes to protect investors against the insolvency of financial firms. Payment services[35] with regard to 'funds'[36] are further governed by the Payment Services Directive (PSD2) and, as one type of 'funds', e-money is governed by EMD.

30 Article 3(1)(9) of MiCA defines utility token as 'a type of crypto-asset that is only intended to provide access to a good or a service supplied by its issuer'.

31 See D. A. Zetzsche *et al.*, 'The Markets in Crypto-Assets Regulation (MiCA) and the EU Digital Finance Strategy', *Capital Markets Law Journal*, 16(2) (2021): 203, 218–21.

32 Article 2(4)(b), (c), and (e) of MiCA.

33 Article 2(2)(c) and (d) of MiCA.

34 Directive 2009/138/EC of the European Parliament and of the Council of 25 November 2009 on the taking-up and pursuit of the business of Insurance and Reinsurance (Solvency II), OJ 2009 No. L335, 17 December 2009.

35 See Article 4(3), cf. Annex I of PSD2.

36 Article 4(25) of PSD2.

3.4.2 *Funds and E-money: Challenges*

In its 2019 report, the EBA demonstrated that cryptoassets backed by fiat money (i.e., stablecoins) may indeed qualify as e-money under EMD.[37] The same is true for less typical token schemes, for instance, where tokens are used for specific payments like charity donations, with the option to redeem the tokens at par value.[38] Following its principle of "technological neutrality", the original MiCA proposal exempted e-money from its scope, unless they qualified as EMTs.[39] This caused difficulties because of the partial overlaps between the EMT and e-money definitions, meaning that the proposal's exemption for e-money was probably superfluous. Hence, under the adopted version of MiCA, all EMTs now qualify as e-money,[40] with the implication that EMD applies to them.

This is important because e-money institutions under EMD need authorisation, for instance, and they are also not banks, so they are not allowed to take deposits,[41] to pay interest,[42] or to grant credit from the funds they receive in exchange for e-money.[43] Moreover, PSD2 applies to firms that want to carry out a 'payment service'[44] with regard to 'funds', which includes e-money.[45] So when EMTs qualify as e-money, they also qualify as funds under PSD2.

Yet, while MiCA thus solves the question of whether EMTs also qualify as e-money and funds, it remains unclear whether the reverse is also true. The conundrum is amplified by MiCA making an exemption for 'funds' as defined by PSD2,[46] unless they qualify as EMTs. Under this definition, funds are defined as 'banknotes and coins, scriptural money or electronic money'.[47] Yet, because cryptoassets that would otherwise qualify under MiCA are probably not banknotes, coins, or scriptural money, they qualify as 'funds' under PSD2 only if they also qualify as e-money. This leaves the question of whether all cryptoassets that qualify as 'funds' also qualify as EMTs, which we discuss further in Section 4.4.3.

3.4.3 *MiCA's Gap-Filling Function*

With regard to banking assets, like deposits and e-money, MiCA complements existing EU financial law in four ways.

First, as shown in Section 4.4.3, numerous cryptoassets have banking asset characteristics but do not qualify as 'funds' under PSD2 or e-money under the EMD definition. These would typically qualify as either EMTs under MiCA, if they purported to maintain a stable value by reference to one fiat currency, or ARTs if referenced to several fiat currencies, commodities,

[37] EBA, 'Report with Advice for the European Commission', p. 13, referring to the following made-up example: 'Company A wishes to create a Blockchain-based payment network. The network is open meaning that both merchants and consumers can participate. Company A explains that it intends to issue a token which is intended to be the means of payment in the network. The token is issued on the receipt of fiat currency and is pegged to the given currency (e.g., EUR 1 to 1 token). The token can be redeemed at any time. The actual payment on this network is the underlying claim against Company A or the right to get the claim redeemed'.

[38] See EBA, 'Report with Advice for the European Commission', p. 13.

[39] See Article 2(2)(b) of MiCA Regulation Proposal, COM (2020) 593 Final.

[40] See Article 48(2) of MiCA.

[41] Article 6(2) of EMD.

[42] Article 12 of EMD.

[43] Article 6(1) of EMD.

[44] See Article 4(3), cf. Annex I of PSD2.

[45] Article 4(25) of PSD2.

[46] Article 2(4)(c), cf. Article 3(1)(14) of MiCA.

[47] Article 4(25) of PSD2.

other cryptoassets, or a combination of such assets.[48] These cryptoassets are regulated under Titles III and IV MiCA, which to a large extent mimic existing EU financial law for banking assets. Title III MiCA on ARTs includes, for instance, requirements for authorisation of issuers, own funds, and reserve assets, while Title IV MiCA on EMTs prohibits the issuer from paying interest and makes EMTs redeemable at par value, just like e-money under EMD.[49] Moreover, Article 48(2) MiCA states that EMTs shall also be deemed e-money, thus making EMD directly applicable to all EMTs.

Second, even if cryptoassets that qualify as funds under PSD2 are exempt from MiCA because they are subject to existing EU financial law, they are still subject to MiCA insofar as they also qualify as EMTs.[50] This means, for instance, that MiCA's disclosure (whitepaper) and marketing communication rules apply, along with the operating conditions for cryptoasset service providers, the market abuse regime, and the system for supervision. As discussed further in Section 4.4.3, we suspect that all or almost all cryptoassets that qualify under the strict EMD definition of e-money, and even those that qualify under the wider PSD2 definition of funds, will also qualify as EMTs under MiCA if the e-money is tokenised. Hence, the entire exemption from MiCA of funds seems to be of little practical value, with the effect that MiCA, EMD, and sometimes PSD2 apply simultaneously. This constitutes an exception from MiCA's "technology neutrality" principle, presumably justified by MiCA's particular aim of regulating stablecoins, which may have economic implications beyond those of conventional e-money and other payment instruments.

Third, cryptoassets with similar characteristics to deposits may still not qualify as such under EU financial law (see Section 4.4.4). Hence, even if many stablecoins certainly have similar characteristics to deposits (and not just to e-money), they typically do not qualify as such, meaning that MiCA steps in as gap-filling legislation.

Finally, as discussed in Section 3.3 with regard to investment assets, the very fact that MiCA applies to all cryptoassets that fall outside the scope of existing EU financial law means that the definitions become less important in practice. Simply put, private parties do not stand to gain much from having their assets classified as one or the other type under EU law when the rules for both are similar.

3.5 HYBRID ASSETS: STRUCTURED DEPOSITS

There are of course hybrid asset types, as all assets cannot fit neatly into one side of the investment asset vs. banking asset divide. The most prominent example in EU financial law is a structured deposit, which is defined in Article 4(1)(43) MiFID and loosely refers to a deposit where the returns (interest or a premium) are linked to external factors such as the value of an index, a financial instrument, or a commodity. Hence, an asset must first qualify as a 'deposit' (see Sections 3.4 and 4.4.4), with additional criteria to be met to qualify as a 'structured deposit'. For example, if or when we see cryptoassets that qualify as deposits, it is easy to imagine the returns on such cryptoassets being linked to the value of other cryptoassets.

Due to its hybrid character, EU financial law on structured deposits contains elements from both investment asset and banking asset legislation. For instance, if combined with

48 Article 3(1), (3), and (4) of MiCA.

49 See Articles 36, 44, and 45 of MiCA, cf. Article 11 of EMD2.

50 Article 2(2)(b) of MiCA.

granting credits, the offering of structured deposits would make the issuer qualify as a 'credit institution' under the CRR,[51] with implications for prudential requirements and more. Similarly, the market for structured deposits is scrutinised by the EBA, as opposed to the ESMA, which monitors the market for financial instruments.[52] Yet, in other respects, rules minted on financial instruments apply. For example, investment firms and credit institutions that sell or advise clients in relation to structured deposits must be covered by an investor compensation scheme (as opposed to a deposit guarantee scheme),[53] prevent conflicts of interest,[54] follow typical investor protection rules,[55] and be supervised by NCAs under coordination by the ESMA (as opposed to the EBA).[56]

For cryptoassets that do not qualify as structured deposits but bear similar characteristics, it would be natural to expect that they qualify as ARTs under MiCA. After all, ARTs are also referenced to other assets, much like structured deposits, and the MiCA rules for ARTs entail both investment asset (e.g., disclosure/whitepaper) and banking asset (e.g., own funds) requirements. However, structured deposits are redeemable at par value, and only the returns are referenced to other assets, while for ARTs, the entire asset 'purports to maintain a stable value by referring to' other assets.[57] Hence, it seems like the entire value of a cryptoasset must follow the reference assets in order to qualify as an ART. The implication of this is that cryptoassets that do not qualify as structured deposits but demonstrate similar characteristics would be considered either MiFID financial instruments or cryptoassets other than ARTs or EMTs, and thereby fall under Title II MiCA together with utility tokens. The latter would make for a light regulatory regime for investment assets, which is not really suitable for hybrids with characteristics of structured deposits. (On the classification of hybrid assets under MiCA, see Section 4.4.5.)

3.6 CONCLUSION

Given its role as gap-filling legislation, MiCA mirrors EU financial law for investment assets and banking assets. Because all cryptoassets have the potential to be traded, basic rules for investment assets apply to all cryptoassets under MiCA – namely, Title V on cryptoasset service providers and Title VI on market abuse. In addition, cryptoassets with banking characteristics would typically qualify as either ARTs or EMTs, with the consequence that banking asset rules apply, such as requirements for authorisation of issuers, own funds, and reserve assets. For ARTs, these rules are entailed in Title III MiCA, while for EMTs, they are partly covered in Title IV MiCA and partly by the fact that EMD applies to EMTs, which qualify as e-money. The banking asset characteristics of ARTs and EMTs are also reflected in the fact that supervisory authority is coordinated by the EBA and, for so-called significant ARTs and EMTs, the EBA is entirely responsible for supervision. Meanwhile, cryptoassets with investment asset characteristics are subject to Title II MiCA (unless they qualify under existing EU financial law), which provides a

[51] Article 4(1)(1) of CRR, Regulation 575/2013, OJ 2013 No. L176.
[52] Article 39(2), cf. 39(1) of MiFIR, Regulation 600/2014, OJ 2014 No. L173.
[53] Article 1(4)(a), cf. Article 14 of MiFID.
[54] Article 1(4)(a) and (b), cf. Articles 23 and 16(2) and (3) of MiFID.
[55] Article 1(4)(b), cf. Articles 23–26, Articles 28 and 29 (excluding the second subparagraph of paragraph 2 thereof), and Article 30 of MiFID.
[56] Article 1(4)(c), cf. Articles 67–75 of MiFID.
[57] Article 3(1)(3) of MiCA.

light disclosure (whitepaper) regime, effectively mimicking EU law for financial assets when combined with the general rules in MiCA Titles V and VI.

In sum, this creates a sound legal framework, where the risk inherent in the different types of cryptoassets are accounted for and mitigated. Of course, cryptoassets also carry risks other than the ones captured by MiCA and EU financial law (see Section 1.3), yet these are largely tech risks addressed by generic risk management requirements of MiCA (see Chapter 7) or the bespoke tech risk rules under the domain of DORA (see Chapter 15).

4

Scope of MiCA

As explained in Chapter 3, MiCA adopts a regulatory approach by which it applies to all 'cryptoassets'[1] but then makes substantial exceptions in light of its gap-filling function in the context of EU financial law (Figure 4.1). Here, in Chapter 4, we discuss first the definition of 'cryptoassets' (Section 4.1), the exemptions that apply thereto (Section 4.2), and MiCA's geographical scope (Section 4.3), before we deep-dive into the regulation's difficult interface in relation to other EU financial law (Section 4.4), how MiCA attempts to solve the issues relating to its scope (Section 4.5), and finally, we conclude in Section 4.6.

4.1 STARTING POINT: ALL 'CRYPTOASSETS'

To determine the scope of MiCA, it is necessary to start with the term 'cryptoasset', which is defined as 'a digital representation of a value or of a right that is able to be transferred and stored electronically using distributed ledger technology or similar technology'.[2] Further specifications of the term 'distributed ledger technology' are also provided.[3] By including both value and rights here, MiCA covers essentially all kinds of cryptoassets – even utility tokens and other cryptoassets where the underlying value may not be obvious, but that still represent a right to something.[4]

Similarly, its DLT definition is deliberately wide so as to encompass new technological innovations. This corresponds to the intention of MiCA's scope being future-proof and able to keep pace with technological developments as cryptoassets and DLT are 'defined as widely as possible to capture all types of cryptoassets that currently fall outside the scope of Union legislative acts on financial services'.[5] It seems to be sufficient that the data are recorded in a

[1] Article 2(1) of MiCA, Regulation 2023/1114, OJ 2023 No. L150.

[2] Article 3(1)(5) of MiCA. See also ESMA, 'Consultation Paper on the Draft Guidelines on the Conditions and Criteria for the Qualification of Crypto-Assets as Financial Instruments', ESMA75–453128700-52, Guideline 7 (2024).

[3] Article 3(1)(1)–(4) of MiCA. See also Section 2.1 of this book regarding the technology.

[4] See Recital 2 of MiCA and the ESAs, 'Consultation Paper: Draft Guidelines on Templates for Explanations and Opinions, and the Standardised Test for the Classification of Crypto-assets, under Article 97(1) of Regulation (EU) 2023/1114' (2024), ESA 2024 12, para. 18.

[5] Recital para. 16 of MiCA (which further notes that the definitions should ensure that entities under the scope of MiCA and existing EU legislation on cryptoassets must also comply with anti-money laundering and counter-terrorist financing legislation. To this end, one can assume that all "cryptoassets" under MiCA are also covered by the term "virtual assets" as defined in the guidance of the FATF. See Fatf-gafi.org, 'Updated Guidance for a Risk-Based Approach to Virtual Assets and Virtual Asset Service Providers' (2021). Website www.fatf-gafi.org/en/publications/Fatfrecommendations/Guidance-rba-virtual-assets-2021.html (last accessed on 1 October 2024).

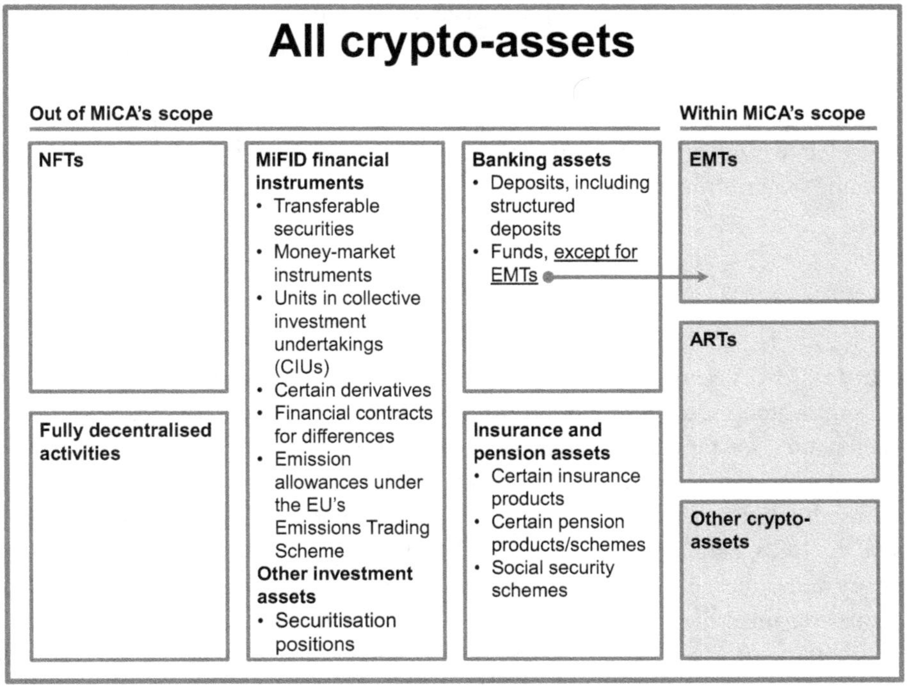

FIGURE 4.1 Scope of MiCA

distributed fashion, synchronised through a consensus mechanism. It is not necessary, for instance, that the data be encrypted or stored in blocks, as commonly used terms such as 'cryptoassets' or 'blockchain' might indicate. The DLT definition has been revised several times, first through the MiCA legislative process, before the final MiCA and PilotR definitions were harmonised.[6] We approve of this relatively future-proof definition eventually arrived at, which focuses on the key aspects of the relevant technology.

As part of the cryptoasset definition, it is a requirement that cryptoassets are 'able to be transferred and stored' by means of DLT or similar technology.[7] On the one hand, it is not sufficient that the cryptoassets may be either transferred or stored/recorded by these means. On the other hand, MiCA has a broader scope than PilotR, which applies only to cryptoassets that are 'issued, recorded, transferred, and stored' using DLT (see Section 12.2.1).[8] Here, the MiCA formulation seems to meet a practical need with respect to the use of DLT for parts of the trading and settlement processes only.[9] The wording also indicates that MiCA applies even to assets that primarily use conventional technologies as long as they are also able to be transferred and stored using DLT or similar technology.

It is, of course, natural to interpret the term 'cryptoasset' as a reference to some kind of cryptography. This was explicitly avoided in the course of the legislative process, however, with

[6] See, for example, some early revisions of the MiCA text proposed in the Committee on Economic and Monetary Affairs (ECON), 'Draft Report, 2020/0267 (COD)', European Parliament (2021), pp. 43–44.

[7] On the term 'transferred', see the ESA's, 'Consultation Paper: Draft Guidelines on Templates for Explanations and Opinions, and the Standardised Test for the Classification of Crypto-assets, under Article 97(1) of Regulation (EU) 2023/1114' (2024), ESA 2024 12, para. 19.

[8] Article 2(11) of PilotR, Regulation 2022/858, OJ 2022 No. L151.

[9] See Committee on Payments and Market Infrastructures, 'Distributed Ledger Technology', p. 11.

typical cryptoassets such as Ether (ETH) not necessarily encrypted.[10] Finally, with the inclusion of cryptoassets using 'similar technology' to DLT, it seems that MiCA covers the use of most, if not all, distributed transfer and recording technology. This means that, in sum, MiCA's definition of cryptoassets is all-encompassing because it covers all types of cryptoassets that we know of, which may use any combination of technologies that includes the option of transferring and recording on a distributed network.

4.2 EXEMPTIONS

4.2.1 *Exempted Entities*

In Article 2(2), MiCA exempts certain entities from its scope for specific reasons. The first such category is intra-group services or 'persons who provide cryptoasset services exclusively for their parent companies, for their subsidiaries or for other subsidiaries of their parent companies'.[11] Here, typical regulatory objectives, like consumer and investor protection, do not apply.

The second category concerns EU and other public authorities. Specifically, the exemption applies to 'the ECB, national central banks of the Member States when acting in their capacity as monetary authorities, or other public authorities of the Member States',[12] as well as 'public international organisations',[13] and specific EU entities.[14] It seems to us that the term 'other public authorities of the Member States' is all-encompassing so that the central banks of Member States would, for instance, be exempted also when acting outside their capacity as monetary authorities. Similarly, the term 'public international organisations' could be read to encompass all EU entities; then the specific listing of exempted EU entities is superfluous.

The exemption of public entities excludes from MiCA's scope the possible launch of CBDCs. With regard to the ECB, it is also explicitly stated that MiCA operates without prejudice to the Single Supervisory Mechanism (SSM Regulation)[15] according to which the ECB is handed specific tasks related to the prudential supervision of credit institutions. The exclusion of public entities also corresponds to most academic definitions of cryptoassets, which tend to explicitly exclude assets that are issued or guaranteed by a central bank or public authority.[16] Instead of excluding these assets from the cryptoasset definition, MiCA exempts such entities from its scope. This has the seemingly intentional consequence of private CBDC service providers being subject to MiCA as CASPs.

Article 2(2)(b) MiCA exempts 'a liquidator or an administrator acting in the course of an insolvency procedure'. Given that liquidation typically does not involve the issuance of cryptoassets, the emphasis of this exemption is on insolvency proceedings where the issuer's operations are ongoing or where CASPs issue tokens as part of their regular business (e.g., liquidity pool managers). Such liquidators or administrators are nevertheless explicitly not exempted from Article 47 MiCA, which regulates the orderly redemption of ART holders in

[10] See Committee on Economic and Monetary Affairs (ECON), 'Draft Report, 2020/0265 (COD)', European Parliament (2021), pp. 6–7.
[11] Article 2(2)(a) of MiCA.
[12] Article 2(2)(c) of MiCA.
[13] Article 2(2)(f) of MiCA.
[14] Article 2(2)(d) and (e) of MiCA.
[15] Council Regulation (EU) 1024/2013 of 15 October 2013 conferring specific tasks on the European Central Bank concerning policies relating to the prudential supervision of credit institutions, OJ 2013 No. L287, 29 October 2013. See Article 2(6) of MiCA.
[16] See Houben and Snyers, 'Crypto-Assets', pp. 16–17.

the event of, for instance, the issuer's insolvency. According to Article 55 MiCA, Article 47 MiCA also applies to issuers of EMTs. If an issuer of EMTs goes into liquidation or enters insolvency proceedings, it seems to us that the same regulatory objectives are pursued so that the liquidator or administrator is subject to Article 47 MiCA (by reference to Article 55) just as if it were an ART issuer going into liquidation or entering insolvency proceedings.

Finally, it is also worth mentioning that specific types of entities are exempted from various authorisation requirements under MiCA because they are already authorised under EU financial law. For instance, credit institutions and managers of collective investment schemes may provide certain cryptoasset services; in some cases, however, they need to expand their existing licence.[17] Similarly, credit institutions are exempted from the authorisation requirement for ART and EMT issuers,[18] and so too are e-money institutions with regard to EMTs.[19]

4.2.2 *The Exemption for NFTs*

MiCA is a piece of financial regulation, so it aims to cover only cryptoassets that raise regulatory concerns similar to those dealt with by other financial regulation.[20] In Article 2(3) MiCA, this is expressed through an explicit exemption for NFTs, which was added during the trilogue process as NFTs became increasingly popular in the marketplace. This makes sense, but it also points to the possibility that other new types of cryptoassets may emerge in the future, which will not fit well with MiCA or financial regulation in general. Even for existing NFTs, it is not obvious how to draw the boundaries of MiCA's scope.

The exemption applies to 'cryptoassets that are unique and not fungible with other cryptoassets'.[21] This extends beyond classical NFTs that represent digital art pieces and would include, for instance, (smart) contracts resulting in tokens tailored to the needs of specific parties. Hence, the exemption may to some extent apply also to so-called financial NFTs, which are tokenised financial products.[22] An insurance contract can be tokenised, for instance, but so too could any other cash-flow-yielding contract like a lending agreement. If the underlying product or service of a *utility token* is unique to the holder, this also makes a difficult distinction between typical utility tokens, which are in scope of MiCA, and NFTs, which are not.[23]

According to the term's original meaning, an NFT is a cryptographic token that cannot be interchanged in a like-for-like manner.[24] In a world where one ETH cryptoasset is equal to another one, cases where a token is not akin to another are an exception. Essentially, an NFT is a type of digitally securitised asset that only exists in one copy, and hence, it is unique. Yet, as is

[17] See Article 59(1)(b), cf. Article 60 of MiCA. For details, see Chapter 7.

[18] Articles 16(1)(b) and 48(1)(a) of MiCA.

[19] Article 48(1)(a) of MiCA.

[20] See F. Annunziata, 'An Overview of the Markets in Crypto-Assets Regulation', EBI Working Paper Series No. 158 (2023), pp. 30-32. Website https://dx.doi.org/10.2139/ssrn.4660379 (last accessed on 1 October 2024).

[21] Article 2(3) and Recital 10 of MiCA. See also ESMA, 'Consultation Paper on the Draft Guidelines on the Conditions and Criteria for the Qualification of Crypto-Assets as Financial Instruments', ESMA75-453128700-52, Guideline 8 (2024); the ESAs, 'Consultation Paper: Draft Guidelines on Templates for Explanations and Opinions, and the Standardised Test for the Classification of Crypto-assets, under Article 97(1) of Regulation (EU) 2023/1114' (2024), ESA 2024 12, para. 21(b).

[22] See Zetzsche *et al.*, 'Remaining Regulatory Challenges in Digital Finance', pp. 96–104.

[23] One could argue that utility tokens that give access to an *existing* good or service has no financial component and should then be exempted from MiCA. This, however, is not sufficient as Article 4(3)(c) and (4) MiCA takes a more nuanced approach and exempts such tokens from parts of MiCA only.

[24] Binance Academy, 'What Is an NFT?' (2023). Website https://academy.binance.com/en/articles/what-is-an-nft (last accessed on 1 October 2024).

found with tokenised music, the underlying asset can be represented multiple times, albeit its use can be restricted to one user at a time. In such instances, the uniqueness may stem from the personalisation of users' rights.

NFTs are also unique in a technical sense, which is achieved through the respective token standard that is used.[25] In particular, while fungible token standards require that each token has the same value as another token created in accordance with the same protocol, the NFT standard ERC-721, for instance, allows for the processing of several tokens that each have a different value compared to other tokens that are created through the same protocol.[26] Each ERC-721 NFT has a token identification code property that must be globally unique, analogous to a postage stamp series where each stamp has a unique number.[27] This does not imply any rareness or scarcity of the underlying asset, but the token can nevertheless be enriched with properties that attribute uniqueness to the NFT within its collection. Often, the combination of different attributes of one NFT is unique but not its individual attributes. For instance, financial NFTs may function as governance tokens allowing holders to vote on, for example, the allocation of rewards to liquidity providers.[28]

Given the broad wording of MiCA and our experience with the crypto industry so far, we expect crypto intermediaries to stretch the limits of MiCA's exemption for NFTs. Yet, according to Recitals 10 and 11 of MiCA, the concept of 'substance over form' must apply. Hence, naming a token an NFT or using an NFT technical standard would not confirm that it falls outside MiCA's scope. But what constitutes substance in this regard? First, it can be derived from these recitals that digital art, collectibles, and cryptoassets representing services or physical assets that are unique and non-fungible, such as product guarantees or real estate, remain outside MiCA's scope, while 'fractional parts of a unique and non-fungible cryptoasset should not be considered unique and non-fungible'. Second, MiCA acknowledges that exempted NFTs may still be traded on the marketplace and be accumulated speculatively. This is logical as a single piece of art may well be traded at prices many would consider unfathomable.

It seems to us that the defining criteria for what qualifies as an NFT under MiCA is whether the 'value of such unique and non-fungible cryptoassets is attributable to each cryptoasset's unique characteristics and the utility it gives to the holder of the token' so that they 'are not readily interchangeable and the relative value of one such cryptoasset in relation to another, each being unique, cannot be ascertained by means of comparison to an existing market or equivalent asset'.[29]

This required standard of a having a unique value applies to all cryptoassets alike, whether they be financial NFTs, art, music, or otherwise. When issuing a collection or series becomes synonymous with fungibility in this sense, it will result in, for example, NFT art collections

[25] K. Garbers-von Boehm *et al.*, 'Intellectual Property Rights and Distributed Ledger Technology with a Focus on Art NFTs and Tokenized Art', Study PE 737.709. European Parliament (2022), p. 13. Website www.europarl.europa.eu/thinktank/en/document/IPOL_STU(2022)737709 (last accessed on 1 October 2024); Zetzsche *et al.*, 'Remaining Regulatory Challenges in Digital Finance', pp. 96–98.

[26] Several other examples of NFT standards are listed in Zetzsche *et al.*, 'Remaining Regulatory Challenges in Digital Finance', pp. 96–98.

[27] See Ethereum, 'ERC-721 Non-Fungible Token Standard'. Website https://ethereum.org/en/developers/docs/standards/tokens/erc-721/ (last accessed on 1 October 2024).

[28] Equalizer Exchange, 'Gauge Voting & Bribes' (2022). Website https://equalizerox.gitbook.io/equalizer-exchange-docs/guides/gauge-voting-and-bribes (last accessed on 1 October 2024); Thena, 'VeTHE' (2023). Website https://thena.gitbook.io/thena/the-tokenomics/vethe (last accessed on 1 October 2024).

[29] Recital para. 10 of MiCA, which further states that '[s]uch features limit the extent to which those crypto-assets can have a financial use, thus limiting risks to holders and the financial system and justifying their exclusion from the scope of this Regulation'.

being included in the scope of MiCA. As a comparison, the works of Rothko or Warhol are, in principle, not fungible even if they are part of a print series of 100 copies since one copy can be in a different state than another one. Yet, different copies of digital art may be identical (such as NFTs where the only difference is the identification number), so they may be subject to MiCA. It is probable that a mere few copies would not make the NFT fungible as part of an NFT series by the standard of MiCA, but at around ten copies, we assume that the value of each copy will be 'ascertained by means of comparison to an existing market or equivalent asset'[30] and may indeed fall within MiCA's scope. When a series reaches this level, typical objectives of financial law (e.g., consumer protection, agency conflicts, and information asymmetry) are better addressed by MiCA than by consumer contract law.

4.2.3 *The Exemption for Assets Covered by Other EU Financial Law*

As discussed in Chapter 3, Article 2(4) of MiCA exempts cryptoassets already covered by existing EU financial law, other than EMTs which are covered both by MiCA and by EMD.[31] Drawing the boundaries between MiCA and other parts of EU financial law is by no means a trivial task, and we discuss the details thereof in Section 4.4.

4.2.4 *The Exemption for Fully Decentralised Services*

As noted in Section 2.1, one of the main aspects in which crypto markets differs from traditional finance is the partial decentralisation of functions within the financial ecosystem. This partial decentralisation results in technical and financial complexities and often a cross-border situation, which renders regulation and enforcement a challenge.

MiCA does not yet address this challenge directly[32] as it applies to 'natural and legal persons and certain other undertakings'.[33] This is further substantiated by Recital 22 of MiCA, by which cryptoasset services that 'are provided in a fully decentralised manner without any intermediary' fall outside of MiCA's scope and cryptoassets with 'no identifiable issuer' are not covered by MiCA's product rules in its Titles II–IV. Bitcoin, for instance, is in our view[34] a cryptoasset with 'no identifiable issuer', which is not covered by Titles II–IV of MiCA.[35] Yet, Title V still applies to providers of cryptoasset services in relation to Bitcoin. We discuss these two situations in Sections 7.2.3.4 and 6.2.4, respectively.

The issue of partial decentralisation will likely lead to legal battles as crypto intermediaries, and in particular, self-proclaimed "decentralised" platforms, often argue that no legal entity is involved in the economic activities resulting from peer-to-peer transactions and smart contracts. Yet, even where crypto platforms pose as DeFi *stricto sensu*, it is far from certain whether they are, in fact, fully decentralised in accordance with MiCA.[36] For instance, some type of legal

[30] Recital para. 10 of MiCA.
[31] See Section 3.1 on MiCA's gap-filling function within existing EU financial law.
[32] This will most likely be more adequately addressed in later amendments to MiCA. See Articles 140(2)(t) and 142(2)(a) of MiCA.
[33] Article 2(1) of MiCA.
[34] Some commentators express doubts of whether Bitcoin may still be covered by Titles II–IV of MiCA. See, for instance, M. Lehmann, 'MiCAR – Gold Standard or Regulatory Poison for the Crypto Industry' *Common Market Law Review*, 61 (2024): 699, 705.
[35] See also Article 4(3)(b) and Recital 26 of MiCA.
[36] See Zetzsche *et al.*, 'Remaining Regulatory Challenges in Digital Finance', pp. 27–29.

entity is often related to such decentralised platforms.[37] While avoiding transaction risks itself, this legal entity typically develops and maintains, directly or indirectly, the platform and markets its services, and it may even exert control through so-called governance tokens. Furthermore, most lending platforms pool assets from various users before lending.[38] This could be understood as centralisation of liquidity similar to what a bank would do prior to lending. Finally, some concentration of influence usually occurs at the governance level as this enables developers to receive compensation for their efforts in stack development and maintenance.[39] Empirical evidence suggests that developers and founders retain control over their protocols after the initial token offering.[40] Such conduct puts the rationale behind regulatory leniency for 'fully decentralised services' in doubt. Depending on the circumstances, 'natural and legal persons' taking part in such schemes may indeed be covered by MiCA, either individually or if they collectively qualify as 'certain other undertakings'.[41] Recital 22 of MiCA acknowledges this by stating that 'partially decentralised services' remain in scope. For details see Sections 7.2.3.4 and 6.2.4, respectively.

4.3 GEOGRAPHICAL SCOPE

MiCA applies 'in the Union'[42] (i.e., EU and European Economic Area (EEA) territory). This is specified further in various sections of MiCA, so, for instance, the rules on cryptoasset issuers apply when cryptoassets are offered to the public or asked for being admitted to trading in the Union irrespective of the domicile of the issuer.[43] In addition, '[a]n e-money token that references an official currency of a Member State shall be deemed to be offered to the public in the Union',[44] irrespective of whether it is issued to the public or is the subject of a request for admission to trading in the EU. Similarly, Title V of MiCA on CASPs applies to such services offered within the Union,[45] unless the services are provided by a third-country firm on the exclusive initiative of the client.[46] Finally, Title VI of MiCA on market abuse applies to acts or omissions committed anywhere in the world, relating to cryptoassets that are traded or are the subject of a request for admission to trading in the EU.[47]

Certainly, it will be difficult to enforce the rules of MiCA on many third-country firms given that the issuance, trading, and provision of services related to cryptoassets take place almost exclusively online. The occurrence of EU brokers forwarding trades to third-country exchanges[48] as well as the prevalence of anonymous accounts, in particular, outside of the EU,

[37] See Zetzsche *et al.*, 'Remaining Regulatory Challenges in Digital Finance', pp. 29–33.

[38] See Zetzsche *et al.*, 'Remaining Regulatory Challenges in Digital Finance', pp. 52–58.

[39] For details, see L. Anker-Sørensen and D. A. Zetzsche, 'From Centralized to Decentralized Finance: The Issue of "Fake-DeFi"' (2021). Website http://dx.doi.org/10.2139/ssrn.3978815 (last accessed on 1 October 2024).

[40] M. Goldberg and F. Schär, 'Metaverse Governance: An Empirical Analysis of Voting within Decentralized Autonomous Organizations', *Journal of Business Research*, 160 (2023): 3–7.

[41] See Article 2(1) of MiCA.

[42] Article 2(1) of MiCA.

[43] Articles 4(1), 5(1), 16(1), and 48(1) of MiCA.

[44] See Article 48(2) para. 2 of MiCA.

[45] Article 59(1) of MiCA.

[46] Article 61 of MiCA; ESMA, 'Consultation Paper on the Draft Guidelines on Reverse Solicitation under MiCA' (29 January 2024). Website www.esma.europa.eu/sites/default/files/2024-01/ESMA35-1872330276-1619_Consultation_Paper_on_the_draft_guidelines_on_reverse_solicitation_under_MiCA.pdf (last accessed on 1 October 2024).

[47] Article 86(3), cf. Article 86(1) of MiCA.

[48] See ESMA, 'Opinion to Support the Convergent Application of MiCA', 31 July 2024, ESMA75-453128700-1048. Website www.esma.europa.eu/document/opinion-broker-models (accessed 6 August 2024).

will not make this task any easier. Hence, both the ESMA and the Commission are, in their respective future reports on the application of MiCA, requested to address specifically the operations of third-country actors in the EU.[49]

4.4 INTERFACE TOWARDS OTHER EU FINANCIAL LAW

Given that Article 2(4) MiCA exempts from its scope a variety of cryptoassets that are in-scope of other EU financial law, we now address the matter of scope for the most important categories of assets.

4.4.1 *A Long-Standing Challenge*

EU financial law has evolved gradually since the process of legal harmonisation started in the 1970s.[50] In particular, driven by the introduction of the Euro, the 1999 Financial Services Action Plan (FSAP) included forty-two legislative and non-legislative measures that were largely completed by the 2004 deadline.[51] Then came the global financial crisis in 2007–8 and the subsequent European sovereign debt crisis, which led to an extensive overhaul of financial legislation globally – including more than fifty legislative and non-legislative measures proposed by the Commission.[52]

This evolvement naturally led to several related pieces of legislation being passed, with associated difficulties emerging with respect to determining which laws apply to cases that do not fit neatly into pre-defined categories. Moreover, the increasing pace of change seen over the past decades has created challenges when it comes to harmonising interpretation and enforcement across the EU's twenty-seven Member States and twenty-four official languages. This complication is further intensified by the fact that much of the existing EU financial law has been passed as directives (most notably MiFID), leaving some discretion to Member States.

The compartmentalised 'box approach' to EU financial regulation, with the related problems in determining and harmonising the boundaries or scope of each 'box', has gone from difficult to near-impossible with the emergence of thousands of new digital asset schemes.[53]

[49] See Articles 140(2)(v) and 141(h), (i), and (m) of MiCA.

[50] Most notably with three Council directives: the First Non-Life Insurance Directive, Council Directive 73/239/EEC of 24 July 1973 on the coordination of laws, regulations, and administrative provisions relating to the taking up and pursuit of the business of direct insurance other than life insurance, OJ 1973 No. L228, 16 August 1973; the First Banking Directive, Council Directive 77/780/EEC of 12 December 1977 on the coordination of the laws, regulations, and administrative provisions relating to the taking up and pursuit of the business of credit institutions, OJ 1977 No. L322, 17 December 1977; and the First Life Insurance Directive, Council Directive 79/267/EEC of 5 March 1979 on the coordination of laws, regulations, and administrative provisions relating to the taking up and pursuit of the business of direct life assurance, OJ 1979 No. L63, 13 March 1979.

[51] See European Commission, 'Communication on Implementing the Framework for Financial Markets: Action Plan', COM (1999) 232 Final.

[52] See R. Parenti, 'Fact Sheet: Financial Services Policy', European Parliament (2023). Website www.europarl.europa.eu\\factsheets\\en\\sheet\\83\\financial-services-policy (last accessed on 1 October 2024).

[53] See ESMA's survey results, which are discussed in Section 3.3.2. See also, more generally, Zetzsche *et al.*, 'The Markets in Crypto-Assets Regulation (MiCA) and the EU Digital Finance Strategy'; F. Annunziata, 'An Overview of the Markets in Crypto-Assets Regulation', EBI Working Paper Series no. 158 (2023), pp. 26–28. Website https://dx.doi.org/10.2139/ssrn.4660379 (last accessed on 1 October 2024).

4.4.2 *Investment Assets: MiFID Financial Instruments*

Article 4(1) MiFID defines 'financial instruments' as those listed in Section C of MiFID's Annex I.[54] Broadly speaking, these are transferable securities, money-market instruments, units in CIUs, a broad range of derivative contracts, financial contracts for differences, and emission allowances under the EU Emissions Trading Scheme. Below, we discuss each of these categories in turn.

4.4.2.1 *Transferable Securities*

'Transferable securities' constitute the most important type of financial instruments. In fact, important pieces of EU financial law apply to transferable securities only, such as the Prospectus Regulation. Transferrable securities are defined as 'those classes of securities which are negotiable on the capital market, with the exception of instruments of payment' such as shares and bonds.[55] These criteria pose difficulties in the classification of cryptoassets, some of which are addressed in the ESMA's guidelines yet most are not.[56]

Negotiability (Transferability and Standardisation)

In order to be 'negotiable', a security must at a minimum be transferable. Importantly, there is no requirement that a transfer actually takes place, only that the security may be transferred. Even if cryptoassets are transferable by design, transferability is frequently restricted by the issuer ('lock-up'), typically by encoding transfer restrictions onto the ledger.[57] The implications of such transfer restrictions under the MiFID definition remain unclear, but mere contractual restraints probably do not strip an asset of its transferability.[58] After all, many companies impose restrictions on share transfers, yet shares are explicitly considered 'transferable securities'.[59] The point here, in our view, is to prevent a path through which EU financial law could be circumvented by first issuing a non-transferable instrument and then later lifting the transfer restrictions.[60] In turn, cryptoassets should still qualify as 'negotiable' unless restrictions permanently disable the possibility of transfers.

Beyond transferability, securities must be standardised in order to be 'negotiable'.[61] This is also suggested by the MiFID definition when it refers to 'classes of securities'.[62] Each class (if more than one) must consist of a clearly distinguishable set of sufficiently equal cryptoassets to enable trading. We have, however, not yet seen this cause any issues with respect to the classification of cryptoassets which are typically either designed to be equal (within each class) or explicitly unique, as is the case with NFTs.

[54] See also ESMA, 'Consultation Paper on the Draft Guidelines on the Conditions and Criteria for the Qualification of Crypto-Assets as Financial Instruments', ESMA75–453128700-52 (2024).

[55] See Article 4(1)(44) of MiFID, Directive 2014/65, OJ 2014 No. L173.

[56] See ESMA, 'Consultation Paper on the Draft Guidelines on the Conditions and Criteria for the Qualification of Crypto-Assets as Financial Instruments', ESMA75–453128700-52, Guideline 2 (2024).

[57] See Hacker and Thomale, 'Crypto-Securities Regulation', 645, 663–64.

[58] See ESMA, 'Q&As on the Prospectus Regulation' (2021), p. 69; Maume and Fromberger, 'Regulations of Initial Coin Offerings', 548, 574; Hacker and Thomale, 'Crypto-Securities Regulation', 645, 663. Some authors argue, however, that significant contractual restrictions may inhibit transferability as required by the MiFID definition of transferrable securities; see M. Hobza, 'ICOs, Cryptoassets and MiFID II: Are Tokens Transferable Securities?' *Charles University in Prague Faculty of Law Research Paper*, 3(1) (2020): 7.

[59] Article 4(1)(44)(a) of MiFID.

[60] See Maume and Fromberger, 'Regulations of Initial Coin Offerings', 548, 574–75; Hacker and Thomale, 'Crypto-Securities Regulation', 645, 663–64; ESMA, 'Annex 1: Legal Qualifications of Crypto-Assets', para. 20.

[61] See ESMA, 'Consultation Paper on the Draft Guidelines on the Conditions and Criteria for the Qualification of Crypto-Assets as Financial Instruments', ESMA75–453128700-52, Guideline 2(ii) (2024).

[62] Article 4(1)(44) of MiFID.

Negotiable 'on the Capital Market'

Transferable securities, to be classified as such, must also be negotiable 'on the capital market'.[63] The latter term is not defined under EU law, and most NCAs apply the broad definition of a place where buying and selling interests meet.[64] This implies a span broader than 'traditional' capital markets and the inclusion of crypto exchanges, for example. However, it does not distinguish *capital* markets from other markets, other than by the circular argument of them being markets for securities (which, according to the MiFID definition, are traded on the capital market). This has caused some confusion among both academics and NCAs, as we now outline.

In particular, some apply a standard of bearing similarity to shares, bonds, or derivatives,[65] which are the (non-exhaustive) examples of transferable securities explicitly listed in the MiFID definition.[66] Others seem to argue that securities are defined by an investment aspect[67] or by an ongoing relationship between the issuer and the investor as opposed to the more transactional relationships seen in other financial markets, like money markets or commodity markets.[68] In our view, the actual MiFID wording must serve as a starting point. By 'capital market', MiFID presumably means markets for capital, as that is where capital today is exchanged for capital tomorrow. Yet, the various standards applied may serve to clarify what this means.

For example, the majority of NCAs in the ESMA's survey thought that an investment component is a necessary characteristic for securities.[69] Moreover, the 'existence of profit rights, without having necessarily ownership or governance rights attached' was typically seen as sufficient to be considered a security.[70] However, there was no common view among the surveyed NCAs as to whether a direct flow of payment from the originators to the holders of cryptoassets is a required characteristic.[71]

In our opinion, for a security to be traded on the 'capital market', it requires a right to some potential capital flow, like dividends, interest payments, share of revenues, or share of the proceeds at the time of liquidation of the underlying business. Otherwise, there is no exchange of capital today (i.e., the purchase of a security from an issuer) and capital tomorrow (the potential future capital flow).[72] This means that Bitcoin, for example, would not qualify as transferable securities in our view, even if it is often purchased with investment in mind and even if the Bitcoin price would indeed prove to appreciate over time.

A practical question in relation to cryptoassets is whether the capital flow involved must take the form of money or money-like instruments or, in the absence thereof, if *any* asset would do. For example, cryptoassets are often purchased from the issuer by payment in other cryptoassets (typically cryptocurrencies), and possible returns may be paid in all kinds of ways – often through access to (digital) products or services, as is the case with utility tokens. The (non-exhaustive) examples of transferable securities listed in the MiFID definition suggest that cash settlement may be required, as it mentions shares, bonds, derivatives of such securities, and derivatives of

[63] See ESMA, 'Consultation Paper on the Draft Guidelines on the Conditions and Criteria for the Qualification of Crypto-Assets as Financial Instruments', ESMA75-453128700-52, Guideline 2(iii) (2024).

[64] ESMA, 'Annex 1: Legal Qualifications of Cryptoassets', para. 23.

[65] See, for example, Hobza, 'ICOs, Cryptoassets and MiFID II', 9.

[66] Article 4(1)(44) of MiFID.

[67] See, for example, R. Veil 'Token-Emissionen im Europäischen Kapitalmarktrecht', ZHR (2019), 346, 361–62; Vandezande, 'Regulating Initial Coin Offerings', 33, 34.

[68] See Maume and Fromberger, 'Regulations of Initial Coin Offerings', 548, 576.

[69] ESMA, 'Annex 1: Legal Qualifications of Cryptoassets', paras. 31–32.

[70] See ESMA, 'Advice – Initial Coin Offerings and Cryptoassets', p. 20.

[71] ESMA, 'Annex 1: Legal Qualifications of Cryptoassets', para. 33.

[72] A similar point of view is raised by Veil, 'Token-Emissionen im Europäischen Kapitalmarktrecht', 346, 363–64.

other assets but only insofar as they give rise to cash settlement. A commodity derivative, for example, is therefore explicitly excluded from the list of examples unless it is settled in cash. This is sensible insofar as commodities delivered in kind clearly belong to the commodities market, as opposed to the capital market, even if they are prepaid, for instance, and thereby include an element of credit.

It seems to us that the distinction here must be drawn between cases where the returns on capital are paid in something that may be used or consumed, as opposed to something that is merely or predominantly a unit of cash-like value. This corresponds to the investment aspect standard discussed above, with the caveat that it is the objective nature of the transaction that matters and not the subjective purpose of the investor. Just as contracts for in-kind delivery of commodities (like iron ore or pork belly) do not constitute securities on the 'capital market' (even if they may indeed be purchased with investment in mind), so pure utility-type tokens that give a right to future (digital) products or services are also not securities on the 'capital market'. The same conclusion is supported by NCAs as revealed in the ESMA's survey results.[73]

Exception for Payment Instruments

The MiFID definition of 'transferable securities' specifically excludes instruments of payment.[74] The term is not defined within MiFID, yet Article 4(14) PSD defines 'payment instrument' as 'a personalised device(s) and/or set of procedures agreed between the payment service user and the payment service provider and used in order to initiate a payment order'. While the PSD definition does not apply directly under MiFID, it could provide some guidance as to what is meant by the MiFID term 'instruments of payment'.[75]

Typical examples of payment instruments are debit or credit cards, cheques, credit transfers, direct debits, and e-money.[76] Payment tokens are similar to e-money (see Section 4.4.3 and Chapter 6) and may qualify as payment instruments as they are typically designed for payment purposes.[77] This is also in line with the *Hedqvist* decision, where the Court of Justice of the European Union (CJEU) considered Bitcoin to be a contractual payment instrument (albeit under the VAT Directive).[78] However, the intended use cannot alone be sufficient. Bitcoin, for instance, was clearly developed with the intention of facilitating payments, but given its massive price fluctuations, it is not suited for that purpose and is increasingly used purely for the purposes of investment and storage of value. It is, therefore, doubtful whether it qualifies as a payment instrument, and this may alter over time as the use and price fluctuations of Bitcoin change. Finally, to distinguish payment instruments from typical utility tokens, we believe that the former must be accepted as means of payment by someone other than the issuer, which corresponds to the definition of e-money (see Section 4.4.3.4).

73 ESMA, 'Advice – Initial Coin Offerings and Crypto-Assets', p. 20.

74 Article 4(1)(44) of MiFID. See also ESMA, 'Consultation Paper on the Draft Guidelines on the Conditions and Criteria for the Qualification of Crypto-Assets as Financial Instruments', ESMA75–453128700-52, Guideline 2 (i) (2024).

75 There is a question of whether the PSD definition's referral to 'device(s) and/or set of procedures agreed between the payment service user and the payment service provider' excludes most cryptoassets altogether. After all, they may possibly qualify neither as a device, a procedure, nor as based on any explicit agreement. We believe, however, that these words should not be interpreted too narrowly. MiFID itself uses the term 'instrument', which must clearly include payment tokens just as the term 'financial instrument' includes financial tokens. Moreover, there is an agreement between the user of tokens and the wallet provider, which facilitates a procedure for crypto payments. The term 'wallet' does also, in itself, indicate that such services indeed are meant at least partly as payment services.

76 See Maume and Fromberger, 'Regulations of Initial Coin Offerings', 548, 581.

77 See Maume and Fromberger, 'Regulations of Initial Coin Offerings', 548, 581.

78 Case C-264/14, *Skatteverket* v. *David Hedqvist* [2015] ECR 718.

4.4.2.2 Money-Market Instruments

'Money-market instruments' are instruments 'normally dealt in on the money market, such as treasury bills, certificates of deposit and commercial papers'.[79] Given the definition's emphasis on what is 'normally dealt with', the first question to be answered is whether this excludes new innovations like cryptoassets. Here, a substance-over-form argument prevails: what is otherwise a money-market instrument qualifies even if it is stored and/or traded on a distributed ledger.

Another question to arise is whether the MiFID definition is exhaustive. In particular, UCITSD has its own definition of money-market instruments, with the additional requirement that such instruments must also be 'liquid and have a value which can be accurately determined at any time'.[80] This is to be understood in light of the UCITSD's particular objectives, in particular ensuring the retail investors' redemption rights. However, many cryptoassets tend to be illiquid even if they are traded on a crypto exchange. In our view, there is no reason to establish an additional liquidity requirement under the MiFID definition.

Finally, money markets, as opposed to capital markets, are typically defined as markets for short-term debt instruments that mature in less than one year.[81] This distinction may become difficult to draw for smart contracts where maturity could be defined by a complex algorithm rather than by a set date, yet such complexities are in themselves an argument for treating the asset more like a security than a typical money-market debt instrument.

4.4.2.3 Units in Collective Investment Undertakings

Cryptoassets qualify as units of CIUs when the capital collected through the cryptoassets is pooled prior to investing it.[82] Most importantly, UCITSD and AIFMD may apply to such cryptoassets.[83] Article 1(2) UCITSD defines UCITS as undertakings that raise money (from the public) with the sole object of collective investment; UCITS units may, at the request of holders, be repurchased, redeemed, or transacted at market values given that the UCITS is an open-ended fund. Article 4(1)(a) AIFMD refers to Alternative Investment Funds (AIFs) as undertakings that 'raise capital from a number of investors, with a view to investing it in accordance with a defined investment policy for the benefit of those investors'.

The CIU qualification is irrespective of the assets invested in by the undertaking.[84] Yet, we see at least three questions arising when determining whether cryptoassets qualify as CIUs.

First, some cryptoassets do not grant redemption rights to holders but rather further secondary trading on crypto exchanges. However, a redemption right is merely a feature of open-ended funds. Even for UCITS, the archetypal open-ended fund, sufficient liquidity at public markets may serve as a substitute for the redemption right.[85]

[79] Article 4(1)(17) of MiFID. See also ESMA, 'Consultation Paper on the Draft Guidelines on the Conditions and Criteria for the Qualification of Crypto-Assets as Financial Instruments', ESMA75–453128700-52, Guideline 3 (2024).

[80] Article 2(1)(o) of UCITSD, Directive 2009/65, OJ 2009 No. L302.

[81] See Vandezande, 'Regulating Initial Coin Offerings', 33, 35; Hobza, 'ICOs, Cryptoassets and MiFID II', 7.

[82] On cryptoassets as CIUs, see ESMA, 'Consultation Paper on the Draft Guidelines on the Conditions and Criteria for the Qualification of Crypto-Assets as Financial Instruments', ESMA75–453128700-52, Guideline 4 (2024).

[83] For a detailed analysis, see Chapter 9.

[84] AlchemyBite provides an example, the value of which is backed roughly three quarters by other cryptoassets and one quarter by crypto-related assets such as shares in cryptoasset-developing companies. A significant majority of NCAs answered to ESMA's survey that they would treat this cryptoasset as a CIU under MiFID and, hence, that it qualifies as a MiFID financial instrument. See ESMA, 'Annex 1: Legal Qualifications of Crypto-Assets', paras. 25 and 52.

[85] Article 1(2)(b) of UCITSD.

Second, the term 'collective' in CIU implies that such funds are managed 'collectively' by a professional third-party manager. Individual investors lack investment discretion.[86] This is unproblematic insofar as there are fund managers or even algorithms that invest on behalf of CIU unit holders. However, some cryptoassets leave this partly or entirely to the CIU (token) holders. For example, the original DAO served as a fund that raised USD 150 million worth of ETH coins in exchange for DAO tokens, whose holders could vote for investment proposals, curated by a set of volunteers. Such cases raise the question of whether the DAO tokens qualify either as CIUs or as a share-like instrument representing ownership in the DAO.[87] In either case, it would qualify as a MiFID financial instrument (either as a CIU unit or a transferable security); hence, MiCA does not apply. The distinction determines, however, whether, for example, AIFMD could potentially apply to the curators. For details, see Section 9.2.

Finally, there is some uncertainty as to whether typical stablecoins qualify as CIUs, given that they tend to be backed by a pool of assets. The determining factor here is whether there is a 'hard balance sheet' in between the holder of the stablecoin and the pool of assets or, to put it another way, whether the issuer of the stablecoin (or someone else) guarantees the value of the coin so that the holder has a claim on the issuer. If this is the case, the holder does not carry the risk of the underlying pool of assets so does not take part in a CIU. Instead, it would likely be considered a holder of e-money or a similar type of payment instrument. Yet, as vividly shown by the struggles of ostensibly asset-backed stablecoins to keep their dollar peg,[88] the amount and composition of reserve assets may be inadequate to uphold a 'hard balance sheet'. These difficulties are amplified by insufficient or even fraudulent reporting, as seen in the case of Tether which was fined by the New York District Attorney's office for covering up around USD 850 million in losses after overstating its reserves.[89] Then, there are so-called algorithmic stablecoins, which seek to keep a stable value against fiat currencies by automatically adjusting coin supply to market events. If you then imagine a hybrid of an algorithmic and asset-backed stablecoin, the question of how much and what type of reserve assets are required to establish a 'hard balance sheet' becomes difficult to answer. The authorization and operating requirements under Title III and IV MiCA for ARTs and EMTs function as a guideline (see Chapter 6). Where these are not met, we suggest erring on the side of caution and applying CIU law.[90]

4.4.2.4 *Derivatives*

Just as the value of CIUs depends on that of an underlying pool of assets, so does the value of a derivative hinge on an underlying asset.[91] Section C of MiFID's Annex I lists a number of derivatives that qualify as financial instruments. The most important categories here are derivatives qualifying as transferable securities, a defined set of other derivatives (including commodity derivatives) that must or may be settled in cash, commodity derivatives for physical settlement if

[86] See D. A. Zetzsche and C. D. Preiner, 'Scope of the AIFMD', in D. A. Zetzsche (ed.), *The Alternative Investment Fund Managers Directive* (Alphen aan den Rijn: Wolters Kluwer, 2020), 3rd ed., pp. 26–61.

[87] The prevailing view among fund lawyers holds that *one* passive investor suffices to establish a CIU. See Zetzsche and Preiner, 'Scope of the AIFMD', pp. 26–61. For a detailed analysis, see Chapter 9.

[88] See R. Browne, 'World's Biggest Stablecoin Regains Dollar Peg after $3 Billion in Withdrawals', CNBC (2022). Website www.cnbc.com\\2022\\05\\13\\tether-usdt-stablecoin-regains-peg-after-3-billion-in-withdrawals.html (last accessed on 1 October 2024).

[89] *Financial Times*, 'Tether Says Its Reserves Are Backed by Cash to the Tune of . . . 2.9%' (2021). Website www.ft.com\ \content\\529eb4e6-796a-4e81-8064-5967bbe3b4d9 (last accessed on 1 October 2024).

[90] On the consequences, see Chapter 9.

[91] On cryptoassets qualifying as derivatives, see ESMA, 'Consultation Paper on the Draft Guidelines on the Conditions and Criteria for the Qualification of Crypto-Assets as Financial Instruments', ESMA75–453128700-52, Guideline 5 (2024).

they are traded on a regulated market, and other derivatives if they 'have the characteristics of other derivative financial instruments'.

This raises a number of questions in relation to cryptoassets, starting with whether payment in cryptoassets qualifies as cash settlement. We hold that 'cash settlement' must be interpreted more widely than just physical cash to include, for instance, bank transfers and cheques. As for the similar question discussed above with regard to transferable securities, it seems to us that the distinction here must be drawn between cases with settlement in something that may be used or consumed, as opposed to something that is merely or predominantly a unit of value. Consequently, settlement in typical cryptocurrencies would count as cash settlement, whereas settlement in utility tokens linked to specific goods or services would not.

Another question to emerge is whether cryptoassets may qualify as commodities, with the consequence that derivatives on such assets classify as commodity derivatives. The closest example that comes to mind is gold, which is clearly a commodity and shares many characteristics with cryptocurrencies. Limited supply and a shared belief in its value turn both gold and Bitcoin into an asset used mainly for investment and storage of value. Still, gold can also be used or consumed, which Bitcoin cannot.[92] Hence, in our view, cryptoassets do not qualify as commodities, but cryptoassets may, of course, refer to an underlying commodity and thereby qualify as commodity derivatives.

There is also the question of whether a crypto exchange qualifies as a 'regulated market', as defined in Article 4(1)(21) MiFID. Crypto exchanges will qualify if they are authorised under Title III MiFID or under regulation of third-countries equivalent to Title III MiFID.[93] Where this is the case, commodity derivatives traded on them also qualify as financial instruments. Yet, in fact, many crypto exchanges are not authorised under Title III MiFID or equivalent regulation of third-countries. For that reason, Title V MiCA foresees a bespoke regime (see Chapter 7). This raises the final question of what is meant by derivatives with 'characteristics of other derivative financial instruments'. This includes at least derivative cryptoassets that trade on an exchange which is not authorised under Title III MiFID, but that resembles a regulated market under its applicable home country rules.[94] An otherwise pure utility token with a derivative component may qualify as a financial instrument under this category.

4.4.2.5 *Other MiFID Financial Instruments*

Cryptoassets also qualify as MiFID financial instruments if they are financial contracts for differences (CfDs) or emission allowances. A CfD is a contract that pays the difference in the value of an underlying asset between two points in time. This may include emission allowances under the EU Emissions Trading Scheme.[95] Financial contracts for differences may, for instance, be coded as smart contracts. In fact, some lending arrangements with regard to cryptoassets take on this form, where the difference in value between two cryptoassets is disbursed to the lending partners. Where the lending assets are not pooled – then CIU law

[92] See also R. Rirsch and S. Tomanek, 'Crypto-Assets: Commodities under European Financial Markets Law?', *Journal of Financial Compliance*, 2(3) (2018): 199.

[93] ESMA maintains a list of regulated markets notified by the EU Member States pursuant to Article 56 MiFID, as well as of markets in third countries that are regulated equivalent to Title III MiFID, pursuant to Article 2a(2) EMIR (referring to Title III MIFID).

[94] Examples include the trading venues defined in Article 50(1)(b), (c) UCITSD to the extent that these do not qualify as regulated markets under Title III MiFID.

[95] See ESMA, 'Consultation Paper on the Draft Guidelines on the Conditions and Criteria for the Qualification of Crypto-Assets as Financial Instruments', ESMA75–453128700-52, Guideline 6 (2024).

applies, see Section 4.4.2.3 – the respective arrangement may qualify as CfD under MiFID, and the arranger as MiFID investment firm.

4.4.3 *Banking Assets: E-money under EMD*

MiCA exempts from its scope funds, unless they qualify as EMTs.[96] Because 'funds' is defined as 'banknotes and coins, scriptural money or electronic money',[97] and because cryptoassets are probably not banknotes, coins, or scriptural money, the definition of e-money is most relevant for determining MiCA's scope in relation to such banking assets.

E-money is linked to payment solutions in the form of hardware or software e-money products and can be seen as 'an electronic surrogate for coins and banknotes, which is to be used for making payments, usually of limited amount and not as means of saving'.[98] They are defined under Article 2(2) EMD as 'electronically, including magnetically, stored monetary value as represented by a claim on the issuer which is issued on receipt of funds for the purpose of making payment transactions ... and which is accepted by a natural or legal person other than the electronic money issuer'.

While all cryptoassets are 'electronically ... stored', many (or possibly most) stablecoins still do not qualify as e-money under EMD, as shown by our analysis below of the remaining criteria under the e-money definition. Yet, if they qualify as EMTs, Article 48(2) MiCA now deems them to also qualify as e-money, with the implication that EMD still applies in parallel with MiCA. Remaining is the question of whether cryptoassets may qualify as e-money under EMD but not as EMTs under MiCA, which we answer in the following.

4.4.3.1 *Monetary Value as Represented by a Claim on the Issuer*

The requirement of a monetary value as represented by a claim on the issuer entails that, in order to qualify as e-money, cryptoassets must be pegged to a conventional fiat currency, and they must be redeemable in that currency at par value. This means that stablecoins that qualify as e-money under EMD presumably also qualify as EMTs under MiCA, rendering the two definitions entirely overlapping (see Section 4.4.3.5).

Yet, many stablecoins do not qualify (but may instead qualify as ARTs under MiCA; see Section 6.2). For instance, the stablecoin PAXG (Pax Gold) would in our view not qualify as e-money even if it is issued on receipt of USD because it is backed by gold and redeemable only in gold or in USD at the prevailing gold price.[99] A pertinent case was brought before the European Free Trade Association (EFTA) Court[100] in a request for an advisory opinion to the Liechtenstein Appeals Board of the Financial Market Authority.[101] Referring to Articles 11(1) and 11(2) EMD on the issuance and redemption of e-money at par value, the court noted that:

> [i]n order to fulfil its function as an electronic surrogate for coins and banknotes, which may be redeemed at any moment and at par value, the electronic money stored must at all times hold a value equivalent to the monetary value of the funds provided in exchange. ... This excludes

[96] See Article 2(4)(c) MiCA.

[97] See Article 3(1)(14) MiCA, cf. Article 4(25) of PSD2.

[98] Recital para. 13 of EMD, Directive 2009/110, OJ 2009 No. L267.

[99] Paxos, 'PAX Gold Terms and Conditions' (2023). Website www.paxos.com\\pax-gold-terms-conditions (last accessed on 1 October 2024).

[100] The European Court of Justice in matters relating to EEA EFTA States.

[101] Case E-9/17, *Edmund Falkenhahn AG v. The Liechtenstein Financial Market Authority (Finanzmarktaufsicht)* [2018] EFTA.

> from the scope of the Electronic Money Directive a business model where the electronic money would be linked to the price of gold at the electronic money holder's risk. ... Accordingly, electronic money cannot be linked to a value other than the monetary value.[102]

Similarly, the original 2019 version of Facebook's Libra coin was intended to be backed by a basket of underlying currencies and securities and, hence, redeemed at the value of the basket,[103] which would, of course, fluctuate relative to each of the underlying currencies. Therefore, this stablecoin would neither qualify as e-money nor EMT under MiCA (but as ART). Neither would coins that are redeemed in other stablecoins, even if these underlying coins seem to be backed by a fiat currency. Despite being 'stable', the value of stablecoins still fluctuates somewhat – both relative to the underlying fiat currency and amongst different USD-backed stablecoins.[104] Stablecoins backed by other stablecoins could probably still qualify under the broader definition of EMTs under Article 3(1)(7) MiCA and thus qualify as e-money pursuant to Article 48(2) MiCA.

Another concern is *how* the stablecoins may be redeemed. For instance, some cryptoassets are redeemable only by verified users or by designated dealers who distribute tokens.[105] Conventional e-money like anonymous pre-paid cards, by comparison, are typically redeemable by anyone upon presentation of the card itself.[106] In our view, a practical path to redemption is sufficient under EMD, even if that may, for instance, require the holder to go through a dealer or a verification process on the issuer's website.

4.4.3.2 *Issued on Receipt of Funds*

The term 'funds' is not defined in EMD, yet PSD defines funds as 'banknotes and coins, scriptural money or electronic money'.[107] Article 3(1)(14) MiCA references the PSD definition. This precludes many stablecoins from qualifying as e-money, unless they qualify as EMTs and thus as e-money pursuant to Article 48(2) MiCA.

DAI tokens, for instance, are issued on receipt of Ethereum-based assets (mainly ETH and Basic Attention Token (BAT)).[108] Since these cryptoassets, again, are not banknotes, coins, or scriptural money, they may be considered as 'funds' only if they qualify as e-money. Because ETH and BAT are not issued on receipt of 'funds' and thereby do not qualify as e-money, neither do the DAI tokens.[109] Similarly, the now discontinued mUSD tokens were issued on receipt of USD-backed stablecoins such as DAI and US dollars by Tether (USDT). Even if DAI does not qualify as e-money and thereby as 'funds', USDT possibly does. However, given that it was impossible to separate mUSD tokens issued on receipt of DAI from those issued on receipt of USDT, we would again argue that no mUSD tokens qualify as e-money.

4.4.3.3 *Purpose of Making Payment Transactions*

This criterion concerns the stated purpose of e-money as 'an electronic surrogate for coins and banknotes, which is to be used for making payments, usually of limited amount and not as

[102] Case E-9/17, *Edmund Falkenhahn AG v. The Liechtenstein Financial Market Authority (Finanzmarktaufsicht)* [2018] EFTA, para. 46.

[103] See M. Sokolov, 'Are Libra, Tether, MakerDAO and Paxos Issuing E-money?' p. 44. Website https://dx.doi.org/10.2139/ssrn.3746250 (last accessed on 1 October 2024).

[104] Sokolov, 'Are Libra, Tether, MakerDAO and Paxos Issuing E-money?' p. 47.

[105] See Sokolov, 'Are Libra, Tether, MakerDAO and Paxos Issuing E-money?' pp. 36–37 and 41.

[106] Sokolov, 'Are Libra, Tether, MakerDAO and Paxos Issuing E-money?' pp. 36–37.

[107] Article 4(25) of PSD2.

[108] Sokolov, 'Are Libra, Tether, MakerDAO and Paxos Issuing E-money?' p. 31.

[109] See Sokolov, 'Are Libra, Tether, MakerDAO and Paxos Issuing E-money?' p. 31.

means of saving'.[110] Consequently, a stablecoin would not qualify as e-money if it can be deposited on an interest-bearing account, or otherwise earn a return from the issuer.[111] Furthermore, the above-mentioned PAXG coin would also not qualify as e-money because its peg to gold allows the holder to speculate on the price of gold. Tether's USDT is, however, a more difficult case: due to the liquid market for USDT on crypto exchanges, these coins can be deposited to earn interest or even be used as collateral for loans through third-party websites. While EMD entails no rules on such third-party services, these USDT use cases clearly go beyond the 'purpose of making payment transactions'. Still, our uncertain conclusion is that the e-money definition refers to the purpose as set by the issuer so that USDT still may qualify as e-money under EMD.[112]

4.4.3.4 *Accepted by Parties Other than the E-money Issuer*

Finally, e-money must be 'accepted by a natural or legal person other than the electronic money issuer'. This implies that the Crypterium cryptoassets do not qualify as e-money because they may only be used to purchase services from the issuing 'cryptobank'. The same is probably true for the PAquarium cryptoasset that may be used only within the company's premises, unless they allow external vendors on the premises. This last example shows that it may sometimes be difficult to determine what counts as a natural or legal person other than the e-money issuer. According to the wording, it should be sufficient that a fully owned subsidiary of the PAquarium issuer accepts the tokens. This would clearly place the tokens closer to conventional gift cards than to typical e-money. Yet, the wording 'natural or legal person' other than the e-money issuer seems deliberate; alternative terms such as 'entity' or 'group of companies' could have been employed instead if that was the intended meaning. However, the objective of the requirement and the term acceptance leads us to require low barriers and ongoing, in contrast to only temporary, acceptance. Our conclusion is, therefore, that acceptance by just one other legal entity is sufficient, even if this entity is related to the issuer, under the condition that the acceptance by that entity is permanent and unconditional.

A further question to consider is whether the cryptoassets must in fact be accepted as means of payment by parties other than the issuer or if the intention of such third-party acceptance is sufficient. Again, the wording 'is accepted by' indicates that actual acceptance by third parties is required. In practice, this means that typical utility tokens may be issued without authorisation as e-money institution under EMD, but that such authorisation may be required if the tokens are then allowed to be accepted by third parties, such as with the Munchee token that serves as a means of payment in a variety of restaurants.[113]

4.4.3.5 *Interaction with MiCA*

Article 48(2) MiCA explicitly states that EMTs also qualify as e-money, meaning that both MiCA and EMD apply in parallel. That still leaves the question, however, of whether the

[110] Recital para. 13 of EMD.

[111] Again, the now-discontinued mUSD coins provide an example as they could be deposited on an interest-bearing account with the issuer, who also facilitated other services, such rewarding holders for allowing their cryptoassets to serve as liquidity for decentralised exchanges. Similarly, eEUR and other single-currency stablecoins by e-Money A/S are not e-money because interest is paid by the issuer. See Sokolov, 'Are Libra, Tether, MakerDAO and Paxos Issuing E-money?' pp. 32 and 47.

[112] See also Sokolov, 'Are Libra, Tether, MakerDAO and Paxos Issuing E-money?' pp. 40–41.

[113] Maume and Fromberger, 'Regulations of Initial Coin Offerings', 548, 560.

reverse is also true so that cryptoassets qualifying as e-money under EMD also qualify as EMTs under MiCA.

The above analysis shows, however, that the strict e-money definition under EMD is probably narrower in all aspects, as compared with Article 3(1)(7) MiCA, which defines EMTs as 'a type of cryptoasset that purports to maintain a stable value by referencing the value of one official currency'.[114] Hence, we suspect that all cryptoassets that qualify as e-money under EMD will indeed also be considered EMTs under MiCA.

This seemingly renders obsolete the entire exemption from MiCA's scope of 'funds', which are defined as 'banknotes and coins, scriptural money or electronic money'.[115] Since cryptoassets are not banknotes, coins, or scriptural money, they qualify as 'funds' only if they also qualify as e-money, and if they qualify as e-money, they will tend to also qualify as EMTs, so MiCA applies nevertheless despite the exception for 'funds'.

4.4.4 *Banking Assets: Deposits*

MiCA exempts from its scope deposits, which loosely refers to a credit balance deriving from funds left in an account or from other normal banking transactions, where its principal is repayable at par value, unless its existence can only be proven by a MiFID financial instrument.[116] Hence, the above analysis of cryptoassets as MiFID financial instruments is also relevant to deposits. Similarly, the above analysis on the term 'funds' and of redeemability at par value as part of the e-money definition is similarly pertinent.

Two specific questions with regard to deposits are whether a tokenised representation of value stored on a distributed ledger may ever constitute a 'credit balance … in an account' or derive from 'normal banking transactions'. Under the conventional view, an account refers to a book entry of credit and debit balances, whereas a cryptoasset on a distributed ledger is a representation of value in itself due to its potential scarcity, regardless of the underlying claim. Similarly, because it is unusual for banks to use tokens, they may not qualify as 'normal banking transactions'. However, there is no reason why credit and debit balances could not be stored on a distributed ledger, just as they are stored on the bank's centralised ledger today. Moreover, the concept of what constitutes a 'normal' banking transaction will certainly change over time as the banking system evolves. We would also argue that the term 'normal' here refers to the type of transaction rather than the way these transactions are stored and executed on a ledger.

4.4.5 *Hybrid Instruments*

Hybrid instruments pose special challenges as they may qualify under several parts of EU financial law simultaneously.[117] Each piece of relevant legislation seeks to address issues arising

[114] Article 3(1)(7) of MiCA.

[115] Article 4(25) of PSD2.

[116] See Article 2(4)(b) of MiCA, cf. Article 3(1)(50) of MiCA and Article 2(1)(3) of DGSD. See also the ESAs, 'Consultation Paper: Draft Guidelines on Templates for Explanations and Opinions, and the Standardised Test for the Classification of Crypto-assets, under Article 97(1) of Regulation (EU) 2023/1114' (2024), ESA 2024 12, para. 22(b), with further references.

[117] For instance, the PAquarium cryptoasset comes with a right to 20 per cent of normal dividends and voting rights specifically on the location of the issuer's proposed aquarium but also provides lifetime free entry to the aquarium and may be used to purchase yet undefined goods at the aquarium premises. Similarly, the Crypterium cryptoasset grants the right to a monthly share of revenues and can be used to purchase yet to be fully defined services from the issuing 'cryptobank'. Such cryptoassets resemble shares so may qualify as MiFID financial instruments, yet they also

from certain asset characteristics, so one solution would be to apply several pieces of legislation simultaneously to such hybrid assets. Yet, this additive approach could bring an excessive regulatory burden and, hence, discourage innovation in new hybrid instruments. In response to this dilemma, we agree that the primary characteristics of the asset should determine the classification insofar as regulatory objectives are reasonably protected.[118] In this regard, we support ESMA's hierarchical approach, whereby cryptoassets that meet the criteria for MiFID financial instruments should be qualified as such, even if they also share other features.[119]

4.5 MICA'S APPROACH TO ADDRESSING THE SCOPE ISSUE

MiCA is not blind to the interface issue towards other EU financial law. It offers no silver bullet but does introduce the following eight different mitigators to harmonise the interpretation of terms relevant to it.

(1) MiCA provides for guideline powers to the ESMA on the criteria and conditions for the qualification of cryptoassets as financial instruments, thus addressing the MiCA/MiFID interface.[120]
(2) When notifying the cryptoasset whitepaper to the NCA, offerors of a cryptoasset, persons seeking admission to trading, or operators of trading platforms, as the case may be, shall add an explanation of why the cryptoasset to be sold in the European Single Market is excluded from the scope of MiCA and is also neither an EMT nor an ART.[121] In a similar vein, the issuers of an ART need to deliver a legal opinion supporting the classification of the cryptoasset as an ART.[122] At the request of the NCA, the ESMA and the EBA shall comment on these explanations; thus, the NCAs may ask for the European Supervisory Authorities' (ESAs') opinion on each case.[123]
(3) To ensure the consistency of such explanations and legal opinions, the ESAs shall jointly develop guidelines to specify the content and form of the explanation.[124] The guidelines shall include a template for the explanation and the opinion itself, as well as a standardised test for the classification of cryptoassets. This test will address the MiCA/PSD/EMD

have characteristics of both payment instruments and utility tokens. See ESMA, 'Annex 1: Legal Qualifications of Crypto-Assets', para. 24.

[118] For instance, four out of twenty-nine NCAs surveyed by ESMA argued that cryptoassets must be intended solely for payment purposes to be considered a payment instrument and thereby excluded from the definition of transferrable securities under MiFID, while others argue that the main purpose of the asset should be the determining factor. We disapprove of subjective and overly narrow interpretations, and we hold that an asset should be exempted as a payment instrument if its primary purpose is to facilitate payments. See ESMA, 'Annex 1: Legal Qualifications of Crypto-Assets', para. 41; Maume and Fromberger, 'Regulations of Initial Coin Offerings', 548, 582.

[119] See ESMA, 'Consultation Paper on the Draft Guidelines on the Conditions and Criteria for the Qualification of Crypto-Assets as Financial Instruments', ESMA75–453128700-52, Guideline 9 (2024).

[120] See Article 2(5) and Recital para. 14 of MiCA.

[121] Article 8(4) of MiCA. See also the ESAs, 'Consultation Paper: Draft Guidelines on Templates for Explanations and Opinions, and the Standardised Test for the Classification of Crypto-assets, under Article 97(1) of Regulation (EU) 2023/1114' (2024), ESA 2024 12, Annex A.

[122] Articles 17(1)(b)(ii) and 18(2)(e) of MiCA. See also the ESAs, 'Consultation Paper: Draft Guidelines on Templates for Explanations and Opinions, and the Standardised Test for the Classification of Crypto-assets, under Article 97(1) of Regulation (EU) 2023/1114' (2024), ESA 2024 12, Annex B.

[123] Article 20(5) of MiCA.

[124] Article 97(1) of MiCA. See the ESAs, 'Consultation Paper: Draft Guidelines on Templates for Explanations and Opinions, and the Standardised Test for the Classification of Crypto-assets, under Article 97(1) of Regulation (EU) 2023/1114' (2024), ESA 2024 12.

interface as well as the distinction between EMTs, ARTs, and other cryptoassets within MiCA's scope.

(4) NCAs may request an opinion on the classification of cryptoassets from one of the ESAs, including NFTs formally exempted pursuant to Article 2(3), which needs to be provided within fifteen working days of receipt of the request from the competent authorities.[125]
(5) NCAs must register cryptoasset whitepapers based on a set of ESMA regulatory technical standards, ensuring the provision of data necessary for their classification.[126]
(6) The ESAs shall jointly draw up an annual report. Based on issues reported by NCAs, it will identify difficulties in the classification of cryptoassets and divergences in the approaches of the competent authorities and consider the information stored in the cryptoasset (service provider) register.[127]
(7) The Commission may adopt delegated acts specifying technical aspects of definitions,[128] including, primarily, the definition of cryptoassets as well as particular terms used in MiCA, such as EMTs, ARTs, utility tokens, and other cryptoassets.
(8) Finally, the matter of classification will be closely monitored. The Commission will draw up a report within 24–48 months after the coming into force of MiCA, which will discuss classification of cryptoassets including possible divergences in approaches by competent authorities.[129]

All in all, through various measures, MiCA establishes a centralised approach linking the classification decision to the competencies of the ESAs. With respect to the guidelines, the ESAs will likely build on their significant work already done on cryptoassets.[130] For the practice of this centralised approach, however, the capacity and expertise of the NCAs, as well as the ESAs, will play a crucial role.[131] In light of the different market sizes and populations of Member States, not all NCAs will be able to develop and focus their resources on cryptoassets and their technical specificities. This will remain particularly true as long as the crypto industry represents a niche sector of the economy. Under these circumstances, the more sophisticated and work intensive a regulatory approach is, the less we expect NCAs to be able to deliver effectively on their obligations to enforce EU financial regulation. Any EU approach should thus be tailored towards facilitating oversight and the efficient, pragmatic application of the law. To this end, we propose a set of policy considerations, outlined in Chapter 16.

[125] Article 97(3) of MiCA.
[126] Article 109(8) of MiCA.
[127] Article 97(4) of MiCA.
[128] Article 3(2) of MiCA.
[129] Article 140(2)(b) of MiCA.
[130] See EBA, 'Final Report on Response to the Non-Bank Lending Request from the CfA on Digital Finance' (2022). Website www.eba.europa.eu\\eba-provides-its-advice-eu-commission-non-bank-lending (last accessed on 1 October 2024); EBA, 'Advice on the Review of the Macroprudential Framework' (2022). Website www.eba.europa.eu\\eba-proposes-simplify-and-improve-macroprudential-framework (last accessed on 1 October 2024); EBA, 'Report with Advice for the European Commission'. Website www.eba.europa.eu\\eba-reports-on-crypto-assets (last accessed on 1 October 2024); ESMA, 'Crypto-Assets and Their Risks for Financial Stability' (2022). Website www.esma.europa.eu\\sites\\default\\files\\library\\esma50-165-2251_crypto_assets_and_financial_stability.pdf (last accessed on 1 October 2024); ESMA, 'Advice – Initial Coin Offerings and Crypto-Assets'. Website www.esma.europa.eu\\sites\\default\\files\\library\\esma50-157-1391_crypto_advice.pdf (last accessed on 1 October 2024).
[131] See, for instance, E. Noble, 'Opening Remarks to the European Economic and Social Committee (EESC) Public Hearing on Crypto-Assets: Opportunities and Challenges', European Economic and Social Committee (2022), pp. 3–4. Website www.eesc.europa.eu\\en\\news-media\\presentations\\crypto-assets-challenges-and-opportunities (last accessed on 1 October 2024).

4.6 CONCLUSION

MiCA was passed as a regulation (as opposed to a directive) and, hence, constitutes binding EU law in all Member States. This reflects a clear agenda to foster harmonisation across the European Single Market.[132] However, because the scope of MiCA relies on references to definitions laid out in MiFID, EMD, and the DGSD, variations across Member States may result from divergences in the implementation of these directives into national law. In fact, when the ESMA revealed significant discrepancies in the understanding of MiFID financial instruments across NCAs in different Member States,[133] this was partly driven not only by different interpretations of the same terms but also by twelve out of twenty-nine NCAs reporting to have national criteria that deviate from the MiFID definition.[134]

Importantly, MiCA refers to the definitions in MiFID, EMD, and the DGSD but not to those transposed into national law. Nevertheless, it would be fair to assume that the broad discrepancies uncovered in the understanding of MiFID financial instruments still represent a significant blow to the European Single Market agenda for cryptoassets. Similar problems likely exist with regard to EMTs, where MiCA is referencing large parts of EMD[135] and where one must also assume some divergence in the transposition into national law. Hence, to deliver on the European Single Market agenda for cryptoassets, MiCA's eight mitigators to addressing the scope issue will be all important.

[132] See MiCA Regulation Proposal, Explanatory Memorandum, COM (2020) 593 Final, p. 5; PilotR Regulation Proposal, Explanatory Memorandum, COM (2020) 594 Final, p. 5; Recital para. 14, DORA, Regulation 2022/2554, OJ 2022 No. L333, p. 4.

[133] See ESMA, 'Advice – Initial Coin Offerings and Crypto-Assets', with the associated ESMA, 'Annex 1: Legal Qualifications of Crypto-Assets'.

[134] ESMA, 'Annex 1: Legal Qualifications of Crypto-Assets', para. 24. For example, German law considers 'units similar to foreign currencies and not of legal tender' as financial instruments, a category that is not recognized by MiFID. This has led the German regulator BaFin to treat cryptocurrencies as financial instruments under this uniquely German category. On the other hand, three of the NCAs in ESMA's survey reported that they have in their national legislation a compulsory book-entry recording requirement, which does not allow them to qualify as 'transferrable securities' other than those explicitly classified as such by law. Similarly, while MiFID itself has no definition of 'instruments of payment' (but explicitly excludes such instruments from the definition of 'transferable securities'), ten NCAs reported to have national definitions, with potential implications for the treatment of cryptocurrencies.

[135] See, for instance, Article 43(1)(b) of MiCA.

5

Prospectus Rules under MiCA and the Prospectus Regulation

5.1 OBJECTIVES AND APPLICABLE LEGISLATION

The purpose of distribution and prospectus rules is to protect retail and consumer investors, and, by enhancing and standardising information, to support the creation of trustworthy and well-functioning financial markets. Distribution and prospectus rules apply to issuers of various assets and typically govern the offering of such assets to the public and the admission of the assets to a trading platform.

An important issue seen in the cryptoasset markets, leading up to the adoption of MiCA, was the lack of information typically provided to cryptoasset investors,[1] compared with the long-standing prospectus requirements for securities that are now laid down in PR.[2] Therefore, MiCA puts forward a comprehensive set of requirements for the publishing of a so-called cryptoasset whitepaper, which are a modified and somewhat simplified version of similar requirements under PR. While the PR rules are comprehensively discussed elsewhere,[3] here in Chapter 5 we compare the prospectus rules for cryptoassets that qualify under PR to those that qualify under MiCA. For simplicity, we use the term "prospectus" also when referring to the whitepapers to be published under MiCA, unless we explicitly want to distinguish the whitepapers under MiCA from the prospectuses governed by PR.

As explained in Chapters 3 and 4, MiCA covers cryptoassets that fall outside of existing EU financial law, as well as EMTs which are covered by both MiCA and EMD. Meanwhile, PR applies to transferable securities as defined by MiFID,[4] which, as one type of MiFID financial instruments, are by design not covered by MiCA.[5] Depending on the legal qualification of the cryptoasset in question, we typically have prospectus rules either in MiCA or in PR, which never overlap. Yet, for some types of cryptoassets, neither MiCA nor PR applies.[6]

[1] See Zetzsche *et al.*, 'The ICO Gold Rush', 267.

[2] Regulation (EU) 2017/1129 of the European Parliament and of the Council of 14 June 2017 on the prospectus to be published when securities are offered to the public or admitted to trading on a regulated market and repealing Directive 2003/71/EC, OJ 2023 No. L168, 30 June 2017.

[3] See M. Lehmann and C. Kumpan (eds.), *European Financial Services Law: Article-by-Article Commentary* (Baden-Baden: Nomos, 2017); D. Busch, G. Ferrarini and J. P. Franx (eds.), *Prospectus Regulation and Prospectus Liability* (Oxford: Oxford University Press, 2020).

[4] Article 1(1), cf. Article 2(a) of PR, Regulation 2017/1129, OJ 2017 No. L168.

[5] Article 2(4)(a) of MiCA, Regulation 2023/1114, OJ 2023 No. L150, cf. Article 4(1)(15) and Section C of Annex I of MiFID, Directive 2014/65, OJ 2014 No. L173.

[6] See Article 2 of MiCA, which excludes more cryptoassets from MiCA's scope than transferrable securities. This is the case, for instance, with all financial instruments other than the sub-category of transferrable securities. See Chapters 3 and 4 for further details on the scope of applicable legislation.

Two notable specific exemptions from the scope of PR are money-market instruments and units and shares issued by open-ended CIUs.[7] While cryptoassets issued as units and shares of closed-ended funds must publish a prospectus under the PR,[8] cryptoassets that qualify as units of open-ended CIUs[9] are typically subject to specific disclosure rules,[10] instead of those laid down in MiCA and PR. Money-market instruments, on the other hand, are not subject to anything similar to a prospectus regime, and the same is true for e-money, unless the e-money qualifies as an EMT under MiCA.

Finally, it is important to note that other EU and national laws may, of course, set expectations for the disclosure of information when cryptoassets are issued or traded, for instance, the general principles of contract law or, specifically in business-to-consumer relations, the Consumer Rights Directive,[11] the Unfair Commercial Practices Directive,[12] or the Unfair Terms in Consumer Contracts Directive.[13] In addition, of course, both MiCA and other EU financial law lay down rules for the distribution of cryptoassets beyond mere prospectus requirements. Yet, in the following, we limit the discussion to rules concerning the cryptoasset prospectus as governed by MiCA and PR.

5.2 RISK-BASED DIFFERENTIATION OF PROSPECTUS RULES

Both MiCA and PR differentiate the prospectus requirements for different types of assets and issuers. Under MiCA, ARTs, EMTs, and other cryptoassets are treated separately in Titles III, IV, and II, respectively. (On the scope of Titles III and IV, see Chapters 3, 4, and 6.) An ART whitepaper must be pre-approved by a competent authority, for instance, as is the case for a prospectus under PR (see Section 5.4.3), while for whitepapers relating to "other cryptoassets"

[7] Article 2(a) of PR; Article 1(2)(a), cf. Article 2(p) and (q) of PR.

[8] See the bespoke items to be disclosed by closed-ended CIUs under Article 5 Annex 4 of Commission Delegated Regulation (EU) 2019/980 of 14 March 2019 supplementing Regulation (EU) 2017/1129 of the European Parliament and of the Council as regards the format, content, scrutiny, and approval of the prospectus to be published when securities are offered to the public or admitted to trading on a regulated market and repealing Commission Regulation (EC) No. 809/2004, OJ 2019 No. L166, 21 June 2019.

[9] Pursuant to Article 2(p) PR CIUs other than the closed-end type include unit trusts and investment companies that (i) raise capital from a number of investors, with a view to investing it in accordance with a defined investment policy for the benefit of those investors, and (ii) where the units are, at the holder's request, repurchased or redeemed, directly or indirectly, out of their assets. For a delineation of the scope of CIU legislation to applications that issue cryptoassets under MiCA, see Chapter 9.

[10] We will not cover these bespoke prospectus rules in this book. For details, see Chapter IX of UCITSD, Directive 2009/65, OJ 2009 No. L302; Article 23 of AIFMD, Directive 2011/61, OJ 2011 No. L174; Article 36 of MMFR, Regulation 2017/1131, OJ 2017 No. L169; Chapter IV of ELTIFR, Regulation (EU) 2015/760, OJ 2015 No. L123; Article 13 of EUVECAR, Regulation (EU) No. 345/2013, OJ 2013 No. L115; Article 14 of EUSEFR, Regulation (EU) No. 346/2013, OJ 2013 No. L115. On top, in the domain of AIFs, national CIU legislation foresees prospectus rules for the issuance of open-ended fund units to retail investors. See the countries' overviews provided in Zetzsche, *The Alternative Investment Fund Managers Directive*.

[11] Directive 2011/83/EU of the European Parliament and of the Council of 25 October 2011 on consumer rights, amending Council Directive 93/13/EEC and Directive 1999/44/EC of the European Parliament and of the Council and repealing Council Directive 85/577/EEC and Directive 97/7/EC of the European Parliament and of the Council, OJ 2011 No. L304, 22 November 2011.

[12] Directive 2005/29/EC of the European Parliament and of the Council of 11 May 2005 concerning unfair business-to-consumer commercial practices in the internal market and amending Council Directive 84/450/EEC, Directives 97/7/EC, 98/27/EC, and 2002/65/EC of the European Parliament and of the Council and Regulation (EC) No. 2006/2004 of the European Parliament and of the Council ('Unfair Commercial Practices Directive'), OJ 2005 No. L149, 11 June 2005.

[13] Council Directive 93/13/EEC of 5 April 1993 on unfair terms in consumer contracts, OJ 1993 No. L95, 21 April 1993.

under Title II (primarily *utility tokens*), the competent authority must simply be notified. Interestingly, while EMTs subject to Title IV MiCA are stablecoins (and in that characteristic, they are similar to ARTs), for them no whitepaper pre-approval is necessary. That is likely due to their similarity to conventional e-money for which no prospectus is required whatsoever; also in other respects, MiCA leans for EMTs on the rules for e-money (cf. Article 48(3) MiCA). Hence, the MiCA prospectus rules for EMTs represent a compromise, as they are stricter than those for e-money yet more lenient than the equivalent for ARTs.

Similarly, PR differentiates between its default prospectus rules, the 'base prospectus' for non-equity securities,[14] the 'EU Follow-on prospectus' for repeated listings (prior to the Listing Act: 'Simplified disclosure regime for secondary issuances' and 'EU Recovery prospectus'), and the 'EU Growth issuance prospectus' for small issuers (prior to the Listing Act: 'EU Growth prospectus'). In addition, under both MiCA and PR, small issuances are typically exempted from any obligation to publish a prospectus whatsoever (see Section 5.3.4).

This differentiated approach creates a risk-adjusted regime, where the prospectus requirements are balanced against both the risk typically faced by investors in any given asset class, the collective risk to investors in any given issuance as determined by its size, and a wish to exempt small issuers from overly burdensome rules. In this context, however, we note that the differentiation between ARTs, EMTs, and other cryptoassets under MiCA is clearly more adjusted to financial stability concerns with stablecoins than to risks faced by individual investors. Hence, the requirements with regard to the content and form of the prospectus are largely similar for all cryptoassets under MiCA but more differentiated under PR.

5.3 SCOPE

5.3.1 *Starting Point*

Although we have outlined how MiCA and PR apply to different types of cryptoassets, the scope of the two sets of prospectus rules is otherwise fairly similar.

As a starting point, both sets of rules apply when cryptoassets are either offered to the public or admitted to trading.[15] A notable difference between them is that PR applies when securities are 'admitted to trading',[16] while MiCA uses the terms 'ask for' or 'seek' with respect to 'admission ... to trading'.[17] This is presumably because MiCA also includes an authorisation regime and other rules beyond mere prospectus requirements, which are meant to apply already by the time the admission to trading is sought or asked for. Meanwhile, the investor protection rationale behind the prospectus requirements, strictly speaking, does not apply before the assets are in fact admitted to trading. Yet, MiCA must be interpreted literally on this point.

Furthermore, PR uses the term 'trading on a regulated market',[18] in comparison to MiCA's 'trading on a trading platform for cryptoassets' or merely 'trading' with no further qualification.[19] This difference is probably of little practical significance, given the similarities shared by the two

[14] Article 8 of PR.
[15] Article 1(1) of PR; Articles 4(1), 5(1), 16(1), and 48(1) of MiCA.
[16] Article 1(1) of PR.
[17] Articles 5(1), 16(1), and 48(1) of MiCA.
[18] Article 1(1) of PR.
[19] See Articles 1(2)(a), 4(1), 5(1), 16(1), and 48(1) of MiCA. It is not entirely clear whether the addition "on a trading platform for cryptoassets" makes any difference, but in our view, this is probably implicit even when the term "trading" is used without such a qualifier.

definitions.[20] Yet, it is worth noting that a 'regulated market' by definition must be authorised, but (notwithstanding the fact that EU crypto-exchanges must be authorised as crypto-asset service providers under Title V MiCA, see Chapter 7) there is no similar requirement for a "trading platform for cryptoassets" under Title II MiCA. This is probably deliberate in order for MiCA to cover crypto exchanges that resemble regulated markets but that (legally or illegally) operate without authorisation.

Finally, the prospectus rules under both PR and MiCA operate within the same geographical scope. PR applies when securities are offered to the public or admitted to trading on a regulated market 'situated or operating within a Member State',[21] while MiCA does likewise in or within 'the Union'.[22]

5.3.2 *Exempted Issuers*

Both PR and MiCA exempt a similar but not identical list of entities from their respective scopes. This is partly because MiCA provides a much broader set of rules than merely a prospectus regime. Hence, MiCA's exemptions for intra-group services and for a liquidator or an administrator of an insolvency procedure are probably meant to exempt from the rules for cryptoasset service providers (see Section 4.2.1), which have no equivalent in PR.

Both PR and MiCA exempt certain EU and Member State entities. Yet, while the exemptions under MiCA are general and seemingly cover all EU and Member State bodies (see Section 4.2.1), the exemptions under PR are more specific: they cover only non-equity securities,[23] unless they are issued by central banks or merely guaranteed (but not issued) by Member State authorities.[24] The real difference here is small or non-existent, insofar as the issuance of equity instruments by EU or Member State entities can probably be conceived of only in rare cases of hybrid institutions performing both business and governmental functions.

While MiCA exempts all 'public international organisations',[25] PR makes a similar exemption only to the extent that 'one or more Member States are members'.[26]

Finally, PR provides an exemption for associations and other non-profit entities,[27] which has no equivalent under MiCA. Presumably, this is intentional and aimed at removing any doubt over MiCA's application to utility token schemes, where the for-profit or non-profit characteristics of the issuing entity can sometimes be rather vague and obscure.

5.3.3 *Exempted Assets*

MiCA covers cryptoassets that fall outside of existing EU financial law, as well as EMTs which are covered by both MiCA and EMD (see Section 4.4.3). In comparison, PR applies to securities with the exception of money-market instruments and units issued by CIUs other than the closed-end type.[28] Hence, there is no overlap between the scope of the two regulations, but some cryptoassets are exempted from both regulations. Beyond money-market instruments and

[20] See Article 2(j) of PR, cf. Article 4(1)(21) of MiFID.
[21] Article 1(1) of PR.
[22] Articles 4(1), 5(1), 16(1), and 48(1) of MiCA.
[23] Article 1(2)(b) of PR.
[24] Article 1(2)(c) and (d) of PR.
[25] Article 2(2)(f) of MiCA.
[26] Article 1(2)(b) of PR.
[27] Article 1(2)(e) of PR.
[28] See Article 1(1), cf. Articles 1(2)(a) and 2(a) of PR.

open-ended CIUs (see Sections 4.4.2.2 and 4.4.2.3 and Chapter 9), this applies, for instance, to all types of financial instruments listed in Annex I, Section C of MiFID that are not transferable securities.

In addition, both PR and MiCA exempt non-fungible assets. This exemption under MiCA is general,[29] as it applies to all NFTs (see Section 4.2.2). The equivalent under PR applies only to 'non-fungible shares of capital' that provide the holder with a right to occupy an apartment or another specific piece of real estate. Yet, this difference is presumably of little practical significance because PR applies to securities, which are fungible by definition.[30]

5.3.4 *Exemption by Size*

PR typically does not apply when an offer to the public is for less than EUR 12 million over twelve months.[31] Moreover, there is no obligation to publish a prospectus when securities are offered to fewer than 150 persons per Member State (other than qualified investors).[32] Similar exemptions do not apply, however, when securities are admitted to trading on a regulated market.[33] By comparison, MiCA applies very similar exemptions for cryptoassets other than ARTs and EMTs,[34] yet with no authority for Member States to increase the threshold beyond EUR 1 million. No similar exemption exists for small issuances of ARTs or EMTs though.[35] These differences are surprising, given MiCA's objective of providing a less burdensome regime than conventional EU financial law, and they seem to counter the Commission's stated goal of boosting 'responsible innovation in the EU's financial sector, especially for highly innovative digital start-ups'.[36]

No such general, size-based exemptions apply when assets are admitted to trading, but PR applies a specific exemption for credit institutions that repeatedly issue non-equity securities offered for less than EUR 150 million per year.[37] No equivalent exemption applies under MiCA, most likely since the legislator assumes there will not be a mass-use of crypto issuances by credit institutions. Conversely, MiCA provides an exemption for cryptoassets other than ARTs or EMTs that are offered for free,[38] which is found neither under PR nor for ARTs or EMTs

[29] Article 2(3) of MiCA.

[30] See the definition in Article 4(1)(44) of MiFID, which by the term "classes of securities" presumably implies that the securities must be fungible within each class.

[31] Article 3(2)(b) of PR as amended by the Listing Act. See Article 1(1)(a) and 1(3)(a) of the European Parliament Legislative Resolution of 24 April 2024 on the Proposal for a Regulation of the European Parliament and of the Council Amending Regulations (EU) 2017/1129, (EU) No 596/2014 and (EU) No 600/2014 to Make Public Capital Markets in the Union More Attractive for Companies and to Facilitate Access to Capital for Small and Medium-Sized Enterprises (COM(2022)0762 – C9-0417/2022 – 2022/0411(COD)).

[32] Article 1(4)(b) of PR.

[33] See Article 1(5) of PR (by omission).

[34] Article 4(2) of MiCA.

[35] Articles 16 and 48 of MiCA (by omission). Please note that the exemptions in Articles 16(2) and 48(4) and (5) of MiCA do not include the obligation to produce a cryptoasset whitepaper. See Article 48(7) and Article 16(2) para. 2 of MiCA.

[36] European Commission, 'Digital Finance Package: Commission Sets Out New, Ambitious Approach to Encourage Responsible Innovation'. Website https://ec.europa.eu/commission/presscorner/detail/en/IP_20_1684 (last accessed on 1 October 2024).

[37] Articles 1(4)(j) and 1(5)(i) of PR, as amended by the Listing Act. See Article 1(1) (b) and (c) of the European Parliament Legislative Resolution of 24 April 2024 on the Proposal for a Regulation of the European Parliament and of the Council Amending Regulations (EU) 2017/1129, (EU) No 596/2014 and (EU) No 600/2014 to Make Public Capital Markets in the Union More Attractive for Companies and to Facilitate Access to Capital for Small and Medium-Sized Enterprises (COM(2022)0762 – C9-0417/2022 – 2022/0411(COD)).

[38] Article 4(3)(a) of MiCA.

under MiCA. We expect innovative crypto firms to exploit this exemption through complex schemes making it appear that the cryptoassets in question were offered for free even if, in reality, compensation is paid in kind, postponed, or concealed in other ways. We also expect courts to see through such attempts over time, and MiCA adds further mitigators through the qualifiers in the second paragraph of its Article 4(3).

5.3.5 *Exemption for Qualified Investors*

PR does not apply when an offer to the public is directed only to qualified investors, to fewer than 150 persons per Member State other than qualified investors, or only to investors that each invest at least EUR 100,000.[39] Under similar circumstances, MiCA exempts ARTs and cryptoassets other than ARTs and EMTs, yet with the additional criterion that the cryptoassets 'can only be held by such qualified investors'.[40] Again, the narrower exemptions under MiCA as compared to PR are surprising given the objective of providing a less burdensome regime than conventional EU financial law and the stated goal of boosting innovation and digital start-ups.[41] It is also unclear why a similar exemption does not apply to EMTs under Article 48 MiCA. One can, of course, assume that EMTs are conceived of as a form of payment instrument, so they are less likely to be offered solely to qualified investors. That said, this same argument should then imply that no prospectus would be necessary whatsoever, in line with the rules applying to conventional e-money under EMD.

5.3.6 *Exemptions Where a Prospectus May Already Exist*

As a starting point, the prospectus regime under PR and the one for cryptoassets other than ARTs and EMTs under MiCA both apply to a subsequent resale of cryptoassets, unless a prospectus already exists.[42] Similar exemptions apply to securities that are already admitted to trading on another market.[43] Yet, no equivalent exemption exists for ARTs and EMTs. Again, MiCA applies strict rules for stablecoins (see Chapter 6), here by offering a narrower set of exemptions than those provided by PR.

In addition, PR makes a number of exemptions from the prospectus requirements when securities are issued or admitted to trading as substitution or in exchange for other securities or dividend paid on such securities.[44] No similar exemptions are found in MiCA presumably because the EU legislators assume that these situations are common to securities and not

[39] Article 1(4)(a)–(d) of PR.

[40] Articles 4(2)(c) and 16(2)(b) of MiCA.

[41] European Commission, 'Digital Finance Package: Commission Sets Out New, Ambitious Approach to Encourage Responsible Innovation'. Website https://ec.europa.eu/commission/presscorner/detail/en/IP_20_1684 (last accessed on 1 October 2024).

[42] Article 5(1) para. 2 of PR; Article 4(7) para. 2 of MiCA.

[43] Article 5(4) of MiCA; Under Article 14a PR, the Listing Act is introducing a simplified 'EU follow-on prospectus'. See Article 1(12) of the European Parliament Legislative Resolution of 24 April 2024 on the Proposal for a Regulation of the European Parliament and of the Council Amending Regulations (EU) 2017/1129, (EU) No 596/2014 and (EU) No 600/2014 to Make Public Capital Markets in the Union More Attractive for Companies and to Facilitate Access to Capital for Small and Medium-Sized Enterprises (COM(2022)0762 – C9-0417/2022 – 2022/0411(COD)).

[44] Articles 1(4)(da)–(h) and 1(5)(a)–(g) of PR, as amended by the Listing Act. See Article 1(1) of the European Parliament Legislative Resolution of 24 April 2024 on the Proposal for a Regulation of the European Parliament and of the Council Amending Regulations (EU) 2017/1129, (EU) No 596/2014 and (EU) No 600/2014 to Make Public Capital Markets in the Union More Attractive for Companies and to Facilitate Access to Capital for Small and Medium-Sized Enterprises (COM(2022)0762 – C9-0417/2022 – 2022/0411(COD)).

important for cryptoassets subject to MiCA. Still, the fact is that once again MiCA offers a narrower set of exemptions compared to PR.

5.4 PROCEDURE

5.4.1 *Obligation to Publish a Prospectus; Voluntary Prospectuses*

When cryptoassets fall within the scope of the prospectus rules, either in PR or in MiCA, they can only be offered to the public or admitted to trading following the publication of a prospectus.[45] Because MiCA provides a bespoke authorisation regime for ARTs, a whitepaper is even a prerequisite for being granted such an authorisation.[46]

Where an offer to the public or admission to trading is exempted from the prospectus regime, there is still a possibility to publish a voluntary prospectus under PR.[47] This is a practical option mostly for issuances that are exempted due to their small size (see Section 5.3.4). Hence, the voluntary publishing of a prospectus under MiCA is an option limited to the issuance of cryptoassets other than ARTs and EMTs,[48] which is the only case for which MiCA offers exemptions for small issuances. So there is a general option to publish a voluntary prospectus under PR, but it is limited under MiCA not only to cryptoassets other than ARTs and EMTs but also to cases of issuance as opposed to admission to trading.

Wondering why we see this distinction in the legislative text, we doubt that anyone will want to use this limited option to publish a voluntary prospectus under MiCA. While, under the PR regime, the voluntary prospectus may be approved by the competent authority of the home Member State,[49] serving as a verification for the issuer to use it for marketing purposes, no such approval mechanism exists for cryptoassets other than ARTs and EMTs under MiCA. It seems that the sole purpose of a voluntary prospectus, then, is that the offeror be subject to the rights and obligations under Title II MiCA.[50] Yet, assuming this refers to the rights for offerors laid out in Article 11 MiCA, it would appear that these rights provide no better protection than the fundamental four freedoms of EU law, so the value of publishing a voluntary prospectus in accordance with MiCA is indeed limited.

5.4.2 *Obliged Entities*

The main rule in this regard under MiCA is that the duty to publish a prospectus lies with the person that offers the cryptoassets to the public or the person seeking admission to trading.[51] The same is implicit under Article 3 PR according to which securities cannot be offered to the public or admitted to trading unless a prospectus has been published. Yet, for cryptoassets other than ARTs and EMTs, an additional rule applies under MiCA, whereby the operator of a trading platform may alternatively be obliged to publish the prospectus.[52] This must be construed in relation to the fact that no authorisation requirement applies to the issuer of such cryptoassets,

45 Article 3 of PR; Articles 4(1)(b), 5(1)(b), 16(2) para. 2, 17(1)(a), 48(1)(b), and 48(7) of MiCA.
46 Article 18(2)(k) of MiCA.
47 Article 4 of PR.
48 Article 4(8) of MiCA.
49 Article 4(2) of PR.
50 See Article 4(8) of MiCA.
51 Articles 4(1)(b) and 5(1)(b), Article 16(2) para. 2, Articles 17(1)(a), 48(1)(b), and 48(7) of MiCA.
52 Article 5(2) of MiCA.

and enforcement is easier to achieve against licensed entities. Operators of trading platforms, meanwhile, need authorisation to operate in the EU (see Section 7.3),[53] so making them responsible promotes effective law enforcement.

5.4.3 *Approval of Prospectuses and Marketing Communications*

Prospectuses under PR, and those for ARTs under MiCA, require pre-approval by the competent authority of the home Member State.[54] Under the bespoke authorisation regime for ARTs, this is included in the authorisation process (see Section 6.3), so the whitepaper must be submitted as part of the application.[55] Meanwhile, for cryptoassets under MiCA other than ARTs, no pre-approval of the whitepaper is required,[56] although the competent authority must be notified.[57] This implies that the entire whitepaper, including any accompanying information, must be sent to the competent authority prior to publication. It is not sufficient to simply issue a notification of the fact that the whitepaper exists; the whitepaper itself must be attached in its entirety. For cryptoassets other than ARTs and EMTs, the notification should also be accompanied by an explanation of why the cryptoasset in question does not qualify as an ART, EMT, or cryptoasset subject to PR or otherwise outside MiCA's scope.[58]

The simplified process for cryptoassets other than ARTs and EMTs is fully in line with the goal of making a simplified framework for such assets. Yet, for EMTs, MiCA is, in fact, more burdensome than the rules for conventional e-money under EMD, under which no prospectus is required whatsoever.

Compared to the prospectus, scrutiny from a competent authority of accompanying marketing communications is never a precondition for offering cryptoassets to the public or seeking admission to trading. Yet, the competent authority of the Member State where the marketing communications is disseminated may exercise control over it, supported by the competent authority of the home Member State.[59]

Both MiCA and PR further facilitate cross-border cooperation. For ARTs under MiCA, where approval of the whitepaper is part of the bespoke authorisation regime for ARTs, this follows already from the authorisation process under that regime (see Section 6.3). Under PR, meanwhile, the competent authority must notify the ESMA once the prospectus is approved[60] and, upon request, also notify the competent authorities of any host Member States.[61] Furthermore, the ESMA shall use its powers under the ESMA Regulation to promote supervisory convergence and conduct at least one peer review of the scrutiny and approval procedures of competent authorities.[62] In addition, Articles 33 and 34 PR provide general rules about the cooperation between competent authorities and with the ESMA. For EMTs and other cryptoassets, MiCA creates a regime by which the competent authority of the home Member State

[53] Article 59, cf. Article 3(1)(16)(b) of MiCA.
[54] Article 20 of PR; Articles 20(1) and 21(1) of MiCA.
[55] Article 18(2)(k) of MiCA.
[56] Articles 8(3) and 51(11) of MiCA.
[57] Articles 4(1)(c) and 5(1)(c), cf. Article 8(1) of MiCA and the ESAs, 'Consultation Paper: Draft Guidelines on Templates for Explanations and Opinions, and the Standardised Test for the Classification of Crypto-assets, under Article 97(1) of Regulation (EU) 2023/1114' (2024), ESA 2024 12, Annex A.; Article 48(1)(b) and 48(7), cf. Article 51(11) of MiCA.
[58] Articles 8(4) of MiCA.
[59] Article 22(6) of PR; Articles 7(3), 8(2), 8(3), 29(4), 29(5), 53(4), and 53(5) of MiCA.
[60] See Article 20(2) last para. of PR.
[61] Article 25(1) of PR.
[62] Article 21(12) and (13) of PR.

notifies the ESMA and, in the case of other cryptoassets, the competent authority of any host Member States.[63]

5.4.4 *Publication of the Prospectus and Marketing Communications*

A prospectus and, where applicable, marketing communications should be published online. Under MiCA, they must simply be published on the website of the issuer, offeror, or person seeking admission to trading for the cryptoassets.[64] This also applies under PR, but with the option to rather publish the prospectus on the website of the financial intermediaries placing or selling the securities or on the website of the regulated market or market operator.[65] The difference in legislation here clearly shows how MiCA is adapting to a disintermediated cryptoasset environment.

Another difference is that the publication rules under MiCA apply both to the whitepaper and to any accompanying marketing communications, while under PR, they apply to the prospectus only, and there is no rule for how advertisements should be published; instead, the marketing rules of MiFID and EU investment fund regulation apply. Presumably, the requirement under MiCA to publish marketing communications on specific websites does not preclude publishing through additional marketing channels.

In addition to being published by the issuer, offeror, or person seeking admission to trading, the prospectus is to be published by the ESMA on its website and, under PR, also by the competent authority of the home Member State.[66] This is a subtle example of how MiCA shifts responsibilities to the EU level compared with past legislation.

5.4.5 *Expiration of the Prospectus*

A prospectus under PR expires twelve months after it has been approved by the competent authority.[67] Hence, an offer to the public cannot continue beyond this time without another approval of a prospectus. If the cryptoassets somehow are still not admitted to trading twelve months after the approval of the prospectus, a new approval is similarly required for such admission. No similar requirement applies under MiCA, but the authorisation for an issuer of ARTs may be withdrawn by the competent authority.[68] Furthermore, Article 4(7) MiCA specifies for cryptoassets other than ARTs and EMTs that a subsequent offer to the public should be deemed a separate offer that may require a separate whitepaper. The same may, of course, implicitly apply also for EMTs, but MiCA's silence on this point may instead reflect the regulatory objectives, which for EMTs are more tilted towards financial stability than investor protection.

5.4.6 *Updating, Modification, and Supplementing of the Prospectus and Marketing Communications*

Aside from any expiration rules for prospectuses, if new information becomes available, the prospectus must be updated. Both MiCA and PR require such updates, yet in slightly different

[63] Article 8(6) and (7) of MiCA; Article 51(14), cf. Article 109(4) of MiCA.
[64] Articles 9(1), 28, 29(3), 51(13), and 53(3) of MiCA.
[65] Article 21(2) of PR.
[66] Article 21(5) and (6) of PR; Article 109 of MiCA.
[67] Article 12, cf. Article 8(11) of PR.
[68] Article 24 of MiCA.

ways. While Article 23 PR requires new information to be added as a supplement to the prospectus, MiCA requires the publication of a new and modified whitepaper. Moreover, MiCA clearly also requires the modification of associated marketing communications, while PR simply requires such advertising to be 'consistent with the information contained in the prospectus'.[69] These discrepancies should not be exaggerated, however. Of course, a prospectus with a supplement is, for most practical purposes, a de facto modified prospectus, and the competent authority may even request a consolidated version of the supplemented prospectus to ensure the comprehensibility of the information therein, if required.[70] In addition, under MiCA, the order of the information in a modified whitepaper or marketing communications should be consistent with that of the original version, so in practice, the two versions would typically be identical except for the added or modified information.[71]

The event triggering the need to update the prospectus is similar for both EMTs and utility tokens under MiCA and securities under PR. Essentially, the requirement is activated whenever there is a significant new factor, material mistake, or material inaccuracy in the prospectus that may affect the assessment of the cryptoassets.[72] Meanwhile, the trigger event for ARTs under MiCA is simply when the issuer intends to make a change to its business model which is 'likely to have a significant influence on the purchase decision' of the ARTs, supplemented by a list of what could count as such a change.[73] The different formulation of the trigger event for ARTs probably makes minimal difference in practice, but it is understandable given that investors in stablecoins such as ARTs face very different risks from investors in transferable securities. The same argument could be made for EMTs, but Article 51(12) MiCA probably takes a simpler approach here because EMTs are a regulated payment product with limited investment risk, which is reflected in the fact that no prospectus is required whatsoever for conventional e-money.

Because the obligation to modify the prospectus is triggered by events that can alter investment decisions, it applies only during the period where investors can indeed subscribe to or purchase the cryptoasset. For cryptoassets under PR and ARTs under MiCA, this means from the approval of the prospectus or, for ARTs, during the time of the authorisation.[74] For EMTs under MiCA, no specific rule applies, but given that the obligation to modify the prospectus applies only when an event is capable of affecting the assessment of the EMTs in question, it is natural to apply a similar rule to that provided for other cryptoassets under MiCA. Here, Article 12(1) makes it explicit that the obligation to modify the whitepaper applies only during the offer to the public or for as long as the cryptoassets are admitted to trading. Interestingly, the equivalent rule under PR puts an end to the obligation when trading of the given cryptoasset begins on a regulated market, so the obligation to modify the prospectus later, while the cryptoasset is still being traded, applies under MiCA only. Then, specifically for utility tokens giving rights to a service that is not yet in operation, a modification of the whitepaper cannot extend the maximum twelve-month duration of the offer to the public.[75]

The process for the publishing of a modified prospectus is similar to that for the original prospectus. Hence, for transferable securities under PR and ARTs under MiCA, the modified

[69] Article 22(3) of PR.
[70] Article 23(6) of PR.
[71] See Articles 12(4) and 25(2) of MiCA.
[72] See Article 23(1) and Article 10(1) para. 2 of PR and Articles 12(1) and 51(12) of MiCA, which use similar wording.
[73] Article 25(1) of MiCA.
[74] Article 23(1) of PR; Article 25(1) of MiCA.
[75] Article 12(8), cf. Article 4(6) of MiCA.

prospectus must be approved by the competent authority.[76] For EMTs and other cryptoassets under MiCA, however, no approval is required, albeit the issuer must notify the competent authority about the modified whitepaper prior to publication.[77]

Both PR and MiCA mandate cross-border collaboration among competent authorities and with the ESAs. Essentially, the same procedure applies for supplements to the original prospectus (see Section 5.4.3). That implies that, under PR, the competent authority must notify the ESMA once the prospectus is approved[78] and, upon request, also notify the competent authorities of any host Member States.[79] Similarly, for EMTs and other cryptoassets, the competent authority of the home Member State shall notify the ESMA about the modified whitepaper and, in the case of other cryptoassets, also to the competent authority of any host Member States.[80] As for the approval of new ART whitepapers (see Sections 5.4.3 and 6.3), more stringent rules also apply to modifications thereof.[81]

The modified prospectus is then published largely in the same way as the original one (see Section 5.4.4).[82] Moreover, presumably because no approval is required for a whitepaper for cryptoassets under MiCA other than ARTs and EMTs, additional requirements apply according to which the issuer, the person seeking admission to trading, or the operator of the trading platform must provide information on its website that the whitepaper has been modified and the reasons therefor.[83] In addition, the modified prospectus must be time-stamped and marked as the applicable version, while previous versions also remain publicly available.[84]

Finally, the main purpose of a modification to the prospectus, of course, is to provide correct and up-to-date details to inform future investment decisions. Yet, PR goes a step further by also giving existing investors some room to withdraw.[85] The issuer or, if applicable, the financial intermediary must inform investors about this right to withdraw.[86] Of note, no equivalent right to withdraw applies under MiCA, although for ARTs and EMTs, the right of redemption fulfils the same purpose.[87] For other cryptoassets under MiCA, *retail holders* have a general fourteen-day withdrawal period.[88] To the contrary, non-retail holders have no right to withdraw and must seek economic compensation instead for any losses endured due to the discrepancy between the original and modified whitepaper (see Section 4.6).

76 Article 23(1) para. 2 of PR; Article 25(2) of MiCA.

77 Articles 12(2) and 51(12) of MiCA.

78 See Article 20(2) last para. of PR.

79 Article 25(1) of PR.

80 Article 12(5) and Article 51(14) para. 2 of MiCA.

81 See Article 25(3)–(5) of MiCA.

82 See Article 23(1) of PR; Articles 12(6), 28, 29(3), 51(12), and 53(3) of MiCA.

83 Article 12(3) of MiCA.

84 Article 12(7) and (9) of MiCA.

85 Article 23(2) of PR as amended by the Listing Act. See Article 1(20) of the European Parliament Legislative Resolution of 24 April 2024 on the Proposal for a Regulation of the European Parliament and of the Council Amending Regulations (EU) 2017/1129, (EU) No 596/2014 and (EU) No 600/2014 to Make Public Capital Markets in the Union More Attractive for Companies and to Facilitate Access to Capital for Small and Medium-Sized Enterprises (COM(2022)0762 – C9-0417/2022 – 2022/0411(COD)).

86 Article 23(3) of PR, as amended by the Listing Act. See Article 1(20) of the European Parliament Legislative Resolution of 24 April 2024 on the Proposal for a Regulation of the European Parliament and of the Council Amending Regulations (EU) 2017/1129, (EU) No 596/2014 and (EU) No 600/2014 to Make Public Capital Markets in the Union More Attractive for Companies and to Facilitate Access to Capital for Small and Medium-Sized Enterprises (COM(2022)0762 – C9-0417/2022 – 2022/0411(COD)).

87 See Articles 39 and 49(4) of MiCA.

88 See Article 13 of MiCA.

5.5 CONTENT AND FORM

5.5.1 *Overview*

While MiCA provides specific rules for ARTs, EMTs, and other cryptoassets, PR covers a wide range of transferable securities under essentially the same framework. Hence, instead, the requirements with regard to the content and form of the prospectus vary under PR with respect to the nature and circumstances of the issuer, the type of securities, and, for non-equity securities, the denomination per unit and whether they are tradable by qualified investors only.[89] For non-equity securities, PR also offers an option to publish only a simplified 'base prospectus'.[90] Similarly, simplified disclosure rules also exist for secondary issuances and for the securities of small issuers.[91] Finally, under MiCA, the whitepaper (prospectus), including its summary, is seen as one document, while under PR, it may be split into a separate registration document, a securities note, and a summary.[92] For simplicity, we refer to all of the above when using the term 'prospectus' in the following, with specific references where deemed necessary. In addition, we cover the content and form of marketing communications (advertisements) separately in Section 5.5.4.

The content and form of the prospectus are regulated in Articles 6, 19, and 51 MiCA and in Articles 6–10 and 13–19 PR. In addition, the content is further detailed in Annexes I–III MiCA, while further details on both content and form are to some extent also to be set out in technical standards.[93] Similarly, PR also to a large extent refers to delegated acts for the content and form of the prospectus.[94] In the following, we focus on the core rules in and main differences between MiCA and PR.[95]

89 See Article 6(1) para. 2 and Article 13(1) of PR with the associated delegated acts.

90 See Article 8 of PR.

91 Articles 14a and 15a of PR, as amended by the Listing Act. See Article 1(11)–(14) and 1(3)(a) of the European Parliament Legislative Resolution of 24 April 2024 on the Proposal for a Regulation of the European Parliament and of the Council Amending Regulations (EU) 2017/1129, (EU) No 596/2014 and (EU) No 600/2014 to Make Public Capital Markets in the Union More Attractive for Companies and to Facilitate Access to Capital for Small and Medium-Sized Enterprises (COM(2022)0762 – C9-0417/2022 – 2022/0411(COD)).

92 See Articles 6(3), 8(6), and 10 and Articles 14a and 15a of PR with annexes, as amended by the Listing Act. See Article 1(1)(11)–(14) of the European Parliament Legislative Resolution of 24 April 2024 on the Proposal for a Regulation of the European Parliament and of the Council Amending Regulations (EU) 2017/1129, (EU) No 596/2014 and (EU) No 600/2014 to Make Public Capital Markets in the Union More Attractive for Companies and to Facilitate Access to Capital for Small and Medium-Sized Enterprises (COM(2022)0762 – C9-0417/2022 – 2022/0411(COD)).

93 Articles 6(11) and (12), 19(10) and (11), and 51(10) and (15) of MiCA. See draft regulatory technical standards (RTS) on sustainability indicators, the data necessary for the classification of whitepapers, and draft implementing technical standards (ITS) on standard forms and templates for the cryptoasset whitepaper in ESMA, 'Final Report: Draft Technical Standards Specifying Certain Requirements of Markets in Crypto-Assets Regulation (MiCA) – Second Package', ESMA75-453128700-1229 (2024), Annexes IV and IX, respectively.

94 See Article 13 of PR; Commission Delegated Regulation (EU) 2019/980 of 14 March 2019 supplementing Regulation (EU) 2017/1129 of the European Parliament and of the Council as regards the format, content, scrutiny, and approval of the prospectus to be published when securities are offered to the public or admitted to trading on a regulated market and repealing Commission Regulation (EC) No. 809/2004. See also Articles 14a(8) and 15a(8), as amended by the Listing Act. See Article 1(12) and (14) of the European Parliament Legislative Resolution of 24 April 2024 on the Proposal for a Regulation of the European Parliament and of the Council Amending Regulations (EU) 2017/1129, (EU) No 596/2014 and (EU) No 600/2014 to Make Public Capital Markets in the Union More Attractive for Companies and to Facilitate Access to Capital for Small and Medium-Sized Enterprises (COM(2022)0762 – C9-0417/2022 – 2022/0411(COD)).

95 For details, we refer to the Annexes of MiCA and to the above-mentioned delegated acts under MiCA and PR and the general literature on PR, e.g., Lehmann and Kumpan, *European Financial Services Law*; Busch *et al.*, *Prospectus Regulation*.

5.5.2 *Content of the Prospectus*

As a general principle, the prospectus must contain the information necessary for an investor to make an informed investment decision.[96] This is then specified in MiCA, PR, and delegated acts, with an emphasis placed on various elements. Specifically, the prospectus must contain information about the issuer, offeror, person seeking admission to trading, operator of the trading platform, any guarantor, and/or any other person engaged in drawing up the prospectus.[97] In addition, it must include information about the offer to the public or admission to trading,[98] the cryptoassets (as well as the rights and obligations attached thereto),[99] the underlying technology,[100] and investment risks specific to the cryptoasset in question.[101] Due to environmental concerns over the energy intensity of proof-of-work consensus mechanisms, under MiCA, the prospectus must also provide information on adverse impacts on the environment deriving from the consensus mechanism used.[102]

The financial condition and prospects of the issuer are naturally of the utmost importance to investors, particularly when investing in equity or equity-like instruments. Hence, Annexes I–III MiCA specify that the information about the issuer should include its 'financial condition'. For cryptoassets other than ARTs and EMTs, which are the most equity-like instruments under MiCA, the prospectus must also contain information about the cryptoasset project and, specifically for utility tokens, state that the tokens may eventually not be exchangeable in the promised goods or services.[103] Meanwhile, for ARTs, which are non-equity-like instruments and backed by reserve assets, the prospectus must contain information on those reserve assets.[104] Under PR, by comparison, the prospectus must outline 'the assets and liabilities, profits and losses, financial position, and prospects of the issuer and any guarantor'.[105] Further detail for different scenarios is then to be provided by delegated act.[106]

5.5.3 *Formal Requirements to the Prospectus*

As a general principle, the prospectus should be concise, comprehensible, fair, and clear, while it should not be misleading or have material omissions.[107] It must also contain a summary that

[96] This is specified in Article 6(1) of PR, but it must be seen as a general principle also under MiCA.

[97] Articles 6(1)(a)–(c), 19(1)(a), 51(1)(a), and Articles 6(1) para. 2, 19(1) para. 2, and 51(1) para. 2 of MiCA; Article 6(1)(a) of PR.

[98] Articles 6(1)(e), 19(1)(c), and 51(1)(c) of MiCA; Article 6(1)(c) of PR.

[99] Articles 6(1)(f) and (g), 19(1)(b) and (d), and 51(1)(b) and (d) of MiCA; Article 6(1)(b) of PR.

[100] Articles 6(1)(h), 19(1)(e), and 51(1)(e) of MiCA.

[101] Articles 6(1)(i), 19(1)(f), and 51(1)(f) of MiCA; Article 16 of PR.

[102] Articles 6(1)(j), 19(1)(h), and 51(1)(g) of MiCA.

[103] Article 6(1)(d) and 6(5)(d) of MiCA.

[104] Article 19(1)(g) of MiCA.

[105] Article 6(1)(a) of PR.

[106] Commission Delegated Regulation (EU) 2019/980 of 14 March 2019 supplementing Regulation (EU) 2017/1129 of the European Parliament and of the Council as regards the format, content, scrutiny, and approval of the prospectus to be published when securities are offered to the public or admitted to trading on a regulated market and repealing Commission Regulation (EC) No. 809/2004.

[107] Articles 6(2), 14, 19(2), 27, 51(2), and 66 of MiCA; ESMA, 'Consultation Paper: Draft Technical Standards and Guidelines Specifying Certain Requirements of the Markets in Crypto Assets Regulation (MiCA) on Detection and Prevention of Market Abuse, Investor Protection and Operational Resilience – Third Consultation Paper' (2024), ESMA75-453128700-1002; Articles 6(2), 7(2), and 8(4) of PR.

provides key information.[108] MiCA further specifies that the prospectus must include the date of its notification and a table of contents and should clearly state that it complies with the requirements under MiCA and that the cryptoassets are covered neither by the EU's investor compensation scheme nor by the EU's deposit guarantee scheme.[109] For EMTs and cryptoassets other than ARTs and EMTs under MiCA, the prospectus must also state that it has not been approved by any competent authority.[110] Furthermore, for ARTs and cryptoassets other than ARTs and EMTs, the whitepaper may not present any assertions about their future value but must clearly state that they may lose their value and become non-transferrable or otherwise illiquid.[111]

The prospectus should be drawn up either in an official language of both the home and, if applicable, the host Member States or, alternatively, 'in a language customary in the sphere of international finance', which for most practical purposes is English.[112] Under PR, however, the summary of the prospectus may have to be translated into the languages of the home Member State and all host Member States.[113]

5.5.4 *Marketing Communications (Advertisements)*

The prospectus is typically not suitable for marketing purposes, so the issuer, offeror, or person seeking admission to trading would usually also seek to reach prospective investors through other channels. To protect investors and ensure consistency with the prospectus, MiCA has rules about such 'marketing communications' and PR regulates 'advertisements', which is essentially the same thing. For simplicity, we refer to both as marketing communications in the following.

Marketing communications should be clearly recognisable as such;[114] they must be fair, clear, and not misleading,[115] as well as consistent with the information contained in the prospectus,[116] and they should state that a prospectus has been or will be published and indicate where investors can access it.[117] In addition, for ARTs and EMTs under MiCA, the marketing communications should state that holders have a right to redemption against the issuer.[118]

Scrutiny of the marketing communications from a competent authority is no precondition for offering the cryptoassets to the public or seeking admission to trading (see Section 5.4.3). However, for cryptoassets other than ARTs and EMTs, where neither the whitepaper nor the

[108] Articles 6(7), 19(6), and 51(6) of MiCA; Articles 7(1) and 8(9) of PR.

[109] Articles 6(5)(e) and (f), 6(6), 6(8), 19(4)(e) and (f), 19(5), 19(7), 51(5), 51(4), and 51(7) of MiCA.

[110] Articles 6(3) and 51(3) of MiCA.

[111] Articles 6(4) and (5) and 19(3) and (4) of MiCA.

[112] See Articles 6(9), 19(8), and 51(8) of MiCA; Article 27(1) and (2) of PR.

[113] See Article 27(2) para. 4 and (2) para. 2 of PR, as amended by the Listing Act. See Article 1(21) of the European Parliament Legislative Resolution of 24 April 2024 on the Proposal for a Regulation of the European Parliament and of the Council Amending Regulations (EU) 2017/1129, (EU) No 596/2014 and (EU) No 600/2014 to Make Public Capital Markets in the Union More Attractive for Companies and to Facilitate Access to Capital for Small and Medium-Sized Enterprises (COM(2022)0762 – C9-0417/2022 – 2022/0411(COD)).

[114] Article 22(3) of PR; Articles 7(1)(a), 29(1)(a), and 53(1)(a) of MiCA.

[115] Article 22(3) of PR; Articles 7(1)(b), 29(1)(b), and 53(1)(b) of MiCA.

[116] Article 22(3) of PR; Articles 7(1)(c), 29(1)(c), and 53(1)(c) of MiCA.

[117] Article 22(2) of PR; Articles 7(1)(d), 29(1)(d), and 53(1)(d) of MiCA.

[118] Articles 29(2) and 53(2) of MiCA.

TABLE 5.1 *Passporting procedure under MiCA and PR*

Topic	MiCA Articles	PR Articles
Required use of either official language in the host Member State or a language customary in the sphere of international finance (typically English)	6(9), 19(8), and 51(8)	27(2)
Notification of ESMA and NCA of the host Member State as precondition for a prospectus and its supplements to be valid in that Member State		24(1), cf. 25
Duty for NCA of the home Member State to notify the NCA of intended host Member States and/or ESMA	7(4), 8(6)–(7), 12(5), 21(5), 25(5), and 51(14)	
Duty for ESMA to make the prospectus available in its register	8(7), 12(5), 21(5), 25(5), and 51(14), cf. 109	
ESMA and NCA of the host Member State may inform the NCA of the home Member State about needs to update a prospectus	General rules in Articles 95 and 96	24(2)
Duty for NCA of the host Member State to notify the NCA of the home Member State and ESMA (and sometimes EBA) of suspected irregularities	102(1)	37(1)
Duty for NCA of the host Member State to take appropriate measures if irregularities persist and amount to an infringement of MiCA, after informing the NCA of the home Member State and ESMA (and sometimes EBA)	102(2)	37(2)
Direct intervention by ESMA/EBA in case of disagreement between NCAs of the host and home Member States.	102(3)	37(3)

marketing communications need approval, the marketing communications must instead clarify to investors that it has not been reviewed or approved by a competent authority.[119]

5.6 LIABILITY

Articles 15, 26, and 52 MiCA and Article 11 PR expressly state that an offeror, person seeking admission to trading, or operator of a trading platform is liable for damages claimed by holders of cryptoassets for information in the whitepaper that is either misleading or not complete, fair, or clear. Also liable under MiCA are individual members of their administrative, management, or supervisory body presumably because the shell entities used for issuance of cryptoassets are often thinly capitalised.[120] MiCA also specifies that any exclusion of civil liability (e.g., through typical 'disclaimer' statements) shall be deprived of legal effect.[121] This strict liability regime is presumably a response to the various frauds observed in the crypto contexts.

MiCA's whitepaper liability is in addition to[122] the possibility of raising civil liability claims under national law. Where the law of Member States provides so,[123] liability may also extend to, for instance, information provided in marketing communications even if that is mentioned neither in MiCA nor in PR.

119 Article 7(1)(e) of MiCA.

120 Article 11 of PR here leaves some discretion to Member States.

121 Articles 15(2), 26(2), and 52(2) of MiCA.

122 See Articles 15(6), 26(5), and 52(5) of MiCA; Article 11(2) of PR.

123 An example is the liability of individual actors under the German Bürgerliches Gesetzbuch for marketing efforts that take the shape and form similar to a prospectus, without relying on a formal prospectus.

One significant deviation, however, between MiCA, on the one hand, and PR and civil liability claims under national law, on the other hand, is that no culpability standard applies under MiCA. Hence, liability is incurred simply when the whitepaper infringes the standards laid out in MiCA, irrespective of any negligence on behalf of the person held liable. This is particularly strict for individual members of the management or supervisory board, who may not even know about the whitepaper, and must be understood in relation to the past difficulties experienced in law enforcement over cryptoassets that MiCA seeks to address. Under Article 11 PR, meanwhile, Member States are free to regulate the conditions for liability, so they are inclined to apply conventional culpability standards.

Finally, both MiCA and PR specify that holders of cryptoassets may not rely solely on the summary of the whitepaper. Hence, they cannot claim damages for information provided in the summary, except where the summary does not provide key information or is misleading, inaccurate, or inconsistent when read together with the other parts of the whitepaper.[124]

5.7 EU PASSPORT

The prospectus is valid throughout the EU, so competent authorities of host Member States must not undertake any approval or administrative procedures relating to it.[125] The person responsible for drafting the prospectus or the NCA of the home Member State must, however, notify the NCAs of intended host Member States and the ESMA in a procedure described further in Table 5.1.

[124] Articles 15(5), 26(4), and 52(4) of MiCA; Article 11(2) para. 2 of PR.

[125] Article 24(1) of PR; Articles 4(1), 5(1), 11(1) and (2), 16(1)–(4), 48(1), and 51(13) of MiCA.

6

Product Regulation of Stablecoins (E-money Tokens and Asset-Referenced Tokens) in Titles III and IV MiCA

6.1 INTRODUCTION

To ensure financial stability, an adequate degree of investor protection, market fairness, and integrity in places where gaps in the traditional EU financial regulation have been identified,[1] MiCA imposes bespoke product regulation, in force since July 2024, for cryptocurrencies (more precisely, so-called stablecoins) under the labels of ARTs and EMTs. Yet, it distinguishes between (partly) centralised and "fully decentralised cryptoassets without an intermediary". MiCA's product regulation extends to centralised and *partly* decentralised digital currencies only and leaves *fully* decentralised currencies like Bitcoin unregulated.

Based on this taxonomy, in this chapter, we provide an overview of the ART and EMT product rules. Section 6.2 lays out the scope of Titles III and IV MiCA, after which Section 6.3 discusses the licensing requirements forming the basis for the token issuer's European Passport. Section 6.4 then covers the rules on redemption rights and reserve management, while Section 6.5 addresses disclosure requirements. Section 6.6 lays out the EBA's supervision of significant ARTs and EMTs, and Section 6.7 concludes.

6.2 SCOPE

6.2.1 *Electronic Money Tokens*

Title IV MiCA provides for the product regulation of EMTs. An EMT is a type of cryptoasset that purports to maintain a stable value by referencing the value of *one* official currency.[2] Examples include the USDC or EURC which are "pegged to" the USD or the EUR, respectively.

EMTs function inside DeFi ecosystems as cryptocurrencies where a DeFi ecosystem seeks to avoid the downside of heavily volatile cryptocurrencies such as Bitcoin. EMTs offer, similar to e-money, immediate finality and settlement paired with potentially low transaction fees.[3] At the same time, they potentially remove the need for bank accounts in transactions due to a type of

[1] Recitals paras. 1, 2, and 4 of MiCA.

[2] Article 3(7) of MiCA.

[3] See, for instance, O. Caudevilla *et al.*, 'Stablecoins – An Introduction and Recommendations for the European Union. Digital Euro Association' (2023). Website www.researchgate.net/publication/363255932_Stablecoins_An_Introduction_and_Recommendations_for_the_European_Union (last accessed on 1 October 2024).

transfer similar to bearer instruments.[4] Since EMTs do not yield interest,[5] they do not have the potential to provide money market returns such as money market funds.

6.2.2 *Asset-Referenced Tokens*

Title III MiCA regulates ARTs. An ART can include cryptoassets that are not EMTs and purport to maintain a stable value by referencing another value or right or a combination thereof, including one or more official currencies.[6]

The best way of understanding this definition is to look at the example of the ART known as Libra (later renamed Diem), a global stablecoin project referenced to a large basket of international treasuries and high-quality debt securities.[7] Yet, ARTs may also be of a smaller scale.

Any project that purports to maintain a stable value qualifies as ART. Stablecoin projects pegged to the value of one or several cryptocurrencies (e.g., Bitcoin or Ether) are not referenced to the value of an *official* currency and qualify as ARTs. Meanwhile, ARTs could further include the tracking of a basket of currencies (such as the International Monetary Fund's Special Drawing Rights[8]), a portfolio of securities, or an index (e.g., Dow Jones or Eurostoxx).

ARTs can become functional equivalents to investment funds (in particular, money market funds, index funds, and exchange-traded funds (ETFs)), hence MiCA's strict approach to regulating ARTs which mimics the rules on index and money market funds. For the same reasons, NCAs shall refuse an authorisation 'where the business model of the applicant issuer of [ARTs] might pose a serious threat to market integrity, financial stability or the smooth operation of payment systems'.[9]

6.2.3 *Stablecoin Characteristics*

To qualify as stablecoin, it is required that the cryptoasset purports to maintain a stable value. The stability referred to here means that the stablecoin does not fluctuate *in relation to the referenced value(s)* (e.g., the USDC seeking to track the USD 1:1). Fluctuation in absolute value may well come despite the stablecoin label, for instance, if the USD exchange rate against another currency or the accumulated value of the tracked portfolio increases or decreases.

MiCA does not stipulate how the functioning of a stablecoin must be expressed. We hold that there are at least the following three different paths towards qualification as EMTs or ARTs:

4 See, for instance, P. Bains *et al.*, 'Regulating the Crypto Ecosystem: The Case of Stablecoins and Arrangements', Fintech Notes, International Monetary Fund (2022).

5 See Article 50 of MiCA.

6 Article 3(6) of MiCA.

7 Cf. Zetzsche *et al.*, 'Regulating Libra', 80–113.

8 See Imf.org, 'Special Drawing Rights' (2023). Website www.imf.org/en/About/Factsheets/Sheets/2023/special-drawing-rights-sdr (last accessed on 1 October 2024). ('The SDR is an international reserve asset. The SDR is not a currency, but its value is based on a basket of five currencies – the US dollar, the euro, the Chinese renminbi, the Japanese yen, and the British pound sterling. (. . .) The IMF created the SDR as a supplementary international reserve asset in 1969, when currencies were tied to the price of gold and the US dollar was the leading international reserve asset. The IMF defined the SDR as equivalent to a fractional amount of gold that was equivalent to one US dollar. When fixed exchange rates ended in 1973, the IMF redefined the SDR as equivalent to the value of a basket of world currencies. The SDR itself is not a currency but an asset that holders can exchange for currency when needed. The SDR serves as the unit of account of the IMF and other international organizations.')

9 Recital para. 45 of MiCA.

- Language indicating the tracking of an official currency, value, or right in the whitepaper or on the project website;
- The description of a stabilisation mechanism in the whitepaper or on the project website; or
- Language indicating a stablecoin or tracking function as part of the name of the cryptoasset (e.g., Euro Stablecoin, Stable Euro, and TrackingStoxx).

Stablecoin projects often seek to maintain a stable value by way of *reserves*, which are typically invested in the best-rated bank deposits and securities (often treasuries or money market instruments in the referenced currency).[10]

So-called algorithmic stablecoins aim to keep a stable value in relation to an official currency and employ protocols that provide for the increase or decrease in the supply of such cryptoassets in response to changes in demand.[11] Algorithmic stablecoins pegged to *one* official currency are subject to Title IV MiCA, while those pegged to anything else are subject to Title III MiCA. Given Title II MiCA deals with "other cryptoassets" (i.e., cryptoassets within the scope of MiCA but not qualifying under Titles III and IV MiCA), algorithmic cryptoassets 'that do *not* aim to stabilise the value of the cryptoassets by referencing one or several assets' must comply with Title II MiCA.[12]

6.2.4 *(Partly) Centralised vs. Fully Decentralised Applications without an Intermediary*

For some cryptoassets, in particular, Bitcoin, it is difficult to identify a single token issuer. Pursuant to Recital 22, 'where cryptoassets have no identifiable issuer, they should not fall within the scope of Title II, III or IV of [MiCA]'. Titles III and IV MiCA provide the context for this statement in the non-binding text. The product regulation for ARTs and EMTs requires an issuer, as the issuer and the whitepaper must be authorised.

The general exemption for fully decentralised services from MiCA's scope is covered in Section 4.2.4. In the following, we focus specifically on the implications for MiCA's product rules.

6.2.4.1 *EMTs: Lack of a Credit or E-money Institution*

For EMTs, the issuer must be a credit institution or an e-money institution and must be a legal entity.[13] In turn, one credit or e-money institution must issue the EMTs; no group of nodes, nor their owners, can assume this role as long as the group does not qualify as a legal entity that can be authorised as a credit or e-money institution.

6.2.4.2 *ARTs: A Legal Entity or "Other Undertaking"*

The situation is more complex for ARTs. Pursuant to Article 16(1) MiCA, a 'person shall not make an offer to the public, or seek the admission to trading, of an [ART], within the Union, *unless that person is the issuer*' of that ART *and* is a credit institution (subject to Article 17 MiCA) or '*a legal person or other undertaking* that is established in the Union and has been

[10] G. B. Gorton and J. Y. Zhang, 'Taming Wildcat Stablecoins', *The University of Chicago Law Review*, 90(3) (2023): 909, 910–24; R. Clements, 'Built to Fail: The Inherent Fragility of Algorithmic Stablecoins', *Wake Forest Law Review Online*, 11 (2021): 131.

[11] Recital para. 41 of MiCA.

[12] Recital para. 41 of MiCA.

[13] See Article 48(1) of MiCA, and Article 1, 33 CRD; Article 1 EMD.

authorised in accordance with Article 21 by the competent authority of its home Member State'. This requirement leads us to three considerations.

The first consideration concerns the use of technology. In fully decentralised systems, technology is deployed to issue the tokens. Yet, in non-traditional fully centralised setups, technology is also at the core of token or share issues; no-one issues tokens by hand. Hence, the use of smart contracts or other automated protocols (such as a mining protocol) alone is insufficient to preclude the existence of an issuer.

This leads to the second consideration, which involves the issuer's legal capacity. Under Article 16(1) MiCA, the issuer may be a legal entity or an "other undertaking". In decentralised systems, one could also consider the owners of the DLT's nodes that collectively issue the tokens as "other undertakings", to reflect the fact that under many laws of EU Member States as well as in US private law, a group of individuals may form a simple partnership with legal capacity, yet without legal entity status.[14] Under MiCA, however, an "other undertaking" qualifies only to the extent that 'their legal form ensures a level of protection for third parties' interests equivalent to that afforded by legal persons and if they are subject to equivalent prudential supervision appropriate to their legal form'.[15] This sentence stems from Article 4(1), second subsection, of MiFID. It allows, for instance, a German *GmbH&Co KG* to function as issuer. If we apply the same principles as those established under MiFID,[16] sole traders, simple partnerships, and loose contractual relationships are entitled to perform authorised functions only if they meet complex requirements aimed at safeguarding client funds in the event of insolvency.

A mere random assembly of token-holders does not meet this prerequisite. Even where the group of node owners qualifies as a simple (general) partnership,[17] Articles 16 and 59 MiCA exclude this group from functioning as issuer. A more permanent establishment of the group is necessary. In turn, to confirm the presence of an issuer, we look for at least one legal entity or individual qualifying under the previously described criteria intended to provide certain safeguards for clients, as a central institution issuing units.

Note that the former does not preclude the possibility of several legal entities (and even qualifying individuals) functioning together as an issuer. On the contrary, MiCA recognises that a stablecoin may be issued by several issuers simultaneously[18] by setting requirements for such cases. Here, legal entities and/or qualified individuals (meeting the prescribed criteria) cooperate in the issuance, as a type of permanently established group.

[14] Cf. Zetzsche *et al.*, 'The Distributed Liability of Distributed Ledgers'. See A. Gilbert, 'Governance Tokens Might Come with Legal Liability, US Judge Says – bZx DAO and Founders Were Sued After $55M Hack', 30 March 2023. Website https://thedefiant.io/gov-tokens-legal-risk (last accessed on 1 October 2024).

[15] Cf. Article 16(1)(a) and second subsection of MiCA (ART); Article 59(3) of MiCA (EMT).

[16] See, for instance, Central Bank of Ireland, 'Guidance Note for Authorisation as an Investment Firm under MiFID: Guidance on Completing an Application for Authorisation under the European Union (Markets in Financial Instruments) Regulations 2017', No. S.I. 375 of 2017 (2021), p. 4 (stating that "Where a natural person provides services (...) he or she ensures that the following conditions are fulfilled: (a) the ownership rights of third parties in instruments and funds must be safeguarded, especially in the event of the insolvency of the investment firm or of its proprietors, seizure, set-off or any other action by creditors of the firm or of its proprietors; (b) the investment firm must be subject to rules designed to monitor the firm's solvency and that of its proprietors; (c) the investment firm's annual accounts must be audited by one or more persons empowered, under the law of the State or another Member State, to audit accounts; (d) where the investment firm has only one proprietor, he or she must make provision for the protection of investors in the event of the investment firm's cessation of business following his or her death incapacity or any other such event.")

[17] Cf. Zetzsche *et al.*, 'The Distributed Liability of Distributed Ledgers'. See Gilbert, 'Governance Tokens Might Come with Legal Liability'.

[18] See Articles 23(3), 43(3), and 45(6) of MiCA (ART); Article 56(2) of MiCA (EMT).

6.2.4.3 *Partial vs. Full Decentralisation: Control Test*

An issuer as a central institution is missing in some cryptocurrency projects, particularly Bitcoin. Yet, many cryptocurrencies have remained in a state of *partial* centralisation; these partially centralised and partially decentralised firms remain, as Recital 22 states, within the scope of Titles III and IV MiCA. This prompts the need to clarify which functions one must identify to distinguish between partial and full decentralisation.

Offering a hint perhaps, Recital 22 refers to the lack of an intermediary. The term "intermediary" is not defined in MiCA. In traditional terms, an intermediary would act either on-balance or off-balance and modify the duration, nature, time, risks, and other features of the asset or cash flow. Within that broad meaning, all DeFi ecosystems come with an intermediary function. After all, their purpose is to "do something" with the clients' funds or cryptoassets. One could try to define intermediaries by looking at the services listed in Article 3(16) MiCA, yet this blurs the CASP functions further specified in Title V MiCA with the issuer function detailed in Titles III and IV MiCA. Only where the same entity issues EMTs/ARTs and offers cryptoasset services must the entity apply Titles III/IV and V MiCA simultaneously.

This prompts us to look at the issue of full vs. partial decentralisation. We hold that the distinction between the two relates to the degree of centralisation: where one person (or a permanently established group of entities and qualifying individuals, as laid out before) controls the issuance process, partial centralisation is given. Control in such a sense derives from an overall assessment of whether someone controls: (1) the algorithm that issues tokens, for instance, due to access codes and other technical modes of access; (2) the governance process over the algorithm (for instance, through "golden tokens" that carry the majority in voting processes);[19] and (3) the distribution of tokens and services to new clients and token-holders, thus indirectly prompting the issuance of new tokens. Where no-one controls the issuance of tokens in this way, an issuer is lacking and full decentralisation is given.

We, thus, propose delineating between partial and full decentralisation by applying the control test by asking whether there is at least one entity or group of entities controlling functions material to the issuance and redemption of new tokens.

6.3 LICENSING REQUIREMENTS AND THE EUROPEAN PASSPORT

6.3.1 *Issuance of ARTs and EMTs as a Regulated Activity*

MiCA defines the issuance of ARTs and EMTs[20] as a regulated activity.

On the one hand, an issuer of ARTs and EMTs is subject to licensing. As credit institutions tend to be licensed, both ARTs and EMTs may be issued by credit institutions (subject to additional MiCA requirements[21]). EMTs may also be issued by electronic money institutions,[22] while ARTs may also be issued by other issuers subject to bespoke requirements set out in Articles 18, 20, and 21 MiCA.

[19] See Anker-Sørensen and Zetzsche, 'From Centralized to Decentralized Finance'.; Goldberg and Schär, 'Metaverse Governance'.

[20] EMTs are deemed e-money under the E-money Directive 2009/110 (Article 48(2) of MiCA), and thus, the rules of Titles II and III of EMD apply (Article 48(3) of MiCA), subject to additional product requirements set out in Title IV of MiCA. The EMD, in turn, refers to the first Payment Services Directive 2007/64/EC (PSD I), which has been repealed by the second Payment Services Directive 2015/2366 (PSD II). This multi-referencing makes the Title IV of MiCA difficult to handle.

[21] Cf. Article 17 of MiCA; Title IV of MiCA (EMTs).

[22] Article 48(1) of MiCA.

On the other hand, the content of the whitepaper for the ART or EMT being issued is meticulously prescribed.[23] Moreover, a number of product rules are specified (including the holders' redemption right, minimum rules on ART and EMT reserves, and reinvestments of funds paid by clients) and thus reviewed by the NCA.

The authorisation is, therefore, a mix of entity and product authorisation, similar to the issuance of EU retail investment funds, like UCITS under UCITSD[24] or ELTIFs under the ELTIF Regulation:[25] where the entity is a credit institution or e-money institution that is already licensed, the authorisation process focuses on the product rules.[26] Where ARTs are issued by other entities, the application for authorisation will also lead to a full review of the issuer.[27] This legislative setup enables credit institutions (and e-money institutions in the case of EMTs) to function as archetype multi-issuers of these tokens, while bespoke vehicles are primarily used for project finance in relation to a single token type.

6.3.2 *Licensing Requirements*

Licensing comes with a set of rules on licensing[28] well known from other EU-regulated activities, including rules on:

- The issuer's programme of operations, organisation, outsourcing requirements, capitalisation, governance,[29] conflict management, complaint handling,[30] as well as the identity and solidity of main shareholders and the fitness and properness of the issuer's directors;[31,32]
- Modification of information provided in support of the application, in particular, the content of the whitepaper[33] and on the (authorised) management body;[34]

[23] Cf. Article 19 and Annex II of MiCA (ART); Article 51 and Annex III of MiCA (EMT) and Regulatory Technical Standards on the approval process for whitepapers for ARTs issued by credit institutions under Article 17(8) of Regulation (EU) 2023/1114, Draft Final Report (2024), EBA/RTS/2024/05.

[24] See on UCITS, D. A. Zetzsche, 'The Anatomy of European Investment Fund Law', in W. A. Birdthistle and J. Morley (eds.), *Research Handbook on Mutual Funds* (Cheltenham, UK: Edward Elgar Publishing Limited, 2018), pp. 305–7.

[25] See D. A. Zetzsche and C. D. Preiner, 'ELTIFR versus AIFMD', in D. A. Zetzsche (ed.), *The Alternative Investment Fund Managers Directive* (Alphen aan den Rijn: Wolters Kluwer, 2020), 3rd ed., Chapter 5, at pp. 95 et seq.

[26] Cf. Article 17(1) of MiCA (ART); Title IV of MiCA (EMT).

[27] Article 18(2) of MiCA (ART) and the ESAs, 'Consultation Paper: Draft Guidelines on Templates for Explanations and Opinions, and the Standardised Test for the Classification of Crypto-assets, under Article 97(1) of Regulation (EU) 2023/1114' (2024), ESA 2024 12, Annex B.

[28] Cf. Regulatory Technical Standards on information for application for authorisation to offer to the public and to seek admission to trading of asset-referenced tokens and Implementing Technical Standards on standard forms, templates, and procedures for the information to be included in the application, under Article 18(6) and (7) of Regulation (EU) 2023/1114, Draft Final Report (2024), EBA/RTS/2024/03 and EBA/ITS/2024/03.

[29] EBA, 'Guidelines on the Minimum Content of the Governance Arrangements for Issuers of Asset-Referenced Tokens', Final Report (2024), EBA/GL/2024/06.

[30] Regulatory Technical Standards to specify the requirements, templates, and procedures for handling complaints under Article 31 of the Regulation (EU) 2023/1114 on Markets in Crypto-assets and amending Directive (EU) 2019/1937 (MICAR), Draft Final Report (2024), EBA/RTS/2024/02.

[31] EBA, ESMA, 'Joint Guidelines on the Suitability Assessment of Members of Management Body of Issuers of Asset-Referenced Tokens and of Crypto-Asset Service Providers, and Joint EBA and ESMA Guidelines on the Suitability Assessment of Shareholders and Members, Whether Direct or Indirect, with Qualifying Holdings in Issuers of Asset-Referenced Tokens and in Crypto-Asset Service Providers', Final Report (2024), EBA/GL/2024/99, ESMA 75-453128700-10.

[32] In particular, see Article 18(2)(d), (f)–(j), (m), (q) and Articles 31–35 of MiCA (ART), Article 48(3) of MiCA in conjunction with Article 3(1) of EMD, and Article 5(a)–(i) of PSD1, Directive 2007/64, OJ 2007 No. L319 (EMT).

[33] Cf. Article 25 of MiCA (ART); Article 51 (12) of MiCA (EMT).

[34] Article 33 of MiCA (ART), Article 48(3) of MiCA, in conjunction with Article 3(1) of EMD, Articles 14 and 5(i) of PSD1 (EMT).

- The granting, refusal, and withdrawal of applications;[35]
- Acquisition of licensed entities;[36] and
- Sanctions in cases of violations and infringements.[37]

6.3.3 *Fiduciaries under Statutory Law?*

Articles 27 and 32 MiCA clarify that ART issuers are fiduciaries. Rather than pursuing their own interests, they must act in the best interests of the ART holders and treat them equally, unless any preferential treatment is disclosed in the whitepaper and, where applicable, the marketing communications.

In line with the fiduciary status, ART issuers are obliged to 'act honestly, fairly, and professionally'. They must communicate with the (prospective) token-holders 'in a fair, clear and not misleading manner' (cf. Article 27 MiCA). Finally, ART issuers are subject to advanced duties to manage conflicts of interest.[38] They must take 'appropriate steps to identify, prevent, manage and disclose conflicts of interest arising from the management and investment of the reserve of assets referred to' in Article 36 MiCA.[39]

For EMT issuers, similarly detailed provisions are lacking. One could argue that the personal claim of an EMT holder against the issuer substitutes for the fiduciary status, similar to credit institutions that do not owe fiduciary duties to deposit clients as preserving their balance sheet is in their own interest rather than that of their client(s). Yet, two aspects push EMT issuers closer to the fiduciary status of ART issuers. First, EMT issuers must safeguard clients' funds shortly after they are paid to them (Article 7(1) EMD). Second, there is the need to set up a recovery and redemption plan (Article 55 MiCA). These duties support behaviour of EMT issuers in the interest of token-holders similar to a fiduciary status, as well as the application *mutatis mutandis* of the wider duties specified in Articles 27 and 32 MiCA.

6.3.4 *European Passport*

The authorisation of issuers and whitepapers is valid for offers all across the EU.[40] Any intent to offer ARTs and EMTs across borders must be specified in the application for authorisation and will be forwarded by the NCA deciding on the authorisation.[41]

[35] Cf. Articles 21 and 24 of MiCA (ART); Article 48(3) of MiCA in conjunction with Article 3(1) of EMD, Articles 10–12 of PSD1 (EMT).

[36] Cf. Title III, Chapter 4 of MiCA (ART); Article 48(3) of MiCA in conjunction with Article 3(3) of EMD. Cf. Regulatory Technical Standards on the detailed content of information necessary to carry out the assessment of a proposed acquisition of qualifying holdings in issuers of asset-referenced tokens under Article 42(4) of Regulation (EU) 2023/1114, Final Report (2024), EBA/RTS/2024/04.

[37] Cf. Title VII, Chapter 3 of MiCA.

[38] Regulatory Technical Standards specifying the requirements for policies and procedures on conflicts of interest for issuers of asset-referenced tokens under Article 32(5) of Regulation (EU) 2023/1114, Draft Final Report (2024), EBA/RTS/2024/07.

[39] Article 32(2) of MiCA.

[40] Article 16(3), (4) of MiCA (ART); the European Passport for issuers of EMTs follows from Article 48(3) MiCA in conjunction with Article 3(1) E-money Directive, referring to the passporting rules of Articles 17 and 25 of the first Payment Services Directive (PSD 1).

[41] Articles 21(5) and 25(5) of MiCA (ART); Article 25 of PSD1 (EMT).

6.4 REDEMPTION RIGHT AND RESERVE MANAGEMENT

Any holder of ARTs and EMTs has an individual redemption right that may be exercised on a daily basis, subject to the conditions laid out in the whitepaper.[42] Prior to MiCA, the redemption right was common practice for large stablecoin offerings, but its details were often subject to hidden and/or not well understood procedural conditions or participation in costs or even fees. Furthermore, stablecoins often lost their stability when the underlying reserves were uncertain, or the custodians that stored the reserves were under pressure.[43]

MiCA seeks to address these issues by putting in place a number of safeguards. First, some conditions for redemptions are statutorily prescribed, while additional conditions set by the issuer must be disclosed in the whitepaper. Second, MiCA prescribes mandatory handling of reserves for all ARTs and significant EMTs. Third, MiCA prescribes the setting into motion of a recovery and redemption plan once the redemption is at risk and the issuer is unable to meet their obligations.[44] The triggering of this plan may lead to the dissolution of the ART/EMT project.

6.4.1 *Redemption Rights*

MiCA grants holders of ARTs and EMTs a statutory redemption right against the issuers, which may be exercised free of charge at all times.[45] Issuers that sell tokens in return for funds[46] other than e-money must provide the option to redeem in the same currency (example: EUR => EUR); other cryptoassets in this case do not qualify as "fund".[47] A stablecoin issuer handing out tokens (e.g., in return for Bitcoin) does not bear the obligation to redeem tokens from token-holders in return for Bitcoin.

Issuers must establish, maintain, and implement clear and detailed policies and procedures with respect to such permanent redemption right and disclose these policies in the whitepaper.[48] With regard to ARTs, stipulations of these policies may include thresholds, exercise periods, and settlement timeframes, as well as liquidity management, reserve management, and a valuation mechanism as to the reserves that shall effectuate the exercise of the redemption right.[49]

When issuers are not able to meet their obligations, the redemption right is activated with respect to the reserve assets.[50] In the case of EMTs a direct claim against the issuer,[51] an

[42] Cf. Articles 39 and 49 of MiCA and on the disclosures in the White Paper Articles 19(6) last sentence and 51(6) last sentence of MiCA.

[43] See N. Baker, 'USDC Stablecoin Depegs, Crypto Market Goes Haywire After Silicon Valley Bank Collapses' (2023). Website www.coindesk.com/markets/2023/03/11/usdc-stablecoin-and-crypto-market-go-haywire-after-silicon-valley-bank-collapses/ (last accessed on 1 October 2024). See also Zetzsche *et al.*, 'Remaining Regulatory Challenges in Digital Finance', pp. 31–32 (on de-pegging of US stablecoins when reserve banks got into financial difficulties).

[44] Cf. Title III, Chapter 6 of MiCA (ART) and Article 55 of MiCA (EMT).

[45] Article 39 of MiCA (ART); Article 49 of MiCA (EMT).

[46] Article 3(14) of MiCA defines funds by reference to Article 4(25) of PSD2, Directive 2015/2366, OJ 2015 No. L337. This definition includes cash, cash substitutes, and e-money and excludes cryptocurrencies and other cryptoassets. This means that a stablecoin handing out tokens in return for Bitcoin does not fall under this provision.

[47] Article 3(14) of MiCA defines funds by reference to Article 4(25) of PSD2. This definition includes cash, cash substitutes, and e-money and excludes cryptocurrencies and other cryptoassets. This means that a stablecoin handing out tokens in return for Bitcoin does not fall under this provision.

[48] Cf. Articles 19(6) last sentence and 51(6) last sentence of MiCA.

[49] Article 39(2) of MiCA (ART).

[50] Article 39(1) of MiCA (ART).

[51] Article 49(2) MiCA (EMT).

e-money institution or credit institution subject to capital adequacy rules substitutes for such a provision.

6.4.2 *Managing the Reserve Assets*

To effectuate the redemption right, MiCA stipulates rules on the management and safeguarding of reserve assets.[52] These are more extensive for ARTs than for EMTs (where some rules of the E-money Directive apply), but the underlying principles are identical. Furthermore, we find that the legislative mechanics on reserve assets are similar to investment fund legislation asking for liquidity of fund assets to allow for an effective redemption right.

First, MiCA requires ART and EMT issuers to have a reserve at all times, sufficient to cover the risks from the underlyings and at a liquidity level in line with EBA guidelines,[53] as well as being adequate to satisfy the holders' redemption request.[54] Similar to sub-funds, each of the token types must have their own reserves: the reserve for each ART and significant EMT must be managed prudently and separately and must be legally segregated from the issuers' own assets as well as the reserve assets with regard to other tokens[55] 'so that creditors of the issuers [and other token reserves] have no recourse to the reserve of assets, in particular in the event of insolvency'.[56] MiCA, however, foresees a pooled reserve in case different ART and EMT issuers offer the same token to the public.[57] For (ordinary) EMTs issued by a credit institution or e-money institution, Article 49(2) MiCA grants a claim against the *issuers* (plural) of those EMTs. This language is open to multiple issuers of *one* type of EMT.

Any issuance and redemption of ARTs and significant EMTs must be matched by a corresponding increase or decrease in the reserve of assets. Based on market prices of reserve assets using mark-to-market pricing as prescribed for EU money market funds,[58] the aggregate value of ART reserves must be at least equal to the aggregate value of the claims made by all holders collectively of that token type.[59]

Second, MiCA focuses on the stabilisation mechanisms of ARTs and EMTs. Again, MiCA requires for ARTs a stabilisation policy setting out the underlyings of the ART, their allocation, methods of repurchase, and a detailed risk assessment, among other aspects relevant to the stability of the DeFi ecosystem.[60]

[52] Cf. Article 36 et seq. of MiCA (ART); see for EMTs, Article 48(3) of MiCA in conjunction with Article 7 of EMD and for Significant EMTs Article 58(1) of MiCA referring to the rules for ARTs in Article 36 et seq. of MiCA.

[53] Cf. Article 36(4) of MiCA (ART) and for Significant EMTs Article 58(1) of MiCA; the same follows for EMTs from Article 48(3) of MiCA in conjunction with Article 7 of EMD. Cf. Regulatory Technical Standards to further specify the liquidity requirements of the reserve of assets under Article 36(4) of Regulation (EU) 2023/1114, Draft Final Report (2024), EBA/RTS/2024/10.

[54] Article 36(1) of MiCA (ART) and for Significant EMTs Article 58(1) of MiCA, pursuant to Article 49(4) of MiCA, EMT holders may redeem their tokens by asking the issuer "at any time and at par value, [to pay] in funds, other than electronic money, the monetary value of the e-money token held to the holder of the e-money token".

[55] Articles 36(2), (5) and 37(2) of MiCA (ART) and for Significant EMTs Article 58(1) of MiCA.

[56] Article 36(2) of MiCA (ART) and for Significant EMTs Article 58(1) of MiCA.

[57] Article 36(5) of MiCA (ART) and for Significant EMTs Article 58(1) of MiCA.

[58] Cf. Article 36(11), (12) of MiCA (ART) and for Significant EMTs Article 58(1) of MiCA. The pricing must be based on good data, follow recognised valuation procedures, and set the price on the conservative end of the spectrum. Where data quality is poor, valuation shall aim at an accurate estimate of the intrinsic value of the reserve assets. For details, see Article 2(8), (9) of MMFR, Regulation 2017/1131, OJ 2017 No. L169.

[59] Article 36(6), (7) of MiCA (ART) and for Significant EMTs Article 58(1) of MiCA.

[60] Article 36(8) of MiCA (ART) and for Significant EMTs Article 58(1) of MiCA.

Third, MiCA tries to make sure that the valuation of reserve assets is accurate by mandating an independent audit of the ART reserves every six months. The audit results must be notified to the NCA without delay and not later than six weeks after the valuation date.[61] This valuation forms the basis for the ongoing disclosure of ART and significant EMT reserve assets as provided for in Article 30 MiCA. The results of the audit of ART and significant EMT reserves must be published, under regular circumstances, two weeks after the notification is issued to the NCA.[62] Exemptions apply for issuers that execute a recovery and redemption plan (see Section 6.4.3), and when delaying, disclosure may be necessary to protect token-holders and ensure the resilience of the financial system.

Fourth, reserve assets must be safeguarded at all times based on adequate policies and procedures, starting not later than five business days upon their receipt.[63] For ARTs and significant EMTs, according to the applicable custody procedures, reserve assets must:

- Not be encumbered nor pledged as a financial collateral arrangement;
- Be held in custody in accordance with Article 37(6) MiCA;
- Be distributed in a manner that prevents the risk of concentration of reserve assets and the concentration of custodians holding the reserve; and
- Be available to issuers promptly to meet any holders' redemption requests.

Reserve assets must be held in custody by qualified custodians with a good reputation for the types of assets in custody that is separate from the issuer and which the issuer's board must select in line with the custody policy and in pursuit of enhanced duties of care,[64] including:

- Credit institutions separate from the issuer;
- For financial instruments only: investment firms under MiFID; and
- For cryptoassets as defined by MiCA only: cryptoasset service providers subject to Title V MiCA.

The custodians must be appointed by way of written contract, act as fiduciaries of issuers and token-holders, and provide custody in a segregated account opened in the custodians' books or registers, and physically delivered where this is possible. For cryptoassets, custodians must hold the private cryptographic keys. Moreover, all assets must be registered in the name of the issuer so that the funds can be clearly identified.[65] Conflicts of interest between the custodian, the issuer, and the token-holders must be avoided, and if they exist, a functional and hierarchical separation is applied, and such potential conflicts are properly identified, monitored, managed, and disclosed by the issuers to the token-holders.[66]

[61] Article 36(9), (10) of MiCA (ART) and for Significant EMTs Article 58(1) of MiCA (modifying the first point in time that this requirement applies).

[62] Article 36(9), (10) of MiCA (ART) and for Significant EMTs Article 58(1) of MiCA.

[63] Article 37 of MiCA (ART) and for Significant EMTs Article 58(1) of MiCA; see also Articles 48(3) and 54 of MiCA, in conjunction with Article 7(1) of EMD (EMT). While the methods of safeguarding for e-money are specified in the law of the Member States (Article 7(5) of EMD), custody is one accepted method of safeguarding.

[64] Article 37(2)–(5) of MiCA (ART) and for Significant EMTs Article 58(1) of MiCA; for EMTs Article 48(3) of MiCA in conjunction with Article 7 of EMD (less pronounced).

[65] For details, see Article 37(6)–(8) of MiCA (ART) and for Significant EMTs Article 58(1) of MiCA; for EMTs Article 48(3) of MiCA in conjunction with Article 7 of EMD (less pronounced).

[66] Cf. Articles 37(9) and 31 of MiCA (ART) and for Significant EMTs Article 58(1) of MiCA; for EMTs, Article 48 (3) of MiCA in conjunction with Article 7 of EMD (less pronounced).

To function on behalf of ART/EMT issuers and token-holders, the custodian must accept liability for the loss of financial instruments or cryptoassets vis-à-vis the issuer and token-holders: the custodian 'shall compensate, or make restitution, to the issuer (. . .) of an identical type or the corresponding value without undue delay'. However, the custodian 'shall not be liable for compensation or restitution where it can prove that the loss has occurred as a result of an external event beyond its reasonable control, the consequences of which were unavoidable despite all reasonable efforts to the contrary'.[67] Disclosure of a private key by the custodian to an inside or outside attacker – which forms the main type of asset misappropriation in relation to custodians – does not constitute such an "external event". At first sight, one would wonder whether issuers of ARTs and EMTs find such custodians ready to assume liability, yet Article 75 MiCA on custody provided by CASPs foresees the same liability clause, and EU fund depositaries are traditionally subject to similar, if not stricter, liability clauses with regard to the loss of financial instruments.[68]

Fifth, MiCA prescribes how reserve assets must be invested.[69] Eligible for ARTs and significant EMTs are 'highly liquid financial instruments (to be held in custody as previously prescribed) with minimal market risk, credit risk, and concentration risk. The investments shall be capable of being liquidated rapidly with minimal adverse price effect'. A UCITS is eligible 'where that UCITS invests solely in assets as further specified by EBA in accordance with paragraph 5 and where the issuer of the ART ensures that the reserve of assets is invested in such a way that the concentration risk is minimised'. Issuers of ARTs and significant EMTs have to bear '[a]ll profits or losses, including fluctuations in the value of the financial instruments, and any counterparty or operational risks that result from the investment of the reserve of assets'. This results in the issuer taking the position of a de-facto guarantor, which is inconvenient for sure. While MiCA's reserve requirements for ordinary EMTs are not as detailed, competent authorities may require to apply the reserve requirements for significant EMTs pursuant to Article 58 (2) MiCA. In the absence of such a requirement, EMD to which Article 48(3) MiCA refers rests on the same principles.[70]

Finally, issuers are prevented from granting interest or any other financial benefit on the token value related to the duration for which the token is held, regardless of whether this is offered by the issuer or any third party.[71] This is to prevent incentivising large-scale investments by offering (overly) generous returns or even fixed interest, which would blur the boundaries even further between ARTs/EMTs, on the one hand, and deposits and money market funds, on the other.

[67] Cf. Article 37(10) of MiCA (ART) and for Significant EMTs Article 58(1) of MiCA; for EMTs, Article 48(3) of MiCA in conjunction with Article of 7 EMD (less pronounced).

[68] Cf. Article 24 of UCITSD, Directive 2009/65, OJ 2009 No. L302; Article 21 of AIFMD, Directive 2011/61, OJ 2011 No. L174. For details, C. Clerc and D. Eckner, 'The AIF Depositary's Liability for Lost Assets', in D. A. Zetzsche (ed.), *The Alternative Investment Fund Managers Directive* (Alphen aan den Rijn: Wolters Kluwer, 2020), 3rd ed., Chapter 17, at 487 et seq.

[69] Cf. Article 38 of MiCA (ART) and for Significant EMTs Article 58(1) of MiCA. For details, cf. Regulatory Technical Standards to specify the highly liquid financial instruments with minimal market risk, credit risk, and concentration risk under Article 38(5) of Regulation (EU) 2023/1114, Draft Final Report (2024), EBA/RTS/2024/11.

[70] Cf. Article 54 of MiCA (EMT) (requiring that at least 30 per cent of the funds received are deposited in separate accounts in credit institutions, while the remaining funds must be invested in "in secure, low-risk assets that qualify as highly liquid financial instruments with minimal market risk, credit risk, and concentration risk, in accordance with Article 38(1) of this Regulation, and are denominated in the same official currency as the one referenced by the e-money token").

[71] Cf. Article 40 of MiCA (ART); Article 50 of MiCA (EMT). On EMTs, see also Section 4.4.3.

6.4.3 *Recovery and Redemption Plans*

Issuers of ARTs and EMTs are required to set up a recovery and redemption plan and notify the NCA[72] within six months of the authorisation of the issuer or the whitepaper pursuant to Articles 17 and 21 MiCA. For EMTs, specifically, authorisation must be obtained for the first initial offering or trading of the token, with a recovery and redemption plan in place in line with EBA guidelines,[73] to be applied thereafter if and when the issue fails to comply with the reserve requirements.[74] In addition, updates are to be filed whenever due.

The main features of a recovery plan include details of how to preserve the issuer's services with regard to the ART/EMT and on how to recover operations as swiftly as possible and fulfil the issuer's obligations where the operations may be at risk of disruption.

To a large extent, recovery plans may foresee a halt to daily redemption, that is, the "closing" of the "open-ended" token system by way of imposing liquidity fees on redemptions; placing limits on redemptions during any working day; and the suspension of redemptions.[75]

The NCA may order the issuer to apply or update any of the measures specified in the recovery plan when the issuer fails to comply with reserve (management) requirements or where the issuer's financial condition is deteriorating.[76] It may also order the temporary suspension of redemption if this is in the interest of the token-holders and/or financial stability. In this regard, we find an analogy to "bank runs" (where the remaining depositors are exposed to the risk of the bank's default) as well as open-ended funds useful, where speedy redemptions of some unitholders may put those staying in the fund at a disadvantage, as these unitholders bear the valuation and liquidity risks related to the assets staying in the fund.[77] For the same reasons, the NCA may suspend redemptions.

The redemption plan shall prepare for a situation where the issuer is unable to or unlikely to meet its obligations, including in the event of insolvency, resolution (where applicable), or withdrawal of authorisation. This state is recognised, and hence, the plan is deemed to be implemented by way of the NCA's order.[78]

The redemption plan shall 'demonstrate the ability of the issuer (...) to carry out the redemption of the outstanding ART issued without causing undue economic harm to their holders or to the stability of the markets of the reserve assets'.[79] All in all, the redemption plan shall ensure both the equitable treatment of all token-holders and that these holders receive their monetary value in a timely manner through the proceeds from the sale of the remaining reserve assets. The plan shall provide for the orderly dissolution of the token system by way of

[72] Where under national law, the NCA is different from the respective resolution and restructuring authorities and prudential supervisory authorities, as the case may be, these authorities are to be informed in parallel. In case of a redemption plan, the authority in charge of resolution and restructuring may make recommendations in regard to the plan.

[73] Cf. EBA, 'Guidelines on Recovery Plans under Articles 46 and 55 of the Regulation (EU) 2023/1114', Final Report (2024), EBA/GL/2024/07.

[74] Cf. Title III, Chapter 5 of MiCA (ART) and Article 55 of MiCA (EMT). Often credit institutions that are already licensed issue ART or EMT. While Article 46 of MiCA on ARTs does not relate to this case, Article 55 of MiCA on EMTs does by specifying the initial date of a public offering or trading as point of reference. We hold that the same date must be the reference date in this case where an already licensed institution offers ARTs.

[75] Article 46(1) of MiCA (ART); Article 55(1) of MiCA (EMT).

[76] Article 46(3) of MiCA (ART); Article 55(1) of MiCA (EMT).

[77] See on runs on money-market funds W. A. Birdthistle, 'Breaking Bucks in Money Market Funds', *Wisconsin Law Review*, 5 (2010): 1155–201.

[78] Article 47(1) of MiCA (ART); Article 55 of MiCA (EMT).

[79] Article 47(2) of MiCA (ART); Article 55 of MiCA (EMT).

contractual arrangements, procedures, and systems, for instance, through the designation of a temporary administrator. It should include measures aimed at maintaining any critical activities by issuers or third-party entities necessary for orderly redemption.

6.5 MANDATORY DISCLOSURE AND STATUTORY LIABILITY FOR WHITEPAPERS

Another focal point of MiCA's product rules is mandatory disclosure (initial and ongoing).

Initial disclosure by way of a whitepaper must provide details on the duration of the offering, the redemption, and background on the issuer and related parties[80] and ought to be available free of charge on the issuer's website.[81] We have discussed the details of prospectus-style whitepapers at length in Chapter 5.

To ensure the effectiveness of disclosure rules, MiCA introduces statutory liability for the whitepaper's content.[82] Contrary to what is known from other EU financial regulation which assigns liability to the issuer as an entity only, the 'members of [the issuer's] administrative, management or supervisory body shall be liable to a holder' for any 'information that is not complete, fair or clear, or that is misleading'. At the same time, any 'contractual exclusion or limitation of civil liability ... shall be deprived of legal effect'. The onus of proof to show incomplete, unfair, or unclear information is on the token-holders. The foregoing does not preclude any culpability or "fault" requirement under the laws of the Member States (see Section 5.6). Nevertheless, the liability of board members is a sharp sword, and even more so as in the case of two-tier boards where potentially both the management body in charge of day-to-day business and the supervisory board may be liable. The national laws of the Member States may provide even more stringent liability rules, which may include a reversed burden of proof regarding culpability/fault; yet in most instances, these laws focus on the entity's liability rather than that of the board members.

Additional rules seek to ensure that marketing information accompanying the whitepaper is identifiable as such and that its language and content is fair, clear, not misleading, and consistent with the information provided in the whitepaper.[83] The issuers must include in all marketing communications that ART and EMT holders have a statutory right of redemption against the issuer at any time.[84] While market sounding is allowed, marketing communications must not be disseminated prior to the publication of the whitepaper.[85] They must be published on the issuer's website, and a notification must be issued to the NCA upon request.[86]

Ongoing disclosure is foreseen in the case of ARTs vis-à-vis the NCAs (or the EBA) by way of quarterly reports.[87] Moreover, ART issuers must disclose at least monthly on their website (accessible to token-holders) the amount of ARTs in circulation and the value and composition of the reserve assets.[88] To ensure that the disclosures on reserve values are accurate, the ART

[80] Cf. Annex II (ART) and Annex III (EMT) of MiCA.

[81] Article 28 of MiCA (ART); Article 51(13) of MiCA (EMT).

[82] Cf. Articles 26 (ART) and 51 (EMT) of MiCA. The same rule applies to White Papers issued under Title II of MiCA, cf. Article 15 of MiCA. For details, see Section 5.6.

[83] Article 29(1) of MiCA (ART); Article 53(1) of MiCA (EMT).

[84] Article 29(2) of MiCA (ART); Article 53(2) of MiCA (EMT). The statutory redemption rights are mandated by Articles 39 and 49 of MiCA disclosed in the White Paper subject to Articles 19(6) last sentence and 51(6) last sentence of MiCA.

[85] Article 29(6) of MiCA (ART); Article 53(6) of MiCA (EMT).

[86] Article 29(3), (5) of MiCA (ART); Article 53(3), (5) of MiCA (EMT).

[87] Cf. Article 22(1), (2) of MiCA (ART).

[88] Cf. Article 30(1) and Recital para. 48 of MiCA (ART).

TABLE 6.1 *Supervisory measures for EMTs in relation to issuing size, transaction numbers, and transaction volume*

Supervisory measure	MiCA Articles	EMT issues affected
Whitepaper + Liability + Marketing Rules	48(4), (5)	All issues
Licence	48(1) i.c.w. Article 9(1) EMD	Issues starting from EUR 5 million
Own funds	48(1) i.c.w. Article 5 EMD	1) The higher of 350,000 EUR or 2% of reserve assets under Article 36 MiCA 2) Risk-based adjustment Risk management processes, risk loss databases, internal controls: ± 20%
EBA supervision (if 3 out of 6 criteria are met)	56 and 43	1) >10 million users 2) > 2.5 million transactions and EUR 500 million transaction value 3) Issuer is the provider of core platform services designated as gatekeepers re. Reg 2022/1925 4) International significance in terms of payments and remittances 5) Interconnectedness with the financial system 6) Issuer to issue at least one more ART/EMT and one cryptoasset service
Significant EMTs	58	1) Additional operating requirements (see Table 6.3) 2) Own funds subject to Tier 1, 20% risk surcharge, stress testing (Article 35(2), (3), and (5) MiCA) 3) Reserve management requirements (Articles 36–38 MiCA)

issuers must also disclose the annual audit report on the reserve assets in full and in summary.[89] ART issuers must further disclose events that have or are likely to have a significant impact on the value of the ART or on the reserve assets; that duty exists even where the ART is not admitted to trading.[90] In addition, Title VI MiCA mandates that issuers of ARTs and EMTs admitted to trading, or about to be traded, disclose inside information that may have an impact on the token value to the public in a manner prescribed by EU regulations and retain all of these disclosures on their website for five years. Prior to this publication, the information must neither be used for trading nor otherwise disclosed.[91]

6.6 SIZE AND SIGNIFICANCE OF EMTS AND ARTS

6.6.1 *Size-Based Intensity of Regulation and Supervision*

In relation to the issuing size, transaction numbers, and transaction volume with regard to a given ART or EMT, the supervisory requirements become increasingly strict, as shown in Tables 6.1 and 6.2.

[89] Cf. Article 30(2) of MiCA (ART).
[90] Cf. Article 30(2) and Recital para. 48 of MiCA (ART).
[91] Cf. Articles 88–90 of MiCA.

TABLE 6.2 *Supervisory measures for ARTs in relation to issuing size, transaction numbers, and transaction volume.*

Supervisory measure	MiCA Articles	ART issues affected
Whitepaper + Liability	16(2)(a)	All issues
Licence	16(1)	Issues starting from EUR 5 million
Own funds (in Tier 1 capital)[92]	35	1) The higher of 350,000 EUR or one-quarter of the fixed overheads of the preceding year or 2% of reserve assets under Article 36 MiCA [increasing to 3% for significant ARTs, cf. Article 45] 2) Risk surcharges: a) Risk analysis: plus 20% b) Stress tests: plus 40%
Reserve management requirements	36	Detailed requirements (see Section 6.4.2)
Quarterly report to the NCA[93]	22(1), (2)	Issues of over EUR 100 million (or lower when stipulated by the NCA)
Automatic issuance stop *plus* plan to reduce volume	23(1)	Where on average in the last quarter per day there were at least 1 million transactions EUR 200 million aggregate transactions value in one single currency area
EBA supervision (if 3 out of 6 criteria are met) resulting status of a significant ART	43	1) Number of holders >10 million 2) ART's total value, market capitalisation, or reserve of assets > EUR 5 billion 3) > 2.5 million transactions and EUR 500 million transaction value per day 4) Issuer is provider of core platform services designated as gatekeepers re. Reg 2022/1925 5) International significance in terms of payments and remittances 6) Interconnectedness with the financial system 7) Issuer to issue at least one more ART/EMT and one cryptoasset service
Significant ARTs	45	Additional operating requirements (see Table 6.3)

6.6.2 *Additional Operating Requirements*

Title III Chapter 5 and Title IV Chapter 2 MiCA foresee a number of additional operational requirements for significant ARTs and EMTs, as

[92] Cf. Regulatory Technical Standards on adjustment of own funds requirements and stress testing of issuers of asset-referenced tokens or of e-money tokens subject to the requirements in Article 35 of regulation (EU) 2023/1114 on markets in cryptoassets, Draft Final Report (2024), EBA/RTS/2024/08.

[93] Cf. Regulatory Technical Standards on the methodology to estimate the number and value of transactions associated to uses of asset-referenced tokens as a means of exchange under Article 22(6) [MiCA] and of e-money tokens denominated in a currency that is not an official currency of a Member State under Article 58(3) [MiCA], Draft Final Report (2024), EBA/RTS/2024/13; Implementing Technical Standards on the reporting on asset-referenced tokens under Article 22(7) [MiCA] and on e-money tokens denominated in a currency that is not an official currency of a Member State pursuant to Article 58(3) [MiCA], Draft Final Report (2024), EBA/ITS/2024/04.

TABLE 6.3: *Additional operating requirements for significant ARTs/EMTs.*

Requirements	ARTs: MiCA Articles	EMTs: MiCA Articles
A remuneration policy that promotes sound and effective risk management	45(1)	58(1)
To ensure that tokens can be held in custody by *different* CASPs authorised for custody under Title V MiCA that are independent from each other	45(2)	58(2)
To assess and monitor the liquidity needs to satisfy requests for redemption of ARTs by their holders by way of advanced liquidity management policy and procedures	45(3)	58(3)
To conduct liquidity stress testing on a regular basis; the EBA may intensify liquidity requirements based on testing results	45(4)	58(4)
Own funds to increase to at least 3% of the reserve assets	45(5)	58(1)

laid out in Table 6.3 and further specified in a set of Technical Standards[94] and EBA guidelines.[95]

6.6.3 *EBA Supervision*

A common feature of both an EMT and an ART is the EBA's supervision of important tokens with a potential impact on the traditional financial system.[96] The EBA's supervision reflects the cross-border nature of large cryptocurrencies in the Union, as well as the EBA's task to prevent systemic risk in the EU.[97] On EBA's supervision and the role of the ECB, see Section 11.3.3.

While most issuers will be subjected to EBA supervision following intense fact gathering and communication with NCAs and the ESAs,[98] issuers can also submit themselves to the EBA's supervision voluntarily.[99] Such an opt-in may increase legal certainty and avoid a lengthy fact-gathering procedure, which will eventually result in a potential reassessment of documents provided before.

94 Cf. Regulatory Technical Standards on the minimum content of the governance arrangements on the remuneration policy under Article 45 of Regulation (EU) 2023/1114, Draft Final Report (2024), EBA/RTS/2024/06; Regulatory Technical Standards to specify the minimum contents of the liquidity management policy and procedures under Article 45(7)(b) of Regulation (EU) 2023/1114, Draft Final Report (2024), BA/RTS/2024/12; Regulatory Technical Standards to specify the procedure and timeframe to adjust its own funds requirements for issuers of significant asset-referenced tokens or of e-money tokens subject to the requirements set out in Article 45(5) of Regulation (EU) 2023/1114 on markets in cryptoassets, Draft Final Report (2024), EBA/RTS/2024/09. In addition the standards specified in note 93 also apply.

95 Cf. EBA, 'Guidelines Establishing the Common Reference Parameters of the Stress Test Scenarios for the Liquidity Stress Tests Referred in Article 45(4) Regulation (EU) 2023/1114', Final Report (2024), EBA/GL/2024/08.

96 Cf. EBA, 'Draft Regulatory Technical Standards on Supervisory Colleges under Article 119(8) of Regulation (EU) No. 2023/1114 (MiCAR)', EBA/CP/2023/33 (2023).

97 See Article 1(5), third para of Regulation (EU) No. 1093/2010 of the European Parliament and of the Council of 24 November 2010 establishing a European Supervisory Authority (European Banking Authority). ("In the exercise of the tasks conferred upon it by this Regulation, the Authority shall pay particular attention to any systemic risk posed by financial institutions, the failure of which may impair the operation of the financial system or the real economy.") As such, the EBA contributes to the European Systemic Risk Board which is the coordinating body within the European System of Financial Supervisors in charge of systemic risk supervision.

98 Cf. Article 43 of MiCA (ART); Article 56 of MiCA (EMT).

99 Article 44 of MiCA (ART); Article 57 of MiCA (EMT).

ARTs and EMTs can fall below the threshold and lose the status of a significant ART or a significant EMT, respectively, following intense communication among the ECB, the NCAs, and the ESAs. In this case, the supervisory responsibilities regarding the token issuer will be transferred to one NCA.[100]

6.6.4 *Strict Approach to ARTs*

The intensity of regulation and supervision increases commensurate to the size and risk involved for both ARTs and EMTs. For instance, the additional operating requirements laid out in Articles 45 and 58 MiCA are preserved for significant ARTs and EMTs. Except for the own funds requirements set out in Article 35 MiCA, these additional operating requirements do not exceed the risk management requirements that Managers of Alternative Investment Funds (AIFMs) have to meet on a regular basis.[101]

A comparison of Tables 6.1 and 6.2 shows, however, that MiCA's rules for ARTs are more severe and strict than those for EMTs. For instance, the reserve management requirements of Articles 36–38 MiCA and the qualifying own funds requirements pursuant to Article 35(2), (3), and (5) apply to all ARTs, but only to significant EMTs. Furthermore, Article 35 MiCA on own funds merely foresees risk-based surcharges and no benefits in the event of well-organised risk management, in contrast to the rules applicable to ordinary EMTs.

A particularly burdensome rule is exclusively applicable to ARTs. Once an ART gains high practical importance in a given currency area, Article 23(1) MiCA imposes a statutory issuance limit preventing the further growth of the ART. This issuance limit is inserted to prevent any single privately issued ART to replace the importance of the central-bank-issued currency, as was supposed to happen if the Libra project had come to life, with all 1.2 billion Facebook users incentivised to use the Libra (later renamed "Diem") coins.[102] Note that any size threshold is most likely to be bypassed within the eurozone, spanning 350 million people and with a GDP exceeding EUR 14 trillion.[103] The size limit here represents a substantial disincentive with regard to setting up an ART in the first place.

6.7 CONCLUSION

The unique feature of MiCA is that it neither follows the approach established in EU law for securities, nor commodities, nor payments, or credit institutions, but that it presents the first, to our knowledge, bespoke set of rules for the two main types of privately issued cryptocurrencies: EMTs (in particular, traditional stablecoins) and ARTs, with the global stablecoin project Libra (later renamed "Diem") being the prime example to date. As such, it combines regulatory elements from other types of financial regulation. The product rules for ARTs and EMTs incorporate features known from payment services and investment

[100] Cf. Article 43(8)–(10) of MiCA (ART); Article 56(8)–(10) of MiCA (EMT).

[101] See Articles 15 and 16 of AIFMD; for details, see D. A. Zetzsche and M. Hanke, 'Risk Management', in D.A. Zetzsche (ed.), *The Alternative Investment Fund Managers Directive* (Alphen aan den Rijn: Wolters Kluwer, 2020), 3rd ed., Chapter 13, pp. 315 et seq. For comparisons to other EU and international significance regimes, see P. Hansen and H. Bauer, 'MiCA's Significance Regime for Stablecoins – A Sledgehammer to Crack a Nut?' (2024). Website: https://dx.doi.org/10.2139/ssrn.4699043 (last accessed on 1 October 2024).

[102] See Zetzsche *et al.*, 'Regulating Libra'.

[103] IMF, 'Euro Area Datasets' (2021). Website www.imf.org/external/datamapper/profile/EURO (last accessed on 1 October 2024).

funds, with the rules for ARTs often mimicking those common to the regulation of money market and index funds, paired with own funds requirements associated with e-money regulation.

The mix of regulatory principles is far from light-touch, as neither the principles set in EU financial regulation for off-balance intermediation nor on-balance intermediation have been followed through, and the ART rules are particularly burdensome. One may understand this strict regulatory response as an effort to all but ban global stablecoin projects like Libra (later renamed "Diem"). We have explained the strict approach taken to some extent by pointing to the fact that ARTs can become functional equivalents of investment funds (in particular, money market funds, index funds, and ETFs) and become systemically important. Hence, MiCA leans on regulatory examples of investment fund product regulation and e-money own funds requirements at the same time. Nevertheless, the size limit for ARTs embedded in Article 23 MiCA is unique. In turn, ARTs will be preserved to products that lack liquidity and/or are unsuitable for securitisations. ART projects discussed so far include ARTs linked to Gold and commodity baskets.

Compared to ARTs, the rules on EMTs are relatively soft, piggy-backing to a large extent on existing EU rules on e-money and resulting in an overall permissive approach even where EMTs become of systemic dimensions.

7

Regulation of Cryptoasset Service Providers (Title V MiCA)

7.1 INTRODUCTION

MiCA's most important set of rules is in its Title V, providing primarily activity-based bespoke rules for CASPs (cryptoasset service provider). Title V MiCA is divided into the following five parts: Chapter 1 concerns the authorisation of CASPs, chapter 2 covers conditions for all CASPs, chapter 3 deals with specific cryptoasset services, chapter 4 focuses on the acquisition of CASPs, and chapter 5 addresses significant CASPs.

Three matters regarding CASPs are regulated outside of Title V MiCA. These concern the scope (which follows from the provisions in Title I MiCA) and the supervision of CASPs by NCAs and the ESMA, which follows partly from Title VII MiCA and partly from Title V Chapter I MiCA.[1] In addition, some additional provisions are foreseen in EU financial law beyond MiCA, in particular, the MiFID/MiFIR framework and EMD.

Table 7.1 provides an overview of the provisions applicable to CASPs.

We discuss these provisions in turn. However, crypto custody is discussed in Chapter 8, while the interplay of MiCA and EU investment fund regulation is the main topic of Chapter 9. Meanwhile, in the current chapter, we start with an analysis of the scope of MiCA's CASP rules (Section 7.2) before proceeding to licensing and authorisation requirements (Section 7.3), followed by the joint conditions for all CASPs (Section 7.4), after which we provide an analysis of the specific conditions for certain cryptoasset services (Section 7.5), and then present a conclusion (Section 7.6).

7.2 SCOPE

A CASP is a legal person or other undertaking whose occupation or business is the provision of one or more cryptoasset services (cf. Section 7.2.1) to clients on a professional basis (cf. Section 7.2.2).[2] Some additional criteria follow from MiCA's scope (cf. Section 7.2.3). The last element of Article 3(14) MiCA, concerning authorisation in accordance with Article 59 MiCA, follows from meeting the previous criteria. Acting as a CASP without authorisation prompts administrative penalties pursuant to Article 111(1)(d) MiCA.

[1] On scope and supervision, see Chapters 4 and 11, respectively.
[2] Article 3(1)(15) of MiCA.

TABLE 7.1 *Provisions applicable to CASPs*

Subject matter	Legislation	Discussed herein
Scope	Title I MiCA	Section 7.2
Conditions for all CASPs (including authorisation and acquisitions)	Title V Chapters 1, 2, and 4 MiCA	Section 7.3
Conditions for certain cryptoasset services	Title V Chapter 3 MiCA and general EU financial law	Section 7.4
Supervision (including rules on significant CASPs)	Title VII and Title V Chapter 5 MiCA	Chapter 11

7.2.1 *Cryptoasset Services (Article 3(16) MiCA)*

Cryptoasset services are defined by way of an exclusive list in Article 3(16) MiCA. If an activity is not included in this catalogue, it is not regulated under MiCA. It may nevertheless be regulated under general EU financial law, for instance, as an investment firm, manager, or depository of collective investment schemes; as a credit, payments, or e-money institution; or as an insurance undertaking.[3]

Recital 21 and Article 3(16) MiCA mention *two categories of services*. The first category of services relates, in the wider sense, to the trading of cryptoassets including the (1) operation of a trading platform, exchanging cryptoassets for (2) funds or (3) other cryptoassets, providing (4) custody and administration and (5) transfer services for cryptoassets on behalf of clients. The second category of services broadly entails brokerage, investment advice, and asset management and includes the (1) placing of cryptoassets, (2) reception or transmission of orders on behalf of clients, (3) execution of orders for cryptoassets on behalf of clients, (4) providing advice on, and (5) portfolio management of cryptoassets.

The catalogue and the respective definitions are in large part taken from similar provisions in Annex I, Sections A and B of MiFID (Directive 2014/65/EU) on "investment services and activities". Even divergences in some minor aspects do not seem to matter, as follows from Article 60(3) MiCA, which states that an investment firm can provide cryptoasset services equivalent to those for which it is authorised under MiFID.

Some cryptoassets meet the definition of transferable securities and/or financial instruments, or their provision is a regulated activity listed in Article 2(4) MiCA.[4] CASPs offering services for a broad range of cryptoassets must comply with both MiFID/MiFIR rules (if the cryptoasset in question qualifies as a financial instrument) and MiCA (with regard to cryptoassets that qualify neither as a financial instrument under MiFID nor as any other regulated activity referred to in Article 2(4) MiCA). In light of this practical challenge, we welcome the fact that MiCA provisions borrow heavily from examples in general EU financial law. More precisely, Title V MiCA on CASPs' authorisation is based on examples provided in payment services legislation (PSD2 and EMD), brokerage, exchange, and asset management legislation (MiFID/MiFIR with implementing acts,[5] AIFMD with AIFMR

[3] Article 2(4) of MiCA refers to some of the products offered or issued by these entities. The list of examples is not exhaustive.

[4] See for details, Chapters 3 and 4.

[5] For instance, Commission Delegated Regulation (EU) No. 2017/2055 of 23 June 2017 supplementing Directive (EU) 2015/2366 of the European Parliament and of the Council with regard to regulatory technical standards for the cooperation and exchange of information between competent authorities relating to the exercise of the right of establishment and the freedom to provide services of payment institutions, OJ 2017 No. L294, 11 November 2017;

TABLE 7.2 *MiCA's reliance on EU financial law with regard to definitions*

MiCA Articles	Subject matter	Provision equivalent to
3(1)(1)	DLT	Article 2(1) PilotR
3(1)(2)	Distributed ledger	Article 2(2) PilotR
3(1)(3)	Consensus mechanism	Article 2(3) PilotR
3(1)(10)	Issuer	Article 2(1) (h) Prospectus Regulation
3(1)(11)	Applicant issuer	Article 2(1) (d) Prospectus Regulation
3(1)(12)	Offer to the public	Article 2(1) (i) Prospectus Regulation
3(1)(13)	Offeror	Annex I, Section B(1) MiFID
3(1)(16)	Cryptoasset service	Annex I, Sections A and B MiFID
3(1)(17)	Custody and administration of cryptoassets on behalf of clients	Annex I, Section B(5) MiFID
3(1)(21)	Execution of orders of cryptoassets on behalf of clients	Article 4(1)(5) MiFID
3(1)(24)	Advice on cryptoassets	Article 4(1)(4) MiFID
3(1)(25)	Portfolio management of cryptoassets	Article 4(1)(8) MiFID
3(1)(27)	Management body	Article 4(1)(36) MiFID
3(1)(39)	Client	Article 4(1)(9) MiFID

(L2),[6] UCITSD with the UCITS Implementing Directive[7]), legislation on credit institutions (CRD/CRR[8]), as well as AMLD/CTF rules (cf. Chapter 14). While in some instances the wording is exactly the same, in other cases, only the rationale is identical.

Throughout this chapter, we lay out the equivalences between the provisions of Title V MiCA and EU financial legislation in tables preceding the relevant sections. Specifically, Table 7.2 contains the scope provisions borrowed from EU financial law.

Commission Delegated Regulation (EU) No. 2017/1943 of 14 July 2016 supplementing Directive 2014/65/EU of the European Parliament and of the Council with regard to regulatory technical standards on information and requirements for the authorisation of investment firms, OJ 2017 No. L276, 26 October 2017; Commission Implementing Regulation (EU) No. 2017/1945 of 19 June 2017 laying down implementing technical standards with regard to notifications by and to applicant and authorised investment firms according to Directive 2014/65/EU of the European Parliament and of the Council, OJ 2017 No. L276, 26 October 2017; and Commission Delegated Directive (EU) 2017/593 of 7 April 2016 supplementing Directive 2014/65/EU of the European Parliament and of the Council with regard to safeguarding of financial instruments and funds belonging to clients, product governance obligations, and the rules applicable to the provision or reception of fees, commissions, or any monetary or non-monetary benefits, OJ 2017 No. L87, 31 March 2017.

[6] Commission Delegated Regulation (EU) No. 231/2013 of 19 December 2012 supplementing Directive 2011/61/EU of the European Parliament and of the Council with regard to exemptions, general operating conditions, depositaries, leverage, transparency, and supervision, OJ 2013 No. L83, 22 March 2013.

[7] Commission Directive 2010/43/EU of 1 July 2010 implementing Directive 2009/65/EC of the European Parliament and of the Council as regards organisational requirements, conflicts of interest, conduct of business, risk management, and content of the agreement between a depositary and a management company, OJ 2010 No. L176, 10 July 2010.

[8] Directive 2013/36/EU of the European Parliament and of the Council of 26 June 2013 on access to the activity of credit institutions and the prudential supervision of credit institutions and investment firms, amending Directive 2002/87/EC and repealing Directives 2006/48/EC and 2006/49/EC, OJ 2013 No. L 176, 27 June 2013; Regulation (EU) No. 575/2013 of the European Parliament and of the Council of 26 June 2013 on prudential requirements for credit institutions and investment firms and amending Regulation (EU) No. 648/2012, OJ 2013 No. L 176, 27 June 2013.

7.2.1.1 *Trading and Exchange Services*

Operation of a Trading Platform for Cryptoassets
MiCA regulates as a trading platform any technical means where a client uses fiat currency, money booked on a payment account, or e-money (collectively dubbed 'funds'[9]) or cryptoassets to acquire a cryptoasset or part thereof. Operating a trading platform requires that the providers 'bring together or facilitate the bringing together of multiple third-party purchasing and selling interests in crypto-assets'. That definition does not require from the CASP to be involved in the execution of the transaction. In the case of peer-to-peer transactions where an entity facilitates, as a multilateral platform, the transactions as arranger, that entity provides a cryptoasset service (cf. Section 14.2.3.3).

Also covered are platforms or CASPs where cryptoassets are swapped, without adding or receiving any funds. However, the acceptance of cryptoassets by the issuer or initial offeror in return for transferring its own cryptoassets to the holder of the transferred cryptoassets does not qualify as a cryptoasset service;[10] these activities are regulated by Titles II–IV MiCA instead.

MiCA defines as a regulated activity the operation of a trading platform for cryptoassets. This is defined in Article 3(1)(18) MiCA as follows:

- the *management* of
- one or more *multilateral systems*, which bring together or facilitate the bringing together of multiple third-party purchasing and selling interests
- in *cryptoassets*,
- in the system and in accordance with its rules,
- in a way that *results in a contract*,
- either by *exchanging cryptoassets for funds or by the exchange of cryptoassets for other cryptoassets*.

Given the proximity of MiCA to Article 4(1) (21) and (22) MiFID, with regard to 'management' and the 'multilateral system' which 'bring together or facilitate the bringing together of multiple third-party purchasing and selling interests in the system', 'in a way that results in a contract', we could rely on the interpretation of Article 4(1) (21) and (22) MiFID. For instance, MiCA does not define multilateral systems. In turn, the definition of Article 4(1)(19) MiFID applies whereby a 'multilateral system' means 'any system or facility in which multiple third-party buying and selling trading interests in financial instruments are able to interact in the system'.

Four deviations are noteworthy here. The first and most obvious is that MiCA applies to cryptoassets, while MiFID focuses on financial instruments.

Second, MiFID limits the operations of regulated markets to market operators and of MTFs to market operators and investment firms. Meanwhile, MiCA's CASP rules apply to all entities managing a trading platform and do not require a regulatory status.

Third, the MiFID definitions refer to acting in accordance with *non-discretionary* rules, but MiCA limits itself to services in accordance with its 'rules'. There are two worthwhile remarks to make here. First, most platforms have operational conditions embedded in the smart contracts operating the system. In particular, the if-then conditions in smart contracts constitute relevant

[9] Article 3(1)(14) of MiCA refers for 'funds' to the definition in Article 4(25) of PSD2, Directive 2015/2366, OJ 2015 No. L337. Funds, thus, means "banknotes and coins, scriptural money or electronic money" as defined in Article 2(2) of EMD, Directive 2009/110, OJ 2009 No. L267.

[10] Cf. Recitals paras. 4 and 87 of MiCA.

rules for the trading system. Second, it is not obvious why MiCA does not refer to "non-discretionary" rules, given that the smart contracts in question are usually quite rigid and non-discretionary. However, the broader wording of MiCA may bring more services in scope than that of MiFID and ensures that discretionary decisions do not impair the application of MiCA.

Fourth, MiCA stresses that both a swap of cryptoassets for cryptoassets and a swap of cryptoassets for funds are in scope. Similar wording is lacking in MiFID, yet the same follows from a reference to Title III and Annex I Section C (4)–(10) MiFID as to financial instruments.

More details on trading platforms are specified in Article 76 MiCA (cf. Section 7.5.1).

Exchange of Cryptoassets for Funds or Other Cryptoassets

Article 3(1)(19) and (20) MiCA defines the exchange of cryptoassets for funds[11] or other cryptoassets as the conclusion of purchase or sale contracts concerning cryptoassets with clients for funds or for other cryptoassets by using proprietary capital. These activities include what Article 4(1)(6) MiFID defines as the 'dealing on own account' (i.e., trading against proprietary capital resulting in the conclusion of transactions with clients). The split into two different activities emphasises that both transactions – cryptoassets for cryptoassets and cryptoassets for funds (and vice versa) – are covered. Exchange services may be found in many crypto applications unrelated to trading, including bridging and mixing tools as well as other anonymity-enhancing product and service features (cf. Section 14.2.4.3 (ii)).

Similar to Article 2(1)(d) MiFID, only the exchange of cryptoassets *with clients* is a regulated activity. An example of this is a CASP's systemic internalisation of client orders. If a person does not serve clients, but merely trades on their own proprietary capital for speculative purposes or as a market maker, that person is not performing an "exchange of cryptoassets". If the person trades using client capital, that person may be performing "portfolio management".

Article 77 MiCA provides further details on the exchange of cryptoassets (cf. Section 7.5.2.).

7.2.1.2 *Custody and Administration*

Article 3(1)(17) MiCA defines 'custody and administration of crypto-assets on behalf of clients' as the safekeeping or controlling on behalf of clients, of cryptoassets, or of the means of access to such cryptoassets, where applicable in the form of private cryptographic keys. We discuss crypto custody in detail in Chapter 8.

7.2.1.3 *Brokerage Services*

Execution of Orders for Cryptoassets on Behalf of Clients

Article 3(1)(21) MiCA defines 'execution of orders for cryptoassets on behalf of clients' as the conclusion of agreements, on behalf of clients, to purchase or sell one or more cryptoassets or the subscription on behalf of clients for one or more cryptoassets, and it includes the conclusion of contracts to sell cryptoassets at the moment of their offer or admission to trading. The definition is akin to Article 4(1)(5) MiFID.[12]

[11] Article 3(1)(14) of MiCA refers for 'funds' to the definition in Article 4(25) of PSD2. Funds, thus, means "banknotes and coins, scriptural money or electronic money" as defined in Article 2(2) of EMD.

[12] '"Execution of orders on behalf of clients" means acting to conclude agreements to buy or sell one or more financial instruments on behalf of clients and includes the conclusion of agreements to sell financial instruments issued by an investment firm or a credit institution at the moment of their issuance'.

Similar to Article 4(1)(5) MiFID in the case of financial instruments, the last half-sentence of Article 3(1)(21) clarifies that MiCA applies where crypto brokers are intermediating in the context of initial token and coin offerings. Article 78 MiCA foresees further details on this.

Placing of Cryptoassets

The 'placing of cryptoassets' is defined in Article 3(1)(22) MiCA as the marketing, on behalf of or for the account of the offeror or a party related to the offeror, of cryptoassets to purchasers.

MiCA refrains from stipulating a definition of "marketing". Other pieces of EU financial legislation provide such definitions. In particular, Article 4(1)(x) AIFMD defines "marketing" as a direct or indirect offering or placement at the initiative of the [fund manager] or on behalf of the [fund manager] of units or shares of an [investment fund] it manages to or with investors domiciled or with a registered office in the Union. We hold that this definition applies to MiCA *mutatis mutandis*.

The use of the term "marketing" is remarkable in light of the alternative term of "distribution" which is used in MiFID. However, it follows from Article 60(3)(e) MiFID[13] that the EU regulator did not see a major difference between marketing and distribution under MiFID.

The practical difficulty here lies in the delineation between activities too imprecise and distant to be seen as an offering or placement of cryptoassets (such as "awareness raising" by discussing new technical features on websites and "market sounding") and the precise provision of information where agreement could establish all elements of a contract. In fact, indirect forms of marketing of cryptoassets have prompted major concerns.[14] They may be addressed either by way of the "placing" definition or by virtue of the market abuse rules of Title VI MiCA (cf. Chapter 10), unless they are exempted as reverse solicitation (cf. Section 7.2.4).

Reception and Transmission of Orders for Cryptoassets on Behalf of Clients

Article 3(1)(23) MiCA defines 'reception and transmission of orders for cryptoassets on behalf of clients' as the reception from a person of an order to purchase or sell one or more cryptoassets or the subscription for one or more cryptoassets and the transmission of that order to a client for execution. While in the case of an "execution", the order to be executed comes from the client, reception and transmission consider cases where a third party's order is received by the crypto broker (for instance, holders of cryptoassets trading via a trading platform or the broker of such a holder).

The service is equivalent to Section A, point (1), of Annex I MiFID on the reception and transmission of orders in relation to one or more financial instruments.

Article 80 MiCA provides further details on the reception and transmission of orders (cf. Section 7.5.3).

7.2.1.4 *Portfolio Management and Advice*

Article 3(1)(24) MiCA defines 'providing advice on crypto-assets' as offering, giving, or agreeing to give personalised recommendations to a client, either at the client's request or on the initiative of the CASP providing the advice, with respect to one or more transactions relating to cryptoassets or the use of cryptoasset services. Subject to Article 3(1)(25) MiCA, 'providing

[13] 'The placing of crypto-assets is deemed equivalent to the underwriting or placing of financial instruments on a firm commitment basis and placing of financial instruments without a firm commitment basis referred to in Section A, points (6) and (7), respectively, of Annex I to Directive 2014/65/EU'.

[14] Cf. Zetzsche *et al.*, 'Remaining Regulatory Challenges in Digital Finance', pp. 74–78.

portfolio management of crypto-assets' means managing portfolios in accordance with mandates given by clients on a discretionary client-by-client basis where such portfolios include one or more cryptoassets.

The provision of advice in relation to cryptoassets and portfolio management is equivalent to investment advice and financial portfolio management under MiFID.[15] The features established under MiFID for delineating these activities among each other and from other regulated activities such as collective portfolio management apply vice versa.

Article 81 MiCA provides further details on these cryptoasset services, which we discuss in Section 7.5.4.

Note that Article 3(1)(25) MiCA includes individual portfolio management only and excludes collective investment management on behalf of investment funds. For instance, where the clients' assets are segregated and investment decisions impact, in principle, only the portfolio value of one client, that constitutes portfolio management under MiCA, while as soon as assets from various clients are bundled and pooled, collective portfolio management materialises. Note that collective portfolio management is not a regulated activity under MiCA, and hence, the EU general legislation (UCITSD and AIFMD) does apply. We discuss MiCA's approach to collective investment schemes in Chapter 9.

7.2.1.5 *Transfer Services for Cryptoassets on Behalf of Clients*

Article 3(1)(26) MiCA defines transfer services as services related to the transfer, on behalf of a natural or legal person, of cryptoassets from one distributed ledger address or account to another. Many CASPs offer these transfer services as part of their custody and administration, exchange, or order execution services. Given that the definition clearly includes the transfer from 'one distributed ledger address or account to another', these services do not require a change *on* the distributed ledger. A swap across two custodial accounts managed by the same crypto custodian holding the assets on the same ledger address also qualifies as transfer service, regardless of whether any of this rebooking takes place on-chain or off-chain. All in all, similar to the exchange of cryptoassets for funds or other cryptoassets in the trading context (see Section 7.2.1.1), the transfer of funds assumes a fall-back function and thus puts services not included in Article 3(1)(16) MiCA in scope of the authorisation requirement of Title V MiCA.

Besides simple transfers, services in scope include, for instance, the switching of accounts, and in our view also the merger and splitting of accounts that come with a transfer (such as many mixing services and other anonymity-enhancing transactions and technologies). In a similar vein, a transfer may cover netting transactions, unless they are covered by other licensed activities, including the exchange of cryptoassets for other cryptoassets (see Section 7.2.1.1). Further, some service models come with a transfer of funds; for instance, some crypto-lending and crypto-staking models require that cryptoassets are transferred from the original holder's address to that of a borrower of cryptoassets. Given that crypto-lending and crypto-staking are otherwise exempted and disregarded by MiCA, as stated in Recital 94 MiCA, the underlying transfer of cryptoassets may put the provider into a scope of Title V MiCA.

Note, however, that all transactions must take place on behalf of clients; in turn, where the former transactions are made in the CASP's own interest, for instance, as proprietary trader, the transaction does not qualify as transfer services. At the same time, the issuer/initial offeror who

[15] See Article 60(3) of MiCA: '(g) providing advice on crypto-assets is deemed equivalent to investment advice referred to in Section A, point (5), of Annex I to Directive 2014/65/EU; (h) providing portfolio management on crypto-assets is deemed equivalent to portfolio management referred to in Section A, point (4), of Annex I to Directive 2014/65/EU'.

transfers their own cryptoassets to the acquirer[16] and the validators, nodes, or miners that contribute to the confirmation of a transaction and to updating the state of the underlying distributed ledger[17] are out of scope.

Besides client protection, the regulatory interest in these transfers is related to AML/CTF concerns. On these questions relating to Article 3(1)(26) MiCA, see the provision of Article 3(9) Transfer of Funds Regulation (TFR)[18] as well as Chapter 14 (on AML/CTF rules applicable). More details on how the transfer of funds are regulated can be found in Article 82 MiCA and are discussed in that context in Section 7.5.5.

7.2.2 *Relevance of MiCA's Limitation of Scope?*

The type of asset may determine whether MiCA's Title V applies.

7.2.2.1 *No Application to NFTs*

As discussed in Section 4.2, MiCA's scope excludes some types of cryptoassets, in particular, certain NFTs (Article 2(3) MiCA). Where the cryptoasset is out of MiCA's scope entirely, the MiCA CASP rules do not apply. However, authorisation may be required even in this case under MiFID or other EU financial law.

7.2.2.2 *No Application to "Other Cryptoassets" Exempted under Article 4(3) MiCA*

If a cryptoasset other than an ART or an EMT meets the requirements of Article 4(3) MiCA, for instance, where it is offered for free, the provision of a cryptoasset service is not subject to authorisation.[19] However, an authorisation is required if that exempt cryptoasset is offered to the public for a second time, but the other offer is not exempted (for instance, because it is not free), or if that cryptoasset is admitted to a trading platform. Note that EMTs and ARTs do not benefit from the exemptions under Article 4(3) MiCA.[20]

7.2.2.3 *Application If There Is No Identifiable Issuer*

MiCA's Titles II–IV do not apply where cryptoassets have no identifiable issuer (Recital 22 MiCA). Meanwhile, Title V MiCA does not require the existence of an issuer of a token. Where a cryptoasset lacks an issuer (such as in the case of Bitcoin), the service provided may nevertheless qualify under Article 3(16) MiCA (cf. Recital 22 MiCA).

7.2.3 *Additional Conditions for a Regulated Activity (Article 3(14) MiCA)*

7.2.3.1 *Occupation or Business*

The mere occasional provision of a cryptoasset service does not open the scope of Title V MiCA. This must be the "occupation or business" of a CASP. We argue that an occupation or business requires some permanency regarding the offering of the services. For instance, running a pilot

[16] Cf. Recitals paras. 4 and 87 of MiCA.

[17] Recital para. 93 of MiCA.

[18] The provision covers 'any transaction at least partially carried out by electronic means on behalf of a payer through a payment service provider, with a view to making funds available to a payee through a payment service provider, irrespective of whether the payer and the payee are the same person and irrespective of whether the payment service provider of the payer and that of the payee are one and the same'.

[19] See Article 4(5) of MiCA.

[20] For details, see Section 4.4.

with informed clients for a limited amount of time or the experimental provision of a cryptoasset service within clear limits does not render the service a regulated activity.

However, Title V MiCA applies to main and side services alike. If a cryptoasset service is provided as a side service, all respective rules apply. The fact that the service (for example, a transfer of cryptoassets) is merely an annex to a main service (for example, custody) has no impact on the need to comply with the rules in full. This follows from MiCA's recitals stressing, *inter alia*, that transfer services are often provided together with custody.[21]

7.2.3.2 *Professional Basis*

If a cryptoasset service is provided on a professional basis, the person is deemed a CASP.[22] The establishment of a professional basis requires neither profitability nor an income scheme. Indeed, a professional basis is confirmed if the cryptoasset service is *oriented towards clients*. This does not require a hierarchical organisation to provide the service. For instance, a regular cooperation among developers that follows a certain scheme or order with a view to attracting clients (for instance, where one developer is in charge of coding, another handles code review, and the third takes care of testing) may meet the requirement of a professional basis.

7.2.3.3 *Legal Person or Undertaking*

Any CASP must be either a legal person or other undertaking or any of the financial institutions mentioned in Articles 59(1)(b) and 60 MiCA. "Legal person or other undertaking" here is the essential precondition for a successful application for authorisation.

If a person provides a cryptoasset service as a business on a professional basis, it is subject to authorisation under Article 59 MiCA. A person cannot avoid the authorisation requirement by claiming that the person is acting as a sole trader or as a group of persons (for instance, developers) by claiming the absence of a legal entity. If they do offer a cryptoasset service without an authorisation, administrative penalties apply pursuant to Article 111(1)(d) MiCA, and criminal prosecution may also follow under the laws of the Member States.

Given that the requirements of "a legal person or other undertaking" are taken directly from Article 4(1) MiFID, European institutions are supposed to apply the same principles as in MiFID. Even though MiCA is a regulation, it is not "complete". Some gaps remain, and these are filled by Member States' laws; for instance, the law of the Member State prescribes which entity is a legal person, or other undertaking, as the case may be.

Where under the law of the Member States, "other undertakings" are not legal persons, they shall only provide cryptoasset services 'if their legal form ensures a level of protection for third parties' interests equivalent to that afforded by legal persons and if they are subject to equivalent prudential supervision appropriate to their legal form'.[23] Even though the additional requirements of Article 4(1)(1) second subsection of MiFID are missing, we expect that the same requirements will be adopted by way of implementing legislation or the NCA's supervisory practice. Under these requirements, an "other undertaking" or sole trader/proprietor may provide cryptoasset services only if:

[21] Recital para. 93 of MiCA.

[22] Recital para. 21 of MiCA.

[23] Article 59(3) of MiCA and Article 1(k) of the Technical Standards specifying certain requirements of the Markets in Crypto-Assets Regulation (MiCA), Draft Final Report (2024) ESMA13-72330276-1634, p. 79.

- The ownership rights of third parties in instruments and funds are safeguarded, especially in the event of the insolvency of the firm (or of its proprietors), seizure, set-off, or any other action by creditors of the firm or of its proprietors;
- The firm is subject to rules designed to monitor the firm's solvency and that of its proprietors;
- The firm's annual accounts are audited by one or more persons empowered, under national law, to audit accounts; and
- Where the firm has only one proprietor, that person must make provisions for the protection of investors in the event of the firm's cessation of business following the proprietor's death or incapacity or any other such event.

7.2.3.4 *Partially vs. Fully Decentralised Provision of Services*

Distinct from the former question of who is entitled to function as a CASP, is the question of what happens if the provision of the cryptoasset service is dispersed and shared among many actors, including developers, nodes, and commercial entities and token-holders assuming part of the risk. Note that Recital 22 (which we discussed in Section 4.2.4 and 6.2) does not provide an answer to this as it deals with the application of Titles II, III, and IV MiCA only.

Similar to what we have laid out in the context of who functions as an issuer for the purposes of Titles III and IV MiCA (cf. Section 6.2), we argue that NCAs shall focus on the question of whether a developer firm, a group of developers, or other persons *control* the platform. If there is control, there is the provision of a cryptoasset service and the firm or group must meet the conditions of Article 59 et seq. MiCA. Where they do not qualify as a legal person, they must meet the requirements for "other undertakings" (cf. Section 7.2.2.3).

Where all the other criteria are met for the application of Title V MiCA (including occupation and professional basis) but no person or group controls the platform, NCAs will find it difficult to single-out one or several developers to qualify them jointly as an "intermediary" for the purposes of applying the CASP rules of Title V MiCA. In this case, fully decentralised platforms are beyond the scope of MiCA, although Recital 22 MiCA, if read strictly, does not support the exclusion of these CASPs. We have aired some doubts as to the policy rationale behind excluding fully decentralised platforms elsewhere and proposed assigning entity status to DAOs to establish a legislative basis on which to submit fully decentralised setups to MiCA.[24]

7.2.4 *Exemption for Reverse Solicitation (Article 61 MiCA)*

Although the wording of Article 61 MiCA seems to indicate otherwise, this article does not constitute an exemption from a licensing requirement but rather ascertains the regional scope of EU financial law. In cases of reverse solicitation (i.e., where cryptoasset services are provided *at the exclusive initiative of the client*), even where the client is established or situated in the EU, a service provider residing in a third country (i.e., a non-EU and non-EEA country) does not require an authorisation by an authority of an EU Member State, as a precondition for the provision of this service. On the contrary, even third-country CASPs need an EU authorisation if they market their services to clients in the Union. The same is true for any EU CASP systemically facilitating transactions with third-country CASPs, for instance by forwarding trades to third-country crypto exchanges.[25]

[24] Cf. Zetzsche *et al.*, 'Remaining Regulatory Challenges in Digital Finance', pp. 115–18.

[25] See ESMA, 'Opinion to Support the Convergent Application of MiCA', 31 July 2024, ESMA75-453128700-1048. Website ESMA75-453128700-1048_Opinion_on_broker_models.pdf (europa.eu) (accessed on 8 August 2024).

In turn, in cases of reverse solicitation, there is not only no authorisation requirement, but the rules attached to authorisation in Title V MiCA also do not apply. Further still, in most such cases, *MiCA does not apply at all*, as these cases are within the exclusive jurisdiction of third countries. An exemption, however, applies to the extraterritorial provisions of MiCA discussed in the context of market abuse and insider trading (Chapter 10).

While this principle is clearly established not only in MiCA but also in other EU financial regulation,[26] the practical difficulty of MiCA stems from the fact that CASPs and issuers of cryptoassets often use internet-based forms of indirect marketing, including the use of "Finfluencers", referral programmes, and other indirect types of social media marketing (for details, cf. Chapter 10). In this regard, MiCA sets out a number of limitations.

First, MiCA prohibits any direct or indirect solicitation of clients or prospective clients *in the Union*, 'regardless of the means of communication used for the solicitation, promotion, or advertising in the Union'. Whenever a client is solicited regionally in the EU, the exemption for reverse solicitation does not apply. Note that the solicitation must take place in the Union; this is the case whenever a client is in EU territory and is contacted by whatever means. The opposite applies where *the client* contacts the provider. The difficulty lies not in the rule but in its execution, given the multiple types of practices attracting clients to visit a CASP's website. We hold that typical forms of modern, online marketing like "Finfluencers", referral programmes, social media, and even some types of search engine optimisation (SEO) preclude invocation of the reverse solicitation exemption under Article 61 MiCA if they target clients within the Union. See also Chapter 10.

Second, contractual stipulations and disclaimers do not influence the assessment of facts. Authorities will rely here on a "substance over form" approach.

Third, where a client has been onboarded by a third-country CASP, this fact does not 'entitle a third-country firm to market new types or categories of crypto-assets or crypto-asset services to that client' (Article 61(2) MiCA).

As previously laid out and further discussed in Chapter 10, there are difficulties when it comes to execution. MiCA grants a strong role to the ESMA in this regard, including through the development of guidelines and joint supervision practices to detect and prevent the circumvention of MiCA (cf. Article 61(3) MiCA).[27] On this basis, implementing a client protection approach, ESMA has defined in which cases MiCA applies where MiCA-licensed CASPs forward trades to third-country crypto exchanges.[28]

7.3 LICENSING AND AUTHORISATION

7.3.1 *Licensing Requirements*

Like most provisions of Title V MiCA, the licensing requirements set out in Articles 59–61 MiCA[29] borrow from EU general financial law, as shown in Table 7.3.

[26] See Article 42 of MiFID II, Directive 2014/65, OJ 2014 No. L173.

[27] Cf. ESMA, 'Guidelines on Reverse Solicitation under the Markets in Crypto-Assets Regulation (MiCA)', Draft version, ESMA35-1872330276-1619, pp. 18–21.

[28] See ESMA, 'Opinion to Support the Convergent Application of MiCA', 31 July 2024, ESMA75-453128700-1048. Website ESMA75-453128700-1048_Opinion_on_broker_models.pdf (europa.eu) (accessed on 8 August 2024).

[29] On the notification to NCAs as well as on the application for authorisation for CASPs, cf. Technical Standards specifying certain requirements of the Markets in Crypto-Assets Regulation (MiCA), Draft Final Report (2024), ESMA18-72330276-1634, pp. 50–112.

TABLE 7.3 *EU financial law orientation of MiCA's authorisation requirements*

MiCA Articles	Subject matter	Provision equivalent to
59(2)	Choice of home country	Article 11(3) PSD2
59(3)	Applicant's legal form	Article 4(1)(1) MiFID
59(4)	Continuing compliance	Article 6(1) AIFMD and Article 21 (1) MiFID
59(5)	Protecting the term "CASP"	Rec. 72 Commission Delegated Regulation No. 2017/565
59(6)	Detailing cryptoasset services	Articles 6(1) and 60 MiFID
59(8)	Expansion of licence	Articles 6(2) and 60 (1) MiFID
59(7)	European Passport	Article 11(9) PSD2, Article 6 (3) MiFID, and Article 32 et seq. AIFMD
60(7)	Essential information to be provided by certain financial entities wanting to provide a cryptoasset service	Article 8(2)(1) CRD, Article 5(1)(k) PSD2, Article 19(1)(b) CRD, Article 10(1)(l) Commission Delegated Regulation No. 2017/2055, Article 6(1)(j) Commission Delegated Regulation No. 2017/1943
61	Cryptoasset services at the exclusive initiative of the client	Article 42 MiFID

7.3.1.1 *Authorisation (Article 59 MiCA)*

Article 59 MiCA sets a licensing requirement for all CASPs. Either the legal person or the undertaking applies for an entirely new authorisation in accordance with Articles 62–64 MiCA, or the holders of certain licenses under EU financial law[30] ask for an extension of their existing licence under the conditions set out in Article 60 MiCA.

The licensing conditions are the usual authorisation requirements and are taken from general EU financial law (mostly, the MiFID/MiFIR framework), cf. Table 7.3.

7.3.1.2 *Right of Licence Holders under EU Financial Law to Provide CAS (Article 60 MiCA)*

Article 60 MiCA provides some relief with respect to the regulatory burden for authorised financial institutions seeking to provide cryptoasset services for the first time: it confers the right on financial institutions already authorised under EU law to provide all[31] or only some cryptoasset services[32] subject to:

- An authorisation covering an activity equivalent to the respective MiCA activity; and
- A notice containing the information pursuant to Article 60(7) MiCA to the NCA of the institution's home Member State at least 40 working days before the initial provision of these services.

Article 60 MiCA, thus, provides a "licence light". The underlying rationale here is that in many respects, the original authorisation will relate to items to be reviewed for the initial authorisation

[30] Qualified entities include subject to Article 59(1) (b) of MiCA: a credit institution, central securities depository, investment firm, market operator, electronic money institution, UCITS management company, or an alternative investment fund manager.

[31] Credit institutions (Article 60(1) of MiCA); investment firms (Article 60(3) of MiCA).

[32] CSDs with regard to custody and administration of cryptoassets on behalf of clients (Article 60(2) of MiCA); E-money Institutions (Article 60(4) of MiCA); UCITS management companies and AIFMs (Article 60(5) of MiCA); market operators (Article 60(6) of MiCA).

as CASPs under Article 59 and Articles 62–64 MiCA. Article 60 MiCA, thus, makes entry into MiCA's scope less expensive and spares both the CASP and the authorities from duplication of work.

As a technical matter, MiCA defines which activities are equivalent to the authorisations under EU financial law and do not extend to cryptoassets. For instance, 'custody and administration of cryptoassets' is equivalent to 'providing, maintaining, or operating securities accounts in relation to the settlement service' pursuant to Annex, Section B, No. (3), CSDR as well as the respective ancillary service pursuant to Annex I, Section B, No. (1) MiFID.[33]

The notice, under Article 60(7) MiCA, must provide information on:

- The potential CASP's programme of operations;
- Advanced AML/CTF measures;
- Technical documentation and a non-technical description of the ICT systems and security arrangements;
- A description of the procedure for the segregation of clients' cryptoassets and funds; and
- Service-specific additional requirements, for instance, the custody and administration policy where the CASP seeks to provide custody and administration, or expertise in cases of cryptoasset advice.[34]

The NCA of the home Member State is to review the notice within twenty days and decide whether or not to ask for additional information (within another twenty days) or, following the consideration that duplication of regulatory duties is undesirable, MiCA grants some relief to entities already authorised under EU financial law.

First, they do not have to resubmit identical information that has been previously submitted. Yet, in practice, this is hardly feasible given that the new activity will require some additional information. We hold that this rule is to be construed to allow for submission of *only the new parts* of the respective documents, so the institution only needs to send, and the authority only needs to review and assess, the respective amendments. A mark-up would also suffice.

Second, already authorised institutions are freed from certain MiCA provisions in the authorisation process regarding cryptoassets (Articles 62–64 MiCA), the prudential requirements (Article 67), and Title V Chapter 4 on the acquisition of the service provider. This follows the logic that the financial regulation applying to the original authorisation covers these items. Following the same logic, the right to provide cryptoasset services hinges on the existence of the authorisation of the original service (Article 60(10) and (11) MiCA).

All rights under Article 60 MiCA are registered with the ESMA, and the granting and removal of the right follow a harmonised process laid down in the implementing legislation.[35]

7.3.2 *Authorisation*

The authorisation framework for CASPs is equivalent to many provisions of general EU financial law (cf. Table 7.4).

In short, the authorisation is subject to a three-step procedure, outlined in the following subsections.

[33] For further examples, cf. Article 60(3) of MiCA.

[34] Article 60(7)(d)–(k) of MiCA.

[35] Article 60(11)–(14) of MiCA.

TABLE 7.4 *Authorisation under MiCA vs. EU financial law*

MiCA Articles	Subject matter	Provision equivalent to
62(1)	Submission of application to the competent authority of the home Member State	Article 7(1) AIFMD
62(3)	Provision of proof by the CASP	Rec. 39 and Articles 91(1) and 62(3) point (b) CRD
63(1)	Acknowledgement of receipt of the application	Article 12 PSD2, Article 15 CRD, Article 3 Commission Implementing Regulation No. 2017/1945, and Article 12(1) MiFID
63(2)	Assessment of the application for authorisation and grant or refusal of authorisation	Article 12 PSD, Article 4 Commission Implementing Regulation No. 2017/1945, Article 15 CRD, and Article 46(4) para. 2 MiFIR
63(4)	Notification of the applicant in case of a complete application	Article 46(4) para. 4 MiFIR
63(6)	Procedure before the granting/refusal of an authorisation	Article 26(2) AMLD/CTF
63(7)	The existence of close links	Article 14(3) para. 1 CRD, Articles 7(2) para. 1 and 29(1)(c) para. 1 UCITSD, Article 11(7) PSD2, Articles 7(2) para. 1 and 29(1)(c) para. 1 UCITSD, and Article 11(7) PSD2
63(8)	Refusal of authorisation in cases of close links/difficulties preventing the effective exercise of supervisory functions	Article 14(3) para. 2 CRD, Articles 7(2) para. 2 and 29(1)(c) para. 2 UCITSD, Article 11(8) PSD2, Article 14 (2) CRD, and Article 10(1) para. 2 MiFID
63(10)	Cases in which authorisation should be refused	Articles 9(4) and 63(5) MiFID and Article 8(1) para. 2 UCITSD
63(12)	Further information necessary to complete the assessment	Article 22(3) CRD and Article 12(2) MiFID
64(1)	Cases in which the granting of authorisation should be withdrawn	Articles 7(5) and 29(4) UCITSD, Article 18 CRD, Articles 8, 43, 44(5), and 62 MiFID, and Article 11 AIFMD
64(2)	Cases in which the granting of authorisation should be withdrawn	Articles 7(5) and 29(4) UCITSD, Article 18 CRD, Articles 8, 43, 44(5), and 62 MiFID, and Article 11 AIFMD

7.3.2.1 *Application*

The first step comprises the entity's initial application with the relevant documents that allow the NCA to assess the firm's operational, financial, and technical setup and resources, the management's fitness and probity[36] for the respective cryptoasset services, as well as the soundness of the

[36] Cf. Article 62(3)(a), (b) of MiCA: the entity must prove 'for all members of the management body of the [CASP], the absence of a criminal record in respect of convictions or the absence of penalties imposed under the applicable commercial law including insolvency law and financial services law, or in relation to anti-money laundering, and counter-terrorist financing, to fraud or to professional liability; (b) that the members of the management body of the [CASP] collectively possess sufficient knowledge, skills and experience to manage the crypto-asset service provider and that those persons are required to commit sufficient time to perform their duties'.

key shareholders[37] (cf. Article 62(1) and (2) MiCA). The information must show additional expertise for certain services, for instance, the investment advice on cryptoassets, and additional safeguards depending on the service provided (e.g., a custody policy for crypto custodians). Furthermore, close links to non-EU countries will be carefully considered,[38] and hence, applicants must provide information on these links.

Information already provided under other EU or domestic law prior to the application must also be considered.

7.3.2.2 *Assessment of Information*

The second step comprises an assessment of the information provided pursuant to Article 63(1)–(4) MiCA. Where necessary, the NCA will ask for additional information (with the application being rejected if the applicant does not provide it); otherwise, it will acknowledge receipt and notify the applicant that their file is complete.

7.3.2.3 *Assessment of Application*

The third step includes an assessment of the application by the NCA (Article 63(5)–(12) MiCA). This assessment shall take place within 40 days of the complete submission of the application. However, the NCA may find that it requires more information, in which case it is entitled to interrupt the proceedings for an additional 20 days.

The following consultative procedures are required prior to the definitive decision being reached on the application:

- The first relates to applicants where they themselves or their subsidiaries or parent or sister undertakings (controlled by the same parent) have any authorisation as a financial institution in another Member State. We hold that NCAs may rely on their response not only for authorisations granted under EU law but potentially also for additional licences granted under national law; however, the applicant's NCA may not know about these additional licences due to a lack of pan-EU registration and thus cannot ask for them directly (cf. Article 63(5) MiCA).
- The second involves AML/CTF authorities. Where links to non-cooperative countries or otherwise high risks exist, the NCA may ask for additional safeguards (cf. Article 63(6) MiCA). For details on AML/CTF requirements, cf. Chapter 14.
- The third relates to close links to third countries that may cast doubt as to whether EU law can be effectively enforced (cf. Article 63(7), (9) MiCA).

Article 63(10) MiCA lists four absolute reasons for rejecting an application.[39] The fact that three of them relate to the quality of management, and the influence of the CASP's shareholders demonstrates the importance attached by MiCA to the CASP's key personnel.

37 Cf. Article 62(3)(c) of MiCA: the entity must prove 'for all shareholders and members that have qualifying holdings in the [CASP], the absence of a criminal record in respect of convictions or the absence of penalties imposed under the applicable commercial law including insolvency law and financial services law, or in relation to anti-money laundering and counter-terrorist financing, to fraud or to professional liability'.

38 Cf. Article 63(7), (8) of MiCA ('7. Where close links exist between the applicant crypto-asset service provider and other natural or legal persons, competent authorities shall grant authorisation only if those links do not prevent the effective exercise of their supervisory functions'; '8. Competent authorities shall refuse authorisation if the laws, regulations or administrative provisions of a third country governing one or more natural or legal persons with which the applicant crypto-asset service provider has close links, or difficulties involved in their enforcement, prevent the effective exercise of their supervisory functions.')

39 These reasons are (1) the management body of the CASP poses a threat to its effective, sound, and prudent management and business continuity, and to the adequate consideration of the interest of its clients and the integrity

7.3.3 *European Passport (Article 65 MiCA)*

CASPs are allowed to provide cryptoasset services throughout the Union, either through the right of establishment, including through a branch, or through the freedom to provide services. CASPs that provide cryptoasset services on a cross-border basis shall not be required to have a physical presence in the territory of a host Member State.

Article 65 MiCA grants, providing the conditions of Title V MiCA are met, a European passport. The preconditions for this include a notification including the list of Member States to be operated in and the type of services to be provided in those Member States. To ensure speedy procedures, the home NCA must forward the relevant notice to all EU Member States within ten days and inform the CASP about this notice. The CASP may begin to provide cryptoasset services in these host Member States from the date of receipt of its NCA's communication.

The European Passport is the main privilege of EU (and EEA) membership as it allows CASPs to offer services to markets much larger than those of its home Member State and thus to capitalise on economies of scale.

7.3.4 *Withdrawal of Authorisation*

Once granted, the authorisation may be withdrawn pursuant to Article 64 MiCA because the applicant has not used it or does not want it anymore or for irregularities and infringements including where:

- The authorisation was obtained by irregular means (e.g., based on false statements);
- The CASP no longer meets the authorisation or operating conditions and could not remedy the deficiencies within a timeframe set by the NCA. As a qualification of the former, MiCA mentions the failure to have in place effective systems, procedures, and arrangements to detect and prevent money laundering and terrorist financing, and/or infringements of AML/CTF law at large. Furthermore, in the case of Article 60 MiCA, the withdrawal of the original authorisation necessarily results in the withdrawal of a right to provide cryptoasset services; or
- The CASP has seriously infringed MiCA.[40]

To allow for proportionate actions, the withdrawal may be limited to certain cryptoasset services.

Again, the withdrawal will be based on a number of consultations with the AML/CTF authorities and within the EU financial supervisory system through single points of contact of the host Member States. Moreover, the withdrawal will be registered with the ESMA.[41]

7.4 JOINT CONDITIONS FOR ALL CASPS

Articles 66–74 MiCA set conditions for all CASPs regardless of the service offered. These conditions are generic organisational and conduct requirements widely inspired by MiFID and other existing EU financial law (cf. Table 7.5). Often joint European Supervisory

of the market, or exposes the applicant cryptoasset service provider to a serious risk of money laundering or terrorist financing; (2) the members of the CASP's management body do not meet the governance standards of Article 68(1) of MiCA (cf. Section 7.4.2); (3) the key shareholders or members cannot show sufficiently good repute, as set out in Article 68(2) of MiCA; and (4) the future CASP will fail any of the authorisation or operating requirements of Title V of MiCA.

[40] Cf. Article 64(1)–(3) of MiCA.

[41] Cf. Article 64 of MiCA.

TABLE 7.5 *Operating requirements of MiCA vs. EU financial law*

MiCA Articles	Subject matter	Provision equivalent to
66(1)	Obligation to act honestly, fairly, and professionally in the best interests of clients	Articles 24(1) and 13d(1) MiFID and Article 29(1) Commission Directive 2010/43/EU
67(6)	The insurance policy shall include coverage against the certain risks	Article 12(2) Commission Delegated Regulation 231/2013
68(1)	Fit and proper members of the management body	Article 91(1) CRD, Article 9(4) MiFID, Article 8(1)(c) AIFMD, and Article 7(1)(b) UCITSD
68(2)	Fit and proper shareholders and members that have qualifying holdings	Article 9(1)(b) EMD, Article 10(1) MiFID, Article 8(1)(d) AIFMD, and Article 8(1) UCITSD
68(3)	Measures to be taken in the event of prejudicial influence of shareholders or members who have qualifying holdings	Article 10(3) MiFID
68(5)	Fit and proper personnel of the CASP	Article 21(1)(d) Commission Directive 2010/43, Article 9(3)(a) MiFID, Article 18(1) AIFMD, and Article 14(1)(c) UCITSD
68(6)	Assessment and periodical review of the effectiveness of the policy arrangements and procedures followed by the management body of the CASP	Article 10(2)(a) Commission Directive 2010/43, Article 60(3) Commission Regulation 231/2013, Article 9(3) in fine MiFID, and Article 76(1) CRD
68(7)	Continuity and regularity in the performance of their cryptoasset services	Article 16(4) MiFID, Article 3 Commission Directive 2010/43, and Recital 23 AIFMD
68(8)	Mechanisms, systems, and procedures to ensure risk assessment	Article 4(5) Commission Directive 2010/43, Article 57(6) Commission Regulation 231/2013, and Article 9(3) in fine MiFID
68(9)	Record-keeping for all services, activities, orders, and transactions of encrypted assets undertaken	Article 16(6) and Article 16(7) para. 8 MiFID
70(1–2)	CASPs that hold cryptoassets of clients must safeguard their ownership	Article 16(8) and (9) MiFID
70(3)	Placement of clients' funds	Articles 2(1)(e) and 4(1) Commission Delegated Regulation 2017/593 and Article 10(1)(1) PSD2
71(1)	Complaint-handling procedures	Article 26(1) Commission Delegated Regulation 2017/565, Article 6(1) Commission Directive 2010/43/EU, and Article 15 UCITSD
71(3)	Record of clients' complaints	Article 6(3) Commission Directive 2010/43/EU
72(1)	Effective policies and procedures to identify, prevent, manage, and disclose conflicts of interest	Article 18(1) Commission Directive 2010/43/EU, Article 31(1) Commission Delegated Reg. 231/2013, Article 34(1) Commission Delegated Regulation 2017/565, Articles 12 (1)(d) and 14 AIFMD, and Article 12(1)(b) UCITSD
72(2)	Disclosure of the general nature and sources of conflicts of interest to their (prospective) clients	Articles 23(2) and 13c(2) MiFID, Article 14 (2) AIFMD, and Article 14(2)(c)UCITSD
72(3)	The format of the disclosure and its context	Article 23(3)(b) MiFID, Article 34(4) Commission Delegated Regulation 2017/565

(continued)

TABLE 7.5 (*cont.*)

MiCA Articles	Subject matter	Provision equivalent to
72(4)	Assessment and review of the conflicts of interest policy by the CASP	Article 34(5) Commission Delegated Regulation 2017/565
73(1)	Outsourcing of services or activities to third parties	Article 31(1) and (2) Commission Delegated Regulation 2017/565, Article 20 AIFMD, and Article 13 UCITSD
73(3)	Rights and obligations through a written agreement in relation to outsourcing	Article 31(3) Commission Delegated Regulation 2017/565 and Article 75(d) Commission Delegated Regulation 231/2013
73(4)	Information to the competent authorities so the latter are able to assess the compliance of the outsourced activities	Article 31(5) Commission Delegated Regulation 2017/565, Article 13(1)(a) UCITSD, and Article 20(1) AIFMD

Authority (ESA) opinions or ESA guidelines on these requirements already exist that may become part of the respective Level 2 legislation.[42]

The heavy borrowing from MiFID, UCITSD, and AIFMD confirms the perspective that CASPs are, by and large, off-balance intermediaries similar to investment firms and managers of investment funds. This stands in contrast to on-balance intermediaries such as credit institutions. The adoption of rules for off-balance intermediaries entails that regulators shall focus on operational and fiduciary risk as well as the risk relating to the intermediary's insolvency as these are the main risk categories of relevance for off-balance intermediaries. MiCA meets these expectations by providing rules on fiduciary duties, governance, safekeeping, and outsourcing, as well as a wind-down plan. Prudential requirements, in turn, are less focused on contractual obligations and oriented more towards operational issues.

We focus in turn on the substantive operating requirements. Details on reporting and supervision are discussed in Chapter 11.

7.4.1 *Fiduciary Duties (Articles 66 and 72)*

7.4.1.1 *The Fiduciary Principle*

MiCA clarifies that CASPs are fiduciaries and as such are in a similar position to investment firms under MiFID and managers of collective investment schemes under UCITSD and AIFMD.

Equivalent to similar provisions for off-balance intermediaries in other EU financial law,[43] Article 66(1) MiCA establishes the basic fiduciary requirement for CASPs whereby they 'shall act honestly, fairly, and professionally in accordance with the best interests of their clients and

[42] For details, see the RTS on complaints handling by cryptoasset service providers; cf. Technical Standards specifying certain requirements of the Markets in Crypto-Assets Regulation (MiCA), Draft Final Report (2024), ESMA18-72330276-1634, pp. 113–25; RTS specifying the requirements for policies and procedures on conflicts of interest for crypto-asset service providers, Draft Final Report (2024), ESMA18-72330276-1634; RTS on content, methodologies, and presentation of sustainability indicators on adverse impacts on the climate and the environment, on measures that cryptoasset service providers must take to ensure continuity and regularity in the performance of services, on trade transparency, on content and format of order book records, as well as on record-keeping by cryptoasset service providers; cf. Technical Standards specifying certain requirements of the Markets in Crypto-Assets Regulation (MiCA), Draft version, ESMA75-453128700-438, pp. 102–215.

[43] See Table 7.4.

prospective clients'. This provision stands at the outset of a number of requirements on fairness, transparency, and conflict management, which follow the principle that the clients' interests shall be paramount, unless they have been explicitly informed and the clients have provided their explicit consent to being treated in a disadvantageous manner.

Fiduciary duties have, on the one hand, a harmonising effect that aligns the position of CASPs with other off-balance sheet intermediaries in the field of finance. On the other hand, they prohibit the setting up of crypto business models resulting in value transfers from clients to CASPs, many examples of which we have seen throughout the Crypto Winter.

In particular, CASPs must:

- Provide clients with fair, clear, and not misleading information;
- Identify marketing communications as such;
- Refrain from deliberately or negligently misleading clients in relation to the advantages of cryptoassets;
- Warn clients of the risks associated with crypto transactions;
- Provide hyperlinks to any cryptoasset whitepapers of relevance to their services; and
- Disclose their policies on pricing, costs, and fees prominently on their website.

7.4.1.2 *Sustainability Impacts*

CASPs must disclose prominently on their website information on climate- and environment-related principal adverse impacts of the consensus mechanism used to issue each cryptoasset in relation to which they provide services. That information may be obtained from the cryptoasset whitepapers.[44]

While this information may be copied from the whitepaper, it provides little guidance if the whitepaper is not sufficiently comprehensive on the matter. For that reason, the whitepaper rules require the same disclosures.[45]

MiCA is silent on the question of what a CASP must do if it finds a whitepaper disclosure dissatisfying.[46] For instance, a whitepaper may hide the sustainability impacts, lack detail thereon, or not provide disclosures on obvious (for instance, operational) risks. This situation is likelier than in the case of financial instruments given that the disclosures of whitepapers relating to "other cryptoassets" are not subject to a review by an NCA, contrary to disclosures laid down in a prospectus for transferable securities. Remaining silent would run counter to the overall fairness principle that governs the CASP–client relationship. At the same time, the CASP lacks the means to calculate sustainability impacts itself, unless it functions as the key stakeholder of the cryptoasset.

We hold that the fiduciary duties of Article 66(3) MiCA indicate that the CASP must in this case issue a warning to clients that it finds a given disclosure within a whitepaper insufficient, and thus, the risk of misleading content is present. The fact that the CASP must repeat the

[44] However, the whitepapers do not have to provide this information. Cf. Chapter 5. This leads to gaps as to the sustainability reporting of CASPs; see Zetzsche *et al.*, 'Remaining Regulatory Challenges in Digital Finance', pp. 70–71.

[45] Cf. Chapter 5.

[46] Cf. the RTS on content, methodologies, and presentation of sustainability indicators on adverse impacts on the climate and the environment (requiring that where information relating to the indicators is not readily available, the persons drawing up the whitepaper and the CASPs shall provide estimates and details of the best efforts carried out to obtain the information by conducting additional research, cooperating with third-party data providers or external experts or making reasonable assumptions), cf. Technical Standards specifying certain requirements of the Markets in Crypto-Assets Regulation (MiCA), Draft version, ESMA75-453128700-438, pp. 85–101.

disclosures on sustainability impacts while it does not have to repeat *all* whitepaper disclosures shows also the limit of that duty: the CASPs must review the disclosures on sustainability impacts, while with regard to other risks, the CASP must warn the client only where it becomes aware of a risk.

Note that clients may agree with the CASP to perform the due diligence of any cryptoasset prior to acting on it on behalf of a fund. We encourage institutional clients to do so as risks posed by the cryptoasset will surface later as risks of the institutional portfolio; if the CASP does not perform the due diligence, an EU financial institution must nevertheless perform it under EU financial law on its own.[47]

7.4.1.3 *Conflicts of Interest*

Article 72 MiCA on identification, prevention, management, and disclosure of conflicts of interest is a more precise variant of the general fiduciary duties laid down in Article 66 MiCA. Again, that provision is modelled on similar provisions in MiFID, AIFMD, and UCITSD (cf. Table 7.4), that is, the provisions establishing the conflicts duty for archetype off-balance intermediaries.

In particular, CASPs shall 'implement and maintain effective [conflicts] policies and procedures' that may be proportionate to the services and firm size 'to identify, prevent, manage, and disclose' all potential conflicts of interest between themselves and various internal and external parties linked to the CASP, its control holder, shareholders, key staff, employees, and clients. These policies and procedures shall be subject to an annual review.

General conflicts are to be disclosed on the CASP's website so that clients can be informed in a meaningful way.

Further details will be determined in the implementing legislation.[48]

7.4.2 *Governance and Complaints Handling (Articles 68, 69, and 71 MiCA)*

Articles 68, 69, and 71 MiCA on governance arrangements and complaints handling aim to effectuate the aforementioned fiduciary duties.

7.4.2.1 *Suitable Executives and Shareholders*

Reliable, skilled ("fit"), honest ("proper"), and engaged executives and key shareholders of good repute are the best assurance for clients of off-balance intermediaries, where fiduciary risks are paramount. This concern is laid down clearly in Article 68 MiCA.[49] Indeed, MiCA extends this principle: compared to other EU law, it puts greater emphasis on AML/CTF measures which may be understood as attributable to the AML/CTF risks various international and EU bodies

[47] Cf. Recitals 33, 40, and 67 and Articles 18 and 19 Commission Delegated Regulation No. 231/2013 (establishing the duty to perform a due diligence on investment assets).

[48] The respective RTS requires the categorisation of conflicts of interest along several categories, including between the CASP and its clients, among individual clients, or groups of clients of the CASP, and internal conflicts of interest. See RTS specifying the requirements for policies and procedures on conflicts of interest for crypto-asset service providers, Draft Final Report (2024), ESMA18-72330276-1634, pp. 27–40.

[49] For clarifications on the suitability criterion, cf. EBA and ESMA, 'Joint EBA and ESMA Guidelines on the Suitability Assessment of Members of Management Body of Issuers of Asset-Referenced Tokens and of Crypto-Asset Service Providers', and 'Joint EBA and ESMA Guidelines on the Suitability Assessment of Shareholders and Members, Whether Direct or Indirect, with Qualifying Holdings in Issuers of Asset-Referenced Tokens and in Crypto-Asset Service Providers', Draft Final Report (2024), EBA/GL/2024/09, ESMA75-453128700-10.

associate with cryptoassets.[50] CASPs must notify any changes among their executives and shareholders to the NCA.[51]

CASPs must also ensure that these requirements are met at all times, requiring, for instance, regular compliance updates on board members and key shareholders. The CASP's management body shall 'assess and periodically review the effectiveness of the policy arrangements and procedures put in place (...) and take appropriate measures to address any deficiencies in that respect'.[52]

7.4.2.2 *Adequate Resources*

CASPs must have adequate resources and people fit for the task. In the words of Article 68(5) MiCA, CASPs must 'employ personnel with the knowledge, skills and expertise necessary for the discharge of the responsibilities allocated to them, taking into account the scale, nature and range of crypto-asset services provided'.

7.4.2.3 *Tech Risk*

One focal point of MiCA is business continuity and tech risk;[53] it addresses instances observed throughout the Crypto Winter's streak of insolvencies.[54] In particular, CASPs 'shall take all reasonable steps to ensure continuity and regularity in the performance of their crypto-asset services.[55] To that end, [CASPs] shall employ appropriate and proportionate resources and procedures, including resilient and secure ICT systems as required by' DORA. As part of the former, CASPs must 'establish a business continuity policy, which shall include ICT business continuity plans as well as ICT response and recovery plans set up pursuant to Articles 11 and 12 [DORA] that aim to ensure, in the case of an interruption to their ICT systems and procedures, the preservation of essential data and functions and the maintenance of crypto-asset services or, where that is not possible, the timely recovery of such data and functions and the timely resumption of crypto-asset services'. The same robustness check is expected with regard to AML/CTF systems and information security as a whole.[56] We discuss DORA requirements in Chapter 15.

7.4.2.4 *Record-Keeping*

Related to the former, yet distinct from it, are the record-keeping requirements of Article 68(9) MiCA.[57] Again, this is a standard rule for regulated intermediaries, which facilitates proper enforcement of financial law by NCAs. A new facete of this is the client's right to ask for the CASP's records of the last five years; the NCA may extend this period to seven years.

[50] Article 68(1), (2) of MiCA.

[51] Cf. Article 68(1)–(4) and 69 of MiCA.

[52] Cf. Article 68(5) of MiCA.

[53] See on TechRisk, Buckley *et al.*, 'Techrisk', 35.

[54] See Zetzsche *et al.*, 'Remaining Regulatory Challenges in Digital Finance', p. 52.

[55] See RTS on measures that CASPs must take to ensure continuity and regularity in the performance of services (requiring specific organisational arrangements, business continuity policies, and plans which are periodically tested, taking into account relevant complexity and risks), cf. Technical Standards specifying certain requirements of Markets in Crypto-Assets Regulation (MiCA), Draft version, ESMA75-453128700-438, pp. 102–9.

[56] Cf. Article 68(7), (8) of MiCA.

[57] The respective RTS requires the retention of records by the CASPs and sets specific rules on the type and content of records in relation to certain cryptoasset services and activities, cf. Technical Standards specifying certain requirements of Markets in Crypto-Assets Regulation (MiCA), Draft version, ESMA75-453128700-438, pp. 157–215.

7.4.2.5 *Complaints Handling*

CASPs must 'establish and maintain effective and transparent procedures for the prompt, fair and consistent handling of complaints received from clients and shall publish descriptions of those procedures'. This includes, on the one hand, the right of clients to complain free of charge. Naturally, this involves the CASPs also having to deal with complaints in a timely manner and public disclosures on how to complain (including a template and records of all complaints filed).[58]

7.4.3 *Safekeeping (Article 70 MiCA)*

Given the incidents during the Crypto Winter (cf. Chapter 1), MiCA's rules on safekeeping are of the utmost importance.

According to its heading, Article 70 MiCA relates to safekeeping. Article 70 MiCA presents general provisions for CASPs holding clients' cryptoassets and funds as part of its regular business or in the course of payments. Thus, Article 70 MiCA on safekeeping extends, in principle, to all CASPs. Yet, each of the provisions set specific requirements on its scope depending on the asset being safekept.

Article 70 MiCA regulates:

- The holding of cryptoassets or means of access to such cryptoassets in Article 70(1) MiCA which we discuss at length in Chapter 8 and therefore only touch upon in Section 7.4.3.1,
- The holding of client funds in Article 70(2) and (3) MiCA (cf. Section 7.4.3.2), and
- Payments initiated by CASPs on behalf of clients in Article 70(4) MiCA (cf. Section 7.4.3.3).

The safekeeping of financial assets other than cryptoassets, funds, and payments is regulated outside of MiCA. In particular, the safekeeping of financial instruments (which may take place by way of custody, or ownership verification, depending on whether they may be held in custody) is subject to MiFID[59] and bespoke investment fund regulation.[60]

7.4.3.1 *Holding of Cryptoassets or Means of Access (Article 70(1) MiCA)*

Article 70(1) MiCA extends to CASPs that 'hold crypto-assets *belonging to clients* or *the means of access* to such crypto-assets [i.e., the private key]' (*emphasis added*). Article 75 MiCA expands Article 70(1) MiCA. Crypto custody under Article 75 MiCA is then a qualified form of safekeeping under Article 70(1) MiCA, and CASPs providing safekeeping in relation to cryptoassets are necessarily subject to Article 75 MiCA on crypto custody.

As follows from Article 60 MiCA, the scope of these provisions extends to crypto custodians, regardless of whether the provision of custody and administration is the provider's core or side

[58] See Article 71 of MiCA and RTS on complaints handling by cryptoasset service providers in Technical Standards specifying certain requirements of the Markets in Crypto-Assets Regulation (MiCA), Draft Final Report (2024), ESMA18-72330276-1634, pp. 113–25.

[59] See Annex I Section B (1) MiFID (defining safekeeping and administration of financial instruments as ancillary service of investments firms) in tandem with Article 3 of Commission Delegated Directive (EU) 2017/593 of 7 April 2016 supplementing Directive 2014/65/EU of the European Parliament and of the Council with regard to safeguarding of financial instruments and funds belonging to clients, product governance obligations, and the rules applicable to the provision or reception of fees, commissions, or any monetary or non-monetary benefits, OJ L 87/500 of 31.3.2017.

[60] For details on investment funds, see Chapter 9.

business. For that reason, Articles 70(1) and 75 MiCA apply, for instance, to asset managers and crypto brokers who also hold clients' cryptoassets. Note that MiCA does not foresee a separation requirement preserving certain types of business for certain types of providers only.[61] Given the link between Article 70(1) MiCA and Article 75 MiCA, we deal with the details in the chapter on crypto custody (Chapter 8).

7.4.3.2 *Holding of Client Funds as a Business Model or Services Prerequisite (Article 70(2) and (3) MiCA)*

While Article 70(1) MiCA is concerned with value represented in cryptoassets, Article 70(2) MiCA deals with the clients' non-crypto values. Article 70(2) MiCA applies to CASPs whose business model or services 'require holding clients' funds other than e-money tokens'. Article 3 (14) MiCA refers to the definition of funds in Article 4(25) Directive (EU) 2015/2366 (PSD2), and hence, funds include banknotes, coins, scriptural money, or electronic money belonging to clients (in sum, all assets traditionally referred to as "fiat"). EMTs are excluded as they are cryptoassets falling under Article 70(1) MiCA (and potentially Article 75 MiCA). Note that the service providers' holding of non-fiat and non-cryptoassets, in particular, financial instruments, is subject to bespoke regulation (*sub specie* MiFID).

Again, the CASPs shall have 'adequate arrangements in place to safeguard the ownership rights of clients and prevent the use of clients' funds for their own account'. These arrangements are specified in Article 70(3) MiCA: CASPs shall place such funds with a credit institution or a central bank, where an account with the central bank is available. The requirement to post funds with an external regulated financial institution ensures *segregation*. In addition, Article 70 (3) MiCA[62] requires that client assets be clearly *earmarked* as such. Segregation and earmarking together allow for the disposal of clients' cryptoassets in the event of the CASP's insolvency, even though a reference to insolvency, as in Article 70(1) MiCA, is missing.

Given that MiFID requires the same safeguards in relation to client funds held by an investment firm, we expect more implementing legislation similar to Article 4 of Commission Delegated Directive (EU) 2017/593 in the MiCA implementing legislation.[63]

For that reason, Article 70(2) and (3) MiCA does not apply to e-money institutions, payment institutions authorised under PSD2, and credit institutions: here, the safeguards in relation to client funds of the EMD and PSD2 apply.[64]

7.4.3.3 *Payments (Article 70(4) MiCA)*

While Article 70(4) MiCA seems to contain an authorisation, it is, in fact, a *restriction*: CASPs may provide payment services *only* if authorised under PSD2, and if they do so, they need to

[61] For instance, the business of 'collective portfolio management' is preserved to fund managers. Credit institutions are not allowed to perform collective portfolio management.

[62] '[CASPs] shall take all necessary steps to ensure that clients' funds other than e-money tokens held with a central bank or a credit institution are held in an account separately identifiable from any accounts used to hold funds belonging to the [CASPs]'.

[63] The respective RTS provides a dedicated set of obligatory information to be included in the application for a CASP's authorisation or the notification of an entity intending to hold clients' cryptoassets or funds, focusing, in particular, on the prohibition of reuse, the segregation, and the deposit of the clients' funds with a central bank (and if not, the disclosure of the reasons taken into account to select credit institutions for the deposit of clients' funds); cf. Technical Standards specifying certain requirements of the Markets in Crypto-Assets Regulation (MiCA), Draft Final Report (2024), ESMA18-72330276-1634, pp. 57–58, 92–93; for an overview of the respective record-keeping obligations, cf. Technical Standards specifying certain requirements of the Markets in Crypto-Assets Regulation (MiCA), Draft version, ESMA75-453128700-438, pp. 161–62, 170–71.

[64] See Article 7 of EMD; Article 10 of PSD2.

inform their clients of (a) the nature and terms and conditions of those services, including references to the applicable national law and to the rights of clients; and (b) whether those services are provided by them directly or by a third party.

Institutions authorised to act under PSD2 (in particular, payment service providers and credit institutions) are deemed to be authorised under Article 70(4) MiCA.

7.4.4 *Outsourcing (Article 73 MiCA)*

Mimicking the MiFID, AIFMD, and UCITSD framework,[65] Article 73 MiCA establishes a framework for delegations of material services to third parties. The purpose here is to ensure the effectiveness of the authorisation requirements and financial supervision even where the authorised CASPs rely on other, potentially not authorised, service providers. This is crucial as delegates tend to depend on someone else's authorisation and are, by law, not tied to the authorised institution's laws and obligations.

7.4.4.1 *Duties of Outsourcing CASPs*

CASPs 'that outsource services or activities to third parties for the performance of operational functions shall take all reasonable steps to avoid additional operational risk. They shall remain fully responsible for discharging all of their obligations pursuant to this Title'.[66]

Moreover, CASPs that outsource need to ensure[67] that the outsourcing:

- Does not result in the delegation of the responsibility of the CASP;
- Does not alter the relationship between the CASP and their clients, nor the obligations of the CASP towards their clients; and
- Does not alter the conditions for the authorisation of the CASP.

As for formalities, CASPs must have an outsourcing policy, including on contingency plans and exit strategies, taking into account the scale, the nature, and the range of cryptoasset services provided. This outsourcing policy is usually a part of the overall plan of operations. In addition, MiCA requires a written outsourcing agreement, with the rights and obligations of each party specified. Outsourcing agreements shall give CASPs the right to terminate those agreements; MiCA prohibits indefinite agreements.[68]

Another bundle of requirements relates to the controls over, and compliance of, the delegate.[69] CASPs must retain the expertise and resources necessary to evaluate the quality of the services provided, to supervise the outsourced services effectively, and to manage the risks associated with the outsourcing on an ongoing basis. For that purpose, CASPs must have direct access to relevant information on the outsourced services. What constitutes relevant information cannot be determined ex ante with certainty; this may vary based on what is necessary for the CASP to deliver its services on behalf of its clients. In turn, the delegate must submit itself to any information request that is reasonable by that standard.

Furthermore, the delegates must meet the EU's data protection standards.[70] CASPs are responsible for ensuring that those data protection standards are set out in the written

[65] See Article 16(5) of MiFID; Article 20 of AIFMD; Article 13 of UCITSD, Directive 2009/65, OJ 2009 No. L302, with respective implementing legislation. We expect implementing legislation similar to the model provisions.
[66] Article 73(1) of MiCA.
[67] Article 73(1)(a)–(c) of MiCA.
[68] Cf. Article 73(2), (3) of MiCA.
[69] Cf. Article 73(1)(e), (f) of MiCA.
[70] Cf. Article 73(1)(g) of MiCA.

outsourcing agreements and need to supervise compliance. An IT audit may be the tool of choice for this requirement.

The CASPs and the outsourcing partner shall make all information available to the competent and all other authorities relevant to the outsourcing agreement, to assess the compliance of the outsourced activities with the outsourcing requirements.[71] This includes, for instance, data protection authorities. Furthermore, CASPs must ensure that the delegate (i.e., the outsourcing provider) cooperates with the CASP's competent authority and the outsourcing does not prevent the exercise of the competent authority's supervisory functions, including on-site access to acquire any relevant information needed to fulfil those functions.[72]

7.4.4.2 *Services or Activities in the Performance of Operational Functions*

The heavy compliance and oversight requirements indicate that the scope of Article 73 MiCA is relevant here. Article 73 MiCA applies where the CASP outsources 'services or activities to third parties for the performance of operational functions'.

A look at similar provisions of EU financial law reveals notable differences: Article 16(5) MiFID, as MiFID's main outsourcing provision, applies where an investment firm relies 'on a third party for the performance of operational functions which are *critical for the provision of continuous and satisfactory service* to clients and the performance of investment activities on a continuous and satisfactory basis', while Article 20 AIFMD applies where AIFMs 'delegate to third parties the task of carrying out functions on their behalf'. There is a common understanding that this provision reads as 'carrying out *material* functions'.[73] Article 73 MiCA, by comparison, omits any materiality criteria. However, we hold that a materiality criterion similar to that under MiFID must be read into Article 73(1) MiCA, as any other construction would lead to unnecessary costs on all sides: everyone loses where the cost burden would be unnecessarily high since CASPs must enter into complex agreements for non-material services too. We, thus, construe Article 73(1) MiCA to cover the outsourcing of 'services or activities to third parties for the performance of operational functions *critical for the provision of continuous and satisfactory service to clients and the performance of crypto-asset services on a continuous and satisfactory basis*'.

We then interpret this wording in line with the MiFID framework: Article 73 MiCA applies to operational functions 'where a defect or failure in its performance would materially impair the continuing compliance of [a CASP] with the conditions and obligations of its authorisation or its other obligations under [MiCA], or its financial performance, or the soundness or the continuity of its [crypto-asset] services and activities'.[74]

Even then, "operational functions" are not used elsewhere in MiCA, while the Recitals of MiCA do not provide any clarification on this term either.[75] Again, a look at the MiFID

[71] Cf. Article 73(4) of MiCA.

[72] Cf. Article 73(1)(d) of MiCA.

[73] See T. Partsch, 'Delegation', in D. A. Zetzsche (ed.), *The Alternative Investment Fund Managers Directive* (Alphen aan den Rijn: Wolters Kluwer, 2020), 3rd ed., Chapter 9, pp. 286–90.

[74] Article 16(5) of MiFID in tandem with Article 30(1) of Commission Delegated Regulation (EU) 2017/565 of 25 April 2016 supplementing Directive 2014/65/EU of the European Parliament and of the Council as regards organisational requirements and operating conditions for investment firms and defined terms for the purposes of that Directive, OJ 2017 No. L87, 31 March 2017, as modified by the authors to reflect MiCA's terminology.

[75] The respective Technical Standards address outsourcing only indirectly in relation to business continuity, the authorisation application, the notification process, the conflicts of interest management, and the record-keeping obligations. In particular, the CASP shall establish a general business continuity plan for the *important* functions that are outsourced via a contractual relationship with a third-party; permissionless DLT shall be considered a 'common good' and not a third-party service provider. Cf. Technical Standards specifying certain requirements of the Markets in Crypto-Assets Regulation (MiCA), Draft Final Report (2024), ESMA18-72330276-1634, pp. 53–54, 80; RTS

framework[76] at least provides some initial guidance by way of a white list. Article 73 MiCA does not apply, first, to advisory services and other services which do not form part of the cryptoasset service business of the CASP, including the provision of legal advice to the firm, the training of personnel of the firm, billing services, and the security of the firm's premises and personnel. Second, the purchase of standardised services, including market information services and the provision of price feeds, is not covered by Article 83 MiCA. Given that MiFID has led the EU lawmakers in relation to MiCA in many respects, we may as well also transfer the underlying rationale to MiCA.[77]

7.4.4.3 *Specific Services and Activities*

Beyond these two cases, there is an open question as to what constitutes an operational function in the cryptoasset service context. We discuss some specific cases here. Note that this discussion is distinct from the question of who constitutes an ICT service provider under DORA, which we discuss in that context (cf. Sections 15.3.2 and 15.5.3).

Developer Firms

An important question in the crypto context is whether software developer firms that develop and maintain the underlying token technology are third-party outsourcing providers. These firms are subject to Article 73 MiCA if the developer firm performs operational functions. Applying the guidance above, tailor-made software development for the crypto platform is neither an advisory nor a standardised service; rather it is often the strategy of the developing firm to draft tailor-made applications that lead the crypto platform to grow and flourish. We then need to ask whether the software development and continuous support by the developer firm are 'critical for the provision of continuous and satisfactory service to clients and the performance of cryptoasset services on a continuous and satisfactory basis'.

The answer depends on the degree of dependence of the CASP on the software developer. Where the CASP has hired in-house staff taking care of most technical issues and maintenance, the answer is in the negative; where the technical intelligence of the cryptoasset services rests with the developer firm, the latter is a delegate subject to Article 73 MiCA. Where a developer firm, in fact, controls the operations of CASPs by legal or technical means,[78] Article 73 MiCA applies to the developer firm.

Oracles

Another important question is whether the use of oracles is a 'service or activity for the performance of operational functions'. Oracles enable smart contracts to access external, real-world data by integrating live feeds of information off-chain into the cryptoasset system. The oracle verifies and then relays critical data from the outside world into the smart contract

specifying the requirements for policies and procedures on conflicts of interest for crypto-asset service providers, Draft Final Report (2024), ESMA18-72330276-1634, pp. 32–40; Technical Standards specifying certain requirements of the Markets in Crypto-Assets Regulation (MiCA), Draft version, ESMA75-453128700-438, pp. 19, 21, 23, 106, 162, 171–72.

[76] Article 16(5) of MiFID in tandem with Article 30(2) of Commission Delegated Regulation (EU) 2017/565.

[77] The guidance is taken from a highly regulated environment for investment services. Any transfer to the cryptoasset sector must be treated with caution and requires a case-by-case assessment.

[78] We have discussed the notion of 'control' in the context of legal person and other undertakings, at Section 4.2.4, Chapter 6, and Section 7.2.3.

(and potentially vice versa as well).[79] We analogise an oracle to an informational intermediary providing crucial data feeds with a high degree of automation.[80] These oracles may be centralised or decentralised themselves; some of them are governed by DAOs whose members hold tokens ("oracle coins").

Whether or not Article 73 MiCA applies depends on the services of the CASP. Where the data transmission is a crucial precondition for the CASP's licensed activities, we hold that the CASP's relationship with the data-feed provider is governed by Article 73 MiCA. Examples here include crypto exchanges and brokerages as well as automated portfolio management and advice, where information gathering, transmission, and processing (as in pricing algorithms) are a necessity of the cryptoasset service. By contrast, the substance of custody is the safekeeping of an asset; here, the data-feed on the *pricing* of a cryptoasset is, in principle, not a crucial precondition of crypto custody. However, crypto custody may rely on other types of oracles that then qualify as crucial preconditions for crypto custody and are subject to Article 73 MiCA.[81] For instance, we can imagine an oracle that gives a signal for the taking-in of a new cryptoasset in custody based on asset flows, counterparties, and operational risks present in that cryptoasset.

In general, wherever the oracle has significant influence over the service, it is subject to Article 73 MiCA.

Joint Token-Holders

The third question of relevance here is whether the joint action of holders of cryptoassets may constitute a 'service or activity for the performance of operational functions'. For instance, if the investment decision of a portfolio manager relies on the collective decision of all token-holders, either as a binding decision or in an advisory capacity, does the transfer of responsibilities to token-holders amount to the outsourcing of an operational function? Note that, in this case, the whitelist exemption for advisory services does not apply given that the services form part of the cryptoasset business. If the same binding decision or advice was provided by one entity instead of a collective of many legal and natural persons, outsourcing would without doubt be constituted, as can be seen from Article 3(16)(h), (i) and (24), (25) MiCA as well as Article 81 MiCA which regulate portfolio management and advice in relation to cryptoassets. The fact that a service is provided by many persons collectively, rather than one person, does not change the result that a material service is provided by someone other than the CASP.

Note, however, that outsourcing is constituted only where the *CASP* offers portfolio management services or similar activities. This hints, again, at the importance of looking at the CASP's licensed activities to determine the operational function. If the CASP's own services are limited to, for instance, custody, the portfolio management decision taken by the token-holders collectively is not one of the CASP's services.

For that reason, we discuss what constitutes an "operational function" as a precondition for the application of Article 73 MiCA separately in the context of CASPs that provide custody services,

[79] Cf. Abdeljalil Beniiche, 'A Study of Blockchain Oracles' (2020), arXiv:2004.07140 [cs.CR]. Website: https://doi.org/10.48550/arXiv.2004.07140 (last accessed on 1 October 2024); K. Mammadzada, M. Iqbal, F Milani, L. García-Bañuelos and R. Matulevičius, 'Blockchain Oracles: A Framework for Blockchain-Based Applications', Business Process Management: Blockchain and Robotic Process Automation Forum (2020). Website: https://link.springer.com/chapter/10.1007/978-3-030-58779-6_2 (last accessed on 1 October 2024).

[80] Prominent examples include Band Protocol, ChainLink, Nest, and DIA.

[81] For instance, in social recovery crypto wallets, the oracle enables the management of a wallet address on the client's behalf and authorises a key recovery for them when they have provided authentication successfully, cf. 'Self-Custody—with a Little Help from Chainlink DECO,' *Chainlink* (26 January 2023). Website: https://blog.chain.link/self-custody-with-a-little-help-from-chainlink-deco/ (last accessed on 1 October 2024).

for instance, in relation to sub-custody (see Chapter 8), as well as in the context of CASPs that provide portfolio management and advice in the crypto-fund context (see Chapter 9).

7.4.5 *Prudential Requirements (Article 67 MiCA)*

The minimum capital of a CASP consists of:

- Minimum capital (between 50,000 EUR and 150,000 EUR depending on the services provided, as set out in Annex IV MiCA) and
- One quarter of the fixed overheads[82] of the preceding year (or the projected first year, in case of new CASPs), reviewed annually.

The prudential safeguards shall take the form of "funds" (see Article 3 (14) MiCA), consisting in principle of Common Equity Tier 1 items and instruments pursuant to Articles 26–30 CRR, or an insurance policy meeting the requirements of Article 71 MiCA.

These prudential requirements are very low when compared to those for credit institutions. We explain these low requirements for CASPs as analogous to those for small- and medium-sized MiFID off-balance intermediaries. Furthermore, issuers of EMTs and ARTs, which are both more bank-like with regard to their commitments, are subject to much stricter prudential capital requirements.[83]

7.4.6 *Burial Plan (Article 74 MiCA)*

Article 74 MiCA requires a burial plan and applies exclusively to CASPs subject to Articles 75–79 MiCA. This includes crypto custodians, operators of a trading platform and exchange services, and certain brokerage services. Article 74 MiCA requires a 'plan that is appropriate to support an orderly wind-down of their activities under applicable national law, including the continuity or recovery of any critical activities performed by those service providers. That plan shall demonstrate the ability of crypto-asset service providers to carry out an orderly wind-down without causing undue economic harm to their clients'. The plan needs to be aligned with national insolvency law, which is, so far, not harmonised in the field of cryptoassets.[84]

7.5 SPECIFIC CONDITIONS FOR CERTAIN CRYPTOASSET SERVICES

Chapter 3 of Title V MiCA provides detailed conditions for certain cryptoasset services that only providers of these services must fulfil. We discuss these operating requirements in turn, except for the rules on crypto custody which are discussed in Chapter 8.

[82] Article 67(3) of MiCA states on the overhead costs: 'crypto-asset service providers shall calculate their fixed overheads for the preceding year, using figures resulting from the applicable accounting framework, *by subtracting the following items from the total expenses* after distribution of profits to shareholders in their most recently audited annual financial statements or, where audited statements are not available, in annual financial statements validated by national supervisors:

(a) staff bonuses and other remuneration, to the extent that those bonuses and that remuneration depend on a net profit of the cryptoasset service providers in the relevant year;

(b) employees', directors', and partners' shares in profits;

(c) other appropriations of profits and other variable remuneration, to the extent that they are fully discretionary;

(d) non-recurring expenses from non-ordinary activities'.

[83] Cf. Chapters 6 and 7 and Article 35 of MiCA.

[84] J. Woxholth, D. A. Zetzsche, R. P. Buckley and D. W. Arner, 'Competing Claims to Crypto-assets', *Uniform Law Review* 28(2) (2024): 226–46.

TABLE 7.6 *MiFID orientation of trading platform and exchange services*

Article 76 MiCA	Subject matter	Provision equivalent to
(1)	Operating rules for the trading platform	Article 18(1–6) MiFID II
(6)	CASPs shall only be allowed to engage in matched principal trading	Article 20(7) MiFID II
(7)	CASPs shall have effective systems, procedures, and arrangements	Article 48(1) MiFID II
(8)	CASPs shall inform the competent authority in the event of market abuse or attempted market abuse	Article 31(3) MiFID II
(9)	CASPs shall make public any bid and ask for prices and the depth of trading interest at those prices	Article 3(1) and Article 8(1) MiFIR
(10)	CASPs shall make public the price, volume, and time of the transactions executed	Articles 6(1) and 10(1) MiFIR
(11)	CASPs shall make the information published available to the public on a reasonable commercial basis and ensure non-discriminatory access	Article 13(1) MiFIR
(13)	CASPs shall ensure that their fee is transparent, fair, and non-discriminatory	Article 48(9) MiFID II
(14)	CASPs shall maintain resources and have back-up facilities	Articles 67(3), 26(7) para. 5, 64(4), 65(5), and 66(3) MiFIR[85]
(15)	CASPs shall keep relevant data at the disposal of the competent authority	Article 25(2) MiFIR

7.5.1 *Operating a Trading Platform (Article 76 MiCA)*

Article 76 MiCA mimics the MiFID rules on trading platforms and exchange services, as further laid out in Table 7.6.

Article 76(2)–(5) MiCA provides bespoke rules for cryptoassets, responding to widespread abuses and cyberattacks throughout the Crypto Winter. Trading platform providers:

- Must ensure compliance with the platform's operating rules and assess suitability prior to admitting any in-scope cryptoasset to trading. In terms of the platform's suitability assessment, 'the reliability of the technical solutions used and the potential association to illicit or fraudulent activities, taking into account the experience, track record and reputation of the issuer of those crypto-assets and its development team'[86] is a key concern;
- Must ensure that the operating rules prohibit the trading of 'crypto-assets that have an inbuilt anonymisation function unless the holders of those crypto-assets and their transaction history can be identified by the crypto-asset service providers operating a trading platform for crypto-assets'.[87] The rationale behind this rule is twofold. It pairs client protection (as the counterparty is identifiable and thus a title remains enforceable) with the effectiveness of AML/CTF measures;
- Must ensure that the operating rules are drawn up in English or an official language of the platform's home or host Member State, respectively;[88] and

[85] All these provisions set out how to offer and maintain their services at all times. Not for reporting purposes. But the rational is similar.
[86] Cf. Article 76(2) sent. 2 of MiCA.
[87] Cf. Article 76(3) of MiCA.
[88] Cf. Article 76(4) of MiCA.

- Must not 'deal on own account on the trading platform (...) they operate, including where they provide the exchange of crypto-assets for funds or other crypto-assets'.[89] While this requirement would have prevented a trading platform operator (e.g., Binance or FTX) from trading as a counterparty of trading clients on an own account, the rule does not prevent trading of group entities on the same platform (such as Alameda, FTX's investment entity, to trade on the FTX exchange). Conflicts deriving from group entities' activities, however, are covered by the general conflict management provision of Article 72(1)(a)(ii) MiCA; for conflicts, the general accord of conflict management (identify, prevent, manage, and disclose) applies.

Details will be specified in implementing legislation.[90]

7.5.2 *Exchange Services (Article 77)*

Article 77 MiCA on exchange services deals with a swap where one party is a commercial provider of swap services (the CASP) and another party is a client. Divided into parts, the service consists of a sale of one type of cryptoasset [CA1] and a purchase of another type of asset: the CASP takes in either "funds" (i.e., cash and highly liquid bankable assets) or other cryptoassets [CA2] in return for granting CA1. From a client protection perspective, accessibility, continuity, and reliability of the service (i.e., avoidance of fraud and insolvency), the fair or at least foreseeable pricing of the asset, and the avoidance of insider trading are key concerns.

In turn, pursuant to Article 77 MiCA, CASPs offering exchange services must:

- Establish a non-discriminatory commercial policy that indicates, in particular, the type of clients they agree to transact with and the conditions that shall be met by such clients;
- Publish a firm price of the cryptoassets or a method for determining the price thereof and execute client orders at the price displayed at the time when the order for exchange was made final;
- Publish any applicable limit determined by that CASP on the amount to be exchanged; and
- Publish information about the transactions concluded by them, such as transaction volumes and prices.

Details will be specified in implementing legislation.[91]

[89] Cf. Article 76(5) of MiCA.

[90] The respective Technical Standard mandates a set of information to be included in the application for authorisation of a CASP or the notification of an entity intending to operate a trading platform, cf. Technical Standards specifying certain requirements of the Markets in Crypto-Assets Regulation (MiCA), Draft Final Report (2024), ESMA18-72330276-1634, pp. 59–61, 94–95. Additionally, the respective Technical Standard imposes rules on the transparency of trading data for CASPs operating a trading platform, on the content and format of their order book records and further dedicated record-keeping obligations, cf. Technical Standards specifying certain requirements of the Markets in Crypto-Assets Regulation (MiCA), Draft version, ESMA75-453128700-438, pp. 110–27, 128–35, 172–73.

[91] The respective Technical Standard mandates a set of information to be included in the application for authorisation of a CASP or the notification of an entity intending to provide exchange services to ensure best execution, cf. Technical Standards specifying certain requirements of the Markets in Crypto-Assets Regulation (MiCA), Draft Final Report (2024), ESMA18-72330276-1634, pp. 60–61, 96. Additionally, the respective Technical Standard mandates dedicated record-keeping, cf. Technical Standards specifying certain requirements of the Markets in Crypto-Assets Regulation (MiCA), Draft version, ESMA75-453128700-438, pp. 173–74.

TABLE 7.7 *MiFID orientation of MiCA's regulation of brokerage services*

MiCA Articles	Subject matter	Provision equivalent to
78(1)	Best possible result for their clients when the CASP executes the order for cryptoassets on behalf of clients	Article 27(1) MiFID II, Articles 25(2) and 26(2) Commission Directive 2010/43/EU
78(2)	Effective execution arrangements	Articles 27(4) and 28(1) MiFID II
78(3)	Appropriate and clear information for clients	Article 27(5) para. 2 MiFID II
78(4)	Execution of orders in accordance with the order execution policy	Article 27(8) MiFID II
78(5)	Prior express consent in the event of order execution outside of a trading platform	Article 27(5) para. 3 MiFID II
78(6)	Monitoring of the order execution	Article 27(7) MiFID II
79(2)	Adequate procedures on conflicts of interest	Article 14(1) para. 2 AIFMD, Article 31(2)(b) Commission Delegated Regulation 231/2013, and Article 23 MiFID II
80(1)	Establishment and implementation of procedures and arrangements for the proper transmission of client orders	Article 27(4) MiFID II (with slightly different wording)
80(2)	Remuneration, discount, or non-monetary benefit are prohibited	Article 27(2) MiFID II
80(3)	Information misuse in relation to pending client orders is prohibited	Article 67(3) MiFID II (regulating the order handling)

7.5.3 *Brokerage Services (Articles 78–80 MiCA)*

The execution of orders on behalf of clients, the placing of cryptoassets, and the order reception and transmission on behalf of clients as regulated in Articles 78–80 MiCA, closely follow the MiFID examples, are set out in Table 7.7.

Articles 78 and 80 MiCA reflect the main content of Article 27 MiFID, the core rule of the MiFID framework on order reception, transmission, and execution. While MiCA does not foresee a detailed entitlement to adopt implementing legislation, we have little doubt that detailed guidance will follow the Level 1 legislation.[92]

As for placement, Article 79 MiCA pronounces the minimum placement information (which is contained under MiFID in the transaction and order records); as compared to MiFID, the wording is more pronounced in order to prevent sometimes uncertain market practices as to whether the CASP performs a regulated cryptoasset service, given that CASPs tend to offer multiple services at the same time. According to Article 79 MiCA, the CASP, prior to entering into the contract when offering the placing of cryptoassets, must communicate and obtain consent for:

- The type of placement including whether a minimum amount of purchase is guaranteed or not;
- An indication of the amount of transaction fees associated with the proposed placement;

[92] On the record-keeping obligations of the CASP in relation to reception, transmission, and execution cf. Articles 11 and 13 and Annex I of the RTS on record-keeping by cryptoasset service providers in Technical Standards specifying certain requirements of the Markets in Crypto-Assets Regulation (MiCA), Draft version, ESMA75-453128700-438, pp. 165–66, 169, 174.

- The likely timing, process, and price for the proposed operation; and
- Information about the targeted purchasers.

The legal nature of these stipulations is uncertain. We hold that MiCA in this case sets relevant rules for private law, in particular, on the minimum conditions for the establishment of a binding contract. Where either this information has not been provided or the CASP cannot show consent by the issuer or person seeking admission to trading, MiCA prevents a contract to be established between the CASP and the issuer/arranger. In turn, the CASP may only ask for compensation for unjust enrichment on the side of the issuer.

The placing of cryptoassets is a service prone to conflicts of interest, as most brokers will try to sell the cryptoassets to their existing clients first, as these carry the greatest likelihood of success, particularly in a hot issue context. In turn, MiCA stresses the need to establish robust conflict procedures,[93] emphasising the content of the general conflict rules laid down in Article 72 MiCA.

Details will be specified in implementing legislation.[94]

7.5.4 *Portfolio Management and Advice (Article 81 MiCA)*

Article 81 MiCA mimics the MiFID rules on investment advice and portfolio management, as laid out in Table 7.8.

While Article 81 MiCA closely follows the MiFID example, it is surprising that the risk characteristics of cryptoassets under Article 81(9) MiCA do not include the significant *operational risks* prevalent in crypto, as one of the main causes for losses. Furthermore, CASPs are prohibited from providing advice and portfolio management where information about clients' suitability is lacking or the cryptoasset is unsuitable for them, while Article 25 (3) MiFID mandates that intermediaries provide in these cases a warning only. In practice, however, intermediaries have refrained from client-oriented services in these cases due to a lack of guidance on how to exercise them; the result of both rules is the same. Article 81 MiCA is of the utmost practical importance for digital asset funds, where AIFMs often outsource the investment decision to specialists. Investment advice and (individual) portfolio management with regard to financial instruments, including DLT-based ones, are carried out by MiFID firms as delegates to the AIFM. Moreover, investment advice and (individual) portfolio management with regard to financial instruments are often carried out by AIFMs as side services to their fund clients (cf. Article 6(4) AIFMD). Yet, neither MiFID nor Article 6(4) AIFMD provides an authorisation requirement for these services with regard to cryptoassets within the scope of MiCA. Here, MiCA's gap-filling function comes into play.

Assume that the AIFM provides the core services of collective portfolio management in relation to cryptoassets, and the AIFM delegates portfolio management or investment advice in relation to cryptoassets to a third party. In this case, the AIFM must comply with Article

[93] Article 79(2) of MiCA explicitly requires to consider conflicts arising from CASPs placing the cryptoassets with their own clients, an overestimate or underestimate of the proposed price, and (non-)monetary incentives offered to the CASPs.

[94] The respective Technical Standard foresees a dedicated set of obligatory information to be included in the application for authorisation of a CASP or the notification process of an entity intending to provide reception, transmission, and execution services, cf. Technical Standards specifying certain requirements of the Markets in Crypto-Assets Regulation (MiCA), Draft Final Report (2024), ESMA18-72330276-1634, pp. 61–62, 97–98, as well as dedicated record-keeping obligations, cf. Technical Standards specifying certain requirements of the Markets in Crypto-Assets Regulation (MiCA), Draft version, ESMA75-453128700-438, pp. 162–67, 169, 174.

TABLE 7.8 *MiFID orientation of MiCA's portfolio management and advice rules*

MiCAArticle 81	Matter regarding portfolio management and advice on cryptoassets	Provision equivalent to
(1)	Suitability for clients	Article 25(2) MiFID II
(2)	Information on independent or restricted advice	Article 24(4) MiFID II
(3)	Duty to consider a broad portfolio for independent advice	Article 24(7) MiFID II
(4)	Information on all costs and related charges	Article 24(4)(c) MiFID II
(5)	Retention of fees, commissions, and any (non-) monetary benefits prohibited	Article 24(8) MiFID II
(6)	Retention of inducements in cases of independent advice	Article 24(9) MiFID II
(7)	CASPs to ensure for knowledge and competence of adviser	Article 25(1) MiFID II
(8)	Inquiry into client's expertise for suitability assessment	Article 25(1) MiFID II
(9)	Mandatory warning on risks of volatility, liquidity, and losses	Article 48(2) Com. Del. Reg. 2017/565 (adjusted to CA)
(10)	Policies and procedures for conducting client assessments	Article 54(7) Com. Del. Reg. 2017/565
(11)	Prohibition on the provision of advice where information is lacking or the cryptoasset product is unsuitable	Article 25(3) MiFID II (warning only)
(12)	Regular reviews of suitability assessment	Article 54(13) Com. Del. Reg. 2017/565
(13)	Report on the suitability test specifying the advice	Article 54(12) Com. Del. Reg. 2017/565
(14)	Periodic statements on activities and performance	Article 60(1) Com. Del. Reg. 2017/565
(15)	ESMA guideline powers	Article 25(9) MiFID II (in part)

20 AIFMD on outsourcing.[95] Article 20(1)(c) AIFMD requires an authorisation of the delegate with regard to the regulated activity's "portfolio management" unless the delegate resides in a country that does not foresee a licensing scheme for portfolio management; then, the AIFM must ask its NCA for approval of the delegation. MiCA now introduces a harmonised licence for portfolio management of EU entities with regard to cryptoassets; the road is, however, blocked for the approval of delegations by any EU NCA under different terms. Where the delegate resides in a third country that does not provide for a licensing scheme of portfolio management in relation to cryptoassets, the AIFM must instead (still) apply to its NCA for approval of the delegation.

Given the uncertainty as to which digital assets qualify as financial instruments and are thus out of the scope of MiCA (cf. Chapters 3 and 4), Article 81 MiCA leads, in practice, to a dual authorisation requirement (and potentially an additional approval requirement): for cryptoassets qualifying as financial instruments, the delegate must have a licence under MiFID, and for cryptoassets in MiCA's scope, the delegate must have an authorisation under Articles 59 and 60 MiCA. Finally, for assets that qualify neither as financial instruments nor as in-scope assets of

[95] For MiCA side services where the UCITS ManCO and AIFM qualify as CASPs in scope of Title V of MiCA, Article 73 of MiCA foresees an outsourcing rule that does not require authorisation of the delegate.

MiCA (in particular, NFTs), the AIFM must ask its NCA for approval of the delegation. Due to the legal uncertainty as to which digital asset qualifies for which category,[96] AIFMs will feel pressed to require their delegates to have both MiFID and MiCA CASP licence and, on top of that, to ask their NCA for a general rather than specific approval of the respective delegation.

Details will be specified in implementing legislation.[97]

7.5.5 *Transfer Services (Article 82 MiCA)*

Transfer services regulated in Article 82 MiCA do not involve a commercial transaction per se, although often a commercial transaction (such as a sale or an asset swap, which may be executed by way of an exchange service) may be the reason underlying the transaction. Here, the accessibility, continuity, and reliability of the service (i.e., the avoidance of fraud and insolvency) are key concerns, in addition to AML/CTF objectives.

Where the cryptoasset qualifies as an EMT, the given EMTs are treated as e-money[98] and e-money transfers are regulated by PSD,[99] and the transfer qualifies as payment services under PSD. Where EMTs (or outright e-money as any other type of "funds") are transferred, the PSD is paramount to the rules of MiCA. PSD governs the transaction, MiCA – in line with its gap-filling function – steps back.[100]

For other transactions, Article 82 MiCA prescribes the minimum content of the transfer contract by requiring CASPs to include:

- The identities of the parties to the agreement;
- A description of the modalities of the transfer service provided;
- A description of the security systems used by the CASP;
- The fees applied by the CASP (note that there may be two types of fees though, one charged by the transferring CASP and another charged by the receiving CASP); and
- The applicable law.[101]

Details will be specified in implementing legislation.[102]

96 See Section 4.4.

97 The respective Technical Standard mandates the provision of certain information as a precondition for the application for authorisation of a CASP or the notification process of an entity intending to provide advice or portfolio management services, seeking to ensure the skills and expertise of natural persons providing advice or portfolio management, as well as the appropriateness of the human and financial resources, cf. Technical Standards specifying certain requirements of the Markets in Crypto-Assets Regulation (MiCA), Draft Final Report (2024), ESMA18-72330276-1634, pp.62–63, 98, as well as dedicated record-keeping obligations, cf. Technical Standards specifying certain requirements of the Markets in Crypto-Assets Regulation (MiCA), Draft version, ESMA75-453128700-438, pp. 174–76.

98 Cf. Article 48(2) of MiCA.

99 According to Recital para. 25 of PSD, the PSD 'lays down rules on the execution of payment transactions where the funds are electronic money as defined in Directive 2009/110/EC'. In turn, Article 4(25) of PSD states that 'funds' include 'banknotes and coins, scriptural money or electronic money as defined in point (2) of Article 2 of Directive 2009/110/EC'.

100 Recital para. 93 of MiCA.

101 Details will be prescribed by ESMA guidelines, cf. Article 82(2) of MiCA.

102 The respective Technical Standards foresees a dedicated set of obligatory information for the authorisation of a CASP or the notification process of an entity intending to provide transfer services, cf. Technical Standards specifying certain requirements of the Markets in Crypto-Assets Regulation (MiCA), Draft Final Report (2024), ESMA18-72330276-1634, pp. 62–63, 98, as well as dedicated record-keeping obligations, cf. Technical Standards specifying certain requirements of the Markets in Crypto-Assets Regulation (MiCA), Draft version, ESMA75-453128700-438, pp. 176–77.

7.6 CONCLUSION

MiCA's CASP rules have been taken to a large extent from existing EU financial law. Proximity to MiFID/MiFIR is desirable to reduce costs of MiFID-authorised intermediaries functioning as CASPs (cf. Article 60 MiCA) and to achieve coherence and convergence with existing EU financial law. Given the proximity to MiFID here, we encourage the ESMA to propose, and the European Commission to adopt, implementing rules very similar to those existing under MiFID/MiFIR.

Similar if not identical rules are desirable given that many CASPs, in particular, those financial institutions relying on for the right to provide cryptoasset services pursuant to Article 60 MiCA, have to apply MiCA *in addition* to MiFID, but also PSD2, or UCITSD/AIFMD, depending on their initial authorisation. Identical rules would also provide a practical solution to the scope conundrum where, for quite some time, uncertainty will prevail as to which digital assets are in-scope for MiCA or rather qualify as another regulated activity subject to Article 2(4) MiCA (see Chapter 4). While the Level 2 legislative text aims to align the MiCA framework with existing financial legislation, namely, MiFID, PSD2, or UCITS/AIFMD, many Level 2 provisions lack the clarity and thoroughness of the existing financial legislation, resulting in (unnecessary) legal uncertainty and enhanced implementing costs.

Nevertheless, while cryptoassets in many respects raise old issues and thus are not special, *some* fields are indeed special and raise new risks[103] which we expect to be addressed by way of somewhat unique implementing legislation. These include (1) valuation, (2) custody, (3) technical risk management, in particular, on operational risks relating to the technology used, (4) decentralisation of functions, and (5) the programme of operations as well as wind-down plans reflecting these unique features of cryptoassets.

[103] See Zetzsche *et al.*, 'Remaining Regulatory Challenges in Digital Finance', pp. 14, 46 et seq.

8

Crypto Custody

8.1 INTRODUCTION

In light of widespread asset misappropriations throughout the Crypto Winter, crypto custody has become a topic of major practical importance.[1] This chapter discusses its regulation in Articles 3 (17), 70(1), and 75 MiCA.

After first examining international developments (Section 8.2), we discuss the scope of MiCA's custody rules (Section 8.3) prior to analysing the impact of MiCA's general requirements for CASPs, in particular fiduciary duties and the safekeeping rule in Article 70(1) MiCA on custody (Section 8.4). We then discuss in detail the requirements of Article 75 on crypto custody (Section 8.5) after which we explore how crypto custodians regulated by MiCA interact with other regulatory intermediaries that safekeep assets either as their main business or as side services to supplement their brokerage or asset management services, including investment firms under MiFID, credit institutions that provide investment services, and fund depositaries regulated by AIFMD (Section 8.6), and then conclude (Section 8.7).

8.2 CRYPTO CUSTODIANS ON THE INTERNATIONAL AGENDA

The Crypto Winter of 2022–23 and the turmoil it has subsequently brought about have led to large-scale losses for many investors, especially retail investors.[2] In turn, regulators worldwide took steps to harmonise crypto-regulation.[3]

[1] For an overview of incidents relating to crypto custody, see D. A. Zetzsche, J. Sinnig and A. Nikolakopoulou, 'Crypto Custody', *Capital Markets Law Journal*, 19 (2024): 207–29, 210–12.

[2] See G. Cornelli, S. Doerr, J. Frost and L. Gambacorta, 'Crypto Shocks and Retail Losses', *BIS Bulletin* 69. Bank for International Settlements (2023). Website www.bis.org\\publ\\bisbull69.htm (last accessed on 1 October 2024) (finding that, in the wake of the Terra/Luna collapse and the FTX bankruptcy, crypto trading activity increased markedly, with large and sophisticated investors selling and smaller retail investors buying. Data on major crypto trading platforms over August 2015 to December 2022 show that, as a result, a majority of crypto app users in nearly all economies made losses on their Bitcoin holdings.).

[3] For a complete overview of global regulators' activities, see Zetzsche *et al.*, 'Crypto Custody', pp. 210–12.

8.2.1 *FSB Work on Financial Stability*

While not addressing custodians explicitly, the Financial Stability Board (FSB)[4] recommended a comprehensive regulation of CASPs with multiple functions, subjecting them 'to appropriate regulation, supervision, and oversight that comprehensively address the risks associated with individual functions and the risks arising from the combination of functions, including but not limited to requirements regarding conflicts of interest and separation of certain functions, activities, or incorporation, as appropriate'. This stance may be attributable to the FSB's focus on stability.

8.2.2 *IOSCO's Recommendations on Crypto Custody*

The International Organisation of Securities Commissions (IOSCO) has been more explicit on crypto custody and provided extensive guidance on custody-related risks and the safeguarding of client monies and assets.[5] Key risks identified include the lack or deficiency of asset segregation, the re-use of assets, a custodian's liability, and ownership considerations. IOSCO issued five recommendations with a view to ensuring that 'where Client Monies and Assets are held by CASPs they are held safely, and transferred securely, and that inappropriate mixing of assets and other potential abuses are avoided'.[6]

IOSCO's starting point is the recognition of large-scale non-compliance, outlined as follows:

> 'Many retail investors conduct their trading activities through, and entrust custody of their cryptoassets to, centralised intermediaries, referred to as CASPs. Many CASPs, including those with the largest market share and highest trading volumes, have demonstrated a consistent lack of willingness to comply with applicable regulatory frameworks that seek to achieve investor protection and market integrity outcomes, and in many cases structured their operations in a way to evade such frameworks. By not complying with such measures, CASPs profit off retail investors while seeking to avoid the crucial safeguards that come with adherence to regulatory requirements.'[7]

While listing a number of abuses involving crypto custodians, IOSCO has also showcased the importance of robust regulation, noting that Japanese laws on crypto custody were quite robust, following the lessons learned from the Mt. Gox insolvency in 2014. In turn, FTX Japan became the first FTX affiliate to allow customers to withdraw cryptoassets and cash in 2023, as a result of its decent holding of client assets in accordance with Japanese regulations.[8]

8.2.2.1 *Cryptoasset Context*

To understand IOSCO's high-level recommendations, some context may be instructive. A particular concern of customer and investor protection is the *technical structure of segregation and custody* in the crypto industry. So far, "hot" custody is common practice, whereby the wallet

[4] Cf. Financial Stability Board, 'High-Level Recommendations for the Regulation, Supervision and Oversight of Crypto-Asset Activities and Markets: Final report', Recommendation 9 (2023).

[5] See IOSCO, 'Policy Recommendations for Crypto and Digital Asset Markets, Consultation Report', CR01/2023 (2023). Website www.iosco.org\\library\\pubdocs\\pdf\\IOSCOPD734.pdf (last accessed on 1 October 2024); and IOSCO, 'Policy Recommendations for Crypto and Digital Asset Markets, Final Report', FR11/2023 (2023). Website www.iosco.org/library/pubdocs/pdf/IOSCOPD747.pdf (last accessed on 1 October 2024).

[6] IOSCO, 'Policy Recommendations for Crypto and Digital Asset Markets, Final Report', p. 7.

[7] IOSCO, 'Policy Recommendations for Crypto and Digital Asset Markets, Final Report', pp. 7 and 11–12.

[8] IOSCO, 'Policy Recommendations for Crypto and Digital Asset Markets, Consultation Report', p. 53.

provider holds the private keys of their clients and thus establishes something akin to omnibus accounts that are permanently online and linked to the distributed ledger. Concurrently, crypto intermediaries often manage clients' private keys, which are the technical means of confirming ownership of the cryptoassets held on the DLT. In this set up, and depending on the technology used, *some* crypto intermediaries storing private keys for their clients represent a single point of failure – contrary to the DeFi philosophy.[9] Cyberattacks, fraud, or malfunctions can expose the private key (which together with the public one allows transactions to be initiated) for some seconds at least and prompt fraudulent transactions from the omnibus account to another controlled by the attacker or fraudster.[10]

Many other concerns have been reported in the context of custody. For instance, some crypto intermediaries have re-used client assets held in custody without clients' consent. This has been facilitated by the unclear division of functions and authority within a crypto ecosystem, so that it is not always transparent who performs key functions such as the contractual party, the liquidity provider, or the margin agent. Note that any of these functions can also be provided by a group of nodes acting on the stack rather than the Systemically Important Crypto Intermediary (SICI) running the ecosystem.[11]

Furthermore, the use of omnibus accounts may result in the blending of an intermediary's own and third-party claims in cryptoassets.[12] For determining ownership, the industry seems not much to use the tracing feature implicit in blockchain and distributed ledgers' endless chain of transactions. The private law on competing claims stemming from the re-use of assets is unsettled, which renders any true assessment of who holds an asset in bankruptcy and fraud cases very difficult.[13]

Some initial inquiries[14] into the terms and conditions of wallet providers have revealed, for instance, that:

- Both providers of custodial and non-custodial wallets contractually exclude, in almost all cases, liability for lost assets.
- There is little information on what happens in cases of distress, malfunctions, and insolvency.
- Whether the provider keeps omnibus or segregated accounts is rarely disclosed clearly to users.
- Whether the provider stores cryptoassets in so-called hot or cold storage is rarely disclosed in the terms and conditions (though it may be disclosed on the website).
- There are no clauses entitling, or obliging, the provider to represent a token-holder in litigation or measures resulting in damage mitigation.

[9] D. W. Arner, D. A. Zetzsche, R. P. Buckley and J. M. Kirkwood, 'The Financialization of Crypto: Lessons from FTX and the Crypto Winter of 2022–2023'. Research Paper No. 2023/19, University of Hong Kong Faculty of Law, and Law Research Paper No. 23–31, UNSW (2023). Website http://dx.doi.org/10.2139/ssrn.4372516 (last accessed on 1 October 2024).

[10] E. Zamani *et al.*, 'On the Security Risks of the Blockchain', *Journal of Computer Information Systems*, 60(6) (2020): 495.

[11] Arner *et al.*, 'The Financialization of Crypto'.

[12] Arner *et al.*, 'The Financialization of Crypto'.

[13] See para. 13 and Woxholth *et al.*, 'Competing Claims to Crypto-Assets', pp. 226–46.

[14] See cf. D. A. Zetzsche and A. Nikolakopoulou, 'Crypto Custody and Crypto Wallets – An Empirical Analysis'. University of Luxembourg Working Paper (2024). Website https://dx.doi.org/10.2139/ssrn.4769396 (last accessed on 1 October 2024).

These insights suggest that terms and conditions are currently drafted in a one-dimensional way and provide little certainty or protection for users. All in all, custody warrants regulatory attention.

8.2.2.2 *Content of Recommendations*

On that basis, IOSCO promoted the adoption of regulation and supervision of crypto custodians, thereby the harmonisation of cryptoasset regulation.

Recommendation 13 requires that a CASP shall be mandated to place client assets in trust or to otherwise segregate them from the CASP's proprietary assets. Meanwhile, Recommendation 14 asks for extensive clear disclosures by CASPs on:

- How client assets are held, and the arrangements for safeguarding these assets and/or their private keys;
- The use (if any) of an independent custodian, sub-custodian, or related party custodian;
- The extent to which client assets are aggregated or pooled within omnibus client accounts, the rights of individual clients with respect to the aggregated or pooled assets, and the risks of loss arising from any pooling or aggregating activities;
- Risks arising from the CASP's handling or moving of client assets, whether directly or indirectly, such as through a cross-chain bridge; and
- Full and accurate information on the obligations and responsibilities of a CASP with respect to the use of client assets, as well as private keys, including the terms for their restitution and on the risks involved.

Recommendation 15 asks that CASPs have 'systems, policies, and procedures to conduct regular and frequent reconciliations of Client Assets subject to appropriate independent assurance'. At the same time, Recommendation 16 asks for regulation seeking the adoption of appropriate systems, policies, and procedures to mitigate the risk of loss, theft, or inaccessibility of client assets.

Articles 70(1) and 75 MiCA on safekeeping and custody constitute the EU's approach to regulation of crypto custody, which we analyse in light of these international experiences and recommendations.

8.3 SCOPE

A CASP is a legal person or other undertaking (Section 7.2.3) who provides one or more cryptoasset services pursuant to Article 3(16) MiCA (cf. Section 7.2.1) as an occupation or a business to clients on a professional basis (cf. Section 7.2.2). Some additional criteria follow from MiCA's scope (cf. Section 7.2.3).

8.3.1 *Custody as Cryptoasset Services (Article 3 (17) MiCA)*

Article 3(1)(16)(a) MiCA regulates 'custody and administration of cryptoassets on behalf of clients' as a cryptoasset service subject to Title V MiCA. Among these two functions, provision of custody is the qualifying factor. Administration as such does not constitute a cryptoasset service as it could also be provided by accounting firms or other advisers in the financial sector.

Of no relevance here is whether crypto custody is provided as a main or ancillary service. In turn, the custody rules apply to crypto exchanges that also provide custody as well as to custodial wallet providers whose sole business is the provision of crypto custody.

Article 3(1)(17) MiCA defines 'custody and administration of cryptoassets on behalf of clients' as 'the safekeeping or controlling, on behalf of clients, of cryptoassets or of the means of access to such cryptoassets, where applicable in the form of private cryptographic keys.' The definition is noteworthy given that prior to MiCA regulatory experts discussed whether cryptoassets may be held in custody:[15] a DLT does not allow for the exclusion of anyone else's rights, but rather the rights themselves depend on their recognition by the other nodes of the DLT. Proponents of the counterview argued that cryptoassets can only be registered in the name of the holder rather than be held 'in custody', as custody would entail a physical element (akin to possession) which is impossible in the crypto context. Article 3(1)(17) MiCA in tandem with Annex II.1 MiFID has since closed that debate for the purposes of EU financial law, with far-reaching repercussions, for instance, in the context of digital assets qualifying as financial instruments. In particular, investment firms and credit institutions functioning as traditional custodians become potentially subject to the rules on custody under Article 75 MiCA when they hold crypto-assets. Beforehand, they were only subject to the rules of safekeeping.[16]

8.3.2 *Control over the Private Keys vs. Non-custodial Wallets*

Given that a cryptoasset is intangible and its existence depends on recognition by the nodes in the DLT, Article 3(1)(17) MiCA defines that custody 'means the safekeeping or controlling ... of the means of access to such cryptoassets, where applicable in the form of private cryptographic keys'.[17] The former is supplemented by Recital 83, stating that the custody agreement shall 'specify, inter alia, the nature of the service provided, which could include the holding of cryptoassets belonging to clients *or* the means of access to such cryptoassets, in which case the client might keep control of the cryptoassets in custody. Alternatively, the cryptoassets or the means of access to them could be transferred to the full control of the cryptoasset service provider' (italics added by authors). The regulatory focus with regard to crypto custody is hence on the control of the means of access to such cryptoassets.

In simple terms, control over their clients' private keys means control of the cryptoassets assigned to those keys.[18] Each user has, typically, a pair or pairs of private–public keys consisting of a private (secret) key from which a public (openly disclosed) key is mathematically derived. The public key is functionally equivalent to a bank account number that "identifies" it to other users so the account can receive or send funds, while the private key is the functional equivalent of the PIN code or the signature in a bank cheque that enables the holder to control and spend the bank account balance. Meanwhile, a crypto wallet is a digital tool that stores these keys.[19]

[15] Cf. S. N. Hooghiemstra, 'Depositary Regulation', in D. A. Zetzsche, *The Alternative Investment Fund Managers Directive* (Alphen aaden Rijn: Wolters Kluwer, 2020), 3rd ed., pp. 465–66.

[16] Cf. para. 9.5. See also D. A. Zetzsche, F. Annunziata and J. Sinnig, 'Digital Assets, MiCA and EU Investment Fund Law' (2023). Website: https://dx.doi.org/10.2139/ssrn.4637019 (last accessed on 1 October 2024) (making the same arguments for UCITS investing in financial instruments).

[17] Article 3(1)(17) of MiCA, Regulation 2023/1114, OJ 2023 No. L150.

[18] For an overview, cf. C. Goforth and Y. Guseva, *Regulation of Cryptoassets*, American Casebook Series (2nd ed.) (Eagan, MN: West Academic Publishing, 2022), pp. 760–81,790; De Filippi and Wright, *Blockchain and the Law*, pp. 14–16, 20–29; S. Small, 'Bitcoin: The Napster of Currency', *Houston Journal of International Law*, 37 (2015): 588 et seq.; P. Maume, L. Maute and M. Fromberger, *The Law of Crypto Assets* (London: Bloomsbury, 2022), pp. 6–10; W. Kaal and H. Howe, 'Custody of Digital Assets', *Jurimetrics*, 63(2) (2023): 169–95.

[19] De Filippi and Wright, *Blockchain and the Law*, p. 21; Small, 'Bitcoin', pp. 588–89; Maume *et al.*, *The Law of Crypto Assets*, p. 10; M. Haentjens, T. De Graaf and I. Kokorin, 'The Failed Hopes of Disintermediation: Crypto-Custodian Insolvency, Legal Risks and How to Avoid Them', *Leiden Law School Research Paper, Hazelhoff Research Paper Series and Singapore Journal of Legal Studies* (forthcoming), (2020): pp. 9–12.

However, MiCA does not specify exactly what "control" over the keys entails. This is an important feature when it comes to defining which wallet providers fall under the definition of Article 3(1)(17) MiCA, thereby delineating providers offering custodial wallet services from those offering a so-called self- or non-custodial wallet outside of MiCA's scope.[20] This distinction is important given that practice has developed a full spectrum of custodial, non-custodial, and middle-ground wallet solutions.[21]

On one side of the spectrum are custodial solutions where clients do not have direct access to either the cryptoassets or the private keys. The custodian generates fresh public–private key pairs (or wallets) for the cryptoassets they accept to hold in custody. The safekeeping and recovery of the keys and assets here are tied to the custodian.[22]

On the other side of the spectrum are custody solutions where *only* the client has possession of the keys (so-called self-custody). For these cases, MiCA's recitals clarify that the service provider is outside the definition of custody and thus does not provide a cryptoasset service under MiCA.[23]

The users will generate and control their own key pairs to hold cryptoassets. This usually happens via a hierarchical deterministic wallet[24] with a seed encoded as mnemonic,[25] where the seed is the master key, randomly generated during the wallet initialisation by the user, and the latter needs to back it up.[26] If the user loses access to their wallet and the seed, their assets are utterly lost.[27]

For that reason, middle-ground custody solutions share control over the keys in some way between the user and the wallet provider. Where self-custody is defined by the users' exclusive key control, these cases are borderline and need to be assessed according to the way in which control over the key is exercised.

We draw the line here based on the risks clients are facing that rely on the custody solution: where clients face the risk that the means of access could be stolen or obtained through 'inside jobs' by parties or persons not entitled to the assets, these typical custodial risks addressed by Title V MiCA do exist. In these cases, MiCA rules (should) apply. In turn, we hold that MiCA applies to the first group of middle-ground custody solutions where all relevant access data (i.e., where all keys are mere datasets) can be obtained from the service providers' staff, servers, and algorithms but not to middle-ground custody solutions where no conduct on the side of the wallet provider or its staff *alone* is sufficient to obtain control over the assets.

[20] Recital para. 83 of MiCA *in fine*.

[21] Examples of custodial wallet providers include CEFFU, Coinbase Custody, Taurus, BitGo, and Seba Bank; non-custodial wallet providers include Trezor, Atomic Wallet, and MetaMask; middle ground solutions include Ledger Recover, Zengo wallet, and Casa 2-of-3 multisig wallet.

[22] For custodial wallet providers' examples, see note 55.

[23] Recital para. 83 of MiCA *in fine*.

[24] See Gemini Cryptopedia, 'What Are HD Crypto Wallets?' (2022). Website www.gemini.com\\cryptopedia\\hd-crypto-wallets-hierachichal-deterministic (last accessed on 1 October 2024) (stating that 'A hierarchical-deterministic (HD) wallet generates a new key pair from a master key pair for each crypto transaction to enhance privacy and security. Its hierarchical structure resembles that of a tree, with the master key "determining" the key pairs that follow it in the hierarchy. [. . .] The vast majority of wallets are hierarchically deterministic.').

[25] The wallet is deterministic because the same seed-master key will always produce the same sequence of keys even when imported to new wallets. The seed is a recovery mechanism. The mnemonic supports information retention or retrieval of the access data to the cryptoasset (the 'keys'). Source: Chapter 5. 'Wallets' in A. M. Antonopoulos, *Mastering Bitcoin: Programming the Open Blockchain* (2nd ed.) (Sebastopol, CA: O'Reilly Media, 2017).

[26] For non-custodial wallet providers' examples, see note 55.

[27] V. Buterin, 'Why We Need Wide Adoption of Social Recovery Wallets' (2021). Website https://vitalik.eth.limo/general/2021/01/11/recovery.html (last accessed on 1 October 2024).

In short, whenever the service provider can present a single point of failure that leads to a potential loss of assets, MiCA applies. By contrast, *truly* shared control, where no-one can ever act without the user's consent, is not "control" for the purposes of Article 3(1)(17) MiCA.[28]

8.3.3 *Legal Person or Other Undertaking*

If a person provides a crypto-asset service (CAS) as a business on a professional basis, it is subject to authorisation under Article 59 MiCA. Note also that a person cannot avoid the authorisation requirement by claiming that the person is acting as a sole trader or as a group of persons (for instance, developers) by claiming a legal entity is lacking.[29]

8.3.4 *Partially vs. Fully Decentralised Provision of Services*

A qualification of highly practical importance is contained in Recital 22 and Article 2(1) MiCA. Pursuant to Recital 22 MiCA, the regulation shall apply to:

> natural and legal persons and certain other undertakings and to the crypto-asset services and activities performed, provided or controlled, directly or indirectly, by them, including when part of such activities or services is performed in a decentralised manner. Where crypto-asset services are provided in a fully decentralised manner without any intermediary, they should not fall within the scope of MiCA (*emphasis added*)

In turn, where cryptoasset services are provided in a partly decentralised manner, as is the case for many decentralised wallet providers, Title V MiCA on CASPs still applies. This leads to the question of determining which of these providers is a legal person or other undertaking, which we have discussed at length in Section 7.2. In summary, we argue that where an entity or group of entities controls the decentralised application by legal, technical, or governance means, Title V MiCA on CASPs applies. This leaves unregulated solely DeFi applications where there is no one controlling the DeFi application. These cases will be rare however, given that in this case, no one would benefit from the development and maintenance of the application.[30]

By contrast, where control is sufficiently dispersed, NCAs will find it difficult to single out one or several developers to qualify them jointly as an "intermediary" for purposes of Recital 22 MiCA. Essentially, Recital 22 MiCA reflects on these difficulties and states that in these cases, Title V MiCA does not apply.

8.3.5 *Licensing of Crypto Custodians*

For details on licensing, see Section 7.3. MiFID investment firms and credit institutions provide custody and administration in relation to financial instruments and are thus likely to expand their authorisation pursuant to Article 60(1), (3) MiCA. Sometimes, also UCITS ManCos and AIFMs provide custody and administration in relation to their own financial instruments as side services for fund investors.[31]

[28] See Zetzsche *et al.*, 'Crypto Custody', pp. 212–16 (providing a taxonomy on the various wallet types).
[29] See on details para. 7.2.3.3.
[30] For details, see Section 7.2.3.4.
[31] See Zetzsche *et al.*, 'Digital Assets' (making the same arguments for UCITS investing in financial instruments).

8.4 FIDUCIARY DUTIES (ARTICLES 66 AND 72 MICA)

From MiCA's general conditions to all CASPs, the fiduciary duties established by Articles 66 and 72 MiCA (see Section 7.5.1) are particularly important to crypto custodians, who are fiduciaries mandated to act in the best interests of their clients. They shall not trade in client assets on own account and risk. While this duty seems self-explanatory, it is justified in light of the abuses described in Section 8.2.

8.5 OUTSOURCING

Crypto custodians will not have access and links ('bridges') to all DeFi systems. In turn, the arrangements with other custodians are of practical importance: instead of creating a bridge to allow for the holding of cryptoasset A while the client holds only cryptoasset B and fiat currency, the crypto custodian can enter into an arrangement with a CASP entitled to provide custody that has access and links to cryptoasset A.

In this case, Article 73 MiCA on outsourcing applies where the crypto sub-custodian provides a 'service or activity for the performance of operational functions'. As we pointed out in Section 7.4.4, which service qualifies as such depends on the cryptoasset service offered. Since the crypto custodian must be licensed for custody, Article 73 MiCA applies if another CASP holds cryptoassets on behalf of the crypto custodian.

By contrast, in our view, Article 73 MiCA does not apply where the crypto custodian does not show the cryptoassets held by the CASP in the account of its client but rather provides a link to the other CASP's account in which the client then holds cryptoasset A. In turn, Article 73 MiCA applies where there is a hierarchy between one CASP and the other CASP. In particular, this is given where crypto custodial networks are modelled akin to account-based custodial networks for securities where the book entry into the accounts of the higher-level custodian determines the holding of assets by the lower-tier custodian.

Yet, the business rationale behind developing such custodial networks requires deeper thought because many cryptoassets can be booked into the DLT by any participating node applying the conditions set by the smart contract; this is different from conventional shares or bonds, the very existence of which needs to be verified by a single CSD. Custodial networks will be developed, in our view, whenever the costs of participating in the respective DLT are higher than those of relying on a sub-custodian; the smaller the holding in a given cryptoasset, the more likely the development of a hierarchical custodial network instead of direct participation.[32]

For the special case of outsourcing between a fund depositary and one or several CASPs, see Section 9.5.

8.6 SAFEKEEPING OF CRYPTOASSETS (ARTICLES 70 (1) AND 75 MICA)

Given the incidents during the Crypto Winter of 2022–23 (see Section 8.2), MiCA's rules on safekeeping are of the utmost importance. These are regulated in Article 70(1) MiCA (following provisions of the MiFID framework[33]) and Article 75 MiCA on custody

[32] For a detailed review of outsourcing arrangements in custody and their impact on market structure, see Zetzsche *et al.*, 'Crypto Custody', pp. 217–18 and 225–26.

[33] See Articles 2–4 of Commission Delegated Directive (EU) 2017/593 of 7 April 2016 supplementing Directive 2014/65/EU of the European Parliament and of the Council with regard to safeguarding of financial instruments and funds

services by CASPs, equivalent to Article 21 AIFMD and Chapter IV of UCITSD on depositary services.[34]

8.6.1 *Scope of Application*

Article 70(1) MiCA extends to CASPs 'that hold crypto-assets *belonging to clients* or *the means of access* to such crypto-assets' [i.e., the private key] (emphasis added). In scope are crypto custodians acting on behalf of clients (individually or collectively by way of investment funds), but potentially also crypto exchanges and portfolio managers that hold client assets as an ancillary service. Note that MiCA does not foresee a separation requirement preserving certain types of business for certain types of providers only.[35]

8.6.2 *Relationship between Articles 70(1) and 75 MiCA*

According to its heading, Article 70 MiCA deals with safekeeping. At the same time, Article 3 (17) MiCA suggests that safekeeping is one of the two types of custody, with controlling the means of access (i.e., the private key) being the second. This reverses the logical order of Article 70 MiCA, which deals with all kinds of safekeeping. Only Article 70(1) MiCA addresses the custody of cryptoassets. Hence, Article 70 MiCA provides general provisions for CASPs holding client cryptoassets and funds as part of their regular business or in the course of payments, while Article 75 MiCA extends Article 70(1) MiCA. Crypto custodians must read Article 75 MiCA in tandem with Article 70(1) MiCA. We follow suit in the subsequent paragraphs.

8.6.3 *Arrangements to Safeguard Clients' Rights and Prevention of Use for Own Account (Article 70 (1) MiCA))*

Analogous to Article 16(8) and (9) MiFID, these CASPs 'shall make adequate arrangements to safeguard the ownership rights of clients, especially in the event of the [CASP's] insolvency, and to prevent the use of clients' crypto-assets for their own account'.

The first requirement depends on what is necessary to protect the holders of cryptoassets under the insolvency laws applicable in the event of the DeFi application's insolvency or going out of business.[36] Given the widespread legal uncertainties regarding ownership, property, and proprietary rights in digital assets,[37] it will be interesting to see how CASPs meet this requirement. At a minimum, they must segregate the clients' assets from their own assets and register

belonging to clients, product governance obligations, and the rules applicable to the provision or reception of fees, commissions, or any monetary or non-monetary benefits, OJ 2017 No. L87, 31 March 2017.

[34] The MiFiD frameworks on the safeguarding of client funds are scattered around a number of provisions, including Article 16(8), (9), and (10) of MiFiD, Articles 2–4 of Commission Delegated Directive (EU) 2017/593 as well as Article 49 and Annex I of Commission Delegated Regulation (EU) 2017/565 of 25 April 2016 supplementing Directive 2014/65/EU of the European Parliament and of the Council as regards organisational requirements and operating conditions for investment firms and defined terms for the purposes of that Directive, OJ 2017 No. L87, 31 March 2017.

[35] For instance, the business of 'collective portfolio management' is preserved to fund managers. Credit institutions are not allowed to perform collective portfolio management. See Article 6(1) plus Annex II.1 of AIFMD, Directive 2011/61, OJ 2011 No. L174.

[36] Under most insolvency laws, only persons and entities can become insolvent, and it is uncertain whether DeFi applications qualify as one of the former.

[37] Cf. Woxholth *et al.*, 'Competing Claims to Crypto-Assets', pp. 230–32. For an argument that streamlining of crypto insolvency laws is a priority, cf. Zetzsche *et al.*, 'Remaining Regulatory Challenges in Digital Finance', pp. 83 and 91.

the cryptoassets in the name of all clients collectively (this may be dubbed an omnibus account, yet some providers use the term "omnibus account" also for accounts that include their own assets in addition to those of their clients, meaning that precise disclosure is key).

The second requirement responds to widespread abuses where crypto intermediaries (e.g., FTX) were treating client assets as their own, for instance, to cover up losses from risky crypto investments in other parts of their crypto empire (e.g., Alameda, FTX's investment subsidiary[38]). At the very least, CASPs must ensure that the cryptoassets remain registered in the name of clients and impose compliance and organisational guidelines that prevent traders of the given CASP from proprietary dealing in the clients' cryptoassets.

The re-use of client assets is also widespread in crypto-lending and crypto-staking arrangements, yet often the assets were re-used in the sense that they were pooled and then transferred to third-party creditors or users of the staked tokens.[39] Given that crypto-lending and crypto-staking are outside MiCA's scope,[40] MiCA is silent on whether the commingling of client assets with a view to lending or staking is good practice in the context of these particular services. Where the crypto lender also provides a transfer or custody service for clients that is linked to the crypto application, it qualifies, however, as a CASP and Article 70(1) MiCA applies. The CASP arranging crypto-lending and -staking would then argue that the re-use of client assets for lending and staking purposes is not for the benefit of the CASP's own account but for all clients collectively and is thus in line with Article 66(1) MiCA (which prevents trading in client assets on the CASP's own accounts) and Article 70(1) MiCA. However, under MiCA's overall fiduciary duties (see Article 66 MiCA), clients can expect fair and comprehensive disclosure on the impact of the business model on their rights in the given cryptoassets.

Yet, MiCA is incomplete with regard to crypto-lending and crypto-staking, so there is room for the application of other EU financial law to fill the gap: where the lending assets are pooled and, in turn, crypto-lending and -staking applications qualify as AIFs,[41] Article 23(1)(a) AIFMD applies, requiring that the re-use of assets is disclosed to professional investors prior to the initial investment; for retail AIFs, many national laws prohibit the re-use of the (pooled) assets entirely.[42]

8.6.4 *Custody Agreement*

CASPs must enter into an agreement with clients with contractual details meticulously prescribed.[43] The most important stipulations of Article 75 MiCA relate to the parties' identities (which may be difficult to ascertain in cases of "fully decentralised systems"); the custody policy; a description of the CASP's security systems; the fees, costs, and charges to be paid by the client; and the applicable law.[44] The custody policy must contain procedures aimed at ensuring the safekeeping or the control of the means of access to the cryptoassets.[45] This rule

38 See Arner *et al.*, 'The Financialization of Crypto'.
39 See Zetzsche *et al.*, 'Remaining Regulatory Challenges in Digital Finance', pp. 52–69.
40 See Recital para. 94 of MiCA.
41 See Zetzsche *et al.*, 'Digital Assets'.
42 Cf. for Luxembourg on Part II funds, see Article 88-3 in combination with Articles 18(6) and 34 (5) of Law of 17 December 2010 relating to undertakings for collective investment; German Sections 81–82 KAGB.
43 Article 75(1) of MiCA. Unlike Article 21(2) of AIFMD, Article 75(1) of MiCA does not require this agreement to be written.
44 Article 75(1) (a)–(g) of MiCA.
45 Article 75(3) of MiCA.

is a response to frequent incidents where private keys administered by custodians were misappropriated.[46]

8.6.5 *Bookkeeping on Clients' Rights*

Furthermore, the clients' rights to cryptoassets as well as any movement, modification, or creation in positions shall be registered in the name of each client,[47] while the client is entitled to receive information on the register entries.[48] This rule shall provide for the transparent handling of the exercise of clients' rights.

8.6.6 *Return Procedures and Operational Segregation on the DLT*

Moreover, CASPs are obliged to provide procedures necessary for the return of cryptoassets to clients[49] as well as (an operational) segregation of the client's assets from the CASP's assets on the distributed ledger.[50] This shall ensure, for instance, that in the event of the CASP's insolvency, the client's assets remain unimpaired. The additional requirement laid down in Article 75 MiCA is best understood as a detailed supplement to Article 70(1) MiCA, which posits more of a mission than a detailed rule.

8.6.7 *Substitution for the Benefit of Clients*

Notably, Article 75(4) MiCA establishes a private law provision mandating substitution: changes to the DLT and other events possibly impacting clients' rights shall lead to the right of clients 'to any cryptoassets or any rights newly created on the basis and to the extent of the client's positions at the time of the occurrence of that change or event'.[51] While these provisions are meant to protect the custodian's clients, they subject CASPs to liability risk for events taking place on the DLT which the CASPs may or may not be able to influence; note that a CASP may have no governance right in relation to the token's creation or modification. This leads us to the custodian's liabilities, which are discussed next.

8.6.8 *Liability of CASPs*

The liability of CASPs for the loss of cryptoassets or the means of access to these assets shall be limited to situations attributable to and under the control of the CASPs[52] and capped at the market value of the lost cryptoasset at the time the loss occurred. Nevertheless, compared to the

[46] See Zetzsche *et al.*, 'Remaining Regulatory Challenges in Digital Finance', pp. 33–41 (overview of incidents); Zetzsche *et al.*, 'Crypto Custody', pp. 208–10.

[47] Article 75(2), (4) of MiCA. An equivalent monitoring of an AIF's cash flows and assets held in custody, with the objective of ensuring investor protection, is foreseen by Article 21 (7) and (8) of AIFMD.

[48] Article 75(5) of MiCA.

[49] Article 75(6) of MiCA.

[50] Article 75(7) of MiCA. An equivalent asset segregation and registration of an AIF's assets is foreseen by Article 21(8) (a) (ii) of AIFMD.

[51] Article 75(4) second sub-paragraph of MiCA.

[52] Article 75(8) of MiCA. The equivalent provisions of investment fund regulation are Article 21(12) of AIFMD, Article 24 of UCITSD, Directive 2009/65, OJ 2009 No. L302.

TABLE 8.1 *Attributable events*

Incidents resulting in cryptoasset loss	Reasoning
Loss of private key(s)	Articles 3(1)(17) and 75(3), (6), and (8)
Wallet vulnerability due to insufficiently random generation of the private keys	Articles 3(1)(17) and 75(3), (6), and (8); Recital 83
Malfunction of the CASP's cybersecurity mechanisms where the attacker impersonates as client	Articles 3(1)(17) and 75(3), (6), and (8); Recital 83
The attacker disables the 2F authentication system of the custodial CEX and extracts assets from clients' accounts	Articles 3(1)(17) and 75(3), (6), and (8); Recital 83
System failure of any hardware or software used by the CASP, a service provider of the CASP, or telecommunications lines or devices used by the CASP or its service provider	Articles 3(1)(17) and 75(3), (6), and (8); Recital 83
The client cannot obtain a new right substituting for their existing rights because the CASP decides not to support the material operating change of the underlying protocols (e.g., forks or airdrops)	Article 75(4), (5), and (8)
Loss of the client's assets held in omnibus wallet addresses on the blockchain due to the insolvency of another client whose assets were commingled in the same wallet and the CASP cannot demonstrate properly segregated records and registers	Articles 70(1) and 75(2) and (8)
Loss of the client's assets because they were held in collective wallet addresses on the blockchain with the custodian's own assets even if the CASP can demonstrate properly segregated records and registers	Articles 70(1) and 75(7) and (8)
Loss of the client's assets because of use by the CASP for their own account even if the client has signed the terms and conditions enabling such a possibility	Articles 70(1) and 75(8); Recital 83
The CASP also providing a transfer service did not forward assets in a way that allowed for the cryptoasset being taken into custody	Articles 70(1) and 82

(*Source*: Zetzsche D. A., Sinnig J. and Nikolakopoulou A. (2024). Crypto Custody. *Capital Markets Law Journal*, 19, 222, Table 2 – permission granted by authors).

current contractual practice of crypto custodians,[53] the statutory liability of crypto custodians under EU law may function as a game changer in an environment characterised by a lack of accountability and resilience when it truly matters. Instances where the loss is attributable include the frequent occurrence of a private key being lost or misappropriated. Recital 83 MiCA clarifies further that liability is given 'for any losses resulting from an incident related to information and communication technology ('ICT'), including an incident resulting from a cyber-attack, theft or any malfunctions'.

Article 75(8) and Recital 83 MiCA limit the liability of CASPs in three respects. First, the CASP is liable for the loss of cryptoassets or the means of access to these assets only. MiCA does not foresee any other damage that the clients may suffer such as the loss of opportunity or reputational damage.[54] Second, liability is capped at the market value of the lost cryptoasset at

[53] Cf. D. A. Zetzsche and A. Nikolakopoulou, 'Crypto Custody and Crypto Wallets – An Empirical Analysis', University of Luxembourg Working Paper (2024). Website https://dx.doi.org/10.2139/ssrn.4769396 (last accessed on 1 October 2024).

[54] Since MiCA is silent regarding other losses, the fall-back is the applicable national law liability regime.

TABLE 8.2 *Non-attributable events*

Incidents resulting in cryptoasset loss	Reasoning
Malfunction of a DeFi algorithm not controlled by the CASP (e.g., the attacker uses flash loans to buy governance tokens and exploits a token issuer, so the client loses the respective tokens)	Article 75(8) subpar. 2
Unpredictable governance decisions in decentralised arrangements not controlled by the CASP (cf. ESMA75–453128700-438, p. 18.)	Article 75(8) subpar. 2
Client gives away password or the private key or seed phrase because they shared it with others or lost their paper backups	Article 75(8) subpar. 2
System failure of the client's mobile phone where the wallet is installed	Article 75(8) subpar. 2
The CASP cannot obtain right substituting for existing rights of client, although the CASP exercised due care in facilitating clients' rights, due to technical malfunctions in the DeFi code	Articles 66, 72, and 75(4), (5), and (8) subpar. 2
The client cannot obtain a new right substituting for their existing rights because the CASP reserved the discretion to decide to support or not any material operating changes of the underlying protocols (e.g., forks or airdrops) in the signed terms and conditions, and the CASP exercised due care in assisting the client with any appropriate administrative actions such as enabling the withdrawal or transfer of cryptoassets (where applicable)	Articles 66, 72, and 75(4), (5), and (8) subpar. 2
The CASP did not receive assets from a separate asset transfer service	Article 75(8) subpar. 2
The loss of the client's assets occurs due to the client instructing the CASP to send them to a wrong blockchain address	Article 75(8) subpar. 2

(*Source*: Zetzsche D. A., Sinnig J. and Nikolakopoulou A. (2024). Crypto Custody. *Capital Markets Law Journal*, 19, 223, Table 3 – permission granted by authors).

the time the loss occurred. Third, liability is limited to situations attributable to, and under the control of, the CASPs.[55]

In this regard, it is noteworthy that ESMA interprets Recital 83 MiCA to mean that CASPs using permissionless DLT infrastructure that they do not control or manage (i.e., no contractual arrangement exists) are exempted from the liability for this infrastructure.[56] (See, however, Section 15.5.1 on liability under DORA.) While this clearly sets incentive to outsource to permissionless rather than the permissioned DLT applications, ESMA tries to remedy this shortcoming by proposing obligations in the event of a disruption involving a permissionless DLT, for instance, to communicate the disruption to the client along with the associated risks and their own liability exclusion for such events and finally to act in the best interest of the clients. Further, CASPs should remain liable for any losses related to their own smart contracts, such as hacks or exploits, regardless of whether they are deployed on a permissionless or permissioned DLT.[57]

Tables 8.1 and 8.2 provide an overview of attributable and non-attributable incidents derived from MiCA's requirements for crypto custodians.

[55] Article 75(8) of MiCA. The equivalent provision is Article 21(12) of AIFMD and Article 24(1) of UCITSD.

[56] According to ESMA's initial proposal, permissionless DLTs shall be considered a form of 'common good' resource, whereas the use of a permissioned DLT operated by a commercial enterprise will likely be based on contracts available for 'white-labelled' blockchain products; in which case, it can be considered as a 'third-party provider'. Cf. ESMA (2023). Consultation Paper on Technical Standards specifying certain requirements of Markets in Crypto-Assets Regulation (MiCA) – second consultation paper, ESMA75–453128700-438, p. 19. Such a qualification encourages outsourcing to applications the provider cannot control nor monitor, in particular, when seen together with privileges, ESMA foresees on liability in these cases.

[57] Cf. ESMA, 'Consultation Paper on Technical Standards', ESMA75–453128700-438, pp. 19, 21 and 22.

8.7 CONCLUSION

The rules on crypto custody counter the many instances in which the "custody" provided did not amount to what had been promised to the client(s). What results therefrom is a robust framework (akin to securities custodians), which aims to ensure solid crypto custodians. We expect that market forces will lead to fewer, better regulated and better capitalised custodians. The market entry of large traditional financial intermediaries (such as Fidelity Digital Assets) is evidence to our claim. In turn, there is hope that custodians apply more rigid operational risk management, fewer custodians become insolvent and those that become insolvent have better abilities to protect clients. At the same time, MiCA also foresees a number of provisions that anticipate a private law not yet in existence. It is here that we expect practical difficulties.[58]

[58] For a detailed assessment, see Zetzsche *et al.*, 'Crypto Custody', pp. 221–29, highlighting the distinction between Institutional Resilience and Asset Resilience and arguing that MiCA focuses on Institutional Resilience, while the European institutional environment renders decisive steps on Asset Resilience a challenge.

9

Crypto Investment Funds

9.1 INTRODUCTION

Investment activity of regulated investment funds in cryptoassets is desirable from a governance, liquidity, and market maturity perspective, yet operational risks and legal uncertainty had until now prevented fund managers from making large-scale investments in cryptoassets.[1]

Before MiCA's inception, investment funds could be set up as either UCITS subject to UCITSD[2] or AIF subject to AIFMD[3] (retail AIFs were potentially subject to additional rules imposed by Member States). Since MiCA's coming into force, a third variant has materialised, combining provisions of AIFMD and Title V MiCA.

The result is a fragmentation of EU fund regulation, depending on the given investment asset, as displayed in Table 9.1.[4]

For UCITS-only investments and AIFMD-only investments in digital assets that either do not qualify as cryptoassets or are outside the scope of MiCA pursuant to Article 4 MiCA,[5] we refer to the literature on the subject matter of digital asset funds as a whole.[6] We focus herein on the third variant alluded to above, where the AIFMD framework applies in tandem with MiCA. For instance, an AIFM invests, on behalf of the fund (an AIF), in cryptoassets within the scope of MiCA as discussed in Chapters 3 and 4 ("In-scope Assets"). CASPs providing services pursuant to Article 3(16) MiCA[7] must then comply with Title V MiCA if they are ordinarily part of the service spectrum characteristic for investment funds.[8]

[1] Cf. Zetzsche et al., 'Digital Assets, MiCA & EU Investment Fund Law' (2023), pp. 3–4. Website https://dx.doi.org/10.2139/ssrn.4637019 (last accessed on 1 October 2024).

[2] Directive 2009/65/EC of the European Parliament and of the Council of 13 July 2009 on the coordination of laws, regulations, and administrative provisions relating to undertakings for collective investment in transferable securities (UCITS) (recast), OJ 2009 No. L302, 1 November 2009, pp. 32–96.

[3] Directive 2011/61/EU of the European Parliament and of the Council of 8 June 2011 on Alternative Investment Fund Managers and amending Directives 2003/41/EC and 2009/65/EC and Regulations (EC) No. 1060/2009 and (EU) No. 1095/2010, OJ 2011 No. L174, 1 July 2011, pp. 1–73.

[4] Cf. Zetzsche et al., 'Digital Assets, MiCA & EU Investment Fund Law' (2023), p. 12. Website https://dx.doi.org/10.2139/ssrn.4637019 (last accessed on 1 October 2024).

[5] See on the delineation, in particular, with regard to financial instruments and NFTs, Chapter 4.

[6] Cf. Zetzsche et al., 'Digital Assets, MiCA & EU Investment Fund Law' (2023). Website https://dx.doi.org/10.2139/ssrn.4637019 (last accessed on 1 October 2024).

[7] See Chapter 7.

[8] For an overview, see D. A. Zetzsche, 'Introduction', in D. A. Zetzsche (ed.), *The Alternative Investment Fund Managers Directive* (Alphen aan den Rijn: Wolters Kluwer, 2020), 3rd ed., Chapter 1, p. 1 et seq.

TABLE 9.1 *Three types of digital asset fund setups*

Investment asset	UCITS	AIFMD	AIFMD plus Title V MiCA
Traditional transferable security (shares, bonds, or crypto firms) or financial derivatives thereof	X	X	(-)
Digital asset = Transferable security	X	X	(-)
Digital asset = UCI unit (UCITS, AIF, or AIF + MiCA)	X	X	(-)
Securitised digital asset or cryptoasset (SPV holding digital assets), listed or unlisted	X; debated for > 10%.	X	(-)
Financial derivative linked to the index on digital assets/cryptoassets	X (subject to requirements of Article 8 EAD)	X (all)	(-)
CBDCs	(-)	X	(-)
Derivatives referenced to digital assets and cryptoassets, and derivative-related benchmarks and indices	(-)	X	(-)
Tokenised provision of regulated activities listed in Article 2(4) MiCA	(-)	X	(-)
NFTs	(-)	X	(-)
Tokens of fully decentralised applications (Bitcoin)	(-)	(-)	X
ARTs (Title III MiCA)	(-)	(-)	X
EMTs (Title IV MiCA)	(-)	(-)	X
Cryptoassets other than ARTs + EMTs (Title II MiCA)	(-)	(-)	X
Cryptoassets offered for free, reward, and utility tokens, for limited access to a network of merchants (Article 4(3) MiCA)	(-)	(-)	X

Source: Zetzsche et al., 'Digital Assets, MiCA & EU Investment Fund Law' (2023), p. 12. Website https://dx.doi.org/10.2139/ssrn.4637019 (last accessed on 1 October 2024); permission granted by authors.

Here, we first discuss the question of which cases the additional MiCA provisions apply to (Section 9.2) and consider the particularities of the general CASP rules laid down in Title V MiCA in the context of investment funds (Section 9.3) before we look into outsourcing (including brokerage and portfolio management and advice) in Section 9.4 and fund-specific questions regarding safekeeping and custody (Section 9.5). In Section 9.6, we conclude.

9.2 SCOPE OF MICA'S CASP RULES

9.2.1 *Interplay between AIFMD and MiCA's Bespoke Regulations*

For funds investing in in-scope assets, MiCA adds *some* rules to the AIFMD framework, yet it is not exhaustive. In particular, MiCA does not regulate collective portfolio management. However, MiCA does provide additional rules on certain ancillary services pursued by AIFMs and their appointed delegates, as well as on fund depositaries and custodians.

This leaves us with a patchy framework where some activities are subject to AIFMD only, while others are subject to a combination of AIFMD and Title V MiCA, as shown in Table 9.2.

TABLE 9.2 *Provisions governing activities under AIFMD vs. AIFMD plus MiCA*

Regulated activity	AIFMD (re. financial instruments)	In-scope MiCA cryptoassets
Collective Portfolio Management (AIFM)	Article 6 AIFMD	(-)
AIFM's side services: • Portfolio management • Investment advice	Article 6(4) AIFMD plus bespoke rules of MiFID/MiFIR framework	Article 6(4) AIFMD plus Article 60, Chapter II of Title V, and Article 81 MiCA
Delegates of AIFM: • Portfolio management • Investment advice • Brokerage	Article 20 AIFMD plus bespoke rules of MIFID/MiFIR framework	Article 20 AIFMD plus Title V MiCA
Depositaries	Article 21 AIFMD plus bespoke rules of MiFID/MiFIR framework	Article 21 AIFMD plus Article 60, Chapter II of Title V, and Article 70 and 75 MiCA
Sub-custodians	Article 21(11)–(14) AIFMD plus bespoke rules of MiFID/MiFIR framework	Article 21(11)–(14) AIFMD plus Title V MiCA (esp. Articles 70 and 75 MiCA)

Source: Zetzsche et al., 'Digital Assets, MiCA & EU Investment Fund Law' (2023), p. 26. Website https://dx.doi.org/10.2139/ssrn.4637019 (last accessed on 1 October 2024); permission granted by authors.

9.2.2 *Carve-Out for Collective Portfolio Management and Administration*

The core business of AIFMs is the provision of "collective portfolio management",[9] which includes fund portfolio and risk management relating to the given fund and its assets. Furthermore, AIFMs are entitled under Annex II.2 AIFMD to provide administration services (such as accounting, evaluation, and fund-related legal services).

Article 3(1)(16) MiCA defines cryptoasset services and thus the scope of Title V MiCA, but it does *not* mention collective portfolio management or fund administration. We speculate that a possible reason for this may be AIFMD's conception as a manager-oriented framework fit for all types of assets.[10] As the reluctance of regulated fund managers to invest in crypto on a large scale indicates, the AIFMD framework on collective portfolio management is sufficiently robust to address risks relating to cryptoassets with respect to investment policies, portfolio composition, diversification, risk management, valuation, redemption rights, and related conflicts of interest.[11] If any need for amendments should arise, these may be incorporated into AIFMD,[12] but none have been either initiated or discussed so far.

9 See Article 6(1) and Annex II.1 of AIFMD, Directive 2011/61, OJ 2011 No. L174.

10 Cf. Zetzsche, 'Introduction', in *The Alternative Investment Fund Managers Directive*, Chapter 1, p. 16.

11 Cf. D. Eckner and D. A. Zetzsche, 'Appointment, Authorization and Organization of the AIFM', in D. A. Zetzsche (ed.), *The Alternative Investment Fund Managers Directive* (Alphen aan den Rijn: Wolters Kluwer, 2020), 3rd ed., Chapter 8, p. 210 et seq.

12 Cf. on AIFMD II, Directive (EU) 2024/927 of the European Parliament and of the Council of 13 March 2024 amending Directives 2011/61/EU and 2009/65/EC as regards delegation arrangements, liquidity risk management, supervisory reporting, the provision of depositary and custody services, and loan origination by alternative investment funds, OJ L, 2024/927, 26.3.2024.

9.2.3 *Bespoke Rules for Cryptoasset Services*

The bespoke rules for CASPs in Title V MiCA cover, however, other services of importance to investment funds, which either the AIFM, the depositary, or the AIFM's delegates provide to the AIF. Where the provision of such a service qualifies as delegation, the AIFM must adhere to the delegation rules of Article 20 AIFMD, which sets a number of requirements for the selection of service providers, contractual provisions, and the AIFM's oversight of its delegates throughout the duration of the outsourcing agreement.[13] Certain delegates are also subject to bespoke rules; these concern, in particular, the depositary[14] and (prime) brokers.[15]

In addition, MiCA sets requirements for services qualifying as cryptoasset services under Article 3(1)(16) MiCA.[16] For instance, where a fund manager relies on an agent arranging transfers of cryptoassets, these agents qualify as CASPs and must meet the conditions of Title V MiCA accordingly. In the investment fund context, the provisions on brokerage services,[17] portfolio management, and advice[18] are the most important given that all AIFMs rely on external brokerage, and many AIFMs delegate the provision of portfolio management to expert managers or receive advice on niche assets (such as cryptoassets) from expert advisors to enhance their investment decisions.

Furthermore, given that every AIF must have a depositary in charge of safekeeping the assets and taking certain asset types into custody,[19] a third item of importance for investment funds is thus MiCA's rules on safekeeping (Article 70 MiCA) as well as the custody and administration of cryptoassets (Article 75 MiCA). As we have discussed the substance of crypto custody in Chapter 8, we are concerned in the current chapter only with the impact of Articles 70 and 75 MiCA on fund depositaries (regulated by Article 21 AIFMD) and (sub-)custodians acting on behalf of investment funds.

Where the list in Article 3(1)(16) MiCA is incomplete, for instance, on crypto-lending and crypto-staking,[20] some service providers of the fund may not be subject to MiCA. In these cases, Article 20 AIFMD remains the only source of regulatory requirements in the investment fund context.

We will discuss the interplay between AIFMD and MiCA on these three items in turn, first taking into account the general requirements for all CASPs (fiduciary duties in Section 9.3 and outsourcing in Section 9.4) prior to a detailed view on the rules on brokerage, portfolio management, and advice (Section 9.4.4), as well as custody and safekeeping (Section 9.4.5).

[13] See on Article 20 of AIFMD; T. Partsch, 'Delegation', in D. A. Zetzsche (ed.), *The Alternative Investment Fund Managers Directive* (Alphen aan den Rijn: Wolters Kluwer, 2020), 3rd ed., Chapter 9, p. 231 et seq.

[14] Cf. Article 21 of AIFMD; see S. N. Hooghiemstra, 'Depositary Regulation', in D. A. Zetzsche (ed.), *The Alternative Investment Fund Managers Directive* (Alphen aan den Rijn: Wolters Kluwer, 2020), 3rd ed., Chapter 16, p. 441 et seq.

[15] Cf. Articles 4(1)(af), 14(3), 21(4), and 23(1)(o) of AIFMD. See D. A. Zetzsche, '(Prime) Brokerage', in D. A. Zetzsche (ed.), *The Alternative Investment Fund Managers Directive* (Alphen aan den Rijn: Wolters Kluwer, 2020), 3rd ed., Chapter 19, p. 545 et seq.

[16] For details, see Section 7.2.

[17] Article 3(16)(e), (f), (g), and (j) of MiCA.

[18] Cf. Article 3(16)(h) and (i) of MiCA.

[19] Cf. Article 21(1) of AIFMD.

[20] On crypto-lending and crypto-staking cf. Zetzsche et al., 'Remaining Regulatory Challenges in Digital Finance and Crypto-Assets after MiCA', pp. 52, 64 et seq. Some of these services may qualify as AIF, cf. Section 9.2.1.

9.3 THE CASP'S FIDUCIARY DUTIES

Among the general operating conditions for CASPs laid out in Title V, Chapter 2 MiCA,[21] the rules on fiduciary duties (with regard to conflict management) are of high practical relevance.

While these fiduciary duties are rather similar to those established in EU investment fund regulation, their perspectives differ: AIFMD and UCITSD regulate a multilateral situation between the fund, the fund manager, the investors, and the depositary, while Title V MiCA regulates the relationships mainly between CASPs and clients (and, in some cases, issuers of cryptoassets). 'Clients' in this case include AIFs, regardless of their legal form.[22] We also note differences in certain details, and in some cases, we note an overlap of similar but not identical provisions.

9.3.1 *Fiduciary Duties (Article 66 MiCA)*

Equivalent to similar provisions in EU financial law,[23] Article 66(1) MiCA establishes that CASPs are fiduciaries, stipulating that they 'shall act honestly, fairly and professionally in accordance with the best interests of their clients and prospective clients'. This provision underpins a number of requirements on fairness, transparency, and management of conflicts of interest, following the principle that clients' interests shall be paramount, unless they have been explicitly informed and have provided their explicit consent to being treated in a disadvantageous manner.

The fiduciary duties, on the one hand, have a harmonising effect that aligns the position of CASPs with other off-balance-sheet intermediaries in the field of finance. They clarify beyond doubt that CASPs must not use clients' assets on their own accounts. On the other hand, they establish limits to crypto business models resulting in value transfers from clients to CASPs. These matters were at the heart of various scandals during the Crypto Winter,[24] and their clarification greatly adds to the protection of cryptoasset investors (including investment funds).

Beyond establishing fiduciary duties, Article 66 MiCA relies on two principles: (1) a general fairness requirement in all dealings and information[25] and (2) disclosure(s) to clients.[26] In particular, disclosures relate to:

- Risks related to the transaction of that type of cryptoasset;
- The access link to the whitepaper(s);
- The CASP's pricing and fees; and
- Principal adverse sustainability impacts of the consensus mechanism used to issue each cryptoasset in relation to which the CASP provides services.

[21] We discussed these in Chapter 7.

[22] Note that under EU investment fund law, an AIF can be set up as contractual fund, trust, in corporate form, as partnership, or other ways (including foundations and cooperatives). See Article 2(2)(b) of AIFMD.

[23] See Article 24 of MiFID; Article 14 of UCITSD; Article 12 of AIFMD.

[24] IOSCO, 'Policy Recommendations for Crypto and Digital Asset Markets, Final Report', Recommendations 7–17; Financial Stability Board, 'High-Level Recommendations for the Regulation, Supervision and Oversight of Crypto-Asset Activities and Markets: Final Report', Recommendations 4–7; IMF, 'Elements of Effective Policies for Crypto Assets', pp. 17–32.

[25] Cf. Article 70(1), (2) of MiCA.

[26] Cf. Article 70(3), (4) of MiCA.

While this information may be copied directly out of the whitepaper, relying on the whitepaper provides little guidance if it is not sufficiently comprehensive on the matter. For that reason, the whitepaper rules require the same disclosures.[27]

MiCA is silent on the question of what a CASP must do that finds a whitepaper disclosure provided by an issuer or trading platform dissatisfying. For instance, a whitepaper may hide the given asset's sustainability impact, be too short on it, or not provide disclosures on obvious (for instance, operational) risks. The same deficiency may come about with regard to transactional risks, while the CASP should be familiar with its own pricing and fees. This situation is likelier in these circumstances than in the case of financial instruments, given that the disclosures of whitepapers relating to "other cryptoassets" are not subject to a review by an NCA, contrary to disclosures laid down in a prospectus for transferable securities.[28] Remaining silent here would run counter to the overall fairness principle that governs the CASP–client relationship. At the same time, the CASP lacks the necessary means to calculate sustainability impacts and assess transactional risks itself, unless it functions as the key stakeholder of the cryptoasset/DeFi application.

We hold that the fiduciary duties of Article 66(3) MiCA indicate that the CASP must in this case issue a warning that it finds a given disclosure within a whitepaper insufficient, thus leaving the risk of misleading content being present in the whitepaper. The fact that the CASP must repeat the disclosures on sustainability impacts but does not need to for all whitepaper disclosures shows the limits of that duty: the CASPs must review disclosures on sustainability impacts, while for other risks, the CASP must warn the client only where it becomes aware of the risk(s).

Note that clients may agree with the CASP to perform due diligence on any cryptoasset prior to acting on it on behalf of a fund. We hold that the CASP itself owes such due diligence as part of its general duties of care.[29] Moreover, we encourage fund managers to do so, as risks created by the portfolio manager will be revealed later as risks of the fund, and if the CASP does not provide due diligence, the EU fund manager must nevertheless provide it under EU law.[30]

9.3.2 *Conflict Management (Article 72 MiCA)*

Article 72 MiCA on conflict management stipulates a qualified form of fiduciary duty. While we have laid out the similarity between MiFID and AIFMD in Chapter 7 more generally, we discuss here particularities which matter in the context of the fund manager's ancillary services and asset managers functioning as the delegated portfolio manager of the fund or the custodian holding cryptoassets on behalf of the fund.

From the perspective of MiFID and AIFMD, it is not new for a delegated portfolio manager or custodian to require a conflict management policy with related disclosure requirements, which integrates the interests of shareholders, control-holders, and executives with those of clients or among clients. Yet, within the cryptoasset industry, these conflicts have until now not been managed effectively. For instance, if a crypto exchange that also functions as a custodian used clients' assets to cover losses at their trading arm,[31] the interests of the control-holders took

[27] Cf. Section 5.5.2.

[28] Cf. Section 5.4.3.

[29] Title V of MiCA is silent on such a due diligence requirement, yet CASPs will have a hard time to comply with Article 66 et seq. of MiCA in the absence of due diligence in relation to the cryptoassets on which they provide cryptoasset services. We will not be surprised if an explicit due diligence becomes part of MiCA's level 2 legislation.

[30] Article 15(3)(a) AIFMD requires an AIFM to adopt and apply a due diligence process on any asset acquired on behalf of the AIF.

[31] This behaviour was reported for FTX. See Arner et al., 'The Financialization of Crypto: Lessons from FTX and the Crypto Winter of 2022-2023', p. 4 et seq.

precedence over the interests of the clients. Meanwhile, the other conflict rules of Article 72 MiCA must be construed in light of the instances reported by IOSCO[32] and other policy bodies[33] prevalent in the crypto industry prior to the inception of MiCA.

Note that MiCA differs with regard to one important feature of financial regulation compared to EU fund regulation: the segregation and separation of services. Under EU law, a fund manager must neither provide brokerage nor depositary services on behalf of the fund it manages. However, MiCA does not contain similar rules. In turn, the same CASP can, in principle, offer exchange, custody, and asset management services as well as transfer services to the fund. The CASP regulation is thus modelled more on MiFID, where the investment firms may also offer a range of services to clients simultaneously. Yet, even MiFID does not go so far as to allow trading platforms to function as asset managers and brokers at the same time.

The fact that CASPs can, in theory, offer a bundle of services simultaneously to the same client (for the purpose of the current chapter, the fund) emphasises from the CASP's perspective the need for a robust conflict management framework, consisting of a conflict policy and detailed conflict management measures for conflicts that have become acute.

Pursuant to Article 72(2)–(4) MiCA, CASPs must disclose on their website, in an easily accessible manner (i.e., in a prominent place) and with sufficient details, the conflicts in abstract and update the disclosures on a regular basis. Examples here include the fact that a cryptoasset manager also operates a trading platform or a custody business. The idea is that the client reads these disclosures and can decide in an informed manner whether or not to accept the risks stemming from these conflicts.

While this approach is likely to be less effective for retail clients, we support it in relation to EU fund managers, who are sophisticated financial intermediaries subject to due diligence requirements when selecting service providers. From the perspective of the fund manager selecting the CASP, however, the existence of such conflicts will often serve as a strong argument to choose a more focused service provider as any of these conflicts will require additional monitoring on the part of the fund manager.

9.4 OUTSOURCING

Also of high practical importance are the rules on delegations and outsourcing. Here, two provisions come together as the AIFM's delegation to brokers, portfolio managers, and advisers in relation to cryptoassets rests on Article 20 AIFMD (with implementing provisions), while their conduct is subject to additional provisions of both AIFMD and MiCA.

9.4.1 *Requirements of Article 20 AIFMD*

The general conditions of an AIFM's outsourcing of any services are laid down in Article 20 AIFMD.[34] That provision applies regardless of whether the delegate is a CASP providing a cryptoasset service under Title V MiCA (for instance, a cryptoasset portfolio manager taking investment decisions on behalf of the fund) or another entity not regulated by MiCA (for

[32] See IOSCO, 'Policy Recommendations for Crypto and Digital Asset Markets, Final Report', pp. 16–18 and 49–51.
[33] See FSB, 'High-Level Recommendations for the Regulation, Supervision and Oversight of Crypto-Asset Activities and Markets: Final Report', pp. 11–12; IMF, 'Elements of Effective Policies for Crypto Assets', Box 3 and pp. 22–23.
[34] On applicable implementing legislation, see Articles 75 et seq. Commission Delegated Regulation (EU) 231/2013, OJ 2013 No. L83.

instance, an external valuation expert, given that valuation is not a cryptoasset service under Article 3(16) MiCA).

The general outsourcing requirements of Article 20(1) AIFMD ask that the AIFM justifies its entire delegation structure based on objective reasons; such a justification includes the AIFM's reliance on the superior expertise of a service provider in terms of the type of asset, the technology, or risk assessment employed. As cryptoassets are non-traditional assets, this justification comes naturally.

Moreover, the delegation must not prevent effective supervision of the AIFM and, in particular, must not prevent the AIFM from acting, or the AIF from being managed, in the best interests of its investors. As long as the delegate is authorised as a CASP subject to Title V MiCA, we see little reason for concern given that Title V MiCA seeks to ensure, as one of several regulatory objectives,[35] protection of the client (in this case, the AIF).

As to the outsourcing agreement, the AIFM must select the delegate with due care, monitor the delegated activity effectively at any time, and be able to instruct the delegate and to withdraw the delegation with immediate effect when in the interest of investors.

The delegate must dispose of sufficient resources to perform the respective tasks, and the persons who effectively conduct the business of the delegate must be of sufficient repute and be sufficiently experienced. Furthermore, the delegate must be 'qualified and capable of undertaking the functions in question'. In principle, we see these requirements as being met where the delegates are licensed under Title V MiCA as meeting these requirements is part of a CASP's authorisation.[36] AIFMs may then question their qualification only where they learn of information to the contrary.

Meanwhile, the AIFM must not delegate its functions to the extent that, in essence, it can no longer be considered the manager of the AIF, in which case it would become a letter-box entity.

The AIFM's delegation (or any further sub-delegation) does not reduce its liability towards the AIF and its investors. The AIFM must also review the services provided by each delegate on an ongoing basis. This requires, in particular, a review of whether all of the requirements of Article 20 AIFMD are fulfilled.

Finally, Article 20(2) AIFMD provides an absolute outsourcing barrier to depositaries and their delegates, as well as any other entities whose interests conflict with those of the AIFM or the investors of the AIF; for other entities, a functional and hierarchical separation of portfolio management and risk management from other tasks, as well as a qualified conflict management framework, may result in such a delegation being granted permission. Article 20(2) AIFMD is relevant in relation to CASPs that qualify as depositaries or sub-depositaries: a credit institution or investment firm functioning as depositary of the AIF may also, by way of notification, extend their authorisation to function as a crypto custodian subject to Article 60(1) and (3) MiCA. CASPs as sub-depositaries may materialise where a CASP is a delegate of the AIF's depositary (Section 9.5).

9.4.2 *Sub-delegation under Article 20(4)–(6) AIFMD and Article 73 MiCA*

The AIFM's delegate is subject to the sub-delegation rules of Article 20(4)–(6) AIFMD. Where the delegate is a CASP, Article 73 MiCA also applies in conjunction with Article 20(4)–(6) AIFMD.

[35] Recital paras. 12, 75, 75, and 108 of MiCA mention investor protection as rationale of MiCA; more often, the Recitals refer to retail holders and consumer protection as legislative rationale.

[36] See Articles 59 et seq. of MiCA.

Comparing AIFMD against MiCA, a number of requirements of AIFMD cannot be found in Article 73 MiCA: the AIFM must consent prior to sub-delegation and notify the NCA prior to the sub-delegation entering into effect. Furthermore, the AIFM must justify the sub-delegation and must pick the sub-delegate with due skill and care; a sub-delegation to a depositary or sub-depositaries is prohibited on the same grounds as in the case of a delegation pursuant to Article 20(2) AIFMD. The AIFM must further monitor, instruct, receive information from, and potentially dismiss the sub-delegate at any time and regularly review the sub-delegation arrangement. While the sub-delegate must have sufficient resources and its management must be of good repute, the sub-delegation as such must not constitute a barrier to effective supervision by the AIFM's NCA. None of these requirements have equivalents in Article 73 MiCA.

Article 73 MiCA on outsourcing (which we discussed in Chapter 7)[37] is modelled on Article 16(5) MiFID. Again, the purpose here is to ensure the effectiveness of the authorisation requirements and financial supervision even where the authorised CASPs rely on other, potentially not authorised, service providers. Yet, the legislative text of Article 73 MiCA diverges in part from Article 20(4)–(6) AIFMD. In particular, CASPs engaging in outsourcing need to ensure that the outsourcing does not: (1) result in the delegation of the responsibility of the CASP; (2) alter the relationship between the CASP and their clients, nor the obligations of the CASP towards its clients; and (3) change the conditions for the authorisation of CASPs.

At the same time, some requirements are similar: CASPs must also retain sufficient capacity for monitoring and risk management and have direct access to information, while the outsourcing must not present a barrier to effective supervision. In particular, the delegate must submit itself for supervision by the CASP's NCA. As these missions are similar, yet not identical, and although the regulatory objective is identical, we see potential for implementing rules to achieve convergence.

9.4.3 *AIFMD vs. MiCA*

As for the most significant differences between MiCA and AIFMD, MiCA does not require that the client (here, the AIFM/AIF) of the CASP that is outsourcing has a say in the outsourcing, nor does it allow for an information flow where the client (i.e., the AIFM/AIF) may involve its own NCA. It is noteworthy that AIFMD's absolute outsourcing barrier in Article 20(2) and (5) of portfolio and risk management to depositaries and sub-depositaries is not present in MiCA.

Yet, MiCA does not contain a rule that sets aside the AIFMD rules. In turn, the CASP whose clients include AIFs/AIFMs must meet the requirements set out in AIFMD, plus the requirements of MiCA. Note then that the regulatory pyramid is as follows: the fund manager relying on a CASP must comply with Article 20 AIFMD[38] and needs to make sure that the CASP follows suit so that the AIFM and depositary can meet their regulatory requirements. While the CASP outsourcing 'services or activities for the performance of operational functions' (see Section 7.4.4) even further to other CASPs, they must adhere to Article 73 MiCA plus the additional restrictions stemming from AIFMD on sub-delegation.

[37] While we have discussed in Section 7.4.2.3, the more general matters on outsourcing in the context of software developing firms, oracles, and token-holders, we discuss here in Chapter 9 how the AIFM's use of crypto brokers, portfolio managers, and advisers is organised as well as how the AIF's depositary cooperates with crypto custodians.

[38] For the depositary outsourcing services, Article 21 of AIFMD provides additional rules. See Section 9.5.

9.4.4 *In Focus: Brokerage*

AIFMD stipulates outsourcing rules in its Article 20, with bespoke rules on prime brokers spread over a handful of provisions throughout the whole Directive: while traditional brokers function as either representatives or trustees of the AIF/AIFM or act on a commission basis, a prime broker subject to Article 4(1)(ah) AIFMD is characterised as an intermediary primarily engaged in financing or executing *as counterparty to the AIF*. Due to the counterparty function, the reliance on prime brokers is subject to a special contract tying the transfer and reuse of AIF assets to the AIF's constituting documents and mandating the AIFM to perform due diligence of the prime broker and to inform the AIF's depositary.[39] At the same time, Article 21(4)(b) AIFMD provides special rules on the prime broker delivering, as the same legal entity, also depositary or sub-depositary services to the AIF.

In this setup, as long as the CASP acts on behalf of clients regarding order execution, placing, as well as the reception and transmission of orders, Article 20 AIFMD and related implementing legislation deal with the selection on the side of the AIFM, while the execution of these services is governed by Articles 78–80 MiCA.[40]

9.4.5 *In Focus: Portfolio Management and Advice*

From the perspective of AIFMD, the outsourcing of portfolio management and advice to CASPs is subject to additional requirements. First and foremost, the AIFM's delegates must be authorised or registered for the purpose of asset management and subject to supervision or, where that condition cannot be met, only subject to prior approval by the competent authorities of the home Member State of the AIFM. Where the delegate resides in a third country, cooperation between the NCA of the AIFM and the supervisory authority of the delegate must be ensured; this requires the existence of a cooperation agreement subject to the ESMA's model MoU.[41] Second, delegation and sub-delegation to depositaries and sub-depositaries are prohibited under Article 20(2) and (5) AIFMD.[42]

In this context, we hold that the CASP's licence for portfolio management under Article 81 MiCA is a licence for "asset management": Article 81 MiCA mimics the MiFID rules on investment advice and portfolio management in relation to financial instruments.[43] We expect the ESMA to propose and the European Commission to adopt, implementing rules very similar to those existing under MiFID/MiFIR. While proximity to MiFID/MiFIR is desirable to reduce the compliance costs of MiFID-authorised intermediaries functioning as CASPs (cf. Article 59 MiCA), some minor differences are worth mentioning. For instance, it is surprising that the risk characteristics of cryptoassets under Article 81(9) MiCA do not include the significant operational risks prevalent in crypto among the main causes of losses.

Article 81 MiCA is of the utmost practical importance for digital asset funds: AIFMs often outsource investment decisions to specialists. Investment advice and (individual) portfolio management with regard to financial instruments, including DLT-based ones, are carried out by MiFID firms as delegates to the AIFM. Furthermore, investment advice and (individual)

[39] Article 14(3) of AIFMD.

[40] For details, see Chapter 7.

[41] Article 20(1)(d) of AIFMD.

[42] For details, see Section 9.4.1.

[43] Cf. Articles 24 and 25 of MiFID and Articles 48(2), 54(12) and (13), and 60(1) of Commission Delegated Regulation 2017/565, OJ 2017 No. L87.

portfolio management with regard to financial instruments are often carried out by AIFMs as side services to their fund clients (cf. Article 6(4) AIFMD). Yet, both MiFID and Article 6(4) AIFMD do not provide an authorisation requirement for these services with regard to cryptoassets in the scope of MiCA. Here, MiCA's gap-filling function comes into play.

Assume that the AIFM provides the core services of collective portfolio management in relation to cryptoassets and delegates portfolio management or investment advice in relation to cryptoassets to a third party. In this case, the AIFM must comply with Article 20 AIFMD on outsourcing.[44] Article 20(1)(c) AIFMD requires an authorisation of the delegate with regard to the regulated activity of "portfolio management" unless the delegate resides in a country that does not provide for a licensing scheme for portfolio management (in that case, the AIFM must ask its NCA for approval of the delegation). MiCA now introduces a harmonised licence for portfolio management of EU entities regarding cryptoassets; however, the approval of delegations by any EU NCA under different terms than a licensing requirement under MiCA is still not allowed. Where the delegate resides in a third country that does not provide a licensing scheme for portfolio management in relation to cryptoassets, the AIFM must instead (still) apply to its NCA for approval of the delegation.

Given the uncertainty as to which digital assets qualify as financial instruments and are thus outside the scope of MiCA,[45] Article 81 MiCA leads, in practice, to a dual authorisation requirement (and potentially an additional approval requirement): for cryptoassets qualifying as financial instruments, the delegate must have a licence under MiFID and for *in-scope assets* an authorisation under Articles 59 and 60 MiCA. Finally, for assets that qualify neither as financial instruments nor as in-scope assets (particularly NFTs), the AIFM must ask its NCA for approval of the delegation. Due to the legal uncertainty as to which digital asset qualifies for which category,[46] AIFMs will likely feel under pressure to require their delegates to have both MiFID and MiCA CASP licences, and, on top of that, ask their NCA for a general (rather than specific) approval of the respective delegation.[47]

9.5 THE DEPOSITARY'S RELIANCE ON CRYPTO CUSTODIANS

A depositary of an AIF rarely itself holds all assets of the AIF. Instead, it often relies on external service providers as sub-custodians. Article 21(11)–(13) AIFMD provides for rules on sub-depositary services. Articles 70(1) and 75 MiCA regulate crypto custody as a qualified form of safekeeping under Article 70(1) MiCA, similarly to Article 21(8) AIFMD.

9.5.1 *Custody Rules under Articles 70(1) and 75 MiCA*

Safekeeping under Article 70(1) MiCA extends to the holding of cryptoassets on behalf of clients, and, in a far more practical sense, the means of access to these cryptoassets (i.e., the private key, see Article 3(17) MiCA).[48] In the investment fund context, the scope extends to

[44] For MiCA side services where the UCITS ManCO and AIFM qualify as CASPs in scope of Title V of MiCA, Article 73 of MiCA foresees an outsourcing rule that does not require authorisation of the delegate.
[45] See Chapter 4.
[46] See Chapter 4.
[47] See Zetzsche et al., 'Digital Assets, MiCA & EU Investment Fund Law' (2023), p. 31. Website https://dx.doi.org/10.2139/ssrn.4637019 (last accessed on 1 October 2024).
[48] For details, see Chapter 8 on crypto custody.

crypto custodians but potentially also to crypto portfolio managers that hold clients' assets as a side service.

Article 75 MiCA on custody services provided by CASPs is the equivalent of Article 21 AIFMD and Chapter IV of UCITSD on depositary services.[49] CASPs must reside within the European Single Market[50] and enter into an agreement with clients characterised by meticulously prescribed contractual details,[51] which we discussed in Chapter 8. Among many other stipulations, CASPs are obliged to provide procedures necessary for the return of cryptoassets to clients[52] as well as (an operational) segregation of the client's assets from those of the CASP on the distributed ledger.[53] This shall ensure, for instance, that in the event of the CASP's insolvency, the client's assets remain unimpaired. Notably, Article 75(4) MiCA inserts a private law provision mandating substitution in the event of changes to the DLT and other events potentially impacting clients' rights. The provision establishes the right of clients 'to any crypto-assets or any rights newly created on the basis and to the extent of the client's positions at the time of the occurrence of that change or event'.[54] While these provisions are meant to protect the custodian's clients, they subject CASPs to liability risk for events taking place on the DLT, which the CASPs may or may not be able to influence. Of note, a CASP may have no governance right in relation to token creation or modification by way of DLT. If the DLT does not allocate the right, or a part thereof, to the respective token, it may never come into the custodian's reach.

These difficult provisions with uncertain private law impacts shift the focus of attention onto the custodian's liabilities, which we covered in detail in Chapter 8 and are of relevance in the investment fund context. To sum up: the liability of CASPs for the loss of cryptoassets or the means of access to these assets shall be limited to situations attributable to, and under the control of, the CASPs.[55] The liability here is limited to the market value of the lost cryptoasset at the time the loss occurred. (See, however, Chapter 15 on liability under DORA.)

9.5.2 *Impact of MiCA on Fund Setup*

When depositary services in relation to cryptoassets in the scope of MiCA are concerned, Articles 70(1) and 75 MiCA must be read in tandem with Article 21 AIFMD (see Figure 9.1).[56]

Subject to Article 21(1) AIFMD, every AIF (with every sub-fund of an umbrella structure constituting one separate AIF) must have one depositary. Moreover, all depositaries must provide *safekeeping* for the AIF's assets subject to Article 21(8) AIFMD. Pursuant to Article 21 (8)(a) AIFMD, for financial instruments that may be held in custody, depositaries must provide

[49] The MiFID frameworks on the safeguarding of client funds are scattered around a number of provisions, including Article 16(8), (9), and (10) MiFID as well as Article 49 and Annex I of Commission Delegated Regulation 2017/565.

[50] Cf. Articles 59(2) and 60(1)–(6) of MiCA.

[51] Article 75(1) of MiCA. Unlike Article 21(2) of AIFMD and Article 75(1) of MiCA does not require this agreement to be written.

[52] Article 75(6) of MiCA.

[53] Article 75(7) of MiCA. An equivalent asset segregation and registration of an AIF's assets is foreseen by Article 21(8)(a)(ii) of AIFMD.

[54] Article 75(4) second sub-paragraph of MiCA.

[55] Article 75(8) of MiCA. The equivalent provision under AIFMD is Article 21(12); under UCITSD Article 24. We discuss this provision in detail in Chapter 8.

[56] The following text is taken from Zetzsche et al., 'Digital Assets, MiCA & EU Investment Fund Law' (2023), pp. 34–37. Website https://dx.doi.org/10.2139/ssrn.4637019 (last accessed on 1 October 2024).

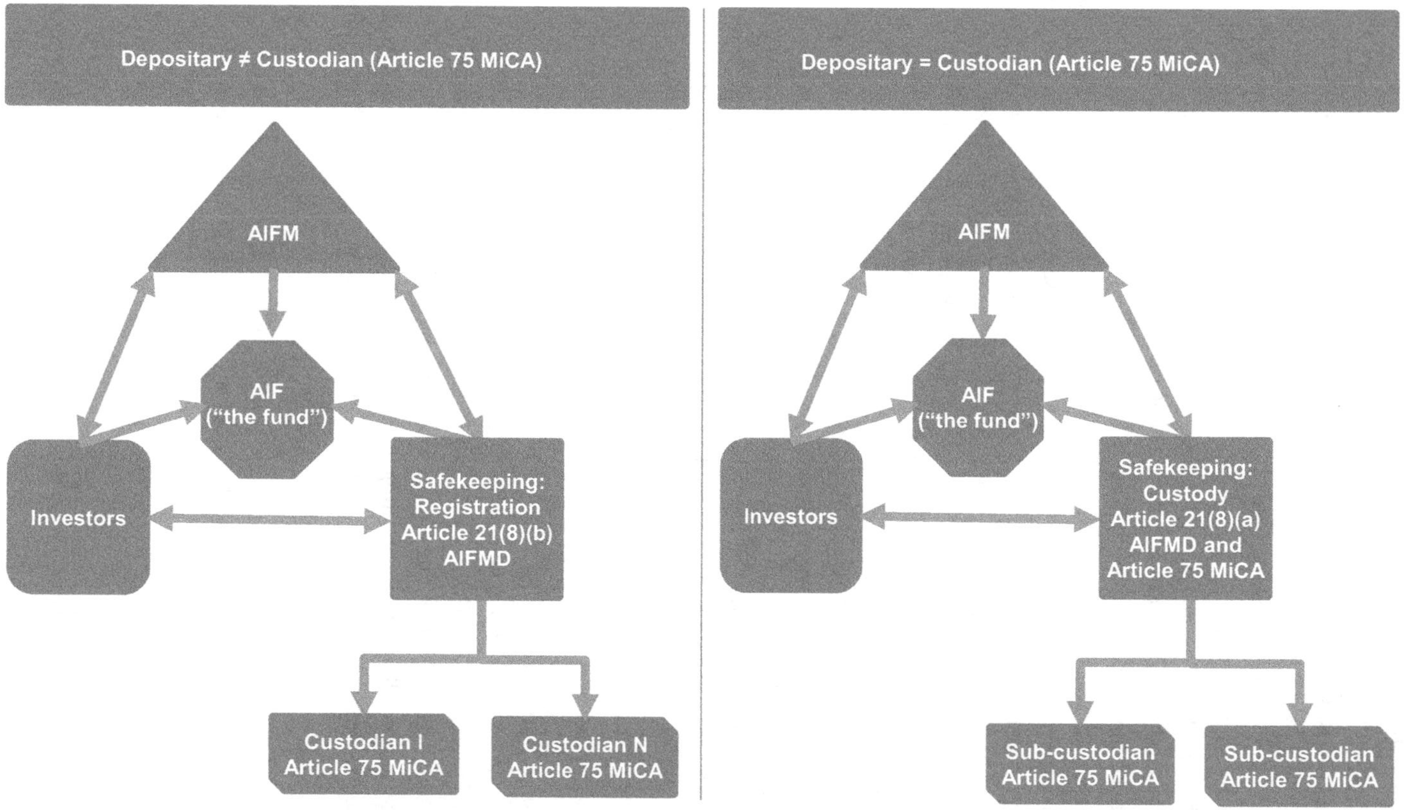

FIGURE 9.1 Custody setups for cryptoassets under AIFMD and Title V MiCA.

that *custody*. For other assets, they must safeguard ownership rights by way of record-keeping. Furthermore, a fund depositary may delegate safekeeping (and thus custody) to sub-custodians pursuant to Article 21(11)–(14) AIFMD.

Articles 70 and 75 MiCA specify safekeeping and custody with respect to cryptoassets but do not regulate depositary relationships under AIFMD. This leaves open a number of questions about the relationship between Article 21 AIFMD and Articles 70 and 75 MiCA. The first question is whether Articles 70 and 75 MiCA amend or merely supplement AIFMD. The answer to that influences the second question, concerning which alternative to Article 21 AIFMD applies to safekeeping of in-scope assets. A third question is linked to the second, which is whether Articles 70 and 75 MiCA widen the catalogue of depositaries listed in Article 21(3) AIFMD.[57]

In answering these questions, the starting point is to establish that Article 21(8)(a) AIFMD was *not* amended. The bifurcation between "financial instruments to be held in custody" and "other assets" in Article 21(8) AIFMD continues to apply.[58] MiCA applies only to cryptoassets that do *not* qualify as financial instruments pursuant to Article 2(4)(a) MiCA. The wording of Article 21 AIFMD does not require the depositary to hold, in addition to financial instruments, cryptoassets in custody. On that basis, we see two likely readings of the law.

Under the first reading, we could stick to MiCA's gap-filling approach: in-scope assets, even with MiCA in force, remain as "other assets" subject to Article 21(8)(b) AIFMD. In turn, the depositary is not obliged to hold in-scope assets in custody. The depositary's duties are then limited to verifying the ownership of the AIF (or the AIFM acting on behalf of the AIF) of such assets and maintaining up-to-date records of those assets where the depositary believes that they are owned by the former.

Under the second reading, we anticipate an implicit amendment of AIFMD, following Article 60(3)(a) MiCA, according to which 'providing custody and administration of cryptoassets on behalf of clients is deemed equivalent to the ancillary service referred to in Section B, point (1), of Annex I to Directive 2014/65/EU'. We can only speculate as to the meaning of "equivalent" in this context, but one interpretation of that clause is to treat in-scope assets in the future as if they were listed in Article 21(8)(a) AIFMD under "financial instruments" as the second asset category to be held in custody. Articles 70 and 75 MiCA would then specify the conditions of crypto custody in a way similar to the MiFID framework's rules on the custody of financial instruments.

Note that both interpretations are consistent with AIFMD. Under the first interpretation, the depositary satisfies the duties of safekeeping in relation to in-scope assets by way of ownership verification and record-keeping. The role of Articles 70 and 75 MiCA then follows that of Article 21(8)(b)(ii) AIFMD: pursuant to that provision, the depositary's assessment of "ownership" shall be based on information or documents provided by the AIF or the AIFM and, where available, on *external evidence*. The crypto custodian holding assets on behalf of the AIF then provides the evidence on which the depositary relies, similar in function to sub-custody, yet different in legal

[57] According to that provisions, depositaries must be credit institutions or MiFID investment firms, or in the case of closed-ended AIFs investing in assets other than those to be held in custody in accordance with Article 21(8)(a) of AIFMD, certain professionals active as depositaries as further defined by law of the Member States.

[58] While we have argued that for financial instruments, Article 3(1)(17) of MiCA clarifies that digital assets may be held in custody, and hence, Article 21(8)(a) of AIFMD applies (see Chapter 8) that this does not include an implicit amendment of the AIFMD; rather it clarifies a question so far unanswered by EU law as to whether digital assets can be held in custody; MiCA's answer is: yes, they can.

form. Under the second interpretation, the depositary satisfies the duties of safekeeping by way of custody, details of which are provided in Articles 70 and 75 MiCA.

The main practical differences between the two readings concern (a) the freedom to choose crypto custodians and (b) the depositary's liability. Under the first interpretation, given that the crypto custodian does not have to function as the AIF's depositary at the same time, fund managers, promoters, and depositaries are fairly free to choose a crypto custodian from among all those authorised under Title V MiCA. This may be beneficial given that some crypto custodians could more effectively safeguard some token types and less effectively protect others depending on regional proximity and the technical features of the token. Depositaries will nevertheless quite strictly review the choice of a custodian since they rely on the custodian's records with respect to establishing the fund's ownership. In this case, pursuant to Article 21(11) third subsection AIFMD, the depositary is liable only for losses suffered by the fund and its investors 'as a result of the depositary's negligent or intentional failure to properly fulfil its obligations'. Most importantly, failures at the custodian's level unrelated to the depositary would not result in the *depositary's* liability. Instead, the custodian would be liable under Article 75(8) MiCA to the fund and its investors (usually represented by the AIFM) for losses attributable to the *custodian*.

Under the second reading, which widens the scope of Article 21(8)(a) AIFMD, any choice of crypto custodian is limited by the depositary's willingness to deliver cryptoasset services. So far, the market of large-scale and professional depositaries offering cryptoasset services has been rather small. And, significantly, the second reading is unlikely to change that: pursuant to Article 21(11) first and second subsections AIFMD, the depositary is liable for any loss of the cryptoasset (other than one prompted by *force majeure*).

The upside of the first interpretation is its openness to innovation courtesy of a balanced approach that mixes established depositary services with a reliance on new authorised and supervised crypto custodians. By contrast, the second reading is consistent with the strict liability that UCITS and AIF depositaries face with respect to funds investing in digital assets that qualify as financial instruments *and* with the core motivation of the original adoption of AIFMD's depositary rules in the aftermath of the Madoff scandal,[59] with the purpose of ensuring investor protection through strong depositaries.

We cannot say with certainty which of the two views will prevail eventually in court. With that in mind, regulators are encouraged to provide further clarity in the upcoming Level 2 legislative process. It should be noted that this decision will be pivotal: whether or not depositaries are liable for the existence of the assets will be a 'game changer' as to whether depositaries are willing to act as fund depositaries, and thus whether EU investment funds investing in cryptoassets under MiCA will exist at all, in an environment characterised by the risks of heavy operational losses and large-scale asset diversion.

In this regard, a reasonable compromise would rely, for in-scope cryptoassets, on Article 21(8)(b) AIFMD. Either the depositary may delegate crypto custody to a CASP which is then subject to Articles 70 and 75 MiCA, and potentially liable for losses under Article 75 MiCA as laid out in Section 8.6.8; or the depositary may decide to hold the cryptoassets itself; then Articles 70 and 75 MiCA apply to the depositary, leading to liability of the depositary for lost assets under Article 75 MiCA. In turn, Article 21(8)(a) AIFMD only applies to crypto-financial instruments but not for cryptoassets subject to MiCA.

[59] On the Madoff scandal, see D. C. Langevoort, 'The SEC and the Madoff Scandal: Three Narratives in Search for a Story', *Michigan State Law Review* (2009): 899–914.

9.6 CONCLUSION

The presence of regulated investment funds and fund managers is desirable for cryptoasset markets, yet this potentially exposes both investors in these funds to operational risk and fund intermediaries to liability. MiCA has created a greater degree of legal certainty and a more robust environment with regard to fiduciary duties and outsourcing by the AIFM, but potential liability risks will discourage traditional intermediaries from functioning as crypto custodians, while AIF depositaries are strongly encouraged to structure crypto custody under Article 21(8)(b) AIFMD with a view to shielding themselves from liability. If this happens, investors will bear the risk of widespread asset diversions and operational risks. When these risks materialise, trust in the robustness of cryptoasset markets will suffer. While the EU legislature could provide a solution here and shift these risks on to AIF depositaries, we are not sure whether they should do so, given that in this case risks from an isolated cryptoasset market would spill over into traditional finance.

10

Market Abuse and Insider Dealing Rules (Title VI MiCA)

10.1 MARKET FAIRNESS AS A CONCERN UNDER MICA

Market fairness mainly focuses on financial misconduct and criminal behaviour, such as manipulative marketing, insider dealing, and market manipulation (i.e., price manipulation), and thus relates to customer protection. The EU's MAR[1] seeks to ensure market fairness in the field of financial instruments, and Title VI MiCA is modelled on the MAR rules.[2]

Beyond the traditional ways of manipulating markets (such as "pump and dump" schemes[3] and churning[4]) and those shared by other technology-driven market environments,[5] crypto is characterised by an extensive use of social media that is widely regarded as "unregulated." Partly, social media[6] serves as a substitute for regulated disclosures, and it also partly serves marketing purposes, attracting new types of clients who could not be reached through traditional sales channels. Indeed, crypto intermediaries and token issuers often use non-formalised information to market their products. This has prompted regulatory attention given that much of the information disseminated have come to be seen, with hindsight, as misleading, overly enthusiastic, or opportunistic in that they have taken advantage of inside information or sudden market

[1] Regulation (EU) No. 596/2014 of the European Parliament and of the Council of 16 April 2014 on market abuse (market abuse regulation), OJ L 173, 12 June 2014, pp. 1–61.

[2] On this topic, see K. Langenbucher, 'Insider Trading in European Law – From Financial Instruments to Crypto-Assets' (2024) ECGI Working Paper No. 763/2024, pp. 53–56. Website https://dx.doi.org/10.2139/ssrn.4771059 (last accessed on 1 October 2024).

[3] By way of "pump-and-dump" perpetrators attempt to boost the price of an asset through fake recommendations based on false, misleading, or greatly exaggerated statements. The perpetrators will sell their positions after the asset price has risen in response to this information. According to Chainanalysis, 24 per cent of new token on-chain trades were suspicious of being part of a "pump and dump" schemes; see Chainalysis, '24% of New Tokens Launched in 2022 Bear On-Chain Characteristics of Pump and Dump Schemes' (2023). Website www.chainalysis.com/blog/2022-crypto-pump-and-dump-schemes/ (last accessed on 1 October 2024).

[4] See Cambridge Dictionary, sub-churning (defining churning as "the illegal practice by [brokers] of buying and selling a client's investments more often than necessary, in order to make more money in commissions"). Website https://dictionary.cambridge.org/dictionary/english/churning (last accessed on 1 October2024). Events of churning have been identified by S. Aramonte *et al.*, 'DeFi Risks and the Decentralisation Illusion' (2021). Website www.bis.org/publ/qtrpdf/r_qt2112b.htm (last accessed on 1 October 2024).

[5] See, for instance, F. Annunziata, *Artificial Intelligence and Market Abuse Legislation – A European Perspective* (Cheltenham: Edward Elgar, 2023).

[6] See A. Canning, 'Bursting the Crypto-Bubble – Why It's Time to Act Against Social Media Platforms' (2023). Website www.beuc.eu/blog/bursting-the-social-media-crypto-bubble/ (last accessed on 1 October 2024).

turns prompted by such information.[7] While the Commission draft of MiCA was less pronounced on this particular matter, the adopted version of Title VI MiCA contains a full chapter on market manipulation and insider trading.

We discuss the related legal questions here in turn, starting with an account of observed informational conduct (Section 10.2), before describing the rules of Title VI MiCA related to market abuse and insider trading (Section 10.3). We then conclude with an assessment of the effectiveness of Title VI MiCA with respect to the issues previously described (Section 10.4).

10.2 INFORMATIONAL PRACTICE IN CRYPTO

Beyond the whitepapers discussed in Chapter 5, a number of informational practices are widely applied throughout the crypto industry.[8] We divide these practices into the following two categories: indirect distribution efforts and market abuse efforts.

10.2.1 *Indirect Distribution Efforts*

10.2.1.1 Referral Programmes and Social Network Expansion

Crypto firms offer incentives to existing users to attract new ones, through so-called referral programmes whereby any user can generate returns (or "earn") from referring new users to the application, regardless of the jurisdictions in which these users reside.[9] For instance, if a third-country user refers an EU contact, the latter may sign up to the given DLT system as a new user. In return for the referral, the existing user responsible for attracting the new user receives part of the revenues generated through the attracted user, resulting in a de facto commission.

Other DLT systems suggest to their users that they form part of a social community rather than being a financial service, 'resulting in community-building efforts, such as newsletter signups (available to mail-addresses from EU countries) and chat groups, such as Telegram groups (available to phone numbers from EU countries)'.[10]

Since existing users prompt new users to contact the crypto firm via its website or often-used communication tools like Discord, the crypto firm can classify that initial contact as "reverse solicitation". In turn, both the commission- and community-based practices result in de facto marketing outside of channels controlled by, yet associated with, the crypto intermediary and contrary to the requirements of EU financial legislation on the cross-border marketing of financial services.

10.2.1.2 Search Engines

Some crypto firms may compensate search engines for paid priority positions (which are on offer for languages, keywords, specific countries, cities, or even a neighbourhood) upon searches for keywords of the industry, such as "cryptoassets", "token", or "stablecoins", or employ SEO

[7] Cf. IOSCO, 'Policy Recommendations for Crypto and Digital Asset Markets Final Report' (16 November 2023), Recommendations 8, 9, 10, and 18 and accompanying text.

[8] This section is borrowing from Zetzsche *et al.*, 'Remaining Regulatory Challenges in Digital Finance and Crypto-Assets after MiCA', para. 3.6, p. 74; we refer for sources and evidence to the statement to that study.

[9] See Zetzsche *et al.*, 'Remaining Regulatory Challenges in Digital Finance and Crypto-Assets after MiCA', para. 3.6.1, p. 74 (stating 'Several websites, accessible to EU citizens, contain marketing of crypto intermediaries. Inspection of the URLs reveals that they contain tracking parameters that are required by affiliate programs to track referrals'.).

[10] See Zetzsche *et al.*, 'Remaining Regulatory Challenges in Digital Finance and Crypto-Assets after MiCA', para. 3.6, p. 74.

techniques to rank high in the organic search results where the search engine takes steps to prevent the advertisement of illicit or otherwise unwanted products and services.[11] This happens even where searches are initiated from areas where the crypto firm is not entitled to either offer cryptoassets or perform financial services.

10.2.1.3 *Social Media*

All large crypto firms have well-promoted social media channels with millions of followers, dubbed "Crypto Twitter."[12] Smaller crypto firms use social media to gather new customers by posting about rewards, high-yielding products, and new listings on crypto exchanges. At the same time, multiple "finfluencers", including world-famous celebrities,[13] promote DeFi applications by detailing technical/fundamental price indicators on their social media channels. A variant of these constitutes affiliate marketing schemes used by "professional" parties to monetise traffic on websites, for instance, by listing "Top 3 crypto exchanges" or "Top 10 hot crypto issues", without disclosing objective criteria for the classification or ranking.

10.2.2 *Market Abuse Efforts*

10.2.2.1 *Non-technical Language*

Switching attention from (manipulative) distribution to outright manipulation, crypto firms often use industry-specific language. In at least one instance, a prominent (now defunct) crypto firm was examined for disclosing on its website information that was neither vetted nor explained. Furthermore, crypto language is often emotional, potentially misleading users to either exert enthusiasm or act with confusion and anxiety.

Crypto's *own language* often 'pretends to apply conduct rules complying with industry standards, yet these assertions (which are frequently found on websites) can hardly be proven. They (. . .) have the potential to mislead users not familiar with crypto'.[14]

10.2.2.2 *Outright Breaches of Laws*

According to the EBA, some crypto firms use misleading and aggressive advertising that may arise from "inadequate" advertising approaches.[15] In the same vein, the Commodity Futures Trading Commission (CFTC) charged the world's largest crypto exchange Binance in the

[11] See Zetzsche *et al.*, 'Remaining Regulatory Challenges in Digital Finance and Crypto-Assets after MiCA', para. 3.6.1, p. 74.

[12] We use the term here as categorisation for any use of informal information exchange in the field of crypto by way of social media. See for that understanding Coinbase. Website www.coindesk.com/tag/crypto-twitter/ (last accessed on 1 October 2024) (defining Crypto Twitter as 'an online community that encompasses individuals, companies, protocols, blockchain networks, and crypto exchanges, all actively engaged in the world of cryptocurrencies on the social media platform Twitter (now "X"). As a hub for discussions, news, and insights, crypto Twitter serves as a resource for those seeking to stay informed about the latest developments in the crypto space. This platform allows people involved in crypto, including enthusiasts, investors, and industry professionals, to connect, share ideas, and collaborate on various projects'.).

[13] U.S. Securities and Exchange Commission, 'SEC Charges Kim Kardashian for Unlawfully Touting Crypto Security', Press release No. 2022-183 (October 2022). Website www.sec.gov\\news\\press-release\\2022-183 (last accessed on 1 October 2024); U.S. Securities and Exchange Commission, 'SEC Charges Crypto Entrepreneur Justin Sun and His Companies for Fraud and other Securities Law Violations', Press release No. 2023-59 (March 2023). Website www.sec.gov\\news\\press-release\\2023-59 (last accessed on 1 October 2024).

[14] See Zetzsche *et al.*, 'Remaining Regulatory Challenges in Digital Finance and Crypto-Assets after MiCA', para. 3.6, p. 74.

[15] See EBA, 'Report with Advice for the European Commission on Crypto-Assets', para. 31. Website www.eba.europa.eu\\eba-reports-on-crypto-assets (last accessed on 1 October 2024).

spring of 2023 for the strategic approach it took to circumvent the respective commodities regulation. Among others, Binance is accused of using several hundred anonymous accounts to manipulate prices for listed tokens.[16]

The FTX's bankruptcy also teaches us a lesson on the risks of insider dealing and market manipulation. While reports state that the FTX's fund Alameda held primarily the FTX's main cryptoasset on its balance sheet – which is equivalent to trading in a regulated entity's own security – Binance, its largest competitor, publicly cast doubt on the FTX's financial reliability. Such behaviour has most likely contributed to the crisis of confidence in the FTX and rendered any rescue efforts by other parties futile from the beginning. Within the regulated securities industry, any such statement would run counter to market abuse legislation.

10.3 MICA'S RULES ON MARKET ABUSE AND INSIDER DEALING

10.3.1 *MAR Orientation*

The market abuse rules in Title VI MiCA heavily borrow from the example provided in the MAR,[17] as shown in Table 10.1.

Title VI MiCA thus constitutes an example of MiCA's leaning on general EU financial law. Assuming that the MiCA implementing legislation will be modelled with MAR provisions in mind, Table 10.1 presents the respective MAR implementing measures.

As follows from the former, MiCA uses the all-encompassing term "market abuse" for the two main types of misconduct, namely, "insider dealing" and "market manipulation".

Insider dealing is inherently linked to the term "inside information" (Article 87 MiCA): Articles 89 and 90 MiCA prohibit both insider dealing (i.e., trading prompted by inside information) and the unlawful disclosure of inside information. To ensure that inside information comes to the public's attention, Article 88 MiCA foresees a lawful way of disclosing inside information. The core question of insider dealing regulation concerns defining the moment at which a piece of information becomes inside information. Article 87 MiCA sets out to define inside information, drawing on concepts established in the context of the MAR.

Market manipulation comprises other types of conduct that influence the market price of a cryptoasset other than insider dealing. The main challenge here is to distinguish lawful ways of communicating about and trading in a cryptoasset from unlawful ways.

Both insider dealing and market manipulation are related: if inside information is present, individuals may seek to manipulate the price downward to build a stake inexpensively prior to the disclosure of positive news. In turn, Article 92 MiCA, supplemented by L2 legislation,[18] prescribes preventive measures aiming to counter both insider dealing and market manipulation. These measures must be performed by professionals involved in crypto transactions.

We discuss each of these elements below.

[16] *Case Commodity Futures Trading Commission (CFTC)* v. *Changpeng Zhao, Binance Holdings Limited, Binance Holdings (IE) Limited, Binance (Services) Holdings Limited, and Samuel Lim.*, US 1:23-cv-01887. Website www.cftc .gov/media/8351/%20enfbinancecomplaint032723/download (last accessed on 1 October 2024).

[17] Regulation (EU) 596/2014 of the European Parliament and of the Council of 16 April 2014 on market abuse (market abuse regulation) and repealing Directive 2003/6/EC of the European Parliament and of the Council and Commission Directives 2003/124/EC, 2003/125/EC, and 2004/72/EC, OJ 2014 No. L173, 12 June 2014.

[18] See ESMA, 'Consultation Paper: Draft Technical Standards and Guidelines Specifying Certain Requirements of the Markets in Crypto Assets Regulation (MiCA) on Detection and Prevention of Market Abuse, Investor Protection and Operational Resilience – Third Consultation Paper' (2024), ESMA75-453128700-1002, pp. 39–56.

TABLE 10.1 *Origin of MiCA's rules on market abuse and insider dealing in the MAR*

MiCA Articles	Subject matter	Equivalent MAR Articles	MAR implementing legislation
86	Scope of the Rules on Market Abuse	2	Commission Delegated Regulation (EU) 2016/1052 of 8 March 2016 (buybacks and stabilisation measures)
87	Inside Information	7	Indirectly, in all other implementing acts
88	Public Disclosure of Inside Information	17	Commission Implementing Regulation (EU) 2016/1055 of 29 June 2016
89	Prohibition of Insider Dealing	14	Commission Implementing Regulation (EU) 2022/1210 of 13 July 2022 (insider lists); Commission Implementing Regulation (EU) 2016/523 of 10 March 2016 (manager's transactions)
90	Prohibition of Unlawful Disclosure of Inside Information	14	Commission Delegated Regulation (EU) 2016/960 of 17 May 2016 (market soundings)
91	Prohibition of Manipulation	15 and 12	Annex I MAR and Annex II of Commission Delegated Regulation (EU) 2016/522 of 17 December 2015
92	Prevention and Detection of Market Abuse	16	Commission Delegated Regulation (EU) 2016/908 of 26 February 2016 (accept market practices); Commission Delegated Regulation (EU) 2016/957 of 9 March 2016 (detection of abusive practices); Commission Delegated Regulation (EU) 2016/958 of 9 March 2016 (investment recommendations)

10.3.2 *Scope (Article 86 MiCA)*

Article 86 MiCA limits its scope to cryptoassets (potentially) admitted to trading. Moreover, Article 86 MiCA covers only cryptoassets within the scope of MiCA (cf. Chapter 4) (e.g., for financial instruments, MAR applies). Note that admission to trading is not qualified here as it is, for instance, in Article 11 MiCA ('admitted to trading on a trading platform for cryptoassets in the Union'); in turn, any listing on a platform that meets the definition of Article 3(1)(18) MiCA[19] for 'operation of a trading platform' suffices. These are platforms that, if located in the EU, would need a licence as a CASP under Article 59 MiCA in tandem with Article 3(16) MiCA (see Chapter 7).

As is the case with regard to MAR, Title VI MiCA claims to have a *global scope*, including actions and omissions in the EU and third countries. In turn, any transaction performed on a third-country exchange may be subject to MiCA, even where (a) the cryptoasset is traded in third countries and (b) the entity is related to that third country. We reconcile this with MiCA's territorial scope in Article 2 MiCA by arguing that EU authorities will exercise powers only

[19] Cf. Article 3(1)(18) of MiCA states: 'operation of a trading platform for crypto-assets' means the management of one or more multilateral systems, which bring together or facilitate the bringing together of multiple third-party purchasing and selling interests in cryptoassets, in the system, and in accordance with its rules, in a way that results in a contract, either by exchanging cryptoassets for funds or by exchanging cryptoassets for other cryptoassets.

where the effects of the conduct are felt on EU territory; the "effects" test to establish jurisdiction is the same here as that in MAR.[20]

With regard to those assets, all transactions, orders, or types of behaviour are in MiCA's scope, even when they take place outside of the trading platform. In turn, acts performed on a DeFi platform (e.g., a token issue or transfer) that impact on the price are also in scope.

Title VI MICA concerns 'acts carried out by any person' thereby excluding merely automated processes such as those performed by smart contracts. Yet, of course, if a smart contract is programmed to take advantage of certain opportunities, this equates to an 'act carried out by any person.'

10.3.3 *Insider Dealing (Articles 87–90 MiCA)*

The provisions on insider dealing are split into three parts: the definition of inside information (Article 87), the lawful ways of disclosing this information (Article 88 MiCA), and the related prohibitions of insider dealing and unlawful disclosure (Articles 89 and 90 MiCA).

10.3.3.1 *Inside Information (Article 87 MiCA)*

Article 87(1) MiCA defines inside information in accordance with Article 7(1)(a) and (d) MAR,[21] addressing on the one hand the self-created information impact on cryptoassets stemming from the inner sphere of issuers, offerors, or persons seeking admission to trading and on the other hand the information stemming from trading activity as a broker or where the order is a side-service (for instance, in addition to (collective) portfolio management).

By including issuers, offerors, or persons seeking admission to trading, the scope is quite far reaching. Note that the execution of orders is not limited to the reception and transmission of orders for cryptoassets on behalf of clients as defined in Article 3(1)(23) MiCA; it can take place in any context where CASPs perform for clients.

The main criterion of inside information is its potential price impact: one must ask whether the information 'if it were made public, would likely have a significant effect on the prices of those crypto-assets or on the price of a related crypto-asset'.[22] Article 87(4) MiCA clarifies that this is the case if 'a reasonable holder of crypto-assets would likely use [that information] as part of the basis of the holder's investment decisions'.

To be classed as inside information, the information must be sufficiently *precise*. Article 87(2) MiCA defines precise information as any information that 'indicates a set of circumstances which exists or which may reasonably be expected to come into existence, or an event which has occurred or which may reasonably be expected to occur, where it is specific enough to enable a conclusion to be drawn as to the possible effect of that set of circumstances or event on the prices of crypto-assets'. The rest of the definition encompasses the criteria of the *Geltl and Lafonta*

[20] See D. A. Zetzsche, in Enzyklopädie Europarecht, Vol. 5, 2nd ed. 2022, Chapter 14, para. 43; D. A. Zetzsche and R. Veidt, in Enzyklopädie Europarecht, Vol. 5, 2nd ed. 2022, Chapter 12, para. 52.

[21] Note that Article 7(1)(d) MAR was amended by the Listing Act, meaning that the wording is no longer identical with MiCA. See Article 2(3) of the European Parliament Legislative Resolution of 24 April 2024 on the Proposal for a Regulation of the European Parliament and of the Council Amending Regulations (EU) 2017/1129, (EU) No 596/2014, and (EU) No 600/2014 to make public capital markets in the Union more attractive for companies and to facilitate access to capital for small and medium-sized enterprises (COM(2022)0762 – C9-0417/2022 – 2022/0411 (COD)).

[22] Some refer to this as the Probability Magnitude test, yet there is uncertainty as to whether the ECJ adopted this test in its judicature on the MAR; cf. ECJ of 28 June 2012 – C-19/11, para. 55; for a detailed discussion, cf. D. A. Zetzsche, in Enzyklopädie Europarecht, Vol. 5, 2nd ed. 2022, Chapter 14, para. 118 et seq.

verdicts developed under the MAR[23] on *protracted processes*, according to which any intermediate step must be evaluated separately as to whether it meets the Probability-Impact test laid out in Article 87(1) MiCA.

10.3.3.2 *Disclosure of Inside Information (Article 88)*

Given that the unlawful disclosure of inside information is prohibited in Article 90 MiCA, there must also be a way to disclose inside information in a lawful way. Article 88 MiCA here leans on the following MAR disclosure concept relating to inside information: 'Issuers, offerors and persons seeking admission to trading [the 'obliged persons'] shall inform the public as soon as possible of inside information referred to in Article 87 that directly concerns them, in a manner that enables fast access as well as complete, correct and timely assessment of the information by the public.' Under the MAR, these requirements are usually fulfilled if the obliged person uses information intermediaries ensuring access through active dissemination to market intermediaries; website disclosures do not suffice. Nevertheless, the issuer must post and maintain the information for five years on their website.[24] What is missing in MiCA though is a reference to the officially appointed storage mechanism for issuers whose securities are listed on regulated markets.

The obliged persons must not use inside information in the marketing of their activities.

Article 88(2) MiCA allows for delayed disclosure under the same conditions as Article 17(2) MAR, requiring that:

(a) immediate disclosure is unlikely to prejudice the legitimate interests of the issuers, offerors, or persons seeking admission to trading;
(b) delay of disclosure is unlikely to mislead the public;
(c) issuers, offerors, or persons seeking admission to trading are able to ensure the confidentiality of that information; and
(d) the competent authority is informed about the delay and the reasons for the delay are explained (cf. Article 88(3) MiCA).

The ESMA is given explicit implementing powers to define relevant details under Article 88 MiCA and has proposed implementing technical standards similar to those under MAR (see Table 10.1).[25]

10.3.3.3 *Prohibitions (Articles 89 and 90)*

Both insider dealing and unlawful disclosure are prohibited. Insider dealing occurs where 'a person possesses inside information and uses that information by acquiring or disposing of, for its own account or for the account of a third party, directly or indirectly, crypto-assets to which that information relates'.

The term "use" is widely understood, and it is assumed to materialise in cases where a person has acquired knowledge of such information (i.e., the acquisition indicates use). MiCA further specifies that use can include an order cancellation, an amendment of an order, or the submission, modification, or withdrawal of a bid.

Insider dealing can take place with an own or third-party account or by way of recommendation or inducement.

[23] ECJ of 28 June 2012 – C-19/11, para. 55 – Geltl/Daimler; ECJ of 11 March 2015 – C-628/13, para. 21 f. – Lafonta/AMF. Cf. D. A. Zetzsche, in Enzyklopädie Europarecht, Vol. 5, 2nd ed. 2022, Chapter 14, para. 110 et seq.

[24] See on the website publication ESMA, 'Final Report: Draft Technical Standards Specifying Certain Requirements of the Markets in Crypto Assets Regulation (MiCA) – Second Package' (2024), ESMA75-453128700-1229, p. 417.

[25] See ESMA, 'Final Report: Draft Technical Standards Specifying Certain Requirements of the Markets in Crypto Assets Regulation (MiCA) – Second Package' (2024), ESMA75-453128700-1229, pp. 413–21 (proposing similar rules to those in Commission Implementing Regulation (EU) 2016/1055 under MAR).

The personal scope of the insider dealing prohibition extends to a group dubbed "primary insiders"[26] including:

- members of the administrative, management or supervisory bodies of the issuer, the offeror, or the person seeking admission to trading;
- holders in the capital of the issuer, the offeror, or the person seeking admission to trading;
- person having access to the information through the exercise of an employment, profession, or duties or in relation to its role in the distributed ledger technology or similar technology; and
- criminals achieving inside information (for instance, cyberattacks).

The prohibition also extends to any other person who obtains inside information where that person knows or ought to know that it is inside information. In these cases, both knowledge and intent matter. Such persons fall under the group "secondary insiders".

Article 90 MiCA builds on the MAR system for the prohibition of the unlawful disclosure of inside information by prohibiting all disclosures unless 'such disclosure is made in the normal exercise of an employment, a profession or duties'. The latter includes, for instance, where inside information is given to an external legal counsel or an M&A consultant subject to conditions of professional secrecy, but also the disclosure of inside information by way of the channels prescribed by law to inform the market at large. Again, we argue that for details, the concepts developed under MAR[27] should also guide the application of MiCA.

10.3.4 *Market Manipulation (Article 91)*

Article 91(1) MiCA stipulates the general prohibition of market manipulation, equivalent to Article 15 MAR.

Determining market manipulation is laden with uncertainties. Some of this uncertainty stems from the fact that the traders' generation of informational advantages is, at its core, desirable to support information efficient markets. That explains why the rest of Article 91 MiCA is devoted to defining market manipulation, a task which in the scope of the MAR in addition to Article 12 MAR is performed by an extensive list of implementing legislation (cf. Table 10.1). Article 91 (2) MiCA provides a general description and Article 91(3) MiCA presents a so-called black list of illicit conduct. We argue that for details, the concepts developed under MAR should also guide the application of MiCA.

According to Article 91(2) MiCA, market manipulation generally includes sending wrong signals to the market and impacting on the price of a cryptoasset. While the bad actor may have intended to impact on the price, where this effort is unsuccessful, the inadequate signal alone constitutes manipulation. Article 91(2) MiCA establishes that manipulation can take place by entering into a transaction, placing an order to trade, or engaging in any other behaviour that leads to the desired effect (i.e., sending a false or misleading signal that has a price impact) or disseminating information through the media, including the internet, or by any other means, including the dissemination of rumours, where the person who engaged in the dissemination knew, or ought to have known, that the information was false or misleading. The latter may cover certain types of conduct observed in the crypto industry (see Section 10.2).

[26] The concept of primary insider vs. secondary insider is akin to Article 8 MAR; cf. D. A. Zetzsche, in Enzyklopädie Europarecht, Vol. 5, 2nd ed. 2022, Chapter 14, para. 126 et seq.

[27] D. A. Zetzsche, in Enzyklopädie Europarecht, Vol. 5, 2nd ed. 2022, Chapter 14, para. 110 et seq.

The "black list" under Article 91(3) MiCA entails:

- securing a dominant position over the supply of, or demand for, a cryptoasset, which has, or is likely to have, the effect of fixing, directly or indirectly, purchase or sale prices or creates, or is likely to create, other unfair trading conditions;
- the placing of orders to a trading platform for cryptoassets, including any cancellation or modification thereof, by any available means of trading, and which either sends a misleading signal or has an impact on the price by:
  - disrupting or delaying the functioning of the trading platform for cryptoassets or engaging into any activities that are likely to have that effect;
  - making it more difficult for other persons to identify genuine orders on the trading platform for cryptoassets or engaging into any activities that are likely to have that effect, including by entering orders which result in the destabilisation of the normal functioning of the trading platform for cryptoassets; or
  - creating a false or misleading signal about the supply of, or demand for, or price of, a cryptoasset, in particular, by entering orders to initiate or exacerbate a trend or engaging into any activities that are likely to have that effect;
- taking advantage of occasional or regular access to the traditional or electronic media by voicing an opinion about a cryptoasset while having previously taken positions on that cryptoasset and profiting subsequently from the impact of the opinions voiced on the price of that cryptoasset, without having simultaneously disclosed that conflict of interest to the public in a proper and effective way.

In particular, Article 91(3)(c) MiCA addresses large liquidity pools dominating the price building of a cryptoasset, while Article 91(3)(b) MiCA addresses artificially created technical interruptions. Article 91(3)(c) MiCA covers the most egregious cases of "pump and dump" schemes and potentially also includes a number of "finfluencer" statements.

Experience with the MAR shows that the general description above will hardly provide legal certainty on details of market manipulation. While Article 91 MiCA does not come with explicit guideline powers, we argue that the ESMA's general guideline powers would nevertheless suffice to coordinate supervisory approaches to market manipulation in crypto. We encourage the exercise of these powers by incorporating the respective MAR guidelines[28] by reference.

10.3.5 *Prevention and Detection of Market Abuse (Article 92)*

Article 92(1) MiCA includes any 'person professionally arranging or executing transactions in crypto-assets' in the prevention and detection measures. These include professional traders, stock exchanges, and brokers, while (collective) portfolio managers may also be in MiCA's scope. The provision is not limited to legal persons.

These entities must put in 'place effective arrangements, systems and procedures to prevent and detect market abuse'. What constitutes such compliance arrangements is determined in Level 2 legislation,[29] which are inspired by the equivalent provisions released under Article 16 MAR.

[28] For an overview of guidelines and implementing legislation, cf. the ESMA webpage. Website www.esma.europa.eu/esmas-activities/markets-and-infrastructure/market-integrity (last accessed on 1 October 2024).

[29] See ESMA, 'Consultation Paper: Draft Technical Standards and Guidelines Specifying Certain Requirements of the Markets in Crypto Assets Regulation (MiCA) on Detection and Prevention of Market Abuse, Investor Protection and Operational Resilience –Third Consultation Paper' (2024), ESMA75-453128700-1002, pp. 39–56.

These arrangements include a far-reaching whistle-blowing duty: the in-scope person must 'without delay report to the competent authority of that Member State any reasonable suspicion regarding an order or transaction, including any cancellation or modification thereof, and other aspects of the functioning of the distributed ledger technology such as the consensus mechanism, where there might exist circumstances indicating that market abuse has been committed, is being committed or is likely to be committed'. Given the abundance of malfunctions in crypto and the large number of cryptoassets, the EU FSAs will likely receive a large amount of notifications.

Upon receiving a suspicious order and transaction report provided by the in-scope person (e.g., a CASP), the authority in charge of the in-scope person must forward the information to the authority supervising the trading platforms. This de facto limits the scope where cryptoassets are traded only on one platform. If, however, several platforms are involved, several EU FSAs may receive the same information.

The effectiveness of Article 92 MiCA will depend on the Level 2 legislation. We predict duplication with the MAR's implementing legislation (cf. Table 10.1),[30] which would be desirable since (a) several professionals authorised as traders, brokers, and others under MiFID will seek to become authorised under MiCA, to the extent that trading in cryptoassets becomes the new normal, and (b) the delineation between cryptoassets and financial instruments is uncertain at times (cf. Chapters 3 and 4).

10.4 ASSESSMENT

10.4.1 *Indirect Distribution Efforts*

We note that MiCA's market abuse rules only address serious cases where misinformation may send misleading signals or impact on the price. Instead of a market abuse solution, we propose a wider understanding of 'solicitation, promotion or advertising in the Union' as defined in Article 61 MiCA. A way of preserving the effective enforcement of EU financial law would be to attribute referrals by existing clients via newsletters or partner programmes, regardless of their name, legally to the crypto firm.

For instance, the implementing provisions for Article 61 MiCA[31] could provide that if any existing client contacts new potential clients, that initial contact is treated as being made by the crypto firm if the crypto firm encourages the client to do so or provides any financial or non-financial incentive. Similarly, relying on existing EU financial law, if products are offered through newsletters and partnership programmes, or if the crypto firm pays search engines to obtain high positions for searches in the EU, the mentioning of products and services is treated as the crypto firm's 'solicitation, promotion or advertising in the Union'. The logic behind such a rule is that the crypto firm initiated the potential clients' "initial contact" through the referral, loyalty, and/or newsletter programmes. See also Section 7.2.4.

[30] This is already happening. See ESMA, 'Consultation Paper: Draft Technical Standards and Guidelines Specifying Certain Requirements of the Markets in Crypto Assets Regulation (MiCA) on Detection and Prevention of Market Abuse, Investor Protection and Operational Resilience – Third Consultation Paper' (2024), ESMA75-453128700-1002, pp. 39–56, which closely resembles Commission Delegated Regulation (EU) 2016/957 of 9 March 2016 supplementing Regulation (EU) No 596/2014 of the European Parliament and of the Council with regard to regulatory technical standards for the appropriate arrangements, systems, and procedures as well as notification templates to be used for preventing, detecting, and reporting abusive practices or suspicious orders or transactions, OJ L 160, 17.6.2016.

[31] See ESMA, 'Consultation Paper on the Draft Guidelines on Reverse Solicitation under MiCA' (2024), ESMA35-1872330276-1619, pp. 18–19 (applying a broad definition of solicitation, including paid search listings, affiliation campaigns, and solicitation by 'any other person acting explicitly or implicitly on behalf of the third-country firm', but without explicitly mentioning referral programs).

10.4.2 *Market Manipulation Efforts*

Title VI MiCA covers a broad range of market manipulation, yet the devil lies in its detail, and the line between marketing and manipulation is sometimes hard to define.

In response to implicit manipulation courtesy of emotional and enthusiastic language, regulations could require the use of plain language (as is the case in securities regulation) and ban the use of unaudited facts.[32]

We hold that a better step would be to select skilled, fit, and proper key staff who are familiar with codes of conduct in the financial sector (through the application of fitness and properness tests of licensing schemes), paired with governance requirements and business conduct rules established in the field of EU financial law. While MiCA has achieved this for centralised crypto intermediaries and issuers of ART and EMD,[33] the remaining issuers and decentralised applications are still outside MiCA's scope (Chapters 3 and 4).

10.4.3 *Adding Crypto to the Scope of the MAR*

While MiCA addresses some of the issues here through a bespoke market abuse regime, the main aim of drafting market abuse legislation is to achieve legal clarity and certainty as to which conduct is abusive. In this regard, the MAR and the respective implementing legislation offers an extensive catalogue of, and comprehensive details on, conduct that may qualify as market abuse (insider dealing and/or market manipulation).[34] Compared to that catalogue, MiCA's text is relatively short and sometimes vague.

To avoid duplications of legislation, an easy solution worth considering would be to include all cryptoassets (as defined and regulated by MiCA) in the scope of the MAR. The addition of cryptoassets to the MAR requires some adjustments given that only *some* token issues are initiated by an issuer (in practice, often a special-purpose vehicle (SPV)). In particular, decentralised protocols claim that a token issuer is lacking. In other cases, the issuer resides outside of the Single Market; in these cases, trading is initiated by token-holders or CASPs.

In this regard, the principle of Article 16(1) MiCA (which is also implemented for cryptoassets other than EMTs and ARTs in Title II MiCA) provides an adequate solution: where an issuer is lacking, the offeror and/or the person seeking admission to trading of the cryptoasset may assume the duties that the MAR imposes on issuers.[35]

[32] Such requirements are, however, not included in the consultation paper for the prospective L2 legislation. See ESMA, 'Consultation Paper: Draft Technical Standards and Guidelines Specifying Certain Requirements of the Markets in Crypto Assets Regulation (MiCA) on Detection and Prevention of Market Abuse, Investor Protection and Operational Resilience – Third Consultation Paper' (2024), ESMA75-453128700-1002, pp. 39–56.

[33] Cf. Recital paras. 51 and 81 and Articles 34 and 68 of MiCA.

[34] See the list of implementing measures at 'Summaries of EU Legislation (Preventing Market Abuse in Financial Markets)' (January 2023). Website https://eur-lex.europa.eu/EN/legal-content/summary/preventing-market-abuse-in-financial-markets.html (last accessed on 1 October 2024). This is supplemented by a myriad of technical standards and guidance as disclosed on the ESMA website. Website www.esma.europa.eu/esmas-activities/markets-and-infrastructure/market-integrity (last accessed on 1 October 2024).

[35] While no such measure is currently made under MiCA or its implementing acts, 'persons professionally arranging or executing transactions in crypto-assets' will need to have appropriate arrangements, systems, and procedures to prevent, detect, and report market abuse. See ESMA, 'Consultation Paper: Draft technical Standards and Guidelines Specifying Certain Requirements of the Markets in Crypto Assets Regulation (MiCA) on Detection and Prevention of Market Abuse, Investor Protection and Operational Resilience – Third Consultation Paper' (2024). ESMA75-453128700-1002, pp. 44–48.

11

Supervision and Supervisory Cooperation

11.1 INTRODUCTION

Financial firms can take on two fundamentally different roles: they can be pure intermediaries, facilitating the issuance and trading of financial assets and cryptoassets issued by others as off-balance intermediaries; or they can carry the risk involved on their own balance sheet and are then on-balance intermediaries. We dub the (crypto-)assets involved in the former as "investment assets" and those involved in the latter as "banking assets".[1] Because of the wholly distinct risks that financial law aims to mitigate for off- and on-balance intermediation, respectively, the type of financial regulation varies accordingly and, at the EU level, so does the ESA in charge. The ESMA handles off-balance intermediation, and the EBA deals with on-balance intermediation. MiCA implements this distinction in the realm of cryptoassets.

Supervision under MiCA is also a result of the compromise inherent in the European supervisory architecture, by which regulation has for decades become more and more centralised at the EU level, and increasingly so in response to the 2007–9 financial crisis and the subsequent European sovereign debt crisis.[2] This reflects hesitancy among EU Member States with regard to transferring their supervisory powers to EU institutions. Consequently, the European supervisory architecture remains a hybrid of national and EU-level supervisory functions.

[1] See Chapter 3.

[2] On the European supervisory architecture, see R. Parenti, 'European System of Financial Supervision (ESFS)', European Parliament (2023). Website www.europarl.europa.eu/factsheets/en/sheet/84/european-system-of-financial-supervision-esfs (last accessed on 1 October 2024); D. Busch, E. Avgouleas and G. Ferrarini (eds.), *Capital Markets Union in Europe* (Oxford: Oxford University Press, 2018); M. Andenas and G. Deipenbrock (eds.), *Regulating and Supervising European Financial Markets* (New York: Springer, 2016); D. Schoenmaker and N. Véron, 'A "Twin Peaks" Vision for Europe', Bruegel Policy Contribution (2017); N. Véron,'Charting the Next Steps for the EU Financial Supervisory Architecture', Bruegel Policy Contribution, Issue n°16 (2017); I. Angeloni, 'The Single Supervisory Mechanism', *European Economy*, 1(3) (2015): 43; E. Ferran and V. S. G. Babis, 'The European Single Supervisory Mechanism', *Journal of Corporate Law Studies*, 13(2) (2013): 255; E. Wymeersch, K. J. Hopt and G. Ferrarini (eds.), *Financial Regulation and Supervision: A Post-Crisis Analysis* (Oxford: Oxford University Press, 2012); M. Rotting and C. Lang, 'Das Lamfalussy-Verfahren im Umfeld der Neuordnung der europäischen Finanzauf sichtsstrukturen', *Europäische Zeitschrift für Wirtschaftsrecht* (2012): 8; P. Braumüller, D. Ennöckl, M. Gruber and N. Raschauer (eds.), *Die neue europäische Finanzmarktaufsicht* (Wien: ZFR-Jahrestagung, 2011, 2012); J. A. Kämmerer, 'Das neue europäische Finanzaufsichtssystem (ESFS) – Modell für eine europäisierte Verwaltungsarch itektur?' *Neue Zeitschrift für Verwaltungsrecht* (2011): 1281; M. Lamandini, 'When More Is Needed: The European Financial Supervisory Reform and Its legal Basis', *European Constitutional Law Review*, 6 (2009): 197.

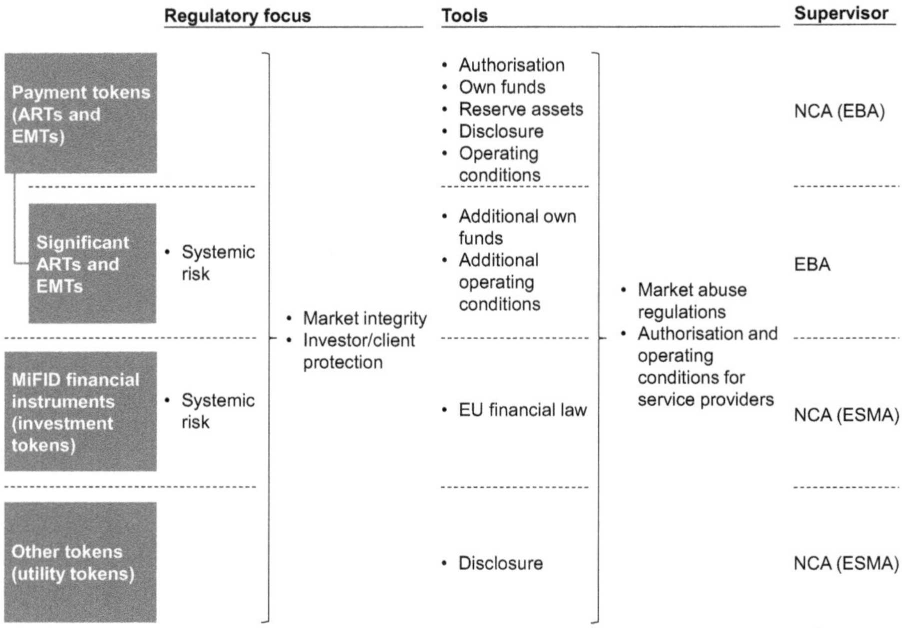

FIGURE 11.1 Regulatory focus and tools along with supervisors for different types of cryptoassets. *(Source: the authors)*

In line with this EU architecture, MiCA assigns the NCAs as primary supervisors yet provides the ESMA and the EBA with important coordination roles inside their respective domains. For ARTs and EMTs that are classified as "significant" (see Section 6.6), MiCA even transfers the supervisory role to the EBA outright, reflecting the EU-level systemic risk caused by such cryptoassets.[3] Yet, even with these deviations, NCAs remain in charge of most supervisory functions concerning cryptoassets (Figure 11.1).

The coordinating and sometimes even supervisory role of the ESMA/EBA aims to ensure a harmonised interpretation of MiCA, thereby mitigating regulatory arbitrage and facilitating a European Single Market for cryptoassets. The most pressing area of such harmonisation relates to MiCA's scope, given the difficulties in determining whether a given cryptoasset is regulated by MiCA or other EU financial law (see Chapter 4). MiCA stipulates eight different mitigators for this problem, many of which rely on close cooperation among NCAs and between NCAs and the ESMA/EBA (see Section 4.5). It remains to be seen whether this approach will work, but its emphasis on supervisory cooperation signals how crucial the supervisory framework is to MiCA's overall success.

11.2 GENERAL SUPERVISION BY NCAS

By default, MiCA assigns general supervisory responsibility to NCAs. Their powers and associated administrative measures and penalties are closely associated with those found elsewhere in EU financial law, as we describe in the following.

[3] With some exceptions. See Section 11.3.

11.2.1 *Designation of NCAs*

The term "competent authority" may refer to two different types of entities.[4] For the supervision of EMT issuers, it refers to those designated by Member States under the EMD. This is due to the stipulation that EMTs qualify as e-money.[5] For all other supervisory tasks under MiCA, the NCAs must be specifically designated by Member States and notified to the EBA and the ESMA.[6] The ESMA will then publish a list of NCAs under MiCA, which we expect to include largely the same NCAs as found under general EU law for investment and banking assets, respectively.[7]

11.2.2 *Powers of NCAs to Perform Their Duties under Titles II–VI MiCA*

To fulfil their supervisory responsibilities under Titles II–VI MiCA (see Chapters 5–10), NCAs are, under Article 94 MiCA and in accordance with national law, provided with a set of supervisory and investigative powers similar to those set out in other parts of EU financial law, as outlined in Table 11.1.

NCAs may exercise these powers directly in collaboration with other authorities and/or by application to the competent courts.[8] Specifically with regard to supervision under Title VI MiCA on market abuse, NCAs are also provided with a set of *additional* powers.[9] On top of that, NCAs may exercise powers provided to them under national law. Beyond the aforementioned proactive supervision exercised by the NCAs, Article 108 MiCA also mandates that NCAs must have in place procedures that allow clients and other interested parties, including consumer associations, to submit complaints regarding alleged infringements of MiCA.

11.2.3 *Administrative Penalties and Other Measures*

In addition to any criminal penalties according to national law, Article 111 MiCA requires the Member States to provide NCAs with appropriate administrative penalties and other administrative measures, which are largely in line with those stipulated in other parts of EU financial law (see Table 11.2).

Some differences here reflect the history and nature of crypto markets. The possibility of banning a natural person from dealing on own account,[10] for instance, probably reflects the now infamous practice of senior CASP executives and their companies trading against the interests of CASP clients.[11] Meanwhile, the possibility under MiFID to ban an investment firm from being a member of a trading platform has no equivalent under MiCA perhaps because of the

[4] Article 3(1)(35) of MiCA, Regulation 2023/1114, OJ 2023 No. L150.

[5] See Article 48(2) of MiCA.

[6] Article 93(1) of MiCA.

[7] Article 93(3) of MiCA. At the time of writing, ESMA had not yet published such a list. See Esma.europa.eu., 'Databases and Registers'. Website www.esma.europa.eu/publications-and-data/databases-and-registers (last accessed on 1 October 2024).

[8] Article 94(4) and (5) of MiCA.

[9] Article 94(3) of MiCA.

[10] Article 111(5)(g) of MiCA.

[11] The most prominent case is that of FTX's founder Sam Bankman-Fried's trading firm Alameda allegedly trading against FTX clients and having unfair advantages. See Coindesk.com, 'Sam Bankman-Fried Wanted to Close Alameda in 2022, Unpublished Posts Show' (2023). Website www.coindesk.com/policy/2023/10/11/sam-bankman-fried-wanted-to-close-alameda-in-2022-unpublished-posts-show (last accessed on 1 October 2024).

TABLE 11.1 *Powers of NCAs compared to MiFID and PR*

Type of power	MiCA Articles	MiFID Articles	PR Articles
Require any person to provide information	94(1)(a), cf. 94(7)	69(2)(a), (b), (d), (g), (j), and (r)	32(1)(b) and (c)
Prohibit or suspend the provision of CAS, an offer to the public, an admission to trading, and the marketing or trading of cryptoassets	94(1)(b), (c), (f), (l)–(q), and (t)	69(2)(f), (m), (n), (s), and (t)	32(1)(d) to (h), (j), (k), and (m)
Require the disclosure of all material information relevant to the provision of CAS or for market participants to assess a cryptoasset	94(1)(d)(s), cf. 94(7)		32(1)(l)
Make public the fact that a CASP, an issuer, an offeror, or a person seeking admission to trading of cryptoassets fails to fulfil its obligations	94(1)(e) and (r)	69(2)(q)	32(1)(i)
Require the transfer of existing contracts to another CASP	94(1)(g)		
Require a person to cease conduct constituting an infringement of MiCA	94(1)(h), (u), (v)	69(2)(k) and (l)	
Require the amendment of a cryptoasset whitepaper or marketing communications	94(1)(i)–(k)		32(1)(a)
Conduct on-site inspections or investigations, including the outsourcing of verifications or investigations	94(1)(w) and (x)	69(2)(c) and (i)	32(1)(n)
Remove natural persons from the management body of an ART issuer or CASP	94(1)(y)	69(2)(u)	
Request any person to take steps to reduce the size of their position or exposure to cryptoassets	94(1)(z)	69(2)(o) and (p)	
Remove, disable, restrict, or alter access to an online interface	94(1)(aa)	69(2)(e)	
Require the introduction of a minimum denomination amount or a limit to the outstanding amount of ARTs or EMTs	94(1)(ab), cf. 23(4), 24 (3), 58(3)		

TABLE 11.2 *Administrative penalties under Article 111 MiCA*

Type of penalties and other measures	MiCA Reference	MiFID Equivalent	PR Equivalent
Issue a public statement about the person responsible and the nature of the infringement	111(2)(a) and 111(5)(a)	70(6)(a)	38(2)(a)
Order to cease conduct constituting an infringement and/or to desist from repeating that conduct	111(2)(b) and 111(5)(b)	70(6)(b)	38(2)(b)
Administrative fines	111(2)(c) and (d); 111(3); 111(5)(h)–(j)	70(6) (f)–(h)	38(2) (c)–(e)
Temporary (or in repeated/serious cases, permanent) ban on natural persons from exercising specific management functions	111(4); 111(5)(e) and (f)	70(6)(d)	
Disgorgement of profits gained or losses avoided from the infringement	111(5)(c)	70(6)(h)	38(2)(c)
Withdrawal or suspension of authorisation	111(5)(d)	70(6)(c)	
Temporary ban for natural persons from dealing on their own account	111(5)(g)		
Additional or higher levels of administrative penalties if decided by Member States	111(6)	70(7)	38(3)
Criminal penalties if decided by Member States	111(1)	70(1)	38(1)

disintermediation embedded in most crypto exchanges, where clients can trade directly or where custody is an embedded service provided by the exchange itself.[12]

The exercise of such powers to impose penalties is further regulated in Article 112 MiCA, and the right to appeal before a court is protected in Article 113. Notably, specific types of organisations may take legal action in the interests and on behalf of consumers.[13] Decisions to impose administrative penalties or other administrative measures must be published on the relevant NCA's website and reported to the ESMA (and sometimes also to the EBA).[14] Meanwhile, criminal penalties shall be reported on an anonymous basis.[15]

11.3 SIGNIFICANT ARTS/EMTS: SUPERVISION BY THE EBA

Given that MiCA assigns the EBA as supervisor for significant ARTs and EMTs (see Section 6.6.3) and because national rules do not apply to the exercise of the EBA's supervisory function, Chapter 4 of Title VII MiCA establishes an entire supervisory framework for this purpose, which we discuss in the following.

11.3.1 *Entry Test*

ARTs are classified as "significant" under Articles 43 and 44 MiCA, while EMTs are classified as "significant" under the similar Articles 56 and 57 MiCA. The classification is based on a defined set of criteria, which is further specified by the L2 legislation.[16]

The EBA is responsible for the classification,[17] while NCAs must report information relevant to the assessment to both the EBA and the ECB at least twice per year.[18] The EBA's draft decision to classify an ART or EMT as "significant" shall then be sent for comments from the ART/EMT issuer, the home Member State NCA, the ECB, and, where applicable, to the home Member State central bank.[19] Upon the EBA's final decision, the home Member State NCA and the EBA shall then cooperate to ensure the smooth transition of supervisory competences.[20] The EBA shall make annual reassessments and, if the EBA proposes reclassifying the significant ART or EMT back to a regular ART or EMT, the same process is set in reverse to transfer supervisory competences back to the NCA.[21] Reflecting MiCA's strict stance on ARTs, the EBA shall also reassess whether the issuer complies with Title III MiCA once an ART is classified as "significant".[22]

While the above process subjects issuers to EBA supervision *ex officio*, issuers may also submit themselves to EBA supervision voluntarily, thus avoiding or limiting the intense fact gathering and communication with NCAs and ESAs (see Section 6.6.3).[23]

[12] See Article 70(6)(e) of MiFID, Directive 2014/65, OJ 2014 No. L173.
[13] Article 113(2) of MiCA.
[14] Articles 114 and 115 of MiCA.
[15] Second paragraph of Article 115(1) of MiCA.
[16] See Article 43(1) and (2), cf. Article 43(11) of MiCA; Article 56(1) of MiCA; Commission Delegated Regulation (EU) 2024/1506 of 22 February 2024 supplementing Regulation (EU) 2023/1114 of the European Parliament and of the Council by specifying certain criteria for classifying asset-referenced tokens and e-money tokens as significant, OJ L, 2024/1506, 30.5.2024.
[17] Articles 43(2) and 56(1) of MiCA.
[18] Articles 43(4) and 56(3) of MiCA.
[19] Articles 43(5) and 56(4) of MiCA.
[20] Second paragraph of Articles 43(7) and 56(6) of MiCA.
[21] Articles 43(8)–(10) and 56(8)–(10) of MiCA.
[22] Article 117(3) of MiCA.
[23] See Articles 44 and 57 of MiCA.

The ECB and other central banks are part of the classification process, not only because of how significant stablecoins may impact the monetary system but also because EMT issuers must be authorised either as credit institutions or as e-money institutions (see Section 6.3). Hence, while their activities as EMT issuers are supervised under MiCA either by the home Member State NCA or by the EBA, other activities undertaken by credit institutions may in fact be supervised by the ECB under the Single Supervisory Mechanism (SSM).[24] We discuss this and other divisions of supervisory responsibilities in the following.

11.3.2 *Supervisory Responsibilities with Regard to Significant ART/EMT Issuers*

When an ART has been classified as "significant", supervisory responsibilities shall be transferred from the home Member State NCA to the EBA.[25] Yet, if the same issuer also provides CAS and/ or issues cryptoassets other than significant ARTs, the responsibility for supervision of these activities remains with the NCA.[26] This makes sense for ART issuers, where MiCA provides a bespoke authorisation regime, but not for EMT issuers who must be authorised as either an e-money or a credit institution (see Section 6.3). Consequently, for issuers of significant EMTs, MiCA stipulates different supervisory regimes depending on whether they are authorised as an e-money or a credit institution.

For e-money institutions that issue significant EMTs, the EBA has the supervisory responsibility specifically for compliance with Articles 55 and 58 MiCA, which entail additional requirements for EMTs compared to e-money, while supervision otherwise remains with the NCA designated by Member States under the EMD.[27] Such dual supervision is an anomaly and seeks to address the very specific risks posed by EMTs at the EU level while otherwise leaving supervision of e-money issuers with the NCA.[28]

The same dual supervision was also suggested for credit institutions that issue EMTs under the European Parliament's first MiCA proposal.[29] Yet, in the consultation over that proposal, the ECB issued an opinion observing that this could lead to the same entity being subject to three different supervisors – the NCA, the EBA, and also the ECB if the issuer qualifies as a "significant" credit institution under the SSM regulation.[30] This is presumably the reason why the dual supervision framework for significant EMT issuers applies only to e-money institutions and not to credit institutions.

One could argue that this difference between credit institution EMT issuers and other issuers of significant ARTs/EMTs implies that the supervisory responsibilities under MiCA at the EU level should be transferred to the ECB for credit institution EMT issuers, while the role of the NCA could remain unchanged. Instead, MiCA seems to strip the NCA entirely of its responsibility to supervise credit institutions in their role of issuing significant EMTs. MiCA is not entirely clear on this point, however, as Articles 56(6) and 57(4) simply state that supervisory

24 See Council Regulation (EU) No. 1024/2013 of 15 October 2013 conferring specific tasks on the European Central Bank concerning policies relating to the prudential supervision of credit institutions, OJ 2013 No. L287, 29 October 2013. MiCA is without prejudice to this Regulation and should be interpreted, so it is not in conflict with it. See Recital para. 15 of MiCA.

25 Article 43(7), cf. Article 117(1) of MiCA.

26 Article 117(2) of MiCA.

27 Article 117(4), cf. Article 3(1)(35)(b) of MiCA.

28 Recital para. 103 of MiCA.

29 See Article 98(4) of MiCA Regulation Proposal, COM (2020) 593 Final.

30 European Central Bank, Opinion on a proposal for a regulation on Markets in Crypto-assets and amending Directive (EU) 2019/1937, CON/2021/4, OJ 2021 No. C152, 29 April 2021, para. 3.1.4.

responsibilities with respect to issuers of significant EMTs 'shall be transferred from the competent authority to EBA in accordance with Article 117(4)', where that article assigns the dual supervision framework to e-money institutions that issue significant EMTs but says nothing about credit institutions. The omission presumably means that supervisory responsibilities under MiCA are transferred outright from NCAs to the EBA for issuers of significant EMTs that are authorised as credit institutions, as suggested by the just cited phrase in Articles 56(6) and 57(4) of MiCA.

This does not change the role of the ECB, however, as MiCA is without prejudice to the SSM regulation and should be interpreted in such a way that it is not in conflict with it.[31] Hence, the EMT issuer still falls under the scrutiny of two different supervisors if it qualifies as a significant credit institution under the SSM regulation. Consequently, Article 117(5) MiCA stipulates that the EBA shall exercise its supervisory powers in close cooperation with other competent authorities supervising the issuer, including not just the NCAs but also prudential supervisory authorities, such as the ECB under the SSM regulation.[32]

11.3.3 *Cryptoasset Committee and Consultative Colleges*

The EBA shall exercise its supervisory powers in close cooperation with other competent authorities, in particular, NCAs and also the ECB given its role as supervisor of credit institutions under the SSM.[33] This principle is operationalised under MiCA through the "cryptoasset committee" and "consultative colleges".

The EBA must establish an internal cryptoasset committee to prepare its decisions.[34] For each issuer of significant ARTs or significant EMTs, the EBA must also establish a consultative supervisory college to facilitate and coordinate the supervision.[35] While the EBA's decision making still follows the procedures laid down by the EBA Regulation, the colleges have supportive and consultative functions. The colleges, moreover, are a clear example of how MiCA seeks to bridge national sovereignty with the need for centralised supervision, as such colleges shall consist of representatives from a variety of EU institutions (the EBA, the ESMA, and the ECB), relevant NCAs, and sometimes also other Member State or even third-country institutions.[36] In this regard, MiCA builds on the same compromise established in international banking supervision.[37] The variety of possible participants reflects the fact that issuers of significant ARTs/EMTs are often central to DeFi schemes that operate across country borders.[38] Cooperation is further strengthened by giving other NCAs a right to request information from the college and an option for the EBA to invite additional members to the college where relevant.[39] The establishment and functioning of the college shall be based on written agreement among its members.[40] Further details about the colleges are specified in regulatory technical standards.[41]

[31] Article 2(6) of MiCA, cf. Recital para. 15 of MiCA. See also Article 94(2) of MiCA.
[32] Article 117(5) of MiCA.
[33] Article 117(5) of MiCA. See also Recital para. 15 of MiCA.
[34] Article 118 of MiCA.
[35] Article 119(1) of MiCA.
[36] Article 119(2) of MiCA.
[37] See Article 116 of CRD (on colleges in cross-border banking supervision, including third-country authorities).
[38] See Recital para. 105 of MiCA.
[39] Article 119(3) and (4) of MiCA.
[40] Article 119(6) of MiCA.
[41] See EBA, 'Final Report: Draft Regulatory Technical Standards on Supervisory Colleges under Article 119(8) of [MiCA]' (2024), EBA/RTS/2024/14.

TABLE 11.3 *Powers and measures of EBA vs. NCAs*

Type of power or measure	MiCA Articles		MiFID Equivalent Articles	PR Equivalent Articles
	EBA supervision	NCA supervision	NCA supervision	NCA supervision
Require persons to provide information	122	94(1)(a), cf. 94(7)	69(2)(a), (b), (d), (g), (j), and (r)	32(1)(b) and (c)
Conduct investigations and on-site inspections, including the outsourcing of verifications or investigations	123 and 124	94(1)(w) and (x)	69(2)(c) and (i)	32(1)(n)
Require NCAs to carry out specific investigatory tasks and on-site inspections	124(7)			

The most important role of the colleges is to issue non-binding opinions,[42] reflecting the "consultative" nature of these colleges, whereby opinions are enforced only through a comply-or-explain logic: when the EBA or an NCA does not agree with an opinion of the college, its decision must include an explanation for any significant deviation from that opinion.[43] Such opinions may be issued by the college in relation to the exercise of a number of specified supervisory powers by the EBA or NCAs and are adopted by a simple majority of college members.[44] The opinions may also include recommendations aimed at addressing the short-comings of measures envisaged by the EBA or NCAs.[45]

11.3.4 *The EBA's Powers and Competences*

Chapter 5 of Title VII MiCA sets out the EBA's powers and competences with regard to the supervision of issuers of significant ARTs and significant EMTs. These include the powers and competences outlined in Table 11.3.

Importantly, the EBA's powers and competences do not include the enforcement of its decisions within the territory of any Member State. For this, NCAs are obliged to assist, where appropriate, with the assistance of the police.[46] Presumably for the same reason, and because the EBA lacks local staff across Europe, the EBA is given the right not only to request the outsourcing of activities to NCAs but to *require* NCAs to carry out specific investigatory tasks and on-site inspections. The lack of enforcement powers also explains why the list of powers and competences provided to the EBA (Table 11.3) is shorter than the comparable list for NCAs (Table 11.1). Partly as a response thereto, the EBA's list of supervisory measures and penalties is correspondingly longer, as we discuss in turn.

11.3.5 *Supervisory Measures and Penalties*

Because the EBA lacks the power to enforce its decisions on the territory of any Member State, its measures and penalties are supervisory in nature, oftentimes framed so the EBA can "adopt a

[42] Article 120, cf. Article 119(5)(a) of MiCA.
[43] Article 120(4) of MiCA.
[44] Article 120(1) and (3) of MiCA.
[45] Article 120(2) of MiCA.
[46] Article 124(8) of MiCA.

TABLE 11.4 *Supervisory measures of EBA vs. NCAs*

Type of power	MiCA Articles		MiFID Equivalent Articles	PR Equivalent Articles
	EBA supervision	NCA supervision	NCA supervision	NCA supervision
Require issuers to transmit supplementary information	122; 130(1)(c) and (2)(c)	94(1)(a), cf. 94(7)	69(2)(a), (b), (d), (g), (j), and (r)	32(1)(b) and (c)
Prohibit or suspend an offer to the public or the trading of cryptoassets	130(1)(d)–(g) and (2)(d)–(g)	94(1)(b), (c), (f), (l)–(q), and (t)	69(2)(f), (m), (n), (s), and (t)	32(1)(d)–(h), (j), (k), and (m)
Require the disclosure of all material information relevant for market participants to assess the cryptoasset	130(1)(j) and (2)(h)	94(1)(d) and (s), cf. 94(7)		32(1)(l)
Require issuers to cease conduct constituting an infringement of MiCA	130(1)(a) and (2)(a)	94(1)(h), (u), and (v); 111(2)(b); and 111(5)(b)	69(2)(k) and (l); 70(6)(b)	38(2)(b)
Prohibit, suspend, or require the amendment of marketing communications	130(1)(h) and (i)	94(1)(i)–(k)		32(1)(a)
Remove natural persons from the management body of an ART issuer	130(1)(m)	94(1)(y)	69(2)(u)	
Require the introduction of a minimum denomination amount or a limit to the outstanding amount of ARTs or EMTs	130(1)(n) and (2)(j), cf. 23(4), 24(3), and 58(3)	94(1)(ab), cf. 23(4), 24(3), and 58(3)		
Issue warnings to the public about the person responsible and the nature of the infringement	130(1)(k) and (2)(i)	94(1)(e) and (r); 111(2)(a); and 111(5)(a)	69(2)(q) and 70(6)(a)	32(1)(i) and 38(2)(a)
Impose fines or periodic penalty payments	130(1)(b) and (2)(b), cf. 131 and 132	111(2)(c) and (d); 111(3); 111(5)(c) and (h)–(j)	70(6)(f)–(h)	38(2)(c)–(e)
Withdraw or suspend authorisation	130(1)(l)	111(5)(d)	70(6)(c)	

decision" which must then be enforced by NCAs and other national authorities (see Section 11.3.4). Consequently, the measures and penalties available to the EBA under Articles 130–132 MiCA correspond to a mix of what would be considered supervisory powers, penalties, and other administrative measures, respectively, under equivalent rules for NCAs. Yet, in sum, the measures are not significantly different from those provided to NCAs in EU financial law more broadly, as shown in Table 11.4.

Some of the measures listed in Table 11.4 apply only to issuers of significant ARTs (as opposed to significant EMTs), namely, the EBA's powers to prohibit, suspend, or require the amendment of marketing communications,[47] withdraw their authorisation,[48] and remove

[47] Article 130(1)(h) and (i) of MiCA.
[48] Article 130(1)(l) of MiCA.

natural persons from their management body.[49] That some of the measures apply to issuers of significant ARTs only reflects partly the fact that EMT issuers must be authorised as credit institutions or e-money institutions, so the authorisation regime for EMT issuers lies outside the scope of MiCA, and partly the particularly strict stance taken by MiCA against ARTs (see Chapter 6).

The exercise of these supervisory powers by the EBA is further regulated in Articles 130–138 MiCA.[50] For instance, the EBA must take into account the nature and seriousness of the infringement, notify the relevant issuer and NCAs concerned as well as the Commission, and publicly disclose the decision on the EBA's website.[51] When taking certain measures, the EBA must even *beforehand* inform the ESMA, the relevant NCA, along with either the ECB or the relevant central bank.[52] Fines and periodic penalty payments shall be within set size limits, disclosed to the public, and of an administrative nature, enforceable in accordance with the rules of civil procedure in the relevant jurisdiction.[53] Article 134 MiCA lays out procedural rules for the exercise of the EBA's supervisory powers, Article 135 provides the rights of the defendant, including the right to be heard, and Article 136 gives the European Court of Justice (ECJ) unlimited jurisdiction to review decisions made by the EBA. Finally, the EBA may charge fees to issuers in order to cover expenditures related to the execution of its supervisory tasks, and it may also delegate specific supervisory tasks to NCAs.[54]

11.4 PRODUCT INTERVENTION: SHARED SUPERVISION OF NCAS, THE EBA, AND THE ESMA

11.4.1 *Primary Supervision by NCAs*

In addition to their supervisory responsibilities under Titles II–VI MiCA, NCAs also have the power to intervene against certain products or activities (known as "product intervention").[55] That is, NCAs may prohibit or restrict either a type of activity or practice in general, or

49 Article 130(1)(m) of MiCA.

50 See also Commission Delegated Regulation (EU) 2024/1504 of 22 February 2024 supplementing Regulation (EU) 2023/1114 of the European Parliament and of the Council by specifying the procedural rules for the exercise of the power to impose fines or periodic penalty payments by the European Banking Authority on issuers of significant asset-referenced tokens and issuers of significant e-money token, OJ L, 2024/1504, 30.5.2024.

51 Article 130(3), cf. Article 131(2) of MiCA; Article 130(6) and (7) of MiCA.

52 Article 130(4) and (5) of MiCA.

53 Articles 131(3) and (4), 132(3) and (4), and 133(1)–(3) of MiCA.

54 Articles 137–138 of MiCA; Commission Delegated Regulation (EU) 2024/1503 of 22 February 2024 supplementing Regulation (EU) 2023/1114 of the European Parliament and of the Council by specifying the fees charged by the European Banking Authority to issuers of significant asset-referenced tokens and issuers of significant e-money tokens, OJ L, 2024/1503, 30.5.2024.

55 See on this topic, P. Iglesias-Rodriguez, 'ESMA as a Residual Lawmaker: The Political Economy and Constitutionality of ESMA's Product Intervention Measures on Complex Financial Products', *European Business Organization Law Review*, 22 (2021): 627; C. Veerle, 'The MiFIR and PRIIPs Product Intervention Regime: In Need of Intervention?' *European Company and Financial Law Review*, 17(1) (2020): 99; K. Tomic, 'Product Intervention of Supervisory Authorities in Financial Services', in S. Grima and P. Marano (eds.), *Governance and Regulations' Contemporary Issues* (Leeds: Emerald, 2018), pp. 229–55; D. Busch, 'Product Governance and Product Intervention under MiFID/MiFID', in D. Busch and G. Ferrarini (eds.), *Regulation of the EU Financial Markets: MiFID II and MiFIR* (Oxford: Oxford University Press, 2017), p. 175; D. Klingenbrunn, 'Produktintervention zugunsten des Anlegerschutzes – Zur Systematik innerhalb des Aufsichtsrechts, dem Anlegerleitbild und zivilrechtlichen Konsequenzen', *WM Zeitschrift für Wirtschafts- und Bankrecht*, 69(7) (2015): 316.

specifically the marketing, distribution, or sale of specific cryptoassets or cryptoassets with certain specified features.[56]

Due to their severe implications, such measures may only be adopted under certain conditions and only by following strict procedural guardrails. The NCA must be satisfied on reasonable grounds that a cryptoasset poses a qualified concern or threat, that the risk cannot be sufficiently addressed through existing regulatory requirements, that the corresponding measure is proportionate, and that the measure does not have a discriminatory effect on services or activities provided by entities from other Member States.[57] An NCA cannot impose such measures earlier than one month after notifying all other NCAs and the ESMA or the EBA, other than in exceptional cases.[58] Meanwhile, NCAs in other Member States that might be significantly affected by the measure must be properly consulted in advance.[59]

Product intervention measures might be implemented on a precautionary basis before the relevant cryptoasset has been marketed, distributed, or sold to clients, but only for activities conducted after said measures have taken effect.[60] Moreover, the measures are meant to be temporary, and they must be revoked when the conditions no longer apply.[61]

11.4.2 *Temporary Intervention Powers of the EBA and the ESMA*

Notwithstanding the primacy of NCAs in supervision under MiCA, Articles 103 and 104 provide the ESMA and the EBA, respectively, with certain temporary intervention powers. These correspond to the NCAs' product intervention powers (see Section 11.4.1) and complement them in the case of inaction by the relevant NCA(s). That is, the ESMA or the EBA may temporarily prohibit or restrict either a type of activity or practice in general or specifically the marketing, distribution, or sale of specific cryptoassets or cryptoassets with certain specified features.[62] Such prohibition or restriction may apply in specific circumstances only or be subject to exceptions, as specified by the ESMA or the EBA.[63] Relevant NCAs must be notified by the ESMA or the EBA, respectively, of such measures, which prevail over any previous measure taken by NCAs on the same matter.[64] The term "previous measure" here probably means that *subsequent* measures by NCAs still prevail over those taken by the ESMA or the EBA, in line with the NCAs' primacy in supervision under MiCA. It is unlikely, however, that NCAs would openly challenge the ESAs in this way and, if they were to, the matter may lead to a political rather than legal resolution.

Because temporary interventions by the ESMA or the EBA constitute an exception to the NCAs' primacy in supervision under MiCA, such interventions may only take place under strict

[56] Article 105(1) of MiCA.

[57] Article 105(2) of MiCA, cf. Article 3 of Commission Delegated Regulation (EU) 2024/1507 of 22 February 2024 supplementing Regulation (EU) 2023/1114 of the European Parliament and of the Council by specifying the criteria and factors to be taken into account by the European Securities Markets Authority, the European Banking Authority, and competent authorities in relation to their intervention powers, OJ L, 2024/1507, 30.5.2024. The term "satisfied on reasonable grounds" alludes to a discretion for the NCA to decide whether the conditions are satisfied, so it cannot be overruled by courts or other administrative bodies, yet this may be reading too much out of the term and may anyway depend on the system for appealing against administrative decisions in each Member State.

[58] Article 105(3) and (4) of MiCA.

[59] Article 105(2)(d) of MiCA.

[60] Second paragraph of Article 105(2) of MiCA; Article 105(5) of MiCA.

[61] Article 105(6) of MiCA.

[62] Articles 103(1) and 104(1) of MiCA.

[63] Second paragraphs of Articles 103(1) and 104(1) of MiCA.

[64] Article 103(4) and (7) of MiCA; Article 104(4) and (7) of MiCA.

conditions. The proposed temporary intervention must address a significant concern or threat that is not adequately addressed either by regulatory requirements under EU law or through actions taken by the relevant NCA.[65] In addition, the ESMA or the EBA, respectively, must ensure that the intervention does not have a disproportionately detrimental effect on market participants or create a risk of regulatory arbitrage.[66]

The product intervention powers of the ESMA and the EBA under MiCA have similarities with the ESMA's intervention powers under Article 28 of the SSR.[67] Because the measures under that Article prevail over those of NCAs, its adoption led to a UK challenge at the ECJ seeking its annulment. The court's decision, however, upheld the ESMA's powers.[68]

So why does MiCA entail similar rules to those challenged under the SSR? It seems to us that the product intervention powers of the ESMA and the EBA under MiCA are meant to serve as a "safety valve" in the case of inaction by the NCA, for instance, due to regulatory competition where certain NCAs deliberately relax their enforcement of MiCA to attract crypto businesses while benefiting from MiCA's EU Passport. We share this concern and admit that the ESMA and the EBA may need certain powers to intervene in this regard.

Their objective as a "safety valve" also explains why the product intervention measures taken by the ESMA or the EBA are meant to be temporary. They must be reviewed at appropriate intervals and at least every six months or, by exception, annually.[69] There is no limit on the number of renewals; however, so in principle, such temporary measures may remain in force for a very long time. This could plausibly become a way for the ESAs to enforce their agenda vis-a-vis Member States that, over time, fail to comply with MiCA or otherwise facilitate regulatory arbitrage.

11.4.3 *The Coordinating Role of the ESMA and the EBA*

The ESMA or the EBA, respectively, shall perform a facilitating and coordinating role in relation to product intervention measures taken by NCAs.[70] They shall ensure that measures taken by an NCA are justified, proportionate, and consistent with the approach taken by other NCAs. After receiving notification from the relevant NCA, either the ESMA or the EBA shall issue an opinion, and they may even take their own measures that prevail over those of the given NCA (see Section 11.4.2). Moreover, if an NCA proposes to take, actually takes, or declines to take measures contrary to an opinion issued by the ESMA or the EBA, the NCA must publish an explanation for this on its website.[71] This is a typical example of how MiCA tries to balance the

[65] Articles 103(2) and 104(2) of MiCA, cf. Articles 1 and 2 of Commission Delegated Regulation (EU) 2024/1507 of 22 February 2024 supplementing Regulation (EU) 2023/1114 of the European Parliament and of the Council by specifying the criteria and factors to be taken into account by the European Securities Markets Authority, the European Banking Authority, and competent authorities in relation to their intervention powers, OJ L, 2024/1507, 30.5.2024.

[66] Articles 103(3) and 104(3) of MiCA.

[67] Regulation (EU) 236/2012 of the European Parliament and of the Council of 14 March 2012 on short selling and certain aspects of credit default swaps, OJ 2012 No. L86, 24 March 2012.

[68] Case C-270/12, *United Kingdom v. Council of the European Union and European Parliament* [2014]. See also Iglesias-Rodriguez, 'ESMA as a Residual Lawmaker', p. 627; E. Howell, 'The European Court of Justice: Selling Us Short?' Website https://eprints.lse.ac.uk/101771/1/The_European_Court_of_Justice.pdf (last accessed on 1 October 2024).

[69] Articles 103(6) and 104(6) of MiCA.

[70] Article 106(1) of MiCA.

[71] Article 106(3) of MiCA.

independence of Member States with the need to promote equal rules across the European Single Market.

11.5 SUPERVISORY COOPERATION

MiCA aims to foster close cooperation between NCAs and with the EBA/ESMA. A general articulation of this is provided in Article 95(1) MiCA, under which NCAs shall cooperate with and render assistance to both each other, to the EBA, and to the ESMA. As discussed in the following, this is further substantiated for the relationships between NCAs of different Member States (Section 11.5.1), their relationships with respect to the EBA and the ESMA (Section 11.5.2), their relationships with other European authorities (Section 11.5.3), their relationships with competent authorities of third countries outside the EU (Section 11.5.4), and the EBA's role as supervisor of significant ART/EMT issuers (Section 11.5.5). Finally, the ESMA will facilitate cooperation by managing a register of CASPs, cryptoasset issuers, and whitepapers (Section 11.5.6).

11.5.1 *Cooperation between NCAs*

Beyond the general rule in its Article 95(1), MiCA adopts specific standards for the level of cooperation between NCAs. For instance, NCAs shall exchange information, provide information upon request, closely coordinate their supervision, promote best practices, foster consistency of interpretation, and provide cross-jurisdictional assessments.[72] Only in specific cases may NCAs refuse to act on a request for information or a request to cooperate.[73]

A specific but highly plausible case for supervisory cooperation presents itself in response to the EU Passport regime under MiCA (see Sections 1.6.6, 4.3, 5.7, 6.3.4, and 7.3.3): the NCA of a host Member State suspects irregularities caused by an entity supervised by the NCA of another EU country (the home Member State). In such instances, if there are clear and demonstrable grounds for suspecting irregularities, then the NCA of the host Member State has a duty to notify the NCA of the home Member State, the ESMA, and, if the matter relates to ARTs or EMTs, also the EBA.[74] If the irregularities persist and amount to an infringement of MiCA, the NCA of the host Member State shall itself take appropriate measures after informing the NCA of the home Member State, the ESMA, and, if relevant, the EBA.[75] This is a significant carve-out from the EU Passport regime, under which the NCA of the home Member State is responsible for supervision. Yet, this carve-out is found also in other EU directives aiming at consumer protection and prevention of systemic risk.[76] Such a fall-back jurisdiction of the host Member State NCA is deemed necessary by EU financial regulation (including MiCA) to offer adequate risk mitigation within any single Member State, for instance, in the service of investor and consumer protection. If the NCA of the home Member State disagrees with any of the measures taken under this procedure, it may bring the matter to the attention of the ESMA or the EBA, the decision of which may be addressed directly towards the relevant cryptoasset market participant.[77]

[72] Article 95(1), (3), and (8) of MiCA.
[73] Article 95(2) of MiCA.
[74] Article 102(1) of MiCA.
[75] Article 102(2) of MiCA.
[76] Article 153(4) of CRD; Article 86 of MiFID; Article 108(5) of UCITSD.
[77] Article 102(3) of MiCA.

The ESMA and the EBA are also given a coordinating role. NCAs may request that the ESMA coordinates an inspection or investigation, for example, or NCAs may bring the matter to the ESMA's attention if a request for cooperation is rejected.[78] Technical standards further specify the information to be exchanged between NCAs, along with corresponding forms, templates, and procedures.[79]

11.5.2 *Cooperation between the NCAs and the ESMA/EBA*

In addition to cooperating with each other, NCAs shall also cooperate closely with the ESMA and the EBA in accordance with the ESMA and EBA regulations.[80] They shall exchange information, and NCAs must 'without undue delay provide EBA and ESMA with all information necessary to perform their duties'.[81] Again, technical standards, with corresponding forms, templates, and procedures, facilitate cooperation and information exchange.[82]

11.5.3 *Cooperation with Other European Authorities*

Where entities supervised under MiCA engage in activities outside of MiCA's scope, NCAs shall cooperate with the authorities responsible for the supervision or oversight of such other activities pursuant to Union or national law.[83] Examples of such entities include tax and AML/CTF authorities.

11.5.4 *Cooperation with Third Countries*

MiCA requires NCAs to cooperate with relevant supervisory authorities of third countries.[84] This, however, often calls for information sharing, and the IOSCO framework and Multilateral Memorandum of Understanding extend to securities and derivatives only.[85] It is as yet uncertain whether cryptoassets fall under that term as it is construed in international securities regulation and, hence, whether NCAs can demand information exchange and on-site visits from third-country competent authorities under that framework.

We propose adding cryptoassets (broadly defined) to the IOSCO cooperation framework so that cooperating authorities provide information that assists in enforcing EU securities regulation. This would facilitate the exchange of information, for instance, on the technical interlinkages and the user/client base, which is crucial to assess the risks for the EU financial sector (traditional or crypto). It would also be helpful in effectively addressing market abuse and insider

[78] Article 95(5) and (6) of MiCA.

[79] Article 95(10) and (11) of MiCA; ESMA, 'Final Report: Draft Technical Standards Specifying Requirements for Cooperation, Exchange of Information, and Notification between Competent Authorities, ESAs, and Third Countries under the MiCA' (2024), ESMA75-453128700-949, Annexes III and IV.

[80] Article 96(1) of MiCA, cf. ESMA Regulation (EU) No. 1095/2010, OJ 2010 No. L331 and EBA Regulation (EU) No. 1093/2010, OJ 2010 No. L331.

[81] Article 96(2) of MiCA.

[82] Article 96(3) of MiCA; Commission Implementing Regulation (EU) 2024/2494 of 24 September 2024 laying down implementing technical standards for the application of Regulation (EU) 2023/1114 of the European Parliament and of the Council with regard to standard forms, templates and procedures for the cooperation and exchange of information between competent authorities and EBA and ESMA, OJ 2024 No. L2494; ESMA, 'Final Report: Draft Technical Standards Specifying Requirements for Cooperation, Exchange of Information, and Notification between Competent Authorities, ESAs, and Third Countries under the MiCA' (2024), ESMA75-453128700-949, Annex V.

[83] Article 98 of MiCA.

[84] Article 98, cf. Article 107 of MiCA.

[85] International Organization of Securities Commissions, 'Multilateral Memorandum of Understanding Concerning Consultation and Cooperation and the Exchange of Information' (2002). Website www.iosco.org/about/?subsection=mmou (last accessed on 1 October 2024).

dealing, bankruptcy, or operational malfunction. The latter was of paramount importance during the Crypto Winter of 2022–23.

Expanding supervisory networks would also complement the work of supervisory colleges for significant ARTs and EMTs. First, such expansion would help to identify NCAs interested in participating in the colleges. Second, Recitals 59–60 MiCA stress the importance of assessing 'the true size and impact' of ARTs and EMTs to ascertain the impact on 'financial stability, monetary policy transmission or monetary sovereignty'.[86] This should pave the ground for the participation of third-country authorities in joint supervisory colleges as is the case in banking supervision. However, even when NCAs will not participate in such a college, they may be more forthcoming in a cooperation framework to share data on the base, market capitalisation, operational risks, number of transactions, and other parameters important when it comes to enforcing EU financial law.

11.5.5 *Significant ARTs/EMTs: Cooperation between the EBA and Other Entities*

MiCA envisages close cooperation between the EBA and NCAs in the exercise of the EBA's supervisory powers towards significant ART/EMT issuers. Most prominently, both the EBA and NCAs are obliged to exchange information on a variety of specified topics, yet the EBA cannot require the disclosure of information which is subject to legal privilege.[87] The EBA may also conclude administrative agreements on the exchange of information with NCAs of third countries, but only if the information disclosed is subject to guarantees of professional secrecy equivalent to those under MiCA, no information is disclosed contrary to the express agreement of the third-country NCA, and any personal data transfers are in compliance with the applicable EU law.[88] Where issuers of significant ARTs/EMTs also engage in activities outside the scope of MiCA, the EBA shall also cooperate with the relevant authorities on these activities, including tax authorities and third-country authorities.[89]

11.5.6 *The ESMA's Register of CASPs, Issuers, and Whitepapers*

Under Article 109 MiCA, the ESMA shall establish a register of CASPs, issuers of ARTs and EMTs, respectively, and of whitepapers for other cryptoassets. For each of the entries, the register shall contain a specified set of information, and NCAs must communicate to the ESMA any initial information gathered throughout the authorisation proceedings as well as changes notified to them regarding the registered information.[90] NCAs must also notify the ESMA of certain supervisory measures taken that affect the provision of cryptoasset services or the issuance, offer to the public, or use of cryptoassets, which the ESMA must then include in the register.[91] Furthermore, to complement the registration of authorised CASPs, the ESMA shall also establish a non-exhaustive register of CASPs that either operates in violation of the

[86] Direct quote from Recital para. 59 of MiCA.

[87] Article 125, cf. Article 121 of MiCA.

[88] Article 126, cf. Articles 127 and 129 of MiCA, and Regulation (EU) 2018/1725 of the European Parliament and of the Council of 23 October 2018 on the protection of natural persons with regard to the processing of personal data by the Union institutions, bodies, offices, and agencies and on the free movement of such data, and repealing Regulation (EC) No. 45/2001 and Decision No. 1247/2002/EC, OJ 2018 No. L295, 21 November 2018.

[89] Article 128 of MiCA.

[90] See Article 109(2)–(5), cf. Article 109(1) of MiCA.

[91] Article 109(6) and (7) of MiCA.

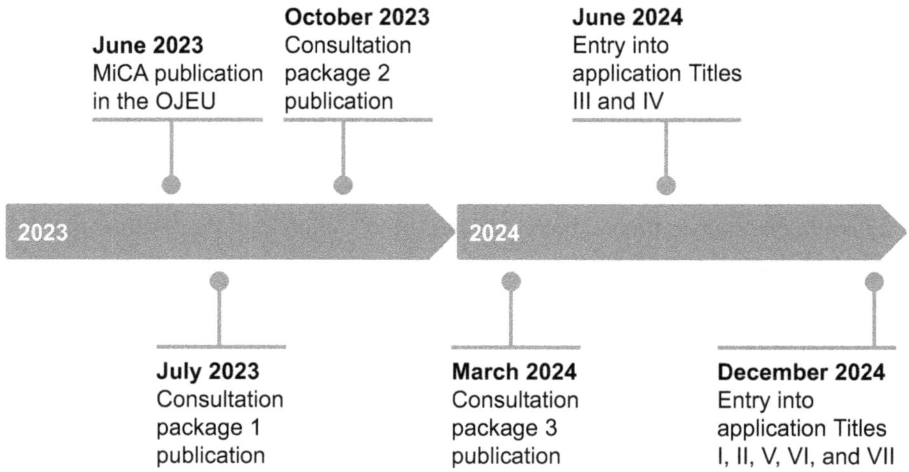

SOURCE: ESMA

FIGURE 11.2 MiCA's implementation timeline.

authorisation requirements or limits as to which third-country firms can service European clients without authorisation.[92]

Given that the register provides an overview of all material measures ever taken by an NCA or an ESA, and in some cases third-country authorities as well, we can understand the register as both the outcome of and the basis for ongoing supervisory cooperation.

11.6 MICA'S IMPLEMENTATION AND IMPLEMENTING MEASURES

11.6.1 *MiCA's Implementation Timeline*

MiCA was published in the Official Journal of the European Union in June 2023 and entered into force 20 days later. Yet, its entry into application is set out in stages, with certain provisions applying already as of 29 June 2023, Titles III and IV (on ARTs and EMTs, respectively) from 30 June 2024, and the remainder of MiCA from 30 December 2024.[93] L2 and L3 legislation is already underway, with the first consultation package published in July 2023, the second in October of the same year, and the third in March 2024, as outlined in Figure 11.2.

11.6.2 *Transitional Measures*

Running parallel to the drafting of L2 and L3 legislation, the ESMA is working with the NCAs on a convergent approach to the authorisation of CASPs during the transitional period to align supervisory expectations and promote consistent practices.[94] On top of that, Article 143 MiCA stipulates transitional measures, some of which leave a level of discretion to Member States to ease the transition from existing national regulatory regimes. This includes, for instance, a

[92] See Article 110 of MiCA.

[93] Article 149 of MiCA.

[94] See ESMA, 'Supervisory Convergence in the MiCA Transitional Phase' (2023). Website www.esma.europa.eu/esmas-activities/digital-finance-and-innovation/markets-crypto-assets-regulation-mica (last accessed on 1 October 2024).

2024		2025	No deadline
By 30 June	**By 30 December**	**By 30 June**	
The EBA ▪ Minimum content of various governance arrangements at ART issuers (in cooperation with the ESMA) (Article 34(13) MiCA) **Joint: the EBA and the ESMA** ▪ Assessment of the suitability of shareholders and members with qualifying holdings in, along with management body members at, ART issuers and CASPs (Articles 21(3) and 63(11) MiCA)	**The ESMA** ▪ Conditions and criteria for crypto-assets to qualify as financial instruments and, thus, be exempted from MiCA (Article 2(5) MiCA) ▪ Union standards for systems and security access protocols for offerors and persons seeking admission to trading of other crypto-assets (in cooperation with the EBA) (last paragraph of Article 14(1) MiCA) ▪ Situations in which a third-country CASP is deemed to solicit clients established or situated in the EU (Article 61(3) MiCA) ▪ CASPs that provide advice and portfolio management, namely on criteria for assessing their clients' knowledge and competence, the information to be obtained about the clients, and the format of the periodic statement to be provided to clients (Article 81(15) MiCA, assuming the reference in Article 81(15)(a) to 'paragraph 2' is a misspelling for "paragraph 1") **Joint: the ESAs** ▪ The content and form of (1) the explanation accompanying the crypto-asset whitepaper outlining why the crypto-asset in question is neither outside MiCA's scope, an EMT, nor an ART, and (2) legal opinions on the qualification of ARTs (Article 97(1) MiCA)	**The ESMA** ▪ Supervisory practices among NCAs to prevent and detect market abuse (Article 92(3) MiCA)	**The ESMA** ▪ Procedures and policies, including the rights of clients, in the context of transfer services for crypto-assets (in cooperation with the EBA) (Article 82(2) MiCA) **The EBA** ▪ Common reference parameters for liquidity stress testing of ART issuers (in cooperation with the ESMA and the ECB) (Article 45(8) MiCA) ▪ Format and content of recovery plans for ART issuers (after consultation with the ESMA) (Article 46(6) MiCA) ▪ Content of redemption plans for ART issuers, the periodicity for review of such plans, and the triggers for implementing them (Article 47(5) MiCA)

FIGURE 11.3 Implementation timeline and responsible agencies for guidelines under MiCA.

"grand-fathering" clause for CASPs to continue operating under national rules until 1 July 2026 or until they are granted or refused a MiCA authorisation. Member States may also apply a simplified authorisation procedure for such CASPs that were already authorised under national rules prior to MiCA's entering into application on 30 December 2024.

11.6.3 *Guidelines and Harmonising Powers*

Beyond the binding rules of MiCA and supplementary L2 legislation, MiCA also mandates the ESMA and the EBA to adopt a set of non-binding guidelines that will promote a harmonised application of MiCA across Member States (see Figure 11.3). In this way, MiCA fulfils the Meroni Doctrine[95] by requiring the ESAs to propose L2 legislation to the Commission, yet the Meroni Doctrine is also partly circumvented by soft law which in practice feels mandatory for NCAs and is sometimes even enforced through "comply or explain" and similar regimes.

11.7 CONCLUSION

Cryptoassets represent an area of rapid financial and technological innovation, which is therefore both difficult to regulate and supervise and provides for an attractive new market. This may easily lead to regulatory arbitrage, where EU Member States compete for crypto business by relaxing the enforcement of MiCA while taking advantage of its EU Passport

[95] The Meroni Doctrine concerns the extent to which EU institutions may delegate their tasks to regulatory agencies, like the ESAs. See *Meroni & Co., Industrie Metallurgiche, SpA* v. *High Authority of the European Coal and Steel Community*, ECJ [1957] Case 9-56; *Meroni & Co., Industrie Metallurgiche, società in accomandita semplice* v. *High Authority of the European Coal and Steel Community*, ECJ [1958] Case 10-56.

regime.[96] To mitigate this anticipated effect, MiCA takes important steps towards coordinating supervisory efforts within the EU's current supervisory framework. This is apparent in its emphasis on cooperation between NCAs and with the ESMA/EBA. It is also visible in MiCA's creative and multi-faceted approach to coordinating the interpretation of the various definitions that determine its scope (see Section 4.5). Yet, as much as we applaud these measures, they are likely to prove insufficient with respect to the challenge at hand. Hence, further supervisory reform is to be expected, including increasing international cooperation through the work of global standard-setters, eventually aiming at joint supervisory colleges.[97]

The global reach of many crypto issuers and intermediaries also means that NCAs, and particularly those of small Member States, may face difficulties in obtaining the information they need to supervise these entities, which may simply not comply and still reach EU citizens through international websites (see Section 7.2.4 on reverse solicitation). Solutions to this problem may include, for instance, providing the ESAs with inquiry rights regarding third-country crypto firms, RegTech initiatives (such as the launch of a "Euro Wallet" that facilitates trade with EU-authorised firms only), or even treating cryptoassets as transferrable securities by default, thus placing the burden of proof on crypto companies that apply for a more lenient regulatory regime.[98]

[96] This was indeed happening pre-MiCA, when several Member States were competing to attract the crypto industry with legislative and supervisory initiatives. See, for instance, France: Autorité des marchés financiers ('AMF'), 'L'AMF lance une consultation sur les Initial Coin Offerings'. Website www.amf-france.org/fr/actualites-publications/communiques/communiques-de-lamf/lamf-lance-une-consultation-sur-les-initial-coin-offerings-et-initie-son-programme-unicorn (last accessed on 1 October 2024); Liechtenstein: Act of 3 October 2019 on 'Token und VT-Dienstleister (Token- und VT-Dienstleister-Gesetz; TVTG)'; and Malta: Act of 1 November 2018 on 'Virtual Financial Assets'.

[97] See Zetzsche *et al.*, 'Remaining Regulatory Challenges in Digital Finance and Crypto-Assets after MiCA', pp. 105–7.

[98] See Zetzsche *et al.*, 'Remaining Regulatory Challenges in Digital Finance and Crypto-Assets after MiCA', pp. 107–14.

12

The Pilot Regime for DLT Market Infrastructures

12.1 OBJECTIVES

Regulation (EU) 2022/858 is establishing a pilot regime for FMIs based on DLT.[1] Hence, it is commonly referred to as the DLT PilotR or even the DLT Sandbox Regulation as it provides for a "sandbox" in which firms can explore DLT market infrastructures under exceptions from otherwise prevailing EU financial law.[2] Accordingly, regulators seek to unlock the benefits of DLT while mitigating the risks (see Sections 1.2 and 1.3).

According to its own recitals, PilotR is based on a belief that 'so-called "tokenisation" of financial instruments ... is expected to open up opportunities for efficiency improvements in the trading and post-trading process'.[3] Meanwhile, these processes are heavily regulated, and EU financial law was obviously not initially developed with DLT in mind. Therefore, existing EU laws include provisions that potentially preclude or limit the use of DLT, and there are regulatory gaps for a variety of peculiarities in relation to issuing, transferring, and storing financial instruments on a distributed ledger.[4] Hence, the PilotR seeks 'to allow for the development of crypto-assets that qualify as financial instruments and for the development of distributed ledger technology, while preserving a high level of investor protection, market integrity, financial stability and transparency, and avoiding regulatory arbitrage and loopholes'.[5] In addition, PilotR should enable the ESMA to 'gain experience of the opportunities and specific risks relating to crypto-assets that qualify as financial instruments and to their underlying technologies'.[6]

PilotR is designed to achieve nothing less than the "squaring of the circle" by ensuring mutual learning, openness to innovation, *and* risk controls all at the same time. To realise these aims, it is establishing a "regulatory sandbox" coupled with an innovative "business plan approach" as a temporary regulatory framework for the European Single Market.

[1] Regulation (EU) 2022/858 of the European Parliament and of the Council of 30 May 2022 on a pilot regime for market infrastructures based on distributed ledger technology and amending Regulations (EU) No. 600/2014 and (EU) No. 909/2014 and Directive 2014/65/EU, OJ 2022 No. L151, 2 June 2022.

[2] See, for instance, D. A. Zetzsche and J. Woxholth, 'The DLT Sandbox under the Pilot Regulation', *Capital Markets Law Journal*, 17(2) (2022): 212 (which this Chapter draws substantially on).

[3] Recital para. 3 of PilotR, Regulation 2022/858, OJ 2022 No. L151.

[4] Recital paras. 4 and 5 of PilotR.

[5] Recital para. 6 of PilotR.

[6] Recital para. 6 of PilotR.

12.2 SCOPE

As a "regulatory sandbox", PilotR offers exceptions from prevailing EU financial law, yet it also retains risk controls by rigorously limiting the scope of the learning environment. Such limits include those placed on the activities that may be performed in the sandbox, the subjects that may be admitted to the sandbox, and the scale of the sandboxed activities, all of which are discussed in the following.[7] In addition, special topics are covered regarding the intersection of PilotR and the SFD, along with the geographic scope and the EU passport regime under PilotR.

12.2.1 *Activities in Scope: DLT Trading and Settlement of Shares, Bonds, and CIUs*

FMIs facilitate the clearing, settlement, and recording of payments, securities, derivatives, and other financial transactions.[8] Therefore, DLT FMIs could in principle include, for instance, payment systems, central counterparty clearing houses, central securities depositories (CSDs), SSSs, and trade repositories.[9] Yet, the first limit placed on the scope of PilotR is that it allows only actors that focus on certain activities – DLT multilateral trading facilities (DLT MTFs), DLT settlement systems (DLT SSs), and DLT trading and settlement systems (DLT TSSs) – to benefit from the regulatory safe space.[10] These three actors are mutually referred to as DLT market infrastructures.[11] A DLT MTF is an MTF as defined in MiFID that admits to trading only DLT financial instruments.[12] Meanwhile, DLT SSs settle transactions in DLT financial instruments against payment or delivery.[13] Interestingly, the DLT SS definition is independent of both the SFD and the SSS definition in Article 2(15) PilotR, which refers to the CSDR definition. Finally, a DLT TSS is simply either a DLT MTF or a DLT SS that combines the services normally offered by the two separate entities.[14]

The second restrictive element to PilotR's scope limits the tradeable and settlement assets to shares, bonds, and some other debt instruments, along with units in UCITSs. This follows from Article 3(1) PilotR, according to which only these instruments can be admitted to trading or recorded on a DLT market infrastructure. With that in mind, PilotR does not extend any privilege to other financial instruments, most notably derivatives. One question to ponder here is whether units of collective investment schemes other than UCITSs, such as AIF units, are covered by PilotR if they are issued as either shares or bonds. This matter was addressed in a draft report by the European Parliament, which suggested explicitly including all DLT exchange-traded fund units in PilotR's scope,[15] yet the final text is limited to UCITS units.[16]

Turning to the third limiting element, PilotR requires a technical feature, meaning that these DLT financial instruments must be 'issued, recorded, transferred *and* stored' (our emphasis)

[7] See also ESMA, 'Questions and Answers on the Implementation of Regulation (EU) 2022/858 of the European Parliament and of the Council of 30 May 2022 on a Pilot Regime for Market Infrastructures Based on Distributed Ledger Technology', ESMA70-460-189 (2023), pp. 17–20.

[8] See Committee on Payment and Settlement Systems, and Technical Committee of the International Organisation of Securities Commission, 'Principles for Financial Market Infrastructures', Bank for International Settlements (2012), p. 7.

[9] See Ibid., p. 5.

[10] See Articles 4(1), 5(1), and 6(1) of PilotR, respectively.

[11] See Article 2(5) of PilotR.

[12] See Article 2(6), cf. 2(13) of PilotR.

[13] See Article 2(7) of PilotR.

[14] See Article 2(10) of PilotR.

[15] See Committee on Economic and Monetary Affairs, 'Draft Report', 2020/0267 (COD), p. 48.

[16] On ETFs, see ESMA, 'Questions and Answers on the Implementation of Regulation (EU) 2022/858', p. 20.

using DLT.[17] Given the use of "and" here as a connector among the requirements, it would seem insufficient to use DLT for *transfer* only while ultimately *recording* on legacy systems or vice versa. We question why this option is restricted, as amid the growing prevalence of DLT, new (currently unforeseeable) modes of transfer and storage could be developed. This feature of PilotR also does not correspond to MiCA's definition of cryptoassets, whereby "transferred and stored" is sufficient.[18] Yet, this may not lead to problems in practice because the terms 'recorded' and 'stored' presumably mean the same in the context of DLT financial instruments, and the ESMA seems to accept under PilotR both the use of existing financial instruments that were initially not issued on DLT and the off-chain *trading* (presumably as opposed to 'transfer') of DLT financial instruments.[19]

The discrepancies to MiCA concern the DLT financial instrument definition, while the definition of DLT as such in Article 2(1)–(4) PilotR is the same as that in Article 3(1)–(4) MiCA (see Section 4.1). Thus, securities covered by PilotR will be cryptoassets under MiCA but exempted from MiCA's scope by virtue of Article 2(4)(a) MiCA since MiCA defers to EU securities law to deal with financial instruments such as shares, bonds, and CIUs.

The first limitation to entities that focus on certain activities is further enforced by a second limitation which relates directly to these sandboxed activities. A DLT MTF can be exempted from rules that otherwise apply to an MTF under MiFIR and MiFID, a DLT SS can be exempted from rules that otherwise apply to a CSD operating an SSS under CSDR, and a DLT TSS can be exempted from both of these sets of rules.[20] Exemptions for rules concerning other activities are not granted under PilotR.

Trading is covered by PilotR to unlock opportunities for DLT-based disintermediation, while the inclusion of settlement is aimed at merging the trading and post-trade environments – a necessity given the envisaged acceleration of a settlement to a "real-time settlement".[21] Beyond trading and settlement, FMIs also execute clearing and recording, as defined by the Committee on Payments and Market Infrastructure Principles.[22] These activities are not explicitly mentioned in PilotR, yet a DLT SS is allowed to also record and provide safekeeping in relation to DLT financial instruments.

We can only speculate as to why clearing and recording are not covered here. One possible explanation is the absence of EU legislation from which exemptions are required for the clearing of shares and bonds: the clearing obligation pursuant to Article 4 EMIR and Article 29 MiFIR extends to derivatives only, which are not covered by PilotR's scope. In a similar vein, recording is largely governed by the rules of EU/EEA Member States. To allow for the smooth functioning of PilotR, Member States' regulators ought to consider whether PilotR should be supplemented by exemptions from national legislation.

12.2.2 *Subjects in Scope: Authorisation Requirements*

Articles 8(1), 9(1), and 10(1) PilotR limit the benefits of the sandbox to legal entities already authorised as investment firms and market operators under MiFID or CSDs subject to CSDR.

[17] Article 2(11) of PilotR.
[18] Article 3(1)(5) of MiCA, Regulation 2023/1114, OJ 2023 No. L150. See Section 4.1.
[19] See ESMA, 'Questions and Answers on the Implementation of Regulation (EU) 2022/858', pp. 17–18, 21.
[20] See Articles 4(1), 5(1), and 6(1) of PilotR, respectively.
[21] See Recital para. 14 of PilotR.
[22] See Committee on Payment and Settlement Systems, and Technical Committee of the International Organisation of Securities Commission, 'Principles for Financial Market Infrastructures', p. 7.

This, of course, implies a risk that PilotR will support innovation by incumbent firms only, and that start-ups will not qualify. It also deviates from most regulatory sandboxes worldwide, which tend to allow (or even prefer) non-authorised entities.[23]

To address this issue, a modification was added to Articles 8, 9, and 10 PilotR during the legislative process, through which a firm can apply for both authorisation and admittance to the sandbox simultaneously without having to fulfil the authorisation requirements from which it requests an exemption under the sandbox regime.[24] It seems that this approach is appealing to already established firms familiar with authorisation and licensing, but it remains to be seen whether this will be sufficient to attract start-ups and other non-authorised firms.

12.2.3 *Size Limits*

Activities covered by PilotR are limited by size in two ways. On the one hand, there is a limit per issuance.[25] Only shares in issuers with less than EUR 500 million (tentative) market capitalisation may be admitted to trading or recorded on a DLT market infrastructure.[26] The equivalent value for bonds (including convertible bonds) and other debt instruments is an issue size of less than EUR 1 billion. While this excludes the shares of large issuers, it does not exclude their bonds, provided that each bond issue is below the limit. For UCITS units, the rule is similar to that for shares, as the market value of assets under management must be less than EUR 500 million. Hence, smaller issuers of both shares and UCITS units can be completely DLT based, with all their shares and bonds covered by PilotR.

There is also a limit per authorised entity.[27] A DLT market infrastructure cannot admit to trading or initially record a new DLT financial instrument if that would take the aggregate market value of all DLT financial instruments on the market infrastructure beyond EUR 6 billion. Moreover, if the aggregate market value for any reason exceeds EUR 9 billion, then the operator of the DLT market infrastructure must notify the NCA and activate its strategy to reduce the activity, transition from DLT to a traditional market infrastructure, or otherwise cease operations of the DLT market infrastructure. Within these limits, large incumbents may operate DLT market infrastructures as a side business to gain experience. However, in the absence of further legislative steps, they will not be able to turn their main business into a DLT market infrastructure.

An NCA may set lower thresholds than the ones mentioned here.[28] Moreover, to monitor the size limits, the DLT market infrastructure must calculate the monthly average aggregate market value and submit monthly reports to the NCA.[29]

12.2.4 *Settlement Finality: PilotR vs. the SFD*

An essential question here relates to how PilotR impacts on the provisions of the SFD.[30]

[23] See Zetzsche *et al.*, 'Regulating a Revolution', 31, 73.

[24] See Articles 8(2) and (3), 9(2) and (3), and 10(2) and (3) of PilotR and Recital para. 11 of PilotR.

[25] Article 3(1) of PilotR.

[26] See on this, ESMA, 'Questions and Answers on the Implementation of Regulation (EU) 2022/858', p. 17.

[27] Article 3(2) and (3) of PilotR.

[28] Article 3(6) of PilotR. The ESMA will issue guidelines on the exercise of this option; see Articles 8(8)(b) and 9(8)(b) of PilotR.

[29] Article 3(4) and (5) of PilotR.

[30] Cf. Directive 98/26/EC of the European Parliament and of the Council of 19 May 1998 on settlement finality in payment and securities settlement systems, OJ 1998 No. L166, 11 June 1998.

Settlement finality – the irrevocable and unconditional transfer of an asset or the discharge of an obligation[31] – is a fundamental concept in risk management, particularly with regard to the event of a participant's insolvency.[32] Hence, according to Principle 8 of the Bank for International Settlements (BIS) Principles for FMIs, '[a]n FMI should provide clear and certain final settlement'. However, some DLT consensus mechanisms, like the one used for Bitcoin, operate with probabilistic finality only. That is, the more nodes that confirm a transaction, the less likely it is that the transaction may be revoked.[33] Accordingly, there could be a need to exempt DLT FMIs from existing legislation on settlement finality, such as the SFD.

Firms that are authorised as investment firms or operators of a regulated market are not subject to the SFD, even if they may facilitate settlement and recording with permission to operate a DLT TSS under Article 10(1) PilotR. CSDs operating a DLT SS or a DLT TSS, however, would normally be subject to the SFD. Therefore, PilotR provides specific exceptions from the SFD for these cases and purposefully uses the term SS instead of SSS to emphasise the difference from a conventional SSS.[34] The exceptions are twofold: first, Article 5(5) PilotR exempts DLT SSs from the intermediation requirement in the SFD so that market participants can interact directly with the DLT SS without the need for an intermediary firm; then, Article 5 (7) PilotR exempts Member States from the duty under CSDR to designate and notify SSSs under the SFD, thereby exempting DLT SSs from the SFD altogether. Instead, Articles 5(7) and 7(1) PilotR simply mandate that a DLT SS provides timely settlement, publicly discloses the rules that it applies to settlement, and mitigates any risk resulting from the exemption from the SFD, particularly with regard to insolvency proceedings. The same rules apply to a CSD operating a DLT TSS.[35] This enables the recognition of probabilistic finality; however, the operator must define "finality" by detailing the working mode of its consensus mechanism, for instance, by a certain number or share of nodes having validated the transaction.

12.2.5 *Geographic Scope and EU Passport*

The most valuable privilege of the European Single Market in financial services is the right to operate across borders. A specific permission to operate DLT market infrastructures is 'valid throughout the Union for a period of up to six years'.[36] Essentially, the operator is granted a time-bound "EU Passport".

Yet, some uncertainties exist as to what activities are covered by this passport; in light of PilotR's objective, we argue that this EU Passport covers all activities necessary to operate the DLT in question. That is, it covers the activities of all nodes and participants of the ledger and their contribution(s) to, for instance, trading, recording, and settlement. In turn, the (potentially several) ledger participants do not require an additional licence, even when these participants may reside in different Member States and even if their business may involve that of an investment firm subject to MiFID or a CSD. This view coincides with PilotR's requirement

31 See Committee on Payment and Settlement Systems, and Technical Committee of the International Organisation of Securities Commission, 'Principles for Financial Market Infrastructures', p. 64.

32 See Committee on Payment and Settlement Systems, and Technical Committee of the International Organisation of Securities Commission, 'Principles for Financial Market Infrastructures', p. 23.

33 See Committee on Payments and Market Infrastructures, 'Distributed Ledger Technology in Payment, Clearing and Settlement', p. 15; Benos *et al.*, 'The Economics of Distributed Ledger Technology', 121, 132 (also noting that other DLT protocols exist that avoid this problem).

34 See Recital para. 33 and Article 2(7) of PilotR.

35 See Article 6(2) of PilotR.

36 Articles 8(11), 9(11), and 10(11) of PilotR for DLT MTFs, DLT SSs, and DLT TSSs, respectively.

that participants need to meet certain qualitative criteria, including good repute.[37] It also coincides with Article 5(4) PilotR, which exempts DLT SSs from the outsourcing rules under CSDR. This may suggest that PilotR treats ledger participants as outsourcing providers, and an exemption from Article 19 CSDR would then explicitly exempt from the authorisation requirement for outsourcing of core services. While Article 5 PilotR applies to CSDs only, the same also holds for DLT MTFs because they are not subject to CSDR and the MiFID rules about outsourcing[38] do not cover settlement activities. However, if the DLT is used for MiFID activities (e.g., to match parties for trading), a question arises as to whether nodes need authorisation subject to MiFID. In this case, we still argue that PilotR must be interpreted as providing an EU Passport covering the activities of all nodes and participants of the ledger so that these do not require separate licences.

The EU Passport addresses the root cause of why regulators have so far refrained from deviating from EU law. In smaller markets, where every transaction is to some extent cross-border, in the absence of an EU Passport very little innovation would take place. In such an environment, PilotR not only grants exemptions from rules that restrain their activities but also allows the inclusion of participants across the European Single Market which are then also covered by PilotR.

12.3 PROCEDURE: MIMICKING MIFID/MIFIR AND CSDR

PilotR is based on the idea that DLT market infrastructures must assign an operator as the authorised legal entity, which may then be granted exemptions from MiFID/MiFIR and CSDR by a competent authority. To be granted these exemptions, certain conditions and compensatory measures apply.

12.3.1 *Operator Requirement*

A market operator 'manages and/or operates the business of a regulated market'.[39] That operator is in charge of the application for running a DLT market infrastructure, functions as an access point for the competent authority, and ensures the compliance of the DLT market infrastructure with all applicable legislation. PilotR refers to the operator as a singular entity, so a scheme where multiple nodes function collectively as operator is impermissible.

This single operator requirement is appealing to established financial intermediaries, but at odds with the idea of decentralised finance, which aims to reduce hierarchies and silo systems; it erects (or, depending on one's perspective, retains) a legal barrier to innovation. This barrier may be explained by PilotR's concept that relies, by way of exemption, on established MiFID/MiFIR and CSDR rules. Any fully decentralised approach would require an entirely novel design relating to jurisdictional competencies, accountability, and responsibility across ledger participants, supervisory cooperation, and the sanctioning powers of competent authorities.[40] In fact, regulators unfamiliar with DLT may find it difficult to allocate jurisdiction over a truly

[37] See Article 5(5) of PilotR, which applies directly to a DLT SS and through Article 6(3)(b) also to a DLT TSS.

[38] Article 16(5) of MiFID, Directive 2014/65, OJ 2014 No. L173, and Article 31(2)(a) of Regulation 2017/565, OJ 2017 No. L87.

[39] Article 2(20) of PilotR, cf. Article 4(1)(18) of MiFID.

[40] See Zetzsche *et al.*, 'Decentralized Finance (DeFi)', 172, 191 (laying out the challenges); D. A. Zetzsche, L. Anker-Sorensen, M. L. Passador and A. Wehrli, 'DLT-Based Enhancement of Cross-Border Payment Efficiency – A Legal and Regulatory Perspective', *Law and Financial Markets Review*, 15(1–2) (2021): 70–115, 103–14.

decentralised DLT country-by-country. PilotR avoids this problem through requiring an operator to apply for approval and exemptions and thus assign jurisdiction over the DLT in question to the operator's home country authority.[41]

That operator must ensure that the DLT market infrastructure has, and applies, a clear and detailed business plan, rules, and terms of use; clear and unambiguous information on their website; sufficient IT and cyber arrangements; operational risk management procedures; segregation of funds; reliable and retrievable records; a strategy for transitioning out of (or winding down) operations; and sometimes also additional prudential safeguards in the form of own funds or an insurance policy (cf. Article 7 PilotR). These elements all contribute to the safe and reliable operations of DLT, and information about them shall accompany the application to operate a DLT market infrastructure.

In particular, the applicant's business plan and the rules and terms of use raise specific questions regarding the governance of DLT market infrastructures, which we discuss separately in Section 12.4.

12.3.2 *PilotR as an Exemption from MiFID/MiFIR and CSDR*

PilotR relies on a system of exemptions from, and requirements set in lieu of, existing MiFID/MiFIR and CSDR requirements.[42] The regulatory technique here is the same for DLT MTFs, SSs, and TSSs: MiFID and MiFIR[43] apply to MTFs and CSDR[44] applies to SSSs, unless the operator (a) has requested and been granted an exemption from certain provisions available for exemption, (b) complies with a set of general obligations to set the rules and meet minimum standards for the DLT market infrastructure operations, and (c) complies with a set of conditions and, at the discretion of the competent authority, additional compensatory measures.[45] For a DLT TSS, MiFID, MiFIR, and CSDR all apply, either directly or *mutatis mutandis*, unless said criteria are met.[46] Hence, DLT MTF, SS, or TSS operators must put forward an exemption request.

An *MTF operator* may ask to be relieved from the MiFID rules governing MTF participants to allow for disintermediation so that persons can trade directly on the DLT MTF without the use

[41] Articles 2(21), 12, and 13 of PilotR.

[42] Recital paras. 15, 54, and 60 of PilotR also allude to the need for updating regulatory technical standards under CSDR and MiFIR to facilitate DLT trading and settlement. Under CSDR, this has led to a suspension of the new buy-in rules. See Commission Delegated Regulation (EU) 2022/1930 of 6 July 2022 amending the regulatory technical standards laid down in Delegated Regulation (EU) 2018/1229 as regards the date of application of the provisions related to the buy-in regime, OJ L 266, 13.10.2022. Under MiFIR, following a call for evidence, ESMA concluded that guidance on the ESMA's expectations would be sufficient and no legislative changed required. See ESMA, 'Report on the DLT Pilot Regime: On the Call for Evidence on the DLT Pilot Regime and Compensatory Measures on Supervisory Data', ESMA70-460-111 (2022); ESMA, 'Questions and Answers on the Implementation of Regulation (EU) 2022/858'.

[43] On the RTS on transparency and data reporting requirements under MiFIR, see ESMA, 'Report on the DLT Pilot Regime on the Call for Evidence on the DLT Pilot Regime and Compensatory Measures on Supervisory Data' (2022), ESMA70-460-111. Regarding exemptions from Article 26 of MiFIR and associated RTS, see ESMA, 'Questions and Answers on the Implementation of Regulation (EU) 2022/858', pp. 10–17; ESMA, 'Report on the DLT Pilot Regime: Study on How Financial Instrument Transactions Are Registered in Various Distributed Ledger Technologies' (2023), ESMA12-2121844265-3183; ESMA, 'Report on the DLT Pilot Regime: Study on Extraction of Transaction Data' (2023), ESMA12-2121844265-3182.

[44] Regarding exemptions from Articles 3 and 40 of CSDR. See ESMA, 'Questions and Answers on the Implementation of Regulation (EU) 2022/858', pp. 23–24.

[45] Articles 4(1) and 5(1) of PilotR.

[46] Article 6(1) of PilotR.

of an intermediary firm.[47] The MTF operator may also be exempted from the requirement to report transactions to the competent authority presumably because the transparency of open distributed ledgers allows the competent authority to access such information directly on the ledger.[48]

CSDs operating a DLT SS can request exemptions from a list of specified CSDR provisions. These are bundled into eight blocks (see Figure 12.1), each of which comes with specific requirements: one block relates to the securities accounts and book entry; one relates to settlement fails; one relates to delegation; one relates to participants in the SS; one relates to transparency; one relates to settlement finality; one relates to cash settlement and delivery-vs-payment; and one relates to access to the DLT SS.[49]

Article 6 PilotR further allows for disintermediation by the integrated delivery of both a DLT MTF and a DLT SS, which is then called a DLT TSS. In such cases, the exemptions and requirements for a DLT MTF and for a DLT SS both apply.[50] Essentially, a DLT MTF is then allowed to expand its services from the facilitation of trading to also covering settlement and the recording of transactions, and the reverse applies to a DLT SS. If the operator of a DLT MTF, for instance, does not ask for relief, it needs to rely on a CSD which may or may not operate a DLT SS subject to Article 5 PilotR. Given the opportunity for disintermediation through the use of DLT, the opening provided for operators to vertically integrate from trading to settlement or vice versa is welcome.

12.3.3 *Conditions and Compensatory Measures*

Exemptions from MiFID/MiFIR and CSDR come with the following three sets of conditions: (1) general conditions; (2) specific conditions for certain exemption requests; and (3) so-called compensatory measures proposed by the applicants and/or induced by the competent authority (see Figure 12.1).

(1) *All exemption* requests must be proportionate, limited to the MTF, SS, or TSS subject to PilotR, and justified to the cause.[51] Some exemption requests must also demonstrate that the rules from which an exception is being sought are incompatible with the use of the DLT in question. This is probably a redundant addition to the general justification requirement. While there is no requirement for operators to provide a genuine innovation, as is the case for some regulatory sandboxes,[52] the justification requirement in PilotR may entail a similar standard. We doubt, however, that regulators are sufficiently qualified to assess the degree of technical innovation as part of a traditional supervisory process.[53]

(2) With regard to *specific conditions*, if exempted from the rules on securities accounts and book entry, for instance, an operator of a DLT SS or a DLT TSS must still ensure that

[47] Article 4(2) of PilotR.

[48] Article 4(3) of PilotR.

[49] Article 5(2)–(9) of PilotR.

[50] Article 6, cf. Articles 4(5) and 5(11) of PilotR.

[51] Articles 4(4) and 5(10), cf. the second sub-paragraph point (b) of Article 6(1) and (2) of PilotR.

[52] See, for example, Financial Conduct Authority, 'Regulatory Sandbox' (2015), para. 3.4. Website www.fca.org.uk/publication/research/regulatory-sandbox.pdf (last accessed on 1 October 2024); Autoriti Monetari Brunei Darussalem, 'Fintech Regulatory Sandbox Guidelines', Guidelines No. FTU/G-1/2017/1 (2017), para. 7.2(a); Bank Negara Malaysia, 'Financial Technology Regulatory Sandbox Framework', BNM/RH/PD 030-1 (2016), para. 5.1(a).

[53] See in the same vein Zetzsche *et al.*, 'Regulating a Revolution', 31, 70.

Topic	CSDR provisions that may be exempted from	Associated specific conditions	General obligations and conditions; additional compensatory measures
Securities accounts and book-entry	▪ Art. 2(1)(4) on dematerialised form, i.e. financial instruments exist only as book entry records ▪ Art. 2(1)(9) on transfer of orders ▪ Art. 2(1)(28) on securities accounts ▪ Art. 3 on book-entry form ▪ Art. 37 on integrity of issue ▪ Art. 38 on the segregation of assets	▪ 'Securities account' or 'book-entry form' are incompatible with the DLT ▪ Proposed 'compensatory measures' ▪ Recording on DLT instead of book-entry ▪ Number of securities admitted to the DLT SS is equal to the number of those recorded on the DLT at any given time ▪ Ability to segregate securities held by one entity from that of another ▪ No overdraft, debit balances, etc.	**Article 7 PilotR** ▪ Clear, detailed business plan ▪ Rules and legal terms ▪ Clear and unambiguous information on website ▪ IT and cyber arrangements ▪ Operational risk procedures ▪ Segregation of funds ▪ Reliable and retrievable records ▪ Investor protection arrangements ▪ Strategy for transitioning out of or winding down operations ▪ Own funds or insurance policy if required by the competent authority **Article 5(10) PilotR** ▪ Requested exemption is proportionate to and justified by the use of the DLT ▪ Requested exemption is limited to the DLT SS and does not apply to other parts of the CSD's business **Article 5(1)(c) PilotR** ▪ 'any compensatory measures that the competent authority deems appropriate'
Settlement fails	▪ Art. 6 on prevention ▪ Art. 7 on addressing settlement fails	▪ Robust procedures and arrangements ▪ Confirmed details of transactions ▪ Prevents/addresses settlement fails	
Delegation	▪ Art. 19 on extension / outsourcing	▪ Legacy rules incompatible with the DLT	
Participants	▪ Art. 2(1)(19) on participants	▪ Participants are of good repute, have given informed consent, and have sufficient ability, competence, experience, and knowledge	
Transparency	▪ Art. 33 on requirements for participation ▪ Art. 34 on transparency ▪ Art. 35 on communication	▪ Proposed 'compensatory measures' ▪ Disclosed and fair participation criteria ▪ Disclosed prices and fees	
Settlement finality	▪ Art. 39 on settlement finality	▪ Proposed 'compensatory measures' ▪ T+2 or shorter settlement time ▪ Disclosed settlement rules ▪ Risk mitigation	
Cash settlement	▪ Art. 40 on cash settlement	▪ Ensured 'delivery versus payment'	
Access	▪ Art. 50 on standard link access ▪ Art. 51 on customised link access ▪ Art. 53 on access between a CSD and another market infrastructure	▪ DLT is incompatible with legacy market infrastructures or integration would be disproportionately costly ▪ Must give access to other DLT operators	

FIGURE 12.1 Exemptions available to DLT SSSs.

the securities are properly recorded on the ledger, that the number of on-ledger securities matches the number of securities circulating, that those securities can be allocated to their owners at all times, and that overdrafts or debit balances are not allowed.[54] The impact on innovation of the latter two conditions rests on the question of who is a 'member, participant, issuer, or client' in the system. If we assume that a custodian is the ledger participant in the reading envisaged by the provision, this condition expresses common sense only; that is, a CSD must identify the custodian only, who again is responsible for identifying its clients. It is unclear, however, whether the operator of a DLT SS or DLT TSS must also allocate DLT financial instruments to the custodian's clients. We do not think that PilotR intends to require that the custodial clients' data must be recorded on the ledger itself, even if PilotR seeks to facilitate disintermediation by having the client as a participant directly in the DLT SS or DLT TSS.

If, however, the custodial client (the 'owner' of DLT financial instruments) is indeed a ledger participant, imposing the requirement that all securities once recorded could be segregated from that of any other member, participant, issuer, or client raises the bar when compared to existing CSDs that operate omnibus accounts where securities held in the CSD's own name are only segregated from those of all clients collectively. This would also mean that each custodial client must opt-in to a new custodial infrastructure to participate in the DLT. As such, we argue in favour of a standard where open terms like "holder of an entitlement" and deference to definitions in the system's business plan would have been preferable and should be considered in a future revision of PilotR.

Furthermore, if a DLT market infrastructure wants to establish new types of participants, it must provide assurances that such participants are of good repute, have given their informed consent, and have a sufficient level of ability, competence, experience, and knowledge with regard to the post-trading and functioning of DLT.[55] Such a requirement de facto excludes custodial clients as ledger participants and as such necessitates some degree of intermediation (which is, again, at odds with the rationale behind employing DLT in the first place).

(3) Finally MTF operators and CSDs must comply with additional 'compensatory measures that the competent authority deems appropriate'.[56] Given that applicants must already meet a number of requirements, it remains dubious as to what additional compensatory measures can be expected and how these measures relate to the existing safeguards. This question is important since certain exemption requests must be accompanied by proposals for such compensatory measures.

12.3.4 *Competent Authorities and the ESMA's Involvement*

Articles 8–10 PilotR require specific permission to operate DLT market infrastructures to be granted by the competent authority of the home Member State. The competent authority is, in principle, the same authority as the one in charge of the authorisation under MiFID/MiFIR and CSDR, yet Member States may enact different provisions to accommodate the special nature of DLT.[57] (Some may, for instance, consider designate the same authority as under MiCA.)[58]

[54] Article 5(2)(b), cf. the second sub-paragraph point (b) of Article 6(1) and (2) of PilotR.
[55] Articles 4(2) and 5(5), cf. the second sub-paragraph point (b) of Article 6(1) and (2) of PilotR.
[56] Articles 4(1)(c), 5(1)(c), and the second sub-paragraph point (c) of Article 6(1) and (2) of PilotR.
[57] The term 'competent authority' is defined in Article 2(21) and further detailed in Articles 12 and 13 of PilotR.
[58] See Section 11.2.1.

Before deciding, the competent authority must give the ESMA the opportunity to provide a 'non-binding opinion on the exemptions requested or on the adequacy of the type of DLT used'.[59] Moreover, the ESMA has issued guidelines and standard templates regarding applications for specific permission under PilotR,[60] and it will develop further guidelines on the exemptions granted and compensatory measures imposed under PilotR.[61] When the application concerns the operation of a DLT SS or a DLT TSS, other authorities under CSDR, such as central banks, must also be consulted.[62]

Furthermore, to promote the consistency and proportionality of the exemptions granted, the 'ESMA shall consult the competent authorities of other Member States and shall take the utmost account of their views when issuing its opinion'.[63] The competent authority then may or may not consider the ESMA's non-binding opinion. In any case, the ESMA will publish on its website a list of all such specific permissions, with their start and end dates, along with the exemptions granted.[64] It is then up to the competent authority to monitor and withdraw the permission if needed.[65]

This involvement of ESMA goes further as compared to the equivalent rules under MiCA, where NCAs are typically entitled to exercise supervisory powers without asking the ESAs for their opinions – with notable exceptions, such as significant ARTs/EMTs and product intervention (see Chapter 11). This involvement of the ESMA under PilotR results in an intense knowledge exchange across competent authorities, as well as some openness to innovation paired with desirable standardisation across the European Single Market. At the same time, collating the opinion(s) is time consuming and therefore slows down innovation.

12.4 GOVERNANCE: THE BUSINESS PLAN APPROACH

12.4.1 *A Novel Approach*

PilotR addresses the issue of governance and accountability in distributed ledgers by requiring the appointment of one operator that holds special permission. It then takes a truly innovative approach to the rights, obligations, and accountability of DLT participants: it leaves it to the operator to determine how functions and obligations are distributed or whether they remain in the hands of the operator or other parties. This is a substantial departure from the status quo where financial market law tends to define the role of each type of intermediary, and each of them is explicitly accountable for their activities as defined by their intermediary activity or entity status.

While Articles 4–7 of PilotR impose a number of obligations on the assigned operator, these obligations are primarily of a procedural nature vis-à-vis the competent authority. With regard to the substance of the DLT operations, the operator itself defines 'the rules under which the DLT market infrastructures and their operators are to operate, including the legal terms defining the rights, obligations, responsibilities and liabilities of operators of the DLT market infrastructures,

59 Articles 8(6) and (7), 9(6) and (7), and 10(7) and (8) of PilotR.

60 See Articles 8(5), 9(5), and 10(6) of PilotR; ESMA, 'Guidelines on Standard Forms, Formats and Templates to Apply for Permission to Operate a DLT Market Infrastructure' (2023), ESMA70-460-213.

61 See Articles 4(6), 5(12), 8(8)(a), and 9(8)(a) of PilotR.

62 Articles 9(6) and (7) and 10(7) and (8) of PilotR.

63 Ibid.

64 Articles 8(11), 9(11), and 10(11) of PilotR.

65 Articles 8(12), 9(12), and 10(12) of PilotR.

as well as those of the members, participants, issuers and clients using their DLT market infrastructure'.[66] All of these matters can and must be defined within the business plan.

Instead of defining the different roles making up the FMI (CSDs, clearing houses, etc.) and regulating the operator of each activity, PilotR grants discretion to the operator (and, in reality, to all DLT participants jointly). Through what we call herein the "Business Plan Approach", PilotR adopts an overall market infrastructure view as opposed to the conventional institutional perspective.

12.4.2 *Openness to Innovation*

The Business Plan Approach bears obvious advantages with regard to openness to innovation and, as such, gains our full support.

For instance, the operator can request an exemption from the authorisation requirement for the outsourcing of core activities in Article 19 CSDR if it demonstrates that this requirement is incompatible with the envisaged use of DLT.[67] This facilitates the outsourcing of core activities to a distributed network of semi-independent nodes, as is integral to DLT. Yet, it marks a stringent reversal relative to the first PilotR Proposal, under which an exemption could also be granted from Article 30(1)(a) and (b) CSDR.[68] This essentially allowed the operator also to free itself of responsibility for tasks allocated to other participants, notably to the nodes in a distributed network. Given the decentralised nature of DLT, it is highly impractical for one operator to be accountable for the actions of largely autonomous nodes. Therefore, we argued in favour of this departure from the conventional financial law 'outsourcing perspective' at the time while also pointing out some associated challenges.[69] Yet, following the adoption of the revised PilotR into law, it is now clear that even an exemption from the outsourcing authorisation requirement in Article 19 CSDR does not relieve the operator of a DLT market infrastructure from its responsibility for the outsourced activities. For instance, Article 7(6) PilotR specifically states that the operator is liable for lost assets.

Under the Business Plan Approach, the operator is asked not only to set the rules but also to outline the sanctions and the enforcement mechanisms in its application: PilotR requires the operator to 'specify the governing law, any pre-litigation dispute settlement mechanisms, any insolvency protection measures under [CSDR] and the jurisdiction in which legal action may be brought'.[70] Of course, a business plan cannot override mandatory law; hence, public intervention powers, administrative sanctions, and criminal law will continue to apply. At the same time, the business plan will be unable to prejudice legal rights granted to third parties not part of the DLT. Yet, the business plan can stipulate intra-ledger rights and obligations as a quasi-contractual tool.

As a safeguard against undesirable opportunism, the governance arrangements proposed by the operator will be reviewed by the competent authority and the ESMA before the specific permission is granted.[71]

66 Second paragraph of Article 7(1) of PilotR.

67 Article 5(4), cf. the second sub-paragraph point (b) of Article 6(1) and (2) of PilotR. See also Recital para. 31 of PilotR.

68 See Article 5(3) of PilotR, Regulation Proposal, COM (2020) 594 Final.

69 See D. A. Zetzsche and J. Woxholth, 'The DLT Sandbox under the Pilot Regulation', *Capital Markets Law Journal*, 17(2) (2022): 212, 225, 227.

70 Second paragraph of Article 7(1) of PilotR.

71 Articles 8(4)(a), 9(4)(a), and 10(4)(a) of PilotR.

Such an approach makes sense in a DLT environment where innovators may be better informed about all the technical opportunities and may know how to best address the challenges resulting from them, when compared to the regulators. Indeed, PilotR may here serve as an example also for other areas where regulators lack the information and insights required to draft suitable legislation.[72]

12.4.3 *Challenges*

Yet, the Business Plan Approach will also bring foreseeable challenges.

One issue is the extent to which other DLT or market participants are legally bound by the rules defined by the operator. Do we apply a contractual or public law perspective for that purpose? Pertinently, do all rights and obligations apply only to DLT or market participants that have signed up to them? Does involvement with the ledger as such come with implicit consent, or do the rules apply as public law whereby consent is not required? Consent can be assumed to have been given only for arrangements sufficiently transparent to be consented to. We doubt that any business plan can be sufficiently detailed for third parties to fully understand their technicalities, and those technicalities will matter if anything goes wrong. In practice, we suggest that the competent authority and the ESMA require the operator to install a mechanism to ensure consent before market participants get involved with the ledger. For that purpose, *operational* details may be stipulated by way of contracts incorporating technical specification sheets. We could further envisage that the operator sets up a technical pilot where nodes test their operational rights and obligations under market conditions in an isolated environment before signing up with binding effect. The situation is different with regard to *legal* details: legal complexity is often present in financial infrastructure contracts, leading to disagreement over their interpretation. To some extent, such disagreement can be remedied through applying the *contra proferentem* doctrine, that is, interpretation against the draftsman where doubts remain, taking into account the technical and financial expertise to be expected from all entities volunteering to function as nodes.

Another pressing question is as follows: to what extent is the operator really entitled to impose sanctions and enforcement mechanisms upon third parties? Here, we draw an analogy to rules and sanctioning regimes prevalent at stock exchanges and other self-regulating financial infrastructures. By and large, if the competent authority and the ESMA require the operator to install a mechanism to ensure consent before market participants get involved with the ledger, general contract law could govern sanctions and penalties assigned to participants for non-compliance.

A matter where we would have expected more legal certainty is what constitutes the default position when the rules defined by the operator are silent. This question is important because even the most expansive business plan would be unable to capture all matters. We argue that for any matter not explicitly addressed in the business plan, the operator remains in charge when it comes to meeting the infrastructure's obligations. This is obvious vis-à-vis third parties, towards whom the operator cannot delegate its responsibility, but should in our view apply also in the relationship between the operator and the other participants in the DLT market infrastructure. This follows from the exemptive nature of PilotR, whereby the operator as a MiFID investment firm, market operator, or CSD needs to comply with all MiFID/MiFIR or CSDR provisions unless PilotR provides otherwise.

[72] See, for example, Zetzsche *et al.*, 'DLT-Based Enhancement of Cross-Border Payment Efficiency', 104–5 (discussing the Business Plan Approach and proposing to implement it for DLTs in the context of cross-border payments).

Finally, we caution that public sanctioning usually requires some written legal text (*nulla poena sine lege scriptum*). Hence, the regulators may lack the competence to enforce business plan duties towards both operators and non-operator DLT participants. This may imply that, on the one hand, conventional financial law cannot be enforced because the operator was exempted from the relevant duty by way of PilotR and, on the other hand, that the competent authority cannot enforce the compensatory rules in the business plan. Even if the market participants have indeed made or accepted the business plan terms, we find it difficult to imagine that they could submit themselves to the sanctioning powers of a competent authority by way of contract. In practice, we expect this issue to be resolved by means of the competent authority withdrawing or threatening to withdraw the specific permission to operate a DLT market infrastructure.[73]

Many of the above-mentioned issues could be remedied if more than one operator took responsibility for the implementation of *some parts* of the business plan. Yet, as mentioned already, PilotR so far refers to the operator as a singular entity meaning the regulation obviously seeks not to deviate too far from the status quo of relying on one operator under the MiFID/MiFIR and CSDR rules.

All in all, we appreciate the PilotR's Business Plan Approach as a bold and innovative step that contributes to a true test-and-learn approach overall. Yet, we would have preferred further clarity on the legal status of ledger participants and the respective sanctioning powers of competent authorities, to ensure more legal certainty and efficient enforcement of any business plan stipulation.

12.5 CONCLUSION

We believe that PilotR marks a significant step in the right direction for EU financial law. Yet, during its first year, PilotR attracted few prospective applicants to its sandbox regime, although there are signs of some improvement.[74] As a pilot regime with learning as a central regulatory objective, PilotR will certainly be amended or otherwise serve as a basis for future legislation. We have earlier identified areas for improvement based on the initial PilotR Proposal,[75] some of which were implemented in the adopted version of the act and some that were not. Subject to what comes out of the learning process, we suggest implementing more of our suggestions in future amended versions of PilotR, in addition to addressing the challenges that have since been identified by ESMA. [76]

[73] This likely requires fulfilment of the requirements under Articles 8(12)(a), 9(12)(a), or 10(12)(a) of PilotR.

[74] See V. Ross (ESMA Chair), 'DLT Pilot Regime Implementation' (2024), ESMA75-117376770-460, pp. 1–2, with reply from M. McGuinnes (EU Commissioner), Ares(2024) 3056562.

[75] See Zetzsche and Woxholth, 'The DLT Sandbox under the Pilot Regulation', pp. 229–33.

[76] See V. Ross (ESMA Chair), 'DLT Pilot Regime Implementation' (2024), ESMA75-117376770-460, pp. 3–4.

13

Private Law of Cryptoassets

13.1 INTRODUCTION

The focus of EU lawmakers with regard to cryptoassets has been largely regulatory. Reflecting the fact that private law is predominantly under the control of the Member States, and without seeking to be comprehensive, this chapter takes a comparative view on the private law topics most relevant to cryptoassets. It covers efforts to harmonise national private laws, refers to principles issued by International Institute for the Unification of Private Law (UNIDROIT) and the European Law Institute (ELI), and considers relevant MiCA provision with private law effects in mind. We address the major fields of private law in turn, namely, property law, contract law, company law, and tort law, along with a look into jurisdiction and law enforcement.

13.2 PROPERTY LAW

The most fundamental private law problems raised by cryptoassets are found in the realm of property law, including (1) whether cryptoassets constitute property and, if so, (2) which rules apply to the title and transfer of cryptoassets. On those foundations, related questions arise with respect to (3) how cryptoassets should be treated in the event of insolvency, (4) custody relationships, and finally (5) security rights in cryptoassets.

13.2.1 *Cryptoassets as Property?*

The first question to consider here is whether cryptoassets constitute property and are subject to either proprietary rights (*in rem* or *things in possession* under common law), contractual rights (*in personam* or *things in action* under common law), or something else.[1] This matters in the event of insolvency, for instance, where proprietary rights generally have priority over claims by creditors. If rights to cryptoassets are neither proprietary (*in rem*) nor contractual (*in personam*), then a question emerges as to whether they are legally enforceable at all because ownership rights typically do not arise in data/information or, more generally, in intangibles that are not

[1] See Woxholth *et al.*, 'Competing Claims to Crypto-Assets', 226, 230–32; K. F. K. Low, 'Third Thing or Sixth Sense? I See Ideational Objects?' in P. Babie and M. Giancaspro (eds.), *Private Law and Digital Assets* (New York: Springer, forthcoming); L. Lee, 'Examining the Legal Status of Digital Assets as Property: A Comparative Analysis of Jurisdictional Approaches' (2024). Website https://dx.doi.org/10.2139/ssrn.4807135 (last accessed on 1 October 2024).

contractual rights.[2] For instance, as authors we may hold the copyright to this book but we do not own the information in it and so cannot prevent anyone from using the information once they have read it.

Most cryptoassets fall neatly into conventional legal categories because they represent conventional rights (see Section 2.2). Typical cryptocurrencies, such as Bitcoin, however, are assets in and of themselves. They neither represent a contractual right (*in personam*) nor are they physical objects, which is traditionally seen as the main characteristic of property (*in rem*). When such cryptoassets consist purely of information stored on a ledger along with information in the form of public and private keys, this information should, in our view, not be seen as constituting the cryptoassets but rather as a record of them and the means of accessing them.[3] This makes cryptoassets profoundly different from other digital assets such as a digital photograph or a copy of this book, the value of which lies in the information itself. Rather, cryptocurrencies are more like physical cash.[4] Since the end of the gold standard, fiat currencies can no longer be seen as a claim on any underlying asset. The value of fiat currencies is also not derived from the metal or paper of which they are made nor from the information printed thereon. In effect, the difference between information, on the one hand, and cryptoassets or cash, on the other hand, lies in scarcity because information can be copied, while cryptoassets and cash are exclusive by design.[5] Therefore, both cryptoassets and cash meet the typical criteria to qualify as property, such as being definable, rivalrous, and identifiable by third parties.[6] After much legal debate, this conclusion now seems to be accepted in most jurisdictions and has been enshrined in the UNIDROIT Principles on Digital Assets and Private Law.[7]

13.2.2 *Rules of Title and Transfer*

13.2.2.1 *Problem*

As explained by the pseudonymous inventor of Bitcoin, Satoshi Nakamoto, '[c]ommerce on the Internet has come to rely almost exclusively on financial institutions serving as trusted third parties to process electronic payments' so '[c]ompletely non-reversible transactions are not really possible, since financial institutions cannot avoid mediating disputes'.[8] He, she, or they go on to propose Bitcoin as an electronic alternative to physical cash by solving "the double-spending

[2] With some exceptions, such as trademarks. See J. D. Michels and C. Millard, 'The New Things: Property Rights in Digital Files?' *Cambridge Law Journal*, 81(2) (2022): 323, chapter 2.1; J. Sarra and L. Gullifer, 'Crypto-Claimants and Bitcoin Bankruptcy: Challenges for Recognition and Realization', *International Insolvency Review*, 28 (2019): 233, 245; H. R. Howe and J. Griffiths (eds.), *Concepts of Property in Intellectual Property Law* (Cambridge: Cambridge University Press, 2013).

[3] See UK Jurisdiction Taskforce, 'Legal Statement on Cryptoassets and Smart Contracts' (2019), para. 60. Website https://lawtechuk.io/explore/cryptoasset-and-smart-contract-statement (last accessed on 1 October2024).

[4] In the same vein, see B. Geva, S. N. Grunewald and C. Zellweger-Gutknecht, 'The e-Banknote as a "Banknote": A Monetary Law Interpreted', *Oxford Journal of Legal Studies*, 41(4) (2021): 1119.

[5] See UK Jurisdiction Taskforce , 'Legal Statement on Cryptoassets and Smart Contracts', paras. 62 and 63; D. Fox, 'Cryptocurrencies in the Common Law of Property', in D. Fox and S. Green (eds.), *Cryptocurrencies in the Public and Private Law* (Oxford: Oxford University Press, 2019), pp. 145–48.

[6] Most jurisdictions have no comprehensive definition of property, yet case law typically points to some characteristics. For digital assets specifically, see Michels and Millard, 'The New Things', 323, chapter 2.1.2.

[7] Principles 3(1) and 4 of the UNIDROIT Principles on Digital Assets and Private Law. See also L. Gullifer and I. Tirado, 'Proprietary Rights and Digital Assets: A "Modest Proposal" from a Transnational Law Perspective', *Law & Contemporary Problems*, 87(2) (2024) (in press).

[8] S. Nakamoto, 'Bitcoin: A Peer-to-Peer Electronic Cash System'. Website https://bitcoin.org/bitcoin.pdf (last accessed on 1 October 2024).

problem".[9] In this sense, cryptoassets were created as a technological solution to the perennial problem of competing claims when the same asset is passed on to multiple parties.

However, DLT can only address claims from transactions *on chain*, not from creditor claims or other rights to cryptoassets arising outside of the DLT network. DLT also comes with the following five side-effects:[10] (1) individual wallets have proven prone to cyberattacks (theft); (2) the pseudonymous nature of private keys implies that transferees cannot validate whether the transferor has legal capacity to conduct the given transaction; (3) the ownership of cryptoassets may easily be hidden from creditors seeking redress; (4) anonymous accounts make it notoriously difficult to identify which courts have jurisdiction and which laws apply; and (5) DLT is designed to be immutable, so it is rarely a viable option to return cryptoassets to their rightful owner by rewriting the ledger.[11] In sum, DLT provides an ingenious solution to the double-spending problem for on-chain transfers, yet the issue of competing claims not only remains unresolved by DLT but is in fact *facilitated* by DLT. This calls for legal solutions.

13.2.2.2 *The Nemo Dat Rule*

The legal starting point can be summarised by the principle of *nemo dat quod non habet* or "no one can give what they do not have".[12] Applied specifically to the double-spending problem, it is typically referred to as "first in time, greater in right". The *nemo dat* rule is now also acknowledged specifically for digital assets in the UNIDROIT Principles.[13]

This is all built on the assumption that multiple parties have claims to the same asset, which is not necessarily the case with on-chain transfers of cryptoassets:[14] when A's private–public key pair is used to send cryptoassets to an account represented by B's public key, typically, no actual transfer of cryptoassets takes place between A and B. When Bitcoins are transferred, for instance, they are simply registered as "spent" by the nodes in the network, so they cannot be spent again, and an equivalent amount of new Bitcoins on the transferee's account is acknowledged by the same nodes as available for new transactions.[15] Thus, the UK Jurisdiction Taskforce argues that no transfer occurs – the implication of which is that no competing claims exist to the same asset so the *nemo dat* rule and other legal principles for competing claims become irrelevant, and whoever has the new cryptoassets recorded on their account in effect prevails.[16] Yet, a substance over form argument should in our view prevail here. Users of cryptocurrencies certainly view their transactions as transferring the same units of value from one to another. This is now also acknowledged by the UNIDROIT Principles on Digital Assets and Private Law.[17]

[9] Ibid.

[10] See Woxholth *et al.*, 'Competing Claims to Crypto-Assets', 226, 229–30.

[11] Yet, this does happen sometimes, for example, following 'the DAO hack': see K. Yeung, 'Regulation by Blockchain: The Emerging Battle for Supremacy between the Code of Law and Code as Law', *Modern Law Review*, 82(2) (2019): 207, 233–35.

[12] This Common Law principle is essentially equivalent to the Civil Law principle of *nemo plus iuris ad alium transferre potest quam ipse habet* or 'one cannot transfer to another more rights than oneself has'.

[13] Principle 9(1) of the UNIDROIT Principles on Digital Assets and Private Law. See also Gullifer and Tirado, 'Proprietary Rights and Digital Assets'.

[14] See Woxholth *et al.*, 'Competing Claims to Crypto-Assets', 226, 232–33.

[15] Fox, 'Cryptocurrencies in the Common Law of Property', pp. 143–45.

[16] See UK Jurisdiction Taskforce, 'Legal Statement on Cryptoassets and Smart Contracts', paras. 44–47.

[17] Principle 2(5) and (6), cf. Principle 6(2) of the UNIDROIT Principles on Digital Assets and Private Law. See also Gullifer and Tirado, 'Proprietary Rights and Digital Assets'.

13.2.2.3 *Bona Fide Purchaser Protection*

The *nemo dat* rule is a mere starting point, and all jurisdictions allow for significant exceptions therefrom, as seen in the cases of property registers and negotiable instruments.[18] Cryptoassets are designed to be negotiable, but this is typically not (yet) reflected in the law because exceptions from the *nemo dat* rule may in most jurisdictions be established only by statute or mercantile usage.[19]

Some countries have adopted statutes that make cryptoassets negotiable, essentially equating recording on a distributed ledger to physical possession or registration in central registries.[20] For jurisdictions without such specific legislation, however, one of the first questions will be whether some cryptoassets may still be treated as negotiable under existing laws. For instance, cryptoassets that represent rights to tangible goods may qualify as electronic documents of title that may be recognised as negotiable in many jurisdictions,[21] following the recommendations of the United Nations Commission on International Trade Law (UNCITRAL) Model Law on Electronic Transferable Records.[22] A second question to emerge is whether existing laws may *prevent* certain cryptoassets from being treated as negotiable if the cryptoassets reference an underlying asset that is already governed by existing rules for title and transfer. In the words of the UNIDROIT Principles on Digital Assets and Private Law, existing laws apply 'to determine the existence of, requirements for, and legal effect of any link between the digital asset and the other asset'.[23]

In the absence of statutory rules, courts may also recognise exceptions from the *nemo dat* rule by mercantile usage. Under English law, for instance, this has been the norm for negotiable documents,[24] and even in codified civil law systems, legislative recognition was typically preceded by mercantile usage.[25] The situation with cryptoassets today is similar to that when negotiable documents were acknowledged by legal systems across medieval Europe.[26] In modern times, the speed of technological and market developments is faster, of course, and thus, mercantile usage can develop more quickly.[27] Even if the duration of a given practice is of relevance to establish mercantile usage, the number of transactions and the perception among participants in the market matter more.[28] A critical element here is what constitutes a relevant market. In our view, we are today much closer to an established mercantile usage in the market for cryptocurrencies like Bitcoin, for instance, than for tokens representing underlying assets with an already established market practice.

[18] See Woxholth *et al.*, 'Competing Claims to Crypto-Assets', 226, 233–37.

[19] See, for example, *Dixon et al.* v. *Bovill* [1856] 3 Macqueen HL 1, 16. Some jurisdictions allow for a more flexible approach. For Norwegian law, for instance, see J. Woxholth, *Kryptoeiendeler i formueretten* (Oslo: Gyldendal 2024) pp. 70–114.

[20] See Woxholth *et al.*, 'Competing Claims to Crypto-Assets', 226, 233–35.

[21] See, for example, UCC, paras. 7-106 and 7-501; paras. 443(III), 475(c), and 516(II) of the German *Handelsgesetzbuch*.

[22] See, for example, 'Article 7 of the UNCITRAL Model Law on Electronic Transferable Records', p. 17. Website https://uncitral.un.org/sites/uncitral.un.org/files/media-documents/uncitral/en/mletr_ebook_e.pdf (last accessed on 1 October 2024).

[23] Principle 4 of the UNIDROIT Principles on Digital Assets and Private Law. See also Gullifer and Tirado, 'Proprietary Rights and Digital Assets'.

[24] See UK Jurisdiction Taskforce, 'Legal Statement on Cryptoassets and Smart Contracts', paras. 112–22.

[25] See UNIDROIT Issues Paper (2021). Study No. LXXXII – WG4 – Doc. 2, p. 61.

[26] See E. Schuster, 'Cloud Crypto Land', *Modern Law Review*, 84(4) (2021): 974, 995.

[27] See UK Jurisdiction Taskforce, 'Legal Statement on Cryptoassets and Smart Contracts', para. 122.

[28] See *Edelstein* v. *Schuler & Co* [1902] 2 KB 144, 154.

Finally, another intriguing question is whether negotiability can be established by contract if *all* the relevant market participants somehow agree. Indeed, one could argue that since blockchains were made to solve the double-spending problem, anyone that voluntarily participates in the network has agreed that "code is law" for this purpose (see Section 13.3.3). This would bind only voluntary participants in the network[29] so that cryptoassets become negotiable with regard to on-chain transactions, but not creditor claims, for instance.

For most practical purposes, competing claims to cryptoassets are today resolved in practice by the "code is law" impact of the software because it is difficult to enforce laws against market participants who hide behind anonymous accounts. While one could take the view that the current de facto negotiability of "code is law" works in the vast majority of cases, as very few legal claims arise relative to the number of cryptoasset transactions, the low number of cases could equally signal legal uncertainty and weak enforcement, as market participants would wonder whether law or technology will eventually prevail. The obvious solution here is to bring the law closer in line with the underlying technology essentially by acknowledging negotiability for cryptoassets and treating "control" of the private key as equivalent to "possession" for negotiable documents. This now also aligns with the UNIDROIT Principles on Digital Assets and Private Law.[30]

13.2.3 *Insolvency*

Insolvency law, of course, applies to cryptoassets as it does to any other property. Essentially, cryptoassets owned by the debtor become part of the bankruptcy estate, which is distributed among the creditors to cover contractual claims made against the debtor. Meanwhile, proprietary rights transferred from the debtor, which have become effective against third parties (see Section 13.2.2), are by default also effective against creditors in the debtor's insolvency proceedings,[31] so the significant uncertainty present in most jurisdictions over the rules of title and transfer for cryptoassets *also* applies to insolvency proceedings.

13.2.4 *Custody*

Even if cryptoassets were designed specifically to bypass intermediaries (see Section 13.2.2.1), many and perhaps most transactions in cryptoassets now occur off-chain by debiting and crediting internal accounts with a custodian.[32] This means that the custodian, through access to the private keys, has factual control over the cryptoassets – either alone, through, or in combination with third parties (sub-custodians).[33] Such intermediary relationships can take on many forms, where an interpretation of the contract between the intermediary and its client (the ultimate owner) determines both whether and what type of relationship is established, unless superseded by mandatory law. This, of course, governs the rights and duties of both parties

29 UK Jurisdiction Taskforce, 'Legal Statement on Cryptoassets and Smart Contracts', para. 134.

30 See Principles 6–9 of the UNIDROIT Principles on Digital Assets and Private Law. In the same vein, see The UK Law Commission, 'Digital Assets: Consultation Paper No. 256' (2022), chapters 11 and 13. See also Gullifer and Tirado, 'Proprietary Rights and Digital Assets'.

31 See Principle 19 of the UNIDROIT Principles on Digital Assets and Private Law.

32 H. Liu *et al.*, 'Client-Intermediary Relations in the Crypto-Asset World', in P. S. Davies and T. Cheng-Han (eds.), *Intermediaries in the Commercial World* (Oxford: Hart, 2022), pp. 213–34; M. Solinas, 'Investors' Rights in (Crypto) Custodial Holdings: *Ruscoe* v. *Cryptopia Ltd* (in Liquidation)', *Modern Law Review*, 84(1) (2021): 156, 162; Haentjens *et al.*, 'The Failed Hopes of Disintermediation', 526, 527.

33 See Woxholth *et al.*, 'Competing Claims to Crypto-Assets', 226, 237–38.

during the normal operations of an intermediary relationship, but it becomes all important in the event of the intermediary's insolvency. Accordingly, a distinction must be drawn between cases where the client has either a contractual or proprietary claim to the cryptoassets. In essence, the situation can fall into one of five of the categories outlined below.

First, the relationship may not constitute custody at all. This is, for instance, the case with many companies providing hardware or software solutions for owners of cryptoassets to undertake self-custody more securely. If these solutions enable the service provider to exercise some type of control over the cryptoassets, however, it can be difficult to distinguish between service and custody agreements.[34] Second, the agreement may establish an outright transfer of title to (or retention of title by) the intermediary. This provides users with no proprietary claim to the cryptoassets, but merely a personal claim against the intermediary firm, equivalent to depositing money in a bank. Third, the agreement may establish a custody relationship under which the custodian holds the cryptoassets *on behalf of* the client, so the assets are protected from the custodian's creditors. Due to its third-party effect on creditors, this typically requires the use of a statutory custody regime, which may apply either directly or by analogy, depending on the jurisdiction.[35] In the EU, when a custody relationship is properly established, Article 67(10) MiCA now specifically states that the client's cryptoassets should be insulated from the custodian's creditors in the event of insolvency.[36] A similar rule is found in the UNIDROIT Principles on Digital Assets and Private Law.[37] Fourth, common law jurisdictions typically also allow for trust-based arrangements, which also protect the client from the custodian's insolvency.[38] Finally, a special question arises as to whether the concept of bailment can be applied to cryptoassets as it traditionally relies on the bailee taking physical possession of the property belonging to the bailor.

Despite the discrepancies in the outcomes of each of these contractual relationships, the underlying contracts are oftentimes extremely vague.[39] Hence, the UNIDROIT Principles suggest that a custody relationship, by which the client retains a proprietary right, should be presumed unless 'it is clear from the agreement that the digital asset is part of the service provider's insolvency estate'.[40] Title V MiCA has put in place further safeguards relating to cryptoasset intermediaries (cf. Chapter 8). For instance, Article 3(1)(17) MiCA clarifies that custody comprises control over the private key, while Article 67 MiCA requires that the client's assets are kept separately from those belonging to the intermediary itself. Similar, yet less specific, obligations for the custodian are also outlined in the UNIDROIT Principles on Digital Assets and Private Law.[41] These may be of little help, however, if there is a shortfall of assets in the custodian's insolvency estate to cover even the proprietary claims of its clients. The

[34] The UK Law Commission, 'Digital Assets: Consultation Paper No. 256', paras. 16.16–16.18 and 16.50–16.51.

[35] Sarra and Gullifer, 'Crypto-Claimants and Bitcoin Bankruptcy', 233, 262.

[36] Article 67(10) MiCA postulates results, not means. The question remains how this provision is integrated into the private law of the EU Member States, and how this regulatory requirement is classified and recognized in international private law. See, for instance, A. Bonomi, M. Lehmann, and S. Lalani (eds.), *Blockchain and Private International Law* (Leiden: Brill, 2023); the UK Law Commission, 'Digital Assets and ETDs in Private International Law: Which Court, Which Law? Call for Evidence' (2024). Website https://lawcom.gov.uk/project/digital-assets-and-etds-in-private-international-law-which-court-which-law/ (last accessed on 1 October 2024).

[37] Principle 13(1) of the UNIDROIT Principles on Digital Assets and Private Law. See also Gullifer and Tirado, 'Proprietary Rights and Digital Assets'.

[38] On trust-based arrangements for cryptoassets, see The UK Law Commission, 'Digital Assets: Consultation Paper No. 256', paras. 16.52–16.91.

[39] See, for instance, the case studies entailed in Haentjens *et al.*, 'The Failed Hopes of Disintermediation', 526.

[40] Principle 10(4) of the UNIDROIT Principles on Digital Assets and Private Law.

[41] Principle 11 of the UNIDROIT Principles on Digital Assets and Private Law.

UNIDROIT Principles on Digital Assets and Private Law Rules suggest rules for the allocation of cryptoassets in this situation.[42]

13.2.5 *Security Rights*

Even if the private key is revealed to the creditor, there is no practical way of preventing the debtor from retaining knowledge of it and thereby spending secured cryptoassets.[43] Hence, in practice, cryptoassets provided as security are routinely transferred to an account controlled by the creditor or an independent third party. Alternatively, as is often the case under DeFi schemes, the cryptoassets are "locked up" by a smart contract (see Section 13.3.2).

From a legal point of view, collateral arrangements can be structured either by means of full title transfer or as a security interest. Under a full title transfer, the title to the cryptoassets is simply transferred to the collateral taker, who undertakes to transfer the title to the same or an equivalent amount of cryptoassets back once the secured obligation is settled. This, however, leaves the collateral provider with only a personal claim for return of the collateralised cryptoassets. Another option is that the arrangement may be established as a security interest, which gives the collateral provider a proprietary right to the return of the cryptoassets upon settlement of the secured obligation. Such security interests, however, may commonly require compliance with statutory formalities and may only be granted in certain types of assets depending on the jurisdiction. The UNIDROIT Principles on Digital Assets and Private Law now suggest that cryptoassets can be the subject of such security rights, as do the ELI's Principles on the Use of Digital Assets as Security.[44] Yet, if the cryptoasset is linked to another asset, then any legal effect upon that underlying asset is a separate question determined by the law governing such assets.[45]

If security can be taken in cryptoassets, then the next matter to address is how to ensure the effectiveness of the security right with regard to third parties. Here, security interests are commonly treated as either possessory or non-possessory, where the former requires a transfer of possession of the collateralised assets, but the latter does not. Because cryptoassets are intangible and thus cannot be possessed in a conventional sense, it is unclear whether security interests can be established by the equivalent of transferring control on the ledger.[46] Meanwhile, it is also unclear whether a non-possessory security interest can be established over cryptoassets. This issue is a derivative of the question discussed in Section 13.2.2 on the rules of title and transfer, to which most jurisdictions provide no clear answer but where rules are now suggested by the UNIDROIT Principles on Digital Assets and Private Law that, along with the ELI's Principles on the Use of Digital Assets as Security, now also suggest equivalent rules for security rights.[47]

13.3 CONTRACT LAW

General contract law naturally applies also to contracts over cryptoassets, yet the following three topics are worthy of specific analysis: (1) the rules that apply to the contractual relationship

[42] Principle 13(6) of the UNIDROIT Principles on Digital Assets and Private Law.
[43] Sarra and Gullifer, 'Crypto-Claimants and Bitcoin Bankruptcy', 233, 249.
[44] Principle 14(1) of the UNIDROIT Principles on Digital Assets and Private Law; Principle 2 of the European Law Institute Principles on the Use of Digital Assets as Security. See also Gullifer and Tirado, 'Proprietary Rights and Digital Assets'.
[45] Principle 14(2) and (3) of the UNIDROIT Principles on Digital Assets and Private Law. On the equivalent question for ownership rights, see Sections 13.2.1 and 13.2.2.
[46] See The UK Law Commission, 'Digital Assets: Consultation Paper No. 256', paras. 18.27–18.43.
[47] Principles 15 and 16 of the UNIDROIT Principles on Digital Assets and Private Law; Principle 4(6) of the European Law Institute Principles on the Use of Digital Assets as Security.

between an issuer of cryptoassets and those who subscribe for those assets; (2) the broader topic of so-called smart contracts, which also raises specific consumer protection concerns; and (3) the possibility of a DLT network as such constituting multi-party contracts between its users.

13.3.1 *Issuance of Cryptoassets*

The contract between issuer and investor is, of course, a contract like any other. Typically, it is partly written in code, so many questions similar to those discussed for smart contracts also arise. Furthermore, MiCA now provides disclosure requirements along with rules for withdrawal periods and claims for wrongful disclosures (see Chapter 5). From a contract law perspective, this implies first that the contract must be interpreted in light of the disclosed information as well as any disclosure requirements disobeyed by the issuer. Second, it means that certain remedies for breach of contract are defined in MiCA, which due to *lex specialis* prevail over general principles of contract law. Third, there must be "an issuer", that is, a (legal) person responsible. This may be lacking in cases of "fully decentralised systems", most notably Bitcoin (see Sections 2.1.3 and 2.1.7).

13.3.2 *"Smart Contracts" and Consumer Protection*

So-called smart contracts are software code facilitating automated transactions, typically with no need or even the possibility for human interaction.[48] This enables automatic and predetermined enforcement of contracts, backed by technology instead of courts. Yet, a variety of questions arise, of course, if the outcome enforced by technology differs from that prescribed in the law.

As pointed out by the ELI's Principles on Blockchain Technology and Smart Contracts, "smart contracts" are not necessarily "contracts" in the legal sense.[49] Under the freedom of form, parties may, of course, enter into legally binding contracts expressed in code,[50] yet often the code is meant simply to be an on-chain enforcement mechanism of conventional, off-chain contracts. This must be determined by assessing the intentions of the parties, which may, of course, also be expressed by a combination of both on-chain and off-chain elements. There may not even be any legally binding contract at all but rather a mere transaction in the technical sense, expressed in code.

The ELI Principles address four general questions arising from the contradiction between computer code and contract law. Principle 9 proclaims that contract terms as expressed by conventional off-chain means prevail over those expressed on-chain in the event of conflict. This is essentially a representation of the general contract law principle according to which courts will apply the natural and ordinary meaning when faced with ambiguous contract terms, unless another interpretation can be shown to better reflect the intentions of the parties. Principle 10 states that the unlawful execution of a smart contract should typically be unwound by a reverse transaction, which is in line with the view we outline here (see Section 13.6.1). This

[48] The Regulation (EU) 2023/2854 of the European Parliament and of the Council of 13 December 2023 on harmonised rules on fair access to and use of data and amending Regulation (EU) 2017/2394 and Directive (EU) 2020/1828 (Data Act), OJ 1/71 of 22 December 2023, defines smart contract as "a computer program used for the automated execution of an agreement or part thereof, using a sequence of electronic data records and ensuring their integrity and the accuracy of their chronological ordering".

[49] Principle 2 of the European Law Institute Principles on the Use of Digital Assets as Security.

[50] See Principles 5–8 of the European Law Institute Principles on the Use of Digital Assets as Security.

must now also be seen in relation to the EU's Data Act, which by means of regulation will require smart contracts to be coded with a "kill switch" so they can be technically disabled, for instance, following a court order or mutual agreement between the parties.[51] Meanwhile, according to Principle 11, businesses (but not consumers) may also consent to arbitration agreements, which are oftentimes embedded in the smart contract itself as on-chain dispute resolution mechanisms. Finally, Principle 12 states that weaker parties should be given protection on-chain that is at least equal to the protection they enjoy off-chain, which is obvious from a legal standpoint but has proven difficult to implement in practice.

The general Principle 12 on weaker parties is complemented in the ELI Principles by the entire Part II on consumer protection. Principles 13–16 and Principle 18 largely specify the application of existing EU consumer protection contract law on smart contracts, including choice of law, information rights, and the prevalence of natural over programming language. Then, Principle 17 goes a step further, suggesting an "obligation to code" by which a legal right for consumers to withdraw from a contract, typically during a reflection period, must be coded into the smart contract itself.

The ELI Principles, of course, do not constitute binding law, yet insofar as they merely specify the application of existing consumer protection contract law to smart contracts, we expect them to serve as a useful guide for courts when interpreting the law in this field.[52] New EU legislation is also on its way, such as the EU Data Act and also MiCA, which is focused on financial regulation yet includes contract law aspects related to the issuance of cryptoassets (see Section 13.3.1). This, naturally, applies also to the issuance of cryptoassets that contain self-executing software code in the form of a smart contract, which further calls into question the definition of "consumer" or the related term "retail holder" used in MiCA.[53] Given the low sophistication of cryptoasset markets relative to conventional financial markets, it is difficult to determine what type and level of trading distinguishes professional from retail investors. The distinction is likely to be even more difficult when applying general consumer protection legislation that is not made specifically for cryptoassets.

13.3.3 *DLT as Multi-party Contracts?*

The fact that computer code can, of course, constitute legally binding contract terms gives rise to the question of whether and to what extent one could see entire DLT networks constituting multi-party contracts between their users. For two examples, see Sections 13.2.2.3 and 13.4.2; we see no reason why this cannot also be the case more generally. In fact, DLT networks are essentially sets of rules (written in code) that users intend to follow as they take part in the network. Different types of users, such as developers, nodes (miners), and end users, even take on different roles, much like in conventional contractual relationships. There is also nothing new in the establishment of legally binding contracts through actions, such as taking a bite of an apple in a store or parking on a metered street – both of which require you to pay.

Some authors still suggest that distributed networks do not give rise to contractual relationships, referring implicitly to a lack of contractual intent on the part of network

[51] See Article 36(1)(b) of the EU Data Act (n 47) (requiring to 'ensure that a mechanism exists to terminate the continued execution of transactions and that the smart contract includes internal functions which can reset or instruct the contract to stop or interrupt the operation, in particular to avoid future accidental execution'.)

[52] See Principle 1(d) of the European Law Institute Principles on the Use of Digital Assets as Security, which makes this point explicit.

[53] Article 3(1)(28) of MiCA, Regulation 2023/1114, OJ 2023 No. L150.

participants.[54] In our view, however, DLT transactions clearly may constitute legally binding contracts. Complex business interactions between many parties that may not know the identity of one another do not, as such, preclude the existence of contractual relationships.[55]

The implications of treating DLT networks as multi-party contracts may be immense. Specifically, such contracts could, of course, lead to joint and several liability depending on the interpretation of the contract terms.[56] Consequently, each node or other party under a DLT multi-party contract may possibly become liable on behalf of the entire network, for instance, if users incur losses due to network failure.

13.4 COMPANY LAW

DLT has so far raised two substantive debates specific to company law, which we discuss here: (1) the legal treatment of organisations that claim to be autonomous of human involvement and (2) the circumstances under which networks facilitated by DLT may constitute partnerships as the default legal form of an organisation.

13.4.1 *Decentralised Autonomous Organisations (DAOs)*

DLT proponents sometimes point to the technology's proclaimed potential to disrupt how businesses are organised altogether.[57] Indeed, this was the objective of the first DAO. Essentially, it was an investment fund coded onto the blockchain, thereby replacing the role of fund managers with a combination of computer code and decentralised human support. It raised USD 150 million worth of Ether coins in exchange for DAO tokens, whose holders could vote for investment proposals, curated by a set of volunteers.[58]

The legal questions, then, concern who should be held to account and under what type of legal organisation form, if the businesses are run without direct human involvement. The former is a question of tort law, as discussed in Section 13.5, unless liability can be based on contract or company law. For the latter question, we believe that partnership would typically apply as the default form of legal organisation, which we turn to next.

13.4.2 *Partnership as the Default Form*

It is tempting to compare DLT with conventional business networks (such as franchise systems, credit card networks, or supply chains involving multiple parties), yet they differ in one critical respect:[59] conventional business networks follow a hub-and-spokes model, where the spokes (e.g., the franchisees) are connected only to the other spokes indirectly through a contractual relationship with the hub (e.g., the franchisor). Essentially, all contracts have only a bilateral

[54] S. Bayern, 'Dynamic Common Law and Technological Change: The Classification of Bitcoin', *Washington and Lee Law Review Online*, 71 (2014): 22, 31–33; M. Dulong de Rosnay, 'Peer-to-Peer as a Design Principle for Law: Distribute the Law', *Journal of Peer Production*, 6 (2015): 1, 3–4.

[55] Zetzsche *et al.*, 'The Distributed Liability of Distributed Ledgers', 1361, 1395–96.

[56] For German law; for instance, see Bürgerliches Gesetzbuch (BGB), para. 421.

[57] Low K. F. K. *et al.*, 'The Company and Block-Chain Technology', LSE Law School Working Paper Series 18/2022. Website https://dx.doi.org/10.2139/ssrn.4258114 (last accessed on 1 October 2024).

[58] See Vandezande, 'Regulating Initial Coin Offerings and DAO Tokens under the EU's Financial Instruments Framework', 33, 34.

[59] See H. Collins, 'Introduction', in G. Teubner (ed.), *Networks as Connected Contracts* (London: Bloomsbury, 2011), pp. 10–13.

effect, so legal action must follow the path of the contractual relationships, and there is no liability on the part of the network as such towards third parties.[60] In contrast, with DLT, all nodes are linked together directly through the software, which can be seen as constituting multi-party contracts (see Section 13.3.3).

Such contracts that organise a business enterprise between two or more people will in most jurisdictions by default constitute a partnership, unless the parties specifically seek out a different organisation form, such as a limited company. The criteria vary somewhat across legal systems, of course, but a joint pursuit of a (joint) objective, possibly with the sharing of profits, is typically sufficient to establish a partnership.[61] (Without the possibility of sharing profits, the entity may still qualify as an unincorporated association.)[62] If the enterprise constitutes a partnership, it will usually result in joint liability. This bears significant repercussions for DLT networks. Take the example where the DAO's code was hacked and USD 60 million worth of Ether coins was misappropriated.[63] The DAO token-holders could qualify as partners and be held personally liable. Furthermore, the volunteer curators could potentially be held to account as a de facto board of directors.

This reasoning can also be expanded to entire DLT networks. Although they vary, such networks typically consist of at least three types of players: developers who build and maintain the code; nodes who typically keep a copy of the ledger and take part in validating transactions; and users who merely transact on the ledger. In general, taking a share in profits or proceeds, influencing the software design, or taking part in business decision-making, all point in the direction of being considered a partner. The developers often function as day-to-day management and as a strategy-setting group, yet few of them are sufficiently well-known and affluent to be exposed to personal liability. Because the nodes are oftentimes awarded for their work, as seen in the case of Bitcoin "mining", they are particularly at risk of being considered partners in a joint enterprise.

13.5 TORT LAW

Tort law becomes important when liability cannot be derived from a contract. This could, for instance, be practical if users of DLT networks suffer losses, and they fail to convince the court that their participation in the DLT network gives rise to a contractual relationship (see Section 13.3.3). Two scenarios seem plausible here. First, the loss could be due to some sort of technical error. If no contractual relationship is established, then this becomes a question of whether the developers or owners of that technology, such as software developers or operators of node/ "mining" hardware, are liable for negligent conduct. This question of whether humans are responsible for machines goes back at least to the Industrial Revolution. The second scenario is where a loss is suffered at least partly also due to human culpability, for instance, if node operators can be blamed for failing to validate specific transactions.

Conceivable losses under the above scenarios tend to be purely economic, which may not give rise to tort claims under many common law and German-law-based civil law jurisdictions. Yet, damages to property are typically protected. Tort law protection against the loss or damage of cryptoassets, then, may well depend on their classification as property (*in rem*), contractual

[60] Zetzsche *et al.*, 'The Distributed Liability of Distributed Ledgers', 1361, 1388–89.

[61] Zetzsche *et al.*, 'The Distributed Liability of Distributed Ledgers', 1361, 1400.

[62] See *Commodity Futures Trading Commission* v. *Ooki DAO* [2022] US District Court, Northern District of California, 3:22-cv-05416-WHO, pp. 5–9.

[63] On the DAO Hack, see, for instance, Yeung, 'Regulation by Blockchain', 207, 233–35.

rights (*in personam*), or a third type of property (see Section 13.2.1). Because this varies across jurisdictions, however, the strictest jurisdiction involved may well set the standard for the entire ledger as lawsuits will be filed there.[64]

13.6 JURISDICTION AND ENFORCEMENT

Bitcoin was created as a peer-to-peer alternative to centralised monetary systems (see Section 13.1), and its proponents regularly see decentralisation not just as a feature but as the entire *purpose* of DLT.[65] In contrast, *any* regulatory intervention other than an outright recognition of "code is law" would go against this purpose of decentralisation because legal systems are centralised by definition.[66] Hence, the question here is one of ideology: code vs. law; decentralised vs. centralised, and trustless vs. trust in legal institutions.[67] This calls for reinforcement of the rule of law in law-governed societies that cannot allow a fully decentralised system of title and transfer.

We see the core elements of this issue as being: (1) how cryptoassets may be returned to their rightful owner; (2) how the holder of cryptoassets may be identified; and (3) how cross-border situations may be resolved. We address each of these questions in the following.

13.6.1 *Reverse Transfer and "Tainting" of Cryptoassets*

Given the de facto immutability of DLT records, the theoretical option that legal title is restored by demanding a rewrite of the ledger from all nodes is unrealistic: too many countries and parties are involved. Instead, enforcement of claims may take place either by the return of the private key(s) or a reverse transfer of the cryptoassets to an account controlled by the rightful title holder. This problem is not unique to cryptoassets but applies also to physical goods, cash, and negotiable documents.[68] When creditors claim the physical belongings of the debtor, for instance, they must be provided with either keys to the storage facility or outright physical possession of the assets.[69] Such court orders are typically enforced through fines for disobedience. The same mechanism can also be used for claims to cryptoassets. An opportunity to go one step further appears here in the transparent transaction history of open blockchains, allowing for the "tainting" of individual cryptoassets. Essentially, unlawfully obtained cryptoassets are added to a public list supported by software to identify prospective transactions in the listed assets, so it would be difficult for anyone to act in good faith and thereby obtain legal title as a bona fide purchaser for value.[70]

64 Zetzsche *et al.*, 'The Distributed Liability of Distributed Ledgers', 1361, 1398–99.
65 See Fox, 'Cryptocurrencies in the Common Law of Property', p. 140.
66 Regulators and courts are central authorities; the legal system as a whole could be conceptualised as some type of centralised ledger for the recording of legal rights and their owners. As noted by *Schuster*, 'under the rule of law, true non-hierarchical decentralisation is impossible because *ruling* always necessitates a hierarchy'. See Schuster, 'Cloud Crypto Land', 993, 998.
67 See Yeung, 'Regulation by Blockchain', 207, 233–35.
68 See M. Lehmann, 'Who Owns Bitcoin? Private Law Facing the Blockchain', *Minnesota Journal of Law, Science and Technology*, 21(1) (2020): 93, 131–32.
69 Of course, the return of a private key for a blockchain account provides no assurance against copies of the same key still being in circulation – as is the case also with the return of physical keys to a storage facility for goods.
70 Fox D., 'Cryptocurrencies in the Common Law of Property' in D. Fox and S. Greed (eds), *Cryptocurrencies in the Public and Private Law* (Oxford: OUP, 2019), pp. 172–74.

13.6.2 *KYC and Licensing of Intermediaries*

Even with perfectly written laws, it is often impossible to know *who* to sue due to the prevalence of anonymous accounts. Hence, the regulatory steps taken by the EU and other lawmakers that we discuss in Chapter 11 (on supervision) and Chapter 14 (on AML/CTF measures) are critical for effective enforcement, with licensing of crypto custodians combined with a strict "know-your-customer" (KYC) requirement to *trace* cryptoasset flows. Essentially, these new tools for *public* enforcement must also be made available for *private* enforcement.

13.6.3 *Jurisdiction and Choice of Law*

As acknowledged by UNIDROIT, 'the usual connecting factors for choice-of-law rules (e.g., the location of persons, offices, activity, or assets) have no useful role to play in the context of the law applicable to proprietary issues relating to digital assets'.[71] Hence, the UNIDROIT Principles on Digital Assets and Private Law leave it largely to either the parties or the forum state to determine the choice of law.[72] Neither DLT networks nor most legislators seem to have taken clear steps to this end, albeit courts tend to find pragmatic solutions and new legislation is on the agenda in some jurisdictions.[73]

Even if the defendant(s) cannot be identified, courts refer, for instance, to the domicile of crypto intermediaries or known defendants other than the persons unknown. We appreciate this pragmatism and are inclined to go even further, for example, by arguing that courts in any country where a node in a DLT network is located can assert jurisdiction. Even more beneficially for claimants, English courts through several cases have applied English law with reference to *lex situs*, meaning the law of the country where the object of a property right ("the thing") is located.[74] For lack of a definitive physical location, the courts have determined the *lex situs* of a cryptoasset to be the domicile or residence of its alleged owner.[75] Law enforcement was facilitated by the English courts' interim proprietary injunction paired with a "Bankers Trust order", meaning that cryptoasset custodians must freeze the assets and disclose information about account holders.[76] While being no panacea, these approaches have yielded some encouraging results.

13.7 TOWARDS A UNIFORM PRIVATE LAW FOR CRYPTOASSETS?

As a response to better law enforcement, we expect to see an increasing prevalence of DLT networks adopting standard terms of use with a clear choice of law provisions in the years to

[71] Commentary 3 to Principle 5 of the UNIDROIT Principles on Digital Assets and Private Law.

[72] Principle 5 of the UNIDROIT Principles on Digital Assets and Private Law.

[73] See Bonomi et al., *Blockchain and Private International Law*; M. Lehmann, 'Digital Assets in the Conflict of Laws: A Comparative Search for The Ideal Rule', *Singapore Journal of Legal Studies* (2024) (in press). The UK Law Commission considers changes on English private international law. See the UK Law Commission, 'Digital Assets and ETDs in Private International Law'. Meanwhile, the Hague Conference on Private International Law, in order to assess the need for law reform, has launched the Digital Tokens Project in June 2024; see www.hcch.net/en/news-archive/details/?varevent=975 (last accessed on 1 October 2024).

[74] See *Ion Sciences Ltd. and Duncan Johns* v. *Persons Unknown and others* [2020], not yet reported; *Osbourne* v. *(1) Persons Unknown and (2) Ozone Networks Inc.* [2022] EWHC 1021 (acknowledging property to non-fungible tokens); *Tulip Trading Ltd.* v. *Bitcoin Association for BSV and Others* [2022] EWHC 667.

[75] According to *Tulip Trading Ltd.* v. *Bitcoin Association for BSV and Others* [2022] EWHC 667, the residence rather than the domicile is the determining factor.

[76] See *Ion Sciences Ltd. and Duncan Johns* v. *Persons Unknown and others* [2020], not yet reported; *Osbourne* v. *(1) Persons Unknown and (2) Ozone Networks Inc.* [2022] EWHC 1021.

come, most likely in favour of *laissez-faire* jurisdictions.[77] This may again be challenged by courts on the basis of consumer protection or *ordre public* limitations.[78] As is so often the case with the law of commerce, the legal certainty that crypto markets so desperately need would be better delivered if national efforts were to follow international coordination and harmonisation of laws along the lines proposed herein. While *full* harmonisation of national private laws is out of reach, some level of international consensus would strengthen the impact of initiatives designed to increase legal certainty. Moreover, efforts that highlight and analyse legal options for harmonisation deserve support.[79]

77 Cf. Lehmann M., 'Who Owns Bitcoin?', 93, 113.

78 See Schuster, 'Cloud Crypto Land', 974, 1002; Principle 14 of the European Law Institute Principles on Blockchain Technology, Smart Contracts and Consumer Protection.

79 See, in particular, the UNIDROIT Principles on Digital Assets and Private Law; The European Law Institute Principles on the Use of Digital Assets as Security; further, the European Law Institute Principles on Blockchain Technology, Smart Contracts and Consumer Protection put forward clauses on court jurisdiction and preference for reverse transactions.

14

AML/CTF Legislation on Cryptoassets

14.1 THE EU'S AML/CTF SYSTEM IN A NUTSHELL

AML/CTF legislation is aimed at combatting money laundering and terrorist financing in order to prevent terrorism, tax evasion, and other illicit activities (most notably fraud, cybercrime, and market abuse), and it can be understood as an enhancement of market integrity at large.

14.1.1 Relevant Legislation

Following the implementation of the AML/Counter-Terrorism Financing (CTF) Action Plan of 7 May 2020,[1] the EU's AML/CTF system comprises four legislative acts.

First, the TFR,[2] with its revision[3] adopted in April 2023 together with MiCA, now covers cryptoassets, effectively enabling the tracing of cryptoasset transfers and thus ensuring alignment with Financial Action Task Force (FATF) recommendations and inhibiting the provision and custody of anonymous cryptoasset wallets.

Second, the EU's "Single Rulebook" Regulation[4] (AML Regulation) which came into force in July 2024 harmonizes rules, formerly included in AMLD, on conducting due diligence on customers, transparency of beneficial owners, and the use of anonymous instruments such as cryptoassets. Third, the AMLD6[5] provides national rules on supervision and financial intelligence units (FIUs), as well as on the access of competent authorities to information, such as beneficial ownership registers and assets stored in free zones. Both the AML Regulation and the AMLD6 replace the previous Anti-money Laundering Directives that embody, until May 2026,

[1] European Commission, 'Communication from the Commission on an Action Plan for a Comprehensive Union Policy on Preventing Money Laundering and Terrorist Financing', C (2020) 2800 Final.

[2] Regulation (EU) 2015/847 of the European Parliament and of the Council of 20 May 2015 on information accompanying transfers of funds and repealing Regulation (EC) No. 1781/2006, OJ 2015 No. L141, 5 June 2015, p. 1.

[3] Regulation (EU) 2023/1113 of the European Parliament and of the Council of 31 May 2023 on information accompanying transfers of funds and certain cryptoassets and amending Directive (EU) 2015/849 (recast) (Text with EEA relevance), OJ 2023 No. L150, 9 June 2023.

[4] See Regulation (EU) 2024/1624 of the European Parliament and of the Council of 31 May 2024 on the prevention of the use of the financial system for the purposes of money laundering or terrorist financing, OJ L, 2024/1624, 19 June 2024.

[5] See Directive (EU) 2024/1640 of the European Parliament and of the Council of 31 May 2024 on the mechanisms to be put in place by Member States for the prevention of the use of the financial system for the purposes of money laundering or terrorist financing, amending Directive (EU) 2019/1937, and amending and repealing Directive (EU) 2015/849, OJ L, 2024/1640, 19 June 2024.

the substantive EU AML/CTF legislation, by virtue of AMLD4[6] as amended by AMLD5[7] (herein referred to as AMLD). We will cite both the forthcoming legislation and the legislation in force to date in turn.

Finally, the regulation establishing the European Anti-money Laundering Authority (AMLA)[8] provides the institutional framework determining the relationship between national FIUs and the AMLA. It equips the AMLA with supervisory and investigative powers to ensure compliance with AML/CFT requirements and shall ensure that the AMLA becomes the focus point of EU AML/CTF activities.

The above-listed legislation is cross-sectorial meaning it covers relevant conduct regardless of authorisation under sectorial financial law. On top of that, certain AML/CTF measures can be found in sectorial legislation, including MiCA. With regard to cryptoassets, the EU AML/CTF framework is spread over the TFR (providing bespoke rules on value transfers across the financial system), AMLD/AMLR (Anti-money Laundering Regulation) (establishing the overall organisation and duties of obliged entities in relation to money laundering), and MiCA (setting out bespoke additions to the general framework). After providing a primer to the EU AML/CTF system, we discuss each of these in turn.

14.1.2 *Risk-Based Approach*

The EU AML/CTF framework implements a risk-based approach: the Member States aim to identify, assess, understand, and mitigate the risks of money laundering and terrorist financing as well as the risks of non-implementation and evasion of targeted financial sanctions and the proliferation of financing-related targeted financial sanctions.[9] Conduct and activities more likely to further money laundering and terrorist financing shall be screened more intensely under this framework, while activities less likely to do so shall benefit from a greater degree of regulatory lenience. The risk-based approach results in a three-step-classification – from high risk to medium risk to low risk; the AML/CTF framework also defines the factors informing an activity's classification as high, medium, or low risk.

Member States are obliged to build and maintain an institutional environment for effective AML/CTF measures through FIUs, adequately staffed law enforcement authorities, effective and proportionate sanctions, and intense cooperation with other competent authorities inside and outside the Member States that may be instrumental with respect to AML/CTF purposes.[10] A part of that environment entails identifying sectors or areas of the economy at lower or greater risk of money laundering and terrorist financing, which may be used to bolster rule-making and enforcement activities, as well as allocation of resources.[11] With AMLAR coming into force,

[6] Directive (EU) 2015/849 of the European Parliament and of the Council of 20 May 2015 on the prevention of the use of the financial system for the purposes of money laundering or terrorist financing, amending Regulation (EU) No. 648/2012 of the European Parliament and of the Council and repealing Directive 2005/60/EC of the European Parliament and of the Council and Commission Directive 2006/70/EC, OJ 2015 No. L141, 5 June 2015, p. 73.

[7] Directive (EU) 2018/843 of the European Parliament and of the Council of 30 May 2018 amending Directive (EU) 2015/849 on the prevention of the use of the financial system for the purposes of money laundering or terrorist financing and amending Directives 2009/138/EC and 2013/36/EU (Text with EEA relevance), OJ 2018 No. L156, 19 June 2018, pp. 43–74.

[8] See Regulation (EU) 2024/1620 of the European Parliament and of the Council of 31 May 2024 establishing the Authority for Anti-Money Laundering and Countering the Financing of Terrorism and amending Regulations (EU) No. 1093/2010, (EU) No. 1094/2010, and (EU) No. 1095/2010, OJ L, 2024/1620, 19 June 2024.

[9] Cf. Articles 6 and 7 of AMLD = Articles 7 and 8 AMLD6.

[10] Cf. VI Sections 2–4 of AMLD = Articles 20–48 AMLR.

[11] Cf. Article 7(4)(b)–(d) of AMLD = Article 8(4)(b)–(d) AMLD6.

these institutional preconditions will be supplemented by a pan-European coordinating – and in parts also supervisory – institution, namely, the European AMLA,[12] that will assume the guideline competencies currently assigned to EBA.[13]

For that purpose, the AML/CTF framework relies on knowledge from private sector entities potentially exposed to, or involved in, activities which, in a state of complete information, may be understood as (support of) money laundering and terrorist financing.[14] Obliged entities must 'take appropriate steps to identify and assess the risks of money laundering and terrorist financing, taking into account risk factors including those relating to their customers, countries or geographic areas, products, services, transactions or delivery channels. Those steps shall be proportionate to the nature and size of the obliged entities'.[15]

Obliged entities are, besides credit institutions and financial institutions at large, a host of professionals involved in financial transactions,[16] including – after the entry into force of TFR[17] – 'providers engaged in exchange services between virtual currencies and fiat currencies', 'custodian wallet providers', and CASPs as defined by MiCA.[18]

14.1.3 AML/CTF Organization and Procedures

Obliged entities are mandated to adopt internal policies, procedures, and controls to mitigate and manage effectively the risks of money laundering as identified at EU, Member State, and firm levels,[19] including:

- model risk management practices;
- customer due diligence (based on a KYC approach);
- reporting;
- record-keeping;
- internal control;
- employee screening; and
- a qualified compliance management (including in larger firms a compliance officer at management level[20]).

In larger firms, an internal audit function must screen and assess the effectiveness of the internal policies, controls, and procedures put in place. As detailed decisions concern the firm's risk

[12] For details as well as a critical discussion, cf. S. Allegrezza, 'The Proposed Anti-Money Laundering Authority, FIU Cooperation, Powers and Exchanges of Information: A Critical Assessment'. Committee on Economic and Monetary Affairs, Policy Department for Economic, Scientific and Quality of Life Policies, European Parliament, Luxembourg (2022).

[13] The European Commission has asked EBA in March 2024 to provide provisional advice until 31 October 2025 on the guidelines AMLA is tasked to issue under the AMLAR.

[14] The AML/CTF framework uses the term 'activities which are particularly likely to be used for the purposes of money laundering or terrorist financing'. Cf. Article 4(1) of AMLD. This is turned into 'money laundering or terrorist financing risks' in Article 3(1) AMLD6.

[15] Cf. Article 8(1) of AMLD = Article 10(1) AMLR.

[16] Cf. Article 2(3) of AMLD = Article 6(1) AMLR. Examples include auditors, accountant, tax advisors, notaries, independent lawyers, trustees, real estate agents, art traders, and many more in certain or all business situations.

[17] Article 38 of TFR amends Article 2 of AMLD.

[18] Up to the TFR, Article 2(3)(g), (i) of AMLD listed 'providers engaged in exchange services between virtual currencies and fiat currencies' and 'custodian wallet providers'.

[19] Article 8(3) and (4) AMLD = Article 9(1) and (2) AMLR.

[20] In Luxembourg, this function is performed by the 'responsable du contrôle du respect des obligations' (RC).

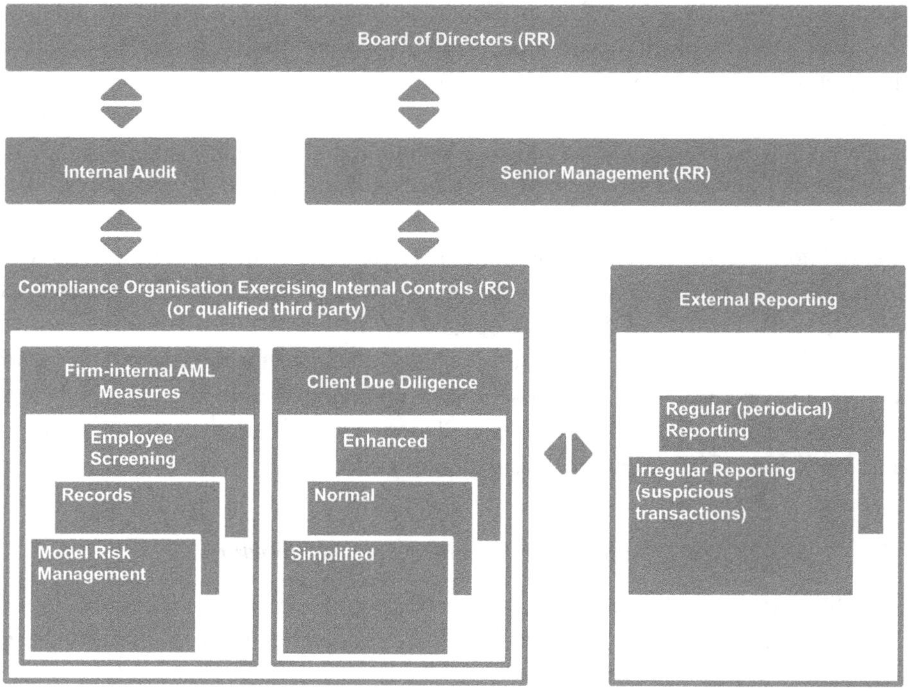

FIGURE 14.1 AML/CTF compliance organisation.

appetite and exposures, the internal policies must be approved, and their effective implementation monitored, by senior management,[21] resulting in the setup laid out in Figure 14.1.

14.1.4 *Simplified, Normal, or Enhanced Screening Commensurate to Risks*

As the AML/CTF framework is risk-based, the intensity of compliance measures is proportionate to the risks present, with the risks depending on factors present or absent relating to the firm, its transactions, and its clients. For instance, depending on the risk of money laundering and terrorist financing identified for the given client and transaction, obliged entities must perform simplified, normal, or enhanced screening of their clients.[22]

The underlying rationale behind this approach is that where clients have no influence to use the transaction for purposes other than for which it was formally set up or have little chance to conceal the transaction, the recipient, or the purpose, and where the legal setups warranting the former are likely to be robust and resilient, the transaction is deemed low risk. Where these criteria are unlikely to be met, the client and their transaction are high risk. In the absence of low- and high-risk indicators, the client and their transaction are medium risk.

Accordingly, as indicators of low risk, EU AML/CTF legislation mentions, for instance, the types of customers, public listed companies subject to transparency requirements on beneficial ownership, public administrations or enterprises, and residents of low-risk countries.[23] Low-risk countries include EU Member States, third countries with effective AML/CFT systems

[21] Article 8(5) of AMLD = Article 9(2)(3) AMLR. In Luxembourg, this function is exercised by the RR ('responsable du respect des obligations'), which is either the board as a whole or a qualified member of senior management.

[22] See Chapter II of AMLD = Chapter III of AMLR.

[23] Annex II AMLD = Annex II AMLR.

(including those having been verified through mutual evaluations and assessment reports in line with FATF recommendations), or those identified by credible sources as having a low level of corruption or other criminal activity. Finally, the legislation lists a number of financial products, services, transactions, or delivery channels over which clients have little influence,[24] where transparency is ensured,[25] or where the overarching objective of financial inclusion outweighs the AML/CTF risks in light of the definitions and limits of the service with regard to certain previously excluded customers. In line with the overall approach, Annex III AMLD = Annex III AMLR defines high-risk factors by stressing the opposite of what Annex II AMLD = Annex II AMLR lays out.

14.2 TFR CONTENT ON CRYPTOASSETS

The anonymity of cryptoassets, together with their global reach and transaction speed, has created a fertile environment for cybercrime and criminal purposes at large.[26] TFR represents the EU's response to the finding of Europol's Internet Organised Crime Threat Assessment[27] that cryptocurrencies have become the default payment method for victim-to-criminal payments in ransomware, as well as criminal-to-criminal payments on the Darkweb. The FATF has recommended mandating institutions involved in payments, banknotes and coins, scriptural and electronic money ('funds'), dubbed 'wire transfer service providers', to accompany transfers of funds with information on the payer and payee engaged in cryptoassets (the so-called travel rule).[28]

The FATF has also expanded these requirements to include new technologies, with the aim of bringing virtual assets and virtual asset service providers (VASPs) into the scope of the travel rule with the purpose of facilitating the traceability of transfers of virtual assets.[29] TFR, as a revision of the 2015 Regulation on Transfers of Funds, has implemented these recommendations[30] with a view to ensuring that certain transactions of relevance to cryptoassets were covered.[31] Its rationale extends to combatting money laundering and terrorist financing, as well as ensuring the effectiveness of restrictive measures, including state sanctions and blacklisting of individuals in the context of armed and political conflicts.[32] In order to ensure the transmission

[24] Annex II of AMLD = Annex II AMLR lists low-amount life insurance policies; insurance policies for pension schemes that are precluded from commercialisation and early termination; and pension, superannuation, or similar schemes for employees, where based on deduction from wages, without discretion or rights granted to scheme members.

[25] Annex II (2)(e) of AMLD = Annex II (2)(e) AMLR mentions products where the risks of money laundering and terrorist financing are managed by other factors such as purse limits or transparency of ownership (e.g., certain types of electronic money!).

[26] See Houben and Snyers, 'Crypto-Assets', p. 25.

[27] EUROPOL Internet Organised Crime Threat ('IOCTA') (2016), pp. 42–43. Website www.europol.europa.eu\\publications-events\\main-reports\\internet-organised-crime-threat-assessment-iocta-2016 (last accessed on 1 October 2024).

[28] See FATF, Recommendation 16 (on transfer of funds), Sections C and D, paras. 6–10. Website www.fatf-gafi.org\\content\\dam\\fatf-gafi\\recommendations\\FATFRecommendations 2012.pdf.coredownload.inline.pdf (last accessed on 1 October 2024) (stating that identity information must be collected from senders and recipients of domestic and cross-border wire transfers).

[29] See FATF, Recommendation 15 and Interpretative Note to Recommendation 15, para. 7 (laying out the obligation to obtain, hold, and transmit required originator and beneficiary information, immediately and securely, when conducting virtual asset transfers), and FATF, 'Updated Guidance for a Risk-Based Approach to Virtual Assets and Virtual Asset Service Providers' (2021). Website www.fatf-gafi.org/en/publications/Fatfrecommendations/Guidance-rba-virtual-assets-2021.html (last accessed on 1 October 2024).

[30] Recital para. 2 of TFR.

[31] Recital para. 4 of MiCA, Regulation 2023/1114, OJ 2023 No. L150.

[32] Recital para. 16 of TFR (referring to Regulations (EC) No. 2580/2001, (EC) No. 881/2002, and (EU) No. 356/201).

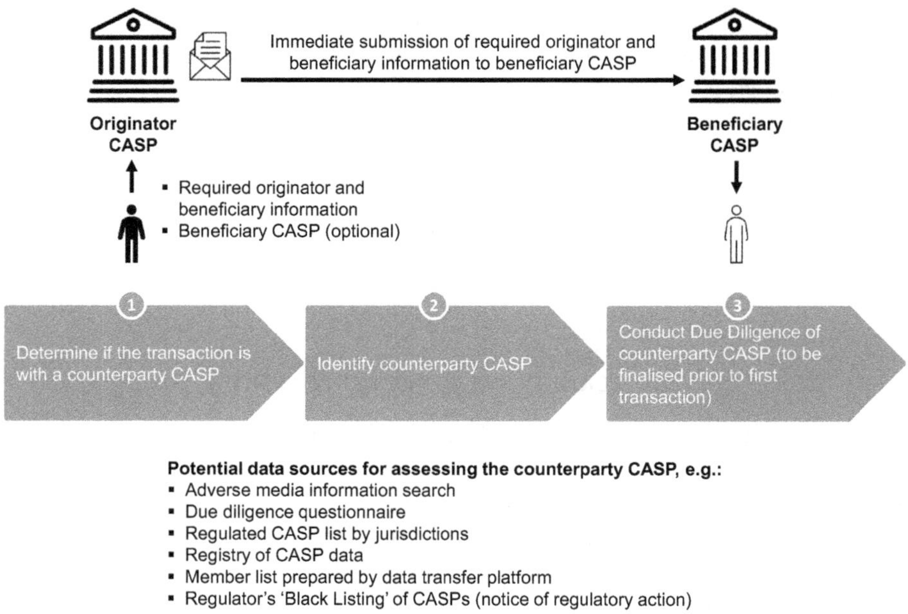

FIGURE 14.2 CASP counterparty due diligence process.
(Own figure, based on FATF, Updated Guidance for a Risk-based Approach to Virtual Assets and VASPs, p. 63)

of information throughout the payment chain or the transfer of cryptoassets chain, TFR imposes 'obligations on PSPs to accompany transfers of funds with information on the payer and the payee and the obligation on CASPs to accompany transfers of cryptoassets with information on the originator and the beneficiary'.[33]

14.2.1 *TFR's Travel Rule*

TFR is directed towards the intermediaries involved: it is aimed at implementing restrictive measures to be applied by the (intermediary) payment service providers (PSPs) and CASPs involved on the side of either the originator (origin) or the beneficiary (destination).[34]

Pursuant to Chapter III Section 1 TFR, CASPs must accompany transfers of cryptoassets with information on the originators and beneficiaries of those transfers: when processing a transaction, the required information must be added to the transaction file or be connected to it. CASPs are also required to obtain, hold, and share that information with their counterpart on the other end of the cryptoassets transfer and make it available on request to the competent authorities.[35]

To comply with the travel rule, the origin CASP must identify the beneficiary CASP, ensuring that it meets certain prerequisites, based on a counterparty due diligence process,[36] as laid out in Figure 14.2.

[33] Recital para. 16 of TFR (referring to Regulations (EC) No. 2580/2001, (EC) No. 881/2002, and (EU) No. 356/201).
[34] Article 1 of TFR.
[35] Recital para. 2 of TFR.
[36] Articles 16–18 TFR; the obligation is based on FATF, 'Updated Guidance for a Risk-based Approach to Virtual Assets and Virtual Asset Service Providers', p. 62, para. 197.

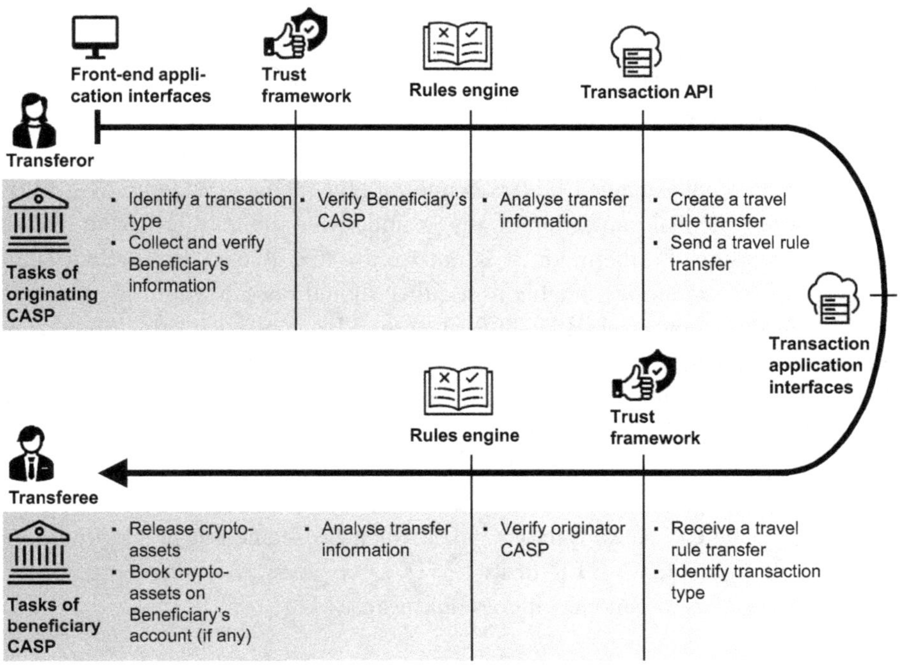

FIGURE 14.3 TFR's travel rule.
(Own figure, inspired Scorechain).

Once the counterparty due diligence leads to satisfactory results, the origin CASP must share the identity of clients and related KYC[37] information for each transaction with the beneficiary CASP.[38] A precondition for this data sharing is that the data on client identity exist and that these data are reviewed by both the origin and beneficiary CASPs; the travel rule rests on the client due diligence prerequisites laid out in AMLD.[39]

All in all, the travel rule results in a complex setup of cryptoasset transactions, as laid out in Figure 14.3.

14.2.2 *Cross-References with MiCA*

TFR foresees two cross-references with MiCA of overarching importance, with regard to cryptoassets and CASPs.

14.2.2.1 ***Cryptoassets***

First, Article 3(14) TFR refers to the definition of "cryptoasset" detailed in Article 3(1)(5) MiCA. TFR also excludes the digital assets that are out of MiCA's scope pursuant to Article 2(2) MiCA (personal exemptions), Article 2(3) MiCA (NFTs[40]), and Article 2(4) MiCA (regulated activities under EU financial law). In turn, the scopes of TFR and MiCA are identical. This is remarkable

37 See H.-J. Haenisch and T. Egner, 'Know Your Customer: Unravelling the Challenges', Journal of Payments Strategy & Systems, 18(1) (2024). https://doi.org/10.69554/KLRO4841.

38 Article 14(1) and (2) of TFR.

39 See Article 13 of AMLD = Article 20AMLR or Articles 14(7)(a) and 16(4)(a) of TFR.

40 According to Recital para. 24 of TFR, cryptoassets 'that are unique and not fungible are not subject to the requirements of [the TFR] unless they are classified as crypto-assets or funds under [MiCA]'.

as it leads to an exemption of transactions in NFTs from TFR's requirements, regardless of the fact that significant value can be transferred this way. It also leads to inconsistencies as larger art traders remain in scope.[41] The exemption of NFTs from MiCA's operating requirements for CASPs and TFR marks a shortcoming of EU law.[42]

Since Article 3(14) TFR does not exempt the assets listed in Article 4(3) MiCA, cryptoassets transferred for free are not exempted. This is in line with the rationale underpinning AML/CTF policies. Which commercial transaction, if any, is underlying the transfer has no relevance in relation to TFR's scope. Furthermore, it is noteworthy that Recital 22 MiCA (stating that "Where crypto-assets have no identifiable issuer, they should not fall within the scope of Title II, III or IV" MiCA) is not repeated by TFR. In turn, TFR applies, in principle, also to fully decentralised cryptoassets. Yet, as TFR addresses intermediaries rather than issuers, limitations stem from the CASP definition where the cryptoasset service is provided in a fully decentralised manner. We discuss these in Section 14.2.2.3 below.

14.2.2.2 *EMTs*

While Article 48(2) MiCA states 'E-money tokens shall be deemed to be electronic money', Article 2(4) fourth subsentence TFR treats EMTs as cryptoassets for the purposes of TFR. Hence, where TFR refers to e-money, it does not mean EMTs.

14.2.2.3 *CASPs*

Article 3(15) TFR refers to the definition of CASPs laid out in Article 3(15) MiCA. It includes inter alia, crypto exchanges, brokers, custody providers and mere transfer services, but it is just as limited as MiCA courtesy of the catalogue of cryptoasset services listed in Article 3(16) MiCA. For that reason, crypto-lending and crypto-staking platforms are out of scope as these are not listed as cryptoasset services in Article 3(16) MiCA, yet a part of their activities may fall under provision of exchange services, order execution, or 'transfer services for cryptoassets on behalf of clients' pursuant to Article 3(16)(d),(e), and (j) MiCA. In particular, the transfer of a cryptoasset from one client's account to another client's account is at the heart of both crypto-lending and crypto-staking.[43]

TFR applies where at least one (intermediary) PSP or CASP involved in the transfer of funds or cryptoassets, respectively, is established or has its registered office in the EU.[44] This raises the issue of which rules apply if one (intermediary) CASP does not reside in the EU. TFR deals with situations of this nature in line with the principles of AML/CTF law, employing the concept of high-risk transactions (Section 14.3.5).

To the extent that a provider of self-custody and self-trading solutions is out of MiCA's scope,[45] that solution is also out of TFR's scope. This is true regardless of whether these solutions are offered by centralised or decentralised DeFi applications.

Furthermore, where a cryptoasset service (for instance, custody) is provided in a fully decentralised manner, that is in our reading where the crypto application is not controlled by a "legal person or other undertaking" due to its fully decentralised setup, it does not qualify as a CASP.[46]

[41] Article 2(1)(i), (j) of AMLD (where transaction values exceed EUR 10,000).

[42] See Zetzsche *et al.* 'Remaining Regulatory Challenges in Digital Finance', p. 83. Website https://dx.doi.org/10.2139/ssrn.4487516 (last accessed on 1 October 2024).

[43] See Section 7.2.

[44] Article 1 of TFR.

[45] For details, see Section 7.2.

[46] For details, see Section 7.2. The reasoning for this limitation of scope is different from Recital para. 22 MiCA exempting cryptoassets that lack an issuer.

For that reason, TFR is criticised for leaving fully decentralised CASPs out of scope,[47] which prompts our inclination to grant regulatory entity status to DAOs.[48]

14.2.3 *Scope of TFR*

14.2.3.1 *Transfer of Funds and Transfer of Cryptoassets*

For the purposes of preventing, detecting, and investigating money laundering and terrorist financing, TFR lays down rules regarding information on payers and payees accompanying transfers of funds and on originators and beneficiaries accompanying transfers of cryptoassets.

For the purposes of TFR, a "transfer of cryptoassets" means 'any transaction with the aim of moving crypto-assets from one distributed ledger address, crypto-asset account or other device allowing the storage of crypto-assets to another, carried out by at least one [CASP] acting on behalf of either an originator or a beneficiary, irrespective of whether the originator and the beneficiary are the same person and irrespective of whether the crypto-asset service provider of the originator and that of the beneficiary are one and the same'.[49]

Such transfers include both direct transfers from PSP to PSP or CASP to CASP, respectively, and indirect transfers involving intermediary PSPs and intermediary CASPs[50] as long as they transfer clients' funds and cryptoassets rather than their own.

Furthermore, TFR applies even where on one side of the transaction there is a self-hosted address,[51] as long as there is a CASP (i.e., *not* a fully decentralised application) involved on one side.

14.2.3.2 *Minimum Amount*

A PSP and CASP in scope of TFR is required to collect information (e.g., name and account number, address, and ID number[52]) of the originator and the beneficiary of any cryptoasset transaction. However, the obligation to check whether information on the payer or the payee is accurate is imposed only in respect of individual transfers of funds worth more than EUR 1,000, unless the transfer appears to be linked to other transfers of funds which together would exceed EUR 1,000, the funds have been received or paid out in cash or in anonymous electronic money, or where there are other specified reasons.[53] In the same vein, while a CASP is in principle not required to verify the information on the user of the self-hosted address, where the transfer to or from a self-hosted address exceeds an amount of EUR 1,000, that CASP must verify whether that self-hosted address is effectively owned or controlled by that client.[54] EUR 1,000 is also the limit for various other stipulations of TFR and implementing options of the Member States.[55]

[47] See Zetzsche *et al.*, 'Remaining Regulatory Challenges in Digital Finance', p. 93.

[48] Chapter 16.

[49] Article 3(10) of MiCA.

[50] Cf. Article 3(16) of TFR, defining intermediary CASPs as a CASP 'that is not the [CASP] of the originator or of the beneficiary and that receives and transmits a transfer of crypto-assets on behalf of the [CASP] of the originator or of the beneficiary, or of another intermediary [CASP]'.

[51] See Recital paras. 38, 39, and 45 and Articles 14(5), 16(2), and 20 of TFR.

[52] See for details Recital para. 29 and Article 2(5) of TFR (subject to the discretion of Member States to apply TFR below that amount).

[53] Article 7(3), (4) and Recital para. 29 of TFR.

[54] Articles 14(5) and 16(2) and Recital para. 39 of TFR.

[55] Articles 2(5)(c), 5(2), and 6(2) TFR.

14.2.3.3 *TFR Carve-Outs*

TFR foresees a number of carve-outs in its recitals and binding text. Note that these carve-outs are in addition to carve-outs coming from the reference to the terms "cryptoassets" and "CASPs" in MiCA, including that a CASP must rest on a "legal person or other undertaking"[56] and thus excludes fully decentralised applications.

The Intermediary's Own Transactions

Transactions between PSPs and CASPs on their own behalf are excluded from TFR's scope.[57] Such a transaction materialises where the PSP and the CASP transfer their own funds rather than clients' funds, for instance, to rebalance their exposure in certain cryptoassets. Yet, where on one side of a transaction the PSP or CASP engages *on behalf of a client,* that PSP or CASP is obliged to perform TFR duties.

Peer-to-Peer Transactions

Of greater practical importance, TFR does not apply to peer-to-peer transactions without the involvement of a CASP. Peer-to-peer transactions are conveyed from one token account to another.[58] A literal reading here suggests that the cryptoasset leaves the account of the originator and is then booked on the account of the beneficiary. Yet, cryptoassets never go anywhere. The transfer is just code rewritten by many nodes in a way indicating that a type of right in the cryptoasset formerly assigned to one person is now assigned to another.[59] Hence, peer-to-peer transactions imply that no-one else gathers rights in that same way in said cryptoassets. This would be the case, for instance, of central counterparty clearing or of a platform provider trading on its own accounts.

Some of these transactions may be facilitated by centralised entities operating trading platforms acting as an arranger but not an executing entity as the carrying out of a transaction implies. These activities shift the focus onto the second element of the exemption, namely, the lack of involvement of a CASP. For instance, we could see an exchange service functioning as a mere arranger between the two parties of the transaction, which is then executed in a peer-to-peer fashion, sometimes even on a separate platform or DeFi solution.

In turn, the carve-out could be read as having one reason (i.e., asking for the two elements cumulatively being given) or as having two reasons (i.e., asking for one of the two elements being given). Given the widespread use of P2P crypto exchanges, this is now of high relevance. We answer this particular puzzle here with a view to the "cryptoasset service" definition stipulated in Article 3(16)(b) and (18) MiCA: for the provision of the operation of a trading platform, it suffices that the providers 'bring together or facilitate the bringing together of multiple third-party purchasing and selling interests in crypto-assets'. That definition does not require from the CASP to be involved in the execution of the transaction. It follows from that definition that peer-to-peer transactions are merely those not facilitated by any CASP acting as arranger of the transaction; in turn, CASPs need to identify clients prior to facilitating the transaction even where afterwards the clients can settle via another venue. See also Section 7.2.

[56] Section 14.3.2.2. Where neither a legal person nor other undertaking is given, as in platforms controlled by no one, we lack a CASP and hence.

[57] Article 2(4), first subsection (c) and second subsection (a) of TFR.

[58] Recital para. 22 of TFR.

[59] See Section 14.2.2.2.

TABLE 14.1 *Cash-like transactions excluded from TFR*

PSD Article	Reasoning
3(a) PSD	Payment transactions made exclusively in cash directly from the payer to the payee, without any intermediary intervention
3(c) PSD	Professional physical transport of banknotes and coins, including their collection, processing, and delivery
3(e) PSD	Cash-to-cash currency exchange operations where the funds are not held on a payment account
3(f) PSD	Cash-to-cash currency exchange operations where the funds are not held on a payment account
3(o) PSD	Cash withdrawal services offered by means of ATM by providers, acting on behalf of one or more card issuers, which are not a party to the framework contract with the customer withdrawing money from a payment account, where those providers do not conduct other payment services

Cash, Cash-Like, and Low-Risk Transactions

TFR does not apply to a number of payment services which are either deemed low risk or out of bounds of wire transfer regulation since they involve cash transactions,[60] as laid out in Tables 14.1 and 14.2.

On top of that, Article 2(3) TFR excludes transfers of funds or transfers of EMTs (but not ARTs and "other cryptoassets") where the transfer is 'carried out using a payment card, an electronic money instrument, a mobile phone or any other digital or IT prepaid or postpaid device with similar characteristics, provided (...) that card, instrument or device is used exclusively to pay for goods or services; and (...) the number of that card, instrument or device accompanies all transfers flowing from the transaction'. The archetypal example is a credit card transaction at the point of sale. However, TFR applies when that transfer device is used for a transfer 'between natural persons acting as consumers for purposes other than trade, business or professional activity'.

14.2.4 *Obligations of the Intermediaries Involved*

In line with AML/CTF principles, the intermediaries' obligations differ with regard to the AML/CTF risks related to the transaction.

14.2.4.1 *Normal Transactions*

Originator CASPs

Originator CASPs must verify[61] the accuracy *ex ante* and transfer afterwards at the latest simultaneously with each transaction concerning both the originator and the beneficiary, the following[62]

- the name of the originator and beneficiary;
- the distributed ledger addresses of the originator and beneficiary, in cases where a transfer of cryptoassets is registered on a network using DLT or similar technology, and the

[60] Cf. Recital para. 23 and Article 2(2) of TFR.

[61] On modes of verification, Article 14(7) of TFR refers to Articles 13 and 14(5) of AMLD.

[62] Article 14(1), (2), (4), (6), and (8) of TFR.

TABLE 14.2 *Low-risk transactions excluded from TFR by reference to PSD*

PSD Article	Reasoning
3(b) PSD	Payment transactions from the payer to the payee through a commercial agent authorised via an agreement to negotiate or conclude the sale or purchase of goods or services on behalf of only the payer or only the payee
3(d) PSD	Payment transactions consisting of the non-professional cash collection and delivery within the framework of a non-profit or charitable activity
3(g) PSD	Certain payment transactions based on cheques, standardised bills of exchange, and promissory notes, as well as paper-based vouchers, cheques, and postal money orders
3(h) PSD	Payment transactions carried out within a payment or securities settlement system between settlement agents, central counterparties, clearing houses and/or central banks, and other participants of the system, and PSPs, without prejudice to Article 35 PSD
3(i) PSD	Payment transactions related to securities asset servicing, including dividends, income, or other distributions, or redemption or sale, *carried out by persons referred to in Article 3(h) PSD or by investment firms, credit institutions, collective investment undertakings, or asset management companies* … and other entities allowed to have the custody of financial instruments
3(j) PSD	Services delivered by technical service providers, which support the provision of payment services, without them entering at any time into possession of the funds to be transferred, including processing and storage of data, trust and privacy protection services, data and entity authentication, information technology (IT) and communication network provision, and the provision and maintenance of terminals and devices used for payment services, with the exclusion of payment initiation services and account information services
3(k) PSD	Services based on specific payment instruments that can be used only in a limited way subject to conditions
3(l) PSD	Certain payment transactions made by a provider of electronic communications networks or services provided in addition to electronic communications services for a subscriber to the network or service for payment transactions up to EUR 50 and up to EUR 300 per month, *for the purchase of digital content and voice-based services; or performed from or via an electronic device and charged to the related bill* within the framework of a charitable activity or for the purchase of tickets
3(m) PSD	Payment transactions carried out between PSPs and their agents or branches for their own account

cryptoasset account number of the originator, where such an account exists and is used to process the transaction;

- the cryptoasset account numbers of the originator and the beneficiary, in cases where a transfer of cryptoassets is not registered on a network using DLT or similar technology;
- subject to the existence of the necessary field in the relevant message format, and where provided by the originator to its CASP, the current Legal Entity Identifier (LEI), or, in its absence, any other available equivalent official identifier of the originator.[63]

These requirements stand at odds with the views of DeFi enthusiasts on anonymity of transactions. The Bitcoin protocol lacks prescribed fields for these data points.[64] In order to ensure compliance, CASPs need to build up proprietary data transmission and verification infrastructure.

Regarding the originator, as the CASP's client, the CASP must deliver the originator's address, including the name of the country of residence or registration, as the case may be, the official

[63] Article 14(1) and (2) of TFR.
[64] See Website https://en.bitcoin.it/wiki/Protocol_documentation#Signatures (last accessed on 1 October 2024).

personal document number, and customer identification number, or alternatively, the originator's date and place of birth; for a legal person the CASP shall also add the commercial registration number.

Where a transfer is neither registered on a DLT network nor made to or from a cryptoasset account, the originator CASP must add a unique transaction identifier to the transfer.

For batch files (where the batch list groups send and receive commands that can be run from the batch file) from a single originator, Article 15 TFR facilitates the bundling of information required by Article 14 TFR.

Beneficiary CASPs

First of all, beneficiary CASPs must monitor incoming transfers and have a compliance organisation in place ensuring that information under TFR is complete.[65] Prior to making the cryptoasset available, the CASP must verify[66] the accuracy of the reported information by way of documents, data, or information from a reliable and independent source (such as an ID database).[67]

Cases of missing or incomplete information are of interest here. In such instances, the beneficiary CASP's compliance organisation must implement 'risk-based procedures, including procedures based on the risk-sensitive basis referred to in [Article 13 AMLD = Article 20 AMLR], for determining whether to execute, reject, return or suspend a transfer of crypto-assets lacking the required complete information on the originator and the beneficiary, and for taking the appropriate follow-up action'. In practice, whenever information is missing and cannot be easily verified by public sources (such as in the case of a person's identity), the beneficiary CASP must reject the transaction for good *or* ask the originator CASP for additional information.[68] Where the originator CASP repeatedly fails to provide the required information, it may be blacklisted and reported to the relevant FIU.[69]

Furthermore, the fact that information on the originator or beneficiary is missing may indicate high risk and/or a suspicious transaction that warrants reporting to the relevant FIU.[70]

Intermediary CASPs

Intermediary CASPs must, through their own effective compliance organisations,[71] check the completeness of the information received, transmit all information received, retain the respective records of such information, and make them available on request to the competent authorities.[72] Where information is missing, they may take the same steps as the beneficiary CASP in relation to the originator CASP.[73]

Compliance Organisation on Restrictive Measures (Sanctions)

All PSPs and CASPs subject to TFR must have in place internal policies, procedures, and controls to ensure the implementation of restrictive measures (i.e., state sanctions) under TFR

[65] Article 16(1) of TFR.
[66] On modes of verification, Article 16(4) of TFR refers to Articles 13 and 14(5) of AMLD.
[67] Article 16(3) of TFR.
[68] Article 17(1) of TFR.
[69] Article 17(2) of TFR.
[70] Article 18 of TFR.
[71] Article 20 of TFR.
[72] Article 19 of TFR.
[73] Articles 21 and 22 of TFR.

and national law[74] in line with EBA guidelines[75] 'to ensure implementation of those restrictive measures, including screening measures against Union and national lists of designated persons'. This shall put the transfer intermediaries in a position where they can 'take appropriate action to freeze certain funds and crypto-assets or that they comply with specific restrictions concerning certain transfers of funds or of crypto-assets'.[76]

14.2.4.2 *Low-Risk Transactions*

For low-risk transactions inside the EU, TFR foresees facilitated information exchange with basic identification devices relying on the PSPs' mandatory use of IBAN and unique transaction identifiers,[77] unless the beneficiaries' PSPs request the full information.[78] We do not find the same easing measures for transfers of cryptoassets in TFR due to the lack of commonly agreed identifiers similar to IBAN and unique transaction identifiers.

14.2.4.3 *Increased Risks*

Generally, for situations of "increased risk", EBA guidelines specify the enhanced due diligence measures for obliged entities to 'mitigate such risks, including the adoption of appropriate procedures such as the use of distributed ledger technology (DLT) analytic tools, to detect the origin or destination of crypto-assets'. In general, the EBA underlined that, concerning the use of advanced analytic tools, while 'firms should determine [independently] the most appropriate controls and tools based on their business and risks associated with their business relationships [and] set this approach out in their policies and procedures',[79] EBA acknowledges the relevance of advanced analytics tools for CASPs.[80] When applying a risk-based approach, CASPs shall consider 'whether the use of advanced analytics tools, like distributed ledger or blockchain analytics tools, is necessary in light of the ML/TF risk associated with the firm's business and with the firm's customers' individual transactions'.[81]

Besides, TFR specifies how to deal with high-risk situations in the case of self-hosted addresses, the use of anonymity-enhancing transactions and technologies, and transactions with exposed persons. We discuss the rules on third countries which may involve high risk in Section 14.2.5.

Self-Hosted Addresses

Article 3(20) TFR defines a "self-hosted address" as a distributed ledger address not linked to a CASP nor a third-country entity providing cryptoasset services. It covers the instances discussed

[74] Article 23 of TFR. Implementing the Single Rule Book approach, national competencies by Member States to issue rules for domestic providers will be abolished.

[75] EBA, Guidelines on customer due diligence and the factors credit and financial institutions should consider when assessing the money laundering and terrorist financing risk associated with individual business relationships and occasional transactions ('The ML/TF Risk Factors Guidelines') under Articles 17 and 18(4) of Directive (EU) 2015/849. Website www.eba.europa.eu/sites/default/files/2024-01/a3e89f4f-fbf3-4bd6-9e07-35f3243555b3/Final%20Amending%20%20Guidelines%20on%20MLTF%20Risk%20Factors.pdf (last accessed on 1 October 2024).

[76] Recital para. 18 of TFR.

[77] See Articles 4(33), 45(1)(a), 52(2)(b), and 88(1), (2) and Recital para. 88 of PSD, referring to the International Bank Account Number ('IBAN'), based on ISO 13616. An IBAN registry coordinating the issuance of IBAN is managed by the payment network SWIFT.

[78] Cf. Article 5 referring to Article 4 of TFR.

[79] Cf. EBA, 'Guidelines on Customer Due Diligence', Section 5.3, Summary of Responses to the Consultation and the EBA's Analysis (referring to the risk-based approach as further described in Guideline 4.74(d) of the Guidelines).

[80] Cf. EBA, 'Guidelines on Customer Due Diligence', Section 5.3, at p. 31 and No. 21(3)(g).

[81] Cf. EBA, 'Guidelines on Customer Due Diligence', p. 16, No. 17, Guideline 4.74(d).

herein as "self-custody". Given that TFR is linked to the CASP definition in MiCA, the delineation we have laid out in Section 8.2 applies: whenever the crypto-service 'custody and administration of crypto-assets for clients' is not given, a self-hosted address as defined by TFR is established. 'Custody and administration of crypto-assets for clients' is an authorized service subject to Title V MiCA. The use of unauthorized cryptoasset services, contrary to MiCA, and, given any service provider needs to show some degree of centralized organization (see Section 7.2), the use of fully decentralised custody applications, leads to the application of the provisions on self-hosted addresses.

The originator CASP sending value to a self-hosted address, as well as the beneficiary CASP that obtains value from a self-hosted address, must obtain and hold the information it usually has to deliver to (or receive from) the counterparty CASP *and* ensure that the transfer of cryptoassets can be individually identified.[82] In this case, there is no requirement on the side of the CASP to *verify* the information on the user of the self-hosted address.[83]

However, where the amount exceeds EUR 1,000, the originator or beneficiary CASP, as the case may be, must take adequate measures[84] to assess whether that address is owned or controlled by the originator (i.e., trying to verify the information obtained). It is not obvious which step this could be where there is no CASP facilitating the transaction. Further risk-mitigating measures[85] may be necessary due to the parallel application of Articles 19a and 19b AMLD = Articles 37 and 40 AMLR, under which the transaction potentially needs to be qualified as "high risk" (see Section 14.3).[86]

Recital 45 TFR provides further guidance on inaccurate information: CASPs must assess which risks are created by transfers to or from self-hosted addresses. If the CASP becomes aware that any information regarding the user of the self-hosted address is inaccurate, or encounters unusual or suspicious patterns, or has other reason(s) to believe that there is a higher ML/TF risk related to the transfers involving self-hosted addresses, the CASP must apply enhanced due diligence measures to manage and mitigate the risks appropriately, and may report the transaction to the relevant FIU.

Yet, the EU legislature ensures further monitoring of the self-hosted address by mandating the European Commission 'to assess the need for additional specific measures to mitigate the risks posed by transfers to or from self-hosted addresses or to or from entities not established in the Union, including the introduction of possible restrictions, and should assess the effectiveness and proportionality of the mechanisms used to verify the accuracy of information concerning the ownership of self-hosted addresses'.[87]

Use of Anonymity-Enhancing Transactions and Technologies

Another example of high-risk transactions is the use of transactions and technologies that enhance anonymity, including privacy wallets, mixers, or tumblers.[88] TFR does not take a stance on these technologies specifically. The related EBA guidelines address the anonymity-

[82] Cf. Articles 14(5) and 16(2) of TFR.
[83] Recital para. 39 of TFR.
[84] Where crypto exchanges are used (such as Coinbase), the intermediary CASP may inquire about the identity of originator and beneficiary. It is not obvious which step this could be if there (a) is no CASP facilitating the transaction and undertaking the originator's client verification and (b) no register of addresses. One option we envisage is the standardised use of chain analytics tracking the transmission data stored on the blockchain.
[85] Example: use of chain-analytics service providers.
[86] Cf. Articles 14(5) and 16(2) of TFR.
[87] Recital para. 58 of TFR.
[88] Cf. Article 18(6) of AMLD.

enhancing transactions and technologies in two ways. Generally speaking, the use of 'an IP address associated with a darknet or a software that allows anonymous communication, including encrypted emails, anonymous or temporary email services and VPN' indicate increased risk regarding the nature of the customer.[89] EBA understands the fact that 'crypto-assets have been subject to "anonymity-enhancing" activities, in particular, processes which obfuscate the transaction on the ledger technology or contain other characteristics similar to those listed' in the s. 21.5.a of the EBA guidelines[90] as indicator of 'increased risk' under Annex III AMLD.[91]

Yet, TFR may have the effect that many CASPs refrain from doing business with anonymity-enhancing transactions and technology platforms, for two reasons. First, in many instances, the anonymity-enhancing transactions and technology providers may not qualify as a CASP because the platform does not provide a cryptoasset service, because the platform is not licensed for the provision of cryptoasset services (as it may be located outside of the EEA or act non-compliantly with EU law), or because there is no identifiable legal person or other undertaking that could be identified as a provider, due to full decentralisation.[92] In these cases, the procedures for self-hosted addresses may apply, which limit the absolute transaction size to EUR 1,000.[93] Second, where the provider of the anonymity-enhancing transactions and technologies qualifies as a CASP (for instance, as the provider of a 'transfer of cryptoassets'[94]), both the originator and beneficiary CASP's ownership verification are likely to fail if the respective counterparty CASP is known for providing these services. In both cases, but also due to the potential qualification as a high-risk transaction, with related duties to notify the relevant FIU about suspicious transactions,[95] we expect CASPs to be restrictive with regard to anonymity-enhancing transactions and technology providers.

Transactions with Politically Exposed Persons

Articles 20–24 TFR require enhanced measures for transactions with politically exposed persons that may hold or receive cryptoassets.

14.2.4.4 *Third Countries*

The AML/CTF framework puts a special emphasis on third countries and third-country providers, as additional elements potentially resulting in high-risk transactions. MiCA does not

[89] EBA, 'Guidelines on Customer Due Diligence', at s. 21.5(a) sub (vi).

[90] EBA, 'Guidelines on Customer Due Diligence', pp. 22–25.

[91] See Recital para. 17 of TFR and Article 18(6) of AMLD, as inserted by TFR (equivalent to = Article 29 AMLR). Cf. Section 14.3.3.

[92] See Sections 7.2 and 14.2.2.

[93] See Section 14.2.4.3.

[94] Whether the anonymity-enhancing transaction or technology depends on the transaction or technology applied. For instance, mixing always requires a transfer from one address to another (or multiple for that matter). While some DLT users may set up their own mixing service for own use (and thus the requirement of Article 3(16) to provide a service 'on behalf of others' is not met), most users will rely on external providers, given that these providers have access to a greater pool of cryptoassets and thus mixing takes places more effectively; in this case, the provider may provide a cryptoasset service pursuant to Article 3(1)(16)(f) MiCA. Where multiple clients commit their cryptoassets to feed the pool operated by a provider on their behalf, the service may qualify under Article 3(1)(16)(d) MiCA (as 'exchange of crypto-assets for other crypto-assets'; this is the case where cryptoasset A is swapped (e.g., via bridging protocols) with cryptoasset B. But even where one Bitcoin is swapped against another Bitcoin, we may see an exchange service: in contrast to fiat, each Bitcoin is identifiable as a separate asset, and thus swapping Bitcoin is not the same as swapping fiat currency. Be this as it may, where a service provider acts on behalf of clients, we may find in any way the "execution of order" pursuant to Article 3(1)(16)(e) MiCA. For a further discussion of cryptoasset services, see Chapter 7.

[95] See Article 33 of AMLD = Article 69AMLR.

apply to third-country providers,[96] hence any reference to CASPs under MiCA ends at the EEA borders. In accordance with the logic of TFR, this should result in the application of the rules on self-hosted addresses (see Section 14.2.4.3).

Article 6(1) TFR stipulates in this case that payment information must be verified and carry the payment account number and unique transaction identifier (if such an identifier exists). Articles 14 and 15 TFR provide for similar rules on cryptoasset transfers but ask for the distributed ledger address of the originator (in the absence of a CASP) and the cryptoasset account number of the originator (where a CASP is present) as well as the unique transaction identifier. Interestingly, Articles 14 and 15 TFR do not provide explicit rules on third-country CASPs nor entities, except on data protection.[97] However, Recitals 33–35 TFR provide basic elements, which if read together with TFR lead to the following situation.

For incoming transfers from originator CASPs outside the EU, the core issue under Article 14 TFR is whether the beneficiary EU-CASP *receives* the relevant information stipulated in Article 14(1) and (2) TFR together with the transfer and whether the beneficiary EU-CASP is, following a risk-based assessment, of the opinion that the information on the originator is accurate. Note that such an assessment is based on the strict standards of Articles 16(1) and 17 (1) TFR referring to Article 13 AMLD, a core provision on customer due diligence. If there is any doubt as to the reliability of the third-country originator CASP, the type of transaction, or the originator applying the risk factors laid out in Annexes II and III AMLD, the transaction may be processed as incomplete or as one with information missing pursuant to Article 17(1) TFR.

For outgoing transfers from originator EU/EEA-CASPs to third-country CASPs, Recitals 33–35 TFR stress that originator EU/EEA-CASPs shall process complete and reliable information to third-country CASPs and support the AML/CTF efforts in that country. Here, complete information includes, in particular, the LEI or any equivalent official identifier provided by the payer to its PSP that allows for better identification of the parties involved in a transfer of funds. Furthermore, this information can easily 'be included in existing payment message formats, such as that developed by the International Organisation for Standardisation for electronic data interchange between financial institutions'.[98] Limited to the purposes of preventing, detecting, and investigating AML/CTF-relevant conduct, third-country FIUs 'should be granted access to complete information on the payer and the payee or on the originator and the beneficiary, as applicable'.[99] In turn, Article 14 TFR applies as if the recipient was an EU/EEA-CASPs. Yet, the lack of abilities of beneficiary CASPs as well as data protection law may justify the limited transfer of information.[100]

This approach is one of equivalence and rests on the cooperation agreements,[101] which we welcome in the borderless reality of cryptoassets. In practice, we expect beneficiary EU/EEA-CASPs to apply a careful approach where the residence of the originator CASPs gives reason to apply a high-risk categorisation.

96 See Chapter 4.

97 Cf. Recital para. 19 and Article 25 of TFR.

98 Cf. Recital para. 33 of TFR.

99 Cf. Recital para. 33 of TFR.

100 Cf. Recital para. 34 of TFR ('When transferring crypto-assets on behalf of a client to a crypto-asset service provider that is not registered in the Union, the crypto-asset service provider of the originator should assess the ability of the crypto-asset service provider of the beneficiary to receive and retain the information required under this Regulation in compliance with [GDPR], using, where appropriate, the options available in chapter V of [GDPR]').

101 See Recital para. 35 and Article 27 of AMLD = Article 49 AMLR. On top, the European Commission may authorise additional agreements under Article 35 of TFR.

The reality will be one of permanent correspondent relationships among CASPs and third-country CASPs. Taking that into account, TFR and AMLD/AMLR provide bespoke rules on correspondent relationships that include cryptoasset services (see Section 14.3.4).

14.3 AMLD/AMLR CONTENT ON CRYPTOASSETS

The first rules on cryptoassets were those adopted under AMLD4. In fact, MiCA was adopted to deal with the situation at that time where 'no rules, other than those in respect of anti-money laundering' existed in the EU for the provision of services related to unregulated cryptoassets.[102] However, AMLD4 has been significantly amended by AMLD5 and TFR (and subsequently, AMLD6 and AMLR). We describe the resulting framework hereafter.[103]

14.3.1 *Scope of AMLD/AMLR*

With the coming into force of AMLR, CASPs under MiCA will be one type of financial institutions, and the respective rules apply unless the framework provides for exemptions.

Up to this point, the regulation on CASPs is less straightforward. The EU AMLD covers – after the introduction of TFR[104] – a host of professionals involved with financial transactions,[105] including 'providers engaged in exchange services between virtual currencies and fiat currencies', 'custodian wallet providers', and CASPs as defined by MiCA.[106]

In that context, a "virtual currency" means a digital representation of value that is not issued or guaranteed by a central bank or a public authority, is not necessarily attached to a legally established currency, and does not possess the legal status of currency or money, but it is accepted by natural or legal person as a means of exchange and which can be transferred, stored, and traded electronically,[107] while a "custodian wallet provider" is 'an entity that provides services to safeguard private cryptographic keys on behalf of its customers, to hold, store and transfer virtual currencies'.

EMTs and ARTs are virtual currencies under that definition. However, depending on how broadly or narrowly one construes the term "means of exchange", digital assets for investment purposes as well as "other cryptoassets" like vouchers and utility tokens will not qualify as virtual currency under AMLD. Furthermore, NFTs, lacking fungibility by definition, will not be accepted as means of exchange. This explains the rationale behind the reference to MiCA terms (see Section 14.2.2), with regard to cryptoassets and CASPs, as implemented by TFR. Moreover, TFR's definition of "self-hosted address" pursuant to Article 3(20) TFR is inserted in Article 3(20) AMLD = Article 2(14) AMLR.

[102] Recital para. 4 of MiCA.

[103] Taking effect on July 2027, and Article 18 AMD6 by July 2029, as part of a Single Rule Book approach, the AMLD minimum rules for the private sector have been expanded and transferred to AMLR, while the remaining AML directive will deal with the organisation of institutional AML/CTF systems at national level in the member states. To reflect on the intermittent period, we cite herein both the AMLD and AMLR provisions.

[104] Article 38 of TFR amends Article 2 of AMLD = Article 3(b)(i) AMLR.

[105] Cf. Article 2(3) of AMLD = Article 6(1) AMLR. Examples include auditors, accountant, tax advisors, notaries, independent lawyers, trustees, real estate agents, art traders, and many more in certain or all business situations.

[106] Up to the TFR, Article 2(3)(g), (i) of AMLD listed 'providers engaged in exchange services between virtual currencies and fiat currencies' and 'custodian wallet providers'. On reasons for repealing that approach, see Recital AMLR, para. 14.

[107] Article 3(18) of AMLD = Article 2(1) point 7 AMLR.

While digital assets qualifying as regulated products and activities pursuant to Article 2(4) MiCA (for instance, investment tokens as financial instruments) will be deemed the business of credit institutions and financial institutions other than CASPs, the insertion of the terms "CASPs" and "cryptoassets" ensures that "other cryptoassets" are in scope.

Under the final concept (AMLR) as much as under the revised AMLD framework, the same three matters that undermine the effectiveness of TFR also undermine the effectiveness of the AMLD framework: (1) NFTs are out of scope (unless the entities involved qualify as large-volume art dealers[108]); (2) it may be difficult to show who is the provider in fully decentralised schemes (similar to the issue of identifying a "legal person or other undertaking" in the case of CASPs); and (3) self-custody solutions are out of scope.[109]

14.3.2 *Supervision and the Fit and Proper Test for VASPs and Crypto Custodians*

VASPs and custodians must be registered (hence, somewhat supervised), and member states' laws require that management and (major) shareholders and beneficial owners are "fit and proper".[110] Article 47 AMLD prompted a large number of VASPs to register across Europe prior to MiCA, yet it did not lead to the provision of a European Passport for financial services. With Articles 4 and 6 AMLD6, replacing Article 47 AIFMD, the MiCA authorisation as a CASP under Title V MiCA will replace the terms "VASPs" and "custodians" in relation to cryptoassets and related authorization requirements. A separate registration as a VASP, which may be required under the laws of some Member States, may retain some meaning for entities that do not qualify as CASPs under MiCA (for instance, for custodians in relation to NFTs only, or token-based payment services), and must then meet the requirements of Articles 4 and 6 AMLR.

The respective EBA guidelines recognise that the transition from a registration requirement to the authorisation as CASP under Title V MiCA presents a challenge: 'as the CASPs sector is new to AML/CFT requirements, with some CASPs having never been regulated or supervised for AML/CFT purposes, additional guidance on different checks that should be implemented by them to mitigate different levels of risk, such as suitable training, enhanced CDD and the use of blockchain analytics tools would be of benefit'.[111]

14.3.3 *Risk Factors for Cryptoassets*

Given the risk-based approach of the EU AML/CTF framework (Section 14.1), TFR has inserted bespoke rules for cryptoassets supplementing the existing AMLD approach.

A closer look reveals that the EU legislature has been relatively light on details, but assigned the task to the EBA to issue guidelines on the risk variables and risk factors to be taken into account by CASPs when entering into business relationships or carrying out transactions in cryptoassets.[112]

In particular, the EBA shall clarify how CASPs ought to take the risk factors listed in Annex III AMLD into account with regard to transactions with persons and entities not covered by AMLD

[108] Cf. Article 2(1)(3)(i) and (j) AMLD = Article 3(3)(i) and (j) AMLR.

[109] We have discussed the matter at length in Chapters 4, 6, and 7 of this book to which we refer.

[110] Article 47 AMLD = Articles 4 and 6 AMLD6.

[111] EBA, 'Guidelines on Customer Due Diligence', p. 35, Title 5.1 (C) ('Cost-benefit analysis/Impact assessment Point').

[112] See Article 18(5), (6) of AMLD as inserted by Article 38 of TFR = Article 19, 20(3) AMLR. See EBA, 'Guidelines on Customer Due Diligence'.

and pay particular attention to anonymity-facilitating products, transactions, and technologies, such as privacy wallets, mixers, or tumblers.[113] The EBA guidelines shall determine the 'enhanced due diligence measures that obliged entities shall consider applying to mitigate [increased] risks, including the adoption of appropriate procedures to detect the origin or destination of crypto-assets'.[114] When setting guidelines, the EBA is encouraged to take into account the classification as a "cryptoasset service" as well as the degree of transparency provided by technical means.

14.3.3.1 *Anonymity-Enhancing Coins and Products*

The AML/CTF framework contains 'measures to limit the misuse of anonymous instruments' (Article 1(c) AMLR). As part of that agenda, it prohibits CASPs to operate anonymous cryptoasset accounts as well as any account otherwise allowing for the anonymisation of the customer account holder or the anonymisation or increased obfuscation of transactions, including through anonymity-enhancing coins (Article 79(1) AMLR). 'Anonymity-enhancing coins' means cryptoassets that have built-in features designed to make cryptoasset transfer information anonymous, either systematically or optionally (Article 2(1)(25) AMLR).

In the view of EU regulators, '[t]he anonymity of crypto-assets exposes them to risks of misuse for criminal purposes. Anonymous crypto-asset accounts, as well as other anonymising instruments, do not allow the traceability of crypto-asset transfers, and make it difficult to identify linked transactions that might raise suspicion or to apply an adequate level of customer due diligence. In order to ensure effective application of AML/CFT requirements to crypto-assets, it is necessary to prohibit the provision and the custody of anonymous crypto-asset accounts or accounts allowing for the anonymisation or the increased obfuscation of transactions by crypto-asset service providers, including through anonymity-enhancing coins. That prohibition does not apply to providers of hardware and software or providers of self-hosted wallets insofar as they do not possess access to or control over those crypto-asset wallets.

'In line with this approach, the respective EBA guidelines[115] state that the use of anonymity-facilitating product features 'such as, but not limited to, mixers or tumblers, obfuscated ledger technology, ring signatures, stealth addresses, ring confidential transactions, atomic swaps and non-interactive zero-knowledge proofs, (...) transfers to and from platforms that obfuscate transactions and foster anonymity, expose CASPs to increased risks. [Also, the] global nature of CASPs' business models may present heightened ML/TF risks, particularly where CASPs' customers are transacting with jurisdictions associated with a high ML/TF risk'.[116]

14.3.3.2 *Self-Hosted Addresses*

Notwithstanding the guideline approach, the EU AML/CTF framework[117] identifies one example of high-risk activities. Specifically, CASPs must 'identify and assess the risk of money laundering and terrorist financing associated with transfers of crypto-assets directed to or originating from a self-hosted address'. CASPs' internal policies, procedures, and controls must be tailored to identify these addresses and 'to apply mitigating measures commensurate with the risks identified', for instance, through:

[113] Article 18(6) AMLD. See also Articles 19 and 20(3) AMLR (less detailed) and Recital para. 160 AMLR.
[114] Article 18(6) AMLD. See also Articles 19 and 20(3) AMLR (less detailed) and Recital para. 160 AMLR.
[115] EBA, 'Guidelines on Customer Due Diligence', p. 8.
[116] EBA, 'Guidelines on Customer Due Diligence', p. 8, para. 23 (Guidelines 21 – Sectoral Guideline for cryptoasset service providers (CASPs)).
[117] Article 19a AMLD = Article 40 AMLR.

- risk-based measures to identify and verify the identity of the originator or beneficiary, or the beneficial owner of the former, of a transfer made to or from a self-hosted address;
- requiring additional information on the origin and destination of the transferred cryptoassets;
- conducting enhanced ongoing monitoring of those transactions; and
- any other measure to mitigate and manage AML/CTF-relevant risks as well as the risk of non-implementation, evasion, and potential proliferation of targeted financial sanctions.

EBA emphasises that 'transactions with self-hosted addresses and decentralised trading platforms present an increased risk due to the lack of a legal framework applicable to them and the lack of identification and verification requirements applicable to their users'.[118] While direct control, increased security, and the ability to engage with many parts of the DLT ecosystems is seen as advantage of self-hosted addresses, EBA rests its notion of increased risks relating to self-hosted addressed on the observation that advanced analytics and other monitoring tools have linked *some* self-hosted addresses to suspicious transactions.[119] This justifies the classification as 'increased risk'.

14.3.3.3 *Other Cases of Increased Risk*

In addition to the former, we hold that a strict approach is advisable for DeFi applications providing cryptoasset services where a legal person or other undertaking controlling the application cannot be identified; the compliance of these entities cannot be trusted given that no-one is accountable for breaches and no-one can be sanctioned for furthering criminal activities.

A more nuanced approach, however, is warranted with regard to crypto-lending and crypto-staking providers. Some of these activities will qualify as transfer services under Article 3(16) MiCA,[120] while others may grant full transparency of transactions by way of access to the DLT on which the transactions are stored. On crypto-lending, the EBA guidelines find that 'customer's behaviour may contribute to an increasing risk in the situation where the customer is investing or exchanging crypto-assets, which it has borrowed via a peer-to-peer or other lending platform that does not fall within the scope of [MiCA], or under any other relevant regulatory framework within or outside the EU and, which is notably a decentralised or distributed application with no legal or natural person with control or influence over it'.[121]

14.3.3.4 *Enhanced Customer Due Diligence*

EBA provides detailed guidance on the minimum action in cases of increased risk, with a focus on self-hosted addresses.[122] For example, CASPs should:

- seek to rely on more than one reliable and independent source in order to verify the customer's and the beneficial owner's identity;[123]
- verify and identify majority shareholders outside of the AMLD's definition of beneficial owner or 'any natural persons who have authority to operate a crypto-asset account or

[118] EBA, 'Guidelines on Customer Due Diligence', p. 37.
[119] EBA, 'Guidelines on Customer Due Diligence', p. 37.
[120] See Sections 14.2.2.3 and 7.2.
[121] EBA, 'Guidelines on Customer Due Diligence', p. 25, s. 21.5(b)(xii).
[122] EBA, 'Guidelines on Customer Due Diligence', pp. 29–31, s. 21.12.
[123] EBA, 'Guidelines on Customer Due Diligence', p. 29, s. 21.12.

distributed ledger address on behalf of the customer or give instructions on the transfer or exchange of crypto-assets or other services relating to those crypto-assets';[124]

- obtain more information about the customer and the nature and purpose of the business relationship via open source or adverse media searches or commissioning a third-party intelligence report;[125]
- obtain more evidence about the source of the funds or wealth and about the source of cryptoassets of transactions where a higher risk is presented;[126]
- increase the frequency of monitoring 'for unexpected behaviours, patterns and indicators of suspicious activity' and also inclusion of a 'consideration of the parties with which the customer is transacting';[127]
- monitor customer's IP addresses and checking them against the IP addresses used by other customers;
- get confirmation of the customer's 'level of knowledge and understanding of crypto-assets to achieve a level of assurance that the customer is not used as a money mule' or
- in the case that the customer has 'multiple distributed ledger addresses or blockchain networks, the CASP should link these addresses to the customer'.

To meet the strict requirements listed above, CASPs should 'apply advanced analytics tools to assess the risk associated with transactions, particularly transactions involving self-hosted addresses, as it allows the CASP to trace the history of transactions and to identify potential links with criminal activities, persons or entities'.[128] Where high-risk non-EU countries are involved in transactions, CASPs must apply the enhanced due diligence requirements for these countries.[129]

14.3.4 *Cross-Border Setups*

14.3.4.1 *Branches*

CASPs are mandated to appoint, on behalf of their branches acting on a cross-border basis by way of a European Passport, permanent contact points for AML/CTF purposes.[130] That central contact point shall ensure, on behalf of the entity operating on a cross-border basis, compliance with AML/CFT rules and facilitate supervision by providing documents and information on request.

14.3.4.2 *Correspondent Relationships*

The cross-chain transfer of cryptoassets requires intense technology links and data sharing: similar to account-based money and debt, cryptoassets are never *truly* transferred. Rather, a bridge protocol creates a corresponding asset value on the new ledger, while the old cryptoassets on the same amount on the old DLT are blocked; thus, the old asset is "wrapped" in a form that can be recognised and transferred between the two networks. For that reason, we expect that

[124] EBA, 'Guidelines on Customer Due Diligence', p. 29, s. 21.12.(a).
[125] EBA, 'Guidelines on Customer Due Diligence', p. 29, s. 21.12.(b).
[126] EBA, 'Guidelines on Customer Due Diligence', p. 29, s. 21.12.(c).
[127] EBA, 'Guidelines on Customer Due Diligence', p. 29, s. 21.12.(d).
[128] EBA, 'Guidelines on Customer Due Diligence', p. 31, s. 21.13.(e).
[129] EBA, 'Guidelines on Customer Due Diligence', p. 31, s. 21.14.(f).
[130] Article 45(9) AMLD = Article 41(1) AMLD6.

stable networks will develop over time that facilitate cross-border and cross-chain transfers, similar to what is observed in the world of cross-border payments.[131]

The law[132] recognises this fact and regulates increased *ex ante* due diligence requirements for setting up a corresponding banking relationship, with the benefit of lower requirements *ex post*. The respective provision[133] allows similar arrangements for transfers of cryptoassets between EU/EEA-CASPs and third-country entities. Relationships between CASPs and third-country entities for cryptoasset transfers 'present similarities to correspondent banking relationships established with a third country's respondent institution. As those relationships are characterised by an ongoing and repetitive nature, they should be considered a type of correspondent relationship and be subject to specific enhanced due diligence measures similar in principle to those applied in the context of banking and financial services. In particular, [CASPs] should, when establishing a new correspondent relationship with a respondent entity, apply specific enhanced due diligence measures in order to identify and assess the risk exposure of that respondent, based on its reputation, the quality of supervision and its anti-money laundering and counter-terrorist financing (AML/CFT) controls. Based on the information gathered, the correspondent [CASPs] should implement appropriate risk mitigating measures, which should take into account in particular the potential higher risk of money laundering and terrorist financing posed by unregistered and unlicensed entities. That is especially relevant as long as the implementation of the FATF standards relating to crypto-assets at global level remains uneven, which poses additional risks and challenges'.[134] The EBA guidelines shall specify on how CASPs conduct enhanced due diligence and which risk-mitigating measures are appropriate when interacting with unregistered or unlicensed entities which provide cryptoasset services.[135] EBA supplemented its Guideline No. 8 on correspondent relationships by way of adding CASPs such that CASPs are subject to the same due diligence standards as PSPs in a correspondent banking relationship.[136]

Furthermore, the provision on correspondent relationships[137] now explicitly mention CASPs. In the same way as credit institutions and other financial institutions, CASPs are prevented from entering into corresponding relationships with shell CASPs. Similarly, it is not permissible for

131 See Zetzsche *et al.*, 'DLT-Based Enhancement of Cross-Border Payment Efficiency – A Legal and Regulatory Perspective'. BIS Working Papers No. 1015. Website www.bis.org/publ/work1015.pdf (last accessed on 1 October 2024).

132 Article 19 AMLD = Article 36 AMLR.

133 Article 19b(1) of AMLD (as amended by TFR) = Article 36(b) AMLR requires CASPs, when entering into a business relationship with a correspondent entity, to: '(a) determine if the respondent entity is licensed or registered; (b) gather sufficient information about the respondent entity to understand fully the nature of the respondent's business and to determine from publicly available information the reputation of the entity and the quality of supervision; (c) assess the respondent entity's AML/CFT controls; (d) obtain approval from senior management before establishing new correspondent relationships; (e) document the respective responsibilities of each party to the correspondent relationship; (f) with respect to payable-through crypto-asset accounts, be satisfied that the respondent entity has verified the identity of, and performed ongoing due diligence on, the customers having direct access to accounts of the correspondent entity, and that it is able to provide relevant customer due diligence data to the correspondent entity, upon request. Where crypto-asset service providers decide to terminate correspondent relationships for reasons relating to anti-money laundering and counter-terrorist financing policy, they shall document and record their decision. Crypto-asset service providers shall update the due diligence information for the correspondent relationship on a regular basis or when new risks emerge in relation to the respondent entity'.

134 Recital para. 60 TFR (referring to Article 19a AMLD, as amended by TFR). The equivalent provision is Article 36(a) AMLR.

135 Recital para. 60 of TFR (referring to Article 19b(3) AMLD = Article 37(3) AMLR, now referring to AMLA).

136 AMLA guidelines to be issued until 10 July 2027 will replace EBA guidelines over time.

137 Article 19b AMLD = Articles 37 and 39(2) AMLR, referring to the definition of correspondent relationships in Article 3(8) AMLD = Article 2(1)(22) AMLR, including a reference to cryptoassets in lit. (b).

CASPs to enter into relationships with entities owned or influenced by a politically exposed person in the absence of qualified risk-mitigation measures.

14.4 AML/CTF CONTENT IN MICA

MiCA adds to the general framework provided by the TFR and AMLDs/AMLR in four respects.

14.4.1 *Reliability of Management and Shareholders*

First, with regard to issuers of ARTs and CASPs, MiCA mandates NCAs to consider the fitness and properness of members of the management bodies as well as the shareholders with qualifying holdings in the applicant issuer or CASP, respectively, not only with regard to concerns of importance from a financial service perspective, like expertise and honesty, but also with regard to overall reliability in terms of AML and CTF. MiCA requires the absence of criminal records or penalties in relation to AML and CTF, to fraud, or to professional liability.[138] These requirements expand the principles laid down in Article 47 AMLD = Articles 4 and 6 AMLD6.

14.4.2 *Cooperation of NCAs with AML Authorities*

Second, MiCA requires NCAs to cooperate with AML authorities prior to granting, refusing, or withdrawing an authorisation as well as the approval of an acquisition of a CASP,[139] in particular, to verify that the applicant CASP has not been the subject of an investigation into conduct relating to money laundering or terrorist financing.

14.4.3 *Ensuring Compliance with AML Law*

Third, in certain situations, the NCAs in charge of supervision under MiCA are in charge of ensuring compliance with the substantive AML/CTF provisions. The process of granting or refusing an authorisation as a CASP involves:

- ensuring that the applicant CASP that operates branches or relies on third parties established in high-risk third countries to comply with the provisions on customer due diligence performed by other obliged entities, branches, and subsidiaries in third countries and countries 'blacklisted' due to significant strategic deficiencies in their national AML/CTF regimes;[140] and
- ensuring that the applicant CASP has put in place appropriate procedures to comply with requirements on enhanced due diligence and other adequate countermeasures where the respective third country involved in the CASP business indicates high-risk.[141]

Both the factors to determine high-risk countries and the procedural requirements have been specified in EBA guidelines.[142]

[138] Cf. Article 18(5)(a) and (c) of MiCA (ARTs) and Article 62(3)(a) and (c) of MiCA (CASPs).

[139] Cf. Article 20(2) of MiCA (ARTs) and Articles 62(6), 64(6), and 83(5) of MiCA (CASPs).

[140] Articles 26(2), 45(3), and 45(5), and Article 9 AMLD = Articles 48(2), 17(1), and 17(2), and Article 29 AMLR.

[141] Article 18a(1) and (3) AMLD = Article 29(4)–(6) and Article 35 AMLR.

[142] EBA, 'Guidelines on Customer Due Diligence', s. 21.13 (referring to Title I of the EBA guidelines on non-EU countries).

14.4.4 *ESMA Reports*

Finally, Article 141 MiCA mandates the ESMA to report annually on market developments. This report must provide, inter alia, 'a mapping of the geographical location and level of know-your-customer and customer due diligence procedures of unauthorised exchanges providing services in crypto-assets to Union residents, including the number of exchanges without a clear domiciliation and the number of exchanges located in jurisdictions included in the list of high-risk third countries for the purposes of Union rules on anti-money laundering and counter-terrorist financing or in the list of non-cooperative jurisdictions for tax purposes, classified by the level of compliance with adequate know-your-customer procedures'.[143] The report must also include the proportion of transactions in cryptoassets made through a CASP and also unauthorised service providers or peer-to-peer arrangements, as well as the relevant transaction volume. This way, the ESMA shall provide sufficient data on which to base further political measures in the field of AML/CTF (on top of providing data on the effectiveness of MiCA, at large).

14.5 REMAINING CHALLENGES

As for the consistency and coherence of the AML/CTF framework, we note four challenges.

14.5.1 *Cross-Reference with MiCA's Scope*

The first challenge relates to the cross-reference in the AML/CTF framework, with MiCA's scope by way of the AMLD's reference to MiCA's definition of "cryptoassets".[144]

Noteworthy in this regard is that the regulatory objectives of MiCA's financial law approach and the AML/CTF framework as embedded in TFR and AMLD/AMLR may not coincide. For instance, MiCA's exclusion of NFTs may be warranted from a financial law perspective, given that EU consumer law ensures some minimum protection of token-holders, while systemic risk is largely absent given the uniqueness of the token.[145] At the same time, unique tokens like NFTs can be utilised to transfer funds from illicit activities into, and out of, the European Single Market. Once value is transferred from NFTs to conventional assets, the tracing of proceeds from a potential sale is increasingly difficult. In this context, we observe some tension with regard to MiCA's Recital 16 stating that 'any legislative act adopted in the field of crypto-assets should also contribute to the objective of combating money laundering and terrorist financing'.

14.5.2 *Cross-Reference with MiCA on CASPs*

We have noted the limitations of MiCA's CASP definition in Chapter 7. Three of them are noteworthy in this context.

First, supervisory authorities may find it difficult to subject fully decentralised applications to MiCA's Title V rules. While we argue that the absence of control shall be the determining feature when establishing whether an application is fully decentralised,[146] whether or not a supervisory authority may establish control strongly depends on the evidence and the authority's

[143] Article 141(i), (j) of MiCA.
[144] See Article 38 of TFR amending Article 3(18) of AMLD = Article 2(1) point 7 AMLR.
[145] We laid out MiCA's scope in detail in Chapters 3 and 4 and Section 14.5.1.
[146] Cf. Section 7.2.4.

capabilities. Second, the catalogue in Article 3(16) MiCA is limited. For instance, CASPs providing crypto-lending and crypto-staking are, in principle, outside of MiCA's scope, unless they qualify under one of the other regulated activities specified in MiCA (e.g., as an exchange or transfer service).[147] By and large, the AML/CTF framework addresses the foreseeable gaps related to the first and second limitations of MiCA by providing bespoke rules for self-hosted addresses and transaction technologies. While some services like crypto-lending may not qualify as anonymity-enhancing transaction or technology, we expect an expansion of MiCA in due course to fill this gap.[148]

Third, Title V MiCA's territorial scope is limited to CASPs residing in the European Single Market;[149] third-country service providers are excluded.[150] Where service providers in third countries hold cryptoassets on behalf of EU/EEA clients, the EU framework is ineffective. Recital 77 MiCA, stressing the need for EU-CASPs to assess the risk related to clients from third countries listed as high-risk (i.e., those with strategic deficiencies in their AML/CTF frameworks), is of little effect where EU clients transact with clients from these blacklisted third countries outside of the European Single Market.

With regard to the last limitation, financial law rationales would naturally demand protection of clients of EU/EEA entities only. Where the clients move outside of the protection of EU/EEA law, they bear the consequences alone. Thus, EU/EEA interests are largely unharmed. In contrast, EU clients' transactions with criminals outside the European Single Market harm the public interest of preventing crime, while international crime may prompt spill-over effects into the EU/EEA. Transactions outside of EU/EEA borders with funds gathered in the European Single Market further, albeit indirectly, these illicit activities.

14.5.3 *International Coordination*

More generally, involving third-country service providers in transactions is far from easy. This raises even more challenges given that most service providers reside a long way from the EU. At the heart of the difficulties is the varying density of regulation prevalent in many third countries. While EU law has moved ahead, in comparative terms, to specify different types of cryptoassets and related services, and then subjected them to regulation, some countries continue to apply securities and payments law to cryptoassets not only in regulatory terms, but also as a component part of their AML/CTF framework. Where the regulatory qualification differs, we may find the regulators specified by MiCA with bespoke competencies on one side of the supervisory system and regulators of a more general background and less focused on cryptoassets on the other side of the regulatory divide. The different scopes and competencies may result in difficulties when it comes to communicating, exchanging information, and agreeing on coordinated regulatory standards and actions.

14.6 CONCLUSION

After the adoption of TFR and the other three measures of the AML/CTF Action Plan, the AML/CTF law on cryptoassets now rests on three pillars: AMLD/AMLR, TFR, and MiCA. Its

[147] Cf. Section 7.2.3 and Recital para. 94 of MiCA.

[148] See the respective recommendations in Zetzsche *et al.*, 'Remaining Regulatory Challenges in Digital Finance', p. 52.

[149] See Article 59(2) of MiCA.

[150] Cf. Section 7.2.4.

focal points include a risk-based approach (AMLD/AMLR), a sensitive screening of permanent and individual relationships (AMLD/AMLR), a special view on information accompanying transfers (TFR), and the overall solidity and reliability of CASPs for AML/CTF purposes (MiCA).

Gaps stem from MiCA's substantial and regional scope, while Title V MiCA has some limits. The AML/CTF framework addresses the relevant risks through taking bespoke approaches on self-hosted addresses and transaction technologies. While many of the details regarding these issues in practice are delegated to EBA guidelines, it is safe to say that none of them work where persons and entities not qualifying as CASPs transact among themselves. In this regard, the EU AML/CTF framework does not provide a solution.

15

Cybersecurity and Digital Operational Resilience in Decentralised Finance

15.1 INTRODUCTION

Where there is money, there is a risk of theft, fraud, and other losses. Hence, when money goes digital, physical bank vaults must be replaced with analogous cybersecurity[1] measures. In fact, finance and insurance have been the most threatened of any industry in three of the last six years, with the highest frequency of such attacks worldwide being in Europe.[2] Each cyberattack in finance is more costly than that in almost any other industry.[3] Yet, there is hope: finance has now been overtaken by manufacturing as the most attacked industry, and the cost per attack is declining, most likely due to better cybersecurity.[4]

This observed improvement is partly driven by regulation, which has undergone unprecedented change in recent years. Cybersecurity is not new, of course, but as one type of operational risk in finance, it used to be covered only by general operational risk requirements along with sector-agnostic rules on data protection.[5] Now, we increasingly see comprehensive regulatory regimes addressing cybersecurity strategy and governance, competence and culture, incident reporting and recovery, threat intelligence sharing, cyber-resilience testing, and third-party dependencies.[6]

In this regard, at least three trends have caught regulators' attention.[7] First, experience shows that even the most advanced institutions cannot prevent all cyberattacks; a new "assume breach"

[1] The Financial Stability Board defines the term as 'preservation of *confidentiality*, *integrity* and *availability* of information and/or *information systems* through the *cyber* medium'. See Financial Stability Board, 'Cyber Lexicon' (2023). Website www.fsb.org/2023/04/cyber-lexicon-updated-in-2023/ (last accessed on 1 October 2024).

[2] IBM, 'X-Force Threat Intelligence Index' (2024), pp. 40, 47, 49. Website www.ibm.com/reports/threat-intelligence (last accessed on 1 October 2024); IBM, 'X-Force Threat Intelligence Index' (2023), pp. 42, 44. Website www.securityhq.com/reports/ibm-x-force-threat-intelligence-index-2023/ (last accessed on 1 October 2024).

[3] IBM, 'Cost of a Data Breach Report' (2023), p. 13.

[4] See IBM, 'X-Force Threat Intelligence Index' (2023), pp. 42, 44; IBM, 'Cost of a Data Breach Report', p. 13; Statista, 'Average Cost of a Data Breach Worldwide from May 2020 to March 2023, by Industry' (2023). Website www.statista.com/statistics/387861/cost-data-breach-by-industry/ (last accessed on 1 October 2024). Note that the cost per breach is in absolute terms, not adjusted for the high inflation observed during the period.

[5] See A. N. Didenko, 'Cybersecurity Regulation in the Financial Sector: Prospects of Legal Harmonization in the European Union and Beyond', *Uniform Law Review*, 25(1) (2020): 125, 127.

[6] See Financial Stability Institute, 'Banks' Cyber Security – A Second Generation of Regulatory Approaches', Bank for International Settlements (2023), pp. 11–24. For the EU, see Section 15.2. The challenge of a fragmented regulatory framework is also under evaluation in the US: see Congressional Research Service, 'Introduction to Financial Services: Financial Cybersecurity' (2023). Website https://crsreports.congress.gov/product/pdf/IF/IF11717 (last accessed on 1 October 2024).

[7] See Didenko, 'Cybersecurity Regulation in the Financial Sector', 125, 128–29.

attitude is required with an increased emphasis on identification, response, reporting, and learning.[8] Second, financial services are becoming increasingly digitalised, and that trend is likely to continue with technologies such as cloud computing and artificial intelligence. Finally, the technology and data used by different financial entities are increasingly complex and interconnected, both within the finance industry and with third parties, in particular, large cloud service providers like Amazon, Microsoft, and Google.[9] This increases the risk of contagion and provides new entry points for hackers – outside the scope of conventional financial regulation.[10]

These trends are particularly acute in DeFi, which typically entails a combination of a lack of institutional rigor and exceptionally digitalised and interconnected financial services. DLT addresses some aspects of cybersecurity, of course, yet even with contracted asset prices during the Crypto Winter, 2022 was still the worst year on record for crypto hacking with USD 3.8 billion worth of cryptoassets stolen.[11] It is also telling that several DeFi platforms have experienced the same types of attack, thus casting doubt on the industry's ability to learn.[12]

Meanwhile, regulatory initiatives seek to address cybersecurity in the financial sector as a whole. In the EU specifically, the new DORA has introduced new requirements to risk management, incident response, cyber-resilience testing, and supervision of third-party providers.[13] As a cybersecurity act for the entire financial sector, DORA makes direct references to MiCA and applies to MiCA-regulated entities. Yet, many of these new, technology-driven companies in finance (FinTechs) lack the institutional capacity to comply. Moreover, distributed financial networks blur the boundaries between internal and third-party technology, and it is not obvious, for instance, how threat-led penetration testing (TLPT) may be enforced in such networks consisting of perhaps thousands of participants worldwide. Constant innovation also

8 See Didenko, 'Cybersecurity Regulation in the Financial Sector', 125, 144–45.

9 See Financial Stability Institute, 'Banks' Cyber Security', p. 22; H. S. Scott, 'The EU's Digital Operational Resilience Act: Cloud Services & Financial Companies' (2021). Website www.pifsinternational.org/wp-content/uploads/2022/08/The-E.U.s-Digital-Operational-Act-Cloud-Services-Financial-Companies-08.06.2021.pdf (last accessed on 1 October 2024).

10 See Recital para. 79 of DORA, Regulation 2022/2554, OJ 2022 No. L333.

11 Chainalysis, '2022 Biggest Year Ever for Crypto Hacking with $3.8 Billion Stolen, Primarily from DeFi Protocols and by North Korea-linked Attackers' (2023). Website www.chainalysis.com/blog/2022-biggest-year-ever-for-crypto-hacking/ (last accessed on 1 October 2024). For examples and implications, see Zetzsche *et al.*, 'Remaining Regulatory Challenges in Digital Finance', pp. 33–41. Website http://dx.doi.org/10.2139/ssrn.4487516 (last accessed on 1 October 2024).

12 Zetzsche *et al.*, 'Remaining Regulatory Challenges in Digital Finance', p. 34.

13 Regulation (EU) 2022/2554 and Directive (EU) 2022/2556 of the European Parliament and of the Council of 14 December 2022 amending Directives 2009/65/EC, 2009/138/EC, 2011/61/EU, 2013/36/EU, 2014/59/EU, 2014/65/EU, (EU) 2015/2366, and (EU) 2016/2341 as regards digital operational resilience for the financial sector, OJ 2022 No. L333, 27 December 2022. In line with common usage, the term 'DORA' is used in the following both as a reference to the Regulation specifically and as a joint reference to the entire Act, that is both the Regulation and the Directive. On DORA, see A. Neumannova *et al.*, 'The Digital Operational Resilience Act for Financial Services: A Comparative Gap Analysis and Literature Review', in M. Papadaki *et al.* (eds.), *Information Systems* (Springer, 2023), pp. 570–85; D. Morgan, 'Coming to Terms with DORA', *Computer Fraud & Security*, 8 (2023); T. Ammann, I. Syed and V. Sanchez, 'Exploring Operational Resilience in Financial Services – The Effects of DORA on Risk and Regulation in Top 3 Financial Markets', *Computer Law Review International*, 24(2) (2023): 43; R. N. Thuama and S. S. Costigan, 'DORA – Understanding the New Regulatory Framework on Digital Operational Resilience' (2023). Website http://dx.doi.org/10.2139/ssrn.4549564 (last accessed on 1 October 2024); K. Avsuvarova, 'Navigating Digital Transformation: Unpacking the Impact of DORA on the Insurance Landscape' (2023). Website http://dx.doi.org/10.2139/ssrn.4549704 (last accessed on 1 October 2024); K. Parchimowicz, 'Do Not Get Lost in the Cloud. How EU Financial Institutions Could Avoid Legal and Practical Problems with Cloud Services Arising under DORA' (2023). Website http://dx.doi.org/10.2139/ssrn.4486264 (last accessed on 1 October 2024); Scott, 'The EU's Digital Operational Resilience Act'.

means that regulators can only hope to address such challenges before technology moves on and creates new ones.

These and other related issues are covered in this chapter, starting with DORA's objectives, approach, and links to MiCA (Section 15.2) and DORA's scope (Section 15.3), before tackling each of DORA's tools (Section 15.4) and analysing DeFi-specific matters (Section 15.5). Section 15.6 concludes.

15.2 DORA'S OBJECTIVES, APPROACH, AND LINKS TO MICA

15.2.1 *Background*

Bespoke cybersecurity regulation at the EU level has emerged over the past decade since the Cybersecurity Strategy of 2013, aiming 'to make the EU's online environment the safest in the world'.[14] Together with this strategy came a new directive on the security of network and information systems (NIS), setting minimum standards across a range of industries.[15] This sparked the still ongoing debate over possible overlaps with existing, sector-specific legislation, such as operational risk management requirements for the financial sector.

Following a massive increase in cyberattacks, a new proposal was launched in 2017,[16] accompanied by a new "Cybersecurity Act" to strengthen the mandate of the European Network and Information Security Agency (ENISA).[17] Simultaneously, cybersecurity provisions were also adopted as part of the GDPR.[18] Then, in 2018, the ECB issued a TLPT framework known as TIBER-EU, which may be applied voluntarily by any sector, but it is designed for the financial industry.[19] The framework is forming the basis of new, mandatory L2 legislation under DORA.[20]

[14] European Commission and High Representative of the European Union for Foreign Affairs and Security Policy, 'Cybersecurity Strategy of the European Union: An Open, Safe and Secure Cyberspace' (2013), p. 3. Website https://edps.europa.eu/data-protection/our-work/publications/opinions/cyber-security-strategy-european-union-open-safe-and_en (last accessed on 1 October 2024). On the current path of EU cybersecurity law, see P. G. Chiara, 'Towards a Right to Cybersecurity in EU Law? The Challenges Ahead' (2023). Website http://dx.doi.org/10.2139/ssrn.4537093 (last accessed on 1 October 2024).

[15] Directive (EU) 2016/1148 of the European Parliament and of the Council of 6 July 2016 concerning measures for a high common level of security of network and information systems across the Union, OJ 2016 No. L194, 19 July 2016, which is repealed with effect from 18 October 2024 and followed by the new Directive (EU) 2022/2555 of the European Parliament and of the Council of 14 December 2022 on measures for a high common level of cybersecurity across the Union, amending Regulation (EU) No. 910/2014 and Directive (EU) 2018/1972 and repealing Directive (EU) 2016/1148 (NIS 2 Directive), OJ 2022 No. L333, 27 December 2022.

[16] European Commission and High Representative of the European Union for Foreign Affairs and Security Policy, 'Resilience, Deterrence and Defence: Building Strong Cybersecurity for the EU', JOIN (2017) 450 Final.

[17] Regulation (EU) 2019/881 of the European Parliament and of the Council of 17 April 2019 on ENISA (the European Union Agency for Cybersecurity) and on information and communications technology cybersecurity certification and repealing Regulation (EU) No. 526/2013 (Cybersecurity Act), OJ 2019 No. L151, 7 June 2019.

[18] Regulation (EU) 2016/679 of the European Parliament and of the Council of 27 April 2016 on the protection of natural persons with regard to the processing of personal data and on the free movement of such data, and repealing Directive 95/46/EC (General Data Protection Regulation), OJ 2016 No. L119, 4 May 2016.

[19] European Central Bank, 'TIBER-EU Framework: How to Implement the European Framework for Threat Intelligence-Based Ethical Red Teaming' (2018). Website www.ecb.europa.eu/pub/pdf/other/ecb.tiber_eu_framework.en.pdf (last accessed on 1 October 2024).

[20] See Article 26(11) of DORA and Joint Committee of the ESAs, 'Final Report: Draft Regulatory Technical Standards Specifying Elements Related to Threat Led Penetration Tests under Article 26(11) of Regulation (EU) 2022/2554' (2024) JC 2024 29.

In addition to the above-mentioned cross-sectorial initiatives, at least eight different EU legislative frameworks cover cybersecurity specifically for the financial sector:[21] (1) operational risk requirements for credit institutions and investment firms;[22] (2) various risk management requirements for PSPs;[23] (3) oversight requirements adopted by the ECB for systematically important payment systems, retail payment systems, and financial market infrastructures;[24] (4) operational risk requirements for market infrastructures under EMIR;[25] (5) operational risk management requirements under the Solvency II Directive for insurance and reinsurance undertakings;[26] (6) requirements for credit rating agencies to have 'effective control and safeguard arrangements for information processing systems';[27] (7) various operational risk requirements for CSDs; [28] and (8) requirements under MiFID and MiFIR for parties engaged in the trading of regulated financial instruments, such as investment firms, trading venues, and data reporting service providers.[29]

[21] See Didenko, 'Cybersecurity Regulation in the Financial Sector', 125, 133–37; P. S. Krüger and J.-P. Brauchle, 'The European Union, Cybersecurity, and the Financial Sector: A Primer. Carnegie Endowment for International Peace', Cyber Policy Initiative Working Paper Series #9 (2021), pp. 7–19. Website https://carnegieendowment.org/2021/03/16/european-union-cybersecurity-and-financial-sector-primer-pub-84055 (last accessed on 1 October 2024).

[22] See Article 4(1)(52) of Regulation (EU) No. 575/2013, OJ 2013 No. L176; Article 85(1) and the pre-DORA version of the now amended Article 85(2) of Directive 2013/36/EU, OJ 2013 No. L176. See also the amendments to Directive 2013/36/EU in accordance with DORA, cf. Article 4 of Directive (EU) 2022/2556. In addition, banks directly supervised by the ECB are subject to cyber-event reporting requirements imposed by the European banking regulator. See European Central Bank, 'IT and Cyber Risk: The SSM Perspective' (2019). Website www.bankingsupervision.europa.eu/press/publications/newsletter/2019/html/ssm.nl190213_4.en.html (last accessed on 1 October 2024).

[23] See the pre-DORA versions of Articles 95 and 96 and regulatory standards under Article 98 of Directive (EU) 2015/2366 (PSD2), OJ 2015 No. L337, accompanied by various EBA guidelines. See also the amendments to PSD2 in accordance with DORA, cf. Article 7 of Directive (EU) 2022/2556.

[24] See Article 15 of Regulation (EU) No. 795/2014, OJ 2014 No. L217, which was later amended to also incorporate new international guidance in subpart V.1 (see Regulation (EU) 2017/2094, OJ 2017 No. L299); European Central Bank, 'Revised Oversight Framework for Retail Payment Systems'. Website www.ecb.europa.eu/pub/pdf/other/Revised_oversight_framework_for_retail_payment_systems.pdf (last accessed on 1 October 2024); European Central Bank, 'Cyber Resilience Oversight Expectations for Financial Market Infrastructures (CROE)' (2018). Website www.ecb.europa.eu/paym/pdf/cons/cyberresilience/Cyber_resilience_oversight_expectations_for_financial_market_infrastructures.pdf (last accessed on 1 October 2024).

[25] See Article 79 of Regulation (EU) No. 648/2012, OJ 2012 No. L201, with more detailed requirements to IT systems in supplementary regulatory technical standards under Commission Delegated Regulation (EU) No. 153/2013, OJ 2013 No. L52.

[26] See Articles 44(2)(e) and 107 of Directive 2009/138/EC, OJ 2009 No. L335. This is further clarified in Guideline 21 (Operational Risk Management Policy) in EIOPA, 'Guidelines on System of Governance, EIOPA-BoS-14/253 EN' (2014). Website www.eiopa.europa.eu/publications/guidelines-system-governance_en (last accessed on 1 October 2024). See also Articles 41(4) and 50(1)(a) and (b) of Directive 2009/138/EC, which are now amended in accordance with DORA, cf. Article 2 of Directive (EU) 2022/2556.

[27] See Annex I, s. 4 of Regulation (EC) No. 1060/2009 of the European Parliament and of the Council of 16 September 2009 on credit rating agencies, OJ 2009 No. L302, 17 November 2009. See also the amending instrument Regulation (EU) No. 462/2013 of the European Parliament and of the Council of 21 May 2013 amending Regulation (EC) No. 1060/2009 on credit rating agencies, OJ 2013 No. L146, 31 May 2013; Commission Delegated Regulation (EU) No. 449/2012 of 21 March 2012 supplementing Regulation (EC) No. 1060/2009 of the European Parliament and of the Council with regard to regulatory technical standards on information for registration and certification of credit rating agencies, OJ 2012 No. L140, 30 May 2012.

[28] See Articles 45 and 47 of Regulation (EU) No. 909/2014, OJ 2014 No. L257. See also Article 4 of Commission Delegated Regulation (EU) 2017/390, OJ 2017 No. L65.

[29] See the pre-DORA version of the now amended Articles 16(5), 17(1), and 48(1) along with Articles 64(4), 65(5), and 66(3) of Directive 2014/65/EU, OJ 2014 No. L173 with supplementing regulatory technical standards in Article 18(4) of Commission Delegated Regulation (EU) 2017/589, OJ 2017 No. L87 and Article 23 of Regulation (EU) 2017/584, OJ 2017 No. L87; Article 26(7) of Regulation (EU) No. 600/2014, OJ 2014 No. L173. See also the amendments to Directive 2014/65/EU in accordance with DORA, cf. Article 6 of Directive (EU) 2022/2556.

This fragmented regulatory framework formed the backdrop to the European Commission's 2018 FinTech Action Plan, which called for a more cyber-resilient financial sector and paved the way for the adoption of DORA in 2022.[30] In conjunction with DORA, the new cross-industry NIS2 and CER Directives were also adopted.[31]

15.2.2 *Objectives and Regulatory Approach*

DORA aims to 'consolidate and upgrade ICT risk requirements as part of the operational risk requirements that have, up to this point, been addressed separately in various Union legal acts'.[32] Hence, it constitutes a comprehensive framework for digital operational resilience in Europe's financial sector, addressing gaps and overlaps in existing EU law.[33] In turn, this enhances confidence in the financial system, preserves its stability, and minimises the impact and costs of ICT disruptions.[34] DORA is aimed to increase the cybersecurity baseline for all financial entities while also allowing for a proportionate application of the requirements.[35]

Emanating from the EU's Digital Finance Package, DORA seeks to balance risk and innovation in a rapidly moving field.[36] One aspect of this is DORA's "assume breach" attitude, which expands the focus from mere prevention to identification, response, reporting, and learning. In addition, reflecting rapid technological innovation, DORA seeks to address cybersecurity strategy and governance, including resilience testing and third-party risk management, rather than setting specific technical standards.[37] To the extent that it still regulates ICT systems, protocols, and tools, DORA demands that these be "appropriate", "reliable", "sufficient", or applies similar regulatory standards.[38]

DORA also marks a step towards increased harmonisation of EU financial law to promote deeper integration of the European Single Market.[39] To that end, and similar to the two other main legislative acts under the FinTech Action Plan, namely, MiCA and PilotR, DORA's main part is embedded by way of a regulation, as opposed to a directive. In turn, it aims to reduce regulatory complexity, foster supervisory convergence, and increase legal certainty – thus reducing compliance costs and competitive distortions.[40]

30 European Commission, 'FinTech Action Plan', at 2–3; Recital para. 6 of DORA.

31 Directive (EU) 2022/2555 (NIS2) came into force in 2023, and the original NIS Directive (EU) 2016/1148 is repealed with effect from 18 October 2024. While NIS2 has a focus on cybersecurity, Directive (EU) 2022/2557 of the European Parliament and of the Council of 14 December 2022 on the resilience of critical entities (CER) and repealing Council Directive 2008/114/EC, OJ 2022 No. L333, aims to create an overarching framework addressing the resilience of critical entities in respect of all hazards. Consequently, DORA constitutes *lex specialis* with regard to these directives: see Recital para. 16 of DORA.

32 See Recital para. 12 of DORA.

33 See Recital para. 10 of DORA.

34 See Recital para. 13 of DORA.

35 See Recital para. 21 of DORA.

36 See European Commission, Proposal for a Regulation of the European Parliament and of the Council on Digital Operational Resilience for the Financial Sector and Amending Regulations (EC) No. 1060/2009, (EU) No. 648/2012, (EU) No. 600/2014, and (EU) No. 909/2014, COM (2020) 595 final, at 0.

37 This is in line with global regulatory trends. See Financial Stability Institute, 'Banks' Cyber Security', pp. 14–16; Didenko, 'Cybersecurity Regulation in the Financial Sector', 125, 139–40.

38 See, for instance, Article 7 of DORA.

39 See Recital paras. 9–11 of DORA.

40 See Recital para. 14 of DORA.

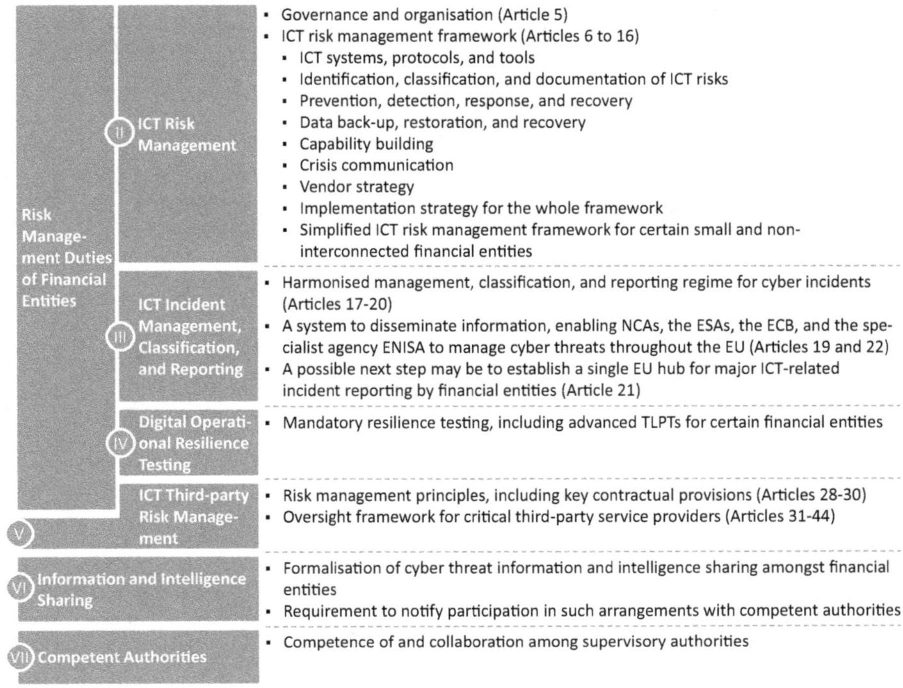

FIGURE 15.1 Overview of tools by DORA chapters.

15.2.3 *Overview of Tools*

DORA formally consists of a regulation and a directive, where the regulation contains a new set of rules, while the directive amends several other EU directives in support of the new regulatory framework.[41] The regulation puts risk management duties on financial entities, including their contractual arrangements with ICT third-party service providers. Notably, DORA also to some extent applies directly to such service providers through a bespoke oversight framework (Figure 15.1).

15.2.4 *Links between MiCA and DORA*

DORA's scope is to some extent linked to MiCA. This is made explicit for CASPs authorised under MiCA (cf. Chapter 7) and ART issuers (cf. Chapter 6), which are specifically listed as entities in the scope of DORA.[42] Competent authorities designated for these entities under MiCA are also responsible for supervision under DORA.[43] Implicitly, we also expect MiCA to be influential in determining DORA's scope with respect to ICT third-party service providers in cryptoasset schemes. Given DORA's substantial regulation of the use of such providers, it becomes paramount to identify which parts of an interconnected DeFi network qualify as ICT third-party service providers for each regulated entity under DORA. In this regard, MiCA's distinction between partly and fully decentralised services (see Section 4.2.4) may, for instance, provide some guidance.

Conversely, MiCA's rules on governance arrangements for ART issuers and CASPs make reference to DORA. In particular, ART issuers must have 'effective control and safeguard

[41] Regulation (EU) 2022/2554 and Directive (EU) 2022/2556.
[42] Article 2(1)(f), cf. Article 3(55) and (56) of DORA.
[43] Article 46(d) of DORA.

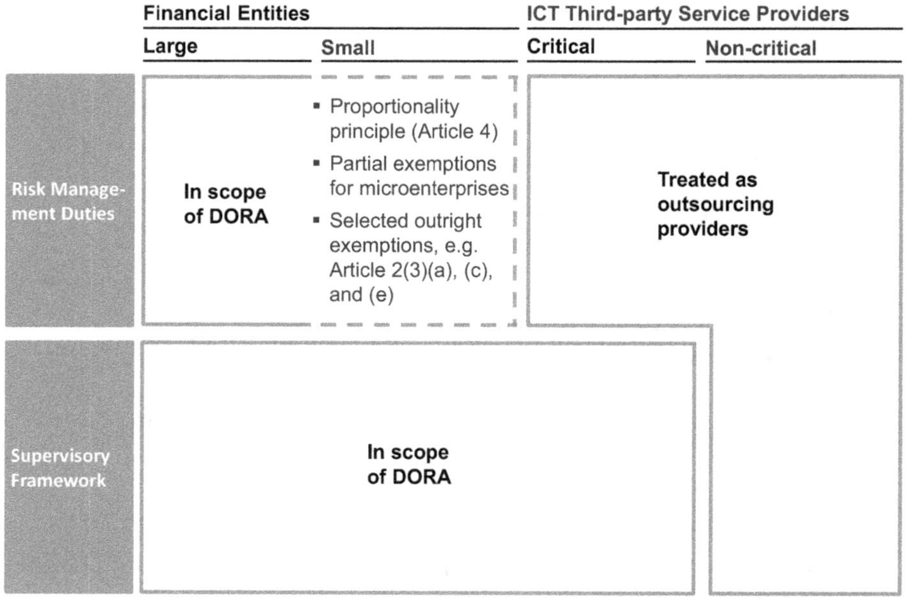

FIGURE 15.2 Scope of DORA.

arrangements for managing ICT systems as required by [DORA]' as well as 'systems and procedures ... that are adequate to safeguard the availability, authenticity, integrity and confidentiality of data as required by [DORA]'.[44] CASPs, meanwhile, must have "resilient and secure ICT systems", "ICT business continuity plans", "ICT response and recovery plans", "mechanisms, systems, and procedures", and specifically "systems and procedures to safeguard the availability, authenticity, integrity and confidentiality of data", all as required by DORA.[45]

15.3 DORA'S SCOPE

DORA applies to the financial entities listed in its Article 2(1)(a)–(t), and it extends to critical ICT third-party service providers through a bespoke supervisory framework. Otherwise, ICT third-party service providers are treated as outsourcing providers and, thus, impacted only indirectly by DORA, while both risk management duties and supervision apply directly to financial entities only. No general size limits apply, but small financial entities face a somewhat more lenient regime through partial and/or selected exemptions, along with a general proportionality principle (see Figure 15.2).

15.3.1 *Financial Entities*

DORA applies to an exhaustive list of twenty-three types of "financial entities".[46] These include ART issuers, credit institutions, and e-money institutions, thereby covering all entities that are

[44] Article 34(10) and (11) of MiCA, Regulation 2023/1114, OJ 2023 No. L150. Infringements against these requirements are also listed under Annex V of MiCA, thus enabling EBA to take measures against significant ART issuers. See Article 130(1) of MiCA and Section 11.3.5.

[45] Article 68(7) and (8) of MiCA.

[46] Article 2(2), cf. Article 2(1)(a)–(t) of DORA. This list will be expanded to twenty-four types with the new Financial Data Access Regulation (FIDA). See European Commission, 'Proposal for a Regulation of the European Parliament and of the Council on a Framework for Financial Data Access and Amending Regulations (EU) No. 1093/2010, (EU) No. 1094/2010, (EU) No. 1095/2010, and (EU) 2022/2554' (2023) COM/2023/360 final, at Article 35 and Recital 32.

entitled to issue ARTs or EMTs under MiCA (see Chapter 6), along with MiCA-authorised CASPs. The list of financial entities in scope is accompanied by eight sub-sets of entities that are exempted, and Member States are entitled to extend the exemptions within their respective territories.[47] The lists of both entities included and excluded from DORA's scope make reference to definitions under other EU financial law, thus transposing into DORA the challenge of applying existing legislation to new realities such as DeFi. We address this issue in Section 15.5.2.

15.3.2 *ICT Third-Party Service Providers*

Beyond "financial entities", DORA also applies to "ICT third-party service providers" defined as an 'undertaking providing ICT services' where such services are defined as 'digital and data services provided through ICT systems to one or more internal or external users on an ongoing basis, including hardware as a service and hardware services which includes the provision of technical support via software or firmware updates by the hardware provider, excluding traditional analogue telephone services'.[48]

DORA's application to such service providers is an overstatement, however, as risk management obligations under DORA apply to financial entities only, who are responsible for the compliance of their service providers. By whom the service is provided matters less in this regard: DORA distinguishes between third-party and intra-group ICT service providers,[49] but the regulated financial entity nevertheless remains responsible for the services.[50]

The only aspect in which DORA applies directly to ICT third-party service providers is the direct oversight framework for such providers that are designated as "critical".[51] This results in an exhaustive list of designated service providers, thus resolving the issue of determining DORA's scope with regard to such providers.

Beyond the oversight framework for critical ICT third-party service providers,[52] DORA treats ICT third-party service providers merely as a term used to establish the rights and obligations of financial entities in their interaction with such service providers. The ramifications are substantial, however, given the broad definition of ICT services.[53] In turn, DORA covers 'a wide range of ICT third-party service providers, including providers of cloud computing services, software, data analytics services and providers of data centre services'.[54] This has profound implications for DeFi: once a participant in a network qualifies as a "financial entity" under DORA, then most or all other parts of the network may qualify as its ICT third-party service providers.

15.3.3 *Geographic Scope*

DORA's defined list of the "financial entities" to which it applies also outlines its geographical scope, as the list of "financial entities" typically refers to other EU financial law with their

47 Article 2(3) and (4) of DORA.
48 Article 2(1)(u), cf. Article 3(19) and (21) of DORA. See also the European Supervisory Authorities, 'Report on the Landscape of ICT Third-Party Service Providers in the EU', ESA 2023 22 (2023).
49 Article 3(19) and (20) of DORA. Intra-group service providers cannot be designated as 'critical'; see Article 31(8)(iii) of DORA.
50 See Articles 6(10), 19(5), and 28(1)(a) of DORA.
51 See Section II of Chapter V of DORA. See also Section 15.4.2.
52 Section II of Chapter V of DORA.
53 See Recital para. 35 of DORA.
54 Recital para. 63 of DORA.

respective scope provisions. When DORA applies to CASPs authorised under MiCA, for instance, this limits DORA's application to CASPs within the scope of MiCA so, essentially, those providers of cryptoasset services (cf. Article 3(16) MiCA) who market their services in the EU.[55] Similarly, when DORA applies to AIFMs, it means those who 'manage and/or market alternative investment funds (AIFs) in the Union' as defined by the scope of AIFMD.[56] By transposing the geographical scope of other EU financial law, DORA typically applies to financial entities that either operate within the EU or market their services to EU citizens.

DORA's application to ICT service providers is wider in two respects. First, once a participant in a DeFi network qualifies as a "financial entity" in scope, then DORA regulates how it must manage its relationships with ICT service providers irrespective of the service provider's own jurisdiction. Second, DORA's direct application to "critical ICT third-party service providers" also has a global reach, as a response to the fact that many such service providers reside outside of the EU.[57] Technically, this is achieved by means of Article 31(12) of DORA, which mandates financial entities to use only those critical ICT third-party service providers who establish a subsidiary in the Union. Beyond effectively regulating all critical third-country service providers, one can speculate that DORA here also aims to support European financial entities in negotiating better terms on cybersecurity in their relationships with American "Big Tech".[58]

In sum, this means that if one or more participants in a DeFi network qualify as a "financial entity", typically by operating or marketing financial services in the EU, then these entities must follow the rules of DORA, including the provisions on third-party risk management – irrespective of where the service providers are located. In this way, indirectly, most or all of a global DeFi network may fall within the scope of DORA.

15.3.4 *Size Limits and Proportionality*

DORA's wide scope reflects the interconnectedness across financial entities and towards their service providers, meaning that even a threat to smaller entities could impact the system as a whole. Hence, instead of exempting smaller entities outright, Article 4 of DORA institutes a broad proportionality principle for the application of DORA,[59] which is in line with the regulatory approach taken on cybersecurity elsewhere.[60]

This is important for many participants in DeFi networks, given that DORA applies to individual financial entities and not to the larger network as such, while the interconnectedness of DeFi must be taken into account when practicing the principle of proportionality in this respect. The simplified ICT risk management framework in Article 16 of DORA applies, for instance, to "small and non-interconnected investment firms", thus rendering investment firms that are interconnected with a larger DeFi network to apply the more comprehensive ICT risk management framework in Articles 5–15 of DORA.

[55] See Article 2(1)(f) of DORA, cf. Article 59(1)(a) of MiCA. See also Chapter 7.

[56] See Article 2(1)(k), cf. Article 3(44) of DORA; Article 4(1)(b), cf. Article 1 of AIFMD, Directive 2011/61, OJ 2011 No. L174.

[57] This is particularly true for cloud services, which are specifically targeted under DORA's new oversight framework. See Recital para. 20 of DORA.

[58] See Recital paras. 28 and 30 of DORA.

[59] That is, Chapters II–IV and Section I of Title V of DORA. For ICT third-party service providers, an even stronger proportionality principle applies by the very fact that DORA applies only to those service providers that are designated as 'significant' according to its Article 31.

[60] See Financial Stability Institute, 'Banks' Cyber Security', p. 27.

The proportionality principle must also be interpreted in light of the dispersed delivery of financial services in DeFi schemes. In fact, DORA recognises that outsourcing enables small financial entities to deliver resilient, digital financial services, hence DORA's emphasis on ICT third-party service providers. Yet, this requires even small financial entities to take care in selecting qualified and compliant service providers, suggesting strict enforcement of DORA in this regard. By implication, small financial entities operating within a DeFi network cannot escape responsibility for the services offered by other parts of the network simply by reference to the proportionality principle.[61]

For the smallest financial entities, DORA applies broader exemptions. Microenterprises, for instance, defined as most financial entities with fewer than ten employees and annual turnover and/or a balance sheet below EUR 2 million,[62] are fully or partly exempt from many of DORA's provisions. They may also rely on independent third parties to inspect and audit their ICT third-party service providers, presumably so that one independent auditor can represent many micro-enterprises vis-à-vis each ICT third-party service provider.[63] Some types of small financial entities are even exempt from DORA altogether.[64] There are few such exemptions, however, and they typically apply to specific types of financial entities rarely seen in DeFi schemes. Hence, in most cases, DORA applies unabridged to financial entities in DeFi networks and, by extension, also to their ICT third-party service providers throughout the network.

15.4 DORA'S TOOLS

15.4.1 *Risk Management Duties of Financial Entities*

15.4.1.1 ICT Risk Management

Chapter II of DORA is aimed at prevention through sound management of ICT risk. This focus on organisational matters is a feature DORA shares with other cybersecurity laws,[65] and it certainly suits DeFi better than the alternative of rigid rules on cybersecurity measures, which would leave little room for innovation. Yet, legal enforcement of hierarchical governance and organisation principles may still pose a challenge to an industry that prides itself on decentralisation.

The "management body" of each financial entity is ultimately responsible for ICT risk management under DORA.[66] The term refers to definitions in other EU financial law, and when identifying the "management body" in DeFi, it is important to note DORA's reference to 'the relevant provision of the Regulation on markets in crypto-assets'.[67] For CASPs and ART issuers under MiCA, one of the requirements for authorisation is to report the identity of their management body members and to notify the competent authority of any changes.[68] EMT issuers under MiCA must be either a credit or an e-money institution,[69] to which similar

[61] See J. Woxholth and D. A. Zetzsche, 'DORA on DeFi' (2024) pp. 16–17, 25. Website http://dx.doi.org/10.2139/ssrn.4874057 (last accessed on 1 October 2024).
[62] Article 3(60) of DORA.
[63] See the last paragraph of Article 30(3) of DORA.
[64] See, for instance, Article 2(3)(a), (c), and (e) of DORA.
[65] See Financial Stability Institute, 'Banks' Cyber Security', pp. 15–16; Didenko, 'Cybersecurity Regulation in the Financial Sector', 125, 139–40.
[66] See Article 5 and Recital paras. 45–47 of DORA.
[67] Article 5(2), cf. Article 3(30) of DORA.
[68] See Articles 18(2)(h), 33, 62(2)(g), 62(3)(a) and (b), and 69 of MiCA.
[69] See Chapter 6.

requirements apply.[70] The same typically applies if participants in DeFi schemes qualify as other types of financial entities under DORA. Otherwise, DORA defines their management body by the catch-all 'equivalent persons who effectively run the entity or have key functions in accordance with relevant Union or national law'.[71] This means, in practice, that whenever there is a financial entity under DORA (see Section 15.3.1), there will be a responsible management body.

The remainder of Chapter II of DORA concerns the "ICT risk management framework",[72] which is outlined in Article 6 and detailed in Articles 7–15. Under this framework, financial entities other than microenterprises must assign an independent control function responsible for ICT risk, document and review its ICT risk management framework at least annually, and subject it to regular internal audits.[73] The framework must also entail an implementation strategy encompassing at least the activities outlined in Article 6(8) of DORA.

The content of the ICT risk management framework must address: ICT systems, protocols, and tools (Article 7 of DORA); identification, classification, and documentation of 'all ICT supported business functions, roles and responsibilities, the information assets and ICT assets supporting those functions, and their roles and dependencies in relation to ICT risk' (Article 8); protection against and prevention of ICT risk (Article 9); detection of anomalous activities and potential material single points of failure (Article 10); ICT incident response and recovery as part of their overall business continuity policy (Article 11), including back-up and recovery procedures (Article 12); methods for learning and continuous improvement (Article 13); and crisis communication and disclosure plans (Article 14).

A feature of all of these requirements for the ICT risk management framework is their widespread use of general, intentionally vague, standards. The framework as such must be "sound, comprehensive and well-documented"[74] for instance, and similar standards apply to each of its components outlined in Articles 7–14 of DORA. This is a necessary component of the legal requirements in a fast-moving field such as cybersecurity, and the implied ambiguity is sought mitigated through regulatory technical standards.[75]

Small and non-interconnected investment firms, along with some other financial entities, are exempt from the above-mentioned requirements and may instead implement a "simplified" ICT risk management framework pursuant to Article 16 of DORA.[76] Yet, the vast majority of DeFi entities are too interconnected to qualify for this exemption.

[70] See Article 13(1) of Directive 2013/36/EU; Article 3(1) of Directive 2009/110/EC, OJ 2009 No. L267, cf. Article 5(i) of Directive 2007/64/EC, OJ 2007 No. L319.

[71] Article 3(30) of DORA.

[72] This is in line with cybersecurity laws elsewhere, even if they may use terms like 'strategy', 'policy', or 'programme' instead of 'framework'. See Financial Stability Institute, 'Banks' Cyber Security', pp. 14–15.

[73] Article 6(4)–(6) of DORA.

[74] Article 6(1) of DORA.

[75] Article 15 of DORA; Commission Delegated Regulation (EU) 2024/1774 of 13 March 2024 supplementing Regulation (EU) 2022/2554 of the European Parliament and of the Council with regard to regulatory technical standards specifying ICT risk management tools, methods, processes, and policies and the simplified ICT risk management framework, OJ L, 2024/1774, 25 June 2024.

[76] See also Title III of Commission Delegated Regulation (EU) 2024/1774 of 13 March 2024 supplementing Regulation (EU) 2022/2554 of the European Parliament and of the Council with regard to regulatory technical standards specifying ICT risk management tools, methods, processes, and policies and the simplified ICT risk management framework, OJ L, 2024/1774, 25 June 2024.

15.4.1.2 *ICT Incident Management, Classification, and Reporting*

The processes of managing, classifying, and reporting cyber threats and incidents are increasingly becoming part of cybersecurity legislation,[77] as seen in Chapter III of DORA, according to which financial entities must 'define, establish and implement an ICT-related incident management process to detect, manage and notify ICT-related incidents'.[78] Financial entities shall also 'record all ICT-related incidents and significant cyber threats' and 'establish appropriate procedures and processes to ensure a consistent and integrated monitoring, handling and follow-up of ICT-related incidents, to ensure that root causes are identified, documented and addressed'.[79]

To support both internal risk management processes and external reporting, ICT-related incidents and cyber threats shall be classified in accordance with the criteria laid out in Article 18 of DORA and specified in regulatory technical standards.[80] In turn, financial entities must report "major ICT-related incidents" to their competent authority and may also voluntarily report "significant cyber threats".[81] The competent authority shall acknowledge receipt of such reports and may provide feedback or high-level guidance.[82] Financial entities may also need to inform their clients about the threat or incident.[83] DORA then stipulates a process for disseminating this information to the relevant authorities that may take action to protect the immediate stability of the European financial system.[84] To instil long-term learning, the ESAs must also report annually on major ICT-related incidents.[85]

The content and format of the reporting will be further detailed in the regulatory technical standards,[86] and the ESAs 'shall prepare a joint report for assessing the feasibility of further centralisation of incident reporting through the establishment of a single EU Hub for major ICT-related incident reporting by financial entities'.[87]

Finally, Chapter III of DORA goes beyond DORA's core scope of cybersecurity in one respect as it also applies to certain *non-cyber*, payment-related operational, or security incidents.[88] This may be relevant to EMT issuers, for instance, and other entities involved in payment transactions.

15.4.1.3 *Digital Operational Resilience Testing*

Article 24 of DORA requires financial entities other than microenterprises to establish a testing programme as part of their ICT risk management framework and to conduct appropriate tests at least annually on all ICT systems and applications that support critical or important

[77] See Financial Stability Institute, 'Banks' Cyber Security', pp. 16–18.

[78] Article 17(1) of DORA.

[79] Article 17(2) of DORA.

[80] Commission Delegated Regulation (EU) 2024/1772 of 13 March 2024 supplementing Regulation (EU) 2022/2554 of the European Parliament and of the Council with regard to regulatory technical standards specifying the criteria for the classification of ICT-related incidents and cyber threats, setting out materiality thresholds and specifying the details of reports of major incidents, OJ L, 2024/1772, 25 June 2024.

[81] Article 19(1), (2), and (4) of DORA.

[82] Article 22(1) of DORA.

[83] Article 19(3) of DORA.

[84] Article 19(6)–(8) of DORA.

[85] Article 22(2) of DORA.

[86] Article 20 of DORA and Joint Committee of the ESAs, 'Final Report: Draft Regulatory Technical Standards on the Content of the Notification and Reports for Major Incidents and Significant Cyber Threats and Determining the Time Limits for Reporting Major Incidents and Draft Implementing Technical Standards on the Standard Forms, Templates and Procedures for Financial Entities to Report a Major Incident and to Notify a Significant Cyber Threat' (2024), JC 2024 33.

[87] Article 21 of DORA.

[88] Article 23 of DORA.

functions.[89] The tests must be undertaken by independent parties, whether internal or external, and be followed up by procedures and policies to prioritise, classify, and remedy all identified issues.

The types of testing entailed in the programme must be proportionate to the risk profile of the financial entity.[90] Special test requirements apply to CSDs and central counterparties, while a simplified test regime applies to microenterprises.[91]

More advanced testing requirements are outlined in Article 26 of DORA, which specifies the type of test to be conducted. Essentially, most financial entities must conduct TLPT at least every three years,[92] which is considered 'the most advanced tool for cyber resilience testing'.[93] The testing scope is wide and must cover 'all relevant underlying ICT systems, processes and technologies supporting critical or important functions and ICT services, including those supporting the critical or important functions which have been outsourced or contracted to ICT third-party service providers'.[94] Given the interconnectedness of DeFi, large parts of the DeFi network may have to participate in such tests to fulfil the legal requirements and yield meaningful outcomes. This is certainly a demanding exercise in a decentralised ecosystem.

15.4.1.4 *ICT Third-Party Risk Management*

Chapter V, Section I of DORA on the management of ICT third-party risk has profound implications for DeFi because other participants in the DeFi network may qualify as ICT third-party service providers to a regulated financial entity. The implications of non-compliance are also substantial, given that the regulated financial entity remains fully responsible for the compliance of its third-party service providers.[95]

Financial entities other than microenterprises must adopt an ICT third-party risk strategy as part of their ICT risk management framework,[96] and they must maintain a register of all ICT third-party service arrangements for reporting to the competent authority.[97] These requirements will be further specified in the regulatory technical standards.[98]

[89] This is largely in line with cybersecurity legislation elsewhere although the details vary substantially. See Financial Stability Institute, 'Banks' Cyber Security', pp. 18–19.

[90] Article 25(1) of DORA.

[91] Article 25(2) and (3) of DORA.

[92] On exempted entities, see Article 26(1), cf. Article 16(1) of DORA. The TLPT requirements will be further detailed in regulatory technical standards. See Article 26(11) of DORA and Joint Committee of the ESAs, 'Final Report: Draft Regulatory Technical Standards Specifying Elements Related to Threat Led Penetration Tests under Article 26(11) of Regulation (EU) 2022/2554' (2024) JC 2024 29.

[93] Joint Committee of the European Supervisory Authorities, 'Joint Advice of the European Supervisory Authorities', JC 2019 25 (2019), p. 10. Website www.esma.europa.eu/sites/default/files/library/jc_2019_25_joint_esas_advice_on_a_coherent_cyber_resilience_testing_framework.pdf (last accessed on 1 October 2024). See also Didenko, 'Cybersecurity Regulation in the Financial Sector', 125, 160–62.

[94] Article 26(2) of DORA.

[95] See Article 28(1)(a) of DORA. See also Articles 6(10) and 19(5) of DORA.

[96] Article 28(2), cf. Article 6(9) of DORA. See Commission Delegated Regulation (EU) 2024/1773 of 13 March 2024 supplementing Regulation (EU) 2022/2554 of the European Parliament and of the Council with regard to regulatory technical standards specifying the detailed content of the policy regarding contractual arrangements on the use of ICT services supporting critical or important functions provided by ICT third-party service providers, OJ L, 2024/1773, 25 June 2024.

[97] Article 28(3) of DORA.

[98] Article 28(9) and (10) of DORA and Joint Committee of the ESAs, 'Final Report on Draft Implementing Technical Standards on the Standard Templates for the Purposes of the Register of Information in Relation to All Contractual Arrangements on the Use of ICT Services Provided by ICT Third-Party Service Providers under Article 28(9) of Regulation (EU) 2022/2554' (2023), JC 2023 85; Joint Committee of the ESAs, 'Register Information Templates Illustration' (2024). Website www.esma.europa.eu/document/register-information-templates-illustration (last accessed on 1 October 2024).

Of particular importance in DeFi settings, given the widespread use of third-party services, are the regulatory requirements when entering into or terminating a "contractual arrangement" with an "ICT third-party service provider".[99] In such instances, DORA may require the financial entity to inform the competent authority *in advance*, make a variety of assessments, including of possible or actual chains of sub-contractors, undertake a due diligence on prospective ICT third-party service providers, ensure that the provider follows appropriate information security standards, pre-determine the type and frequency of audits and inspections, and facilitate termination of and exit from the contractual arrangement.[100]

Article 30 of DORA further regulates the contractual provisions between financial entities and their ICT third-party service providers. This entails, for instance, that '[t]he rights and obligations of the financial entity and of the ICT third-party service provider shall be clearly allocated and set out in writing ... and be documented in one written document'.[101] This does not preclude the use of smart contracts, in our view, but requires them to be replicated in plain natural language. They must also meet the detailed content requirements in Article 30(2) of DORA, including the location of operations and data processing, along with access, recovery, and return of data. For "ICT services supporting critical or important functions", contractual provisions must also cover full service-level descriptions, notice periods, reporting obligations, contingency plans, ICT security, testing regimes, continuous monitoring, and exit strategies.[102]

15.4.2 *Direct Supervision of Significant ICT Third-Party Service Providers*

Chapter V of DORA has received much attention for its innovative Section II,[103] which ensures direct supervision of critical ICT third-party service providers.[104] Yet, DORA contains no operational requirements applicable directly to ICT third-party service providers, so the financial entity is responsible for compliance.[105] Hence, the direct application of DORA to ICT third-party service providers relates to supervision only.

Subject to this direct oversight framework are ICT third-party service providers that are designated as "critical".[106] Such designation does not alter the operational requirements applicable to financial entities under DORA but merely acts as an entry gate for the service provider to DORA's direct supervision framework. For non-critical ICT third-party service providers, in contrast, only the financial entity is supervised under DORA so that DORA relies on the financial entity to enforce its operational obligations vis-à-vis its service providers. For critical

[99] See Woxholth and Zetzsche, 'DORA on DeFi', 24, 25–28.

[100] Article 28(3)–(8), cf. Article 29 of DORA.

[101] Article 30(1) of DORA.

[102] Article 30(3) of DORA. See also Joint Committee of the ESAs, 'Final Report on Draft Regulatory Technical Standards to Specify the Elements which a Financial Entity Needs to Determine and Assess When Subcontracting ICT Services Supporting Critical or Important Functions as Mandated by Article 30(5) of Regulation (EU) 2022/2554' (2024), JC 2024 53.

[103] See, for instance, Financial Stability Institute, 'Banks' Cyber Security', p. 21.

[104] Article 39 of DORA uses the terms 'ICT third-party service provider' and 'critical ICT third-party service provider' interchangeably, thereby possibly applying also to non-critical service providers. The context suggests, however, that the Article still applies to critical service providers only.

[105] One exception may be Article 30(4) of DORA, by which 'financial entities and ICT third-party service providers shall consider the use of standard contractual clauses developed by public authorities for specific services', thereby assigning this duty also to the service provider and not only to the financial entity.

[106] See Article 31 of DORA and Commission Delegated Regulation (EU) 2024/1502 of 22 February 2024 supplementing Regulation (EU) 2022/2554 of the European Parliament and of the Council by specifying the criteria for the designation of ICT third-party service providers as critical for financial entities, OJ L, 2024/1502, 30 May 2024.

ICT third-party service providers, however, DORA acknowledges the fact that (small) financial entities often struggle to negotiate and enforce contracts vis-à-vis large service providers, such as American "Big Tech". Direct supervision at the EU level also seeks to mitigate 'the insufficiency of national mechanisms in providing financial supervisors with adequate tools to quantify, qualify and redress the consequences of ICT risk occurring at critical ICT third-party service providers'.[107]

To conduct oversight, the ESAs through their Joint Committee[108] shall designate the ICT third-party service providers deemed "critical" and appoint a "lead overseer" responsible for the oversight of each such critical ICT third-party service provider.[109] The Joint Committee of the ESAs shall also establish an "oversight forum" as a sub-committee to support the work of both the joint committee and the lead overseer in this regard.[110] This oversight forum shall represent both the ESAs, all Member State NCAs, the Commission, the European Systemic Risk Board, the ECB, the ENISA, and, where applicable, competent authorities under the NIS2 Directive.[111] The ESAs have also issued guidelines on cooperation with NCAs and the detailed procedures for the execution of the oversight functions.[112]

The lead overseers are provided with a set of supervisory powers vis-à-vis their respective critical ICT third-party service provider, which will be further specified in the regulatory technical standards.[113] This does not include enforcement powers, but the lead overseer can issue recommendations to which the critical ICT third-party service providers must respond under a comply-or-explain framework.[114] If the recommendations are not followed, competent authorities can take a set of actions, including, as a last resort, requiring financial entities to temporarily suspend the use or deployment of services provided by, or even terminate the contract with, the critical ICT third-party service provider.[115] The lead overseers may charge their respective critical ICT third-party service provider with oversight fees and establish a joint oversight network (JON) to coordinate the oversight activities.[116] Meanwhile, the ESAs may conclude arrangements to collaborate with third-country authorities to foster international cooperation, and they shall submit a report every five years on the findings gleaned from this cooperation.[117]

[107] Recital para. 31 of DORA.

[108] See Article 3(62) of DORA, cf. Article 54 of the ESMA Regulation (EU) No. 1095/2010, OJ 2010 No. L331, EBA Regulation (EU) No. 1093/2010, OJ 2010 No. L331, and EIOPA Regulation (EU) No. 1094/2010, OJ 2010 No. L331.

[109] Article 31(1), cf. Article 33 of DORA.

[110] Article 32 of DORA.

[111] Article 32(4) of DORA.

[112] Article 32(7) of DORA and Joint Committee of the ESAs, 'Final Report: On Joint Guidelines on the Oversight Cooperation and Information Exchange between the ESAs and the Competent Authorities under Regulation (EU) 2022/2554' (2024), JC 2024 36.

[113] Articles 35–40, cf. Article 41 of DORA and Joint Committee of the ESAs, 'Final Report: Draft Regulatory Technical Standards on Harmonisation of Conditions Enabling the Conduct of the Oversight Activities' (2024), JC 2024 35.

[114] See Article 42(1), cf. Article 35(1)(d) of DORA.

[115] See Article 42(3)–(8) of DORA.

[116] Articles 43 and 33(4), cf. Article 34 of DORA, and Commission Delegated Regulation (EU) 2024/1505 of 22 February 2024 supplementing Regulation (EU) 2022/2554 of the European Parliament and of the Council by determining the amount of the oversight fees to be charged by the Lead Overseer to critical ICT third-party service providers and the way in which those fees are to be paid, OJ L, 2024/1505, 30 May 2024.

[117] Article 44 of DORA.

15.4.3 *Information and Intelligence Sharing*

Cyber intelligence sharing is a practice of high practical importance given the diversity of cyberattacks and technical malfunctions, but a global best practice for such sharing has not yet emerged.[118] Hence, one option for regulators is to rely on industry-led initiatives.

To that end, Article 45(1) of DORA states that '[f]inancial entities may exchange amongst themselves cyber threat information and intelligence ... *to the extent that* such information and intelligence sharing' (emphasis added) aims to enhance their digital operational resilience, takes place within trusted communities, and protects sensitive information, business confidentiality, and personal data in accordance with GDPR and competition policy. Because information sharing is free by default, the real implication of the rule is the emphasised caveat: this type of information can be shared *only* by following the rules laid out in Article 45 of DORA, which include further requirements for such information-sharing arrangements and notification of competent authorities in Article 45(2) and (3). An objective thereof is to facilitate learning and cooperation in addressing cyber threats while preventing malicious actors from getting hold of sensitive information that reveals potential cybersecurity vulnerabilities.[119]

This points to a challenge with many DeFi protocols, which make use of open-source code and/or informal networks of software developers. In turn, participants in DeFi networks that qualify as financial entities under DORA must identify information shared with other participants in the network that qualifies as "cyber threat information and intelligence", for which they must adhere to the sharing restrictions in Article 45 of DORA.

15.5 CRYPTO-SPECIFIC MATTERS

15.5.1 *MiCA plus DORA Situation*

MiCA and DORA are both new and comprehensive regulatory frameworks that apply to DeFi, bar size limits, and exemptions for fully decentralised services.

In the case of DORA, size limits matter less because most financial entities operating as part of DeFi networks are too big to qualify as "microenterprises" and too interconnected to qualify under other exemptions. In fact, the interconnectedness of DeFi leads to *increased* scrutiny under DORA's proportionality principle.

MiCA's exemption for fully decentralised services (see Section 4.2.4) has its equivalent in DORA's emphasis on the "financial entity" as a subject for regulation: while critical ICT third-party service providers may be subject to direct supervision under DORA, only financial entities are subject to risk management duties.

This regulatory approach forces a hierarchical worldview onto an industry that prides itself on decentralisation based on DLT as a technology characterised by its lack of any central authority. While DORA shares this approach with MiCA, PilotR, and financial law more broadly,[120] its emphasis on the underlying technology, rather than the provision of financial services as such, has profound implications for DeFi: just as financial entities remain responsible for the compliance of outsourced *financial* services under MiCA and other EU financial law,[121] they

[118] See Financial Stability Institute, 'Banks' Cyber Security', pp. 17–18.
[119] See Recital paras. 32–34 of DORA.
[120] On PilotR, see Section 12.3.1.
[121] See Section 7.4.2.2.

remain responsible for outsourced *ICT* services under DORA. This is a profound departure from the past, when financial entities could safely rely on third parties to take responsibility for infrastructure services (e.g., telecommunications and computers), and the impact of DORA thus correlates with the role of technology in providing any given financial service.

This difference between MiCA and DORA is put to test in the question of whether CASPs are liable for losses incurred from failures in the underlying DLT on which their clients' cryptoassets are registered. The ESMA interprets Recital 83 and Article 75(8) of MiCA in a way that makes CASPs liable for failures of permissioned DLT networks, but not of permissionless networks that they do not control or manage.[122] We agree with this interpretation under MiCA, but we see DORA's objectives to go further, essentially forcing financial entities to take control through contractual relationships also with ICT infrastructure providers. In support of this reasoning, we point to the analogy to conventional cloud services that also provide data storage infrastructure and which are clearly in scope of DORA. Thus, we believe CASPs in this situation could be held liable under DORA, which as *lex specialis* prevails over MiCA in this regard.

In turn, this leads to four distinct DeFi relationships under the DORA framework: (1) a financial entity interacts through a DeFi network with an ICT third-party service provider; (2) a financial entity interacts through a DeFi network with another financial entity; (3) two ICT third-party service providers interact through a DeFi network; and (4) no regulated financial entity can be identified.

The type of relationship determines the regulatory implications under DORA. In the first instance, the financial entity is responsible for both its own compliance and that of its ICT third-party service provider. In the second instance, each financial entity is responsible for its own compliance and that of its own ICT third-party service providers, but not that of the other financial entity. (Note here that due to the interconnectedness of DeFi, the same entity may play the role of both financial entity and other financial entities' ICT third-party service provider.) In the third instance, neither ICT third-party service provider has risk management obligations under DORA, which rest with financial entities only. Finally, in the fourth instance, the network is fully decentralised and thus unregulated. This leaves the challenge of defining "financial entity" and "ICT third-party service provider" in a DeFi context, which we discuss next.

15.5.2 *Financial Entities*

Given that risk management duties under DORA lie with "financial entities" only, identifying one or more such entities is a prerequisite for the application of DORA to any DeFi network.

15.5.2.1 *Cryptoasset Issuers*

ART issuers under MiCA are "financial entities" under DORA, along with credit institutions and e-money institutions that may issue EMTs. For other cryptoassets under MiCA's Title II, any "legal person" can offer or seek admission to trading of such assets,[123] meaning that the issuer is a financial entity under DORA only if it happens to qualify as one of the listed types of such entities. The same applies to issuers of cryptoassets that are exempt from MiCA, for instance,

[122] See Section 8.6.8 and ESMA, 'Consultation Paper on Technical Standards Specifying Certain Requirements of Markets in Crypto Assets Regulation (MiCA) – Second Consultation Paper', ESMA75-453128700-438 (2023), p. 19.

[123] See Articles 4(1)(a) and 5(1)(a) of MiCA.

because the cryptoassets qualify as MiFID financial instruments or assets otherwise covered by EU financial law beyond MiCA.[124]

In practice, most cryptoassets in DeFi will either be "other" cryptoassets subject to Title II MiCA or be exempted from MiCA altogether, and their issuers will not qualify as a "financial entity" under DORA. Stablecoins are often used to pay for such cryptoassets, however, and also serve multiple other purposes in DeFi, such as in lending schemes. If the stablecoin qualifies as an ART or EMT under MiCA, then its issuer is a financial entity under DORA, and other parts of the DeFi network may qualify as its "ICT third-party service providers".

15.5.2.2 *CASPs*

MiCA-authorised CASPs are considered financial entities under DORA which, due to MiCA's broad CASP definition, encompasses many participants in typical DeFi ecosystems (see Section 7.2) who thus become subject to DORA.[125] Yet, because only authorised CASPs are covered by DORA, providers of cryptoasset services that operate illegally without a MiCA authorisation are probably not.[126] This could be the situation for many participants in DeFi schemes, where competent authorities must then enforce both MiCA's authorisation requirement and DORA at the same time.

15.5.2.3 *Other Financial Entities*

Even if many DeFi participants are covered by MiCA's broad CASP definition, it is not all-encompassing. Yet, because DeFi protocols typically replicate the services of conventional financial entities, many services in a DeFi network may nevertheless be subject to EU financial law in one way or another. When, in turn, DORA covers a broad set of financial entities under EU financial law, then the provision of DeFi financial services may lead to "financial entity" status being granted under DORA. This even applies to services provided in a decentralised fashion, where those who develop or operate the software risk being subject to EU financial law and may, as such, qualify as a "financial entity" (or at least an "ICT service provider") under DORA.

The CASP definition does not include insurance, for instance. Hence, DORA's application to insurance and reinsurance undertakings and intermediaries could become relevant to DeFi schemes where an entity offers or facilitates a guarantee or the carrying of risk in a form that qualifies as insurance.[127] DeFi schemes may also include some type of mechanism to evaluate the creditworthiness of its participants, which may potentially be subject to DORA as a "credit rating agency".[128] Similarly, cryptoasset lending and borrowing are exempt from MiCA[129] but could lead to qualification as a credit institution in scope of DORA.[130]

Even when certain broad activities are in principle covered by the CASP definition, the definition may be limited in various respects. The CASP definition's reference to portfolio management, for instance, extends only to "mandates given by clients on a discretionary client-by-client basis".[131] Yet, managers of cryptoasset investment funds are subject to DORA if they

[124] See Sections 4.2.3 and 4.4.
[125] See Article 2(1)(f) of DORA.
[126] See Article 2(1)(f) of DORA.
[127] See Article 2(1)(n) and (o), cf. Article 2(2)(b) and (e) and Article 3(47)–(51) of DORA, with further references to Directive 2009/138/EC and Directive (EU) 2016/97 of the European Parliament and of the Council of 20 January 2016 on insurance distribution, OJ 2016 No. L26, 2 February 2016.
[128] See Article 2(1)(q), cf. Article 3(54) of DORA.
[129] MiCA Recital para. 94.
[130] Article 2(1)(a) of DORA.
[131] Article 3(1)(16)(i), cf. Article 3(1)(25) of MiCA.

qualify as AIFMs.[132] Similarly, the CASP definition's reference to "placing of cryptoassets" may not extend to all types of crowdfunding service providers, yet these are explicitly covered by DORA.

Finally, DeFi schemes may involve entities that deal with conventional, non-cryptoassets. This could be, for example, an operator of the payment leg when cryptoassets are exchanged for fiat currency or the manager of reserve assets for stablecoin issuers; Article 70(4) MiCA requires that these services are provided by PSPs subject to the PSD framework (see Section 7.4.3.3). PSPs are not necessarily CASPs under MiCA but may still be subject to DORA, which covers a long list of financial entities across different asset classes.

15.5.3 *"ICT Third-Party Service Provider" in Crypto*

Once a financial entity is identified in a DeFi network, the next question is whether other parts of the network may qualify as its "ICT third-party service provider", which is defined under DORA as an "undertaking providing ICT services". The term "undertaking" implies that legal entity status is not required, so a financial entity is responsible for the compliance of ICT services delivered by other parts of the DeFi network, even when such services are delivered in a fully decentralised way.[133] It also follows from DORA's objectives that financial entities cannot avoid responsibility by using fully decentralised ICT services.[134]

This means having to scrutinise the term "ICT services" to determine which parts of a DeFi network qualify as a financial entity's ICT third-party service providers. DORA defines the term as 'digital and data services provided through ICT systems to one or more internal or external users on an ongoing basis, including hardware as a service and hardware services which includes the provision of technical support via software or firmware updates by the hardware provider, excluding traditional analogue telephone services'.[135]

The definition is wide and deliberately seeks to blur the boundaries between financial entities and their service providers in order to also retain responsibility with the financial entity for outsourced services, hence the reference to both "internal and external" users.[136] This lessens the importance of separating the interconnected service delivery in DeFi, as the regulated financial entity is responsible nevertheless.[137] Note, however, that only services provided "on an ongoing basis" may qualify as "ICT services" meaning that mere sporadic service delivery does not. Yet, we hold that services forming part of a broader DeFi stack still qualify even if they are used only sporadically by any given financial entity.[138]

The terms "financial entity" and "ICT third-party service provider" are also not mutually exclusive, in the sense that the same entity can be both a financial entity under DORA and simultaneously the ICT third-party service provider of another financial entity. This is practical in DeFi, where both ICT and financial services of multiple providers are often interconnected. We see no need to identify the dominant service element or to use a similar threshold for the

[132] See Articles 2(1)(k) and 3(44) of Dora, cf. Article 4(1)(b) of AIFMD.

[133] See Woxholth and Zetzsche, 'DORA on DeFi', 19–20.

[134] Ibid., pp. 20–21.

[135] Article 2(1)(u), cf. Article 3(19) and (21) of DORA.

[136] DORA distinguishes between third-party and intra-group ICT service providers. See Article 3(19) and (20) of DORA. Intra-group service providers cannot be designated as 'critical'; see Article 31(8)(iii) of DORA.

[137] See Articles 6(10), 19(5), and 28(1)(a) of DORA.

[138] Hence, in our view, it is the availability rather than the use of the service that must be provided on an ongoing basis. Nodes, for instance, provide the service of storing a copy of the ledger and of validating transactions on an ongoing basis even if each node may only occasionally add new blocks to the ledger.

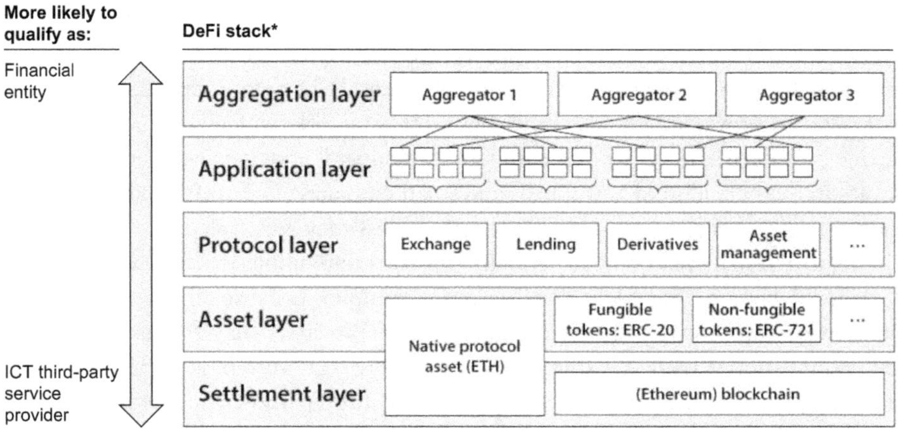

* DeFi stack framework from F. Schär, "Decentralized Finance: On Blockchain- and Smart Contract-Based Financial Markets" (2021) 103(2) *Federal Reserve Bank of St. Louis Review* 153, 156.

FIGURE 15.3 The DeFi stack.

ICT component to qualify as an "ICT service". If the service meets DORA's definition and it is provided to a third party, then the provider qualifies as an "ICT third-party service provider".

This means that the provision of "digital and data services" to a third party that is a "financial entity" will in practice lead to an "ICT third-party service provider" qualification. This can entail most or even all parts of the DeFi stack, but the higher layers of the stack are, by definition, more customer-focused, so are more likely to deliver financial services and thus qualify as a financial entity under DORA. By extension, the lower layers of the DeFi stack are more likely to qualify as their ICT third-party service providers. This does not mean, of course, that a customer-facing service or even a financial entity as part of a DeFi stack cannot also be the ICT third-party service provider of another financial entity, but it may serve as a mental guide to determine the application of DORA in the DeFi context (see Figure 15.3).

The settlement layer provides the underlying digital infrastructure of DeFi, which qualifies as an "ICT service" in our view. Hence, the Ethereum Foundation may possibly qualify as an ICT third-party service provider of DeFi financial entities operating on the Ethereum network.[139] The same can be true for participants in the broader Ethereum ecosystem, including software developers who develop and maintain the network code.[140] When it is clear, moreover, that DORA applies to conventional cloud computing and data centre services, this presumably implies that mining and similar activities of nodes in the operation of a DLT network are also considered "ICT services" under DORA. Many of these contributors in the ecosystem may be considered subcontractors of, or otherwise represented by, the Ethereum Foundation or a similar entity, yet this distinction matters less, as the financial entity is anyway responsible for their ICT services. Given that any "undertaking" may qualify as an "ICT third-party service provider" under DORA, this may possibly even cover the entire Ethereum ecosystem as such. In practice, however, financial entities must identify one or more counterparties with whom to perform the contracting mandated by DORA.

[139] On the Ethereum Foundation, see Ethereum.org, 'About the Ethereum Foundation' (2023). Website https://ethereum.org/foundation (last accessed on 1 October 2024).

[140] On the Ethereum ecosystem, see Ethereum.org, 'Ethereum Community Hub' (2023). Website https://ethereum.org/community (last accessed on 1 October 2024).

The Ethereum Foundation may possibly also act as an ICT third-party service provider on the asset layer of the DeFi stack because developers associated with the foundation have built popular standards like ERC-20 for the creation of new cryptoassets.[141] The same applies, of course, to other technical standard providers. We also hold that most issuers of cryptoassets qualify as ICT third-party service providers, as their use of the underlying standards adds new code and functionality to the software in their creation of new tokens and smart contracts. The same holds true for software developers who create or maintain such software, unless they are treated as subcontractors, but again the regulated financial entity nevertheless remains responsible for their services.

The protocol layer of the DeFi stack is more complex because this is where the actual financial services are created. Some of these service providers may themselves qualify as a "financial entity" under DORA, while others are merely ICT third-party service providers, and some financial entities are simultaneously the ICT third-party service provider of another financial entity. In practice, they all add "digital and data services" to the DeFi stack, so they will typically qualify as an "ICT third-party service provider" to the extent that their services are used by another regulated financial entity. These "digital and data services" are oftentimes partly outsourced, such as in the case of *oracles* that feed real-world data into the DeFi protocol. The *oracles* then become either ICT third-party service providers to the financial entity operator of the DeFi protocol or its subcontractor if the operator itself is an ICT third-party service provider to another financial entity.

The application and aggregation layers create a user-friendly interface, thus making the financial services more available to customers. Depending on how the service is delivered, providers of such applications and aggregation services may typically qualify either as a "financial entity" under DORA or as an "ICT third-party service provider" of another financial entity.[142] Specific challenges arise when applications or aggregators tap into open data or application programming interfaces (APIs) of a financial entity further down the DeFi stack. In this case, the financial entity may risk becoming responsible for a third party of which it is not even aware and may not even want to interact with. Whether this still counts as the provision of an "ICT service" to the financial entity depends, in our view, partly on the significance of such third-party applications and aggregators in the delivery of the underlying financial service and partly on the extent to which the financial entity has set up its data and APIs to facilitate third-party applications and aggregators. A trading venue that relies heavily on third-party interfaces for customers to conduct trades may, for instance, be responsible for a provider of such interfaces as its ICT third-party service provider, while an issuer of cryptoassets that merely happen to be traded through the same interface may not.

15.5.4 *Fully Decentralised Crypto Networks*

By assigning risk management obligations to "financial entities" only, so-called fully decentralised services are presumably exempt from DORA because no financial entity can be identified.

[141] See Cointelegraph, 'ERC-20 Inventor Discusses Origins, New Blockchains, BRC-20 and More' (2023). Website https://cointelegraph.com/news/erc-20-inventor-discusses-origins-new-blockchains-brc-20 (last accessed on 1 October 2024).

[142] They may, for instance, qualify as "financial information service providers" under the forthcoming Financial Data Access Regulation (FIDA) and thus be a financial entity under DORA. See European Commission, 'Proposal for a Regulation of the European Parliament and of the Council on a Framework for Financial Data Access and Amending Regulations (EU) No. 1093/2010, (EU) No. 1094/2010, (EU) No. 1095/2010, and (EU) 2022/2554' (2023) COM/2023/360 final, at Article 35 and Recital 32.

By extension, no parts of the network can then qualify as ICT third-party service providers, as these by definition provide services to a financial entity. Just as we expect many participants in DeFi networks to seek shelter under MiCA's exemption for fully decentralised services (see Section 4.2.4), we expect to see the same in relation to DORA.

We doubt that many DeFi services actually qualify from a functional perspective as fully decentralised under MiCA, however, because they rely on crypto exchanges or other intermediaries for at least part(s) of the services offered and developers or other persons tend to exercise some level of control.[143] The same is presumably true under DORA because the list of financial entities in scope is so wide that most financial services are covered. As we have seen, it is also enough to identify just one financial entity, and then most other parts of the DeFi stack may qualify as its ICT third-party service providers. Hence, we expect to see battles between industry and supervisors, but eventually at least one financial entity can be identified in the vast majority of DeFi networks.

15.6 CONCLUSION

The prevalence of cyberattacks highlights the need for better cybersecurity in the financial sector which, due to interconnectedness and possible systemic consequences, cannot be left to the discretion of financial firms. DORA is a comprehensive response from EU lawmakers in this regard and includes innovative elements, such as mandatory testing and the direct supervision of critical ICT third-party service providers. It also contributes to lower compliance costs through harmonised rules across the EU and could well serve as a global standard-setter.

This comes at a time of massive technological innovation in finance, which brings solutions and new problems alike. DeFi is a case in point: it is built on supposedly secure DLT, yet crypto hacks remain prevalent, so DORA must facilitate further innovation while mitigating risk at the same time.

Because the core risk-mitigating aspect of DeFi comes from its distributed service delivery, this may seem at odds with DORA's hierarchical approach, with regulated financial entities responsible for their ICT third-party service providers. Indeed, we expect many DeFi networks to claim that they are fully decentralised with no financial entity present, thus trying to escape DORA altogether, yet we believe that regulated financial entities can be identified in the vast majority of DeFi networks.

DORA is certainly made with CeFi in mind and may pose a challenge to many DeFi business models. While innovation-friendly in some aspects, such as the freedom to apply bespoke ICT risk management frameworks, in particular the detailed contracting requirements when financial entities interact with service providers seem ill-suited to a DeFi network.[144]

[143] See Section 2.1.7; Zetzsche *et al.*, 'Remaining Regulatory Challenges in Digital Finance', pp. 115–18.
[144] See Woxholth and Zetzsche, 'DORA on DeFi', 24, 25–28.

16

Remaining Regulatory Challenges in Digital Finance and Cryptoassets after MiCA

16.1 THE CONCENTRATION EFFECT OF DECENTRALISED FINANCE

Assessing the impact of MiCA and its related legislation adopted in the context of the EU's Digital Finance Strategy (PilotR, DORA, and the revision of TFR in tandem with the revision of the EU AML/CTF framework) on the EU's Single Market requires, first, taking a step back. It is important to acknowledge that there is not one universal DeFi model. Instead, the degree of decentralisation in DeFi varies wildly throughout the industry. Some DeFi platforms organise peer-to-peer finance by matching lenders and borrowers together in a decentralised manner, while other platforms pool users' funds to bundle liquidity. A third type of platforms books transactions on the balance sheet of a single intermediary. Each of these models come with their own risks and challenges and, as we have shown throughout the book, the DFS legislation spearheaded by MiCA addresses only some of them.

Yet, common to all these forms of DeFi is the risk of platform centralisation arising from large market shares or assuming roles as critical valuation services. These concentrated DeFi platforms have led to the rise of SICIs.[1] Such a finding is of immediate concern given DeFi's unusual idealisation as a safer alternative to concentrated intermediaries in traditional finance and the consequential too-big-to-fail risks. Indeed, these fears were realised in the period now dubbed the Crypto Winter from the second half of 2021 onwards, beginning with widespread operational malfunctions and asset diversions and culminating in the collapse of the Luna/Terra stablecoin system in May 2022, eventually bringing down many large crypto-intermediaries, including FTX.[2]

16.2 SUPERVISORY AND REGULATORY CHALLENGES OF CRYPTO

16.2.1 *Same Risks, Same Rules*

These events not only prompted thoughts that technology is not a "silver bullet" against the risks presented by humans but also showed that human-created operational risks, in particular, deficient system design, programming, and cybersecurity features, malfeasance of system

[1] Cf. Arner *et al.*, 'The Financialization of Crypto', pp. 15–18. Website http://dx.doi.org/10.2139/ssrn.4436852 (last accessed on 1 October 2024).

[2] Zetzsche *et al.*, 'Remaining Regulatory Challenges in Digital Finance', pp. 33–41.

participants, and large-scale cyberattacks, can bring down any DLT system.[3] Such events have encouraged a policy shift from a lenient or even pro-DeFi approach (that was at the core of the European Commission's draft MiCA from October 2020) looking at strengthening the EU's crypto industry and enhancing the efficiency of the EU Single Market to a more risk-control-oriented approach, which has been implemented throughout MiCA's trilogue procedure and resulted in MiCA's significant expansion.

Although DeFi is indeed innovative in its decentralised approach to finance, the realisation has settled in that crypto risks closely resemble those associated with traditional finance.[4] Risks identified here include agency risks, conflicts of interest associated with the bundling of intermediary functions, hidden leverage in crypto-lending, crypto-stacking, and crypto-staking, and concentration risks in SICIs – each of which justifies a regulatory response under the "same risks, same rules" principle.[5]

16.2.2 *New Risks, New Rules*

At the same time, some risks created by crypto are unique. These warrant further regulation under the complementary "new risks, new rules" principle.

In particular, the decentralisation of finance presents difficulties in defining the regulatory scope (with MiCA being a striking example[6]), applying existing financial regulation, managing risks, and ensuring business continuity in insolvency.[7] Furthermore, the severe negative environmental externalities unique to crypto evade traditional disclosure rules required under the SFDR, the CSRD, and Taxonomy Regulation.[8]

16.3 IMPACT OF DFS LEGISLATION ON CENTRALISED CRYPTO

Before the implementation of the DFS 2020, the EU's financial regulation regime contained gaps arising from its inconsistent application across Member States. Ambiguity and legal uncertainty in standard terms like "transferable securities", "financial instruments", and "e-money" often served as a source of regulatory arbitrage. Moreover, the prevailing uncertainty in the application of basic EU financial regulation and the opaqueness of business models rendered supervisory enforcement difficult.

16.3.1 *Robust Supervisory Framework for Centralised Token Issues and CASPs*

Against this background, we find that MiCA along with its accompanying legislation addresses the main challenges relating to the *centralised* issues and provision of crypto services. This combined regime provides a robust framework for the proper ordering of CASPs if extended by virtue of bespoke implementing legislation. The bespoke licensing scheme for issuers of EMTs

[3] Zetzsche *et al.*, 'Remaining Regulatory Challenges in Digital Finance', pp. 33–41.

[4] Cf. Arner *et al.*, 'The Financialization of Crypto', pp. 15–18. A somewhat different and nuanced perspective is apparent in M. Lehmann, 'MiCAR – Gold Standard or Regulatory Poison for the Crypto Industry', *Common Market Law Review* 61 (2024): 699, 708–11.

[5] Cf. Arner *et al.*, 'The Financialization of Crypto', pp. 18–22

[6] See our arguments in Chapter 4 and Sections 6.2 and 7.2.

[7] Cf. Arner *et al.*, 'The Financialization of Crypto', pp. 22–25.

[8] Cf. Zetzsche *et al.*, 'Remaining Regulatory Challenges in Digital Finance', pp. 70–73.

and ARTs[9] and CASPs,[10] as well as the enhanced disclosure requirements and whitepaper registration in Titles II–V MiCA,[11] combines to fill the prior gaps in the EU's financial regulatory landscape. In particular, considering that one of MiCA's key drivers was the launch of Libra (later renamed "Diem"), it is safe to say that Title III MiCA on ARTs provides a robust supervisory environment (which was partly inspired by the regulation of open-ended investment funds, in particular, money market funds, and partly by regulation of e-money) that could potentially address the risks presented by any significant ART issuances within the EU Single Market. Yet, we doubt that under these strict conditions, any global stablecoin project would subject itself to EU financial law as provided in MiCA.

16.3.2 *MiCA's Scope Conundrum*

At the same time, several challenges remain. The main one is the lack of delineation between MiCA's scope and the established terms of EU financial regulation.

Rather than providing clear-cut definitions, MiCA rests on a mere procedural response, building on multiple legal opinions provided by private and public bodies, reports, and guidelines.[12] We expect that the implementation of this procedural approach will take some time, and until it is completed, legal certainty with regard to crypto will be lacking, scarce resources at FSAs will be focused on gathering information widely spread through the internet, and the issuance of cryptoassets will be costly and time-consuming due to the costs incurred obtaining legal opinions and expert advice on various levels.[13] A strict default rule under which all cryptoassets are treated as transferable securities unless qualified under a different framework or exempted, paired with a more generous exemption for small crypto projects (instead of MiCA's EUR 1 million, we find EUR 5–8 million to be adequate), would provide a practical alternative to the definition problem.[14]

16.3.3 *Patchy Disclosure, Uncertain Crypto Insolvency Law*

Other gaps with regard to centralised crypto relate to the lack of periodic disclosure and accounting of entities subject to Titles II–V MiCA,[15] and a patchy framework for the restructuring and resolution of defaulting entities.[16]

16.3.4 *Reverse Solicitation*

We also see further factual challenges concerning the provision of services from third countries to the EU as MiCA focuses on EU entities assisting in the offering or trading. Experiences with the largest crypto exchanges worldwide have shown a strong emphasis on the exemption provided for reverse solicitation, paired with a number of indirect marketing efforts such as the emergence of "Finfluencers", creation of networks, and apparently unrelated blogposts.[17]

9 See Chapter 6.

10 See Chapters 7–9.

11 See Chapters 5–7.

12 See Chapter 4.

13 Zetzsche *et al.*, 'Remaining Regulatory Challenges in Digital Finance', pp. 89–90.

14 Zetzsche *et al.*, 'Remaining Regulatory Challenges in Digital Finance', pp. 110–14.

15 Zetzsche *et al.*, 'Remaining Regulatory Challenges in Digital Finance', pp. 90–91.

16 Zetzsche *et al.*, 'Remaining Regulatory Challenges in Digital Finance', p. 91.

17 Zetzsche *et al.*, 'Remaining Regulatory Challenges in Digital Finance', pp. 107–10.

In addition to a revised approach to reverse solicitation,[18] these instances are to some extent addressed by MiCA's rules on market abuse.[19] In this regard, we hope for robust implementing legislation and enforcement.

16.3.5 *Sustainable Finance*

We further note that the relationship of the EU's sustainable finance framework with the framework for centralised crypto firms in MiCA is unsettled at best.

Centralised token issuers and CASPs are required to disclose impacts on sustainability factors,[20] yet the details in the Level 1 legislation are less burdensome compared to financial market participants under the SFDR or issuers and financial institutions under the CSRD. Whether a level playing field between MiCA-subjected and other financial institutions will be achieved depends to a large extent on the robustness of the implementing legislation[21] and its enforcement. At the same time, an overly inclusive set of datapoints on environmental impacts may force issuers and CASPs to make up data they do not have.

While issuers of cryptoassets qualifying as financial instruments will fall in the scope of expansive and costly disclosure rules on top of risk management and fiduciary requirements including sustainability risks and impacts on sustainability factors, issuers and CASPs under MiCA walk free with regard to sustainability risks.[22] Sustainability risks, however, could be included in the traditional risk management categories; this approach is feasible in light of the fact that sustainability risks, like all other financial and operational risks, concern (potential) internalised risks.

While MiCA thus provides some grounds to deal with sustainability topics for centralised crypto, fully decentralised token issues and services are entirely out of its regulatory scope and thus its sustainability regulation. This is unfortunate in light of the fact that the energy consumption of decentralised tokens like Bitcoin is estimated to be excessive.[23] Yet, it also sheds light on the remaining challenges facing MiCA, discussed in the next section.

16.4 REMAINING CHALLENGES

One of the inherent difficulties in regulating crypto is the speed at which the crypto services environment outpaces the scope of existing regulation. The constant influx of innovative new variants of crypto, most notably illustrated by the rise of "fully decentralised services" and NFTs,[24] clearly demonstrates this point. Despite a number of improvements laid out in Section 16.3, the crypto world today no longer reflects the environment in which the DFS 2020 was drafted.

16.4.1 *MiCA*

While robust in most aspects with regard to centralised crypto, we observe gaps stemming from the scope limitations of MiCA, in particular, the exclusion of "fully decentralised services" and certain NFTs (cf. Chapter 4). This leaves the following significant regulatory challenges to be addressed:

18 See Article 61 of MiCA and Chapter 7.

19 See Chapter 10.

20 See Articles 6(11, 12), 19(10, 11), 51(14, 15), and 66(5, 6) of MiCA.

21 See ESMA, 'Final Report: Draft Technical Standards Specifying Certain Requirements of the MiCA' (2024), ESMA75-453128700-1229, Annex IV.

22 Zetzsche *et al.*, 'Remaining Regulatory Challenges in Digital Finance', pp. 70–72.

23 Zetzsche *et al.*, 'Remaining Regulatory Challenges in Digital Finance', pp. 70–72.

24 Cf. Chapters 2 and 4.

- legal uncertainty as to the applicability of EU law to different types of cryptoassets (Chapter 4);
- issues surrounding whether an NCA retains jurisdiction (Chapter 11);
- difficulties in determining whether a cryptoasset qualifies as an NFT or a "financial NFT" (Chapter 4);
- a lack of coverage of crypto-lending and crypto-staking (Chapters 4 and 7);
- evasion of particularly energy-intensive decentralised platform protocols from existing sustainability-oriented reporting requirements (Chapters 5 and 7 and Section 16.3.5);
- outstanding legislation that implements various MiCA rules including business continuity concepts for both technical malfunctions and the bankruptcy of core intermediaries (Chapter 7);
- narrow disclosure requirements (Chapter 5); and
- the exclusion of private law matters from the scope of MiCA, especially in the context of insolvency and private-law-based enforcement that would be an important supplement to financial regulation (Chapter 13).

16.4.2 *AML/CTF, Particularly the Revised TFR*

With respect to the AML/CTF framework, due to the fact that TFR, the AMLDs and AMLR rely on MiCA's concepts, we find similar limitations in the exclusion of "fully decentralised" crypto services (Section 14.2.2) and in challenges regarding the feasibility of the proposed tracing rules. Techniques such as merging, repackaging, and reuse of cryptoassets, decentralisation of wallets, and transfer into non-cooperative jurisdictions will continue to be problematic and require an expansion of the scope of EU financial regulation. At the same time, the qualification of self-hosted addresses and the use of transaction technologies as high-risk factors (Section 14.2.4.3) pave the way for a more robust AML/CTF framework for transactions taking place with EU-licensed CASPs acting on behalf of clients.

The forthcoming concentration of supervisory powers in the AMLA and the creation of a single rulebook by virtue of the AMLR will, at least, require significant resources and time for capacity and organisation building. Whether the ex-post status is then more effective depends on many factors independent of MiCA, AMLR, AMLD, and TFR, such as budget availability, technical expertise, and overall investments into crypto. Needless to say, more serious and better regulated entities becoming active in the field raises its level of sophistication, meaning that the crypto industry will benefit from the overall trends in AML/CTF, particularly the implementation of RegTech solutions.

16.4.3 *PilotR*

During its first year, PilotR attracted few prospective applicants to its sandbox regime, although there are signs of some improvement.[25] As a pilot regime with learning as a central regulatory objective, PilotR will certainly be amended or otherwise serve as a basis for future legislation, and ESMA has already pointed out some challenges.[26] Our analysis in Chapter 12 also highlights certain quandaries and opportunities for improvement:

[25] See V. Ross (ESMA Chair), 'DLT Pilot Regime Implementation' (2024), ESMA75-117376770-460, pp. 1–2, with reply from M. McGuinnes (EU Commissioner), Ares(2024) 3056562.

[26] See V. Ross (ESMA Chair), 'DLT Pilot Regime Implementation' (2024), ESMA75-117376770-460, pp. 3–4.

- PilotR is limited to select few asset classes, thus missing significant opportunities for learning and innovation.
- PilotR exemptions apply mostly to the CSDR and the Settlement Finality Directive (SFD), while exemptions are supposedly needed from MiFID's outsourcing rules and possibly other parts of EU financial law.
- Rigid exemptions and compensating measures prevent regulatory arbitrage, which discretionary powers for the ESMA could yield in a more flexible way once politically feasible.
- Increased flexibility allows for a wider scope, thus enabling innovation that spans technological and supervisory boundaries.
- Removing the authorisation requirements, or even the need for a designated operator altogether, would stimulate innovative organisational models and level the playing field for start-ups; so far, primarily established firms benefit from the PilotR, thus limiting the effectiveness of regulatory learning.

16.4.4 *DORA*

DORA comes at a time of massive technological innovation in finance, bringing solutions as well as new problems, and DeFi is a case in point: it is built on supposedly secure DLT, yet crypto hacks and malfunctions remain prevalent, so DORA must facilitate further innovation while mitigating risk at the same time.

While DORA entails several innovative aspects that live up to this expectation, by subjecting financial institutions to tech-specific risk management requirements, they are not consistently applied. Harmonisation requirements in the EU reduce compliance costs; the proportionality principle, direct supervision of critical ICT third-party service providers, and "pooled testing" all level the playing field; and DORA's emphasis on procedural approaches paired with governance and continuous improvement courtesy of prescriptive requirements enables new business models. Yet, rigid rules on third-party risk (and risk management) stifle innovation where it hurts most because the use of third-party services is probably the most efficient path towards new and innovative cybersecurity solutions.[27] These rigid rules favour incremental innovation over the disruptive kind offered by DLT, for instance.

16.5 FIVE KEY POLICY CONSIDERATIONS

When it comes to addressing the main challenges remaining after MiCA and its accompanying legislation, we recommend five policy steps.

First, it would be desirable to implement a default rule that deems all cryptoassets "transferable securities" subject to issuers or CASPs proving that their conduct fits into a different type of, or is even exempt from the scope of, EU regulation. Such a default rule provides legal certainty, reduces direct costs for entrepreneurs, and shifts the onus of fact gathering and argument from the NCAs and ESAs (and hence the public) onto the private actors most interested in adequate categorisation.

Second, there is an enhanced need to deal with reverse solicitation in a cross-sectorial harmonised manner, potentially by the ESAs.

[27] In the same vein, see Scott, 'The E.U.'s Digital Operational Resilience Act', pp. 24–26; See J. Woxholth and D. A. Zetzsche, 'DORA on DeFi' (2024), pp. 24, 25–28. Website http://dx.doi.org/10.2139/ssrn.4874057 (last accessed on 1 October 2024).

Third, crypto is a cross-border phenomenon, bypassing EU and EEA borders. There is an intensified need for cross-border cooperation of regulators beyond the EU and the EEA, to address what is labelled "reverse solicitation" from third countries, by way of an international concerted approach based on equivalent regulation and supervision, similar to what is established for derivatives.

Fourth, since MiCA's coverage of fully decentralised applications is uncertain at best, we propose granting regulatory entity status to DAOs involved in financial services, to make them the focal point of existing financial regulation, including MiCA, CRR/CRD, MiFID, and others. As soon as they are in scope of financial regulation, we expect the internal governance of DAOs to follow suit and adjust to regulatory necessities. The main advantage over MiCA's approach is that it relieves regulators from the onus of proof regarding whether a person or group of persons controls the DeFi scheme.[28]

Finally, we see the need to expand Title V MiCA on CASPs to address the additional operational and financial risks concerning NFTs. Exempting, for instance, the custody of NFTs from MiCA draws a line that is hardly feasible in practice. While including cryptolending and cryptostaking in the cryptoasset service definition would provide legal certainty on the application of MiCA.

We note that the solutions here could be regulatory or technical. In particular, all of the steps listed above could be furthered by way of a "EURO wallet" with key compliance features embedded in the technology applied; such a "EURO wallet" could also pave the way for applications relating to the Digital Euro. The first steps to that approach were presented by EU lawmakers as part of the Digital Euro initiative.[29]

[28] On the relevance of 'control' for establishing the function of issuer or CASP cf. above at Sections 6.2 and 7.2.

[29] ECB, 'A Stocktake on the Digital Euro – Summary Report on the Investigation Phase and Outlook on the Next Phase' (2023), pp. 9 and 36. Website www.ecb.europa.eu/paym/digital_euro/investigation/profuse/shared/files/dedocs/ecb.dedocs231018.en.pdf?6fbcce71a4be7bb3b8fabc51fb5c7e2d (last accessed on 1 October 2024).

Bibliography

AFM, 'AFM waarschuwt voor grote risico's bij Initial Coin Offerings' (2017). Website https://perma.cc/JE4R-ZWXW (last accessed on 1 October 2024).

Allegrezza S., 'The Proposed Anti-Money Laundering Authority, FIU Cooperation, Powers and Exchanges of Information: A Critical Assessment'. Committee on Economic and Monetary Affairs, Policy Department for Economic, Scientific and Quality of Life Policies, European Parliament, Luxembourg (2022).

Ammann T., Syed I. and Sanchez V., 'Exploring Operational Resilience in Financial Services: The Effects of DORA on Risk and Regulation in Top 3 Financial Markets', *Computer Law Review International*, 24(2) (2023), 43–48. Website https://doi-org.proxy.bnl.lu/10.9785/cri-2023-240203 (last accessed October 1 2024).

Andenas M. and Deipenbrock G. (eds.), *Regulating and Supervising European Financial Markets* (Springer, 2016).

Angeloni I., 'The Single Supervisory Mechanism', *European Economy*, 1(3) (2015).

Anker-Sørensen L. and Zetzsche D. A., 'From Centralized to Decentralized Finance: The Issue of "Fake-DeFi"'. (2021). Website https://dx.doi.org/10.2139/ssrn.3978815 (last accessed on 1 October 2024).

Annunziata F., 'Speak If You Can: What Are You? An Alternative Approach to the Qualification of Tokens and Initial Coin Offerings', *European Company and Financial Law Review*, 17(2) (2020).

'An Overview of the Markets in Crypto-Assets Regulation', EBI Working Paper Series no. 158 (2023), pp. 30–32. Website https://dx.doi.org/10.2139/ssrn.4660379 (last accessed on 1 October 2024).

Antonopoulos A. M., *Mastering Bitcoin: Programming the Open Blockchain*, 2nd ed. (Sebastopol, CA: O'Reilly Media, 2017).

Arner D. W. *et al.*, 'Cryptocurrencies, Blockchain and ICOs: Policy and Regulatory Challenges of Distributed Ledger Technology and Digital Assets in Asia', in C. Brummer (ed.), *Cryptoassets: Legal, Regulatory, and Monetary Perspectives* (Oxford: Oxford University Press, 2019).

'Stablecoins: Risks, Potential and Regulation', Working Paper No. 905. Bank for International Settlements (2020). Website www.bis.org\\publ\\work905.htm (last accessed on 1 October 2024).

Arner D. W., Zetzsche D. A., Buckley R. P. and Kirkwood J. M., 'The Financialization of Crypto: Lessons from FTX and the Crypto Winter of 2022–2023'. Research Paper No. 2023/19, University of Hong Kong Faculty of Law, and Law Research Paper No. 23-31, UNSW (2023). Website https://dx.doi.org/10.2139/ssrn.4372516 (last accessed on 1 October 2024).

Arner D. W., Buckley R. P., Zetzsche D. A. and Didenko A. N., 'Monetary Hegemony, Technological Evolution and the International Monetary System', *Boston University Journal of International law*, 42 (2024) (in press).

Athanassiou P., 'Impact of Digital Innovation on the Processing of Electronic Payments and Contracting: An Overview of Legal Risks', Legal Working Paper Series No. 37, 16. European Central Bank (2017).

Autorité des marchés financiers (AMF), 'L'AMF lance une consultation sur les Initial Coin Offerings et initie son programme UNICORN', Press Release (2017). Website https://perma.cc/G75E-88JT (last accessed on 1 October 2024) and Website www.amf-france.org/fr/actualites-publications/communi

ques/communiques-de-lamf/lamf-lance-une-consultation-sur-les-initial-coin-offerings-et-initie-son-programme-unicorn (last accessed on 1 October 2024).

Autoriti Monetari Brunei Darussalem, *Fintech Regulatory Sandbox Guidelines*, Guidelines No. FTU/G-1/2017/1 (2017).

Avsuvarova K., 'Navigating Digital Transformation: Unpacking the Impact of DORA on the Insurance Landscape' (2023). Website https://dx.doi.org/10.2139/ssrn.4549704 (last accessed on 1 October 2024).

Bains P. *et al.*, 'Regulating the Crypto Ecosystem: The Case of Stablecoins and Arrangements'. Fintech Notes, International Monetary Fund (2022).

Bank Negara Malaysia, 'Financial Technology Regulatory Sandbox Framework' (2016). Website https://perma.cc/9G8M-7R9E (last accessed on 1 October 2024).

Barsan I. M., 'Legal Challenges of Initial Coin Offerings', *Revue Trimestrielle de Droit Financier*, 3 (2017).

'Regulating the Crypto World: New Developments from France', *Revue Trimestrielle de Droit Financier*, 4 (2019).

Bayern S., 'Dynamic Common Law and Technological Change: The Classification of Bitcoin', *Washington and Lee Law Review Online*, 71 (2014).

Bech M. *et al.*, 'On the Future of Securities Settlement', in *Bank for International Settlements Quarterly Review*, 7th ed. (2020), pp. 67–38.

Belinky M. *et al.*, 'The FinTech 2.0 Paper: Rebooting Financial Services'. Santander InnoVentures, Oliver Wyman, Anthemis Group (2015).

Benos E., Garratt R. and Gurrola-Perez P., 'The Economics of Distributed Ledger Technology for Securities Settlement', *Ledger*, 4 (2019).

Berman A., 'France Finalizes New ICO Framework to "Attract Innovators Globally"'. Cointelegraph (2018). Website https://perma.cc/AG6C-BUJ2 (last accessed on 1 October 2024).

Binance/The News Crypto, 'X (Twitter) Gets License for Crypto Wallet Services in One U.S State' (20 August 2023). Website www.binance.com/en/square/post/1052807 (last accessed on 1 October 2024).

Binance Academy, 'What Is an NFT?' (2023). Website https://academy.binance.com/en/articles/a-comprehensive-guide-to-nft-categories# (last accessed on 1 October 2024).

Birdthistle W. A., 'Breaking Bucks in Money Market Funds', *Wisconsin Law Review*, 5 (2010).

Bitcoin.com, 'Hackers Have Stolen $100 Million from Defi Projects This Year' (2020). Website https://news.bitcoin.com/hackers-stole-100-million-defi-projects/ (last accessed on 1 October 2024).

Bitcoin Exchange Guide News Team, 'Top 5 Biggest 2018 ICO Scams, Ponzi Schemes, Crypto Thefts & Hacks So Far', Bitcoin Exchange Guide (2018). Website https://perma.cc/UPY4-FT8M (last accessed on 1 October 2024).

Bitcoin.org, 'A Peer-to-Peer Electronic Cash System' (2008). Website www.sec.gov/comments/s7-04-23/s70423-290181-707862.pdf (last accessed on 1 October 2024).

Bitcompare.net, 'Tether Lending Rates: Compare Best USDT APY' (2024). Website https://bitcompare.net/coins/tether/savings-interest-rates (last accessed on 1 October 2024).

Bonomi A., Lehmann M., and Lalani S. (eds.), *Blockchain and Private International Law* (Leiden: Brill, 2023).

Boreiko D. and Risteski D., 'Serial and Large Investors in Initial Coin Offerings'. *Small Business Economics*, 57 (2021).

Braumüller P., Ennöckl D., Gruber M. and Raschauer N. (eds.), *Die neue europäische Finanzmarktaufsicht* (Vienna: ZFR-Jahrestagung 2011, 2012).

Browne R., 'World's Biggest Stablecoin Regains Dollar Peg after $3 Billion in Withdrawals'. CNBC (2022). Website www.cnbc.com/2022/05/13/tether-usdt-stablecoin-regains-peg-after-3-billion-in-withdrawals.html (last accessed on 1 October 2024).

Brummer C. and Yadav Y., 'Fintech and the Innovation Trilemma', *The Georgetown Law Journal*, 107 (2019).

Buckley R. P., Arner D. W., Veidt R. and Zetzsche D. A., 'Building Fintech Ecosystems: Regulatory Sandboxes, Innovation Hubs and Beyond', *Washington University Journal of Law and Policy*, 61 (2020).

Buckley R. P., Arner R. P., Zetzsche D. A. and Selga E., 'Techrisk', *Singapore Journal of Legal Studies* (March, 2020), pp. 35–62.

Burilov V., 'Regulation of Crypto Tokens and Initial Coin Offerings in the EU', *European Journal of Comparative Law and Governance*, 6(2) (2019).
Busch D., 'Product Governance and Product Intervention under MiFID/MiFID', in D. Busch and G. Ferrarini (eds.), *Regulation of the EU Financial Markets: MiFID II and MiFIR* (Oxford: Oxford University Press, 2017), pp. 123–46.
Avgouleas E. and Ferrarini G. (eds.), *Capital Markets Union in Europe* (Oxford: Oxford University Press, 2018).
Busch D., Ferrarini G. and Franx J. P. (eds.), *Prospectus Regulation and Prospectus Liability* (Oxford: Oxford University Press, 2020).
Buterin V., 'Why We Need Wide Adoption of Social Recovery Wallets' (2021). Website https://vitalik.eth.limo/general/2021/01/11/recovery.html] (last accessed on 1 October 2024).
Central Bank of Ireland, 'Guidance Note for Authorisation as an Investment Firm under MiFID: Guidance on Completing an Application for Authorisation under the European Union (Markets in Financial Instruments) Regulations 2017', No. S.I. 375 of 2017 (2021).
Chainalysis, '2022 Biggest Year Ever for Crypto Hacking with $3.8 Billion Stolen, Primarily from DeFi Protocols and by North Korea-linked Attackers' (2023). Website www.chainalysis.com/blog/2022-biggest-year-ever-for-crypto-hacking/ (last accessed on 1 October 2024).
Chapman J. *et al.*, 'Project Jasper: Are Distributed Wholesale Payment Systems Feasible Yet?' Bank of Canada Financial System Review (2017).
Chen L. Y. and Lee J., 'Bitcoin Tumbles as PBOC Declares Initial Coin Offerings Illegal'. Bloomberg (2017). Website www.bloomberg.com/news/articles/2017-09-04/china-central-bank-says-initial-coin-offerings-are-illegal (last accessed on 1 October 2024).
Chiara P. G., 'Towards a Right to Cybersecurity in EU Law? The Challenges Ahead' (2023). Website https://dx.doi.org/10.2139/ssrn.4537093 (last accessed on 1 October 2024).
Cohney S., Hoffman D. A., Sklaroff J. and Wishnick D. A., 'Coin-Operated Capitalism', *Columbia Law Review*, 119(3) (2019).
Coindataflow.com, 'What Is An ICO – Initial Coin Offering Meaning – The Best Full 2021 Guide' (2021). Website https://coindataflow.com/clue/what-is-an-ico (last accessed on 1 October 2023).
Coindesk.com, 'Sam Bankman-Fried Wanted to Close Alameda in 2022, Unpublished Posts Show' (2023). Website www.coindesk.com/policy/2023/10/11/sam-bankman-fried-wanted-to-close-alameda-in-2022-unpublished-posts-show/ (last accessed on 1 October 2024).
CoinMarketCap.com., 'Today's Cryptocurrency Prices by Market Cap'. Website https://coinmarketcap.com/ (last accessed on 1 October 2024).
Cointelegraph, 'ERC-20 Inventor Discusses Origins, New Blockchains, BRC-20 and More' (2023). Website https://cointelegraph.com/news/erc-20-inventor-discusses-origins-new-blockchains-brc-20 (last accessed on 1 October 2024).
Collins H., 'Introduction', in G. Teubner (ed.), *Networks as Connected Contracts* (Bloomsbury, 2011).
Committee on Economic and Monetary Affairs (ECON), 'Draft Report, 2020/0265 (COD)'. European Parliament (2021).
'Draft Report, 2020/0267 (COD)'. European Parliament (2021).
Committee on Payment and Settlement Systems, and Technical Committee of the International Organisation of Securities Commission, 'Principles for Financial Market Infrastructures'. Bank for International Settlements (2012).
Committee on Payments and Market Infrastructures, 'Distributed Ledger Technology in Payment, Clearing and Settlement, No. 157'. Bank for International Settlements (2017).
Committee on Payments and Market Infrastructures and Markets Committee, 'Central Bank Digital Currencies', Papers No. 174. Bank for International Settlements (2018). Website www.bis.org/cpmi/publ/d174.pdf (last accessed on 1 October 2024).
Congressional Research Service, 'Introduction to Financial Services: Financial Cybersecurity' (2023). Website https://crsreports.congress.gov/product/pdf/IF/IF11717 (last accessed on 1 October 2024).
Cornelli G., Doerr S., Frost J. and Gambacorta L., 'Crypto Shocks and Retail Losses', BIS Bulletin 69. Bank for International Settlements (2023). Website www.bis.org/publ/bisbull69.htm (last accessed on 1 October 2024).

Davidson S., De Filippi P. and Potts J., 'Blockchains and the Economic Institutions of Capitalism', *Journal of Institutional Economics*, 14(4) (2017).

De Filippi P. and Wright A., *Blockchain and the Law: The Rule of Code* (Cambridge, MA: Harvard University Press, 2018).

Didenko A. N., 'Cybersecurity Regulation in the Financial Sector: Prospects of Legal Harmonization in the European Union and Beyond', *Uniform Law Review*, 25(1) (2020).

Directorate-General for Financial Stability, Financial Services and Capital Markets Union, 'Communication on the Digital Finance Package'. European Commission (2020). Website https://ec.europa.eu/info/publications/200924-digital-finance-proposals_en (last accessed on 1 October 2024).

Dulong de Rosnay M., 'Peer-to-Peer as a Design Principle for Law: Distribute the Law', *Journal of Peer Production*, 6 (2015).

DuPont Q. and Maurer B., 'Ledgers and Law in the Blockchain', *King's Review* (23 June 2015). Website www.kingsreview.co.uk/essays/ledgers-and-law-in-the-blockchain (last accessed on 1 October 2024).

EBA, 'Opinion on Virtual Currencies', EBA/Op/2014/08 (2014).

'Report with Advice for the European Commission on Crypto-Assets' (2019). Website www.eba.europa.eu/eba-reports-on-crypto-assets (last accessed on 1 October 2024).

'Advice on the Review of the Macroprudential Framework' (2022). Website www.eba.europa.eu/eba-proposes-simplify-and-improve-macroprudential-framework (last accessed on 1 October 2024).

'Final Report on Response to the Non-Bank Lending Request from the CfA on Digital Finance' (2022). Website www.eba.europa.eu/eba-provides-its-advice-eu-commission-non-bank-lending (last accessed on 1 October 2024).

Eckner D. and Zetzsche D. A., 'Appointment, Authorization and Organization of the AIFM', in D. A. Zetzsche (ed.), *The Alternative Investment Fund Managers Directive*, 3rd ed. (Alphen aan den Rijn: Wolters Kluwer, 2020), pp. 181–230.

EIOPA, 'Guidelines on System of Governance', EIOPA-BoS-14/253 EN (2014). Website www.eiopa.europa.eu/publications/guidelines-system-governance_en (last accessed on 1 October 2024).

Equalizer Exchange, 'Gauge Voting & Bribes' (2022). Website https://equalizerox.gitbook.io/equalizer-exchange-docs/guides/gauge-voting-and-bribes (last accessed on 1 October 2024).

Esma.europa.eu., 'Databases and Registers'. Website www.esma.europa.eu/publications-and-data/databases-and-registers (last accessed on 1 October 2024).

'Markets in Crypto-Assets Regulation'. Website www.esma.europa.eu/esmas-activities/digital-finance-and-innovation/markets-crypto-assets-regulation-mica (last accessed on 1 October 2024).

ESMA, 'Report on Distributed Ledger Technology Applied to Securities Markets', ESMA50-1121423017-285 (2017).

'Advice – Initial Coin Offerings and Crypto-Assets', ESMA50–157-1391 (2019). Website www.esma.europa.eu/document/advice-initial-coin-offerings-and-crypto-assets (last accessed on 1 October 2024).

'Annex 1: Legal Qualifications of Crypto-Assets – Survey to NCAs', ESMA50–157-1384 (2019). Website www.esma.europa.eu/document/annex-legal-qualification-crypto-assets—survey-ncas (last accessed on 1 October 2024).

'Q&As on the Prospectus Regulation' (2021) Website https://www.esma.europa.eu/document/qas-prospectus-regulation (last accessed on 1 October 2024).

'Crypto-Assets and Their Risks for Financial Stability' (2022). Website www.esma.europa.eu/sites/default/files/library/esma50-165-2251_crypto_assets_and_financial_stability.pdf (last accessed on 1 October 2024).

'Final Report: Guidelines on Standard Forms, Formats and Templates to Apply for Permission to Operate a DLT Market Infrastructure', ESMA70–460-206 (2022). Website www.esma.europa.eu/document/final-report-dltr-gl-application-permission (last accessed on 1 October 2024).

'Supervisory Convergence in the MiCA Transitional Phase' (2023). Website www.esma.europa.eu/esmas-activities/digital-finance-and-innovation/markets-crypto-assets-regulation-mica (last accessed on 1 October 2024).

'Consultation Paper on Technical Standards Specifying Certain Requirements of Markets in Crypto Assets Regulation (MiCA) – Second Consultation Paper', ESMA75–453128700-438 (2023) Website www.esma.europa.eu/sites/default/files/2023-10/ESMA75-453128700-438_MiCA_Consultation_Paper_2nd_package.pdf (last seen 1 October 2024).

'Final Report: Draft Technical Standards Specifying Certain Requirements of Markets in Crypto-Assets Regulation (MiCA) – Second Package', ESMA75–453128700-1229 (2024), Annexes IV and IX.

'Consultation Paper on the Draft Guidelines on Reverse Solicitation under MiCA' (29 January 2024). Website www.esma.europa.eu/sites/default/files/2024-01/ESMA35-1872330276-1619_Consultation_Paper_on_the_draft_guidelines_on_reverse_solicitation_under_MiCA.pdf (last accessed on 1 October 2024).

'Opinion to support the convergent application of MiCA' (31 July 2024), ESMA75-453128700-1048. Website: www.esma.europa.eu/document/opinion-broker-models (accessed 6 August 2024).

Ethereum.org ,'About the Ethereum Foundation' (2023). Website https://ethereum.org/foundation (last accessed on 1 October 2024).

'Ethereum Community Hub' (2023). Website https://ethereum.org/community (last accessed on 1 October 2024).

'Proof-of-Stake (POS)' (2023). Website https://ethereum.org/en/developers/docs/consensus-mechanisms/pos/ (last accessed on 1 Octover 2024).

Eur-lex.europa.eu, 'Summaries of EU legislation (Preventing Market Abuse in Financial Markets)' (2023). Website https://eur-lex.europa.eu/EN/legal-content/summary/preventing-market-abuse-in-financial-markets.html (last accessed on 1 October 2024).

European Central Bank, 'Revised Oversight Framework for Retail Payment Systems'. Website www.ecb.europa.eu/pub/pdf/other/Revised_oversight_framework_for_retail_payment_systems.pdf (last accessed on 1 October 2024).

'Cyber Resilience Oversight Expectations for Financial Market Infrastructures (CROE)' (2018). Website www.ecb.europa.eu/paym/pdf/cons/cyberresilience/Cyber_resilience_oversight_expectations_for_financial_market_infrastructures.pdf (last accessed on 1 October 2024).

'TIBER-EU Framework: How to Implement the European Framework for Threat Intelligence-Based Ethical Red Teaming' (2018). Website www.ecb.europa.eu/pub/pdf/other/ecb.tiber_eu_framework.en.pdf (last accessed on 1 October 2024).

'IT and Cyber Risk: The SSM Perspective' (2019). Website www.bankingsupervision.europa.eu/press/publications/newsletter/2019/html/ssm.nl190213_4.en.html (last accessed on 1 October 2024).

'Opinion on a Proposal for a Regulation on Markets in Crypto-Assets and Amending Directive (EU) 2019/1937', CON/2021/4, OJ 2021 No. C152, 29 April 2021.

European Commission, 'Communication on Implementing the Framework for Financial Markets: Action Plan', COM (1999) 232 Final (1999).

'Communication on a FinTech Action Plan: For a More Competitive and Innovative European Financial Sector', COM (2018) 109 Final (2018).

'Communication on a Digital Finance Strategy for the EU', COM (2020) 591 Final (2020).

'Communication from the Commission on an Action Plan for a Comprehensive Union Policy on Preventing Money Laundering and Terrorist Financing', C (2020) 2800 Final (2020). Website https://eur-lex.europa.eu/legal-content/EN/TXT/?uri=CELEX%3A52020XC0513%2803%29 (last accessed on 1 October 2024).

'Digital Finance Package: Commission Sets Out New, Ambitious Approach to Encourage Responsible Innovation to Benefit Consumers and Businesses', Press Release (2020). Website https://ec.europa.eu/commission/presscorner/detail/en/IP_20_1684 (last accessed on 1 October 2024).

'Proposal for a Directive on the Mechanisms to Be Put in Place by the Member States for the Prevention of the Use of the Financial System for the Purposes of Money Laundering or Terrorist Financing and Repealing Directive (EU) 2015/849', COM/2021/423. Website https://eur-lex.europa.eu/legal-content/EN/TXT/?uri=CELEX%3A52021PC0423 (last accessed on 1 October 2024).

'Proposal for a Regulation of the European Parliament and of the Council on Digital Operational Resilience for the Financial Sector and Amending Regulations (EC) No 1060/2009, (EU) No 648/2012, (EU) No 600/2014 and (EU) No 909/2014', COM (2020) 595 final. Website https://eur-lex.europa.eu/legal-content/EN/TXT/?uri=CELEX%3A52020PC0595 (last accessed on 1 October 2024).

European Commission and High Representative of the European Union for Foreign Affairs and Security Policy, 'Cybersecurity Strategy of the European Union: An Open, Safe and Secure Cyberspace' (2013). Website https://edps.europa.eu/data-protection/our-work/publications/opinions/cyber-security-strategy-european-union-open-safe-and_en (last accessed on 1 October 2024).

'Resilience, Deterrence and Defence: Building Strong Cybersecurity for the EU', JOIN (2017) 450 Final (2017). Website https://eur-lex.europa.eu/legal-content/en/TXT/?uri=CELEX%3A52017JC0450 (last accessed on 1 October 2024).

Fahlenbrach R. and Frattaroli M., 'ICO Investors', *Financial Markets and Portfolio Management*, 35 (2021).

FATF, 'Updated Guidance for a Risk-Based Approach to Virtual Assets and Virtual Asset Service Providers' (2021). Website www.fatf-gafi.org/en/publications/Fatfrecommendations/Guidance-rba-virtual-assets-2021.html (last accessed on 1 October 2024).

'Updated Guidance for a Risk-Based Approach to Virtual Assets and Virtual Asset Service Providers' (2021). Website www.fatf-gafi.org/en/publications/Fatfrecommendations/Guidance-rba-virtual-assets-2021.html (last accessed on 1 October 2024).

FCA, 'Regulatory Sandbox' (2022). Website www.fca.org.uk/firms/innovation/regulatory-sandbox (last accessed on 1 October 2024).

Federal Financial Supervisory Authority ('BaFin'), 'Consumer Warning: The Risks of Initial Coin Offerings' (2017). Website https://perma.cc/JM49-XZEN (last accessed on 1 October 2024).

Ferran E. and Babis V. S. G., 'The European Single Supervisory Mechanism', *Journal of Corporate Law Studies*, 13(2) (2013).

Ferrarini G. and Giudici P., 'Digital Offerings and Mandatory Disclosure: A Market-Based Critique of MiCA', in E. Avgouleas and H. Marjosola (eds.), *Digital Finance in Europe: Law, Regulation and Governance* (Berlin and Boston: De Gruyter, 2022).

Fidelity Digital Assets, 'Digital Asset Custody and Trading Platform Built for Institutions'. Website www.fidelitydigitalassets.com/trading-custody (last accessed on 1 October 2024).

Financial Conduct Authority, 'Regulatory Sandbox' (2015). Websites www.fca.org.uk/publication/research/regulatory-sandbox.pdf (last accessed on 1 October 2024).

Financial Conduct Authority ('FCA'), 'Consumer Warning about the Risks of Initial Coin Offerings' (2017). Website https://perma.cc/Y69C-SLLB (last accessed on 1 October 2024).

Financial Stability Board, 'Regulation, Supervision and Oversight of "Global Stablecoin" Arrangements' (2020). Website www.fsb.org/2020/10/regulation-supervision-and-oversight-of-global-stablecoin-arrangements/ (last accessed on 1 October 2024).

Financial Stability Board, 'Cyber Lexicon' (2023). Website www.fsb.org/2023/04/cyber-lexicon-updated-in-2023/ (last accessed on 1 October 2024).

'High-Level Recommendations for the Regulation, Supervision and Oversight of Crypto-Asset Activities and Markets: Final Report' (2023). Website www.fsb.org/2023/07/high-level-recommendations-for-the-regulation-supervision-and-oversight-of-crypto-asset-activities-and-markets-final-report/ (last accessed on 1 October 2024).

Financial Stability Institute, 'Banks' Cyber Security – A Second Generation of Regulatory Approaches'. Bank for International Settlements (2023). Website www.bis.org/fsi/publ/insights50.htm (last accessed on 1 October 2024).

Financial Times, 'Tether Says Its Reserves Are Backed by Cash to the Tune of... 2.9%' (2021). Website www.ft.com/content/529eb4e6-796a-4e81-8064-5967bbe3b4d9 (last accessed on 1 October 2024).

Finck M., *Blockchain Regulation and Governance in Europe* (Cambridge: Cambridge University Press, 2019).

FINMA, 'Regulatory Treatment of Initial Coin Offerings' (2017). Website https://perma.cc/VB7B-L259 (last accessed on 1 October 2024).

Fisch C., Masiak C., Vismara S. and Block J. H., 'Motives and Profiles of ICO Investors', *Journal of Business Research*, 125 (2021).

Foley S., Karlsen J. R. and Putnins T. J., 'Sex, Drugs, and Bitcoin: How Much Illegal Activity Is Financed through Cryptocurrencies?', *The Review of Financial Studies*, 32(5) (2018), 1798–1853.

Fox D., 'Cryptocurrencies in the Common Law of Property', in D. Fox and S. Green (eds.), *Cryptocurrencies in the Public and Private Law* (Oxford: Oxford University Press, 2019).

Garbers-von Boehm K. *et al.*, 'Intellectual Property Rights and Distributed Ledger Technology with a Focus on Art NFTs and Tokenized Art, Study PE 737.709'. European Parliament (2022). Website www.europarl.europa.eu/thinktank/en/document/IPOL_STU(2022)737709 (last accessed on 1 October 2024).

Gemini Cryptopedia, 'What Are HD Crypto Wallets?' (2022). Website www.gemini.com/cryptopedia/hd-crypto-wallets-hierachichal-deterministic (last accessed on 1 October 2024).

Geva B., 'Cryptocurrencies and the Evolution of Banking, Money, and Payments', in C. Brummer (ed.), *Cryptoassets: Legal, Regulatory, and Monetary Perspectives* (Oxford: Oxford University Press, 2019).

Geva B., Grunewald S. N. and Zellweger-Gutknecht C., 'The e-Banknote as a "Banknote": A Monetary Law Interpreted', *Oxford Journal of Legal Studies*, 41(4) (2021).

Goforth C. and Guseva Y., *Regulation of Cryptoassets*, American Casebook Serie, 2 ed. (Eagan, MN: West Academic Publishing, 2022).

Goldberg M. and Schär F., 'Metaverse Governance: An Empirical Analysis of Voting within Decentralized Autonomous Organizations', *Journal of Business Research*, 160 (2023). Website www.sciencedirect.com/science/article/pii/S0148296323001224 (last accessed on 1 October 2024).

Gullifer L. and Tirado I., 'Proprietary Rights and Digital Assets: A "Modest Proposal" from a Transnational Law Perspective', 87(2) Law & Contemporary Problems (2024) (in press).

Hacker P. and Thomale C., 'Crypto-Securities Regulation: ICOs, Token Sales and Cryptocurrencies under EU Financial Law', *European Company and Financial Law Review*, 15(4) (2018).

Haentjens M., De Graaf T. and Kokorin I., 'The Failed Hopes of Disintermediation: Crypto-Custodian Insolvency, Legal Risks and How to Avoid Them', *Singapore Journal of Legal Studies* (September 2020), pp. 526–63 (2020).

Hansen P. and Bauer H., 'MiCA's Significance Regime for Stablecoins – A Sledgehammer to Crack a Nut?' (2024). Website https://dx.doi.org/10.2139/ssrn.4699043 (last accessed on 1 October 2024).

Hobza M., 'ICOs, Cryptoassets and MiFID II: Are Tokens Transferable Securities?', *Charles University in Prague Faculty of Law Research Paper*, 3(1) (2020).

Hooghiemstra S. N., 'Depositary Regulation', in D. A. Zetzsche (ed.), *The Alternative Investment Fund Managers Directive*, 3rd ed. (Alphen aan den Rijn: Wolters Kluwer, 2020), pp. 441–85.

Houben R. and Snyers A., 'Crypto-Assets: Key Developments, Regulatory Concerns and Responses'. Committee on Economic and Monetary Affairs (ECON) (2020).

Howe H. R. and Griffiths J. (eds.), *Concepts of Property in Intellectual Property Law* (Cambridge: Cambridge University Press, 2013).

Howell E., 'The European Court of Justice: Selling Us Short?'(2014). Website https://eprints.lse.ac.uk/101771/1/The_European_Court_of_Justice.pdf (last accessed on 1 October 2024).

IBM, 'Cost of a Data Breach Report' (2023).

'X-Force Threat Intelligence Index' (2023). Website www.securityhq.com/reports/ibm-x-force-threat-intelligence-index-2023/ (last accessed on 1 October 2024).

'X-Force Threat Intelligence Index' (2024). Website www.ibm.com/reports/threat-intelligence (last accessed on 1 October 2024).

Iglesias-Rodriguez P., 'ESMA as a Residual Lawmaker: The Political Economy and Constitutionality of ESMA's Product Intervention Measures on Complex Financial Products', *European Business Organization Law Review*, 22 (2021).

IMF, 'Euro Area Datasets' (2021). Website www.imf.org/external/datamapper/profile/EURO (last accessed on 1 October 2024).

'Special Drawing Rights' (2023). Website www.imf.org/en/About/Factsheets/Sheets/2023/special-drawing-rights-sdr (last accessed on 1 October 2024).

'Global Financial Stability Report' (2021). Website www.imf.org/-/media/Files/Publications/GFSR/2021/October/English/text.ashx (last accessed on 1 October 2024).

Investopedia.com (2022)., 'All about NEM (XEM), the Harvested Cryptocurrency' (2022). Website www.investopedia.com/tech/meet-nem-xem-harvested-cryptocurrency/ (last accessed on 1 October 2024).

IOSCO, 'Multilateral Memorandum of Understanding Concerning Consultation and Cooperation and the Exchange of Information' (2002). Website www.iosco.org/about/?subsection = mmou (last accessed on 1 October 2024).

'Global Stablecoin Initiatives', OR01/2020 (2020). Website www.iosco.org/library/pubdocs/pdf/IOSCOPD650.pdf (last accessed on 1 October 2024).

'Policy Recommendations for Crypto and Digital Asset Markets', Consultation Report, CR01/2023 (2023). Website www.iosco.org/library/pubdocs/pdf/IOSCOPD734.pdf (last accessed on 1 October 2024).

'Policy Recommendations for Crypto and Digital Asset Markets', Final Report, FR11/2023 (2023). Website www.iosco.org/library/pubdocs/pdf/IOSCOPD747.pdf (last accessed on 1 October 2024).

Joint Committee of the ESAs, 'Joint Advice of the European Supervisory Authorities', JC 2019 25, 10 (2019). Website www.esma.europa.eu/sites/default/files/library/jc_2019_25_joint_esas_advice_on_a_coherent_cyber_resilience_testing_framework.pdf (last accessed on 1 October 2024).

Kaal W. A., 'Digital Asset Market Evolution', *Journal of Corporation Law*, 46(4) (2021).

Kaal W. A. and Evans S., 'Blockchain-Based Securities Offerings', *UC Davies Business Law Journal*, 20(1) (2020).

Kaal W. and Howe H., 'Custody of Digital Assets', *Jurimetrics*, 63(2) (2023).

Kämmerer J. A., 'Das neue europäische Finanzaufsichtssystem (ESFS) – Modell für eine europäisierte Verwaltungsarchitektur?', *Neue Zeitschrift für Verwaltungsrecht* (2011).

Klingenbrunn D., 'Produktintervention zugunsten des Anlegerschutzes – Zur Systematik innerhalb des Aufsichtsrechts, dem Anlegerleitbild und zivilrechtlichen Konsequenzen', *WM Zeitschrift für Wirtschafts- und Bankrecht* (2015).

Krüger P. S. and Brauchle J.-P., The European Union, Cybersecurity, and the Financial Sector: A Primer. Carnegie Endowment for International Peace', Cyber Policy Initiative Working Paper Series #9 (2021). Website https://carnegieendowment.org/2021/03/16/european-union-cybersecurity-and-financial-sector-primer-pub-84055 (last accessed on 1 October 2024).

Lamandini M., 'When More Is Needed: The European Financial Supervisory Reform and Its legal Basis', *European Constitutional Law Review*, 6 (2009).

Langenbucher K., 'Insider Trading in European Law – from Financial Instruments to Crypto-Assets', ECGI Working Paper N° 763/2024 (2024). Website https://dx.doi.org/10.2139/ssrn.4771059 (last accessed on 1 October 2024).

Langevoort D. C., 'The SEC and the Madoff Scandal: Three Narratives in Search for a Story', *Michigan State Law Review*, 899 (2009).

Lee L., 'Examining the Legal Status of Digital Assets as Property: A Comparative Analysis of Jurisdictional Approaches' (2024). Website: https://dx.doi.org/10.2139/ssrn.4807135 (last accessed on 1 October 2024).

Legislation.mt., 'Virtual Financial Assets Act'. Website https://legislation.mt/eli/cap/590/eng/pdf (last accessed on 1 October 2024).

Lehmann M., 'Digital Assets in The Conflict of Laws: A Comparative Search for The Ideal Rule', *Singapore Journal of Legal Studies* (2024) (in press)

'MiCAR – Gold Standard or Regulatory Poison for the Crypto Industry' *Common Market Law Review*, 61 (2024).

'Who Owns Bitcoin? Private Law Facing the Blockchain', *Minnesota Journal of Law, Science and Technology*, 21(1) (2020).

'National Blockchain Laws as a Threat to Capital Markets Integration', *Uniform Law Review*, 95 (2021).

Lehmann M. and Kumpan C. (eds.), *European Financial Services Law: Article-by-Article Commentary* (Baden-Baden: Nomos, 2017).

Liechtenstein Government, 'Vernehmlassungsbericht betreffend die Schaffung eines Gesetzes über auf vertrauenswürdigen Technologien (VT) beruhende Transaktionssysteme' (Blockchain-Gesetz; VT-Gesetz; VTG), 16 November 2018.

Liu H. *et al.*, 'Client-Intermediary Relations in the Crypto-Asset World', in P. S. Davies and T. Cheng-Han (eds.), *Intermediaries in the Commercial World* (New York: Bloomsbury, 2022), pp. 213–35.

Low K. F. K. *et al.*, 'The Company and Block-Chain Technology', LSE Law School Working Paper Series 18/2022 (2022). Website https://dx.doi.org/10.2139/ssrn.4258114 (last accessed on 1 October 2024).

'Third Thing or Sixth Sense? I See Ideational Objects?' in P. Babie and M. Giancaspro (eds.), *Private Law and Digital Assets* (New York: Springer, forthcoming).

Maas T., 'Initial Coin Offerings: When Are Tokens Securities in the EU and US?' (2019). Website www.researchgate.net/publication/331706212_Initial_Coin_Offerings_When_Are_Tokens_Securities_in_the_EU_and_US (last accessed on 1 October 2024).

Magee T., 'Biggest Initial Coin Offerings Techworld' (2018). Website https://perma.cc/W4WL-FXXW (last accessed on 1 October 2024).

Mainelli M. and Milne A., 'The Impact and Potential of Blockchain on the Securities Transaction Lifecycle', Working Paper No. 2015-007 (2016). SWIFT Institute.

Maume P. and Fromberger M., 'Regulations of Initial Coin Offerings: Reconciling U.S. and E.U. Securities Laws', *Chicago Journal of International Law*, 19 (2019).

Maume P., Maute L. and Fromberger M., *The Law of Crypto Assets* (New York: Bloomsbury, 2022).

Michels J. D. and Millard C., 'The New Things: Property Rights in Digital Files?', *Cambridge Law Journal*, 81(2) (2022).

Mills D. *et al.*, 'Distributed Ledger Technology in Payments, Clearing, and Settlement', Working Paper No. 2016-095. Federal Reserve Board, Finance and Economics Discussion Series (2016).

Moloney N., Ferran E. and Payne J. (eds.), *The Oxford Handbook of Financial Regulation* (Oxford: Oxford University Press, 2015).

Monetary Authority of Singapore, 'MAS Clarifies Regulatory Position on the Offer of Digital Tokens in Singapore', Media Release (2017). Website https://perma.cc/W9KS-BLX6 (last accessed on 1 October 2024).

Morgan D., 'Coming to Terms with DORA', *Computer Fraud & Security*, 8 (2023).

Munchee Inc., 'Securities Act of 1933 Release No. 10445'. U. S. Securities and Exchange Commission (2017). Website https://perma.cc/ET52-T99G (last accessed on 1 October 2024).

Nakamoto S., 'Bitcoin: A Peer-to-Peer Electronic Cash System'. Website https://bitcoin.org/bitcoin.pdf (last accessed on 1 October 2024).

Nakamura Y. and Kim S., 'Cryptocurrencies Drop as South Korea Bans ICOs, Margin Trading'. Bloomberg (2017). Website https://perma.cc/V5XB-HYXR (last accessed on 23September 2023).

Neumannová A. *et al.*, 'The Digital Operational Resilience Act for Financial Services: A Comparative Gap Analysis and Literature Review', in M. Papadaki *et al.* (eds.), *Information Systems* (New York: Springer, 2023), pp. 570–85.

New York Times, 'Silicon Valley Bank Collapse Sets Off Blame Game in Tech Industry' (2023). Website www.nytimes.com/2023/03/11/technology/silicon-valley-bank-crypto-investing.html (last accessed on 1 October 2024).

Noble E., 'Opening Remarks to the European Economic and Social Committee (EESC) Public Hearing on Crypto-Assets: Opportunities and Challenges'. European Economic and Social Committee (2022). Website www.eesc.europa.eu/en/news-media/presentations/crypto-assets-challenges-and-opportunities (last accessed on 1 October 2024).

Parchimowicz K., 'Do Not Get Lost in the Cloud. How EU Financial Institutions Could Avoid Legal and Practical Problems with Cloud Services Arising under DORA' (2023). Website https://dx.doi.org/10.2139/ssrn.4486264 (last accessed on 1 October 2024).

Parenti R., 'Regulatory Sandboxes and Innovation Hubs for Fintech'. European Parliament (2020). Website www.europarl.europa.eu/thinktank/en/document/IPOL_STU(2020)652752 (last accessed on 1 October 2024).

'European System of Financial Supervision (ESFS)'. European Parliament (2023). Website www.europarl.europa.eu\\factsheets\\en\\sheet\\84\\european-system-of-financial-supervision-esfs (last accessed on 1 October 2024).

'Fact Sheet: Financial Services Policy'. European Parliament (2023). Website www.europarl.europa.eu/factsheets/en/sheet/83/financial-services-policy (last accessed on 1 October 2024).

Partsch T., 'Delegation', in D. A. Zetzsche (ed.), *The Alternative Investment Fund Managers Directive*, 3rd ed (Alphen aan den Rijn: Wolters Kluwer, 2020), pp. 285–311.

Paxos, 'PAX Gold Terms and Conditions' (2023). Website www.paxos.com/pax-gold-terms-conditions (last accessed on 1 October 2024).

Private Digital Euro Working Group, 'Stablecoins – An Introduction and Recommendations for the European Union'. Digital Euro Association (2022).

Rohr J. and Wright A., 'Blockchain-Based Token Sales, Initial Coin Offerings, and the Democratization of Public Capital Markets', *Hastings Law Journal*, 70 (2019).

Rotting M. and Lang C., 'Das Lamfalussy-Verfahren im Umfeld der Neuordnung der europäischen Finanzaufsichtsstrukturen', *Europäische Zeitschrift für Wirtschaftsrecht* (2012).

Russo C. and Khrennikov I., 'Big Investors Circle Telegram's ICO While Veteran Crypto Insiders Pass'. Bloomberg (2018). Website www.bloomberg.com/news/articles/2018-02-02/big-investors-circle-telegram-offering-as-crypto-insiders-pass#xj4y7vzkg (last accessed on 1 October 2024).

Sarra J. and Gullifer L., 'Crypto-Claimants and Bitcoin Bankruptcy: Challenges for Recognition and Realization', *International Insolvency Review*, 28 (2019).

Schoenmaker D. and Véron N., 'A "Twin Peaks" Vision for Europe'. Bruegel Policy Contribution (2017).

Schuster E., 'Cloud Crypto Land', *Modern Law Review*, 84(4) (2021).

Scott H. S., 'The E.U.'s Digital Operational Resilience Act: Cloud Services & Financial Companies' (2021). Website www.pifsinternational.org/wp-content/uploads/2022/08/The-E.U.s-Digital-Operational-Act-Cloud-Services-Financial-Companies-08.06.2021.pdf (last accessed on 1 October 2024).

Securities and Exchange Commission, Thailand, 'SEC Thailand's Viewpoint on ICO' (2017). Website https://perma.cc/T77N-6HES (last accessed on 1 October 2024).

Shardeum, 'Top 10 DeFi Hacks You Should Know in 2023' (2023). Website https://shardeum.org/blog/defi-hacks/ (last accessed on 1 October 2024).

Small S., 'Bitcoin: The Napster of Currency', *Houston Journal of International Law*, 37 (2015).

Sokolov M., 'Are Libra, Tether, MakerDAO and Paxos Issuing e-Money? Analysis of 9 Stablecoin Types under the EU and UK e-Money Frameworks' (2020). Website https://dx.doi.org/10.2139/ssrn.3746250 (last accessed on 1 October 2024).

Solinas M., 'Investors' Rights in (Crypto) Custodial Holdings: Ruscoe v Cryptopia Ltd (in Liquidation)', *Modern Law Review*, 84(1) (2021).

Statista, 'Average Cost of a Data Breach Worldwide from May 2020 to March 2023, by Industry' (2023). Website www.statista.com\\statistics\\387861\\cost-data-breach-by-industry (last accessed on 1 October 2024).

Supaat S., 'Reply to Parliamentary Question on the Prevalence Use of Cryptocurrency in Singapore and Measures to Regulate Cryptocurrency and Initial Coin Offerings', Notice Paper No. 869. Monetary Authority of Singapore (2017). Website https://perma.cc/W9KS-BLX6 (last accessed on 1 October 2024).

Swiss Financial Market Supervisory Authority ('FINMA'), 'FINMA Closes Down Coin Providers and Issues Warning about Fake Cryptocurrencies', Press Release (2017). Website https://perma.cc/B8TD-TW7N (last accessed on 1 October 2024).

The Corporate Finance Institute Team, 'Initial Coin Offering (ICO)?' The Corporate Finance Institute. Website https://corporatefinanceinstitute.com/resources/knowledge/trading-investing/initial-coin-offering-ico/ (last accessed on 1 October 2024).

The Economist, 'America's Aggressive Use of Sanctions Endangers the Dollar's Reign'. *The Economist* (2020). Website www.economist.com/briefing/2020/01/18/americas-aggressive-use-of-sanctions-endangers-the-dollars-reign (last accessed on 1 October 2024).

The Luxembourg House of Financial Technology, 'Understanding Initial Coin Offerings: Technology, Benefits, Risks, and Regulations' (2017). Website www.lhoft.com/bloockchain/understanding-initial-coin-offerings-technology-benefits-risks-and-regulations/ (last accessed on 1 October 2024).

The World Bank, 'Global Experiences from Regulatory Sandboxes' (2020). Website https://documents.worldbank.org/en/publication/documents-reports/documentdetail/912001605241080935/global-experiences-from-regulatory-sandboxes (last accessed on 1 October 2024).

Thena, 'VeTHE' (2023). Website https://thena.gitbook.io/thena/the-tokenomics/vethe (last accessed on 1 October 2024).

The U. K. Law Commission, 'Digital assets and ETDs in private international law: which court, which law? Call for evidence' (2024). Website https://lawcom.gov.uk/project/digital-assets-and-etds-in-private-international-law-which-court-which-law/assets-and-etds-in-private-international-law-which-court-which-law/ (last accessed on 1 October 2024).

'Digital Assets: Consultation Paper No. 256' (2022). Website https://cloud-platform-e218f50a4812967ba1215eaecede923f.s3.amazonaws.com/uploads/sites/30/2022/07/Digital-Assets-Consultation-Paper-Law-Commission-1.pdf (last accessed on 1 October 2024).

The World Bank, 'Key Data from Regulatory Sandboxes across the Globe' (2020). Website www.worldbank.org/en/topic/fintech/brief/key-data-from-regulatory-sandboxes-across-the-globe (last accessed on 1 October 2024).

Thuama R. N. and Costigan S. S., 'DORA – Understanding the New Regulatory Framework on Digital Operational Resilience' (2023). Website https://dx.doi.org/10.2139/ssrn.4549564 (last accessed on 1 October 2024).

Tomasicchio A., 'Top 5 Cryptocurrency Scams'. Bitcoin Chaser (2017). Website https://perma.cc/34G5-4CCM (last accessed on 1 October 2024).

Tomic K., 'Product Intervention of Supervisory Authorities in Financial Services', in S. Grima and P. Marano (eds.), *Governance and Regulations' Contemporary Issues* (Emerald, 2018), pp. 229–56.
TrackICO, 'RedCab (REDC)'. Website https://perma.cc/N7AA-K8T5 (last accessed on 1 October 2024).
Uhlig H., 'A Luna-tic Stablecoin Crash', Working Paper No. 2022-95. Becker Friedman Institute for Economics, University of Chicago (2022). Website https://dx.doi.org/10.2139/ssrn.4163038 (last accessed on 1 October 2024).
U. K. Jurisdiction Taskforce, 'Legal Statement on Cryptoassets and Smart Contracts' (2019). Website https://lawtechuk.io/explore/cryptoasset-and-smart-contract-statement (last accessed on 1 October 2024).
UNIDROIT Issues Paper, 'Study No. LXXXII – WG4 – Doc. 2' (2021).
U. S. Securities and Exchange Commission, 'SEC Exposes Two Initial Coin Offerings Purportedly Backed by Real Estate and Diamonds', Press Release (2017). Website https://perma.cc/4GJW-QSWU (last accessed on 1 October 2024).
'SEC Emergency Action Halts ICO Scam', Press Release (2017). Website https://perma.cc/SG8A-YXRY (last accessed on 1 October 2024).
'SEC Statement Urging Caution Around Celebrity Backed ICOs', Public Statement (2017). Website https://perma.cc/2Q69-KJ73 (last accessed on 1 October 2024) (demanding compliance with U.S. disclosure rules).
'Investor Bulletin: Initial Coin Offerings', Press Release (2017). Website https://perma.cc/7G6M-PUT4 (last accessed on 1 October 2024).
'SEC Charges Kim Kardashian for Unlawfully Touting Crypto Security', Press release No. 2022-183 (2022). Website www.sec.gov/news/press-release/2022-183 (last accessed on 1 October 2024).
'SEC Charges Crypto Entrepreneur Justin Sun and His Companies for Fraud and Other Securities Law Violations', Press release No. 2023-59 (2022). Website www.sec.gov/news/press-release/2023-59 (last accessed on 1 October 2024).
Vandezande N., 'Regulating Initial Coin Offerings and DAO Tokens under the EU's Financial Instruments Framework', *Law and Financial Markets Review*, 14(1) (2020).
Van Steenis H. *et al.*, 'Blockchain in Banking: Disruptive Threat or Tool?' Morgan Stanley Global Insight (2016).
Veerle C., 'The MiFIR and PRIIPs Product Intervention Regime: In Need of Intervention?', *European Company and Financial Law Review*, 17(1) (2020).
Veil R., 'Token-Emissionen im Europäischen Kapitalmarktrecht'. ZHR (2019).
Véron N., 'Charting the Next Steps for the EU Financial Supervisory Architecture'. Bruegel Policy Contribution, Issue n°16 (2017).
Walch A., 'The Bitcoin Blockchain as Financial Market Infrastructure: A Consideration of Operational Risk', *New York University Journal of Legislation and Public Policy*, 18 (2015).
Weber R. H., 'Neue Blockchain-Gesetzgebung in der Schweiz', *Recht Digital*, 4 (2021).
Welfare A., *Commercializing Blockchain: Strategic Applications in the Real World* (Chichester: Wiley, 2019).
WorldBank.org, 'Key Data from Regulatory Sandboxes across the Globe' (2020). Website www.worldbank.org\\en\\topic\\fintech\\brief\\key-data-from-regulatory-sandboxes-across-the-globe (last accessed on 1 October 2024).
Woxholth J., *Kryptoeiendeler i formueretten* (Oslo: Gyldendal 2024).
Woxholth J., Zetzsche D. A., Buckley R. P. and Arner D. W., 'Competing Claims to Crypto-assets', *Uniform Law Review*, 28(2) (2024).
Woxholth J., Zetzsche D. A., 'DORA on DeFi' (2024). Website https://dx.doi.org/10.2139/ssrn.4874057 (last accessed on 1 October 2024).
Wymeersch E., Hopt K. J. and Ferrarini G. (eds.), *Financial Regulation and Supervision: A Post-Crisis Analysis* (Oxford: Oxford University Press, 2012).
Yeung K., 'Regulation by Blockchain: The Emerging Battle for Supremacy between the Code of Law and Code as Law', *Modern Law Review*, 82(2) (2019).
Zamani E. *et al.*, 'On the Security Risks of the Blockchain', *Journal of Computer Information Systems*, 60(6) (2020).
Zetzsche D. A., 'The Anatomy of European Investment Fund Law', in W. A. Birdthistle and J. Morley (eds.), *Research Handbook on Mutual Funds* (Cheltenham, UK: Edward Elgar Publishing Limited, 2018), pp. 302–59.

'European Financial Law: Financial Intermediaries', *Encyclopedia on European Law*, VI (2022).

Zetzsche D. A., Buckley R. P., Arner D. W. and Barberis J. N., 'Regulating a Revolution: From Regulatory Sandboxes to Smart Regulation', *Fordham Journal of Corporate and Financial Law*, 23 (2017).

Zetzsche D. A., Buckley R. P. and Arner D. W., 'The Distributed Liability of Distributed Ledgers: Legal Risks of Blockchain', *University of Illinois Law Review*, 4 (2018).

Zetzsche D. A., Buckley R. P., Arner D. W. and Föhr L., 'The ICO Gold Rush: It's a Scam, It's a Bubble, It's a Super Challenge for Regulators', *Harvard International Law Journal*, 63(2) (2019).

Zetzsche D. A., Arner D. W. and Buckley R. P., 'Decentralized Finance (DeFi)', *Journal of Financial Regulation*, 6(2) (2020).

Zetzsche D. A., Anker-Sorensen L., Passador M. L. and Wehrli A., 'DLT-Based Enhancement of Cross-Border Payment Efficiency – A Legal and Regulatory Perspective', Working Paper No. 1015. Bank of International Settlements (2021).

Zetzsche D. A. and Woxholth J., 'The DLT Sandbox under the Pilot Regulation', *Capital Markets Law Journal*, 17(2) (2022): 212.

Zetzsche D. A. *et al.*, 'Remaining Regulatory Challenges in Digital Finance and Crypto-Assets after MiCA'. Committee on Economic and Monetary Affairs (ECON) (2023). Website https://dx.doi.org/10.2139/ssrn.4487516 (last accessed on 1 October 2024).

Zetzsche D. A., Annunziata F. and Sinnig J., 'Digital Assets, MiCA and EU Investment Fund Law' (2023). Website https://dx.doi.org/10.2139/ssrn.4637019 (last accessed on 1 October 2024)

Zetzsche D. A., Buckley R. P. and Arner D. W., 'Regulating Libra', *Oxford Journal of Legal Studies*, 41(1) (2021): 80.

Zetzsche D. A. and Nikolakopoulou A., 'Crypto Custody and Crypto Wallets – An Empirical Analysis'. University of Luxembourg Working Paper (2024). Website https://dx.doi.org/10.2139/ssrn.4769396 (last accessed on 1 October 2024).

Zetzsche D. A., Sinnig J. and Nikolakopoulou A., 'Crypto Custody'. *Capital Markets Law Journal*, 19, 207–29 (2024).

Zetzsche D. A. and Preiner C. D., 'Scope of the AIFMD', in D. A. Zetzsche (ed.), *The Alternative Investment Fund Managers Directive*, 3rd ed. (Alphen aan den Rijn: Wolters Kluwer, 2020), pp. 25–61.

Zetzsche D. A. and Hanke M., 'Risk Management', in D. A. Zetzsche (ed.), *The Alternative Investment Fund Managers Directive*, 3rd ed. (Alphen aan den Rijn: Wolters Kluwer, 2020), pp. 315–74.

Zetzsche D. A. and Preiner C. D., 'ELTIFR versus AIFMD', in D. A. Zetzsche (ed.), *The Alternative Investment Fund Managers Directive*, 3rd ed. (Alphen aan den Rijn: Wolters Kluwer, 2020), pp. 95–128.

Zetzsche D. A., '(Prime) Brokerage', in D. A. Zetzsche (ed.), *The Alternative Investment Fund Managers Directive*, 3rd ed. (Alphen aan den Rijn: Wolters Kluwer, 2020), pp. 545–79.

Zetzsche D. A., 'Introduction', in D. A. Zetzsche (ed.), *The Alternative Investment Fund Managers Directive*, 3rd ed. (Alphen aan den Rijn: Wolters Kluwer, 2020), pp. 1–22.

Index

For EU product safety concerns, contact us at Calle de José Abascal, 56–1°, 28003 Madrid, Spain or eugpsr@cambridge.org.

www.ingramcontent.com/pod-product-compliance
Lightning Source LLC
LaVergne TN
LVHW081938200926
848484LV00009B/2461